CORELDRAW 8:
THE OFFICIAL GUIDE

Foster Coburn
and Peter McCormick

Osborne/**McGraw-Hill**

Berkeley New York St. Louis San Francisco
Auckland Bogotá Hamburg London Madrid
Mexico City Milan Montreal
New Delhi Panama City Paris São Paulo
Singapore Sydney Tokyo Toronto

D1484655

Osborne/**McGraw-Hill**
2600 Tenth Street
Berkeley, California 94710
U.S.A.

For information on translations or book distributors outside the U.S.A., or to arrange bulk purchase discounts for sales promotions, premiums, or fund-raisers, please contact Osborne/**McGraw-Hill** at the above address.

CORELDRAW 8: THE OFFICIAL GUIDE

Copyright © 1998 by The McGraw-Hill Companies. All rights reserved. Printed in the United States of America. Except as permitted under the Copyright Act of 1976, no part of this publication may be reproduced or distributed in any form or by any means, or stored in a database or retrieval system, without the prior written permission of the publisher, with the exception that the program listings may be entered, stored, and executed in a computer system, but they may not be reproduced for publication.

4567890 AGM 90198765432109

ISBN 0-07-882447-8

Publisher: Brandon A. Nordin
Editor-in-Chief: Scott Rogers
Acquisitions Editor: Megg Bonar
Project Editor: Jennifer Wenzel
Associate Project Editors: Heidi Poulin, Cynthia Douglas
Editorial Assistant: Stephane Thomas
Technical Editors: Joe Donnelly, Debbie Cook
Copy Editors: Deborah Craig, Judith Abrahms
Proofreaders: Pat Mannion, Sally Engelfried, Stephany Otis
Indexer: Valerie Robbins
Computer Designer: Roberta Steele, Michelle Galicia
Illustrator: Arlette Crosland

Information has been obtained by Osborne/**McGraw-Hill** from sources believed to be reliable. However, because of the possibility of human or mechanical error by our sources, Osborne/**McGraw-Hill**, or others, Osborne/**McGraw-Hill** does not guarantee the accuracy, adequacy, or completeness of any information and is not responsible for any errors or omissions or the results obtained from use of such information.

CONTENTS

PART 5   ADVANCED TOPICS

PART 6 APPENDICES

CorelDRAW™ 8: The Official Guide is the newest addition to the CorelPRESS™ library of books, and represents the most recent in this series of important collaborations between Corel and Osborne/McGraw-Hill. The CorelPRESS line of books features expert authors who provide both a solid grounding in product fundamentals and the knowledge necessary to master advanced features of the products.

This book provides a first look at CorelDRAW™ 8, Corel's latest version of its award-winning graphics and image-editing suite. Now revised for more intuitive, interactive and innovative work, the enhancements to CorelDRAW 8 offer maximum productivity. Whether you're designing for print and presentations or publishing to the Web, this outstanding tool set facilitates creativity and job efficiency. New CorelDRAW users, as well as those already familiar with the program, will find significant value in this book, and will benefit from the in-depth knowledge these authors have developed from their experience with CorelDRAW.

Corel's 1997 World Design Contest Winners are featured in this book's full-color insert—we salute all the artists who work in CorelDRAW to create each of the masterpieces entered in this year's design contest, and we appreciate the opportunity to show off some of the creativity and talent.

The CorelPRESS series represents an important step in the ability of Corel to disseminate information to users with the help of Osborne/McGraw-Hill, the authors, tech reviewers, editors and designers involved in the series. Congratulations to the entire CorelPRESS team at Osborne on the creation of this excellent book!

Dr. Michael J. Cowpland
President and CEO
Corel Corporation

FOREWORD

It only seems appropriate to thank all of the people who helped us to complete this book. The hardest part in putting this book to bed is that we never feel that it is finished. There is always one more tip or technique that needs to be added. And as soon as this book hits the shelves, we know we'll find a great feature hidden beneath the surface. Each user will find a way that works best for him or her, so, as we find these new gems, we'll add them to our Web site at **http://www.unleash.com**.

On the color pages you'll see some really incredible images from Corel's World Design Contest. This book will show you how to use the tools and effects that were used to create these images, the time and talent is up to you. Even those of us who are "artistically challenged" can create some great work thanks to the power of CorelDRAW.

We are always eager to hear what you think of our books. We want to know what you liked and what we've missed. This allows us to continue building on this book so that the next book can be ever bigger and better. Visit our Web page, send us a letter, fire off an e-mail or just give us a call. The more we hear from you, the more that we can give back in future editions and on our Web site.

The number of people who must be thanked is enormous. Some of them don't even realize how important their help has been. Sue McCormick has known exactly where to find Pete the past few months and he can finally emerge from his cave for a little bit of relaxation and golf. And Foster can now resume his search for someone to coax him out of his cave. Our friends and families have been extremely patient as we made excuses for working nights and weekends. We can finally turn off the computers for a few hours and enjoy ourselves for a little while.

Jodi, our office manager, has been wonderful throughout this whole ordeal. We even made her read many of the chapters to find our typos. So thank you Jodi. Enjoy the many years to come with your beautiful daughter, Julia!

INTRODUCTION

Debbie Cook worked through each chapter to make sure that what we had written was correct. In doing so, she also provided lots of helpful tips. Thanks Debbie for the great work!

"Doctor" Dickson is responsible for getting a decent picture out of us. Doug Dickson has educated us tremendously on the printing and pre-press industry. We are probably his most irritating client and he still accepts our jobs and gets them off press looking fantastic.

The crew at Corel has been wonderful. Without their help, the book couldn't have been written. Joe Donnelly and Warren Tomlin not only had to get CorelDRAW 8 out the door, but also had to deal with our many questions. They did a great job with both projects. Mike Bellefeuille and Michelle Murphy at Corel are together responsible for authors, seminars, and user groups. This book is really their project and they did a tremendous job. Even though we didn't directly cover PHOTO-PAINT, Doug Chomyn was extremely helpful in answering questions. And we must single out Rus Miller, the engineer extraordinaire that handles the print engine. Not only does he write great code, but he is always willing to explain it to us mere mortals. Thanks to all those we mentioned and to the many others who we've accidentally missed. Keep up all the great work, eh?

To our fellow betazoids, thanks for all of your input. You'll undoubtedly find something in this book that you provided in one way or another. Reading through the beta newsgroups provided a much needed break from writing, but was also an inspiration as new features were deciphered. Get some rest, as it's about time to start the beta cycle all over again!

Each year we marvel at the work of the artists who use CorelDRAW. Thanks to all of the artists whose work is featured within our color pages. It is your work that inspires all of us to use the product and maybe one day we can join you on the winner's platform.

Most of all, we must thank you for purchasing this book. We sincerely hope that we've been able to enlighten and inspire you to push CorelDRAW to its limits and beyond.

PART
1

THE BASICS

1

INSTALLING CORELDRAW 8

Before you begin the installation process, be sure to check CD1 to see if it includes a readme file. The first release of CorelDRAW 8 contains a readme file with the file name CorelDRAW 8 README. Readme files often contain last minute information about the programs and any special instructions on installation or hardware compatibility. Pay particular attention to the section on video display problems and the section on fonts or installing multilingual fonts. The remainder of the readme file primarily contains portions of the Help files that are in the various other programs that come with CorelDRAW.

Before you insert the installation CD, you may want to look at what's included on the three CD-ROMs. The contents of each CD are listed here:

► *CD1* Programs, templates, fonts, Font Navigator, symbols, photo edges, and samples

► *CD2* Clipart images (approximately 40,000)

► *CD3* Photos, tiles, images, image lists, brush textures, objects, and 3D models

You need to know what's on the CD if you want to be able to find a certain clipart or photo CD image.

INSTALLING THE PROGRAMS

Before you begin the installation process be sure to close any open programs and any TSRs running in the background, especially virus checkers and crash utilities.

Whether you're installing CorelDRAW for the first time or adding programs and files you didn't install the first time, start by inserting CD1. The auto-run program will begin the installation process by displaying the initial screen of the Corel Setup Wizard.

If for some reason the auto-run program does not start the Setup Wizard, follow these steps:

1. Click the Windows Start button and choose Settings from the Start menu. When the Settings flyout appears, choose Control Panel.

2. In the Control Panel dialog box, double-click the Add/Remove Programs icon. The Add/Remove Programs Properties dialog box will appear.

3. Click the Install button. The Install Program from Floppy Disk or CD-ROM Drive dialog box will appear.

4. Click the Next button to go to the Run Installation Program dialog box. If the CD is in the correct drive, the drive letter of your CD will appear along with the Setup.exe command in the Command Line for Installation box. If it doesn't appear, type the correct path to the CD plus the words **Setup.exe** in the Command Line for Installation box.

When the initial setup screen appears, you are given a choice of installing either CorelDRAW 8, Corel PHOTO-PAINT 8 and Utilities, or CorelDREAM 3D 8. If you want to install all the programs, you'll have to do two separate installs. After you choose which programs to install, the Corel Setup Wizard will appear. Click the Next button to view the License Agreement. Click the Accept button to go to the next screen. The next two screens ask for registration information, including the serial number of your program.

The sixth screen, shown in Figure 1-1, is the beginning of the installation process. The Setup Options screen offers four choices: Typical Setup, Compact Setup, Custom Setup, and Run from CD-ROM drive. Don't choose the CD-ROM option unless you have very little hard disk space available. If you choose this option, you won't be able to access the clipart and other files located on the other CDs because CD1, which contains the programs, will be in the CD-ROM drive.

If you don't want to get involved making choices during the setup procedure, you should choose the Typical Setup installation option. This option asks you only two questions during the installation process.

USING THE TYPICAL SETUP OPTION

If you choose the Typical Setup option, the first screen asks you to choose a destination folder (see Figure 1-2). The top parameter box lets you enter the drive letter and name of the folder where you want CorelDRAW 8 and all its other programs and utilities to reside. A drive letter and directory will appear

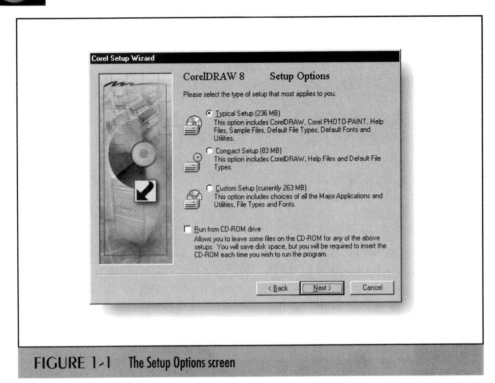

FIGURE 1-1   The Setup Options screen

by default. If the drive letter and directory are acceptable, you don't need to make any changes.

The second parameter box on the Destination Folder screen shows the amount of free space available in the drive on which you chose to install the programs and the amount of space the programs require. If you chose a drive other than drive C, this box will still show a small amount of space used on the C drive.

The last screen to appear is the Ready to Install screen, shown in Figure 1-3. It simply verifies the name of the registered owner and the destination folder you designated earlier. If any information is incorrect, click the Back button to return to the previous screens and make corrections. You can review the components that will be installed by putting a check mark in the Show Selected Components box. Expanding the various folders will reveal all the

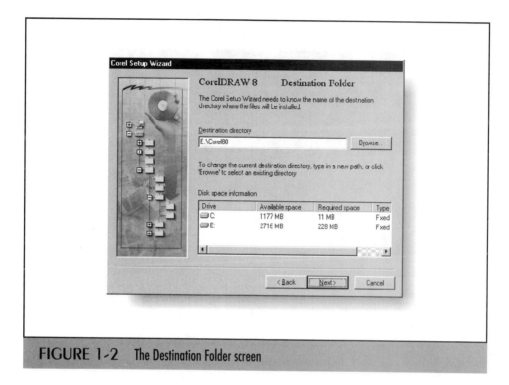

FIGURE 1-2   The Destination Folder screen

components. You can't make any changes to the component list. It is merely there to show you what is being installed. If you see a component that you don't want or one that is missing, use the Custom Setup option. When everything is correct, click the Install button.

The programs, graphic utilities, productivity tools, and filters that will be installed automatically when you choose the Typical Setup option are listed next.

Programs

▶ CorelDRAW

▶ Corel PHOTO-PAINT

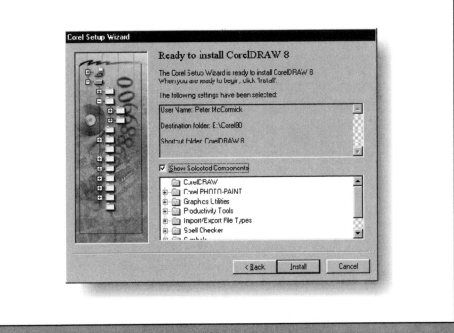

FIGURE 1-3 The Ready to Install CorelDRAW 8 screen

Graphics Utilities

▶ Corel OCR-Trace

▶ All plug-in filters

▶ Corel Color Profile Wizard

▶ CorelSCAN

▶ Corel Media Folders

Productivity Tools

▶ Writing tools (English components only)

▶ Fifty-five default fonts

► Help files for each component

► All tutors

► Approved partners and technical support

► Corel Uninstall

► Readme files

► Labels (North America only)

► Corel Barista

► Duplexing Wizard

Filters

► *Bitmap filters*   CPT, TIF, PCX, BMP, GIF, JPG, PCD, PSD, MAC, PP5, TGA, SCT, EXE, ICO, CUR, WVL, FPX, PNG, RAW

► *Vector filters*   WPG, AI, DXF, CGM, CMF, CMX, CDR, CPX, CDX, CCH, AI (Trace), EPS, EMF, HPGL/PLT, PCT, Interpreted PostScript, WMF, PDF, PSF, DWG, 3DMF

► *Animation filters*   All

► *Text filters*   WP6, WP7, WP8, DOC (V6 and 7), RTF, TXT, SAM

► *Internet filters*   HTM

USING THE COMPACT SETUP OPTION

The Compact Setup option installs only the basic CorelDRAW application along with the readme files and the Uninstall utility. This option is designed for the laptop user or the user with very little hard disk space. The application includes all import and export filters as well as the bitmap filters. This installation requires approximately 83 megabytes.

   *No fonts will be installed if you use the Compact Setup.*

USING THE CUSTOM SETUP OPTION

If you are comfortable navigating around in Windows 95 or Windows NT 4.0, you may want to use the Custom Setup option. This option allows you to decide what will be installed. For example, the Typical Setup option installs many filters, but most users use only a few of these filters. Installing all of them serves no purpose other than taking up valuable hard disk space. Additionally, you may want to install only one or two of the applications that come with CorelDRAW 8 instead of the entire suite.

If you choose the Custom Setup option on the Setup Options screen, the next screen you see is the Components screen, shown in Figure 1-4. This is where you decide which components of CorelDRAW you want to install. Click the + icon next to each program to see the list of components within the program. Remove any component you don't feel you will need. For example, Figure 1-4 shows the Productivity Tools folder expanded to reveal its various components. If you do not want to install the Barcode Wizard, for example,

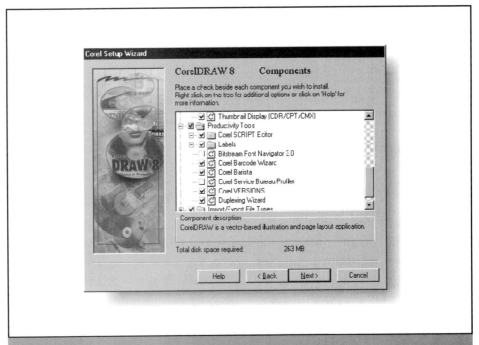

FIGURE 1-4   The Components screen

remove the check mark from its box. You may decide you don't want an entire program, in which case you should remove the check mark from the box next to the name of the program.

 *We highly recommend installing the Font Navigator program located in the Productivity Tools folder. This is a fantastic program for managing your fonts.*

Be sure to click the + box next to each Import and Export file type category name to see the list of available file types. The Import and Export file types is an area where you can save some hard disk space. Look through each category for file types you know you won't ever use. For example, if you know you will never handle a file created in WordStar, you can remove the check mark next to that file type's name. If you are not familiar with a particular file type, it is best to install it, to be safe.

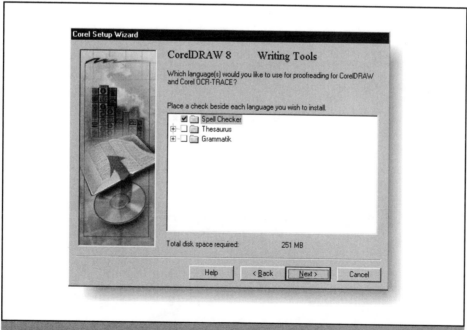

FIGURE 1-5   The Writing Tools screen

The next screen following the Components screen is the Writing Tools screen, shown in Figure 1-5. You're instructed to put a check beside each language you wish to install. The spell checker defaults to the language of the program. If you bought the English version the spell checker will default to English. If you choose to install either the thesaurus or grammar checker Grammatik, be sure to click the + to expand the folders to deselect the languages you don't want. If you just check the box, you will end up installing eight languages in the thesaurus and four languages in Grammatik.

The Color Profile screen shown in Figure 1-6 follows the Writing Tools screen. Place a check mark in the Monitor Profiles check box and then click on the + to expand the folder. Choose your monitor from the list. Place a check mark in the Input Profiles check box and then click the + to expand the folder. Choose the name of your scanner from the list provided. Place a check mark in the Printer Profiles check box and expand its folder. Choose the desired printer profile from the list. These could include the printer on your desktop or the printer your service bureau uses.

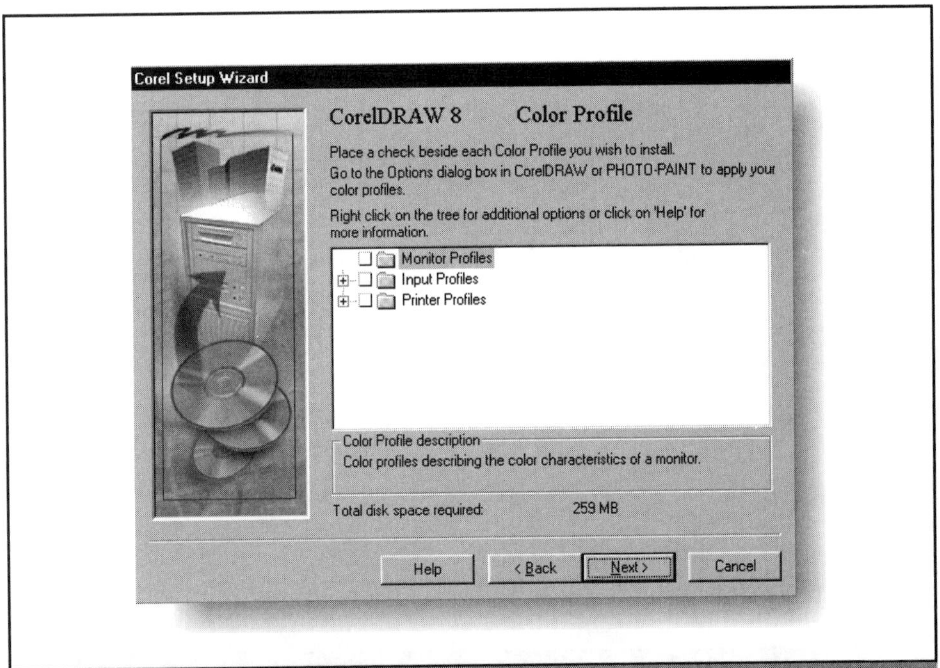

FIGURE 1-6   The Color Profile screen

 *If you forget to install a profile during the installation process, you can always install it later either with the setup program or when using the Corel Color Management Wizard discussed in Chapter 24.*

Next you will see the Fonts screen, shown in Figure 1-7. We recommend installing only the Symbols by removing the check mark from the Default check box ensuring that no fonts are installed in the installation process. We suggest not installing any fonts at this point because we feel the better way to install fonts is from within Windows or through a font management system such as Font Navigator. Refer to Chapter 38 for a detailed explanation of how to install fonts. If you have very few fonts currently installed, you may want to install the default fonts. Selecting the default fonts will install 55 new fonts in your Windows Fonts folder. You can also select additional fonts from categories provided in this screen.

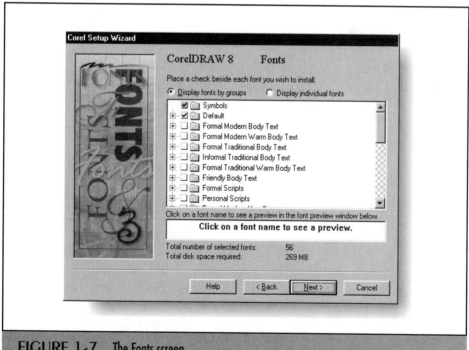

FIGURE 1-7   The Fonts screen

>CAUTION: *If you do install fonts during the installation process, do not install every available font in the list. If you did you could easily overload your system. Additionally, if you install fonts using the Install program, only TrueType fonts will be installed.*

After you have made your font choices, the Destination Folder screen (see Figure 1-8) appears. The top parameter box lets you enter the drive letter and name of the directory (folder) where you want CorelDRAW 8 and all its other programs and utilities to reside. A drive letter and directory will appear by default. If the drive letter and directory are acceptable, you don't need to make any changes.

The second parameter box on the destination directory screen shows the default fonts directory. If you are operating under Windows 95, the directory will be C:\Win95\fonts. If you are operating under Windows NT, the directory will be C:\WINNT\fonts. Unless you have a specific reason to change this directory, do not change the default settings.

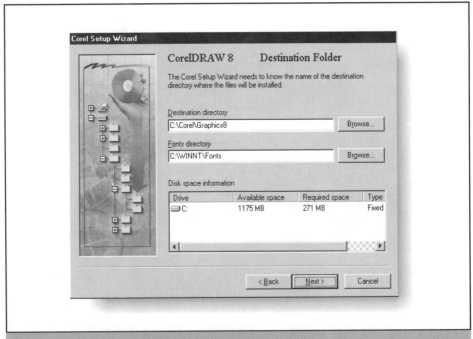

FIGURE 1-8   The Destination Folder screen

The next screen that appears is the Temp Folder Selection screen (see Figure 1-9). This screen shows each of your nonremovable drives and displays the amount of space that is available. Temp files are files CorelDRAW creates when the program is running. At times these temporary files can become quite large. Therefore, it is generally best to choose the drive letter that has the most available space. In the example in Figure 1-9, the E drive has almost 3 gigabytes of available space. Here, the E drive would be the drive best suited as a temporary drive. This example may not reflect the average user's available hard disk space.

The next screen (see Figure 1-10) is the Shortcut Folder screen, where you choose the folder where all the CorelDRAW 8 related applications will be stored. You can choose the default CorelDRAW 8 folder, choose a name of an existing folder or type a new name in the parameter box.

The last screen to appear is the Ready to Install screen (see Figure 1-11). This screen simply verifies the destination folder and fonts folder you designated earlier. If you check the Show Selected Components box you can

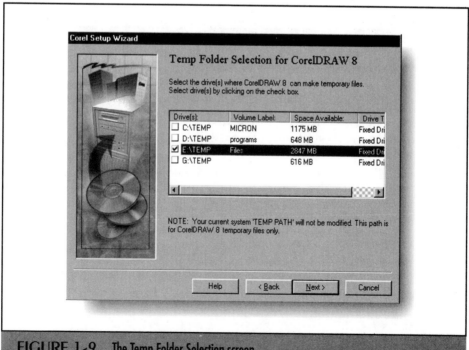

FIGURE 1-9   The Temp Folder Selection screen

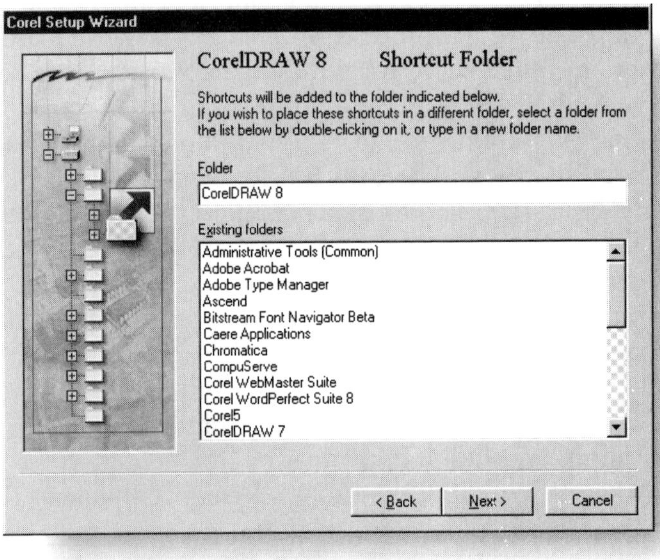

FIGURE 1-10   The Shortcut Folder screen

review the choices you made in the previous screens. If the information is incorrect, click the Back button to return to the previous screens and make corrections. When everything is correct, click the Install button. From this point forward, the Installation Wizard takes over and completes the installation process.

If you installed every program and every available component, you would end up adding all the programs, graphics utilities, productivity tools, and filters installed in the Typical Setup plus the following:

▶ Corel Capture

▶ Corel Texture

▶ Corel Texture Batcher

▶ Corel Script Editor

▶ Corel Script Converter

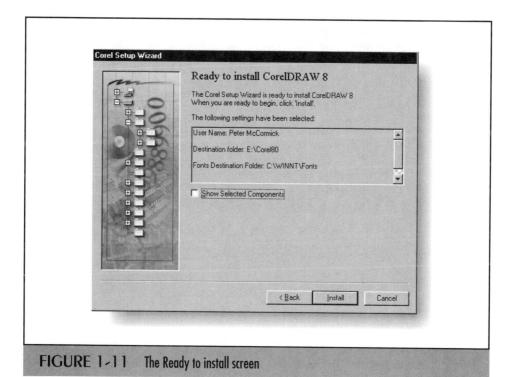

FIGURE 1-11   The Ready to install screen

► Corel Bar Code

► Corel Media Folders Indexer 8

► Duplexing Wizard

When the installation is complete, you will be told to reboot your system so all of the newly selected components can be installed correctly. You will have the option to reboot as soon as the installation process is complete or at a later time. Unless you have a specific reason for not rebooting, you should reboot as soon as the installation process is complete.

Use the Custom Setup option when you are installing additional applications or components that may not have been installed during the initial installation.

As you have seen, there are several choices to make when installing CorelDRAW on your system. If you feel you have minimal technical expertise, we recommend using the Custom Setup method; this will conserve hard disk space by not installing something you may never use. If you decide later you want to use a particular program or add additional fonts, you can run the installation program again.

Chapter 2 is called "Getting Started." It will begin your introduction to CorelDRAW by discussing just what's in the box. You'll learn how to get help when you can't find the answer on your own by using either the Help files or the CorelTUTOR. For the more experienced user, a list of what's new in CorelDRAW 8 is provided at the end of the chapter.

2

GETTING STARTED / NEW FEATURES IN CORELDRAW 8

The purpose of this chapter is two-fold. First, it's to introduce some basic principles of the CorelDRAW program to first-time users and discuss areas where they can get answers to their questions. Second, it's to point out to the experienced user, the many new features introduced in CorelDRAW 8 and to direct them to the chapters where these features are discussed.

WHAT'S IN THE BOX

CorelDRAW 8 is really a suite of applications, beginning with the flagship illustration program CorelDRAW. Also included is Corel PHOTO-PAINT, the image editing and pixel based paint program. The third program is CorelDREAM 3D 8, the three-dimensional rendering program. Besides the three main applications, there are various other graphic utilities and tools. Because of the complexities of the three main programs, this book covers CorelDRAW 8 only. To incorporate the other applications into a single book would make the book unmanageable for the reader.

WHAT IS CORELDRAW?

CorelDRAW is a vector-based drawing and illustration program. This means when you draw an object on the CorelDRAW drawing page, the shape of the object displayed onscreen is defined by a mathematical formula. In fact, its accuracy can be measured to one tenth of a micron. Sounds complicated, doesn't it? Forget the technical definition. What it really is, is a program that lets you draw shapes to illustrate ideas in a graphical and text-based fashion. The capabilities and potential of the program are limited only by your own imagination.

BEGIN AT THE BEGINNING

If you're completely new to CorelDRAW, you may feel intimidated when you first open the application. If you're like most of us, your concern will grow when you try to draw your first object on the screen. The anxiety will become even greater when you try to color your object with something other than a color from the palette on the right side of the screen. After trying one tool and another, many first-time users feel that a degree in rocket science is required to use the program. Before you start looking for the receipt so you can return the box for a refund, remember one thing: we've all been where you are and we got through it. What most of us didn't have was a book like this to make the learning process easier.

WHAT'S ON THE SCREEN

When you first open CorelDRAW 8, the screen will look like the one shown in Figure 2-1. Before you can begin, you must select one of the options on the

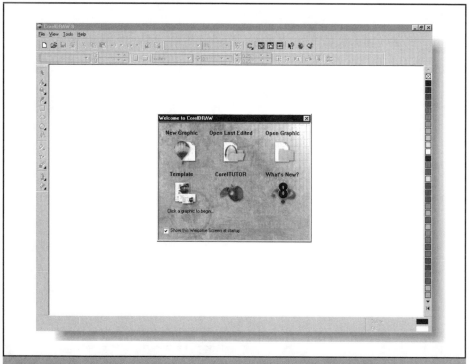

FIGURE 2-1   The default CorelDRAW screen when Typical Install is used

Welcome screen. Select New Graphic and the default screen shown in Figure 2-2, displaying the drawing page, will appear. The remaining options are self-explanatory. If you have used the program before, you may wish to choose the What's New? option first.

The following is a brief description of the CorelDRAW screen. The entire area below the Title bar with the exception of the actual drawing page in the center of the screen, is called the Workspace. Down the left-hand side of the screen is the toolbox. The color palette is displayed on the right-hand side.

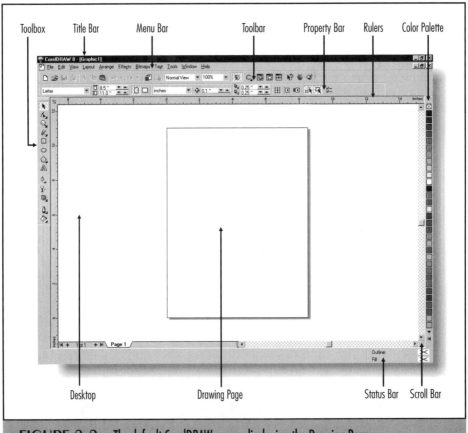

FIGURE 2-2 The default CorelDRAW screen displaying the Drawing Page

2

Across the top of the screen are displayed the Title Bar, Menu Bar, Toolbar, and Property Bar in descending order. The bottom of the screen displays the scroll bar and below that the Status Bar. In the center of the screen is the Drawing Page. The drop shadow around the page is called the Page Border. The white area surrounding the page is called the Desktop. Each of these elements that make up the screen will be covered in the following chapters as they are introduced. This chapter will begin by introducing the Toolbox, the Hints page, and CorelTUTOR.

The Toolbox

The toolbox, shown in Figure 2-3, contains the tools you'll need to create the shapes to illustrate your ideas. There are additional tools in the toolbox that

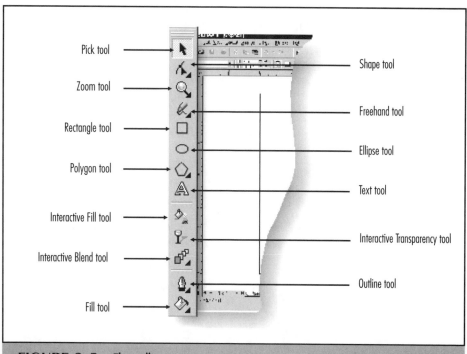

Pick tool

Zoom tool

Rectangle tool

Polygon tool

Interactive Fill tool

Interactive Blend tool

Fill tool

Shape tool

Freehand tool

Ellipse tool

Text tool

Interactive Transparency tool

Outline tool

FIGURE 2-3   The toolbox

allow you to modify the basic shapes and to change the fill and outline colors of those shapes. Some icons in the toolbox have small black triangles at the lower right corner. If you click and hold on the triangle with the left mouse button, a flyout will appear, containing either additional shape creation tools, or, in some cases, icons that provide access to roll-ups and dialog boxes. You can create a floating toolbar from a flyout by left-clicking and dragging the flyout out onto the drawing window. This technique is called tearing off a flyout. There will be certain tools whose flyouts contain additional tools that you find you use frequently. Creating a floating toolbar from these flyouts will provide quicker access to them.

The following table lists each tool in the toolbox, including any additional tools on their respective flyouts; it includes a description of each tool's basic function. Also noted is the chapter number where a complete description of each tool's functions can be found.

Tool	Flyout	Basic Function
Pick (Chapter 7)		Select and transform objects
Shape (Chapter 8)		Change shapes of objects by node manipulation
	Knife	Cut away portions of objects and line welding
	Eraser	Erase portions of objects
Zoom (Chapter 12)		View an object from close up or farther away
	Pan	Move the page within the drawing window
Freehand (Chapter 5)		Draw shapes freehand as if you had a pencil in your hand
	Bézier	Draw shapes in a "Connect the Dots" style while also controlling the shape
	Natural Pen	Draw shapes with variable thickness
	Dimension	Draw measurement lines on or between objects, including Callouts
	Connector Line	Draw connecting lines between objects
Rectangle (Chapter 4)		Draw rectangles of all sizes

Tool	Flyout	Basic Function
Ellipse (Chapter 4)		Draw ellipses of all sizes
Polygon (Chapter 4)		Draw polygons and stars with varying numbers of sides
	Spiral	Draw spirals with varying revolutions
	Graph Paper	Draw graph paper with varying numbers and sizes of cells
Text (Chapter 6)		Type Artistic or Paragraph text
Interactive Fill (Chapter 10)		Interactively fill objects onscreen
Interactive Transparency (Chapter 21)		Apply transparency to object interactively onscreen
Interactive Effects (Chapter 20)	Interactive Blend	Blend objects interactively onscreen
	Interactive Distortion	Distort objects interactively onscreen
	Interactive Envelope	Warp objects interactively onscreen
	Interactive Extrude	Add 3D effects to objects interactively onscreen

NOTE: *The Fill and Outline tools at the bottom of the toolbox were not included in the preceding table because they are not technically considered tools. The Fill tool allows you to fill the inside of a shape with various colors, patterns, and textures using roll-ups and dialog boxes. The Outline tool allows you to control the color, size, and style of the outline of shapes, also through the use of roll-ups and dialog boxes. Both tools are described in complete detail in Chapters 9 and 10.*

CHANGING THE WORKSPACE VIEW FOR NEW USERS

As was pointed out in the beginning of the chapter the entire area below the Title bar with the exception of the drawing page is considered the Workspace. Notice that none of the buttons on the toolbar, Property Bar, and toolbox have descriptive words telling you what happens if you click on one. CorelDRAW 8 now allows you to change the Workspace view to display this information.

Click on Tools | Options and the Workspace dialog box shown here will display.

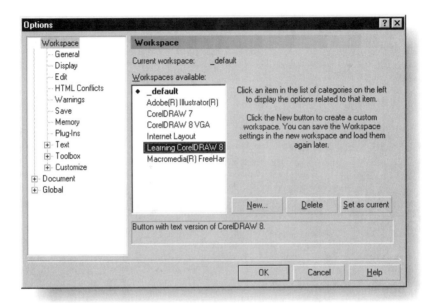

Click on Learning CorelDRAW 8 in the Workspace available list. Click the Set as current button at the lower right of the Workspace dialog box, then click the OK button. Your screen display will now look like the one shown next. All the buttons on the toolbar, Property Bar, and toolbox now display either the name of the button or the action taken if you click the button.

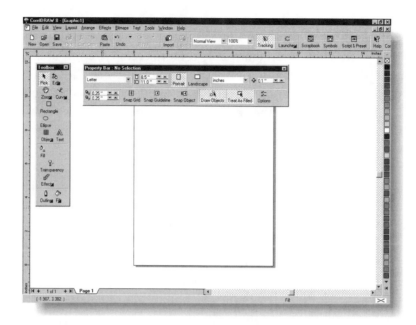

 The actual size of the toolbar, Property Bar, and toolbox will vary depending on the screen resolution you are using.

If you find that the increased size of the toolbar, Property Bar, and toolbox takes up too much screen space, you can still get the information about the button by holding the cursor over the button for a few seconds. Holding the cursor over a button will display a Tool Tip telling you the function of the button.

USING THE HELP SYSTEM

The Help menu, shown in Figure 2-4, offers access to seven areas of help. They are: Help Topics, What's This?, CorelTUTOR, Hints, Technical Support, Corel on the Web, and About CorelDRAW. The following is a description of all these headings and how they can be used to help you learn CorelDRAW.

HELP TOPICS

Clicking Help | Help Topics will bring up the Help Topics tabbed dialog box. The first tab shows the Contents page, displaying a list of primary topics for which you can choose to get help. When you choose one of these topics, the title subject will expand in a hierarchical order, offering you additional topics related to your first choice. This list will let you narrow the focus on the subject you're interested in until you find the answer.

The second tab is the Index tab. This tab provides an alphabetical list of topics that you can choose to find help on. It also provides a parameters box above the list box that lets you type in key words you may be looking for. For

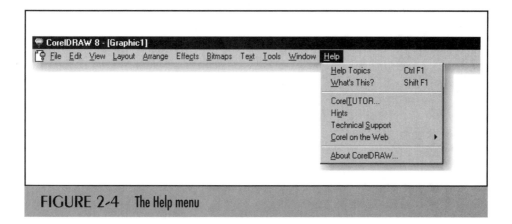

FIGURE 2-4 The Help menu

example, if you wanted to know how to blur an object, you would type the word "blur." The list box would move down with the words Blur effects highlighted. You would then click the Display button to learn how to use the Blur effect.

The third tab on the Help dialog box is the Find tab. When you choose this tab, the Find Setup Wizard screen is displayed, letting you create a database of every word in the Help files. You will be given a choice as to how extensive this database is. We would not recommend creating this Find database unless you are unable to find the help you need using the first two Help methods.

WHAT'S THIS?

When you click What's This? (SHIFT-F1) in the Help menu, the cursor is replaced by a cursor with a question mark. You then use this cursor to click on various elements of the CorelDRAW screen. For example, if you clicked on the Rectangle tool in the toolbox, a Tool Tip would pop up, telling you how the tool is used. If you clicked on the drawing page in the center of the screen, a message would tell you that this is the area that can be printed by your printer. This tool is great for getting fast feedback about certain elements of the screen. It can also be accessed by clicking the What's This? button on the toolbar.

USING CORELTUTOR

CorelTUTOR, shown here in its default configuration on the right side of the screen, is an online tutor that is activated by either choosing it from the Help menu, Help | CorelTUTOR (ALT-H-T), or by clicking the Apple button on the toolbar. The Tutor provides step-by-step instructions, and in many cases interactive instruction, on how to complete specific tasks. You can learn something as simple as creating a simple shape or more complex tasks that require several steps. It's an excellent learning tool for the new user and a good quick review source for the experienced user.

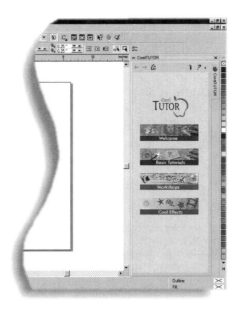

By default, CorelTUTOR is displayed as a docked sizable window. This means that you can undock the window and make it into a floating window on the desktop. To undock the window, click at the top of the docked window and drag it out onto the desktop. To redock the window, click the Title bar of the floating window and drag the window over to either side of the desktop until it docks. In addition, the window can be minimized or maximized by clicking the double arrows next to the words "Corel Tutor" at the top of the window.

USING THE HINTS WINDOW

The Hints window, shown in Figure 2-5, is accessed by clicking its name in the Help menu. Its primary purpose is to provide hints on how to use the tools in the toolbox. It is also context-sensitive, so when a tool is selected, a hint on how to use the tool is displayed. Figure 2-6 shows the Hints window when the Rectangle tool has been selected.

2

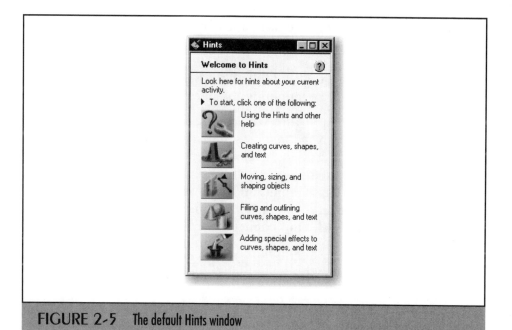

FIGURE 2-5   The default Hints window

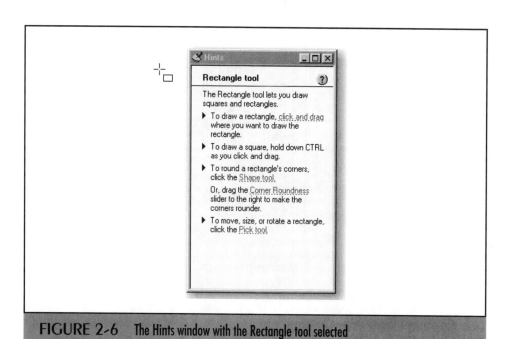

FIGURE 2-6   The Hints window with the Rectangle tool selected

Practice drawing a rectangle with the Hints window displayed while following these steps:

1. Click the Rectangle tool and follow the first instruction on the Hints window telling you how to draw a rectangle.

2. After you have drawn the rectangle, drag the crosshair portion of the cursor over the X in the middle of the rectangle (the cursor will change to a pair of crossed double-headed arrows). The Hints window will change to look like the one shown in Figure 2-7. In this configuration, additional hints are given on how to transform the rectangle you just created. Practice the first three instructions on the Hints window while in this configuration. If you followed the

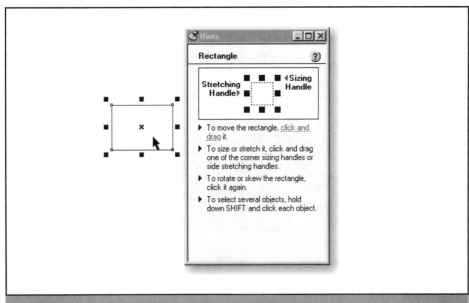

FIGURE 2-7   The Hints window when the rectangle has been selected with the Pick tool

instructions correctly, you will have learned how to move, stretch, resize, rotate, and skew your rectangle.

If you want more information pertaining to the tool you are using or the object you have selected, click the question-mark button at the upper right of the Hints window. This action will display the CorelDRAW Help screen with even more information about the tool or object.

As you can readily see, the Hints window can provide a wealth of information on how to use the various tools in CorelDRAW. If you take advantage of this storehouse of information, it will make your learning curve much shorter.

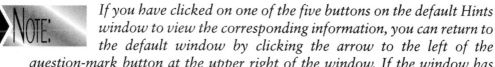 *If you have clicked on one of the five buttons on the default Hints window to view the corresponding information, you can return to the default window by clicking the arrow to the left of the question-mark button at the upper right of the window. If the window has changed configuration because a tool has been selected, you must close and reopen the Hints window to display the default Hints window again.*

TECHNICAL SUPPORT

Technical support is much like the Help topics discussed earlier, but focuses on the more technical aspects of the program. Clicking Help | Technical Support will bring up the Corel Technical Support tabbed dialog box. The first tab shows the Contents page, displaying a list of technical topics from which you can choose to get help. When you choose one of these topics, you will be taken to a second dialog box, which offers additional topics related to your first choice.

The second tab is the Index tab. This tab provides an alphabetical list of topics that you can choose to find technical help on. It also provides a Parameters box above the list box that lets you type in the key words you are looking for.

The third tab on the dialog box is the Find tab. It offers the same options as the Find page in the general Help dialog box. As before, we would not recommend creating the Find database unless you are unable to find the help you need using the first two Help methods.

COREL ON THE WEB

Corel on the Web is a new method of providing up-to-date help. It allows you to go to Corel's Web site while actually working in CorelDRAW. When you click the Help menu and then hold the cursor over the words "Corel on the Web," a flyout is revealed, offering several Help topics that can be found on Corel's Web site. When you click one of these topics, your default Web browser will be activated. If you're currently connected, it will take you directly to the specific page you clicked on. If you're not connected, you'll need to connect (on some systems your dial-up networking dialog box will appear, asking if you want to connect). There are a total of six areas on Corel's Web site that you can visit.

Located at the bottom of the Web flyout is Edit Links. When you click Edit Links, an Edit Links dialog box appears (see Figure 2-8). You will notice that

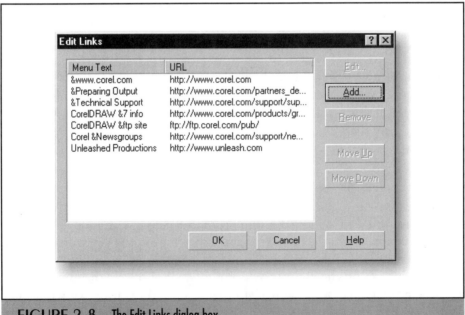

FIGURE 2-8 The Edit Links dialog box

it lists the URLs corresponding to the names in the flyout. An additional benefit of this dialog box is that you can also add your own favorite links. Practice adding a link to the author's Web site by following these steps:

1. Click the Add button at the upper right of the Edit Links dialog box. The Link Details dialog box will appear.

2. Type "Graphics Unleashed" in the Menu Text for Link: parameters box.

3. Type **unleash.com** in the Corresponding URL parameters box after the prefix http://.

4. Click the OK buttons in both the Link Details and the Edit Links dialog boxes.

5. Click the Help menu and then click Corel on the Web to see your added link listed on the flyout.

ABOUT CORELDRAW

When you click Help | About CorelDRAW, the About CorelDRAW 8 dialog box, shown in Figure 2-9, appears. At first glance, this dialog box may not appear to be very interesting-looking. However, it is a very important dialog box that contains information that can be very helpful when you're troubleshooting a problem or simply requesting tech support from Corel itself.

To begin, this dialog box shows the current version of the program you're using. This can be extremely important information to have if you're experiencing problems with the program. Often-times, Corel sends out revised versions of the program to fix problems that surface in early versions. Knowing which version you have will tell you if you are using the most current version. The lower portion of the dialog box lists the name of the person to whom the program is registered, along with the serial number and Pin number. This information is required when you are asking for tech support.

Perhaps the most import information to be found in this dialog box appears when you click the button labeled System Info at the upper right. Clicking this button displays the System Info dialog box, shown in Figure 2-10. This dialog box, by default, shows you a list containing complete system information about your computer system. When you click the down arrow of

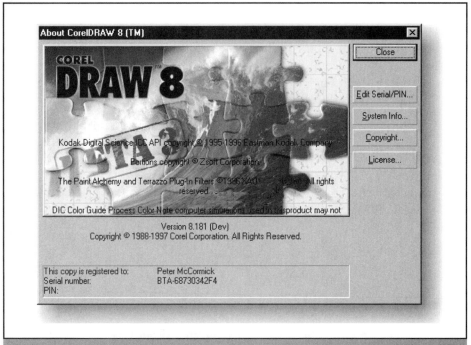

FIGURE 2-9   The About CorelDRAW 8 dialog box

the Choose a Category list box, you can display information about four more areas pertaining to your system and to the CorelDRAW program itself. These include

▶ Your computer's display data

▶ A listing of the printers installed on your system

▶ A complete list of all Corel .exe and .dll files

▶ A complete list of all the System .dll files

This information can be vital in troubleshooting a problem. Bet you didn't know how important this dialog box really was!

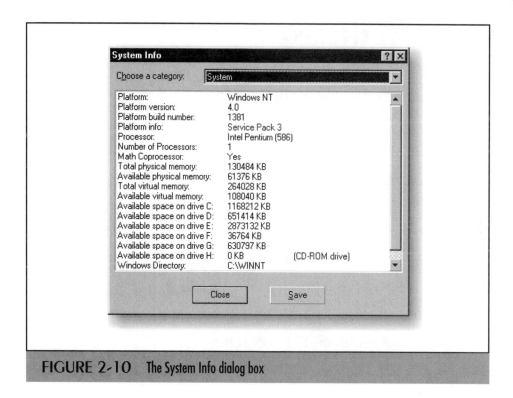

FIGURE 2-10   The System Info dialog box

NEW FEATURES IN CORELDRAW 8

We will end this chapter with a list of the new features that have been included in CorelDRAW 8. Next to each new feature will be the number of the chapter that describes it's use or function.

SHAPE MODIFICATION

► Trim, Intersection, and Weld functions Applied to Groups (Chapter 16)

► Curve Welding (Chapter 8)

► Line Welding with Knife Tool (Chapter 8)

► Drop Shadow (Chapter 20)

INTERACTIVE EFFECTS

► Distortion Tool (Chapter 18)

► Envelope Tool (Chapter 18)

► Extrude Tool (Chapter 18)

► Improved Interactive Blend Tool (Chapter 18)

► Transform Tools (Chapter 7)

OBJECT MANIPULATION

► Move Objects with Drawing Tools (Chapter 4)

► Lock Objects on the Drawing Page (Chapter 7)

► Smart Duplication (Chapter 17)

► Node Editing with the Pick Tool (Chapter 7)

► Accelerated Alignment Using Shortcut Keys (Chapter 17)

► IntelliMouse™ Support (Chapter 12)

► Layers and Object Manager combined into one (Chapter 13)

FILLS AND COLOR

► Interactive Fountain Fills (Chapter 10)

► Color Mixing (Chapter 10)

► Interactive Tints (Chapter 10)

► Interactive Fill Tiling (Chapter 10)

► Palette Editor (Chapter 9)

► Color Harmonies Options (Chapter 9)

► Fill Open Curves (Chapter 40)

2

▶ 49 New Custom Palettes (Chapter 9)

▶ Create a New Palette from an Open Document (Chapter 9)

▶ Create a New Palette from Selected Objects (Chapter 9)

▶ A New Pop-up Palette (Chapter 10)

▶ Fit Text to Frame Command (Chapter 6)

▶ Paragraph Text Linked to Path (Chapter 6)

▶ 3D Text (Chapter 6)

BITMAPS

▶ Bitmap Inflation (Chapter 23)

▶ Duotone Support (Chapter 23)

▶ Working with 3DMF Files (Chapter 23)

UTILITIES

▶ Font Navigator (Chapter 38)

▶ CorelSCAN (Chapter 25)

FILE IMPORT/EXPORT

▶ Improved AI Export Filter (Chapter 27)

▶ Import Option to 3DMF (Chapter 26)

INTERNET FEATURES

▶ Improved .gif Export (Chapter 39)

▶ Improved .jpeg Export (Chapter 39)

▶ Improved Animation (Chapter 39)

▶ Direct Export to HTML (Chapter 39)

Chapter 3 will continue your introduction to CorelDRAW by discussing the menus, standard toolbar, Property Bar, and dialog boxes.

3

USING THE MENUS, STANDARD TOOLBAR, PROPERTY BAR, AND DIALOG BOXES

The CorelDRAW menus, standard toolbar, Property Bar, and dialog boxes are all discussed in this chapter because they share a commonality: each contains tools or commands that allow you to change or modify objects.

MENU BAR

The menu bar, shown in Figure 3-1, is located at the top of the screen, just under the title bar. It is the only one of the various bars in CorelDRAW that you cannot move from its default position on the screen. The menu bar provides 11 default menus. In addition, you can add your own personalized menus to the menu bar (see Chapter 40).

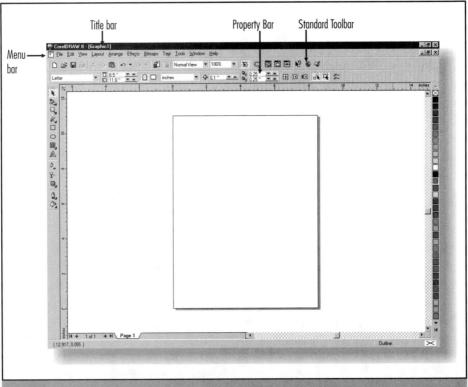

FIGURE 3-1   The CorelDRAW menu bar

When you click a menu, a drop-down menu of commands appears. For example, if you click the Effects menu, the drop-down menu displays all of the available Effects commands. To select a command when the drop-down menu is displayed, you can either use the mouse or simply press the underlined letter in the command name. For example, if you want to open the Object Manager dialog box, you can click the Layout menu and press the letter N. Not all items in the menus have an underlined letter, so this shortcut method is not always available.

You can select many menu items using only shortcut keys. For example if you want to display the blend roll-up discussed in Chapter 20, press ALT-C-B (C is for Effects and B is for Blend). If you are new to shortcut keys, for the shortcut just described you would press and hold the ALT key, then press the C key, and then press the B key. As you become more familiar with the contents of each menu you may find you can work more quickly using the shortcut keys.

You use the three buttons at the far right end of the menu bar in the following manner. If you click the leftmost button, the current graphic is minimized at the bottom of the CorelDRAW window. The middle button toggles between maximizing the screen so it fills the entire CorelDRAW window and reducing the screen to half its original size. The rightmost button closes the current image file.

WINDOWS CONTROL MENU

The Windows control menu is located on the far left end of the menu bar, next to the File menu, and is represented by the Corel balloon icon on a page. The Windows control menu contains the basic Windows commands Restore, Move, Size, Minimize, Maximize, Close, and Next. You can also access this menu by clicking the Corel balloon next to the word "CorelDRAW" on the title bar or by holding down the ALT key and pressing the spacebar.

MENU ACCESS USING A RIGHT MOUSE CLICK

In Windows 95, users can right-click almost anything on the screen and something will happen. CorelDRAW 8 uses this feature extensively. For example, you can right-click to open menus. Figure 3-2 shows the Document

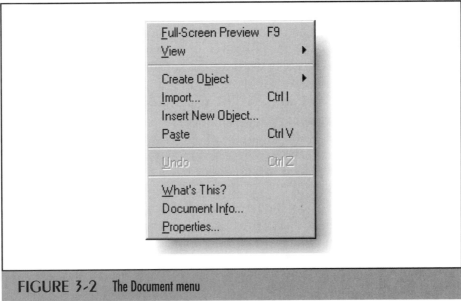

FIGURE 3-2   The Document menu

with nothing selected. Figure 3-3 shows the Object menu displayed when you right-click a group of objects. This menu is context sensitive, so the items it contains will vary depending on the objects selected when you click the mouse; the menu shown in Figure 3-3 appears when a group of objects has been selected.

TOOLBAR MENU

One of the more useful menus is the toolbar menu, which is shown in Figure 3-4. You open it by right-clicking either the standard toolbar, the Property Bar, or the toolbox. This menu lets you choose various toolbars to display on screen. Figure 3-5 shows the Workspace toolbar, which you access from the toolbar menu. The Workspace toolbar offers access to all the other toolbars

3

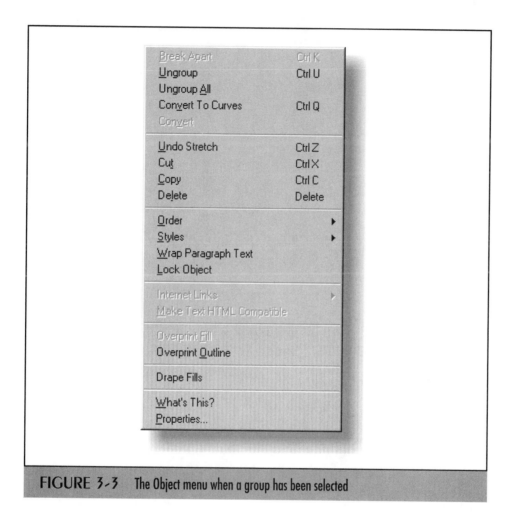

FIGURE 3-3   The Object menu when a group has been selected

and allows you to toggle the various screen elements on and off. For example, if you don't want the rulers displayed, simply click the ruler icon on the Workspace toolbar. Remember, you can dock any extra toolbar underneath existing toolbars or vertically along the sides of the desktop area.

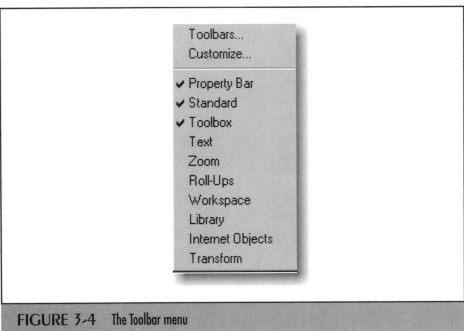

FIGURE 3-4   The Toolbar menu

STANDARD TOOLBAR

The standard toolbar is located just underneath the menu bar (see Figure 3-6). This toolbar includes many shortcut buttons that perform various functions in CorelDRAW. In the center of the toolbar are two list boxes: the View Quality and Zoom list boxes.

FIGURE 3-5   The Workspace toolbar

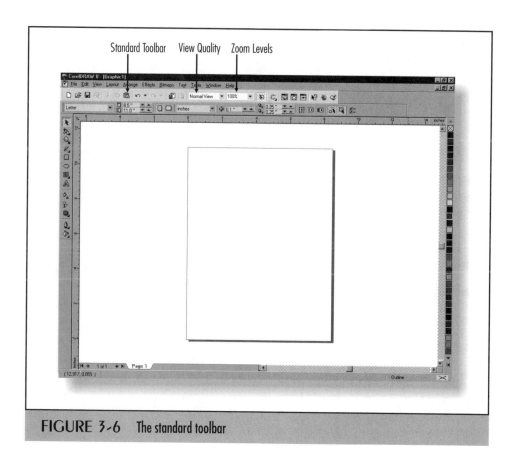

FIGURE 3-6   The standard toolbar

The View Quality list box lets you choose the quality of the active view. Five views are available: the default view, Normal, plus four more, as follows:

▶ *Simple Wireframe* This view shows only basic objects. It does not show fills, extrusions, contours, and blends. Bitmaps appear in monochrome.

▶ *Wireframe* This view does not show fills, but it does show extrusions, contours, and blends. Bitmaps appear in monochrome.

▶ *Draft* This view shows solid fills, and low-resolution texture or bitmap fills. High-resolution bitmap fills, vector fills, Fountain Fills and lenses appear as solid colors. PowerClip contents are hidden.

▶ *Normal*   This view displays all fills except PostScript fills, including high-resolution bitmaps.

▶ *Enhanced*   This view uses 2X oversampling to display a superior image called Supersampling. This is also the only view that displays PostScript fills

The Zoom list box lets you select from 12 different Zoom levels:

▶ To Selected

▶ To Fit

▶ To Page

▶ To Width

▶ To Height

▶ 10%

▶ 25%

▶ 50%

▶ 75%

▶ 100%

▶ 200%

▶ 400%

You can also type in custom zoom levels directly in the Zoom Levels list box. Simply type in a zoom percentage and press the ENTER key. For more information on creating custom zoom levels see Chapter 12.

The standard toolbar is completely customizable, letting you add to or remove the shortcut icons to suit your particular way of working in CorelDRAW. For information on customizing the toolbar, see Chapter 40.

When you hold the cursor over a shortcut icon, a ToolTip appears with a short description of the tool's function. Additional information about the function of the tool appears in the status line at the bottom of the screen.

Table 3-1 lists the default shortcut icons—in the order in which they appear on the toolbar from left to right—and the functions they perform. If an icon is grayed out it is unavailabe in the current context.

Icon	Function
New	Opens a new graphic.
Open	Opens an existing graphic.
Save	Saves the current file you are working on. If the file has never been saved before, the Save As dialog box appears.
Print	Displays the Print dialog box.
Cut	Deletes the selected objects from the screen and puts them on the Clipboard.
Copy	Places the selected objects on the Clipboard without deleting them.
Paste	Places the contents of the clipboard on the CorelDRAW page.
Undo	Reverses the most recent operation.
Undo Multiple actions	Displays an Undo list box allowing you to select the previous actions to undo in the sequence in which they were applied.
Redo	Reverses the most recent Undo operation.
Redo Multiple actions	Displays a Redo list box allowing you to select the previous actions to redo in the sequence in which they were applied.
Import	Opens the Import dialog box.
Export	Opens the Export dialog box.
View Quality list box	See the explanation earlier in this chapter.
Zoom list box	See the explanation earlier in this chapter.
Enable Node Tracking	Enables node editing state when the cursor tracks over nodes when certain drawing tools are in use. This lets you node edit an object without having to select the Shape tool. The tools that will enable an object to function in node editing state are the Pick (Freehand, Bezier, Dimension, and Callout), Rectangle, Ellipse, Polygon, and Spiral. To learn more about this subject see Chapter 7. You can toggle this button on and off to suit the way you work.
Application Launcher	Opens a drop-down list that lets you open another CorelDRAW application or utility.
Scrapbook	Opens the Scrapbook Docker (see Chapter 33).
Symbols Docker	Opens the Symbols Docker (see Chapter 37).

TABLE 3-1   Default Toolbar Icons

Icon	Function
Script and Preset Docker™ Window	Opens the Script and Preset Manager Docker™ window (see Chapter 41 regarding scripts and Chapter 11 regarding presets).
What's This Help	Invokes context-sensitive help by adding a question mark to your cursor. You can then use the cursor to get help information from various parts of the screen and dialog boxes.
CorelTUTOR	Runs the CorelTUTOR program, an interactive program that runs on top of the CorelDRAW window. You select the subject you want to learn about and the CorelTUTOR program guides you through the process of creating the effect or locating the information you need.
Hints	Opens the Hints widow. Its primary purpose is to provide hints on how to use the tools in the toolbox. It is also context sensitive, so when you select a tool you receive a hint on how to use it.

TABLE 3-1   Default Toolbar Icons (*continued*)

PROPERTY BAR

The Property Bar is a context-sensitive command bar. The settings and options available on the bar change depending on the tool or object selected. The Property Bar, shown in Figure 3-7, is located just below the standard toolbar.

The biggest benefit of the Property Bar is that it diminishes the need to use the menu commands or access many of the dialog boxes. As you work in CorelDRAW, you will soon discover the real value of this incredible tool.

Because the Property Bar changes every time you change tools, this chapter doesn't discuss the dozens of possible configurations. The versatility of this toolbar will be apparent as you learn about the commands and effects in the chapters that follow.

DIALOG BOXES

A *dialog box* is a window that appears when CorelDRAW needs additional information before it can perform an action or carry out a command. You can

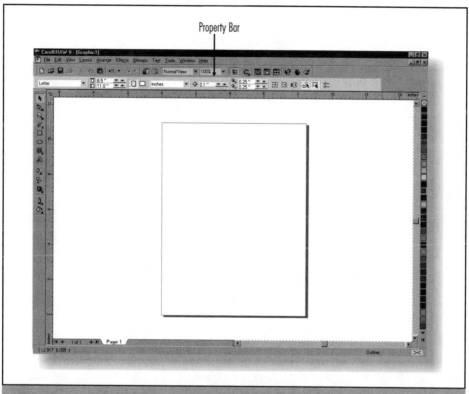

FIGURE 3-7   The Property Bar located under the standard toolbar

navigate through these dialog boxes with either the mouse or the keyboard. Most people find it easier to move around in dialog boxes using the mouse. You simply click a button or check box and then, where applicable, use the appropriate keystrokes to complete the task.

The second way to navigate through dialog boxes is to use the TAB key. When a dialog box is on the screen, pressing TAB cycles through the various radio buttons, check boxes, and so on. When a particular button or parameter box is highlighted, you can use various keys to toggle the item on or off or enter data. Table 3-2 lists the proper keystrokes to use for the various types of items.

Item	Keystrokes
Buttons (OK, Cancel, etc.)	Press the ENTER key to activate.
Radio buttons (choice buttons)	Press the spacebar to toggle on and off.
Check boxes	Press the spacebar to toggle on and off.
Num boxes	Press the UP or DOWN ARROW key to change numbers.
List boxes	Press the UP or DOWN ARROW key to select a name.
Parameter boxes	Type in data.

TABLE 3-2   Keystrokes for Various Types of Dialog Box Items

TABBED DIALOG BOXES

In keeping with Windows 95 and Windows NT conventions, CorelDRAW uses tabbed dialog boxes quite often. The difference between a standard and a tabbed dialog box is that a tabbed dialog box offers a choice of several different dialog boxes. Press CTRL-TAB to highlight the individual tabs or simply click a tab; once you have selected a tab, you can use just the TAB key to move around in the active dialog box. A good example of a tabbed dialog box is the Guidelines Setup dialog box (Layout | Guideline Setup), shown in Figure 3-8.

DOCKER WINDOWS

Docker windows, new to CorelDRAW 8, have replaced many of the dialog boxes and roll-ups used in previous versions of CorelDRAW. Figure 3-9 shows the Script and Preset Manager Docker window. By default, these windows are docked on the right side of the desktop, next to the color palette. You can redock the window elsewhere on the desktop or "tear" it off into a standard dialog box on the desktop, as shown in Figure 3-10. To tear off a Docker window you must drag the top of the window out onto the desktop. You can also redock the dialog box after it's been torn off by dragging it by its title bar to the side of the desktop.

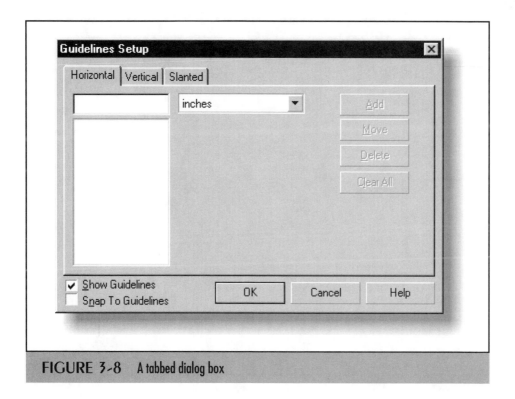

FIGURE 3-8   A tabbed dialog box

You can access all Docker windows but the Scrapbook Docker window found on the standard toolbar by clicking View | Dockers. These windows include

- ► Object Manager
- ► View Manager (CTRL-F2)
- ► Graphic and Text Styles (CTRL-F5)
- ► Color Styles
- ► Symbols (CTRL-F11)
- ► Internet Bookmark Manager
- ► HTML Object Conflict

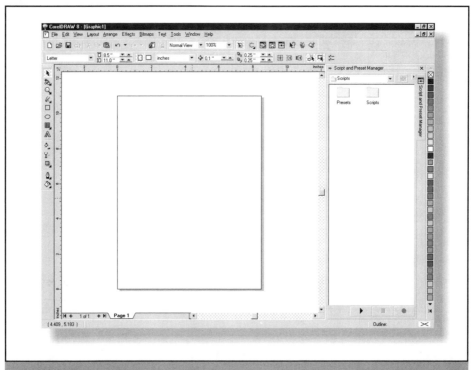

FIGURE 3-9   The Script and Preset Manager Docker window

Script and Preset Manager

► Object Data

► Object Properties

Hopefully, this chapter has given you the knowledge that will help you as you learn how to locate and use the many commands and features contained in the CorelDRAW program. Being able to move within a dialog box or knowing where to look for a certain roll-up or Docker window can make your life an lot easier when you're working in CorelDRAW.

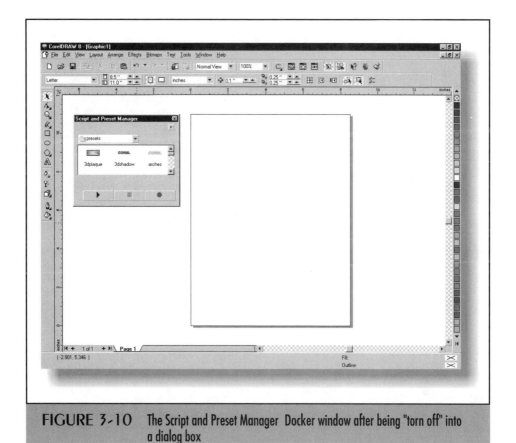

FIGURE 3-10   The Script and Preset Manager Docker window after being "torn off" into a dialog box

The following chapters will teach you how to use the many tools and Effects so you can take advantage of the many features in the program.

4

DRAWING RECTANGLES, ELLIPSES, POLYGONS, STARS, SPIRALS, AND GRAPH PAPER

M ost CorelDRAW users want to create something as fast as possible. Often they will turn to the Freehand tool (see Chapter 5) and be disappointed with the results. This chapter starts with the tools for creating the primitive shapes. As you continue to use the program, you'll find these tools to be much more valuable than you originally thought. Although the primitive shapes may not be that interesting by themselves, you can use them to create many other shapes that are both interesting and useful.

DRAWING RECTANGLES

The rectangle is the most basic of the primitive shapes provided in the toolbox. Plain and simple, it draws rectangles of all shapes and sizes.

Select the Rectangle tool by clicking its icon in the toolbox, by pressing the F6 function key, or by right-clicking the drawing window and choosing Create Object | Rectangle (F6) from the pop-up menu that appears, as shown here.

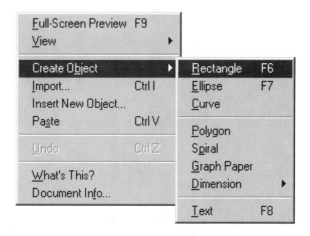

Once the Rectangle tool is selected, your cursor will change into a small crosshair to indicate where the rectangle will be drawn. At the lower-right corner of the crosshair, a small rectangle reminds you which tool is currently selected, as shown here.

To draw a rectangle, simply click where you want to begin a rectangle and drag your mouse (or pen) to the opposite corner. When you release the mouse button, the rectangle will be drawn on the screen. As you draw the rectangle, the Status Bar gives you feedback on the width, height, starting point, ending point, and center point of the rectangle in progress. Once you release the mouse button, the Status Bar indicates that a rectangle is selected and shows its width, height, and center point. Here are examples of the Status Bar while you are drawing a rectangle and after you've finished.

Width: 4.801 Height: 2.197 inches
Start: (1.127 , 10.474) End: (5.929 , 8.277) Center: (3.528, 9.376)

Rectangle on Layer 1
Width: 4.804 Height: 2.212 Center: (3.528 , 9.369) inches

Just drawing rectangles won't garner you any praise as an artist, but you can modify the rectangle in several ways to make it a bit more useful. To do this, you'll need to use the modifier keys: CTRL and SHIFT.

If you hold down the CTRL key while drawing a rectangle, it will be constrained to a perfect square. A good way to remember this is that CTRL means constrain throughout CorelDRAW—for example, if you hold down the CTRL key while drawing an ellipse, it will be constrained to a perfect circle. Holding down the SHIFT key while drawing a rectangle allows you to draw from the center point outward rather than from corner to corner. This approach can be especially handy if you know where the center point should be located. You can also use the modifier keys together to draw squares from the center out. Note that you can change the default behavior of these modifier keys in DRAW 8, as described in Chapter 40. They also work differently by

default on the Macintosh. For Mac users, SHIFT will constrain and Command will draw from the center.

When you've finished drawing a rectangle, it will look something like this.

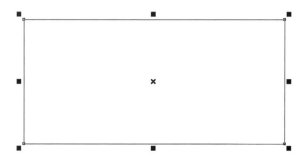

New to CorelDRAW 8 is the X that appears in the center of the object. Grabbing and dragging this X with your cursor allows you to quickly move the object without having to select the Pick tool first. You'll also note that each of the nodes is visible. For those who are new to CorelDRAW, they are the tiny unfilled squares that appear on each corner of the rectangle. You'll learn how these nodes can be useful a little later in this chapter.

ROUNDING THE CORNERS

Magazine reviews have claimed that CorelDRAW doesn't have a tool for drawing rounded rectangles. Clearly those writers haven't read the books on CorelDRAW, as this capability has been in the program since the first version. It is true that there is not a special tool labeled the Rounded Rectangle tool, as in other programs. However, it's easy to draw rounded rectangles by first drawing a rectangle and then rounding the corners. This method actually gives you more control over the final shape.

The original way to round a rectangle's corners is by using the Shape tool. Each corner has one node. Click any of these nodes with the Shape tool and drag away from the corner. All of the corners will become rounded as you drag. The Status Bar indicates the radius of the corner for those who like numerical feedback. When you are done, simply release the mouse button. If the rectangle has been stretched since being originally drawn, the Status Bar will indicate that the corners are "distorted." This means that they won't be perfectly round but, rather, stretched in the same proportions as the rectangle. Using this old method allows you to create a corner radius of an exact amount.

You can also round the corners as one of an object's properties. To bring up the Object Properties dialog box, simply right-click the rectangle with the Pick tool (or the Rectangle tool) and choose Properties from the pop-up menu. A quicker way to access Properties is to use the Windows shortcut key ALT-ENTER while the rectangle is selected.

The Object Properties Docker window contains a tab labeled Rectangle with a single slider on it, as shown here. The slider value can range from 0 to 100. A value of zero indicates that there is no roundness, and a value of 100 indicates that the shortest side of the rectangle will be perfectly round. The slider value is simply a percentage of the shortest side.

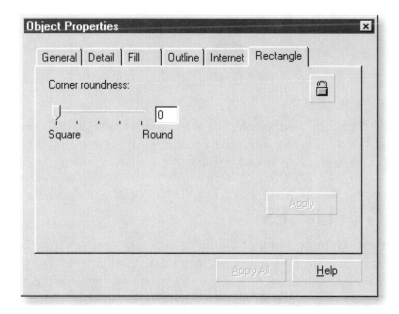

When a rectangle is the active object, the Property Bar has the same slider you saw in the Object Properties dialog box, as shown here. You simply modify the slider on the Property Bar until the roundness is what you want. To the right of the slider is a text box for entering the numerical value. For an exact percentage, simply type the number and press ENTER to make the roundness take effect.

 *There is no way to enter a value for the radius of the corner.*

As we pointed out earlier, there are visible nodes on the rectangle immediately after you draw it. If you move your cursor over one of the nodes while the Rectangle tool is still selected, the cursor changes to this shape.

It will now behave just like the Shape tool. So without changing tools, you can round the corners of the rectangle interactively. This method is certainly faster than those from previous versions.

DRAWING ELLIPSES

The ellipse is the most useful of all the primitive shape tools. You can use it as a starting point for almost any free-form shape imaginable.

When drawing ellipses, you need to understand how their size is determined. You will draw a rectangular shape that is invisible, commonly referred to as the bounding box. The extreme points of the ellipse will be tangent to the midpoint of each side of the invisible bounding box. This sounds a little bit complicated, but after you draw a few ellipses, it will seem very natural.

Select the Ellipse tool by clicking its icon in the toolbox. Alternatively, you can use the F7 shortcut key or right-click the page with the Pick tool and choose Create Object | Ellipse (F7) from the pop-up menu. Note that your cursor will change to the one shown here.

4

Once you've selected the tool, click one corner of the imaginary rectangle and drag to the opposite corner. As you do this, the Status Bar reports the width, height, starting point, ending point, and center point of the ellipse. Release the mouse button to complete the ellipse. The Status Bar will report that you have an ellipse with a certain width, height, and center point. Here are examples of the Status Bar as you are drawing the ellipse and after it is completed.

> Width: 4.138 Height: 2.126 inches
> Start: (1.576 , 10.517) End: (5.714 , 8.390) Center: (3.645, 9.453)

> Ellipse on Layer 1
> Width: 4.141   Height: 2.129   Center: (3.645 , 9.453) inches

As with the Rectangle tool, you can use the modifier keys when drawing ellipses. Holding down the CTRL key constrains the new ellipse to a perfect circle. Holding down the SHIFT key causes the ellipse to be drawn from the center outward. Holding down both keys draws a circle from the center out. Remember to release the mouse button before releasing the modifier key.

As with rectangles, after you've drawn an ellipse, you can move it simply by clicking the X in the middle and dragging it to the desired location.

CREATING PIE WEDGES AND ARCS

Just as there is no rounded rectangle tool, there are no special tools in CorelDRAW for creating arcs and pie wedges. Nevertheless, they are very easy to create with some minor editing of an ellipse.

Each ellipse has one node. The node will be at the top of the ellipse if you drew the ellipse from top to bottom. If you drew the ellipse from the bottom to the top, the node will be at the bottom. To create an arc, select this single node with the Shape tool and drag your cursor around the outside perimeter of the ellipse. To create a pie wedge, drag the node around the inside perimeter of the ellipse. Remember that you can select the node without changing to the Shape tool in CorelDRAW 8. If you hold down the CTRL key while dragging the node, the arc or wedge will be constrained to an angle that is a multiple of the angle you set in the Options dialog box that is described in Chapter 40. This will normally be 15 degrees unless you've changed the default setting. This original way to create arcs and wedges gives you lots of visual feedback, but it is not the quickest way to get the job done, especially if you are trying to create exact angles.

CorelDRAW 6 allowed you to specify the beginning and ending angles, whether to create an arc or a wedge, and the direction in the Object Properties dialog box. The quickest way to access these properties is by selecting the ellipse and pressing ALT-ENTER to select Properties. However, that is still not the quickest way to change the attributes. CorelDRAW 7 made this same information available on the Property Bar any time an ellipse is selected, as shown here. Remember that after you type an angle in the text boxes, you'll need to press the ENTER key to make the changes take effect.

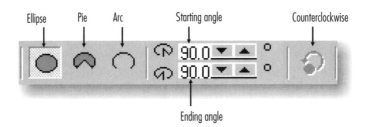

Here are examples of an ellipse, a pie wedge, and an arc.

DRAWING POLYGONS AND STARS

The polygon is the most complex of the primitive shapes included in CorelDRAW. You can choose the number of points or sides it will have, whether it will have flat sides or points, and how those points will be constructed and shaped.

Let's start with the simple polygon. In the default configuration, it has five flat sides. Click the Polygon tool in the toolbox (it is on the Object Flyout shown here), or right-click in the drawing window and choose Create Object | Polygon from the pop-up menu.

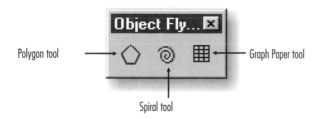

Polygon tool ⟶ ◇   ⟵ Graph Paper tool

Spiral tool

Your cursor will change to reflect that you are drawing a polygon, as shown here.

Now drag out an imaginary rectangle while holding down the left mouse button. You should have a plain old polygon with five sides, as shown here. If you want to constrain the aspect ratio (so the width and height are the same), just use the CTRL modifier key while drawing the polygon. And, yes, the SHIFT key allows you to draw from the center out, as with the other tools.

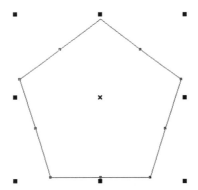

Now that you've seen the basic polygon, you will start changing the attributes. You can do this either before or after you draw the polygon. First you'll change the number of sides. You can change attributes in the Object Properties dialog box or right on the Property Bar, as shown here. Using the Property Bar is by far the easiest method. Type the number 8 in the text box just to the right of the star and press ENTER. The polygon will change into an octagon (like a stop sign). If you're having trouble seeing this shape, just color it red and it should look more familiar. For those who like to push the limits, you can create polygons with as many as 500 sides.

Lowering the number of sides to 3 allows you to easily draw triangles.

Number of points on polygon

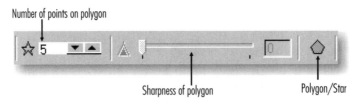

Sharpness of polygon   Polygon/Star

If you change these values while no object is selected, you automatically change the default values.

If you'd rather create a star, simply click the Polygon/Star button on the Property Bar. If you have a polygon selected, the icon will be a polygon. Click once, and the icon will change into a star—as will the polygon you had selected. Notice that inside of the star are construction lines. If you want a star without these lines, you can use another method that will be described a little later in this chapter.

Just to the left of the Polygon/Star button is a slider that controls the sharpness of the points in stars. If you still have only five points in your star, you'll notice that this slider is dimmed. It becomes undimmed when the selected star has at least seven points. If the star has seven points, you can set the sharpness to either 1 or 2. As the number of points increases, the number of sharpness levels also increases, as this number specifies the number of points in between the points that are joined. Basically, the higher the sharpness level, the more pointy your star will be. Here are two 12-pointed stars. The left star has a sharpness level of 1 and the right one has a sharpness level of 4.

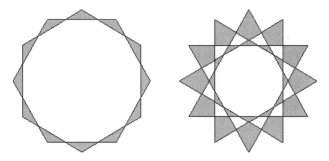

By now, you can see that the Polygon tool can create the shapes you always tried to create with a Spirograph as a child. However, the really interesting behavior of the Polygon tool becomes apparent when you edit the polygon with the Shape tool. You'll learn the basics in this chapter, and in Chapter 8 you'll learn some really awesome techniques.

When you draw a polygon, it has a single node where each of the sides meet and another node in the middle of each side. Thus, the standard five-sided polygon has ten nodes. When you move one node, all the other "similar" nodes move by the same amount. Moving the node in the center of the polygon's side therefore affects the nodes in the middle of the other sides.

With the Polygon tool still selected, click one of the nodes. Move it toward the center of the polygon and watch how the other nodes behave the same way. Now rotate the nodes counterclockwise inside of the polygon. Again the other nodes do the same. You'll see that the simple polygon has now become much more interesting (or at least more intricate) than the original. As you move the nodes, you might notice a very light outline of the original polygon.

This is the bounding box and its display is new to CorelDRAW 8. Don't worry; it is just visual feedback and will not print. Holding down the CTRL key constrains the movement of the nodes so they can only be moved closer or farther from the center of the polygon. One of the side effects of this behavior in polygon editing is the time you will spend just playing with the many cool shapes that you can create—and the more points to the polygon, the more nodes you have to manipulate! If you finish by filling the modified polygon, it becomes even more interesting.

 *Because it is quite easy to draw a polygon with many overlapping paths, you can run into problems with complexity when printing. Chapter 29 describes various ways to decrease the complexity of a drawing.*

DRAWING SPIRALS

When spirals were first introduced in CorelDRAW 6, they seemed pretty neat, but it was difficult to find a use for them. Their behavior was enhanced greatly in CorelDRAW 7, and there are some really interesting ways to use them in your projects.

The Spiral tool is the middle of the three tools on the Object Flyout. When you select the Spiral tool, your cursor changes into the one shown here.

Before drawing your spiral, make sure to change the settings on the Property Bar, shown here, to your desired settings. Spirals are elliptical in shape, so drawing them is similar to drawing an ellipse. Drag from one corner of the imaginary box to the opposite corner. As you draw, the Status Bar reports the width and height of the spiral. If you wish to constrain the width and height so they are the same, simply hold down the CTRL key as you draw the spiral. Of course, the SHIFT key allows you to draw from the center outward. Note that if you have a slow system, it may be nearly impossible for you to use these modifier keys because of the irregular redrawing of the screen.

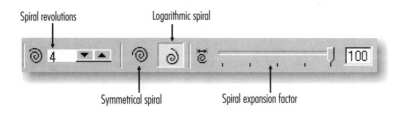

Spiral revolutions   Logarithmic spiral

Symmetrical spiral   Spiral expansion factor

In CorelDRAW 6, the only control you had over spirals was the number of rotations. This setting still exists, and you can specify anything from a single rotation to 100 rotations. Changing the number of rotations only affects new spirals, not spirals that you've already drawn.

Next to the number of rotations on the Property Bar are two buttons for defining the type of spiral. The default is a symmetrical spiral, and this is the only choice you had in CorelDRAW 6. Each rotation of a symmetrical spiral is spaced evenly from the previous rotation. The button on the right allows you to create a logarithmic spiral. Each rotation of a logarithmic spiral is increasingly farther away from the previous rotation. The rate at which the rotation increases is based on the spiral expansion factor, which you control by using the slider just to the right of the Logarithmic Spiral button.

There are no special editing properties associated with spirals. However, you can do some interesting things with spirals and the Shape tool, as described in Chapter 8.

CREATING GRAPH PAPER

The Graph Paper tool actually creates a grid of a specified number of rows and columns. You can access the tool by selecting its icon from the Object Flyout or by right-clicking your drawing and choosing Create Object Graph Paper from the pop-up menu. After you've selected the Graph Paper tool, your cursor will change into the one shown here.

Before drawing the grid, you need to set the number of rows and columns that you want. You can easily do this on the Property Bar, as shown here; the maximum number of rows or columns is 50. Then simply drag out a rectangle, just as you've done with the Rectangle tool. Within that rectangle will appear a grid containing the exact number of rows and columns you specified. Note that the Status Bar will say that you have a group of objects. That is because the Graph Paper tool is nothing more than an automated way to draw a group of rectangles.

Graph Paper columns

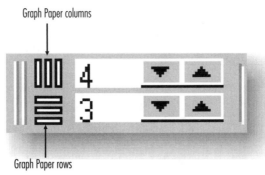

Graph Paper rows

Once you've drawn the grid, you cannot change the number of rows or columns without deleting the entire grid and starting over. If you want to work with the individual rectangles, you'll need to ungroup them, as described in Chapter 15. At that point, each cell in the grid will be a separate rectangle and will behave just like any other rectangle you draw.

5

DRAWING LINES OF ALL SHAPES AND SIZES

In the previous chapter you learned how to create various shapes. This chapter explains how you can create your own freehand shapes from scratch. Many users gravitate to the Freehand tool as the obvious way to draw, but if you don't understand exactly how it works it can be rather frustrating. You'll also find that your skills will be hampered if you choose to draw with a brick on a string or a billiard ball (a mouse or trackball). Using a graphics tablet will give you much greater control over the shapes you create, and it is, essentially, the only way to take advantage of the Natural Pen tool.

Activate any of the tools on the Curve flyout, shown here, by pressing the F5 key. The tool selected on the flyout will be the last tool used. There is no shortcut to get to any of the individual tools.

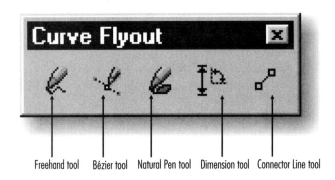

Freehand tool   Bézier tool   Natural Pen tool   Dimension tool   Connector Line tool

FREEHAND TOOL

The Freehand tool works very much like a pencil. When you drag, a line will follow your cursor. If you've had too much coffee to drink, the line will show the shakiness in your hand. It's extremely difficult to draw smooth lines without using a graphics tablet because of the inaccuracy of a mouse. And if you really want to drive yourself nuts, try to draw with the little red eraser tip found on laptops! When you select the Freehand tool, your cursor will look like this.

As you draw, CorelDRAW adds nodes at various intervals along the line. The technical details of nodes are described fully in Chapter 8. But for now you should understand that fewer nodes along the curve are usually good. There are exceptions to this rule, but a curve with more nodes is less smooth because each node adds another point of inflection. How closely the line tracks your movement is also controlled by the Freehand tool settings, which are discussed further in Chapter 40. As you draw a line, the Status Bar shows the start and end point of the line. After you complete the curve, the number of nodes will be displayed, as shown here.

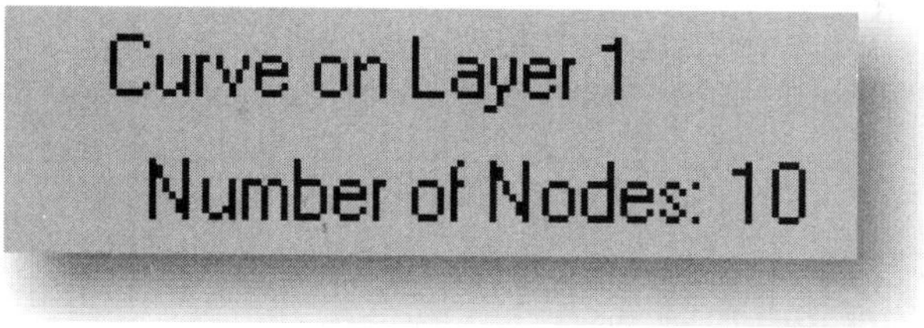

> Curve on Layer 1
> Number of Nodes: 10

Hold down the SHIFT *key while drawing a line and you can backtrack to erase part of the line. Once you release the* SHIFT *key, you can resume drawing.*

You create straight lines in a slightly different way. Instead of dragging, you click at the start of the line, move your cursor to the end of the line, and then click again. This generates a straight line between those two points. Many users want perfectly horizontal or vertical lines and mistakenly call them straight lines. You create such lines in the same manner, except that you hold down the CTRL key before and during the second click. This constrains the line to a multiple of the constrain angle set in the Options dialog box, which is discussed fully in Chapter 40.

You can also switch between drawing a curved line and a straight line. Begin drawing the line freehand and when you get to the place where the straight line should begin, just press the TAB key. The straight line will end when you either release the left mouse button or press the TAB key again. If you press the TAB key to end the straight line, you will still be drawing with a freehand line.

AUTO-TRACING BITMAPS

If you have imported a bitmap into your drawing, it is quite easy to convert it into a vector drawing. First, select the bitmap with the Pick tool and then activate the Freehand tool. The Status Bar will indicate that you are auto-tracing. Click the Freehand tool just outside of the shape you want auto-traced and a vectorized version of it will soon appear. This functionality is intended for simple line art and not photographs. In addition, the quality of the resulting vector shape leaves a lot to be desired and will require some clean-up work. To completely vectorize an image, you may need to click several areas on the bitmap until all lines have been created. Figure 5-1 shows a scanned image and its vectorized counterpart side by side so that you can see the difference.

> *So that it is easier to see the lines created by auto-tracing, you may want to change the color of the "black" part of the bitmap. Right-click a color swatch on the palette while the bitmap is selected and you can change the color.*

There are other ways to trace bitmap artwork. In many instances, re-creating the artwork can work much better. Another way is to use the OCR-Trace program that is included in the CorelDRAW suite. See the online help for more information on how to use OCR-Trace to convert your images from bitmap to vector form.

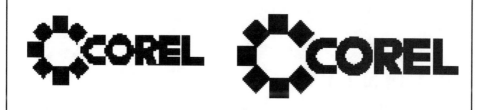

FIGURE 5-1   On the left is some scanned artwork and on the right is a vectorized version of it

BÉZIER TOOL

The first time you use the Bézier tool, you might think it is difficult to understand. This tool definitely takes a little practice to master, but the benefits are worth it. The Bézier tool gives you the most control over the shaping of a curve while drawing. Each time you click, it creates a node and connects the node with the previous node. But by clicking and dragging, you can shape the curve entering the node. This technique will make more sense after you've completed Chapter 8 on shaping objects. But you are actually moving the bézier control handle of the node when you click and drag. It is what controls the angle of the line entering and exiting the node. To change the last node to a cusp node, just press C. In fact, you can hold down the C key while drawing and all the nodes will be cusps. When you are finished drawing the line, either press the SPACEBAR or select another tool.

You can move any of the nodes created previously while the Bézier tool is still creating a line. Just move the cursor over the node until it changes into the Interactive Shape cursor and edit away.

One area where the Bézier tool really shines is in the manual tracing of bitmaps. Earlier you saw how crude CorelDRAW's built-in auto-tracing features are. But by using the Bézier tool and adding nodes at each inflection point on a curve, you can quickly and accurately re-create the scanned artwork. Although it may seem to take longer to do it manually, it is almost always quicker than auto-tracing and then cleaning up the mess of extra nodes

that CorelDRAW created. Even if you don't shape the curves as you create the nodes, you can place them quickly and then use the Shape tool to modify them later.

NATURAL PEN TOOL

Those of you who've had a few versions of CorelDRAW may now have noticed that PowerLines have disappeared. The Natural Pen tool has taken their place. PowerLines never did seem to work as desired because they created a large number of objects with an overwhelming number of nodes. This approach allowed you to change the line dynamically.

The Natural Pen tool doesn't allow you to change the line dynamically and to apply presets to an existing line, but the shapes it creates are much easier to work with since they are all single objects that contain a reasonable number of nodes.

When you select the Natural Pen tool from the Curve flyout, the Property Bar changes to one similar to the one shown here.

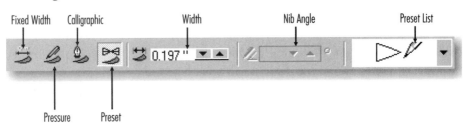

The first four buttons allow you to select which type of pen you would like to use. Choices include Fixed Width, Pressure, Calligraphic, and Preset. Each of these pen types are discussed in detail a little later in the chapter.

Just to the right of the buttons is a parameter box that gives the maximum width of the line (or shape) being created. This value is used in different ways, depending on which type of pen you are using. The next parameter box contains the Nib Angle options. It is only available when you have the calligraphic pen selected. In all other cases it is grayed out. On the far right is a drop-down of the various available presets. This is only available when the preset pen type is selected.

GRAPHICS TABLETS

To get the most out of the Natural Pen tool, you need a graphics tablet. You can create some of the effects without one, but you can't easily simulate the Pressure effect.

Tablets are something that we've been recommending for years. Sure, they cost more than a standard mouse, but they also deliver much more in terms of accuracy. Obviously, using a pen to draw is much more natural than a bar of soap. It is something that you've used your whole life, so you can create lines that are much smoother than those drawn with a mouse.

Tablets are also better for you ergonomically. They decrease your chances of getting Carpal Tunnel Syndrome, which is commonly attributed to using a mouse. The savings in health costs alone can make the tablet a very worthwhile addition.

Most tablet manufacturers offer tablets in three sizes of interest to graphic designers. The smallest tablet is usually in the neighborhood of 4"×5" and is also the cheapest at less than $150. Many users are attracted by the price, but you do get what you pay for. A bit larger is the 6"×8" tablet. This one gives you much more room to work with, and you can commonly find these tablets for under $300. Lastly, there are the 12"×12" tablets. If you are tracing artwork from a full 8.5"×11" page, these tablets can be useful. But most CorelDRAW users will find that the 6"×8" size is optimal.

Tablets all have at least two buttons, just like a mouse. The "left mouse button" is typically the tip of the pen. Pressing down on the tip is the same as left-clicking with a mouse. Nowadays, the tips measure the amount of pressure you use when drawing. This information is used by almost all paint programs, including PHOTO-PAINT, and also by the Pressure Natural Pen type. The "right mouse button" is found on the barrel of the pen. This you press with your finger. Many pens have another button on the barrel that you can program for a double-click. This feature is especially handy since it can be difficult to tap the tip twice in the same place. The latest trend is to add an "eraser" to the other end of the pen. Turn the pen over and this "tip" will

truly act as an eraser in CorelDRAW. In Corel PHOTO-PAINT, you can program it to activate the tool of your choice.

So, next time you have a little extra money for computer "toys," put a graphics tablet at the top of your list and you won't be disappointed.

FIXED WIDTH

Selecting the Fixed Width pen allows you to create shapes that twist and turn, but are always the exact width you specify in the Natural Pen Width parameter box. After you draw a "line," it will automatically change into a two-dimensional shape. You can edit this shape with the Shape tool, but you can't manipulate it as a line. Here is an example of a fixed width line.

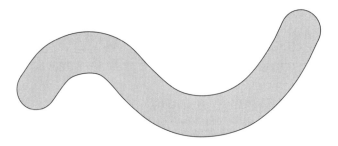

Like the Freehand tool, the Natural Pen tool lets you draw straight lines by double-clicking at the beginning and clicking at the end of the line instead of dragging. Holding down CTRL constrains the line to 15 degree increments and the TAB key allows you to toggle between freehand lines and straight lines.

PRESSURE

Drawing pressure lines requires a graphics tablet. Yes, you can draw them with a mouse, but since there is no pressure, the line will have a minimum amount of width to start. You can use the UP ARROW and DOWN ARROW keys on your keyboard to increase and decrease pressure as you draw with the mouse. The Natural Pen width will be used as the width of the line when the maximum pressure is applied. If you apply less pressure, the line will be thinner. Here is an example of a pressure line.

CALLIGRAPHIC

With the Calligraphic pen, you control the thickness of the line by the angle of the line you draw in relation to the nib angle that has been set on the Property Bar. When you draw perpendicular to the nib angle, the line will be at the maximum thickness specified by the pen width on the Property Bar. Lines drawn at the nib angle will have little or no thickness. The line will get thicker as the angle of the line drawn gets farther from the nib angle. An example of the Calligraphic pen is shown here.

PRESET

The Preset pen allows you to choose a preset shape from the drop-down list shown here.

So, as an example, the first shape is triangular. This means that the beginning of the line you draw will be the maximum width and the end will have no width. In between these two points, it will evenly get thinner. As you draw the line, this will be hard to understand because the display will show the full width until you release the left mouse button. Here are two different examples of preset lines.

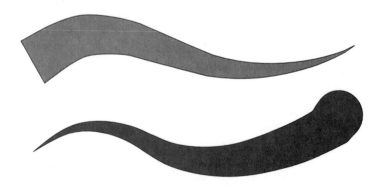

DIMENSION TOOL

When you select the Dimension tool from the Curve flyout, you can actually create several types of dimensions. The Property Bar has a series of icons for each of the dimension types, as shown here.

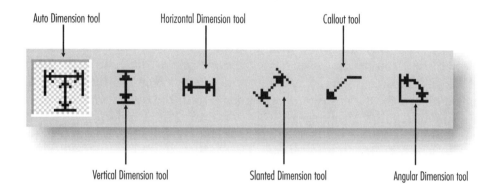

Auto Dimension tool   Horizontal Dimension tool   Callout tool

Vertical Dimension tool   Slanted Dimension tool   Angular Dimension tool

Most of the time, you'll want to link a dimension line with another object. By selecting Layout | Snap to Objects, you activate the linking. By default, it is automatically selected when you choose the Dimension tool. If Snap to Objects has been previously activated, then there is no need to select it again. With auto, vertical, horizontal, and slanted dimension lines, three clicks are required to complete the line. The first left mouse click is where the line begins measuring. Next, click where the line ends measuring. Finally, click where you would like the text of the measurement. Here is an example dimension line.

 *If you use an inappropriate dimension line type, the amount may be zero. As an example, if you use the vertical dimension line to measure the width of an object, it will display zero since there is no change in the vertical direction. The new Auto Dimension tool is a way to avoid this problem. It can draw either Vertical, Horizontal or Slanted based on your mouse movement. You can also press the TAB key to toggle between the three states.*

Once a dimension line has been drawn, you can't modify it by selecting the line itself. You can, however, move the text closer or farther from the linked object and the dimension line will adjust automatically. Also, if you resize the linked object, the dimension line will update to fit the object and change the measurement value. To change the font of the text, simply select it and change it just like any other text.

 *Dimension Text uses the properties of default Artistic Text.*

When the dimension line is selected, you can make several changes to the way the measurement is represented. The Property Bar will include several drop-down lists and buttons, as shown here.

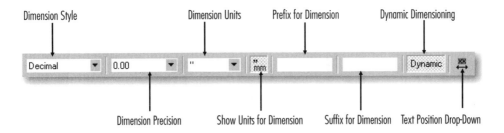

The Dimension Style drop-down lets you choose between Decimal, Fractional, US Engineering, and US Architecture. Decimal represents the amount as a whole number followed by a decimal point and up to ten significant digits. The number of significant digits is selected from the Precision drop-down list. Fractional represents the amount as a whole number followed by a fraction that can have a precision to 1/1024 of a unit that is specified in the Precision drop-down list. US Engineering shows the amount in feet and inches with a precision of up to ten decimal places on the inches. No matter what unit is selected, US Engineering is always measured in feet and inches. US Architecture is similar in that it shows feet and fractional inches. The precision can be as small as 1/1024 of an inch.

The Dimension Units drop-down list allows you to choose any of the units that are available in CorelDRAW. Several of the units are available in more than one form. For example, inches can be represented with the double-tick symbol, the abbreviation "in," or "inches." Remember that you cannot specify units if you've chosen US Engineering or US Architecture for the style.

At times you will not want the units to be displayed. If so, simply deselect the Show Units for Dimension button. When the Dynamic Dimensioning button is selected, the amount shown as part of the dimension line will change any time you resize the dimension line. If you want the amount to remain static, deselect the Dynamic Dimensioning button. You can place text before or after the dimension by typing text in the Prefix for Dimension and Suffix for Dimension boxes. Note that if you want space between the text and the amount, you must add it manually. Lastly, you can control the position of the text relative to the dimension line through the options in the Text Position drop-down list shown here.

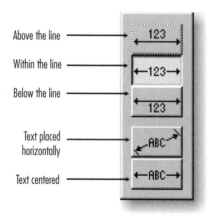

Above the line

Within the line

Below the line

Text placed horizontally

Text centered

If you want to show a unit abbreviation other than one listed, turn off Show Units for Dimension and type your own abbreviation in the Suffix for Dimension box.

ANGULAR DIMENSION

The main difference between angular dimensions and the others is that they require four distinct clicks rather than three. The first click is at the origin of the angle, the second click at the starting point, the third click at the ending point, and the last click where the text should appear. The Units drop-down will only allow degrees, radians, and gradians since the other units don't apply to measuring angles. Here is an example of an angular dimension.

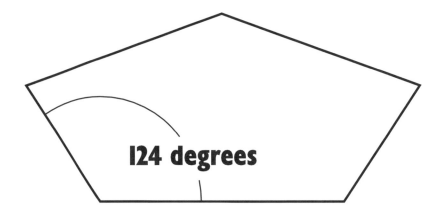

CALLOUTS

Callouts are not dimension lines. It's unclear why they are located on the Dimension Property Bar rather than the Curve flyout, which just makes them hard to find. They do require three clicks just like dimension lines, though. The first click should be near the point that the callout will reference. This end quite often will have an arrow added. The second click creates an elbow in the line if it is a single click. Double-clicking for the second click will leave the line as straight rather than having an elbow. The third click or the previous double-click produces a text cursor for the description of the callout. Callouts automatically link the line and the text so that they move together. You can format the text and line just as you would format any other lines and text. Here is an example of a callout.

We are here!

ARIZONA

 *Callouts can be dynamically linked to an object if Snap to Objects is selected when they are drawn. So if you move the object to which the callout is linked, the callout line will update as well.*

5

CONNECTOR LINE TOOL

The Connector Line tool is at the end of the Curve flyout. You use it to draw a line between two objects that dynamically changes when either or both of the objects are moved. When the tool is selected, Snap to Objects is activated automatically, without having to be selected. The line will snap to any of the nodes on a nearby object. If you click away from any objects, you will simply draw a straight line. Once you've connected two objects, you can specify whether the line is to be locked to the initial node you clicked or whether it can float freely to the closest node to the connected object. To control this, simply select or deselect the Lock to Connector Node button on the Property Bar shown here.

Connector lines are especially useful when drawing a flow chart or organization chart that changes frequently. Simply moving one of the boxes will automatically move the lines. Here is an example of a drawing with connector lines.

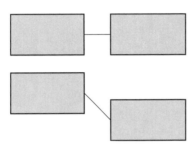

Each of the tools on the Curve flyout allows you to create some form of line. Some of these lines are free-form lines, some have a "thickness," and some are associated with a measurement. Most of the time you will be using either the Freehand tool or the Bézier tool to create a free-form shape. The other tools each are used under special circumstances.

6

CREATING AND MANIPULATING TEXT

The Text tool was changed in CorelDRAW 7 so that it behaves as it did in CorelDRAW 3. Gone are the two separate tools for Artistic and Paragraph Text. No longer are the Symbols accessed through the Text tool; they are now accessible from the View | Dockers menu instead.

ARTISTIC TEXT

Artistic Text is used when you have a short block of text that will have a special effect applied. Quite often you will use it without applying special effects, but you must first have Artistic Text before even attempting most effects. You can have no more than 32,000 characters in a single block of Artistic Text. Older versions of CorelDRAW had a 250-character limit on text blocks that could receive an effect. That limit is gone, but remember that the longer the block, the more time consuming the effect will be to implement.

CREATING ARTISTIC TEXT

To create a block of Artistic Text, you first need to select the Text tool from the toolbox or right-click the drawing window and choose Create Object | Text from the pop-up menu. An even quicker way to select the Text tool is with the F8 shortcut key.

Once the Text tool is selected, click anywhere in the drawing window and begin typing. By default, the text is 24-point Avant Garde Bk BT. As you type, the text will not automatically wrap to the next line. If you want a new paragraph or line, you must press the ENTER key.

You can change the default font for the current document by changing the font name and size on the Property Bar when no text object is selected. After you select the new attributes, you will be presented with the Text Attributes dialog box, shown here, asking whether the change applies to Artistic Text, Paragraph Text, or both.

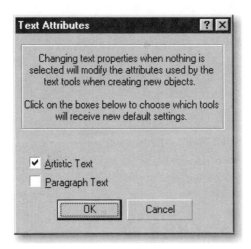

 *You can also change the default font in the Tools | Options dialog box as described in Chapter 40.*

6

Artistic Text behaves like any other graphical object. It can be stretched, mirrored, rotated, extruded, contoured, and placed on a path. If you wish to directly edit the shapes of text characters, you need to convert the text to curves. You can also break apart and arrange blocks of Artistic Text. You can use Arrange | Break Apart (CTRL-K) to make each line of text a separate object. If you apply this command to a single line of text, each word will become a separate object. This can all be very handy when converting text blocks to curves to ensure that they do not become too complex. If you wish to put separate lines of text together, simply use the Arrange | Combine (CTRL-L) command. This will place the text in a single block, with the first block selected being the top line in the block. And separate words can be combined into a line of text.

 *When converting text to curves, do not allow any object to exceed 500 nodes. Doing so can lead to serious printing problems.*

If you wish to edit the text, you can simply click with the Text tool anywhere within the text block, and a cursor will appear. If you'd rather edit the text in a dialog box, choose Text | Edit Text or use the CTRL-SHIFT-T shortcut key. Often it is easier to edit the text within the dialog box because it will automatically wrap the lines for editing purposes; for tiny text using the dialog box is a must, since the text will always be presented in a readable size in the correct font. An example of Artistic Text on screen is shown here.

Artistic Text

ARTISTIC TEXT ATTRIBUTES

You can change the attributes of Artistic Text in two places: the Property Bar and the Format Text dialog box. Not all of the attributes are available on the Property Bar, so this chapter discusses the procedures for using the Format Text dialog box. In many instances, however, when an attribute is available, it is much quicker to use the Property Bar. You access the Format Text dialog box by choosing Text | Format Text (CTRL-T).

If you select the text with the Pick tool, all formatting changes will apply to the whole block of text. You can also select individual characters with either the Shape tool or the Text tool. Both tools allow you to change the attributes of only the selected characters.

A nice change to the Format Text dialog box in CorelDRAW 8 is that it is modeless. This means that you can continue working with text objects on screen while the dialog box is active. You could then easily apply formatting changes to separate text objects or even separate characters within a text block. In addition to the OK button, there is now an Apply button to use in these instances.

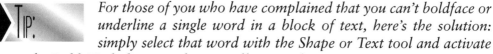

For those of you who have complained that you can't boldface or underline a single word in a block of text, here's the solution: simply select that word with the Shape or Text tool and activate the Bold, Underline, or whatever effect you desire.

FONT

The first tab in the Format Text dialog box is the Font tab, as shown in Figure 6-1. The left side of the dialog box presents a drop-down list of all available fonts. PostScript fonts are preceded by a T1 symbol, and TrueType fonts are preceded by a TT symbol. If the icons are dimmed, the font has been temporarily installed by Font Navigator (see Chapter 38). Just above the list of fonts is the name of the currently selected font. You can manually type in a name. With each letter that you type, you are moved down the list to the first font that matches. For instance, if you're looking for Zapf Dingbats, simply type the Z, and you'll be moved to the first font that begins with the

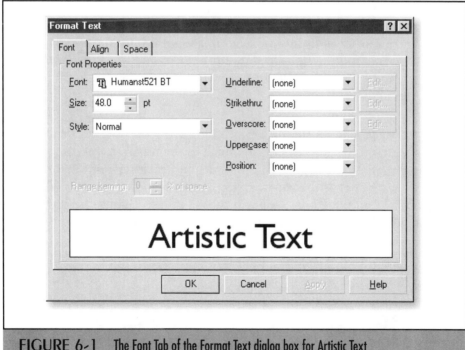

FIGURE 6-1   The Font Tab of the Format Text dialog box for Artistic Text

letter Z. Then use the mouse to click the desired font. The typing method just makes it easier to get to fonts farther down the list. Note that a preview of the chosen font is shown at the bottom of the dialog box.

Below the Font is the Size spin box. Font sizes by default are shown in points. The up arrow increases the value by 1 point, and the down arrow decreases it by 1 point. The smallest point size possible is .001 point, and the largest is 3,000 points.

The next value is the font's weight. Up to four values are available in the Style list, depending on the font chosen. Only weights that exist will be shown, unlike in word processing programs, where the program will "fake" a bold or italic weight. The four possible weights are Normal, Italic, Bold, and Bold Italic. These names are based upon attributes set within the font rather than the font's actual name.

 *The weight names are always reported as Normal, Italic, Bold, and Bold Italic even though this nomenclature is not correct for many fonts. Although this may seem to be just an irritation, it can lead to problems when exporting files to other programs that work with the correct font names.*

On the right side of the dialog box are three drop-down lists labeled Underline, Strikethru, and Overscore. Each of them has an option for Single Thin, Single Thick, or Double Thin outline, and each type of outline can be applied to just words or to the whole text block (including spaces). When you choose any of the ruling lines, you can choose Edit to change the appearance of the lines in the Edit Underline dialog box shown here.

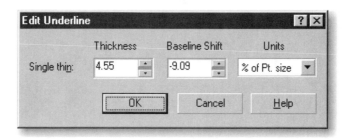

The Thickness and Baseline Shift values are originally a percentage of the font's point size, but they can also be specified in specific points using the Units drop-down list.

Below the three types of lines is the Uppercase drop-down list. By default, it is set to none. But you can change it to either Small Caps or All Caps. The nice thing about using the two different features for converting the text to capital letters is that they are just effects and not permanent changes to the text itself. To make the conversion permanent, you can use the Text | Change Case command discussed later in this chapter.

The Position selection for a font allows you to make the selected text a superscript or subscript. In most instances, you will use these options only when you have selected characters within a text block rather than the text block as a whole. Note that there is no way to customize the percentage of these effects in relation to the rest of the text.

Alignment

When you select the Align tab, six types of alignment are available for Artistic Text, as shown in Figure 6-2. The default alignment is None. This selection does exactly what is says: nothing. Many people assume it is the same as left justification, but it is not. When you have None selected, you can use the Shape tool to move individual characters past the left margin of the text block. Left alignment justifies everything to the left margin, leaving the right edge ragged. Center alignment centers all of the text. Initially, the centering will be relative to where the text cursor was first clicked in the drawing window. As you move the center-aligned text, however, it will be relative to the center of the text block. Right alignment justifies everything to the right margin, leaving the left edge ragged. Again, the initial alignment is relative to where the text cursor was first clicked in the drawing window.

Full justify justifies both the left and right edges of the text. If the last line is only one word, that word will remain just left justified. Unfortunately, this format looks really strange when two words are fully justified with a huge white area between them. Use this form of alignment with great caution. Force justify takes full justification one step further: it forces everything to be justified to both left and right margins. So if only one word appears on a line, a lot of space will be added between characters to justify the word to both the left and right margins. Again, use this option with great caution.

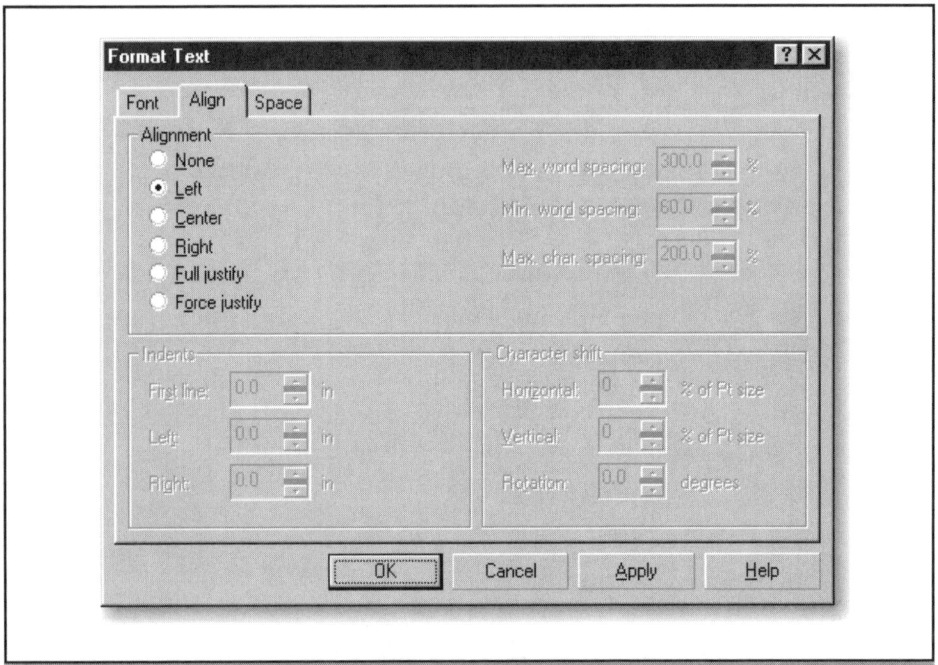

FIGURE 6-2 The Format Text dialog box with the Align tab selected

When you select individual characters within a text block using either the Shape or Text tool before or while accessing the Align tab of the Format Text dialog box, extra controls will be available, as shown in Figure 6-3. These extra controls are described next.

You can control the character shift of the selected characters by moving them a certain percentage in either the Horizontal or the Vertical direction. By character shift, we are referring to the amount that a character is moved above or below the normal baseline for text. These characters can also be rotated individually.

Spacing

The Space tab of the Format Text dialog box, shown in Figure 6-4, is used to control text spacing and alignment. With Artistic Text, you have three spacing

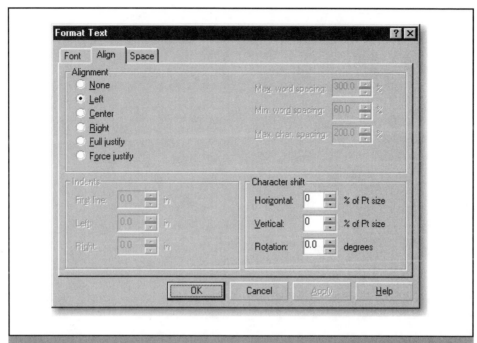

FIGURE 6-3   The Align tab of the Format Text dialog box for selected characters

controls: Chara**ct**er, **W**ord, and **L**ine. Character spacing is measured as a percentage of the space taken up by the space character in the font. By default, it is set to zero so that no extra space is added between characters. By clicking the spin arrows, you can increase or decrease the value by 1 percentage point; you can also simply type a value. Word spacing is measured in the same way, but since you generally want a full space between words, this value defaults to 100 percent.

Line spacing by default is measured as a percentage of the character height. You can also measure line spacing in points or as a percentage of the point size. Plain and simple, the default selection is probably the worst way to measure line spacing. Line spacing (or leading) traditionally is measured in points. Typically, spacing is the font size plus two points. Thus, for 10-point text, the leading would be 12 points. For point sizes over about 24 points, the point size itself tends to work fine as the line spacing measure; in fact, you

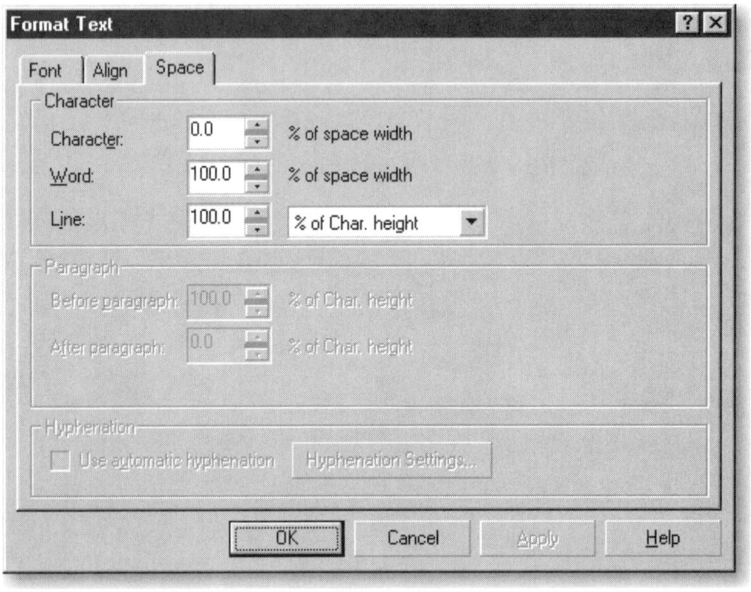

FIGURE 6-4   The Format Text dialog box with the Space tab displayed

may even want the leading to be less than the point size. It is a good habit to start measuring text in points if you do not already do so. You can make that your default selection if you select Points in this dialog box when no text is selected and then save that as your default font, as previously described.

PARAGRAPH TEXT

Paragraph Text is used for larger blocks of text that contain multiple paragraphs, multiple columns, or multiple frames. Because its purpose is to handle long blocks of text, only the enveloping effect can be applied to Paragraph Text. Each paragraph of text can have up to 32,000 characters. Each frame of Paragraph Text can contain up to 32,000 paragraphs, and up to 32,000 frames can be linked together. If you need that much text, you sure as heck shouldn't be using CorelDRAW for that particular project! For projects of that size, we highly recommend that you use CorelVentura.

CREATING PARAGRAPH TEXT

Since there is now only one Text tool in CorelDRAW, you need to actually draw the Paragraph Text frame. Select the Text tool as described earlier in this chapter. Use the text cursor to drag out a marquee box that is the size of the frame where the Paragraph Text will appear. Once the frame exists, start typing. If you have a large amount of text that already exists in your favorite word processor, you can use the File | Import (CTRL-I) command to bring it into CorelDRAW.

When text is imported from a word processing file, it will create a frame that is the same as the page size. If all of the text does not fit on the first page, additional pages and frames will be added until all text appears. There is another way to import text so that the text does not automatically flow. This method will be explained a little bit later in this chapter.

When you are working with a Paragraph Text frame, it will have handles like other objects. If you resize the frame, however, the text inside it is not resized. Instead, only the container into which the text flows is resized. An example of a Paragraph Text frame is shown here.

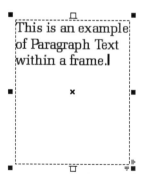

 *If you wish to resize the text at the same time as the frame, hold down the ALT key while resizing.*

6

PARAGRAPH TEXT ATTRIBUTES

Changing the attributes of Paragraph Text is much like changing Artistic Text except that many more options are available.

Font

The Font tab of the Format Text dialog box for Paragraph Text is exactly the same as that for Artistic Text, as shown in Figure 6-1.

Align

The Align tab of the Format Text dialog box is the same as for Artistic Text, with the addition of more controls, as shown in Figure 6-5. Max. word

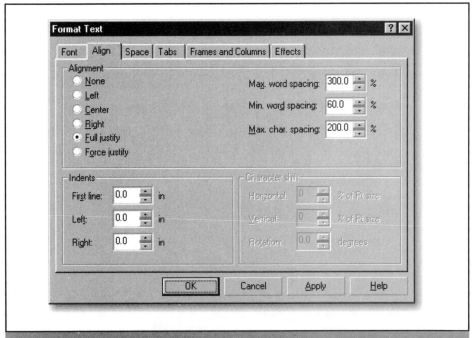

FIGURE 6-5   The Align tab of the Format Text dialog box for Paragraph Text

spacing, Min. word spacing, and Max. char. spacing allow more control when Full justify and Force justify are used. The problem we described earlier of Artistic Text creating large areas of white space can be eliminated by adjusting these settings. Since Artistic Text was not designed for large blocks of text, it doesn't include these controls. But Paragraph Text is geared more towards page layout tasks and you therefore have much greater control over the text flow within the frame.

To change the indents, use the spin boxes labeled First line, Left, and Right. Note that the Left value indicates the left indentation of the paragraph as a whole. None of these values can be negative, but if the First line indent is less than the Left, you will actually be creating an outdent.

Spacing

All of the spacing options that are available to Artistic Text are also available for Paragraph Text. In addition, the Format Text dialog box includes many other options, as shown in Figure 6-6.

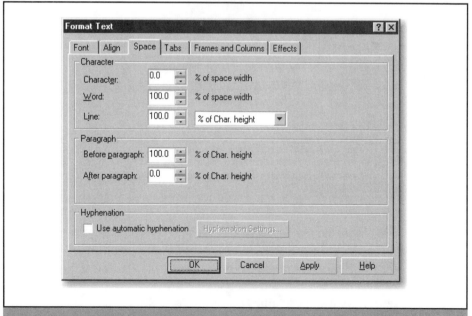

FIGURE 6-6   The Space tab of the Format Text dialog box for Paragraph Text

The Before paragraph and After paragraph settings specify the amount of extra leading, or line spacing, that will be added before or after a paragraph. By default, the setting for spacing before a paragraph is the same as the line spacing. If line spacing has been changed, however, this will not be true. If the setting for spacing before a paragraph is decreased, the end of one paragraph could overlap the beginning of the next one. Thus, this setting should be a value at least equal to the line spacing value. To add extra space, simply increase the Before paragraph value by the amount of extra space you desire.

After paragraph works in much the same way as Before paragraph. But instead of adding the space before a paragraph, it will add it to the bottom of a paragraph. Depending on the layout of your document, each of these values much be carefully adjusted to get just the right "look."

By default, the Hyphenation controls are turned off. You can activate them by checking the Use automatic hyphenation check box. Clicking the Hyphenation Settings button displays the Hyphenation Settings dialog box, shown here.

By default, a break cannot occur between capital letters. To allow this type of break, you check the Break capitalized check box. The Hot zone value indicates the size of the area at the end of the line where hyphenation can occur. The smaller the zone, the more likely that hyphenation will occur. Changing the default to .3 inch will produce more pleasing right margins in most applications. Min. word length specifies the shortest word that can be hyphenated. The default is six letters. Min. characters before and Min. characters after specify the number of letters that must appear before and after a hyphen. This will prevent a single letter from being stranded on a line somewhere. If you don't want two letters to stand alone, for example, simply change the setting to a higher value.

Tabs and Indents

When working with Paragraph Text, you have control over the tab settings. These settings can be controlled either graphically on the ruler or by entering values in the various parameter boxes. Figure 6-7 shows the Tabs tab of the Format Text dialog box.

The left side of the dialog box presents a list of all the existing tabs. The first column in the table indicates the position of the tab. Double-clicking a value allows you to edit it either by typing a new value or using the spin controls. Clicking any of the values in the Alignment column displays a drop-down list from which you can choose Left, Right, Center, or Decimal alignment. Left, Right, and Center tabs align text exactly as you would expect. The Decimal option aligns the decimal point in a number at the tab position.

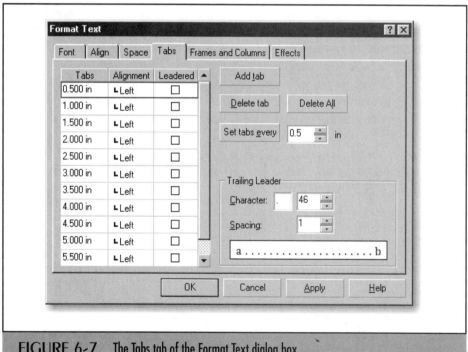

FIGURE 6-7 The Tabs tab of the Format Text dialog box

This allows you to easily align a column of numbers. The numeric characters in a font are usually not proportionally spaced as are the alphabetic characters. This is so that the numbers will line up properly. You will occasionally come across a font that does have proportional spacing for numbers. If so, you may have to change fonts if you need to accurately line up columns of numbers.

The Leadered column indicates whether a particular tab stop uses leaders. Leaders provide actual characters for a tab rather than just a blank space. The most common type of leader is a dot leader, which provides a series of dots or periods within the tab area.

You specify the leader character either by typing it directly in the Character box or by entering its ASCII value in the second Character box. Note than extended characters are not available as leaders. The default leader character is a space. You use the Spacing parameter box to indicate the spacing between leader characters. Spacing can vary from a very tight setting of 0 to an extremely loose setting of 10; the smaller the value, the closer together the characters in the leader line will be. As you adjust the value, a preview just below the Spacing box will show you exactly how the leader will look. Note that even though you can set leaders on more than one tab stop, all leader characters in a paragraph will be the same.

You can set up to 64 tabs for each paragraph—not that you would ever need that many. To set them so they are evenly spaced, use the Set tabs every button. Type the spacing value in the spin box and click the button. Tabs will automatically be added at the interval you specified.

To simply add a single tab, click the Add tab button. If you wish to delete a single tab, you must first select the tab in the table and then click the Delete tab button. To eliminate all of the tab stops, click the Delete All button.

Frames and Columns

All Paragraph Text is in a frame. Inside of that frame, the text can flow into columns. This value is the first value you set on the Frames and Columns tab of the Format Text dialog box, shown in Figure 6-8. Each frame can contain up to eight columns.

The dialog box displays values only for up to three columns, but a scroll bar will appear next to the column numbers if more than three are selected. The Width column controls the width of a single column of text within a frame. The Gutter column controls the amount of white space between

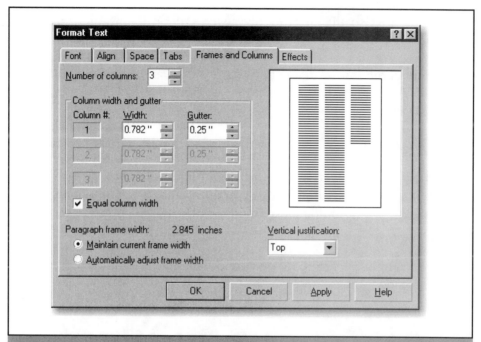

FIGURE 6-8   The Frames and Columns tab of the Format Text dialog box

columns. If the Equal column width check box is checked, you can change these values only for the first column, and all other columns will use identical values. Otherwise, you can enter column widths for each individual column and gutter widths between every pair of columns. Note that there will always be one less gutter width than the number of columns.

At the bottom of the dialog box, the total value of the paragraph frame width is shown. This value is simply the column and gutter widths added together. If you select the Maintain current frame width radio button, the value of the paragraph frame must equal the current frame width. If it doesn't, the values will be adjusted accordingly. Selecting the Automatically adjust frame width radio button resizes the frame to match the values you've entered.

The Vertical justification value indicates how the text fits within the paragraph frame from top to bottom. You can align text at the top, center, or bottom, or you can choose the Full option, which will add leading between

the lines of text so that it is evenly spaced to fill the whole frame. Full justification can be useful for fitting ad copy into an ad, for example.

As you are making the various changes, the preview window in the upper-right corner of the dialog box will give you an idea of how the frame will look. Remember that it is only a rough preview and is not entirely a WYSIWYG view.

Effects

The last tab in the Format Text dialog box is Effects. This is a rather deceiving name as it is used for creating bullets and drop caps. By default, none is select in the Effect Type drop-down list and the dialog box is completely dimmed. If you select Bullet or Drop cap, however, the tab will become usable.

SPECIFYING BULLET EFFECTS Figure 6-9 shows the dialog box displayed when you choose Bullet.

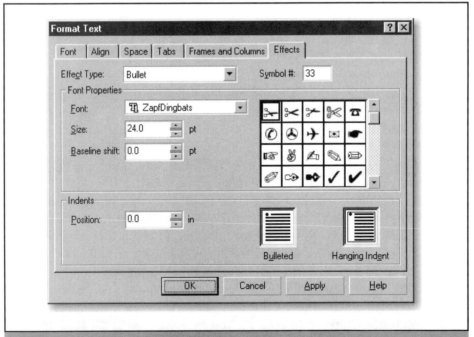

FIGURE 6-9   The Effects tab of the Format Text dialog box when Bullet is selected

A bullet is a character that precedes a paragraph to give it a special emphasis. Normally, it is represented by a symbol character rather than an alphabetic character. The name comes from the filled circle that is the most common type of bullet used. Since it resembles a bullet hole, it is called a bullet.

When you choose a font, all of the characters in the font will be displayed in the grid. Click the character you desire, and it will become the bullet character for the paragraph. If you'd rather enter the character's number, you can use the Symbol # text box. This number is simply the character's ASCII value. ASCII values for the most common fonts used for bullets are provided in the back of the Libraries Catalog that comes in your CorelDRAW box.

Just below the Font drop-down list, you can adjust the Size and Baseline shift. The size of the bullet defaults to the same size as the rest of the text in the paragraph. The baseline shift indicates how far above or below the baseline the bullet character is placed. Some bullet characters need to be shifted up or down so that they "look right." Either enter a value for the shift or use the spin buttons to change the current value. Negative values will shift the bullet below the baseline while positive values will move it above the baseline.

The Position indicates how far the bullet character itself will be from the left margin. If the paragraph has a first-line indent larger than the bullet indent, there will be white space between the bullet and the rest of the text; the text begins at the position that is specified by the first-line indent value.

You also have two placement options. Bulleted places the bullet within the paragraph so that the second line aligns with the bullet rather than the rest of the text. Hanging Indent leaves the bullet "hanging" in the margin so that the text in the paragraph is left-aligned on all lines.

SPECIFYING DROP CAP EFFECTS   Selecting Drop cap from the Effect drop-down list displays the dialog box shown in Figure 6-10.

A drop cap is normally an alphabetical character that is much larger than the size of text within the paragraph. Commonly, it is used at the beginning of a section or chapter to place extra emphasis on the first paragraph. It also can provide a nice graphical touch. The name is derived because the character is normally a capital letter that "drops" over several lines of the paragraph.

In the Dropped lines box, you can select the number of lines the first character will be dropped. Thus, if you use the default setting of three lines, the first character will grow to the height of the first three lines of text. Distance from text determines the amount of space between the right edge of

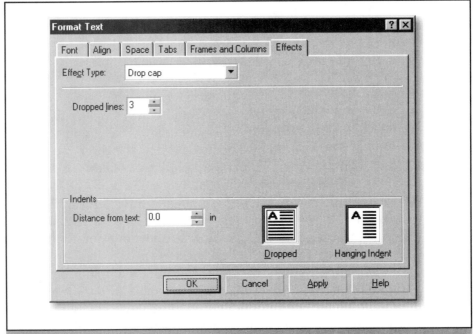

FIGURE 6-10 The Effects tab of the Format Text dialog box when Drop Cap is selected

the drop character and the rest of the text block. The right side of the Indents section allows you to specify whether the character is dropped within the text block or hanging outside of the text block.

FLOWING PARAGRAPH TEXT

Since Paragraph Text is usually a large block of text, quite often it will span more than one page or two areas on the same page. In this case, text will automatically flow from one frame to another. When the text extends beyond the bottom of a frame, the bottom-middle handle will have a downward-pointing arrow in it. Click the handle, and your cursor will look like the cursor shown here.

Go to the place in your drawing where you want more text to appear. If you want a paragraph frame to be created automatically, just click. Automatically created frames will be drawn the same size as the page. You can also drag out a frame instead, to create a paragraph frame of the size you want. Text will flow into the new frame from the previous frame. If there is still more text, the bottom-middle handle will again have a downward-pointing arrow inside of it. You'll also notice that the top-middle handle of this new frame will have "greeked text" inside of it to indicate that it is linked to another frame above it. If you check the first frame, you'll notice that it now has the same symbol in the bottom-middle handle, indicating that there is text in a frame following it. When frames are linked, a small line will be drawn between them to indicate the link. This line is purely for informational purposes and will not be printed. Here is an example of text flowing between two frames.

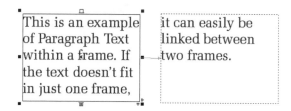

If you have two frames linked and you wish to break the link, use the Arrange | Separate command. There is no way to link paragraph frames without redrawing them.

Text can easily flow around a graphic object. Select the graphic object or group of objects that you wish the text to flow around. Bring up the Object Properties dialog box using the ALT-ENTER shortcut key. The General tab contains a Wrap paragraph text check box. When it is checked, you can specify the Text wrap offset. Click the Apply button and adjust the offset until you are satisfied. At that point, click OK.

Other methods for wrapping Paragraph Text are discussed in Chapter 18.

CONVERTING BETWEEN ARTISTIC AND PARAGRAPH TEXT

In the past, if you created the "wrong" kind of text, you usually had to re-create it to convert it to the other kind of text. Now CorelDRAW provides the Text | Convert command. It will convert Artistic Text to Paragraph Text and vice versa. The conversion is not always perfect, but it sure does save a lot of work.

Note that if you have Paragraph Text selected and not all of the text is displayed in a single frame, the Convert command will be dimmed. Also, text that has been wrapped or in columns will not look the same after conversion. It will be changed to flush left in a single column.

CHANGING CASE

You can change the case of either form of text. Choose the Text | Change Case command. The Change Case dialog box shown here will be displayed.

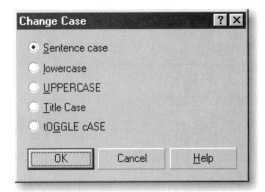

Five options are available. Sentence case will capitalize the first word of every sentence. The lowercase option will make all of the characters lowercase. UPPERCASE will capitalize all of the characters. Title Case will capitalize the first letter of each word. The tOGGLE cASE option will change the case of each character to the opposite of its current setting.

SYMBOLS

Symbols are found in the Symbols Docker. Choose View | Dockers | Symbols (CTRL-F11) to display the Docker-up on screen, as shown here. Note that we've undocked it.

6

Many users get confused about the symbols and assume that they are clipart. They are, but they are stored as fonts and therefore must be installed as fonts in order to be used. At the top of the window is a drop-down list that shows each of the fonts that can be accessed as symbols. Normally, this is only fonts that notify themselves to Windows that they contain symbols. So, you won't see alphabetical fonts in the list without changing the default settings of CorelDRAW.

Just below the drop-down list are the graphical characters of the selected symbol font. A scroll bar at the right side of the window lets you scroll through the characters until you find just the one you desire. If you know the ASCII value of the symbol you need, you can type it directly into the # parameters box below the character showing.

Once you've selected the symbol you want, simply drag it into the drawing window. It will become a graphic within your drawing at the size specified in the Size parameters box in the Docker window.

If your cursor is within a text block, you can drag the symbol and drop it onto the cursor to automatically insert it into the text. To take this one step further, copy any graphic to the clipboard, place your cursor within text, and then select Paste. This will insert the graphic into the text.

By default, you'll only get a single symbol. But you can get several symbols tiled onto your page by checking the Tile check box. If you do choose to tile a symbol, you can control the Horizontal and Vertical grid size of each tile by clicking the Tile Options buttons and choosing the appropriate values in the Tile Options dialog box shown here.

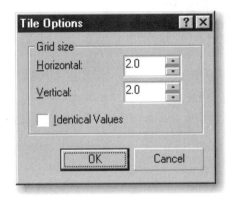

7

SELECTING AND TRANSFORMING OBJECTS

The Pick tool doesn't create anything, yet it is the most versatile tool in the CorelDRAW toolbox. It is used to select, position, resize, rotate, and skew objects. All of these functions can be accomplished in a variety of ways.

SELECTING OBJECTS

Before you can work with an object, you must select it. You select objects in CorelDRAW in four basic ways: using the mouse, marquee selection, tabbing, and the menus.

SELECTING OBJECTS WITH THE MOUSE

The simplest way to select an object is to click it using the left mouse button. Even if the object has no fill, you can click within the object to select it. This is different than the default for previous versions where you needed to click its outline rather than inside the object. Once selected, the object will have eight object handles surrounding its bounding box and an x in the center. (Note that the bounding box of an object may extend beyond the edges of the object.) Four of the handles are at the middle of each side and are the stretching handles, and four of them are at the extreme corners and are the sizing handles. The following illustration shows examples of the object handles on a selected object.

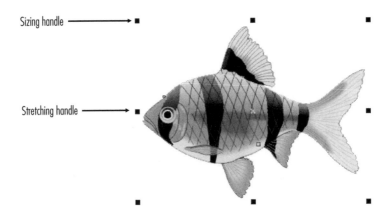

Sizing handle

Stretching handle

> *If you do not want to select unfilled objects by clicking inside of them, select Tools | Options | Workspace | Toolbox | Pick Tool and make sure the "Treat all objects as filled" check box is not checked under the Pick tool. You can also toggle the settings on the Property Bar using the button shown here.*

When an object is selected, the Status Bar supplies valuable information about the object, such as the height, width, and center point or the number of nodes. The information provided depends on the type of object you have selected. An example of the Status Bar for a selected rectangle is shown here:

> *Notice that we only show a portion of the Status Bar. This is because of the high level of customization that can be done with the Status Bar and the fact that it can be positioned at either the top or the bottom of the screen. We want to show you the information it displays and how important it can be to understanding CorelDRAW.*

Rectangle on Layer 1
Width: 3.548   Height: 2.589   Center: (3.525 , 8.443) inches

To select more than one object, hold down the SHIFT key while clicking the object or objects that you wish to add to the selection. With each object added, the object handles change so that they surround all of the selected objects, and the Status Bar reports the number of objects that have been selected, as shown here.

312 Objects Selected on Layer 1

If you find that you have selected more objects than you want, simply click the object you wish to remove from the selection while holding down the SHIFT key. If you watch the Status Bar, you will see that you now have one less object selected than before.

Sometimes you will want to select an object that is within a group. You can ungroup and then select the object you want, but a simpler way is to select the group and then the object while holding down the CTRL key. When you do this, the object handles will be round instead of square, and the selected object will be referred to as a *child object* on the Status Bar. Here is an example of a selected child object.

Child Object handle ────────▶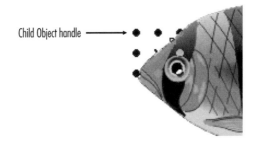

 *Another way to select an object within a group is to select it in the Object Manager, which is described in Chapter 13.*

 *Neither method allows you to select multiple objects within a group.*

Sometimes you will have nested groups—that is, a group within a group. In those cases, a CTRL-click may result in the selection of another group. Continue to use CTRL-click until you get the object you want.

CTRL-click can also work with some effect groups. Unfortunately, it does not work with Blend or Contour groups. Those groups must first be separated before anything other than the whole group can be selected. You can select the control objects, but not the objects created by these effects.

You can now easily select objects that are hidden behind other objects. Hold down the ALT key and click the area where the hidden object is located.

As you click, the X in the middle of the object and the object handles appear. If the object is several levels deep, continue to hold down the ALT key and click until it is selected. You can also use this method to select multiple hidden objects. Hold down ALT-SHIFT while clicking and the newly selected objects will be added to the previously selected objects. Lastly, you can select hidden objects within a group by holding down ALT-CTRL while clicking. If all else fails, you might want to change into Wireframe view (described in Chapter 12) or use the Object Manager (described in Chapter 13).

MARQUEE SELECTION

Selecting objects by clicking them is great if you just have one or two objects. Often, however, you'll want to select a bunch of objects that are adjacent to one another. In this case, you'll want to *marquee select* the objects.

Creating a marquee selection is very similar to drawing a rectangle that encloses all of the objects you wish to select. However, instead of drawing the rectangle with the Rectangle tool, you draw it with the Pick tool. As you draw, a blue dotted box is displayed. Once all of the objects are within the blue dotted box, simply release the mouse button to select all of the objects.

When marquee selecting objects, quite often you may select an extra object or two. Remember that you can SHIFT-click an object to deselect it. Hold down the ALT key while marquee selecting to select any object within the marquee and any objects intersected by the marquee. Using the CTRL key constrains the marquee to a square.

You can also use marquee selection to deselect objects. Simply hold down the SHIFT key while marquee selecting, and any selected objects within the marquee will be deselected. This technique can be very handy if there is a small area of objects you need to deselect within a larger area of objects that you do want selected.

TABBING AROUND

Yet another way to select objects is by using the TAB key on your keyboard. Pressing TAB selects the next object forward in the stacking order. (Chapter 13 provides more information on stacking order.) Tabbing is a great way to move through your drawing one object at a time to search for a problem object or a particular fill. SHIFT-TAB moves you through the stacking order backward.

 If you tab through a group of objects, only objects within the group will be selected if you've already selected a child object.

USING THE MENUS

If you just want to select all of the objects, you can use the Edit | Select All command. A shortcut is simply to double-click the Pick tool itself.

 *To deselect all objects, use the ESC key.*

MANIPULATING OBJECTS

Rarely will you select objects just for the sake of selecting them. Usually you will want to make a change to the object. That change could be moving the object, changing its size, rotating it, or skewing it. As with most functions in CorelDRAW, there are a variety of ways to accomplish these tasks. The best method to use depends on the results you desire.

POSITIONING OBJECTS

Simply put, if you want to position a selected object somewhere else in your drawing, push it there. Clicking a selected object or objects and then dragging them to the desired destination is all you need to do. Once you release the mouse button, the objects are dropped into place. As you move the objects, you'll notice that a blue outline appears to show you where the object is currently located. If you pause briefly, the objects are redrawn completely. You can set the speed at which they are redrawn in the dialog box displayed when you choose Tools | Options | Workspace | Toolbox and select the Pick tool. Change the Delay amount to the time in seconds that elapses before the objects are redrawn.

Some of you may see something other than a blue line showing the new position of the object. That is the simplest rendering. But if you click the TAB key while repositioning the object, it will toggle between three different modes, as shown in Figure 7-1. If you hesitate slightly on the object after selecting it but before moving it, the object will render as XOR when being moved.

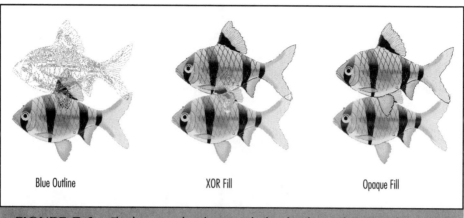

Blue Outline   XOR Fill   Opaque Fill

FIGURE 7-1   The three ways that objects are displayed as they are being moved

The first method we've already discussed and that is the blue outline. The next method is a kind of transparent fill (actually an XOR), which allows you to partially see the objects behind the object you are moving and doesn't require that the screen be redrawn. Thus, it is fast. Lastly, there is the opaque fill. This gives the highest quality rendering of the object, but you can't see what is behind it and it does take a while to redraw. You will see a grid pattern on the object being moved that represents other objects below it. Our recommendation is to use the transparent fill.

If you need to know the distance the objects are moving, the Status Bar tells you the distance of the move horizontally (in the x direction) and vertically (in the y direction), the distance of the move in a straight line, and the angle of the movement, as shown here.

Group of 312 Objects on Layer 1
DX:1.851 in DY:2.319 in Distance: 2.967 Angle: 51.407

During a move, you may notice that the objects begin to snap or stick at certain intervals. This happens because objects can snap to a grid, to guidelines, or to other objects, depending on the settings in the Layout menu. Chapter 14 contains more information on these options.

To make a duplicate of the objects being moved, simply press the + key on the numeric keypad or click the right mouse button. You must be sure to do this before you release the left mouse button. You can also move an object by right-clicking it and dragging. When you release the right mouse button, you'll see a pop-up menu, as shown here. One of the options is to copy the object. Note that there are other options that may come in handy as well. Depending on where you drop the object, the menu choices you see may be different than those shown here.

Although graphics tablets have a right mouse button, it can't always be used to create a duplicate as it is instead used to lock the pressure level of the pen tip. In this situation, you must use the + key on the numeric keypad. If you're using a laptop computer that lacks a numeric keypad, as a last resort you can use the mouse buttons built in to the laptop.

Using the methods described so far, you may find it difficult to place objects in an exact location. If you want to place objects in an exact place in your drawing, you can use the Property Bar. Whenever an object is selected and the Pick tool is the active tool, the far left side of the Property Bar shows the absolute x and y coordinates of the object's center, as shown here.

If you change these numbers, the selected objects are moved automatically when you press the ENTER key. You can use the TAB key to move to the next text box, or you can simply click it, but the changes will not be reflected until you press the ENTER key.

> *After typing the number, type the abbreviation of the number's measurement system, and you can use any available system regardless of the system used for the rulers. Note that the value you enter will automatically be converted into the ruler units after you press the ENTER key.*

Relative Positioning

Many times you'll want to move an object an exact amount in a particular direction. In this case, you want the positioning to be relative to the current position. You can achieve this by moving the object with your mouse, but it can be difficult to move the exact amount you desire. Select Arrange | Transform | Position (ALT-F7) to bring up the Position roll-up shown here.

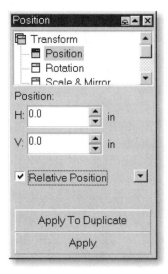

You can enter any amount you desire for relative movement. At the bottom of the roll-up is the Relative Position check box. When this check box is checked, all values you enter in the H (horizontal) and V (vertical) boxes will be a relative amount of movement from the current position relative to the 0, 0 position on the page. To execute the movement, simply click the Apply button at the bottom of the roll-up or press the ENTER key. To leave a duplicate object behind, click the Apply to Duplicate button instead.

Absolute Positioning

The Position roll-up can be expanded so that you can specify the absolute coordinates of any of nine locations on the objects. These positions are the four corners of the selection box, the four midpoints of the sides of the selection box, and the center of the selection box. Click the down arrow just to the right of the Relative Position check box to reveal a coordinate grid, as shown here.

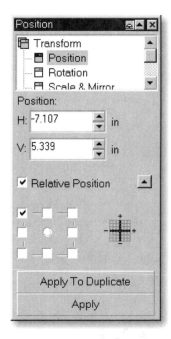

When you are working in the absolute positioning mode, choosing a different check box in the coordinate grid will not move the object, but will change the coordinates shown to the current position of the chosen location in the grid. The idea here is that you will enter the exact H and V coordinates of where you want a particular part of the object to be located. If you are working with a rectangular object, this is quite easy to understand. However, if you choose the upper-left check box in the grid and the selected object is an ellipse, then you'll be positioning the upper-left corner of the selection box instead.

Consider an example in which several objects are selected whose selection box is exactly 2 inches square. Currently the objects are near the center of your drawing page.

1. Disable The Relative Position checkbox.

2. Select the upper-left check box in the grid.

3. Type **0** for H and **11** for V.

4. Click Apply.

Notice that your objects are in the upper-left corner of the page. Now try another example:

1. Disable The Relative Position checkbox.

2. Select the lower-right check box in the grid.

3. Type **8.5** for H and **0** for V (assuming that your page size is 8.5"×11"). If necessary, modify these numbers so that they equal your page size.

4. Click Apply.

Now the objects will be in the lower-right corner of the page. You might want to experiment a little further with this dialog box before moving on as it can take a little while to get used to.

Nudging

There is yet another way to move objects: by nudging. Nudging is extremely useful when you just need to push the selected objects into place. To nudge objects, you simply press the arrow key on your keyboard that corresponds to the direction you want to move the selection. Each press of the arrow moves the objects by the amount specified in the Tools | Options | Workspace | Edit | Nudge box.

The default value is 0.1 inches, which you may find too large. Modify this number to your liking, and it will be used on all drawings using the current

Workspace. Note that you can save multiple Workspaces, which can each have different nudge settings. This is explained in detail in Chapter 40. A quick way to change your nudge setting is on the Property Bar. Make sure that no objects are selected and change the value in the text box shown here to the desired setting. Remember to press ENTER when you're done.

Another variation is the Super nudge. This allows you to use the CTRL key to multiply the amount of nudge. Again you can set the amount of multiplication with the Tools | Options | Workspace | Edit | Super Nudge command. Now hold down the SHIFT key as you press the arrow keys on your keyboard. Notice that the amount of movement has increased. If this isn't clear to you, increase the amount of multiplication. This is one of those features that won't look great in the ads, but sure will save you a lot of work!

LOCKING OBJECTS

In previous versions of CorelDRAW, you could place objects on a Layer and then lock that layer. But there was no way to lock an individual object. When an object is locked, it can't be moved, transformed, filled or outlined. It can, however, be selected so that it can be unlocked.

To lock an object, select the object and then choose Arrange | Lock Object. An alternative is to right-click the object and select Lock Object from the pop-up menu. After the object is locked, you'll notice that the square object handles are now small lock icons. If you attempt to do anything with a selected, but locked, object, CorelDRAW will behave as if you don't have any objects selected.

To unlock an object, you first need to select it. Then choose Arrange | Unlock Object or right-click and choose Unlock Object from the pop-up menu. You can easily unlock all objects in a drawing by selecting Arrange | Unlock All Objects. Before selecting the command, you do not need to select any of the objects. After you select the command, all of the previously locked objects will be selected.

RESIZING OBJECTS

When you create objects in your drawing, very rarely will they be the exact size you need; you were more worried about making the object look correct than getting the exact size. There are several ways that you can resize an object in CorelDRAW.

When an object is selected, you simply need to grab one of the object handles around the perimeter of the selection box and drag it in the direction you want to increase or decrease the size of the object. If you grab a corner handle, the resized object will retain its original aspect ratio. If you instead grab a center handle, then the object will be stretched in only one direction and will thus become distorted.

You can also use the modifier keys to help control the resizing. Hold down the CTRL key while resizing to constrain the size to 100 percent increments of the original size. Dragging across the object in either the horizontal or vertical direction creates a mirror image of the object. You can use the right mouse button or + key before you release the left mouse button to make a duplicate of the object. Pressing the SHIFT key resizes the selection from the center outward. Pressing CTRL and SHIFT together resizes the object from the center outwards in 100 percent increments.

7

In trying to follow Windows standards, Corel provides the ability to use "standard" Windows conventions for the CTRL and SHIFT keys. By default, they work as described here, but you can change this behavior by using the dialog box that appears when you select the Tools | Options | Workspace | Toolbox command and choose the Pick tool so that CTRL leaves a duplicate, SHIFT constrains, and ALT stretches from the center. Those of you using the Macintosh versions of CorelDRAW will note that the modifier keys follow the Macintosh conventions.

Exact Sizing

Sometimes you'll need to make an object an exact size. This is especially important for technical drawings, but can also apply to making an ad fit in a specified area. The quickest way to resize the selected objects is to use the controls found on the Property Bar, shown here.

Type the size you desire in the text box and press the ENTER key. Remember that you can use the TAB key to move between the text boxes on the Property Bar. If you want to retain the aspect ratio, you can use the small lock icon on the Property Bar. When the lock icon is raised, the aspect ratio is constrained. Therefore, changing the number in one box will automatically change the number in the other box.

Similar functionality is available in the Size roll-up, which you can display by choosing Arrange | Transform | Size (or ALT-F10), shown here.

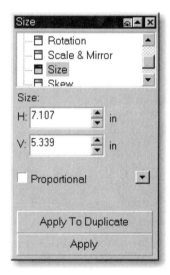

Type the desired size in the H and V text boxes and then click Apply. If you want to apply the changes to a duplicate object, click Apply to Duplicate instead. To retain the aspect ratio of the object being resized, simply check the Proportional check box. When you enter a number in one of the text boxes, the other will change automatically to a proportional value.

You can also expand the Size roll-up by clicking the small down arrow in the lower-right corner of the roll-up. This will allow you to use the coordinate grid when resizing, as shown here.

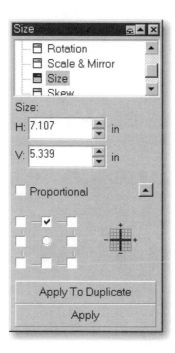

The check box you select in the coordinate grid will remain anchored when you apply the resizing. This is similar to grabbing the handle opposite the point and dragging with the mouse.

Scaling Objects

When resizing objects you can also scale them as a percentage of their current size. As usual, you can do this in more than one way. The easiest way is to again use the Property Bar's scaling controls that were shown a bit earlier.

Instead of entering the exact measurement of the object, now you are entering a percentage by which the object will be scaled. Thus, if you typed 50 percent for each value, the object would be half of its original size, and if you typed 200 percent for each value, the object would double its size. Again, the lock icon next to the scaling boxes can be used to constrain the aspect ratio of the object. Note that when you type a value, you must press ENTER to make it take effect.

> **CAUTION:** *After you press ENTER, both scaling boxes return to 100 percent rather than reflecting the exact amount of cumulative scaling. While this isn't technically a bug, it can be very frustrating if you want to know how much an object was previously scaled.*

These same transformations can be performed in the Scale & Mirror roll-up shown here.

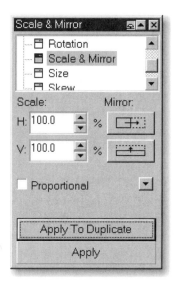

Activate the roll-up with the Arrange | Transform | Scale command (ALT-F9). Type a value in the H and V text boxes and click Apply to implement the changes. Again, you can constrain the aspect ratio by checking the Proportional check box.

As with the other transformation functions, you can expand the roll-up to show the coordinate grid. This allows you to select an anchor point for the scaling. Whichever check box you have checked will remain stationary, and the object will be scaled from that point.

Mirroring Objects

A true mirror requires that the size of the original object be retained. Often, however, you'll use this feature to create a shadow or reflection of the object that is a different size. In those cases, you can create the effect with the mouse. Simply grab one of the side handles (not a corner handle) and drag across the object in the direction you want the mirror to appear. When you are satisfied, release the mouse button. Click the right mouse button or press the + key to create a duplicate, just as with the other transformations. As you drag, the Status Bar tells you the exact scale, and the word "Mirrored" indicates that you are mirroring. You can mirror the object at the exact same size by holding down the CTRL key while dragging.

 *Mirroring is nothing more than using a negative scaling value.*

Entering a negative value into the scaling boxes also creates the mirroring effect. Thus, you can simply use the Property Bar and Scale & Mirror roll-up that were previously discussed. If you want an exact mirror, both the Property Bar and the Scale & Mirror roll-up provide buttons for this. The Scale & Mirror roll-up clearly labels these buttons for mirroring. The Property Bar buttons are shown here.

ROTATING AND SKEWING OBJECTS

To rotate or skew an object manually, you need to click the selected object a second time or double-click it as you select it. This changes the object handles to rotation handles on each corner and skew handles in the middle of each side. You'll also see a thumbtack representing the center of rotation. An example of an object selected in this way is shown here.

Rotation handle ⟶

Skewing handle ⟶

Thumbtack

Drag any of the rotation handles, and the selected object will begin to rotate. As the object rotates, the Status Bar specifies the amount of rotation. When you release the left mouse button, the object will be dropped. You can constrain rotation to a particular angle by holding down the CTRL key while rotating the object. By default, it will be constrained to multiples of 15 degrees, but you can change the amount by choosing Tools | Options | Workspace | Edit and selecting Constrain angle. You can make a duplicate of the object by clicking the right mouse button or using the + key before releasing the left mouse button.

By default, an object rotates around its true center, but you can move the center of rotation to any place inside or outside of the object's selection box. Simply drag the thumbtack (the circle with the dot in the middle) to where you want the center of rotation to be. If you hold down the CTRL key while dragging, the thumbtack will snap to any of the places where a handle appears or to the true center of the object's bounding box.

PRECISION ROTATION

You can also rotate objects by using the Property Bar. You simply type the exact value of rotation you desire and click ENTER. The Property Bar controls are shown here. Remember that immediately after the rotation, the amount will be reset to zero, so there is no way to know how much an object has been previously rotated.

You can also use the Rotation roll-up, accessed with the <u>A</u>rrange | <u>T</u>ransform | <u>R</u>otate command (ALT-F8). The roll-up allows you to type a numeric value for the center of rotation along with the rotation angle, as shown here.

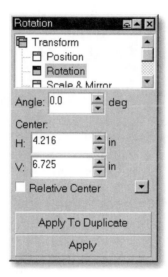

As with the other transformation roll-ups, you can expand the roll-up and work with the coordinate grid when measuring the position of the center of rotation. Clicking any of the nine check boxes will automatically move the center of rotation to that point on the selected object. If you check the Relative Center check box, the center of rotation will be measured relative to the true center of the object's bounding box.

Skewing

Skewing refers to distorting an object in either the vertical or horizontal direction. It makes an object look as if it is leaning. When using the mouse, simply grab one of the skew handles and drag it. Remember that you click twice on an object to display the rotation and skew handles. To skew vertically,

use one of the handles on a horizontal side. As you skew, the Status Bar displays the angle of skew. This angle can be either positive or negative, depending on the direction and the handle you've chosen to use. The following table gives you an idea of which handle to drag in which direction to get a particular angle.

Direction	Left	Right
Top Handle	Positive	Negative
Bottom Handle	Negative	Positive
Direction	**Up**	**Down**
Left Side Handle	Negative	Positive
Right Side Handle	Positive	Negative

As when you rotate objects, you can hold down the CTRL key to constrain the skew to an angle that is a multiple of 15 degrees (unless the default has been changed). Unlike all of the other transformations, there are no skew controls on the Property Bar.

To access the Skew roll-up, select Arrange | Transform | Skew (ALT-F11). As shown here, you can type the horizontal and vertical skew angles.

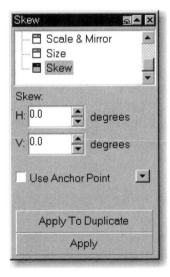

By default, the skew is relative to the center of the object, but by checking the Use Anchor Point check box and expanding the roll-up, you can select any of the check boxes in the coordinate grid.

MANIPULATING OBJECTS WITH OTHER TOOLS

When you learned how to create objects in Chapters 4, 5, and 6, you learned about the X that appears in the center of each object and the handles that surround it. So as you are creating objects, you can easily transform them without having to use the Pick tool.

Drag the X at the center of the object to move it to the desired location. This is slightly different than using the Pick tool as you can only click the X itself and not anywhere within the object. The handles work just the same as with the Pick tool. The corner handles size the object and retain the aspect ratio while the side handles distort the shape.

If you quickly click the X, the handles change into rotation and skewing handles and the X changes into a thumbtack. So you can easily rotate and skew the object by clicking and dragging on the appropriate handle.

You can even select multiple objects by holding down the SHIFT key and clicking on another object. So with all this new functionality, the Pick tool becomes less important and you'll become more productive since you will switch tools less often.

FREE TRANSFORMATION TOOLS

As if there weren't already enough ways to transform objects, Corel added a series of free transformation tools to CorelDRAW 8. At first glance, they seem to just be a duplication of the existing tools. But a longer look reveals that they provide a set of very useful tools. When you select the Free Transform tool from the Shape Edit flyout, the Property Bar changes to the one shown here.

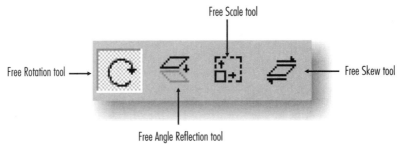

Free Scale tool

Free Rotation tool ——→

Free Skew tool

Free Angle Reflection tool

Each of these tools requires you to click and drag. As you drag, you'll see a preview of the transformation (unless you've disabled this feature, as described earlier). The initial click sets the anchor point and the transformation will be relative to that point. It may take you a while to get the hang of this if you are familiar with the other methods of transforming objects.

FREE ROTATION TOOL

With the Free Rotation tool, the initial click sets the center of rotation for the object. As you drag, a line appears to indicate the angle of rotation relative to the original object along with a preview of the rotated object, as shown here. When you release the mouse button, the rotation is completed.

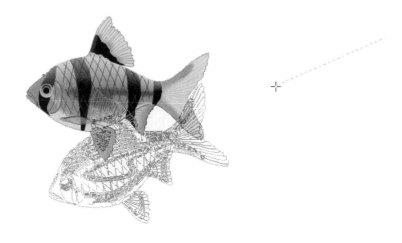

Free Angle Reflection Tool

The initial click of the Free Angle Reflection tool sets the point around which the object is reflected. So if this point is several inches from the objects, the result will be twice that amount in the direction in which you drag your cursor. Here you can see the original object, the plane around which the object is being reflected, and the dotted outline indicating the transformed object.

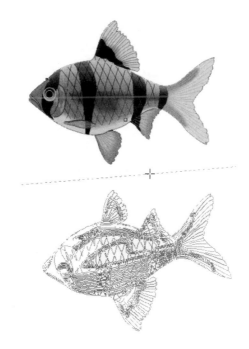

7

Free Scale Tool

You'll probably find the Free Scale tool the hardest to initially understand. The first click sets the position from which the object will scale. As you drag, the shape resizes itself based on the original point and the direction in which you drag. By default, the scaling is not proportional and so the object will become rather distorted, as shown here. You can hold down the CTRL key to constrain the aspect ratio of the original object.

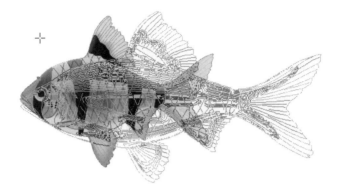

 *After the initial click, the further your cursor is from the object, the more control you'll have over the transform.*

Free Skew Tool

When using the Free Skew tool, as when using the other free transformation tools, you begin by clicking to set the anchor point for the skew. As you drag, you are skewing in both the x and the y axis so it is quite different from using the skew handles, which only affect one direction. Holding down the CTRL key while dragging constrains the skewing to only one direction. Here you'll see the original object and the transformation.

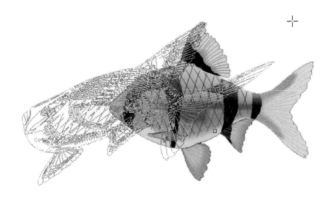

THE TRANSFORM TOOLBAR

You saw earlier how many of the transform commands are available on the Property Bar. But there are a few that are not available. There is a separate toolbar, the Transform toolbar shown here, that contains the same tools as the Property Bar plus some additional tools.

To access the Transform toolbar, select View | Toolbars and place a check in the Transform check box. Or right-click the gray area within any existing toolbar and select Transform from the pop-up menu that appears.

The Center of Rotation Position text boxes allow you to precisely place the center of rotation for an object. You would do this in place of moving the thumbtack. You can also enter the skew angles as exact values rather than using the skew handles to do your skewing interactively.

Probably the most important benefit of this toolbar is the Apply to Duplicate button. This means that any transformations you apply will be to a new object and the existing object will be retained. The last button, Relative to Object, controls whether the values shown on the toolbar are relative to the page or to the object. When the button is up, they are relative to the page and that is how the Property Bar will always work. But with the button depressed, all measurements are relative to the object.

UNDOING ALL TRANSFORMATIONS

With all the various transformations you can apply, there will be times that you decide that the original object was the best. You always have the Edit | Undo (CTRL-Z) command to undo the last few things you've done. But that

won't always save you if you've done many other things in the drawing since transforming the object. But CorelDRAW does remember what you've done and it is quite easy to get rid of these transformations. Simply choose Arrange | Clear Transformations to return the object to its original shape even after the drawing has been saved, closed and reopened. And if you now choose Edit | Undo, the object will return to its fully transformed state.

8

SHAPING OBJECTS

After you've created an object, you'll inevitably need to make changes to it. You'll want to mold the shape so it is just perfect. You may need to make only a minor change or two, but you'll soon discover that fully understanding how to shape objects is essential to using CorelDRAW. The Shape Edit flyout, shown here, includes four tools: the Shape, Knife, Eraser, and Free Transform tools. The most comprehensive of these is the Shape tool, commonly referred to as the Node Edit tool. We previously discussed the Free Transform tool in Chapter 7.

Shape tool ———— ➤   ◄ ———— Free Transform tool

Knife tool   Eraser tool

THE SHAPE TOOL

There is no tool that you'll use more than the Shape tool. It can be used on curves, rectangles, ellipses, polygons, stars, text, bitmaps, envelopes, and more. With each type of shape, it works just a little bit differently.

UNDERSTANDING NODES

Nodes are the building blocks of vector artwork. A node is nothing more than a point in space that has a set of x,y coordinates. We will examine why you need to use nodes and then see how to begin using them.

VECTORS VERSUS BITMAPS

To fully understand nodes, you need to understand how CorelDRAW creates objects. All of the shapes you create are vector objects. That means that they are drawn using vector geometry (you know, that class you hated). Anything you create can be resized without a loss of quality, and large drawings take no more file space than small ones. All of the things you draw are created using mathematical equations. When a graphic is resized, the equations are simply updated for the new size and therefore, there is no loss of quality.

Now consider bitmaps, the domain of CorelPHOTO-PAINT. Everything you see on the screen is composed of thousands of tiny pixels (picture elements). Each of those dots can be one of 16.7 million colors. So to create a drawing with thousands of pixels in full color, you need a lot of memory and hard drive space. Consider a simple program icon that you might find on the desktop. It may look pretty bland, but every such icon is composed of 1,024 tiny dots. Just imagine how many dots are required for artwork that needs to be printed! With bitmaps, resizing can either leave lots of information that is unused or a great lack of information, which leads to jaggies.

Thus, any time you create artwork as a vector image rather than a bitmap, you'll get higher quality and save lots of hard drive space. Some images, such as full-color photos, are nearly impossible to re-create as vector images and work much better as bitmaps.

A common graphic that can easily be represented in either format is a logo. To properly use a logo in bitmap format, you'll need to have it available in many different sizes. However, in vector format, the logo can be resized at will without any loss of quality. If a logo was originally created in CorelDRAW, you already have it as a vector, but if the logo was scanned or is in a bitmap file, you'll need to convert it.

8

Two Types of Lines

Although you can have a single point in space, no node can exist by itself. When another node is added, a segment is created between the two. This segment can be either a line or a curve. The first node will always be displayed larger than the second, and when it is selected, the Status Bar will indicate that it is the first node.

LINES   A line segment is a plain old straight line between any two nodes. Just because a line is straight does not mean it is a line segment. At the end of a line segment is a node called a line node, and this node will not have a bézier control handle on the segment side of the node. Remember that if the overall path contains more than two nodes, some of the segments can be lines and some can be curves, so the nodes are what separate the segments.

CURVES   A curve segment can be straight, but what differentiates it from a line segment is that it has bézier control points, so the curve can be shaped. Here is an example of a curved path with nodes and bézier control points.

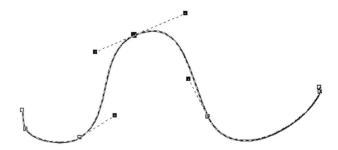

Just as the node itself is a point in space, so is each bézier control point. You'll see a dotted line between the control point handle and the node itself. This line forms a tangent with the curve entering the node. Remember that since there are two control handles for each node, the "launch angle" of the curve entering the node can be quite different from the angle exiting the node.

Three Types of Nodes

There are three types of nodes: cusp, smooth, and symmetrical. The behavior of the two bézier control handles entering and exiting a node is controlled by the type of node. When you understand the behavior of each of these node types, you will be able to fully control the shape of the curve you are creating.

You can move the bézier control handles toward or away from the node, and you can rotate them about the node. Moving the handle closer to the node produces a very tight curve, and moving it farther away makes the curve wider.

CUSP NODES   In situations where a curve needs to come to a point, use a cusp node. You can move the handles in and out to adjust the curve's shape. You can also rotate each handle independently around the node. Here are some examples of cusp nodes.

You can rotate the handles so that the curve will cross itself. This may create the effect you desire, but it can cause problems when printing and so should be avoided if possible.

SMOOTH NODES   Smooth nodes cannot be used where two line segments meet since they will require a cusp node. You can use a smooth node to connect a line segment to a curve segment, but the results can be rather strange. Most of the time when you want a smooth curve, you'll use a smooth node.

The two bézier control handles of a node always remain in a straight line for a smooth node. This means that rotating the handle on one side of a node automatically rotates the handle on the opposite side of the node by the same amount. You can, however, move the handles in and out independently of one another. Just be careful as you move the handles so as not to accidentally rotate them. Here are some examples of smooth nodes.

SYMMETRICAL NODES   Symmetrical nodes cannot be used with a line segment on either side of the node. They can be used only with curve segments since the bézier control handles on either side of the node must be on a straight line and must be equidistant from the node. Moving either control handle causes the opposite handle to mimic that movement. Symmetrical nodes are useful when you want perfectly symmetrical curves—but you probably won't use them very often. Here are some examples of symmetrical nodes.

8

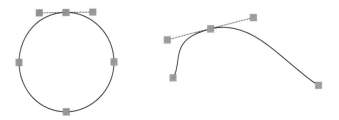

SELECTING AND MOVING NODES

Many of the same techniques used to select objects can be used when selecting nodes. First you need to select the Shape tool itself by clicking its icon in the toolbox or pressing the F10 shortcut key.

 *Remember that in CorelDRAW 8, each of the tools will behave like the Shape tool when the cursor is over a node.*

Selecting Nodes

You can select any individual node simply by clicking it with the Shape tool. If you hold down the SHIFT key, you can select several nodes or deselect nodes if they are already selected. You can marquee select with the Shape tool: Select all nodes of the current object within the marquee box, and all of the nodes within the rectangle will be selected. If you hold down the SHIFT key while marquee selecting, you will toggle the current selection status of each node within the marquee box. The CTRL key will constrain the marquee box to a square.

For those of you who are real keyboard fans, the HOME key takes you to the first node of a curve, and the END key takes you to the last node. If the path is closed, the first and last nodes will be the same node. The TAB key moves you to the next node on the path, and SHIFT-TAB moves you to the previous node on the path. SHIFT-HOME toggles the selection status of the first node, and SHIFT-END toggles the selection status of the last node. Either CTRL-SHIFT-HOME or CTRL-SHIFT-END selects all of the nodes on the path.

 *When all nodes on a path have been selected, line segment nodes will be hollow and curve nodes will be solid.*

Moving Nodes

Once you have selected a node, you can simply drag it to a new location. If multiple nodes have been selected, they will all move in unison. The movement of the nodes can be constrained to only horizontal or only vertical by holding down the CTRL key while moving the nodes.

Just as you can nudge and super nudge objects, you can do the same thing with nodes. This technique is especially useful when you are fine-tuning the shape of a curve. Use the arrow keys on the keyboard to nudge nodes in the direction of the arrow. Use the SHIFT key in conjunction with the arrow keys to supernudge a node.

 *You can also use nudge and supernudge in conjunction with a selected bézier control handle.*

 *If you are unable to grab a bézier control handle because it is on top of the node itself, simply hold down the SHIFT key while dragging it away from the node.*

NODE EDITING TOOLS

So far, we've covered a lot of the theory behind nodes. Now you'll see how you can begin modifying things. All of the node editing tools are found in three different places: the Node Edit roll-up, the Node pop-up menu, and the Property Bar.

You can double-click the Shape tool itself to activate the Node Edit roll-up, shown here.

If you right-click a node with the Shape tool, or any other Shape | drawing tool, CorelDRAW displays the pop-up menu shown here.

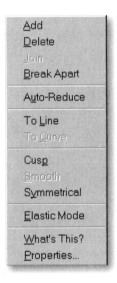

CorelDRAW 8 displays all of the same commands on the Property Bar when the Shape tool is selected. The Property Bar is shown here.

The various commands will be described here using the Property Bar. However, feel free to use whichever tool is most comfortable for you.

Adding and Deleting Nodes

When you are shaping curves, you'll find that often more nodes are needed to get the exact shape that you desire. To position a new node at an exact position, click the path where you wish the new node to appear. A round black dot will appear where you clicked. Click the + icon on the Property Bar or press the + key on the numeric keypad and a node will appear where the circle was located.

Double-click with the Shape tool anywhere on the line where you'd like a node and presto, it will appear!

You can also select an existing node before clicking the + icon. This will create a new node that is located at the midpoint of the segment preceding the selected node. Note that after a node is added, both nodes will be selected. Clicking the + icon a second time will therefore add two more nodes at the midpoints of each of the preceding segments, and then four nodes will be selected. Thus, clicking the + icon several times quickly adds many nodes.

You can delete nodes in much the same manner. Highlight the node or nodes you wish to delete and click the - icon on the Property Bar or simply press the DEL key.

Double-click an existing node with the Shape tool and it will be deleted.

AUTO-REDUCING NODES   As you are creating artwork, sometimes you'll come across a situation where there is an overabundance of nodes. This can be caused by auto-tracing bitmaps, using the Natural Pen tool or Eraser tool, or just plain node craziness. You can spend a lot of time selecting the least important nodes and manually deleting them—or you let the Auto Reduce button can do this for you.

To fully understand the Auto-Reduce function, you need to understand another math term: standard deviation. If you choose Tools | Options | Workspace | Toolbox | Shape tool, you will encounter an Auto-reduce setting that defaults to 4 thousandths of an inch. This value indicates the amount of

8

standard deviation that will be allowed for a node to be deleted—or for you nonmathematicians, the largest distance the node can be from the path that will exist after the node is deleted. The larger the amount of standard deviation, the more nodes that will be deleted. However, deleting more nodes can compromise the integrity of the path. You will find that the default setting works very well under all but the most extreme circumstances.

Breaking Apart and Joining Nodes

Select any node and click the Break Curve icon. This will create two nodes on top of one another and automatically split the path into two subpaths. Move either of the nodes out of the way and you'll see that they are no longer connected. If the path had been closed (and therefore able to be filled), it will now be open, and any fill will be gone. There is still only one path, however, even though there may appear to be two, as shown here.

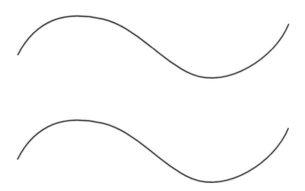

A good example of a single object with two subpaths is the letter O. The outside ellipse is one subpath, and the inside ellipse is a second subpath; when combined, they are a single object with two subpaths. Subpaths don't have to overlap one another. They can be anywhere in a drawing.

When an object contains two or more subpaths, sometimes you will want to combine them into a single path. Select one of the end nodes from each subpath and click the Join Two Nodes icon. The combined node will appear equidistant between the original locations of the separate nodes; therefore, it is a good idea to position the two nodes together in the area where you want the combined node to appear.

Stretching and Rotating Nodes

In Chapter 7 you saw how whole objects could be stretched and rotated. This can also be done with selected nodes. The commands for stretching and rotating nodes are available only when two or more nodes are selected.

The best way to see how these commands work is to complete a simple project:

1. Draw a circle (remember to hold down the CTRL key).

2. Convert the circle to curves using the CTRL-Q shortcut keys.

3. Marquee select all four nodes and click the + key on the numeric keypad twice so that there are a total of 16 nodes.

4. Select every other node by SHIFT-clicking them.

5. Click the Stretch and Scale Nodes icon on the Property Bar.

6. You'll now see handles around the selected nodes just as if they were a selected object. Hold down the SHIFT key and stretch them about two-thirds of the way toward the center of the circle. You should now have a shape similar to the one shown here.

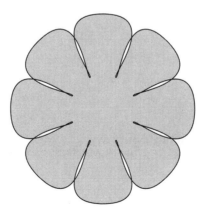

7. Click the Rotate and Skew nodes icon on the Property Bar.

8. The familiar rotation handles should appear. Hold down the CTRL key and rotate the nodes 90 degrees.

9. The final shape should look similar to the one shown here.

Note that the shape you just created has lines that overlap quite a bit, so it may be difficult to print on some printers.

All of the same concepts you learned when stretching and rotating objects also apply when working with nodes.

Closing Open Paths

Suppose you draw this really cool shape and then realize that it isn't closed. Sure, you could grab the Freehand tool and close the shape, but just as easily you can select the end nodes of the open path and click the Extend Curve to Close button on the Property Bar. This will create a straight line between the two end nodes. This button is available only when you have the two end nodes selected. Just selecting one of them will not make the button available.

Another way to accomplish the same feat is to click the Auto-Close Curve button on the Property Bar. It will be available when any nodes of an open path are selected.

Extracting Subpaths

When a curve consists of more than one subpath, there are several ways to make a subpath separate again. The traditional way is to use the Arrange | Break Apart (CTRL-K) command. A problem arises, however, if the curve has more than two subpaths. You may want to separate just one subpath from several others, but Break Apart separates them all.

You can now simply select a node from the subpath that you wish to extract and then click the Extract Subpath button on the Property Bar. This will extract only the selected subpath (or subpaths) and leave the others intact.

Aligning Nodes

When two or more nodes are selected, you have the option of aligning them with one another. Selecting the Align Nodes button on the Property Bar will produce the Node Align dialog box shown here.

You can align the nodes in either the horizontal or the vertical direction. Deselect the option you don't want and then click OK. You can also align the nodes in both the horizontal and vertical directions. This will place all selected nodes on top of one another, but the curve will look very strange because the control points will not be aligned. Therefore, when aligning nodes in both directions, you'll probably want to align the control points as well so the curve remains smooth. The following examples show the results of aligning nodes in the vertical direction, in the horizontal direction, and in both directions, and of aligning the control points.

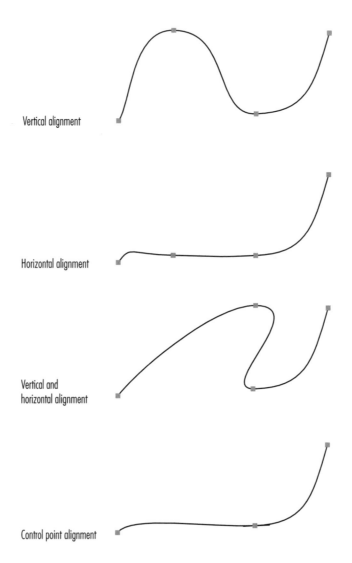

Vertical alignment

Horizontal alignment

Vertical and
horizontal alignment

Control point alignment

Working in Elastic Mode

Normally, when two or more nodes are moved together, they all move the exact same distance. When Elastic Mode is activated, the nodes closest to the node being selected will move proportionally farther. The distance is measured not in a straight line, but along the path itself. A great example of this movement is the "explosion" of a spiral.

1. Draw a spiral with eight rotations, constraining it by holding down the CTRL key.

2. Select all of the nodes.

3. Select Elastic Mode from the Property Bar.

4. Click and drag the outermost node of the spiral to an area above the spiral.

This should provide a twister, as shown here in a before and after view.

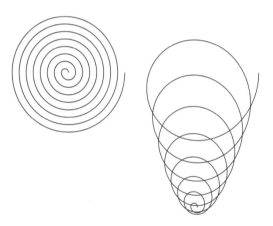

ADVANCED ELLIPSE SHAPING

In earlier chapters, you saw various methods for creating shapes. One of the best ways is to start with an ellipse and then use the Shape tool to mold it into the shape you desire. Before you begin to manipulate the ellipse, make sure to convert it to curves (CTRL-Q). If you don't, you will instead be creating arcs and pie wedges, as described in Chapter 4.

Once you have an ellipse that has been converted to curves, just begin pushing and pulling on nodes, adjusting the bézier handles, and even adding more nodes until the shape begins to take form. Usually you'll need to add many more nodes to the standard ellipse since it only has four to begin with.

This method is so desirable because it often give you curves that are much smoother than what you would get if you drew them using the Freehand tool. In addition, you may find it easier to visualize shapes with this method.

Here is a scene that was created using this method. Some of the shapes are still somewhat elliptical, but others have changed dramatically from the originals. Take a little time to try this method; we think you'll find it quite useful.

In Chapter 15, you'll see how a dolphin was creating from reshaping ellipses.

ADVANCED POLYGON SHAPING

In Chapter 4, you saw how to create some incredible designs by using the Shape tool with a polygon. At that time, you just used the polygon's existing nodes and moved them around a bit. However, you aren't limited to just the existing nodes, and the lines don't have to be straight.

Now that you understand how the Shape tool works, draw another polygon and begin to adjust the nodes. If you want a line to be curved, convert that segment to a curve segment and adjust the bézier control handles. If you want more nodes, add however many you desire. Notice that all of these changes are reflected all the way around the polygon.

With this capability, you can create even more incredible shapes for your projects. Here is an example of a shape created by adding a couple of nodes to a polygon and just playing for a few minutes.

SHAPING BITMAPS

Prior to CorelDRAW 6, when you used the Shape tool on bitmaps, you could crop the edges of the bitmap only in a straight line. There was a single node at each corner of the bitmap, and you could crop the bitmap to any shape—as long as it was rectangular.

Now the rules have changed. You can add nodes, change segments to curves, and basically create any shape you wish. Remember that you are only cropping the bitmap, so the extra information is still contained in your file; it is just hidden from view. This is very similar to using the PowerClip effect described in Chapter 21, but for some bitmaps, it is just as easy to crop the bitmap as it is to PowerClip it.

Here is an example of a bitmap before and after cropping.

8

Before cropping

After cropping

> *The best way to alter the parts of a bitmap that are visible is to mask the bitmap in Corel PHOTO-PAINT, save the file as a CPT (PHOTO-PAINT's native format) file and import into CorelDRAW. Only the area of the bitmap within the mask will display. For more information on importing bitmaps, see Chapter 26.*

THE KNIFE TOOL

The Knife tool is the second tool on the Node Edit flyout. It is similar to the Break Curve button, except that you don't select a node prior to using the Knife tool. Anywhere you click on a path with the Knife tool will create a node and break the curve. If you are working with a closed path, you will need to make two separate cuts to break it into two objects: the first cut will turn the closed path into an open path; the second cut will break the path into two pieces. By default, each object will be closed automatically after that second cut.

You can change the defaults in Tools | Options | Workspace | Toolbox | Knife tool to keep the chopped-up object as a single object. You can also choose not to close additional objects that are created by the Knife tool.

FREEHAND KNIFING

Prior to CorelDRAW 8, you could click the outline of the object to cut it, as described earlier. But you couldn't cut a freehand line with the Knife tool. Now things have changed. Let's work on a little project to see how it works by cracking an egg.

1. Draw an ellipse that looks something like an egg and color it yellow.

2. Select the Knife tool and place it over one side of the egg. The Knife cursor should rotate to indicate that it is ready to cut.

3. Drag the Knife across the object in somewhat of a zigzag pattern until you reach the other side of the object. Note that the cursor will again rotate when it reaches the opposite edge.

4. Before releasing the left mouse button, press the TAB key. You'll notice that half of the egg has been removed. Press TAB again and the other half is removed instead. Press TAB yet again and the whole egg will be retained, but it will be cracked in two. Keep pressing TAB until the piece or pieces you wish to keep are displayed, and then release the left mouse button.

8

Here is the egg prior to cracking and then each of the three stages that can be achieved after cracking. Although this is just a simple addition, it sure can help you to create some cool stuff!

THE ERASER TOOL

A few years back, someone at one of our seminars commented that it would be nice to have an Eraser tool in CorelDRAW. We looked at the person strangely and thought to ourselves that this is a vector program, not a bitmap program. If you want to erase something, just delete it. Then Corel went and added an Eraser tool, and we can see its usefulness. It just goes to show you that some of the best ideas don't always make sense at first.

When you select the Eraser tool from the Shape Edit flyout, the Property Bar will have two different settings that are relevant to the Eraser tool, as shown here.

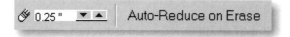

The first setting controls the thickness of the eraser. Just as you can buy different sizes of erasers at your favorite art supply store, you can work with different sizes of erasers in CorelDRAW. Your cursor will change to reflect the size currently chosen so you'll know exactly how big an area you will erase.

The other setting is controlled by the Auto-Reduce on Erase button. Because the Eraser tool can cause quite a few extra nodes to appear, you will probably want this button depressed. It is just an automated way of using the Auto-Reduce function (described earlier in this chapter) immediately after you finish erasing.

To use the Eraser tool, you must first select the object you wish to erase. New to CorelDRAW 8 is the ability to select the object with the Eraser tool. If you have more than one object selected, you will receive an error message. When you have only a single object selected and the Eraser tool is active, simply start erasing the object. As you do this, the parts of the object you've erased will disappear. This can be somewhat misleading as the true erasing doesn't take place until after you release the mouse button. Then the area you've erased will be subtracted from the object.

At times, you may miss certain areas and leave pieces behind. Just continue to erase those areas until you are pleased with the result.

NOTE: *If you have a graphics tablet with an eraser, the Eraser tool is automatically invoked when you turn over your pen—or at least it should be. You may need to make some changes in the tablet's control panel so that it is context sensitive.*

Here is an example of an object before and after parts of it were erased.

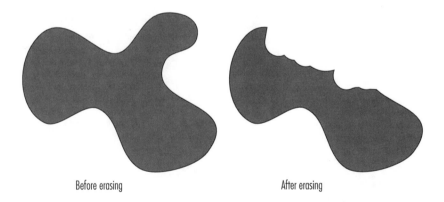

Before erasing   After erasing

As you are creating artwork, you'll find that the Shape tool is the most often used tool in the toolbox. So if you are at all unclear about how nodes work, you might want to go over this chapter again until you fully understand this important concept.

9

COLORS, MODELS, COLOR PALETTES, AND UNIFORM FILLS

Before you can use any of the fill types in CorelDRAW, you have to decide whether to use colors selected from a color palette or a color model. For many CorelDRAW users, a lack of understanding of when to use a color from a palette or a model has lead to disappointing results when a project is printed or displayed on the Internet. To help you make this important decision, the first sections describe the difference between color models and color palettes.

The chapter concludes with a discussion on filling objects using the Uniform Fill dialog box, Color roll-up, and Property Bar. You won't want to miss the section on the new Interactive Tints near the close of the chapter.

COLOR MODELS

Color models contain colors that are either subtractive or additive. Both types of models are made up of colors derived from a mathematical formula. This formula provides a basis for measurement using a color standard.

CorelDRAW supplies seven color models plus a grayscale model. Each color model contains slightly different colors, giving you millions of colors to choose from.

SUBTRACTIVE MODELS

Subtractive models use inks to create color. The more pigment in the ink, the darker the color, and the darker the ink, the less light is reflected off the paper.

Subtractive colors are used for printing to process-color printers using cyan, magenta, yellow, black (CMYK) transparent inks. When using process colors, you can produce millions of colors simply by mixing colors together.

Spot colors are subtractive colors as well, but they are made from opaque inks. These inks cannot be mixed with other spot colors, but tints of a specific ink color can be used. When printing spot colors, a separate plate is required for each spot color used in the image.

When printing process colors, only four plates are required to print the entire color range. Some desktop printers can use only CMY colors. These printers simulate the color black by mixing 100 percent of each of the CMY colors together. Blacks created using this method generally are not as black as those created using the fourth plate containing the black ink.

ADDITIVE MODELS

Additive models use light to create color. Additive colors are made from red, green, blue (RGB) colors. Your computer monitor uses RGB to display colors. The greater a color's intensity, the darker the color. If you use the highest intensity setting, 255, for each of the three colors, you will produce the color white. Conversely, if you use the lowest intensity setting, 0, for each of the colors, you will produce the color black.

Colors can be displayed using the hue, saturation, brightness (HSB) color values of red, green, and blue. The human eye sees colors displayed in HSB more accurately than those using any other color model. Hue is the actual color, saturation is the purity of the color, and brightness is the amount of white in the color.

The additive color models available in CorelDRAW are RGB, HSB, HLS, Lab, and YIQ. These color models differ mainly in that they were developed by different companies, each using its own formula.

The model of choice in most cases is the Lab model. The Lab model uses the color ranges of both the CMYK and RGB color models. The Lab model is device independent and represents the way the human eye sees color, similar to the HSB color model. Because it is device independent, in theory it produces more predictable results than any of the other models. Device independence means that the colors are displayed without any bias toward a particular monitor.

Table 9-1 lists the eight models available, the type of colors used in each model, and the best use of each model.

COLOR PALETTES

An electronic color palette is like the artist's palette except it contains many more separate colors than an artist could place on a palette. The electronic palette displays the many individual colors in color wells. Each of the many color palettes in CorelDRAW contains a different set of colors. These color sets are either CMYK, RGB, or spot colors.

Color palettes contain individual colors that have either been mixed from a color palette or have been specifically supplied by a particular provider. The best examples of colors supplied by a provider are the Pantone spot and process colors.

Color Model	Colors Used in Model	Best Use
CMY	Cyan, magenta, yellow	Four-color printing
CMYK	Cyan, magenta, yellow, black	Four-color printing
RGB	Red, green, blue	Screen presentations, Web display, and slides
HSB	Hue, saturation, brightness	Screen presentations, Web display, and slides
HLS	Hue, lightness, saturation	Screen presentations, Web display, and slides
Lab	Encompasses the range of both CMYK and RGB color models	Four-color printing
YIQ	Luminance and chromatic values (NTSC American video standard)	Television broadcast images
Grayscale	256 shades of gray	Black to white printing

TABLE 9-1   Color Models

There are four basic RGB color palettes, seven spot color palettes, and a basic CMYK color palette. The Lab color palette is in a category of its own because it combines elements of both RGB and CMYK colors.

The default palette docked on the right side of the drawing window is called the Custom palette, which contains the CMYK color palette. To view one of seven basic palettes other than the default palette, choose View | Color Palette. When the flyout appears, click one of the palette types. The benefit of being able to replace the default palette is that when you want to work exclusively with another palette, you can display these other palettes onscreen for easy access. We will discuss the Load Palette option at the bottom of the flyout later in this chapter.

Spot colors are most often used when you need a specific color or when your project contains only one or two colors. A *spot color* is a premixed printer ink that prints the same each time it is used. Spot colors are used in conjunction with a swatch book that contains all the colors in the particular palette. You begin by choosing the color you want from the swatch book. Each color has a corresponding name and number assigned to it. You simply choose the color you want and then choose its matching name or number from the palette in the Uniform Fill dialog box or choose its name on the Color roll-up.

Some projects require the use of both process colors and spot colors. For example, a sales brochure may use process colors for the main brochure and a spot color for the client's logo. Keep in mind that a separate plate is used for each spot color, adding to the cost of the project.

> *A new process color palette called Pantone Hexachrome is now available. Hexachrome color uses six different process inks (cyan, magenta, yellow, black, orange, and green) to produce full-color images. Ask your service bureau and your printer whether you should use hexachrome colors. For you to use them, your service bureau must be able to produce a match print using the six process colors. Remember that using this palette will require two more color plates, which will add to the cost of the project. However, the increase in the quality of the final print may be worth it.*

THE DEFAULT CUSTOM PALETTE

The default Custom palette docked on the right side of the drawing window contains 89 CMYK colors, 10 grays, and white—for a total of 100 choices. The default palette contains CMYK colors because most color printing is done using process colors. It's important to understand that you don't have to use the colors in this palette to print with CMYK process colors. In fact, you can select a color from any of the available color models and palettes and still print in CMYK colors. This is possible because the print engine in CorelDRAW treats all colors except spot colors as CMYK colors. You can even print spot colors as CMYK colors if you check the Convert Spot Colors to CMYK box on the Separations page in the Print dialog box.

> *Although you can use RGB colors when creating your drawings, if your final output is to paper, don't count on the conversion to CMYK process. Use the CMYK color models and palettes to start with to ensure optimum results.*

You may be wondering why there are so many "brand name" palettes to choose from if, when you print, everything is printed in process colors or spot

colors. The answer is that many of the process color palettes and all the spot color palettes provide color swatch books that contain printed colors corresponding to every color in their respective palettes. Choosing your colors from the swatch book ensures that the colors will print the same in your projects.

This brings up the subject of screen color versus the color that is actually printed. Until recently, screen color rarely came close to the actual color printed on paper or film. CorelDRAW includes a Color Profile Wizard 8 that allows you to create a color profile based on your scanner and monitor as well as the desktop printer or separations output device (refer to Chapter 24 to learn how to create color profiles for your system). These color profiles go a long way toward matching the screen colors to the final printed color by using a built-in artificial intelligence system. You notice we say these color profiles go a long way toward matching colors; we don't say they match them perfectly. If you wonder why the color management system can't perfectly match the colors on your screen to the printed colors, it's because your screen uses additive colors, and the printer uses subtractive colors. Additive colors are represented by the light from your monitor (RGB colors), and subtractive colors are made up of the inks the printer uses (CMYK colors). The only absolute way to match CMYK colors is to use the swatch books referred to earlier.

After learning that you can't really trust the screen color, you should be asking, "Then what's the purpose of the default Custom color palette?" The primary purpose of this color palette is to provide a place to store custom colors. The Custom color palette in previous versions was the only palette that allowed you to add your own custom colors. You will learn how to create your own custom palettes using the new Palette Editor later in this chapter.

DETERMINING WHICH PALETTE TO USE

Before you decide which palette to use in a project, you need to know how the image will be used. Will it be printed with process colors or spot colors? Will it be used for screen presentations or slides? Will it be used on the Internet? CorelDRAW lists all the available palettes in the new Color Palette Docker window, which you access by choosing View | Color Palette | Load Palette. When you select one of the palettes from the Docker window, it replaces the existing palette. By default, the CorelDRAW Custom palette, using CMYK colors, is displayed when you open CorelDRAW.

Table 9-2 lists the 16 basic palettes available, the type of colors included in each palette, and the best use of each palette. CorelDRAW 8 includes an additional 49 custom theme palettes for both RGB and CMYK colors.

Palette Type	Colors Used in Palette	Best Use
Uniform	RGB	Screen presentations and slides
Custom (the default palette)	CMYK	Four-color printing
RGB	RGB	Screen presentations and slides
FOCOLTONE colors	CMYK	Color matching system for four-color printing
CMYK	CMYK	Four-color printing
PANTONE MATCHING SYSTEM®	Spot color	Color matching system (spot colors)
PANTONE HEXACHROME™	CMYKOG O = Orange; G = Green	Color matching system (spot colors)
PANTONE Process Color	CMYK	Color matching system for four-color printing
TRUMATCH Process Color System	CMYK	Process color specifier
Netscape Navigator™	RGB	Screen presentations on the Internet using Netscape Navigator™
Microsoft® Internet Explorer	RGB	Screen presentations on the Internet using Microsoft® Internet Explorer
Spectramaster® colors	LAB	Color matching system (spot colors)
TOYO Color Finder system	CMYK	Color matching system (spot colors) for automobile paint
DIC colors	CMYK	Color matching system for four-color printing
LAB colors	LAB	Four-color printing
Grayscale RGB and K	256 and 100 shades of gray	Black and white printing

TABLE 9-2   Color Palettes

9

COLOR MATCHING SYSTEM COLORS AND SPOT COLORS PALETTES

The term "color matching system" in Table 9-2 may be new to you. The common name for colors contained in a color matching system is spot and process colors. These spot colors contain the colors from universally accepted color matching systems such as PANTONE Process Colors. Companies that produce these spot color inks offer swatch books that show the colors as they would appear when printed. The benefit of using a spot color is that you can select a color from the swatch book and then choose the corresponding color in the color palette; you know what the color will look like when it's printed. You will want to use a spot color when, for example, your client tells you that you must match the company colors exactly. You do not need to use spot and process colors for all your projects, but note that the color you see on your monitor is not what is going to print on paper whether you're using spot or process colors. Also available on the third-party market is a swatch book for CMYK process colors. This author uses one produced by AGFA called PostScript™ Process ColorGuide. You can reach them at 1-800-395-7007 or their Web site at agfahome.com.

 *If you are producing files that are being sent to a service bureau or printer, you should buy one of the color matching system swatch books. Onscreen colors can provide a fairly accurate representation of what the colors will look like when printed. However, their accuracy depends on several variables, especially your video card and monitor. A swatch book provides an accurate representation of each color in the color matching system. Being able to compare the colors in the swatch book to the colors you see on your screen can save you time and money at printing time.*

CREATING YOUR OWN SWATCH BOOK FROM THE CUSTOM COLOR PALETTE

If the only purpose for custom palettes was to store custom colors, they would not have much value, but if you could choose a color from a swatch book that related to the colors in your custom palettes, you could then have confidence in the colors being printed. There are no swatch books for CorelDRAW's default palette or for any custom palettes you create, but you can create your own.

Creating a swatch book for the default palette is not a gimmick dreamed up for inclusion in this book. It's an extremely important step in ensuring that the colors you choose from the Custom palette print correctly.

Creating a swatch book, which will actually be a single sheet of paper, involves drawing small rectangles on the page, one for each custom color, and filling each one with a color in the Custom color palette. Underneath the colored squares, you type the CMYK values that make up each color. You then print the file on the paper you will use for your projects.

You can use this pseudo-swatch book to choose your colors for each project that will use the same paper as the swatch book. Make additional swatch books for every medium on which you will be printing. For example, if you will be printing on cups using the sublimation method, create a print using the colors you will be using and print it on a cup. The next time you will be printing on cups, pick the colors from those on the cup, and you will be assured that the colors will print correctly. If you are outputting to film, spend the money and have a match print made of the Custom color palette.

If you don't create custom swatch books, you will have to rely on the colors displayed on your monitor. If you use a color profile created by the Color Profile Wizard, you will have to trust the accuracy of the artificial intelligence of the color management system. Since most users will probably procrastinate and put off creating a custom color swatch file for printing on various media, we have created a .cdr file of all 100 colors in the CorelDRAW Custom palette that you can download from our Web site at unleash.com. Print this palette with the corresponding CMYK values on the medium you will be printing to and use it as your Custom palette swatch book. A sample of the color palette is printed in the color pages of this book.

USING COLOR MODELS AND PALETTES

Now that you understand the differences between color models and palettes and know about the different colors contained in them, it's time to put this knowledge to use.

The average CorelDRAW user tends to pick colors from the default Custom palette displayed on the right side of the CorelDRAW window. With all the new palettes in CorelDRAW 8, it's time to be adventuresome. To change

9

to another palette you have two options. The first option is to choose View | Color Palette and choose one of the listed palettes from the child menu (see Figure 9-1). This option will display the most frequently used palettes. The second option is, instead of choosing one of the palettes listed, choose Load Palette at the bottom of the child menu to display the Color Palette Docker™ window shown in Figure 9-2. This Docker window lets you choose from all the palettes available in CorelDRAW 8.

When you choose a palette from this Docker window, the new palette is immediately displayed. Figure 9-3 shows a close-up view of the Docker window with the CMYK\Misc folder expanded to show the various theme palettes available in this category. The Load button at the bottom of the

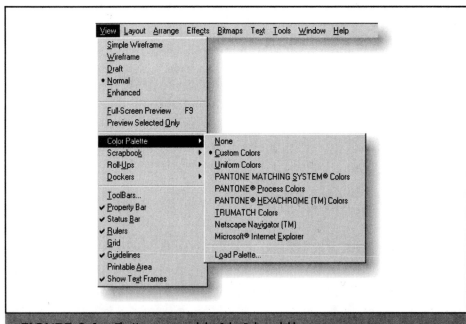

FIGURE 9-1   The View menu and the Color Palette child menu

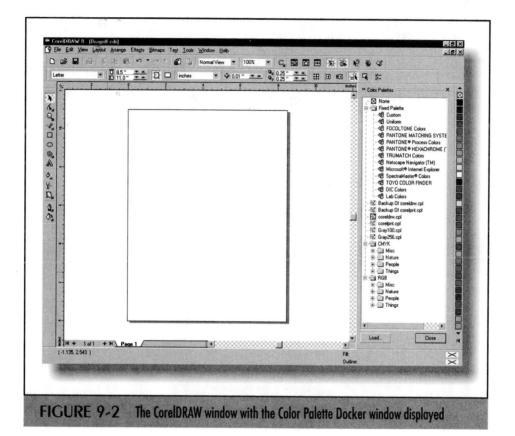

FIGURE 9-2   The CorelDRAW window with the Color Palette Docker window displayed

9

Docker window lets you access any custom palettes you may have stored in a folder other than the default palette folders.

This method of choosing new palettes should be the preferred method for most users.

USING THE POP-UP TINT PALETTES

The new pop-up tint palette, shown in Figure 9-4, lets you select tints from selected colors. To use the new pop-up palette, follow the same steps you

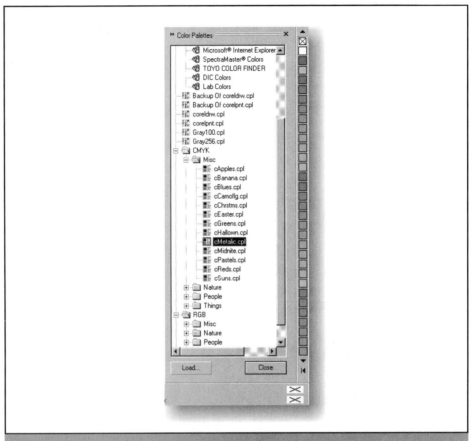

FIGURE 9-3   The Color Palette Docker window showing the CMYK\Misc folder expanded

would normally use to select a color but instead of clicking and immediately releasing the mouse button, click and hold down the mouse button for a second or two. A palette of 64 tints of the color you clicked will appear. Click one of the 64 tints to use as your fill. This pop-up palette is HSL-based, with the hue of the color being used horizontally and a combination of saturation and lightness used vertically. The original color from the palette is the center color in the pop-up, unless the color is at the extreme end of the scale. For

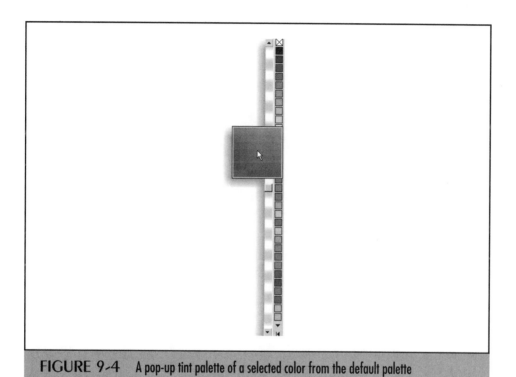

FIGURE 9-4   A pop-up tint palette of a selected color from the default palette

9

example, 100 percent black, grayscale, and spot colors will be a
one-dimensional grid of density (represented by a bar rather than a box).
Figure 9-5 shows the Pantone Matching System Colors palette and the pop-up
palette displaying the ten different tints available for the selected spot color.
The tints on this flyout range from 100 percent closest to the main palette to
0 percent at the left end of the tint palette.

NOTE: *It's OK to use the pop-up palettes with spot colors because, unlike
the* CTRL-*click mixing method described earlier, the pop-up
palette contains only percentages of the spot color, not tints from
different colors.*

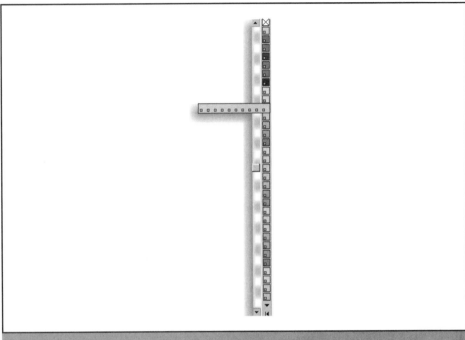

FIGURE 9-5   The pop-up tint palette of a selected spot color

USING THE PALETTE EDITOR

The new Palette Editor in CorelDRAW 8 solves many past problems. Many designers had asked for the ability to create custom palettes containing only a few colors. Although this capability has always been available, knowing how to and where to create a custom palette was difficult. The Palette Editor's primary purpose is to let you create custom palettes. Creating a custom palette could also include modifying an existing palette. You access the Palette Editor, shown in Figure 9-6, by choosing Tools | Palette Editor. You create a custom palette by choosing colors from the Color Models, Fixed Palettes and by using the mixers. You access these various sources by clicking their respective

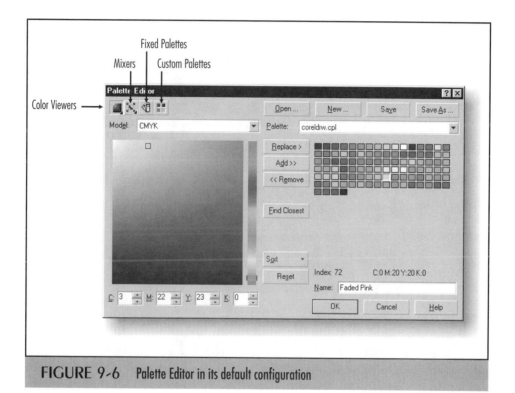

FIGURE 9-6   Palette Editor in its default configuration

9

buttons in the upper-left corner of the Palette Editor. You access the Color models, however, by clicking the Color Viewers button.

CREATING CUSTOM PALETTES

Practice creating a custom palette by choosing Tools | Palette Editor. When the Palette Editor appears, click the New button at the top of the dialog box. The New Palette dialog box shown here will appear. Choose a folder in which to store your custom palette. We chose Palettes\CMYK\Misc. We named the palette My Special and then clicked the Save button to save the palette. As soon as you save the name of your new palette the Palette Editor will reappear, displaying the name of your custom palette. The Palette area that will ultimately contain your custom colors will be empty.

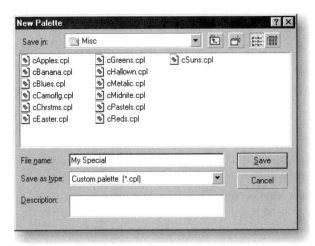

To learn the process of collecting colors from the various models, palettes, and mixers, you will add colors from all these sources into this one custom palette. In the real world, you would most likely create separate palettes from each source. Follow these steps to create a custom palette:

1. Click the down arrow of the Model list box and choose the CMYK model.

2. Click the Color Viewers button and choose CMYK -3D Subtractive.

3. Click the 3D color box to choose a color.

4. Click the Add button and the color you picked will be added to the new palette area. Pick several more colors, but remember to click the Add button each time. The Palette Editor should now resemble the one shown in Figure 9-7.

   You can give your new colors names by typing the names in the Name box at the bottom of the Palette Editor. Pretty easy so far, eh? Now let's add some more colors from the Mixers.

5. Click the Mixers button and choose Color Blend from the drop-down menu.

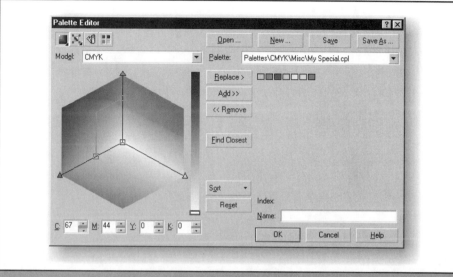

FIGURE 9-7   The Palette Editor with the My Special palette loaded and the CMYK- 3D Subtractive model selected

6. Use the cursor to select additional colors from the grid, each time clicking the Add button.

7. If you want to select from a different set of blended colors, click a down arrow on one of the corner buttons and select a new color from the drop-down palette.

   The Palette Editor should now look something like Figure 9-8.

8. Click the Mixers button again and select Mixing Area.

9. Use the Eyedropper tool to sample colors from the colors in the mixing area. You can also interactively mix the colors by clicking the brush button and smearing colors together.

10. After you select a few more colors from the mixing area, the Palette Editor should look similar to Figure 9-9.

11. Click the Fixed Palettes button in the upper-left corner of the Palette Editor and select the PANTONE MATCHING SYSTEM colors. Normally, you wouldn't add spot colors to a CMYK palette, but let's pretend that you always use a particular spot color for every project. Here's the way to do it.

9

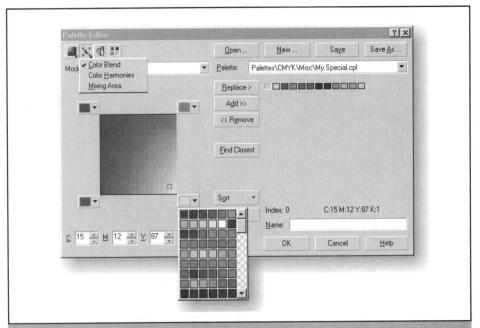

FIGURE 9-8   The Palette Editor with the My Special palette loaded and the Color Blend grid selected

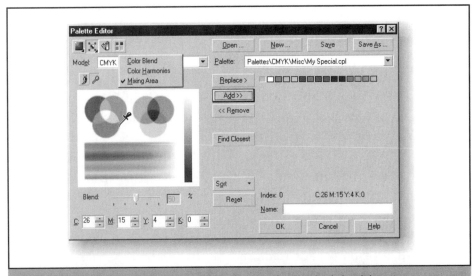

FIGURE 9-9   The Palette Editor with the My Special palette loaded and the Mixing Area selected

12. Select a spot color from the palette and click the Add button as before.

13. To make sure you have the correct color, click the Sort button and choose Name from the drop-down list. This choice will show the name of the spot color selected. The Palette Editor should now look like the one in Figure 9-10.

14. Now, for the last step in creating your custom palette, click the Custom Palettes button and select the coreldrw.cpl palette. This is the default palette.

15. Choose a few colors from this palette to complete your custom palette.

16. Click the Save button to save the palette. If you forget this step, everything you just did will be lost. The Palette Editor should now resemble the one shown in Figure 9-11.

The next time you want to use your custom palette, simply choose View | Color Palette and choose Load Palette. The Palettes Docker window will appear. Select the folder where you stored your custom palette and your new custom palette will replace the existing palette.

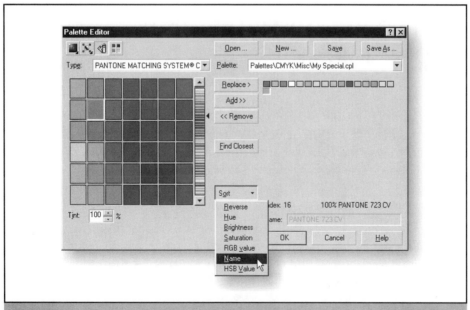

FIGURE 9-10   The Palette Editor with the My Special palette loaded and the PANTONE MATCHING SYSTEM palette selected

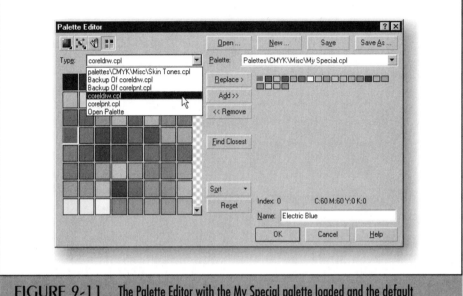

FIGURE 9-11   The Palette Editor with the My Special palette loaded and the default coreldrw.cpl palette selected

CREATING A CUSTOM PALETTE USING COLOR HARMONIES

Now that you've learned how to create a custom palette, let's create another one. This time you will select colors from the Color Harmonies in the Palette Editor. The Color Harmonies list lets you select up to 20 colors that go well together. This approach can be very useful for those of you who need a little help choosing colors that harmonize. Figure 9-12 shows the default setting. Follow these steps to create a new custom palette:

1. Create a new custom palette (see the section "Creating Custom Palettes" earlier in the chapter).

2. With the Palette Editor open and your custom palette loaded, click the Mixers button and choose Color Harmonies from the list. The Palette Editor will look like Figure 9-12.

3. Add two or three colors from the palette beneath the color wheel to your custom palette.

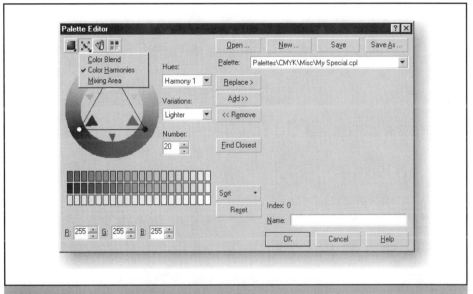

FIGURE 9-12   The Palette Editor with Color Harmonies displayed

4. Change the look of the wheel by selecting Harmony 3 from the Hues drop-down list.

5. Click one of the corner circles of the rectangle on the color wheel and spin it around. Notice that the colors in the palette change as you spin the rectangle.

6. Click the first color in the palette (the upper-left color well). Hold down the SHIFT key and select the last color in the palette (the lower-right color well). This will select all the colors in the palette.

7. Click the Add button and all 20 colors will be placed in your custom palette. If you want a harmonizing palette of fewer than 20 colors, change the number by choosing a lower number in the Number box. As mentioned, you can name each of your custom colors. We named one of the colors in the new palette Arizona Green (see the bottom of the Palette Editor). Your custom palette should now look like Figure 9-13.

8. Remember to save your new palette before you click the OK button.

9

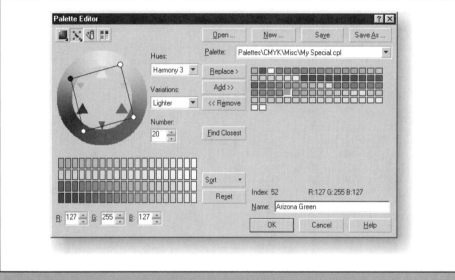

FIGURE 9-13   The Palette Editor with Color Harmonies 3 displayed and 20 more custom colors

By now you should be an expert using the Palette Editor. You should find this ability to create custom palettes a real benefit when working in CorelDRAW.

CREATING PALETTES FROM OPEN DOCUMENTS AND SELECTED OBJECTS

We have just about reached the end of this interesting subject of color palettes. Before the topic can be considered complete, we will cover one of the newest and best features, which we saved for last.

For years, CorelDRAW users have asked to be able to create a custom palette using the colors in an existing document. Well, miracles do happen; now you can. Not only can you create a palette using the colors from an existing document, but you can also create a palette using the colors from within a selection.

The process of creating these unique palettes is extremely simple. Follow these steps to create both of these palettes:

1. Open an existing drawing or import a clipart image into a new document. We used a clipart image from the CorelDRAW 7's clipart CD Clipart\Fantasy folder (we did not have a version 8 CD at the time of this writing.) The file name is Fants016.cdr.

2. Choose Tools | New Palette from Document.

3. The New Palette dialog box will appear (see Figure 9-14).

4. Give your new palette a name and save it to a folder of your choice.

To use your new palette, choose View | Color Palette and choose Load Palette. The Palette Docker window will appear. Select the folder where you stored the palette and your new palette containing only the colors from the

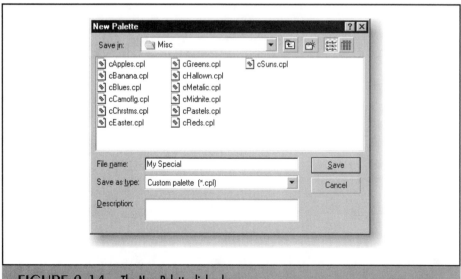

FIGURE 9-14   The New Palette dialog box

document will magically appear. If you used the same .cdr files as we did, your palette will look like Figure 9-15. We have circled the new custom palette.

Now that you've created a palette containing colors from a document, you can create a palette containing colors from only a selected portion of a document. Follow these steps:

1. Open an existing drawing or import a clipart image into a new document. We used a clipart image from the Clipart\Actives folder. The file name is Activ009.cdr (also from CorelDRAW 7's clipart CD). Our goal is to capture the colors used in creating the boy's skin tones.

2. Select all the objects making up the boy by using the SHIFT-click technique (see Chapter 7).

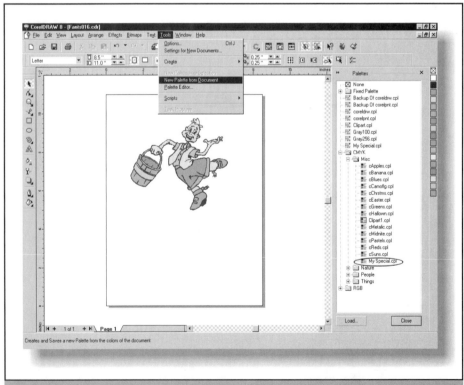

FIGURE 9-15   A custom palette created from an existing document

3. Choose Tools | New Palette from Selection.

4. The New Palette dialog box will appear.

5. Give your new palette a name and save it to a folder of your choice.

6. Load this new palette as before by choosing View | Color Palette and choosing Load Palette. The Palettes Docker window will appear. Select the folder where you stored the palette and your new palette containing only the colors from the selected objects will appear. Your new palette should look like the one in Figure 9-16 if you used the same file that we did. We have circled the Skin Tones Custom palette in the figure.

9

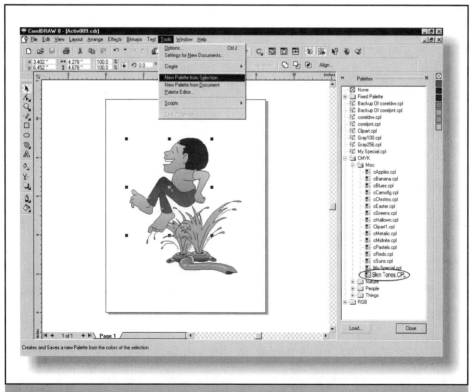

FIGURE 9-16   A custom palette created from selected objects

UNIFORM FILLS

Uniform fills are considered solid fills. These are the colors found in the color palettes and color models discussed earlier. This chapter concentrates on uniform fills whereas Chapter 10 covers special fills. Once you have learned how to use the uniform fills it will be easier to create special fills.

SETTING THE DEFAULT FILL COLOR

The first thing you should learn about fills is how to change the default fill. It's important to know how to do so in case a default value is changed accidentally (this happens more often than you might think). By default, No Fill is set for all objects and Black CMYK is set for text. These values are recommended. If the defaults are changed, follow these steps to reset them:

1. Make sure no objects are selected. Then click the No Fill button (the one with the X) on the Fill tool flyout.

2. The Uniform Fill message box shown here appears. Check the Graphic check box and leave the Artistic Text and Paragraph Text check boxes unchecked.

3. Click the OK button.

4. Click the Fill Color Dialog button on the Fill tool flyout (the leftmost button on the flyout.)

5. The Uniform Fill message box appears again. This time remove any check mark from the Graphics check box and put check marks in the Artistic Text and Paragraph Text check boxes.

6. Click the OK button.

7. The Uniform Fill dialog box will now appear. Click the More button to expand the dialog box. (see Figure 9-17).

8. Click the Color Viewers button and choose CMYK from the Model drop-down list.

9. Enter the number 100 in the K num box and 0 in the C, M, and Y num boxes. The word "Black" will appear in the Name box.

10. Click the OK button.

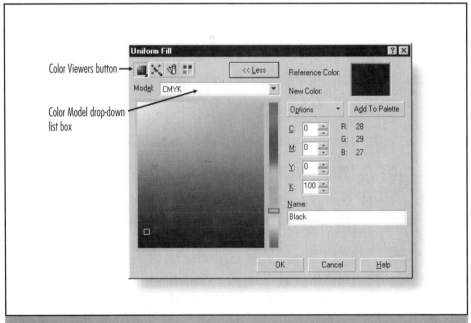

FIGURE 9-17   The expanded Uniform Fill dialog box with the CMYK color model displayed

That's it. You just reset the defaults to No Fill for graphic objects and Black CMYK fill for Artistic and Paragraph Text.

THE UNIFORM FILL DIALOG BOX

You learned all about color models and palettes at the beginning of this chapter. Now you will learn how to use them. The Uniform Fill dialog box is one way to access the many color models and palettes described in the beginning of this chapter. (You can also access the color models and palettes from the Color roll-up and Property Bar, as described later. In addition, as you learned, you can access dozens of color palettes by choosing View | Color Palette | Load Palette.)

You can use the Uniform Fill dialog box to select colors to fill newly created objects or to edit existing fills. To access the Uniform Fill dialog box, select the object you want to fill or edit and click the Fill Color Dialog button (the one at the far left) on the Fill tool flyout. Figure 9-18 shows the Uniform Fill

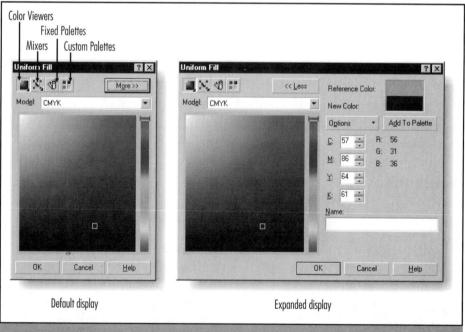

FIGURE 9-18   The Uniform Fill dialog box in the default and expanded display

dialog box displaying the CMYK color model. The first time you access the dialog box it will display as shown on the left side of Figure 9-18. Click the More button in the upper-right corner of the default dialog box to view the expanded dialog box shown on the right side of the figure. The four buttons in the upper-left corner of the dialog box provide access to all the color models and palettes available in CorelDRAW 8. Figure 9-19 shows the expanded dialog box with the Fixed Palettes button selected displaying the PANTONE MATCHING SYSTEM color palette.

Using Color Models in the Uniform Fill Dialog Box

When you first open the Uniform Fill dialog box, one of the color models or color palettes will be displayed. The one displayed depends on the fill of the object selected. If the object has no fill or is filled with a fill other than a solid color, the CMYK color model is displayed. Click the down arrow on the Model drop-down list box to select other color models.

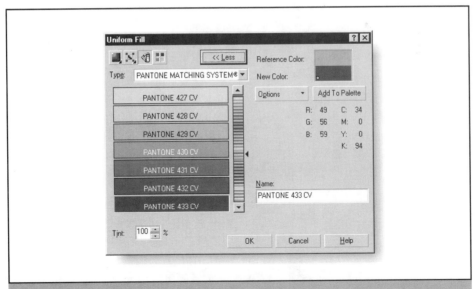

FIGURE 9-19   The Uniform Fill dialog box when the Fixed Palettes button is selected

When you click and hold down the mouse button on the Color Viewers button in the upper-left corner of the dialog box, you'll see a child menu (Figure 9-20) that offers a choice of seven visual representations of the visible color spectrum. Choose a color spectrum of choice to select your colors. When you select a color from one of the color views, the color appears in the preview box in the upper-right corner of the dialog box, adjacent to the words "New Color." If there is an international no symbol next to the color, as shown in Figure 9-21, the color will not print exactly as it displays (see the section "Using the Gamut Alarm" later in this chapter.) Figure 9-21 shows the Uniform Fill dialog box when the RGB color model is selected along with the HSB Wheel Based color viewer.

Using Color Palettes in the Uniform Fill Dialog Box

To change to a color palette, click the Custom Palettes button in the Uniform Fill dialog box. When you click the down arrow of the Type drop-down list

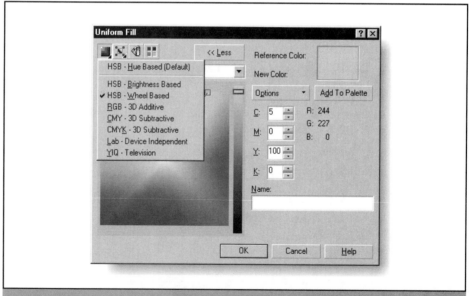

FIGURE 9-20   The Uniform Fill dialog box when the Fixed Palettes button is selected

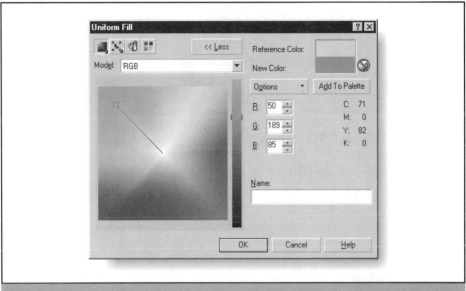

FIGURE 9-21   The Uniform Fill dialog box with an RGB color model and HSB Wheel Based color viewer displayed

box, you will be offered four choices. The first choice is coreldrw.cpl, which is the default CMYK palette. The second choice is corelpnt.cpt, which is the default RGB Corel PHOTO-PAINT palette. The third choice is the User Defined Inks palette discussed later in this chapter. The fourth choice is Open Palette. When you choose this option you can open any of the CorelDRAW 8 custom palettes by choosing them from the Custom\Palettes folder. Figure 9-22 shows the Uniform Fill dialog box when the default coreldrw.cpl palette is selected.

USING THE COLOR HARMONIES PALETTES   Color harmonies are custom palettes made up of 60 or 80 colors that harmonize. These palettes are provided for users who may have difficulty choosing colors that work well together. To access these custom palettes, press the Mixers button (hold down the mouse button) in the Uniform Fill dialog box and choose Color Harmonies from the child menu (see Figure 9-23).

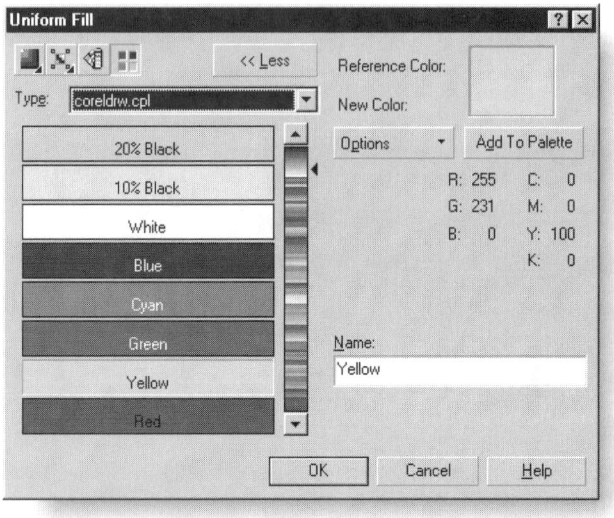

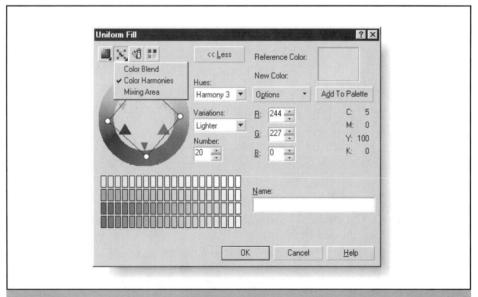

FIGURE 9-22   The Uniform Fill dialog box when the default palette is selected

FIGURE 9-23   The Uniform Fill dialog box when Color Harmonies is selected

Using User-Defined Inks to Fill Objects

Filling an object with the designation of user-defined inks is a way to create a custom color plate in addition to any others created during the color separation process. The colors contained in this plate are used as "stand-in colors" for the colors that will actually be used when the project is printed. This means that if you wanted to use one of the more exotic inks, such as "Gold Foil," you would fill the object in CorelDRAW with one of the user-defined inks fills. When the printer gets to the plate containing the objects with the user-defined inks, he or she simply uses the real Gold Foil ink on the press.

To fill an object with a user-defined ink fill, follow these steps:

1. Click the Custom Palettes button in the upper-left corner of the Uniform Fill dialog box (see Figure 9-24).

   Click the down arrow of the Type list box and choose User Defined Inks. Five user-defined inks are displayed.

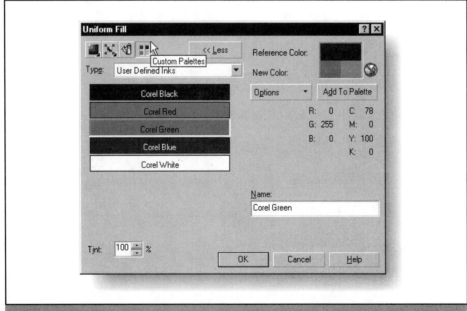

FIGURE 9-24   The Uniform Fill dialog box showing the User Defined Inks colors

2. Choose any of the inks. If you're going to use several, you might start at the top and choose Corel Black (we used Corel Green in our example; see Figure 9-24). Click the OK button to finish.

Figure 9-25 shows the Separations page of the Print dialog box. Notice the user-defined ink color at the bottom of the Separations page, identified as Corel Green.

USING THE COLOR ROLL-UP

As mentioned, solid fills are the single colors found in the many color palettes and color models available in CorelDRAW. The color palette at the right side

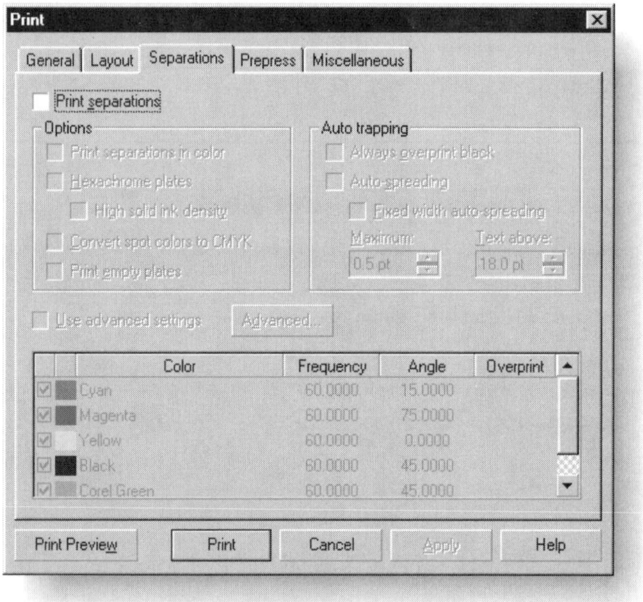

FIGURE 9-25 The Separations page of the Print dialog box, showing a user defined ink identified as Corel Green

of the CorelDRAW window is the primary source for selecting colors to fill your objects. You can change this palette to any one of the CorelDRAW palettes. For many users, this palette is all they ever need. Others prefer to use the Color roll-up to select their colors.

The Color roll-up provides a special convenience in that from this one roll-up, you can access all the color models and palettes, as well as Color Blend and Mixing Area features. An added bonus is that you can apply the selected color to the outline as well as to the fill. To open the Color roll-up, click the Color Roll-up button on the Fill tool flyout.

You can use the Eyedropper tool at the bottom of the roll-up to select an existing object's fill or outline. When you click the Eyedropper, the cursor is replaced by an arrow. Use the arrow to click the object whose color you want to change. When the object is selected, the color model or color palette corresponding to the selected color will automatically appear in the roll-up.

Figure 9-26 shows the Color roll-up displaying the CMYK color model. Remember, to display a color model or color palette, click the down arrow on the Category list box at the top of the Color roll-up. For example, if you want to display a color palette instead of a color model, click the Category list box and choose Palette from the bottom of the list. Figure 9-27 shows that the PANTONE® Process Colors palette is selected and the color Pantone S232-1 is selected from the palette. If you want to view the Pantone colors by name, click the flyout button and choose Show Color Names from the menu.

To change to a different color palette, click the down arrow on the Palette list box under the Name list box. This list box will be displayed only if Palette has been selected from the Category list box at the top of the roll-up.

The CMYK color values displayed under the Category list box show the individual color values of the selected color depending of the color model or palette selected. If you know the values for a specific color you would like to use, you can enter them in the appropriate num boxes.

The Name box lets you type a name for a color selected from a color model. The name will not be assign to the color until you add the color to the palette. To add a color to the currently displayed palette click on the flyout arrow at

9

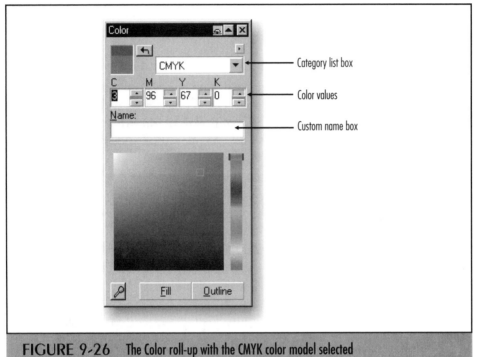

FIGURE 9-26 The Color roll-up with the CMYK color model selected

the upper right of the color roll-up and choose Add Color to Palette from the menu. The new color will be displayed as the last color in the palette.

Using the Gamut Alarm

No discussion on using colors from the Color roll-up would be complete without mentioning the Gamut Alarm. Its function is to warn you if you have selected a color that won't print within the CMYK color range. This doesn't mean it won't print at all; it simply means the color you select will not print in the color you see onscreen. The alarm is not a sound; instead, it warns you by displaying the nonprintable area in green in the color model window. This tells you not to select any colors within the green area if you expect them to print correctly. The Color roll-up is shown here with the flyout displayed and the Gamut Alarm enabled.

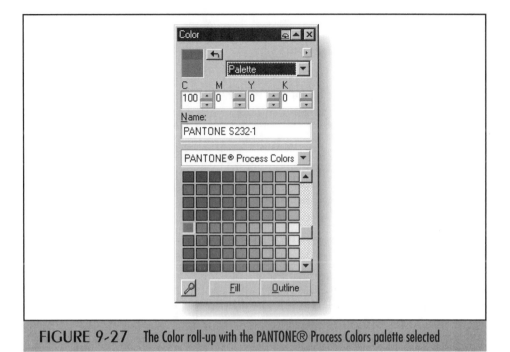

FIGURE 9-27   The Color roll-up with the PANTONE® Process Colors palette selected

Notice the flat gray area in the preview window in the black and white illustration. This is the green area put there by the Gamut Alarm. Any color

9

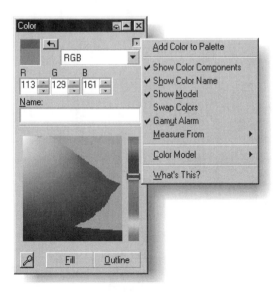

that falls under the green area will not print exactly as it displays on screen.

Using the Mixing Area

Mixing Area is one of the options in the Category list box at the top of the Color roll-up. The Color roll-up, displaying the mixing area, is shown in Figure 9-28.

The Mixing Area option lets you play artist and mix your own colors. You can mix the colors in the mixing area window by using the Brush and Eyedropper tools below the mixing area window. You click the Eyedropper tool and use it to sample a color in the mixing window. Then you select the Brush tool and drag in the mixing area window to paint the color you selected onto a different color or colors. You use the Blend slider control to control the opacity of the color you are painting with. You can select the Eyedropper tool again to sample the colors you painted over. If the color you select is not quite what you want, you can manually change the RGB value in the num boxes near the top of the roll-up. Once you are satisfied with the color, select the object you want to fill and click the Fill button.

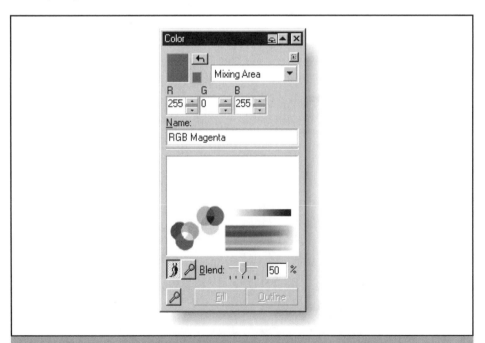

FIGURE 9-28   The Color roll-up displaying the mixing area

If you want to permanently save your new color, type a name for it in the Name box above the mixing area window and click the flyout button at the top of the roll-up. When the flyout appears, select Add Color to Palette. Your new color will be saved, along with its name, at the bottom of the Custom Colors palette.

LOADING A NEW IMAGE IN THE MIXING AREA WINDOW   Using the mixing area window to create custom colors is admittedly a crude method. The real value of this mixing area is that it enables you to load a new image to replace the default colors in the mixing area window. The new image can be any bitmap image. For example, you may want to use a special color from a bitmap image of your own. If the image is very large, crop the portion of the image that contains the colors you want and save it as a separate bitmap image with a .bmp extension. Now click the flyout arrow at the top of the roll-up and select Load Bitmap. The Load Mixing Area File dialog box will appear. Change to the folder where your bitmap is stored and select it. Now click the Open button. Your new bitmap image will replace the default colors in the mixing area window. Use the Eyedropper tool to select the color you want. As with all the options in the Color roll-up, click either the Fill button or the Outline button to apply the selected color.

You can save your new bitmap so that it is stored in the same folder as the default mixing window bitmap, Pntarea.bmp, by clicking the Save Bitmap option in the flyout.

Using the Color Blend Option

Figure 9-29 shows the Color roll-up displaying the Color Blend option. You access it by selecting Color Blend from the Category drop-down list. Like the Mixing Area option, the Color Blend option allows you to create custom colors. It provides perhaps a better way of creating colors than the color mixing method, except that it does not let you load new bitmap images.

When you choose the Color Blend option, a grid of blended colors is generated from a combination of the colors in the four squares at the four corners of the grid. The default grid is 16 squares. The more squares in the grid, the more custom colors you can generate. Click the flyout arrow at the top of the roll-up to select a larger grid size.

To change the colors in the grid, click the corner color buttons and select new colors from their drop-down palettes. After you have selected new colors, a new blend will automatically be generated.

9

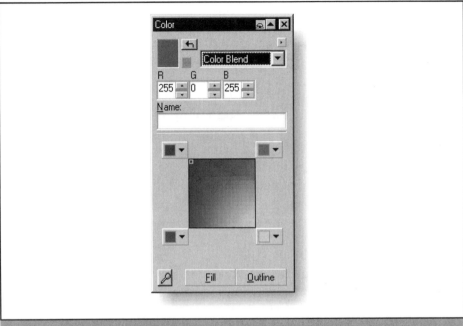

FIGURE 9-29   The Color roll-up displaying the Color Blend display

To select a color from a newly generated blend, click a grid square with the normal cursor. The selected color will appear in the upper-left corner of the roll-up. To use the new color, select an object and click either the Fill button or the Outline button. You can save your new color in the Custom Colors palette by selecting the color and choosing Add Color to Palette in the Color Blend flyout.

It is better to use the Palette Editor if you plan to save a custom color created with the Color Blend display, because it gives you the option of saving the custom color in any of the available color palettes.

Using Registration Color

Registration marks are used to help the printer align the plates on the press. You can have the default registration marks automatically placed on every plate of a color separation when you enable the Print Registration Marks check box in the Prepress page of the Print dialog box.

Registration color refers to user-placed registration marks. There will be times when you want your own custom registration marks to print on each plate of the color separation in place of or in addition to default registration marks. Examples of this would be dotted lines in the drawing that indicate a fold line. You may feel it's more important to align the plates using these dotted lines than using the default registration marks, or you might simply want to use your own registration marks instead of the default marks.

CorelDRAW lets you assign a registration color to objects in your drawings so they will print on all plates of a color separation. If you make up your own registration color containing all four CMYK colors, it won't print on a plate containing spot or user ink colors (see the section on user-defined inks earlier in this chapter).

To fill an object with a registration color, follow these steps:

1. Select the object you wish to fill with a registration color.

2. Click the down arrow of the Category list box in the Color roll-up and choose Registration Color.

3. Click the Fill button to apply the color. The Status Bar will indicate that the object is filled with a registration color.

That's all there is to it. When the separations are printed, the object filled with the registration color will print on all plates, no matter how many plates are created.

9

INTERACTIVE TINTS

An exciting new feature in CorelDRAW 8 lets you tint objects with colors from the onscreen Color palette. As long as the object is not filled with a Pattern fill, Bitmap fill, or Postscript fill, it can be tinted. Practice using this new feature by following these steps:

1. Draw two rectangles on the page. Fill one with the default Yellow from the default palette.

2. Select the first rectangle.

3. Hold down the CTRL key and click the Cyan color well in the default color palette. Each time you click, the yellow rectangle will be given a 10 percent tint of Cyan.

4. Continue holding down the CTRL key and click a total of ten times. The yellow rectangle should now be a teal green.

 *Perhaps the most exciting feature of all regarding color mixing is that you can apply a tint to groups of objects. Remember, groups include vector clipart images. Think how long it would take if you had to individually tint each object in a clipart image made up of five hundred plus objects. You can also apply tints using fountain fills which are described in Chapter 10.*

You can use this tinting technique on spot colors but if you do, the spot color will be converted to an RGB color.

USING THE PROPERTY BAR TO ACCESS UNIFORM FILLS

After explaining both the Uniform Fill dialog box and the Color roll-up to fill objects, we will end this chapter by showing you how to do many of the same things using the Interactive Fill tool and the Property Bar. We won't describe everything over again, but will simply show you how you can access the various color palettes from the Property Bar.

To access the different color palettes from the Property Bar, follow these steps:

1. Select an object to fill.

2. Click the Interactive Fill tool on the toolbox and click the down arrow on the Fill Type list box.

3. Click the down arrow from the Uniform Fill Type list box and choose Palette from the list.

4. Click the down arrow from the Uniform Fill Palette list box and choose Uniform Colors from the list.

5. Click the down arrow of the Uniform Fill Palette Color list box and select a color.

It just took you five steps to fill an object. It would have taken you four to fill the object with the same color using the Fill roll-up. You judge whether this method of filling objects works better than the other methods described. The one benefit of using the Property Bar is that you don't have a roll-up or dialog box taking up screen space.

Figure 9-30 shows the Property Bar with all the drop-down menus displayed when Uniform Fill is selected from the Fill Type list box and Palette is selected from the Uniform Fill Type list box. Notice that you have the additional choices of palettes and colors from the two remaining menus.

Figure 9-31 shows the Property Bar displaying the RGB num boxes when an object has been selected and RGB has been selected in the Uniform Fill Type list box. This configuration allows you to enter the RGB values directly in num boxes. Clicking the Color Model button displays the Color roll-up.

Figure 9-32 shows the Property Bar display when an object has been selected and the PANTONE MATCHING SYSTEM has been selected from

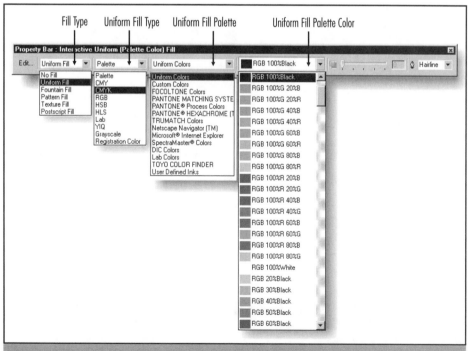

FIGURE 9-30   The Property Bar showing the various drop-down menus when Uniform Fill and Palette have been selected

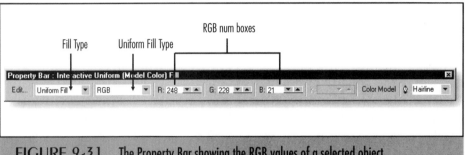

FIGURE 9-31   The Property Bar showing the RGB values of a selected object

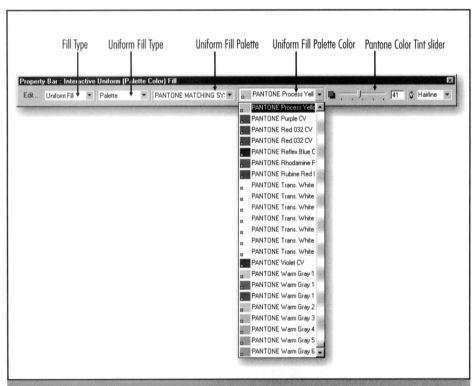

FIGURE 9-32   The Property Bar displaying the PANTONE MATCHING SYSTEM palette colors

the Uniform Fill Palette menu. Notice that all the Pantone colors are available in the Uniform Fill Palette Color menu. The Pantone color tint slider next to the menu lets you control the tint of each color by selecting a value from 0 to 100.

In this chapter, you learned about color models and color palettes and discovered how to create your own. In addition, you found out that your file will be printed in process colors unless you specify spot colors, and you learned that it can be difficult to match the colors on your monitor to those in the printed piece. This chapter also explained how to fill objects using the Uniform Fill dialog box, the Fill roll-up, and the Property Bar. Chapter 10 teaches you how to fill objects with fills other than solid colors. The subjects of color and color printing can be confusing. If you want to learn more about color models and color palettes, refer to the online help files in CorelDRAW.

9

10

SPECIAL FILLS

Y ou can design a great-looking layout or draw an exquisite flower, but without a complementary fill, the objects remain nothing more than outlines. This chapter will teach you where to find the many special fill types and the methods for applying them.

Reading about the numerous special fills can be confusing. We have tried our best to simplify the material so that you can easily understand this important subject.

THE FILL TOOL

CorelDRAW provides seven fill types:

▶ Uniform fill (solid fill)

▶ Fountain fill

▶ Two-color pattern fill

▶ Full-color pattern fill

▶ Bitmap pattern fill

▶ Texture fill

▶ PostScript fill

All these fills can be accessed from the Fill Tool flyout and the Object Properties dialog box, shown in Figure 10-1. You can also access these fills from the Fill drop-down list on the Property Bar, shown in Figure 10-2. All of the aforementioned fill types are covered in this chapter with the exception of the Uniform (solid) fills. Uniform Fills are covered in Chapter 9.

THE FILL FLYOUT

The Fill flyout appears when you click and hold the Fill tool in the toolbox. The flyout can be permanently displayed for ready access by clicking the title bar of the flyout and dragging the flyout into the CorelDRAW window. Clicking a button on the flyout opens the corresponding dialog box or roll-up. For example, the Pattern Fill button opens the Pattern Fill dialog box.

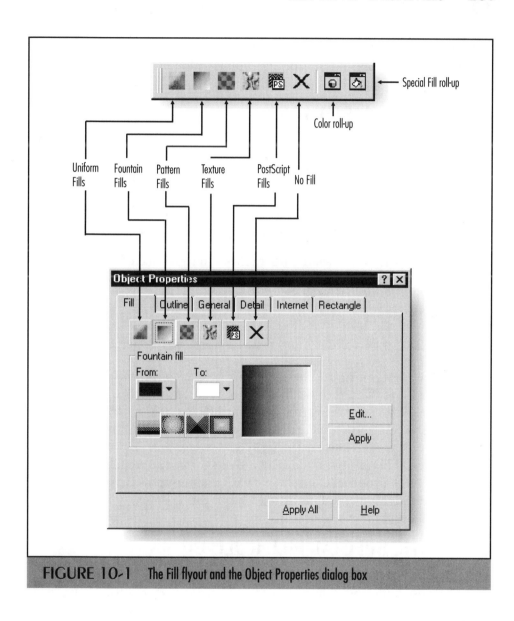

FIGURE 10-1   The Fill flyout and the Object Properties dialog box

THE OBJECT PROPERTIES DIALOG BOX

The Object Properties dialog box is accessed by right-clicking an object and choosing Properties from the bottom of the object menu. When the dialog box is displayed, click the Fill tab to display the Fill page. Just as on the flyout, clicking a button brings up the corresponding dialog box or roll-up.

SPECIAL FILL METHODS

There are four basic methods for filling objects with Special fills. We recommend that you use the Fill flyout as your primary means of accessing the various methods. As you become more proficient at working with fills, we suggest using the Interactive Fill tool in conjunction with the Property Bar as your primary means of filling objects.

Figure 10-2 shows the four ways to access a special fill, they are:

▶ The Property Bar with the Interactive Fill tool selected.

▶ The Object Properties dialog box

▶ The Fill flyout

▶ The Special Fill roll-up (after it has been accessed from the Fill flyout)

We encourage you to use the Fill flyout to access the various fill dialog boxes and roll-ups. We feel this is the best approach; however, for new projects that don't require color editing from previously filled objects, you may be able to work faster and more efficiently by using the Special Fill roll-up, which includes all fill types except PostScript fills.

The Special Fill roll-up provides a kind of shortcut approach for applying special fills. When you feel comfortable with the roll-up, you can easily move on to the interactive method discussed later in this chapter.

USING THE SPECIAL FILL ROLL-UP

The Special Fill roll-up, shown in Figure 10-3, contains three of the most commonly used fills: fountain fills, pattern fills, and texture fills. Click the far right button on the Fill flyout to access the Special Fill roll-up. The following paragraphs describe the different fill types found on the Special Fill roll-up.

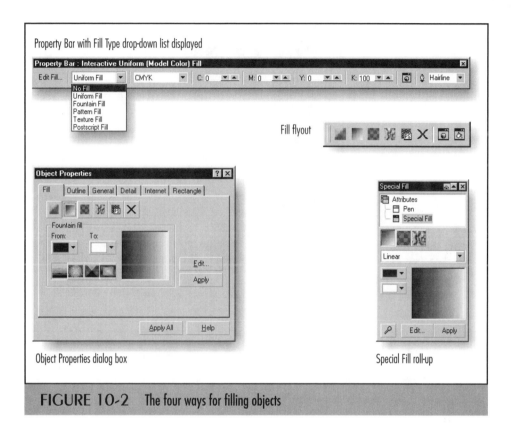

FIGURE 10-2   The four ways for filling objects

Filling Objects Using Fountain Fills in the Special Fill Roll-Up

Click the first button on the left in the roll-up to access fountain fills. A large preview window in the lower right of the roll-up displays the currently active fountain fill. The default is a linear fountain fill ranging from black to white. The Fill Type list box is directly under the fill buttons. Click the down arrow to select a type. Your choices are Linear, Radial, Conical, and Square.

The two color buttons to the left of the preview window represent the starting and ending colors of the fountain fill. When you click a button, a

10

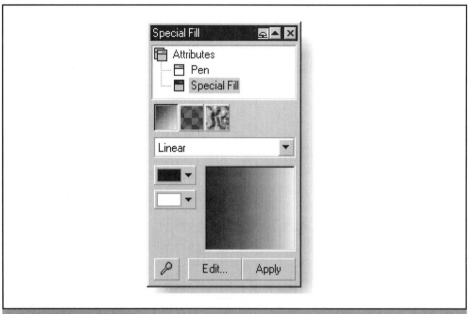

FIGURE 10-3   The Special Fill roll-up

drop-down color palette appears. Practice changing the color of the default fill by clicking the black color button and selecting red from the drop-down palette. It you want to change the angle of the linear fill, click and drag inside the preview window. Practice creating fountain fills using the Special Fill roll-up. When you want to use a different type of fountain fill, simply select it from the list box above the preview window.

Here are a few tips for creating fountain fills: Hold down the CTRL *key while dragging in the preview window to constrain the angles in a linear fill to 15-degree increments. When you're creating a conical fill, holding down the* SHIFT *key while dragging changes the way the colors radiate from the centers of the objects. You can also move the center point of a conical fill to different locations in the preview window just as you can with a radial fill. When you're creating square fountain fills, holding down the* SHIFT *key while dragging rotates the square to a diamond configuration.*

CREATING A CUSTOM FOUNTAIN FILL USING THE SPECIAL FILL ROLL-UP   Follow these steps to create a basic radial fill that looks like a marble:

1. Draw a perfect circle on the page by selecting the Ellipse tool and dragging out the ellipse while holding down the CTRL key.

2. Select Radial from the fill type list box.

3. Select a red from the first color's button drop-down list.

4. Select a light green from the second color button's drop-down list.

5. Click and drag in the preview window until the light green highlight color is in the upper-left corner.

6. Click the Apply button to see the results. Your radial fill should look something like the one shown here.

7. With the circle still selected, remove the outline (to make your marble look like a real marble).

8. Deselect the circle. You could leave the circle selected, but deselecting it shows you that objects don't need to be selected to make changes in the Special Fill roll-up.

9. Click the Edit button in the Special Fill roll-up to bring up the Fountain Fill dialog box, shown in Figure 10-4. This is the same dialog box you would see if you selected the Fountain Fill button from the Fill Tool flyout. Examine the various options in the dialog box. You'll learn more about them later.

10. Click the Custom radio button to display the Fountain Fill dialog box in its custom configuration. Notice that the Custom preview ribbon replaces the area that was occupied by the mid-point slider. The two small squares at the beginning and end of the ribbon are

10

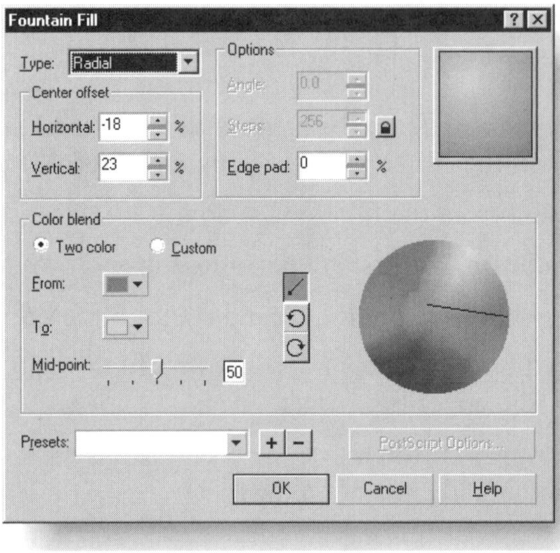

FIGURE 10-4 The Fountain Fill dialog box

the beginning and ending colors of the fountain fill. You can change their colors by clicking a square and choosing a new color from the palette on the right. You can add up to 99 additional colors to the ribbon.

11. Double-click inside the preview ribbon. A marker will be placed above the ribbon at the point where you double-clicked. You can move the marker by clicking and dragging the pointer along the top of the ribbon. To remove a marker, simply double-click it.

12. For this exercise, move the marker to the left, using the leftmost marker in Figure 10-5 as a guide. With the marker still selected, choose a medium blue from the color palette. The new color will be added to the ribbon at the point of the marker.

13. Add three more markers as you did in step 12. Place them approximately as they are in Figure 10-5. As you add each marker, select a different color from the color palette.

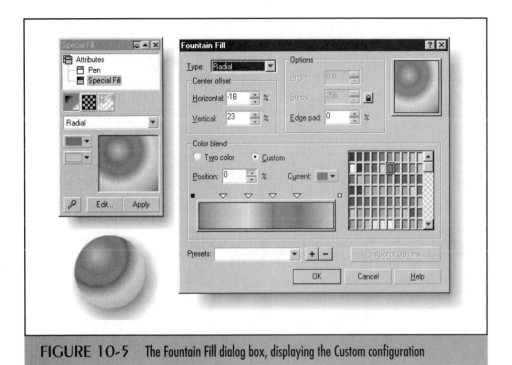

FIGURE 10-5   The Fountain Fill dialog box, displaying the Custom configuration

14. Click the OK button. Your new custom fill will now appear in the preview window of the Special Fill roll-up.

15. Select the circle and click the Apply button on the roll-up to fill your circle with your custom fountain fill. Depending on the colors you used, your circle should look something like a marble.

REUSING A CUSTOM FILL   Now you will see how you can reuse a custom fill you've created:

1. Select the Ellipse tool and draw an egg-shaped ellipse.

2. With the egg-shaped ellipse selected, click the Apply button on the Special Fill roll-up again. The new egg-shaped object you drew will be filled with the custom fill you created for the circle.

10

You can see the advantage of using the Special Fill roll-up to create a custom fill. Had you created your custom fill by accessing the Fountain Fill dialog box from the Fill Tool flyout, you would have had to use the Edit | Copy Properties From command to fill the egg-shaped object, which would require two extra steps.

> *You can copy an existing special fill by first selecting the object you want to fill and then clicking the eyedropper button on the Special Fill roll-up. Use the arrow that replaces the cursor to click another object's fill. The fill of the object you clicked will now fill the first object you selected.*

Using the Interactive Fill Tool to Create Fountain Fills

Now that you've learned how to create fountain fills using the Special Fill roll-up, it's time to learn how to create fountain fills interactively.

The Interactive Fill tool, located in the toolbox, shown next with the Interactive cursor, works in combination with the Property Bar. The purpose of the Interactive Fill tool is to eliminate the need to use dialog boxes and roll-ups when filling objects.

To fill an object using the Interactive Fill tool, first select the object you want to fill and then select the Interactive tool in the toolbox, then select the type of fill you wish to use from the Fill Type list box on the Property Bar (see Figure 10-6). The fill types available are Uniform, Fountain, Pattern, Texture, and PostScript.

If you select the Interactive Fill tool and then select a fill type with no object selected, the default message box appears just as it does when you select the Fill tool at the bottom of the toolbox without an object selected. This means you can set the default fill using the Interactive Fill tool instead of using the Fill tool at the bottom of the toolbox (setting a solid color default fill is discussed in Chapter 9).

The No Fill option at the top of the Fill Type list box removes the fill of any selected object.

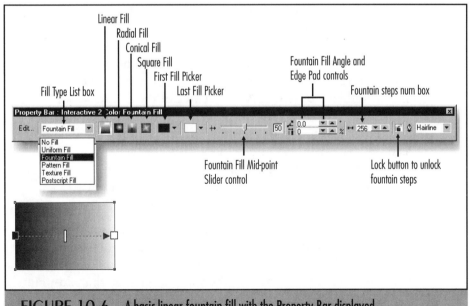

FIGURE 10-6   A basic linear fountain fill with the Property Bar displayed

10

You can create all four Fountain Fill types using the Interactive Fill tool, including custom fountain fills. The best way to learn how to use this powerful tool is through practice. The following steps will teach you how to create all four fountain fills, beginning with the linear fountain fill.

CREATING LINEAR FOUNTAIN FILLS   Follow these steps to create a linear fountain fill.

1. Draw a rectangle on the page.

2. Click the Interactive Fill tool.

3. Using the Interactive Fill tool, click and drag inside the rectangle. By default, you will automatically create a linear fountain fill. You can also click the Fill Type list box on the Property Bar and select Fountain Fill from the drop-down list. Your rectangle should look like the one shown at the lower left of Figure 10-6, filled from left to right with a black-to-white linear fountain fill.

   The Linear fountain fill is the default fill. Notice that a dotted line with an arrow at the end points in the direction of the fill. At each end of the line are small squares that can be moved with the Interactive tool. In the middle of the dotted line is a mid-point slider. If you click and drag the slider, you can control the position of the mid-point on the fountain fill. For example, the default fountain fill blends from black to white. At the center of the fill, the color would be measured at fifty percent black. When you move the slider along the dotted line, you change the point where the value become fifty percent black. When you're dealing with colors other than black and white, the value at the mid-point is the average of the two end colors. This slider is present only when two colors are used in a fountain fill.

4. Using the fountain fill you just created, click the left square and drag it up and inside the rectangle. Click the right square and drag it down and inside the rectangle. Your fountain fill should look like the one shown here. Try moving the slider to change the mid-point.

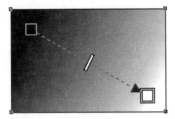

Now comes the fun part. *(Read this entire paragraph before you begin the next step or you will have to start all over.)* Click the red color in the default color palette at the right of the CorelDRAW window. Hold down the left mouse button, drag the color out onto the page, and place it directly on the dotted line of the interactive fill. If you don't click and drag in one continuous motion, you will fill the rectangle with solid red, and you will have to go back to step 1 and begin again. You'll know when to drop the new color onto the dotted line when your cursor shows a box with a plus sign.

5. Continue dragging additional colors and placing them on the dotted line. If you clicked and dragged correctly, your fountain fill should look something like the following illustration. You can also replace the starting and ending colors by dragging and dropping new colors onto the squares or by clicking the First and Last Fill Picker drop-down color palettes on the Property Bar.

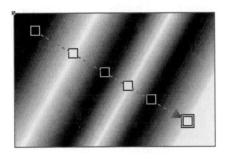

10

6. Now remove all the extra colors you placed on the line while practicing, by right-clicking the extra squares. You're removing the added colors just to see how this is done.

That's it; you've just learned how to create a linear and custom fountain fill using the Interactive Fill tool.

CREATING RADIAL FILLS   Now let's create a radial fountain fill.

1. Draw a circle on the page using the Ellipse tool.

2. Click the Interactive Fill tool and click and drag inside the circle. Your circle will be filled from left to right with a black-to-white linear fill, just as before.

3. With the Interactive Fill tool still selected, click the Radial Fill button on the Property Bar. Your circle should now look like the one shown here. Notice that because only two colors are used, the mid-point slider is present.

4. Click the dotted line of the interactive fill and drag it to the upper-left corner of the circle. The reason you click and drag on the dotted line is to maintain the relationship between the start and end points. Drag the mid-point slider a little closer to the white square to darken the lower portion of the circle. Your circle should now look like the one shown here.

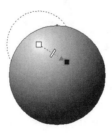

5. Click the right black square and drag it down and to the right, toward the bottom of the circle.

6. With the Interactive Fill tool selected, click the red color from the color palette and drag it onto the page, placing it on the dotted line of the interactive fill. Using the example shown here as a guide, drag the new red square toward the white square. Your circle should now look like the three-dimensional-looking sphere shown next. Practice dragging more colors onto the dotted line and see if you can create a marble look, as you did earlier in this chapter.

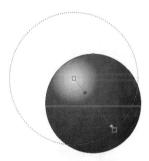

7. Remove any additional colors you may have added by right-clicking the unwanted squares. Leave the original black beginning square and white ending square, as well as the red square you added at the beginning of step 6 in preparation for creating conical fills in the next set of steps.

CREATING CONICAL FILLS   Now use your work in the preceding steps as the basis for creating conical fountain fills:

1. Using the radial fill from step 7 in the preceding sequence of steps and with the Interactive Fill tool selected, click the Conical Fill button on the Property Bar. Your radial fill will turn into a conical fill of black, red, and white, and should look like the one shown next. Added to the dotted straight line is a dotted arc line. All the colors will appear on the arc. The remaining straight line still has squares at its beginning and end, but the beginning square is now the apex of the conical fill and does not contain a color. Notice that there is no mid-point slider because more than one color is used.

10

2. Click and drag out a new color from the color palette and place it on the arc, just as you did when you added a color to the radial fill. Practice dragging the added colored square along the arc. Your new conical filled circle should now look something like the one shown next.

3. Choose another color from the palette and place it on the arc. Now select the empty square at the beginning of the dotted straight line and drag it to the center of the circle. Your conical filled circle should now look something like the one shown here.

CREATING SQUARE FILLS Now let's create square fountain fills.

1. Click the Rectangle tool in the toolbox and draw a square on the page.

2. Select the Interactive Fill tool and click and drag inside the rectangle. As with the previous exercises, the square will be filled from left to right with a black-to-white linear fill.

3. With the Interactive Fill tool selected, click the Square Fill button on the Property Bar. Your square should now look like the one shown next. Notice that the mid-point slider is again present, because there are only two colors used.

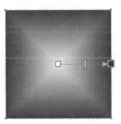

4. Referring to the previous illustration as an example, click the square on the right of the dotted line and drag it to the lower left of the rectangle. Now click the square on the left of the dotted line and drag it to the left edge of the rectangle. Your square should look something like the one shown next.

EDITING FOUNTAIN FILLS There will be times when you'll need to edit an existing fountain fill—one you have just created or one that was created earlier

by you or by someone else. The easiest way to edit a fountain fill is first to select the object with the Interactive Fill tool and then to click the Edit button of the Property Bar. This will display the Fountain Fill dialog box, shown on the left in Figure 10-7. You can also display this box by selecting the object with the Pick tool and then clicking the Fill flyout. With the flyout displayed, click the fountain fill button.

The Fountain Fill dialog box lets you manually change all the attributes that can be applied to a fountain fill. These attributes are described below, beginning at the upper left of the dialog box.

► *Fill Type* Click the down arrow to choose from the four fountain fill types.

► *Center Offset* These controls are active when all but the Linear fill are selected. Entering numbers in the number boxes will change the horizontal and vertical positioning of the center on Radial, Conical, and Square fills.

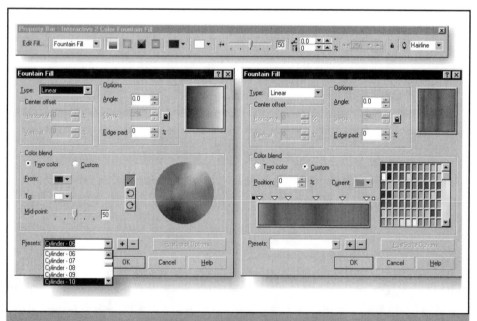

FIGURE 10-7   The Property Bar and the Fountain Fill dialog box, displayed in both default and custom configuration

▶ *Angle Number Box*   Entering numbers here will affect the directional angle of all but Radial fills. This would take the place of doing it interactively.

▶ *Steps*   The steps box defaults to 256 steps. This is the maximum number of steps allowable in a fountain fill. If you wish to use a smaller number of steps, click the adjacent Lock button to enable the number box, then enter your new number.

▶ *Edge Pad*   The Edge Pad setting controls how long the first fill color and the last fill color in a fountain fill remain solid before they begin blending into the next color. It could be used effectively on a circle filled with a radial fill to maintain a solid color on the outside of the circle for a longer period of time, thereby giving the illusion of a darker shadow. The illustration shown next shows a standard radial-filled circle on the left and one with an edge pad setting of 15 on the right. Notice that the one on the right appears more spherical than the one on the left.

▶ *Preview Window*   The preview window shows the direction of the fountain fill. You can change the direction of a linear fill interactively by placing the cursor in the window and dragging in a circular motion. When you click and drag in the window with a Radial, Conical, or Square fountain fill, you change the position of the center of the fill. If you click and drag while holding down SHIFT, you change the angles of the highlights radiating from the center on Conical and Square fountain fills.

▶ *Color Blend*   The Color Blend section shows two radio buttons, Two Color and Custom. The default is Two Color. Below these radio button are the From and To color buttons, which, when you click them, reveal color palettes. It is from these color palettes that you choose the first and last color of a two-color fountain fill. The

10

Mid-point slider control is beneath the color buttons. It functions in the same way described in step 3 of the "Creating Linear Fountain Fills" section. As you may remember, the position of the slider controls the point at which the two colors in the fountain fill meet. This point represent the average of the two colors.

▶ *Color Direction* In the center of the Color Blend section of the Fountain Fill dialog box are three buttons. These buttons control the direction in which the two colors in the fountain fill blend. The button at the top is the Straight Line blend. For example, if we blend red to blue, the fountain fill will be composed of solid red, solid blue, and shades of red and blue. The second button is a rotation button. It directs the fountain fill in a counterclockwise direction, using the color wheel at the right of the buttons. Using the same example, the colors contained in the fountain fill would be solid red, solid blue, and shades of orange, yellow, and green, because those are the colors the blending fountain fill would pass through on the color wheel. A dark line is displayed on the color wheel, indicating the path of the fountain fill when a rotation button is used. The last button is the Clockwise button. Using the same colors as an example, the blended colors of the fountain fill would be solid red, solid blue, and shades of blue, purple, and pink.

▶ *Presets* The Presets list box at the bottom of the Fountain Fill dialog box contains many custom preset fountain fills. To use one of these fills, click the down arrow and select a custom fill from the drop-down list. The list box is empty by default so that you can enter a custom name of your own and save it along with the other custom fills. These will be discussed below.

▶ *Custom* When you click the Custom radio button in the Fountain Fill dialog box, the dialog box display changes to the configuration shown on the right in Figure 10-7. It is in this dialog box that you can create a fountain fill containing more than two colors. When you create custom fills interactively, you drag colors from the palette onto the dotted line of the interactive fill; here, you manually place markers on the color bar at the lower left of the Fountain Fill dialog box. Follow the steps below to create a custom fountain fill by adding colors to the color bar:

1. Draw a rectangle on the page.

2. Click the Fill tool in the toolbox to reveal the fill flyout, then click the Fountain Fill button (the second from the left).

3. When the Fountain Fill dialog box appears, click the Custom radio button. The dialog box should look like the one on the right in Figure 10-7.

4. Place the cursor on the color bar at the bottom of the dialog box and double-click. When you double-click, a marker will be placed above the bar at the point you double-clicked. The position number box just above the color bar will indicate the marker's position by showing a percentage from 0 to 100. For example, if you want a new marker positioned along the bar at 20 percent, but when you double-clicked the marker was added at 34 percent, you could click the down arrow in the number box to move the marker to the desired 20 percent position. You can add up to 99 new markers on the color bar. Each time you add a marker, you select the color for the desired position from the palette on the right of the color bar. The colors in the palette are the same as those in the currently used palette at the right of the CorelDRAW window. (For information on changing palettes, see Chapter 9.) If you would like to save your custom palette, give your palette a name by typing it in the empty Presets list box. With the name entered, click the plus (+) button next to the list box. Your new custom fountain fill will be added, in alphabetical order, to the list of Presets.

10

The first and last colors of a custom fountain fill are represented by the black and white squares at each end of the color bar. To change their colors, click one of the squares and then click the Current color button above and to the right of the color bar. A palette will drop down, offering you the same choice of colors as the larger palette on the right of the dialog box.

Filling Objects with Pattern Fills Using the Special Fill Roll-Up and the Interactive Fill Tool

Click the middle button in the Special Fill roll-up to bring up the pattern fills. By default, the two-color patterns appear first. The list box directly under the button row contains the three types of pattern fills: 2 Color, Full Color, and Bitmap. Figure 10-8 shows the pattern fills found on the Special Fill roll-up.

USING THE TWO-COLOR PATTERN FILLS Follow these steps to fill an object with a two-color pattern:

1. Select 2-Color from the pattern list box.

2. Click the down arrow and select the Polka-dot pattern from the drop-down list (the default pattern).

3. When the pattern appears in the preview window, click the top color button and choose the color red from the drop-down palette. Leave the bottom color white.

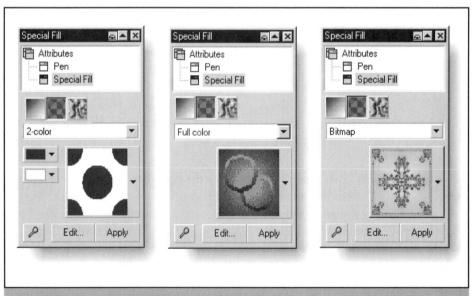

FIGURE 10-8 The three types of pattern fills found on the Special Fill roll-up

4. Draw a rectangle on the page and click the Apply button.

You have just created your first pattern fill. It should look like the one shown at the upper left in Figure 10-9. Yours won't have the dotted lines and handles showing; that part comes next.

Now it's time to learn how to edit your new pattern fill. Editing can be done by clicking the Edit button on the Special Fill roll-up and using the Pattern Fill dialog box, but it can be accomplished much faster by using the Interactive Fill tool.

Follow the steps below to interactively change the look of the default two-color pattern fill.

1. After applying the default fill in step 4 above, click the Interactive Fill tool.

FIGURE 10-9   The special fill roll-up and the first of four two-color pattern fills in the upper left corner

2. When the tool is selected, a dotted bounding box will be placed in the center of the fill. Click the diamond-shaped box in the center to move the bounding box. Click the top center or middle right handles to stretch or skew the bounding box. Click the circle handle to rotate the bounding box.

3. Practice moving the handles in various positions until you get the feel of interactively changing the pattern.

4. When you've finished interactively modifying the fill, click somewhere on the page to deselect the object and your fill will become permanent. You don't need to click the Apply button in the Special Fill roll-up.

Figure 10-9 shows three variations of the default pattern fill that were accomplished by using the Interactive Fill tool.

USING THE TWO-COLOR PATTERN FILL DIALOG BOX   You have just learned that using the Interactive Fill tool lets you create some unusual two-color pattern variations. However, there will be times when you need to create a specific pattern. This is accomplished by clicking the Edit button on the Property Bar, when an object with a pattern fill is selected with the Interactive Fill tool. This action will display the Pattern Fill dialog box, shown in Figure 10-10.

When you're asked to click a specific area on the Property Bar, refer to the callouts in Figure 10-10.

Practice using this dialog box by following the steps below:

1. Draw a three-inch square rectangle on the page.

2. Click the Interactive Fill tool in the toolbox.

3. Click the down arrow on the Fill Type list box on the Property Bar and choose Pattern (it will default to the 2-Color pattern fill).

4. Click the First Fill Picker drop-down arrow and choose the pattern of concentric squares shown in Figure 10-11.

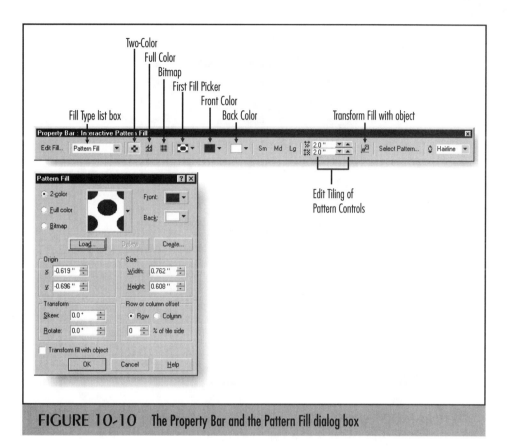

FIGURE 10-10   The Property Bar and the Pattern Fill dialog box

5. Click the Front color button and choose a new color from the drop-down palette.

6. Click the Edit button on the Property Bar to display the Pattern Fill dialog box.

7. Change the Width and Height settings to .5 inch in the Size section of the dialog box.

8. Look in the lower right of the dialog box for the Row or Column Offset section. Click the up arrow in the % of Tile Size number box until you reach the number 50. Leave the radio button with the default setting of Row enabled in the Row or Column Offset portion of the dialog box.

10

Pattern Fill

- ○ 2-color
- ○ Full color
- ○ Bitmap

Front:

Back:

Load...   Delete   Create...

Origin

x: 2.75 "

y: 4.5 "

Size

Width: 0.25 "

Height: 0.25 "

Transform

Skew: 0.0 °

Rotate: 0.0 °

Row or column offset

○ Row   ○ Column

50   % of tile side

☐ Transform fill with object

OK   Cancel   Help

FIGURE 10-11   The Pattern Fill dialog box

9. Click the OK button to see the results on the right of the illustration shown next. The image on the left is the default fill, with the squares larger and lined up in perfect rows. The image on the right contains smaller squares, based on the lower settings entered, and the squares are offset 50 percent displaying a brick-wall pattern.

 *When you enable the Transform Fill with Object button on the Property Bar, the tiling pattern will be stretched or reduced proportionately when you scale the pattern-filled object using a corner selection handle.*

 *The Edit Tiling of Pattern controls on the Property Bar are used to stretch the pattern horizontally or vertically, not to offset the rows or columns.*

USING THE FULL COLOR PATTERN FILLS   You apply the Full Color pattern fills to objects in exactly the same way as the Two-Color fills, using the Special Fill roll-up or the Property Bar, with one exception. There are no Front and Back color drop-down color palettes on the Property Bar or in the Special Fill roll-up, because Full Color pattern fills are Vector Patterns that use more than two colors (see Chapter 37 on how to create vector patterns). Figure 10-12 shows a Full Color pattern fill in its default display and three variations created with the Interactive Fill tool.

USING THE BITMAP PATTERN FILLS   The Bitmap pattern fills are used in the same way as Full Color pattern fills. For a little extra practice, follow the steps below to fill an object with a bitmap pattern.

1. Draw a rectangle on the page.
2. With the rectangle selected, click the Interactive Fill tool.
3. Select Pattern from the Fill Type list box on the Property Bar.
4. Click the Bitmap button on the Property Bar.
5. Click the First Fill Picker button next to the Bitmap button on the Property Bar.
6. Click a Bitmap fill from the drop-down palette.

It gets easier each time. Your bitmap pattern should be similar to the one shown at the upper left in Figure 10-13.

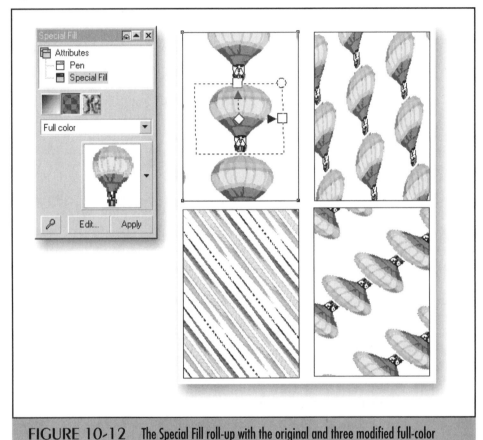

FIGURE 10-12   The Special Fill roll-up with the original and three modified full-color pattern fills

As before, practice stretching, skewing, and rotating the pattern fill using the Interactive Fill tool to see the many possibilities that can be achieved. We have modified three, as before, in Figure 10-13.

USING THE TRANSFORM FILL WITH OBJECT CONTROL   Figure 10-14 shows the same Bitmap pattern used in Figure 10-13. The larger rectangle on the left was filled using the Interactive Fill tool. Two duplicates of the rectangle were made and placed to the right of the original. The Transform Fill with

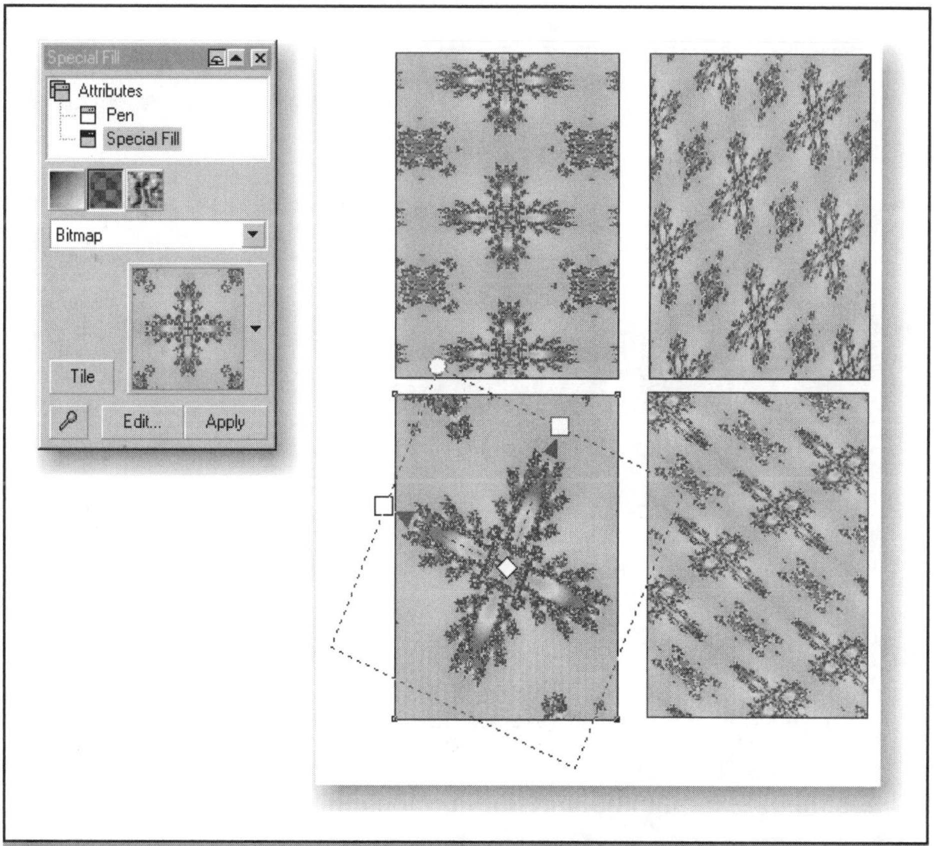

FIGURE 10-13 The special fill roll-up with the original and three Bitmap pattern fills modified with the Interactive Fill tool

10

Object button was enabled and the first duplicate was made smaller by dragging a corner selection handle inward. Notice that the pattern in the first duplicate (center rectangle) was also scaled down proportionately. The Transform Fill with Object button was then disabled when the third rectangle on the right was scaled down. The results are obvious: you can see less of the pattern in the second duplicate rectangle.

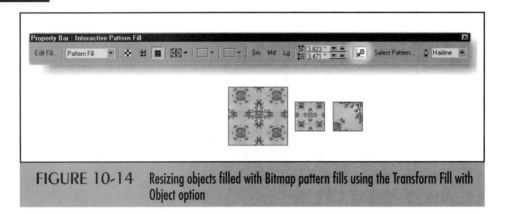

| FIGURE 10-14 | Resizing objects filled with Bitmap pattern fills using the Transform Fill with Object option |

Filling Objects Using Texture Fills from the Special Fill Roll-Up

Follow these steps to fill an object with a texture fill.

1. Select the Texture Fill button in the roll-up.

2. Click the down arrow on the Library list box located beneath the fill buttons and select the Styles library.

3. Click the down arrow on the preview window and select the texture pattern at the upper left of the drop-down list.

4. Draw an ellipse on the page and click the Apply button.

Your ellipse should now be filled with a texture fill called Blue Lava. An example of the fill is shown next.

Creating Interactive Texture Fills

It is just as easy to use the Interactive Fill tool to apply texture fills, so the remainder of this section will cover its use. Before we continue, we must explain what texture fills are.

Texture fills are a special kind of bitmap image. There are more than 100 default texture fills to choose from, and each of these can be modified to look completely different from its defaults. The number of variations that can be assigned to each texture can reach into the millions.

Very few CorelDRAW users take advantage of these splendid fills. A common complaint is that texture fills are jagged when printed. The jagged appearance is caused when the resolution and tile values are not set high enough. Read on and you will get good results.

To fill an object with a texture fill using the Interactive Fill tool, follow these steps:

1. Click the Ellipse tool in the toolbox and draw a circle on the page.

2. Select the Interactive Fill tool and click the Fill Type list box on the Property Bar. Select Texture Fill from the drop-down list. Your ellipse will be filled with the default texture fill. If your texture fill is different from the one shown in Figure 10-15, don't worry; it's not important which fill appears first.

3. Click the down arrow on the Texture Library list box and choose the Styles library.

4. Click the down arrow on the First Fill Picker button, shown in Figure 10-15, to display more of the texture fills available in the library.

5. Click the thumbnail that looks like flames located in the lower right of the first display. Your ellipse will now be filled with the Flames texture, shown in Figure 10-16. Notice that the interactive controls are now available.

6. Click and drag with the square handles to stretch the fill horizontally and shrink the fill vertically. Then click the circle

10

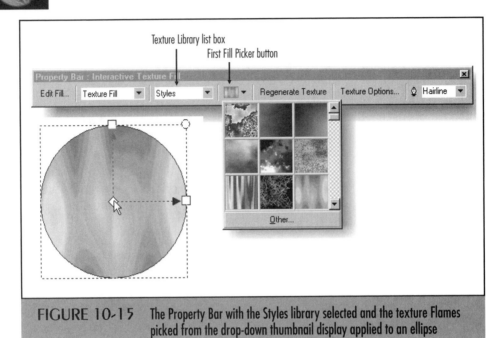

FIGURE 10-15   The Property Bar with the Styles library selected and the texture Flames picked from the drop-down thumbnail display applied to an ellipse

handle and rotate the fill. Your texture fill should now look similar to the one shown next.

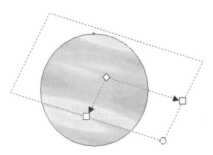

7. Click the Edit button on the Property Bar to display the Texture Fill dialog box shown in Figure 10-16. At the top left of the dialog box is the Texture Library list box. The same libraries are available that are provided in the Library list box on the Property Bar. The Styles library contains original texture styles; the Samples libraries contain variations on the original styles.

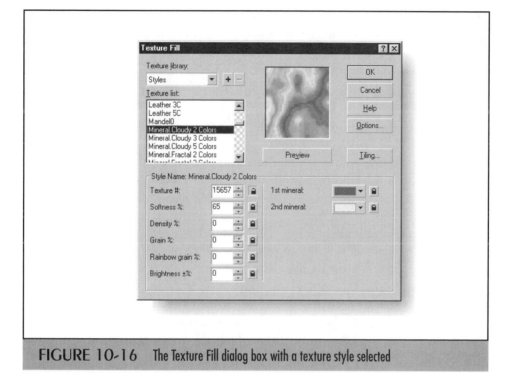

FIGURE 10-16   The Texture Fill dialog box with a texture style selected

8. Click the down arrow in the Texture Library list box and choose the Styles library. Directly below the Texture Library box is the texture list box, containing the names of the individual textures within each library. To select a texture, scroll in the list box. When you click a name, a preview of the texture is displayed in the preview window. When you are satisfied with the texture, click OK. If you're following along, choose the texture Mineral Cloudy 2 Colors.

The dialog box contains a number of parameter selection boxes that enable you to change various attributes of the selected texture. Each texture contains one common parameter box, called Texture #. This box shows the identification number of the displayed texture. In it, you can scroll to or type any number from 1 to 32,767. Each change of the texture number will change the look of the texture to some degree. To see the effect of the changes made in the parameter boxes, you must click the Preview button.

As with the other fills previously described, you can tile texture fills in rows and columns. See the section on using the Two-Color Pattern Fill dialog box earlier in this chapter.

Practice making different texture fills by changing the numbers in the various parameter boxes. Try changing the softness and density settings and then the brightness settings.

Notice the small lock buttons next to each parameter box. By default, all but the Texture # parameter are locked. The buttons default to locked mode so that when you click the Preview button beneath the preview window without making any changes in the parameter boxes, the texture number will change in a random order. This behavior is very helpful when you want to see other variations of a texture without manually typing a new number every time. Simply keep clicking the Preview button and the numbers will change. If you click any of the lock buttons, you will unlock them. The next time you click the preview button without making any changes, all the unlocked buttons and their respective settings will randomly change along with the texture number. A reverse variation on this method might be to lock the texture number and unlock all the other parameters. This would keep the texture number the same but randomly change all the other parameters.

The Regenerate button of the Property Bar acts like the Preview button in the Texture Fill dialog box if no attribute changes have been made to the existing texture. This means you can click the Regenerate Texture button and each time you click, the texture will randomly change.

When you edit a particular texture and want to save it for future use, click the + button next to the texture library name. This will bring up the Save Texture As dialog box, where you can give your new texture a name and then save it in one of the Samples libraries or overwrite the library name to create a custom library of your own.

To delete a texture, simply select the texture and click the minus (–)button next to the library name.

You cannot save an edited texture in the Styles library.

Clicking the Options button in the Texture Fill dialog box, or on the Property Bar, brings up the Texture Options dialog box, shown here. This dialog box allows you to set the resolution and maximum tile size of the texture fill. The settings you make here are the key to texture fills without jaggies.

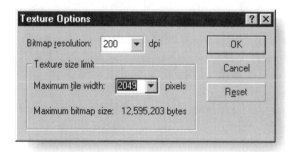

▶ *Resolution* The default setting is 120 dpi. Change the number for the resolution to twice the line screen of your final output device. Here is an example. A common line screen used for outputting to a high-resolution Image Setter is 133 lpi. Therefore, in this case, you would set the resolution to 266.

▶ *Maximum Tile* This setting is as important as the resolution setting. The number you use is based on the size of the object you are filling. Use the following formula: longest dimension of object (LDO) × lines per inch (LPI) = tile size. When you have determined the tile size, choose the next higher setting from the drop-down list box.

Suppose you are outputting an image measuring 3 × 5 inches with a 133-line screen. Using the preceding formulas, the correct number to type in the resolution parameters box would be 266 (133 × 2). Then you would multiply 5 (the longest dimension of the object) by 266 (the resolution). This gives you 1,330. The next higher setting in the maximum tile parameters drop-down list box is 2,049.

CREATING INTERACTIVE POSTSCRIPT TEXTURE FILLS

To fill an object with a PostScript fill using the Interactive Fill tool, follow these steps.

1. Click the Rectangle tool in the toolbox and draw a rectangle on the page.

2. Select the Interactive Fill tool and click the Fill Type list box on the Property Bar. Select PostScript from the drop-down list. Your rectangle will be filled with the default Archimedes PostScript fill shown in Figure 10-17. Notice that the rectangle is filled with hundreds of PS's instead of the actual fill itself. You can see the actual fill if your monitor supports 24-bit (16 million colors) and you have selected Enhanced View in the View Quality list box on the toolbar. PostScript fills are defaulted to display in this manner

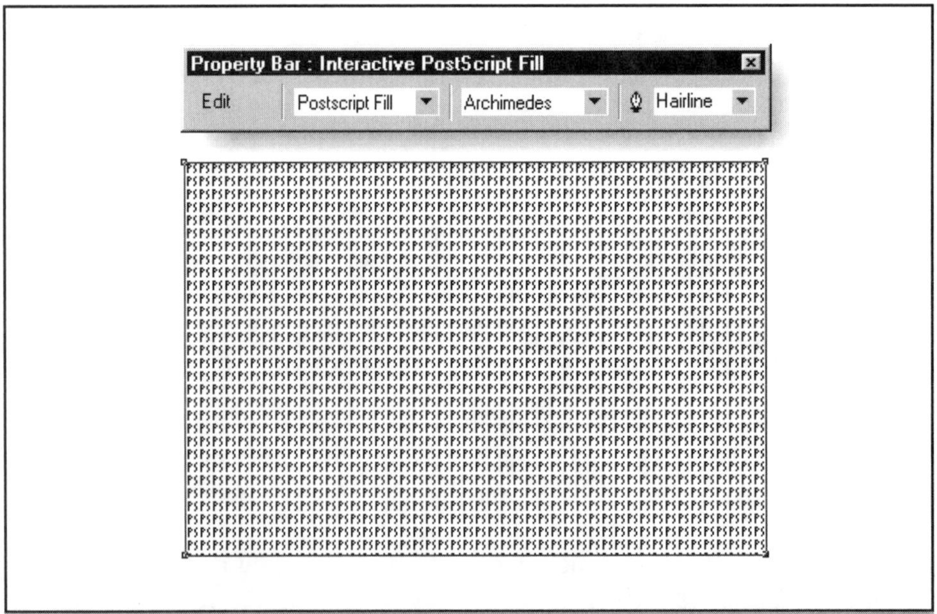

FIGURE 10-17 The Property Bar displaying the PostScript configuration and an object filled with a PostScript fill

because showing the actual fill usually requires a long time for generation and display on the average system.

NOTE: *PostScript fills in versions earlier than Version 7 required a PostScript printer. They can now be printed on any printer that CorelDRAW supports. CorelDRAW 8 converts the PostScript fills to bitmaps for use in non-PostScript printers.*

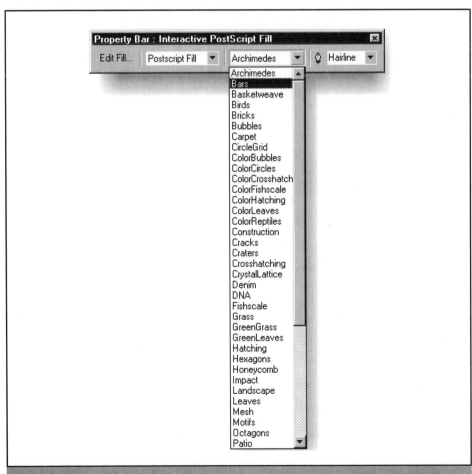

FIGURE 10-18   The PostScript drop-down list box

10

3. To see all the PostScript fills available, click the down arrow on the PostScript list box to display the drop-down list shown in Figure 10-18. As you can see, quite a few PostScript fills are available.

4. Clicking the Edit button brings up the PostScript Texture dialog box, shown in Figure 10-19. Scroll through the list to quickly view the entire list of PostScript fills. If you want to see what a PostScript fill looks like, click the Preview Fill button in the dialog box. There are also various parameter settings you can experiment with to vary the look of the PostScript texture. Use the Refresh button under the preview window to see the results of any changes made in the parameter boxes.

Figure 10-20 shows several PostScript texture fills. These fills have been named so that you can locate them in the drop-down list if you wish to use them in your projects.

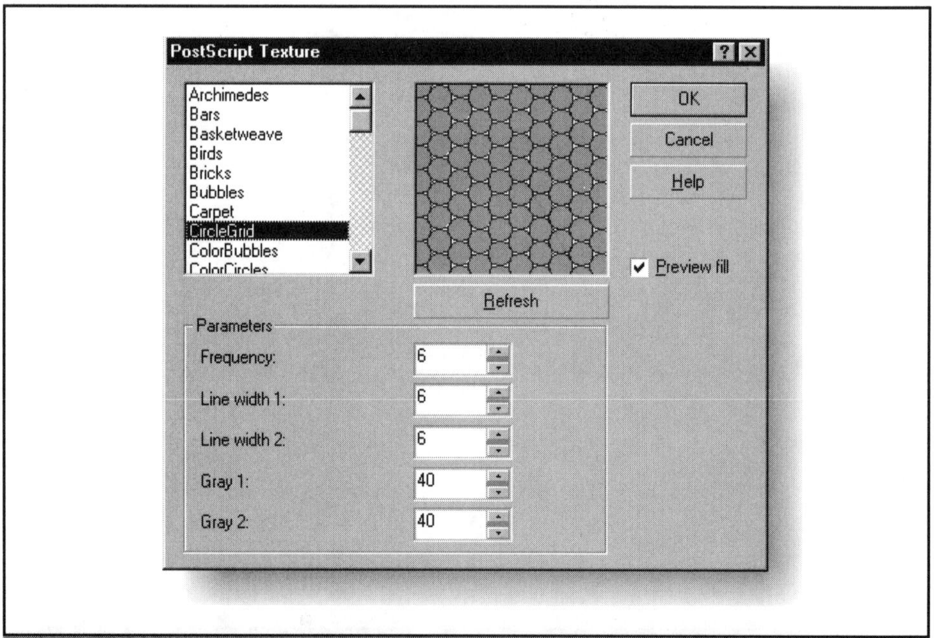

FIGURE 10-19   The PostScript Texture dialog box

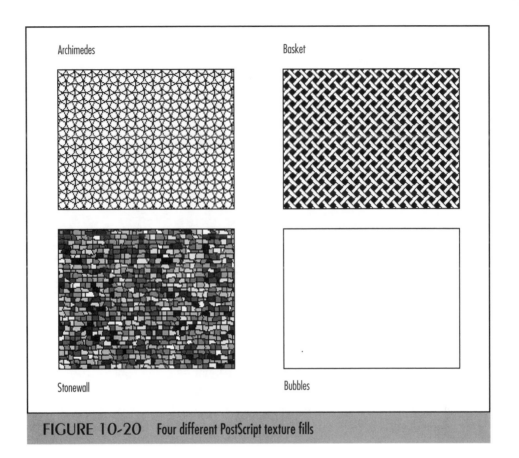

Archimedes

Basket

Stonewall

Bubbles

FIGURE 10-20   Four different PostScript texture fills

10

PostScript fills can be viewed on the screen using the Enhanced view selected from the View Quality list box on the toolbar. Remember that before you can use Enhanced view, it must be turned on by choosing Tools | Options and then checking the Display tab in the Options dialog box. Once you're on the Display page, put a check mark in the Enable Enhanced View while Editing box.

A FINAL NOTE

You have reached the end of a very long chapter. The most important part of this chapter for you to understand is the section on the Interactive Fill tool. This feature has made filling objects easy and intuitive. We recommend that you master the use of this feature and thereby eliminate the confusion of deciding which of the other six methods to use when you want to fill an object.

11

OUTLINING OBJECTS

The settings you make in the Outline Pen dialog box or Pen roll-up control the look and style of the lines you draw and any outlines that are attached to objects and text. Outlines and lines can be changed into dotted and dashed lines and even can have arrowheads attached to them. This chapter describes how to set the attributes used by the Outline tool.

METHODS OF SETTING OUTLINE ATTRIBUTES

As with the Fill tool, there is more than one way to change the attributes used by the Outline tool, and the same advice applies to keep your sanity: choose one or two main methods for changing outline attributes and use the others only when you need to. We recommend using the Pen roll-up or the Property Bar to change most of the outline attributes. We describe both methods in detail. When you learn the differences between the two, you can choose which method you prefer.

Figure 11-1 shows the six different ways to control outline attributes: the Property Bar, the Outline Pen dialog box, the Outline page of the Object Properties dialog box, the Pen roll-up, the Outline flyout, and the Favorite Outlines Docker window.

SETTING THE OUTLINE DEFAULTS

Before we get into the various settings in the Pen roll-up, you should know how to set the default values for the outline width and color in case they are accidentally changed. If the defaults are accidentally changed, you could find yourself scratching your head at the unusual results on your screen.

Most users prefer not to use outlines when they enter text or import Paragraph Text because if the outline width is set too large, a black blob something like this may be the result:

SETTING THE
OUTLINE DEFAULT
TOO WIDE

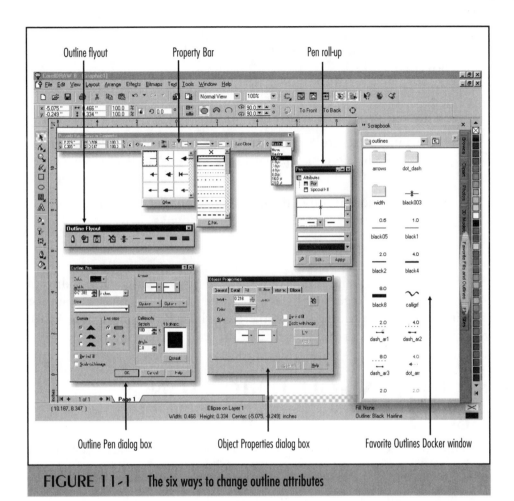

Outline flyout   Property Bar   Pen roll-up

Outline Pen dialog box   Object Properties dialog box   Favorite Outlines Docker window

FIGURE 11-1   The six ways to change outline attributes

Worst of all, if the outline width is set too large and the default color is changed to white, the text on the page will not be visible.

By default, outlines are set to black, and outlines are not applied to Artistic Text or Paragraph Text. You should retain these default settings.

Practice setting the outline defaults by following these steps:

1. Make sure no objects on the page are selected (press the ESC key if anything is selected). Then click the Outline tool in the toolbox. When the Outline flyout appears, click the Pen icon (the first icon on the left).

11

2. In the Outline Pen message box that appears, check the Graphic check box and leave the Artistic Text and Paragraph Text check boxes unchecked.

3. Click the OK button. The Outline Pen dialog box will appear.

4. In the Width parameter box, enter **0.216**.

5. In the units box, scroll to choose Points. Although the default setting is Points, you may prefer to use inches. If you choose inches, the setting in the Width parameter box will change to .003 inches.

6. Click the Color button in the upper-left corner of the dialog box and choose the black well from the drop-down palette.

7. Click the OK button.

That's all there is to it. You just set the defaults so that when you draw a line or object on the page, it will have a black outline that is 0.216 points or .003 inches wide (depending on whether you chose points or inches). When you type Artistic Text or Paragraph Text, the text will have no outline.

USING THE PEN ROLL-UP TO CHANGE ATTRIBUTES

Now that you know how to change the default settings, it's time to learn about the rest of the setting and options. The Pen roll-up, shown here, provides easy onscreen access for most of the attribute changes you will need to make. It functions much like the Special Fill roll-up (see Chapter 10).

You can do the following using the Pen roll-up:

► You can change the outline width by clicking and holding the up and down arrows in the Line Width spin box (an extra advantage to using the roll-up when changing line widths is that you see a visual representation of the actual line width when you change the size).

► You can add arrowheads to the ends of lines by clicking the arrowhead buttons and selecting an arrowhead from the drop-down list. To learn how to create your own arrowheads, see Chapter 37.

► You can click the down arrow in the Line Style box and choose a dashed or dotted line from the pop-up list. To learn how to create your own line patterns, see Chapter 37.

11

► You can change the color of the outline by clicking the color button and choosing a new color from the drop-down palette. If you want to change to a different color model or color palette, click the Other button at the bottom of the drop-down palette. The Select Color dialog box will appear. This dialog box is identical to the Uniform Fill dialog box accessed from the Color Wheel icon on the Fill Tool flyout. For information on how to use the Select Color dialog box, read the discussions of the Uniform fill dialog box in Chapter 10.

► You can copy the attributes of another outline by clicking the Eyedropper icon in the lower-left corner of the roll-up. Select the object to which you want to copy the outline. When you click the Eyedropper, the cursor will change to a pointing arrow. Use the pointing arrow to click the object that contains the outline you want to copy and then click the Apply button. Your selected object will take on the attributes of the object to which you pointed.

The benefit of making these changes from the roll-up is that you can make them right on the screen. For example, if a line width is not the right size, simply use the spin box to increase the size. Changing the line width using the other methods would require additional steps.

As you can see, using the Pen roll-up is fairly easy and straightforward. After you make your changes, you simply select the object to which you want to apply the attributes and then click the Apply button.

When you click the Edit button at the bottom of the roll-up, the Outline Pen dialog box appears. This dialog box contains all the settings that are in the roll-up plus all other settings for outline attributes.

USING THE OUTLINE PEN DIALOG BOX TO CHANGE ATTRIBUTES

The Outline Pen dialog box, shown in Figure 11-2, contains all the attribute settings that can be applied to an outline. Although you should use the Pen roll-up for your everyday projects, when you need to choose special settings, the Outline Pen dialog box is the place to go.

The top half of the dialog box contains the settings found in the Pen roll-up. The only difference is that the dialog box contains two arrowhead Options

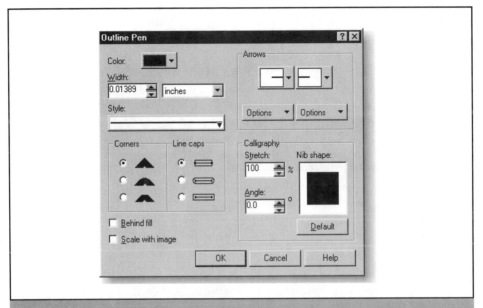

FIGURE 11-2 The Outline Pen dialog box

buttons (for information on these buttons, see Chapter 37). You already learned about the Color button and the Width and units boxes when you learned how to set the defaults. To learn about the Style settings, see Chapter 37.

The bottom half of the dialog box contains the additional settings not available in the Pen roll-up. (The Outline page of the Object Properties dialog box also contains two of these additional settings, Behind Fill and Scale with Image, but for simplicity, stick to the Outline Pen dialog box because it contains all the settings available.) The following sections discuss these additional settings.

11

CORNERS

There are three corner attribute settings:

▶ *Square corners* This is the default setting and the most often used because it provides a look that fits most shapes.

▶ *Rounded corners* This setting can be used when you want a smoother look to lines that bend.

▶ *Beveled corners* This setting can be used when you want a more symmetrical look to your lines.

The rectangles shown here are examples of each type of corner setting applied to a single line:

Square corners   Rounded corners   Beveled corners

LINE CAPS

There are three line cap settings. The line cap settings determine how far the end of a line extends beyond the termination point of the line. Examples of the three different line cap styles are shown here:

BEHIND FILL

Use the Behind Fill option when you want to apply an outline to a stylized font such as a script font. Normally, outlines are applied after the fill is applied. Half of the outline lies inside the object, and the other half lies outside the object. When you enable the Behind Fill check box, the outline is drawn first, and the fill is then placed on top of the outline. This method results in half of the outline being covered by the fill.

A good example of the use of the Behind Fill option is shown here. The font EnglischeSchT was used. The letter *P* on the left used a 5-point outline without the Behind Fill option checked. The letter *P* on the right used a 10-point outline with the Behind Fill option checked. You can see the obvious difference between the two examples. When the Behind Fill option was applied to the letter on the right, an outline width was used that is twice as wide as the one on the left, yet the quality is better. This is because the outline is behind the fill, thereby preserving the quality of the font.

SCALE WITH IMAGE

The Scale with Image option scales the size of the outline when you resize an object with an outline using any of the corner selection handles. This can be an important feature. For example, if an object has a 4-point outline and you later decide to reduce the size of the object by selecting a corner selection handle, you will probably want to reduce the outline width in proportion to the new size of the object. This will happen automatically if you place a check mark in the Scale with Image box. However, if you resize an object with any of the four middle selection handles, the outline will be distorted.

The following examples show the difference when a rectangle is reduced with and without the Scale with Image check box enabled. The top row displays the original rectangles. The rectangle in the left column in the second row was scaled down by using a corner selection handle with the Scale with Image option checked. The rectangle in the right column in the second row was also scaled down but without the Scale with Image option checked. Notice the outline on the smaller rectangle in the left column has been reduced proportionally. The outline on the smaller rectangle in the right column did not change in size and is out of proportion.

11

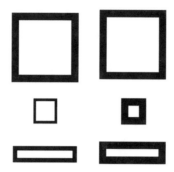

Left column, Scale with Image on   Right column, Scale with Image off

The rectangle in the left column in the third row was scaled down using the top middle selection handle. Notice that the top and bottom outlines were scaled proportionally but the outlines on the side stayed the same. The rectangle in the right column in the third row was scaled down using the top middle selection handle as well, but because Scale with Image was not checked, all four sides again, stayed the same.

 *The Scale with Image check box is not enabled by default. This could cause problems if you add outlines to objects and then stretch the objects proportionately.*

CALLIGRAPHY

The Calligraphy section of the Outline Pen dialog box provides settings to change the rectangular shape and angle of a line. You change the settings in the Stretch and Angle num boxes. To the right of these boxes is a preview window that shows you the size and angle of the line based on the settings in the num boxes. The calligraphy examples shown here all use a point size of 16 and settings of 10 in the Stretch box and 40.2 degrees in the angle box.

You can interactively rotate the nib angle by placing the cursor inside the Nib Shape preview box and dragging. When you use the interactive method, the stretch amount will default to 10 percent. If you manually change the stretch amount number after interactively changing the angle and then interactively adjust the angle again, the stretch amount will go back to 10 percent. The workaround to this is, once you are satisfied with the angle, adjust the stretch percentage to your liking by changing the numbers in the

Stretch num box. Figure 11-3 shows the Outline Pen dialog box with the Nib angle being changed interactively. Also shown are some examples of adjusting the Nib angle and stretch amount on various objects.

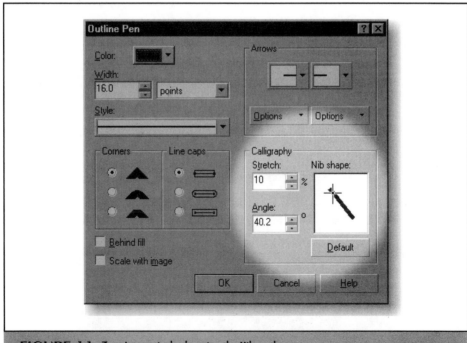

FIGURE 11-3   Interactively changing the Nib angle

11

USING THE PROPERTY BAR TO CHANGE OUTLINE ATTRIBUTES

The Property Bar contains three outline settings that can be used only with single lines and curve objects. The three settings are Arrowheads, Line Styles, and Line Width. Figure 11-4 shows the Property Bar with each setting's drop-down list displayed. The line widths will use the units that you set as the default. The settings will not appear on the Property Bar when normal rectangles, ellipses, and text objects are selected. Again, because of the limited number of settings and types of objects to which these settings can be applied, you should use the Pen roll-up for most of your work.

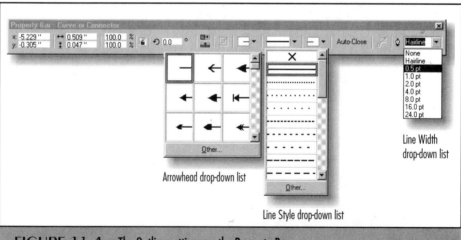

Arrowhead drop-down list

Line Style drop-down list

Line Width drop-down list

FIGURE 11-4　The Outline settings on the Property Bar

REMOVING OUTLINES

There are three ways to remove an outline:

▶ Click the No Outline button on the Outline flyout shown here:

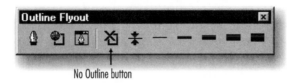

No Outline button

▶ Click the down arrow on the scroll bar in the Pen roll-up until the preview window displays a large X, as shown here:

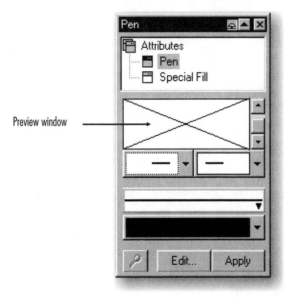

Preview window

▶ Click the word "None" in the Line Width drop-down list on the Property Bar (see Figure 11-4) to remove the outlines from open path objects. This last method's only practical purpose would be to remove the outline from open paths. Interestingly enough, if you close an open path using the Auto-Close button on the Property Bar or manually close an open path using the Shape tool and clicking the Join Two Nodes button on the Property Bar, the None outline option is also available.

As you have just seen, there is more to outlines than you may have thought. The most important lesson you can take from this chapter is knowing how to set the default outline settings. With the default settings in place, you can now proceed without having to change the outline attributes on everything you draw.

COLORING OUTLINES

The quickest way to color an outline is to right-click the color palette on the right side of the drawing window. Realistically, if you're using a certain palette to fill an object, you would use the same palette to color the object's outline. Therefore, you don't really need to change palettes in this roll-up.

There is an Outline Color dialog box, shown here in its default and expanded mode, which you access from the Outline flyout. Other than the name on the Title Bar, this roll-up is identical the Uniform Fill dialog box, which was discussed in Chapter 9. This dialog box is where you select a color for lines and outlines. To learn the intricacies of this dialog box, refer to Chapter 9.

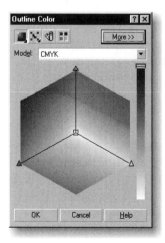
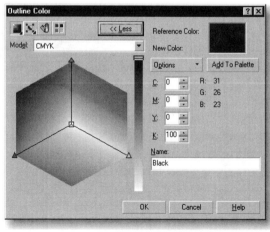

You can also color an outline by using the Color roll-up shown here. This roll-up can only be accessed from the Fill flyout. For instructions on using this roll-up, see Chapter 9.

USING PRESET OUTLINE ATTRIBUTES

You can drag and drop preset outline attributes onto objects by using the presets supplied in the Favorite Outlines folder found in the Scrapbook.

To access these presets, click the Scrapbook folder on the Property Bar. The Docker window should look like the one shown next.

11

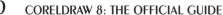

Select the Fill_out folder in the Scrapbook Docker window. The Docker window will now display the Fills and Outlines folders. Double-click the Outlines folder to expand the window. The Docker window will now look like the next illustration:

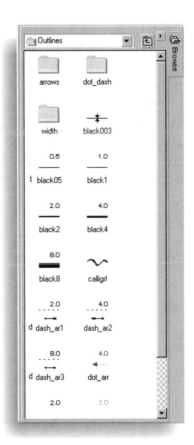

To use the presets, simply select the one you wish to use by dragging it onto the object you wish to apply the outline attributes to. As you can see, there are outline widths, dotted and dashed lines, calligraphy, and arrowheads to choose from—quite an array to make working in CorelDRAW easier.

11

SAVING YOUR OWN PRESETS

It's very easy to save presets of outline attributes that you have created on your own. To save a custom outline, right-click and drag the object with the outline into the Scrapbook Docker window. When you're inside the window, a pop-up menu will give you a choice of the attributes you wish to save. You have only one opportunity to save a choice. If you left-click and drag the object into the window, the Save a Favorite dialog box appears, letting you pick the various attributes you wish to save. The pop-up menu and Save a Favorite dialog box are shown here:

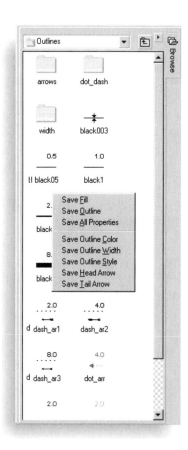

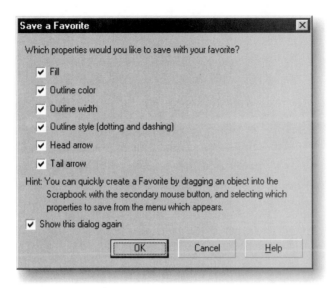

After you have saved an outline preset, it will appear in the Scrapbook Docker window along with the others. You can then give your preset a name that describes its attributes by right-clicking the default name and choosing Rename from the Pop-up menu. This action will highlight the preset name so that you can type in your own words.

As you have just read and seen, there is more to outlines than you may have thought. Perhaps the most important lesson that been covered here is knowing how to set the default outline settings. With the default in place, you can proceed without having to change the attributes on everything you draw.

12

VIEWING, ZOOMING, AND PANNING

If you are upgrading from CorelDRAW 5 or an older version, you'll certainly notice that many more view types are available and the Zoom tool seems quite different. The new types of views that were added in CorelDRAW 7 are a dramatic improvement over those in all past versions in both functionality and speed. Although the new Zoom tool may seem confusing at first, you'll find that it offers lots of added functionality, and you'll find the Pan tool a great tool.

VIEWING TYPES

Some of the previous versions of CorelDRAW had only two viewing types; there are five in this version: Simple Wireframe, Wireframe, Draft, Normal, and Enhanced. You'll examine each type here, from the crudest display to the best. The quality can be set on the standard toolbar using the View Quality drop-down list shown here.

Simple Wireframe view does not show the fill of any objects but, rather, an outline. The outlines all appear in the layer color, regardless of the color of the outline. Normally, the layer color is black. For any effects such as extrusions, contours, and blends, only the control objects appear. All bitmaps are displayed in grayscale, except monochrome bitmaps which are displayed in monochrome.

Wireframe view displays all objects as outlines using the layer color. Bitmaps are all displayed in grayscale, except monochrome bitmaps which display in monochrome. Long-time CorelDRAW users know this view; this is the Wireframe view that has been around since the first version.

Draft view shows all objects. Solid fills are displayed normally. Fountain fills are displayed as solid colors. Texture fills, two-color pattern fills, distinguishing default pattern. Bitmaps are displayed in low resolution. Lenses are displayed as a solid color. The contents of PowerClips are not displayed at all.

Normal view displays all objects and fills without any changes. Bitmaps are displayed in high resolution. This full-color preview has been available since CorelDRAW 3. Note that PostScript fills are displayed as a series of PS characters.

Enhanced view creates a fully anti-aliased version of all objects using 2X Supersampling (Corel's official name for oversampling). Enhanced view can even display PostScript fills on the screen, but they will cause the display to take a long time to appear. The viewing of PostScript fills is turned on by default, but it can be turned off in the Tools | Options | Workspace | Display dialog box.

When you want to see only your drawing and nothing else, you can select View | Full Screen Preview (F9), and the preview will cover your whole computer screen. Even if CorelDRAW is not using the whole screen normally, other applications will now be covered. The view quality used by Full-Screen Preview can be set in Tools | Options | Workspace | Display. By default it is set to Normal. Further details about Full-Screen Preview are discussed in Chapter 40.

ZOOMING

As you are creating a drawing, you'll want to zoom in to work on details and zoom out to see the whole image. You may change views hundreds of times before a particular drawing is finished, so using these tools efficiently is very important.

USING THE ZOOM FLYOUT

The Zoom flyout was reduced dramatically in CorelDRAW 6. Since Microsoft decreed that one-shot tools did not belong in the toolbox, Corel decided to change the behavior of the Zoom tool. Unfortunately, this makes working with the Zoom tool seem much more difficult than in the past. After using it for a while, though,

12

tool seem much more difficult than in the past. After using it for a while, though, you will find that the changes are rather nice. The default Zoom flyout is shown here, but it can be changed to the old version, described later.

The Zoom tool works just like the Zoom In tool of old. If you simply click with your left mouse button, the screen will zoom in by a factor of 2 centered around the point where you clicked. The other option is to drag a marquee box with the left mouse button. The drawing window will zoom to encompass as much of the marquee box as possible.

Clicking the right mouse button with the Zoom tool active will zoom out to the last view or by a factor of 2 or display a menu. You can change the behavior of the right mouse button in Tools | Options | Workspace | Toolbox | Zoom Pan Tool. If you select Default Action, right-clicking will give you the menu shown here. Otherwise, you can select Zoom Out. By default, you will see the menu, which is opposite the default action of CorelDRAW 6.

Zoom/Pan One-Shot		
Zoom Out	F3	
Zoom In		
Zoom	▶	400 %
		200 %
Zoom 1:1		100 %
Zoom To Page	Shift F4	
Zoom To Width		75 %
Zoom To Height		50 %
Zoom To Selection	Shift F2	25 %
Zoom To Fit	F4	10 %

An extra click or two will be required to zoom out, but this method gives you excellent control of the drawing window. The Zoom tool now has functionality that didn't exist in the "old" Zoom tool.

The right-hand tool on the flyout is the Pan tool; it will be discussed later in this chapter.

USING THE ZOOM TOOLBAR

The Zoom toolbar is available in several different places. You can display it as a toolbar by right-clicking the gray area around any existing toolbar and selecting Zoom from the pop-up menu. You can also make it the default Zoom flyout by choosing Tools | Options | Workspace | Toolbox | Zoom Pan Tool and checking Use Traditional Zoom Flyout. Last, it is available at the top of the View Manager Docker discussed later in this chapter. Regardless of how you choose to display it, it is by far the best method for using the Zoom tool. The Zoom toolbar is shown here.

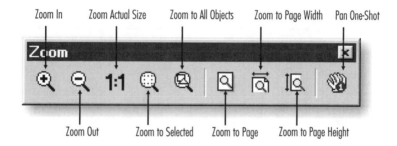

ZOOM IN

The Zoom In tool works very much like the newfangled Zoom tool described previously. The cursor will change to a magnifying glass with a + in the middle, just like on the tool itself. Clicking the screen with the left mouse button will zoom to 200 percent of the current view. Dragging a marquee box will zoom to the area within the marquee box. You can also access this tool from the keyboard by using the F2 shortcut key.

ZOOM OUT

Selecting the Zoom Out tool will instantly zoom out to the previous zoom level or show twice as much information if there is no previous zoom level. Note that if you've made several slightly tighter zooms, the Zoom Out tool

12

may seem to have little effect since there wasn't much change in views. You can also Zoom Out from the keyboard by using the F3 shortcut key.

Zoom Actual Size

To properly use the Zoom Actual Size tool, you need to calibrate your rulers. Select Tools | Options | Workspace | Toolbox | Zoom Pan Tool | Calibrate Rulers. This will bring up the screen shown in Figure 12-1.

You'll see two text entry boxes: for the Horizontal and Vertical resolution of the rulers. These numbers need to be adjusted until the rulers on the screen

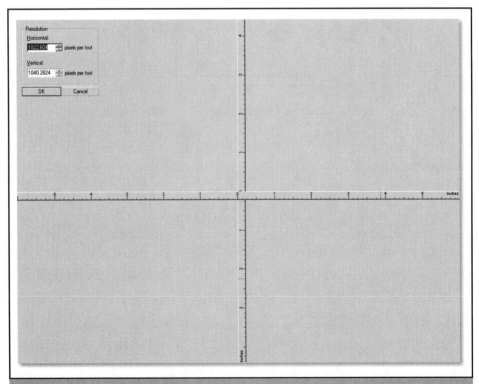

FIGURE 12-1   The screen used for calibrating the rulers

line up perfectly with a real-life ruler. The best way to do this is to get a plastic ruler (like the one that used to be supplied in the CorelDRAW box) and hold it up to the screen. Adjust the resolution values for each ruler separately until the onscreen rulers' tick marks line up with the ones on your plastic ruler. When everything is all set, click OK.

Now that you have the rulers calibrated, Zoom Actual Size will zoom your drawing in or out so that the units on the rulers are life size. Thus, if you are designing an ad that is 4.5 inches square, you'll see it on the screen in the exact size it will appear in print.

Zoom to Selected

Using the Zoom to Selected tool requires that you first select an object or objects. Otherwise, nothing will happen since there is not an object around which to zoom. When you do have something selected, this tool will change the zoom level so the selected objects completely fill the drawing window. You can also access this tool from the keyboard using the SHIFT-F2 shortcut key.

Zoom to All Objects

The Zoom to All Objects tool zooms in or out until all objects in the drawing fill up the drawing window. Every now and then objects get placed quite a ways from the page itself and cause frustration when printing. You know they exist, but you can't find them. Using the Zoom to All Objects tool can help you to locate them so you can move or remove them. You may also see this command referred to as Zoom to Fit. It can be accessed from the keyboard using the F4 shortcut key.

Zoom to Page

In the drawing window is a graphical representation of the page size you've selected. Using the Zoom to Page tool will zoom the drawing in or out so that the page will be as large as possible in the drawing window. You can also access this tool from the keyboard using the SHIFT-F4 shortcut key.

12

Zoom to Page Width

Zoom to Page Width will zoom in or out so that the width of the onscreen page fills up the drawing window. You will not necessarily see the top of the page, but rather, a part of the page relative to the previous view. This means that if you were zoomed in near the bottom of the page, the bottom part of the page will be represented.

Zoom to Page Height

Zoom to Page Height works just the same as the Zoom to Page Width tool except that it will adjust the zoom so that the entire height of the page will fit in the drawing window.

Pan One-Shot

The Pan tool will be discussed later in this chapter. The one-shot nature of this tool means that it works once and then is deselected, and the previously selected tool becomes active again.

USING THE STANDARD TOOLBAR

The standard toolbar has a drop-down list of zoom levels, shown here.

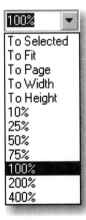

Many of these zoom levels have been previously described. Some of the other levels that are available here are common ones, such as 25 percent, 50 percent, 200 percent, and 400 percent of the page. The current zoom level will always be the first choice and will not necessarily be a round number. You can also type in any level you want, using a value as small as 1 percent or as large as 405651 percent. When zoomed to 1 percent, you can see nearly 100 feet in both the horizontal and vertical directions, while at 405651 percent, you can see only a few thousandths of an inch in both directions.

 *If you are at a zoom level you wish to save, type a name into the drop-down list and it will be saved in the list for later use.*

ZOOMING WITH AN INTELLIMOUSE

You may have seen an Intellimouse. It is the latest variation of a rodent from Microsoft. Between the two buttons is a roller. Initially, the roller simply enabled you to scroll through a document in a word processor or Web page. But Corel has added support for the Intellimouse as a way to zoom in and out of your drawing.

If you roll the roller towards you, the display will zoom out by 10 percent for each click of the roller. For those who are unfamiliar with the Intellimouse, the roller will give a definite click after a certain amount of rotation. Roll the roller away from you and the display will zoom out by a factor of 50 percent for each click of the roller. And if you roll it faster than half a second between clicks, the zoom will double itself. OK, so that is the technical description. But the best way to understand how it works is to roll the roller in each direction and watch what happens. Although a graphics tablet is still the best input medium for CorelDRAW users, for those using mice the Intellimouse does have this cool feature.

PANNING

Panning is used to move the drawing window so that the objects you are working with are displayed. If the screen is zoomed out for all objects, you won't need to pan, but if it is zoomed in tight, you'll frequently need to move around to see other objects or to move the object you are working with.

12

In older versions of CorelDRAW, panning was accomplished by moving the thumb buttons on the scrollbars or simply by zooming out and zooming back in on something else. CorelDRAW 6 added the Pan tool, CorelDRAW 7 added the ability to pan with the keyboard and made the Pan tool behave as many users originally expected it to do, and CorelDRAW 8 added panning support with the Intellimouse.

USING THE PAN TOOL

The Pan tool (either the tool on the flyout or the one-shot tool on the toolbar) will change your cursor into a hand, which is appropriate. Simply use the hand to push (drag) the page where you want it. Thus, if you dragged from the bottom of the screen toward the top, the drawing would move upward on the screen to show the part farther down on the actual page.

USING KEYBOARD PANNING

If you are familiar with the nudge actions available in previous versions of CorelDRAW, keyboard panning will be extremely easy. Hold down the ALT key and press one of the arrow keys on the keyboard. This will scroll the screen in the direction of the arrow you selected. You can even call it a nudge for the whole page.

PANNING WITH AN INTELLIMOUSE

Again, the special roller on the Intellimouse will activate a special mode of panning. Remember, you can roll the special wheel in the middle of the Intellimouse to zoom in and out. To pan, depress the roller, just as with the other mouse buttons. Your cursor will change to a four-headed arrow. Now move the mouse in the direction you want the screen to pan. The four-headed arrow will change into an arrow pointing in the direction you are moving and the screen will begin to pan.

Once you've moved to the desired view, click the roller wheel again and the screen will stop panning. Basically, you're just treating this roller as a third mouse button that will activate and deactivate the panning mode.

THE VIEW MANAGER

The View Manager provides an easy way to store the views of a drawing that you use often. The information stored includes the zoom level and page number. Figure 12-2 shows the View Manager floating in an undocked state with several saved views. The View Manager is accessed by choosing <u>V</u>iew | <u>D</u>ockers | <u>V</u>iew Manager or by pressing CTRL-F2.

To create a new view, first you need to select the page and zoom to the magnification level you want to save. Then click the + icon in the View Manager Docker or select <u>N</u>ew from the flyout. The view will be added to the main display window of the Docker. To delete a view, simply click the - icon or select <u>D</u>elete from the flyout.

 *If you added a view by typing a name in the standard toolbar's drop-down list of zoom values, it will automatically appear in the View Manager.*

In the leftmost column in the View Manager is a Page icon. This controls where the specific page of the view will be applied when the view is selected.

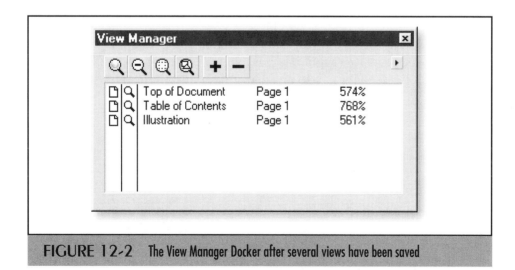

FIGURE 12-2   The View Manager Docker after several views have been saved

12

If the page icon is dimmed, only the magnification of the view will be used. If you needed to zoom in on the lower-left corner of every page, you would definitely want to turn off the Page icon. Similarly, the Magnification icon controls whether the magnification information of the saved view is used. If all you need is a view of page 5 and you've saved a view of page 5, deselect the Magnification icon so that it is dimmed.

Initially, a new view will be named View *x*, where *x* represents the number of the view created. Click the name to highlight it or right-click and select Rename from the pop-up menu, and you can then type a more descriptive name, as in Figure 12-2. The next two columns show the page number and magnification level of the saved view.

By dragging a particular view, you can rearrange the order in which views are listed. Right-clicking any of the views displays the same menu as on the flyout except that it will appear right at your cursor. If you double-click a view or select Switch to View from the menu, your main display window will change to the selected view.

If you will be sharing a drawing with others, creating saved views would be a great way for you to point out certain items in the drawing.

Without the Zoom tool, it would be very tough to work on a drawing. Sometimes you'd only see a tiny part of what you needed and other times you'd see so much that you couldn't work with a detailed area. Understanding the Zoom tool will allow you to always work at exactly the view you need.

PART
2

MANIPULATION

13

OBJECT ORDERING, LAYERS, AND THE OBJECT MANAGER

This chapter discusses the various methods for controlling and modifying the relationship of objects to each other. Object Ordering lets you change objects in their stacking order. Layers allow you to place objects on separate layers, which themselves can be placed in a stacking order. Object Manager provides a hierarchical display of the entire document, showing the stacking order of all the objects and layers within the document. Object Manager also lets you change the stacking order of objects and layers as well as modify objects within Object Manger itself. CorelDRAW has brought together the control of Layers and Objects into a single Object Manager.

ORDERING OBJECTS

Remember that each time you draw a new object on the page, it is placed on top of the other objects on the page, in a *stacking order*. The last object you draw is considered to be at the top of the stacking order. Do not confuse stacking order with *layers* (discussed later in this chapter).

The Arrange | Order command allows you to select and move objects to different levels within your document. When you access the Arrange | Order child menu, you are given seven different choices of how to move an object or objects in the stacking order:

▶ *To Front* Choose this option to move the selected object or objects to the front of all the other objects on the page. This command comes in handy when you are rearranging objects in your document.

▶ *To Back* Choose this option to move a selected object or objects behind all other objects on the page.

▶ *Forward One* Choose this option to move the selected object or objects forward one level at a time in the stacking order.

▶ *Back One* Choose this option to move the selected object or objects backward one level at a time in the stacking order.

▶ *In Front Of* Choose this option to move an object or objects in front of a specific object in your document.

▶ *Behind* Choose this option to move an object or objects in back of a specific object in your document. The following illustration shows a good example of the use of this option. If you would like to follow along, the file name is Travel0096.cdr and it is on the Clipart CD under Clipart\Travel\Misc. Suppose you want to move the dog looking out the window in the back seat to the front seat between the driver and the passenger. There are many objects in this document, and it would be hard to know where in the stacking order to move the dog so it is behind the driver's shoulder but in front of the passenger. To move the dog behind the shoulder you would first ungroup the clipart image and then select and group just the elements that make up the dog. To move the dog to the new location in the document choose Arrange | Order | Behind. The cursor will change into an arrow. Use the arrow to point to the driver's shoulder; the dog will be placed behind his shoulder. If the dog is not in the perfect position, use the arrow keys on the keyboard to nudge the dog into the position of choice.

The dog in the back seat looking out the window   The dog in the front seat between the driver and passenger

▶ *Reverse Order* Choose this option to reverse the order of two or more selected objects. The following illustration shows a good example of the use of the Reverse Order option. The positions of the elephant and zebra on the left have been reversed in the image on the right. The elephant is moved up in the stacking order, and the zebra is moved down in the stacking order.

13

Original images   Images in reverse stacking order

There are two other ways to move objects in their stacking order besides using the Order child menu accessed from the Arrange menu: You can use the Object menu or the Property Bar.

You can access the Order options child menu by right-clicking an object or objects and choosing Order from the pop-up Object menu. The Order child menu will appear displaying all the various options, as shown in Figure 13-1. You may find using the Object pop-up menu a faster way to choose Order options than using the Arrange menu. The To Back and To Front commands found in the menus are also available on the Property Bar when objects are selected.

 *If your document contains different layers, any changes in order will affect only the objects within their respective layers. For example, if you want to move an object on layer 1 behind an object on layer 2, you will first have to move the object on layer 1 to layer 2 (see "Working with Layers" a little bit later in the chapter).*

If you move a small object behind a larger object so that it is completely hidden by the larger object, you will not be able to visually select the hidden object again. To solve this problem, use the new Digger functionality by ALT-clicking the object that is obscuring the hidden object until the hidden object is selected. Groups will be perceived as one object if you're using just the ALT key. Using the CTRL-ALT key combination will allow you to select a hidden object within a group. Using the SHIFT-ALT key combination will let you selected multiple hidden objects.

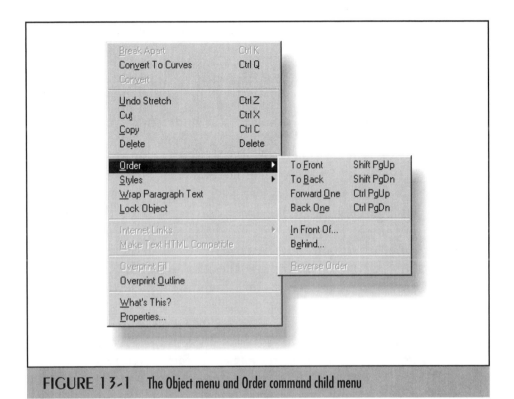

FIGURE 13-1   The Object menu and Order command child menu

THE OBJECT MANAGER

The new and improved Object Manager displays the hierarchical tree structure of all objects, layers, and pages in your documents. Its Docker window displays the stacking order of objects and layers on each page in the document. Each object in the document is represented by a small icon along with a description of the object's fill and outline properties. In past versions of CorelDRAW, the Object Manager was a separate dialog box containing information on only the objects and pages in a document.

The Object Manager now includes information on individual layers within a document. In previous versions, layers were displayed in the Layers Manager

13

dialog box. This combining of objects and layers into a single Docker window simplifies the organization of objects and layers. Although the Object properties section appears above the Layers section in the Object Manager Docker, we will describe the Layers section first.

WORKING WITH LAYERS

Every time you draw an object in CorelDRAW, in effect you create a new layer on the page. Understanding this basic fact will help you understand the complex world of layers. The layers discussed in this section are not like the layers you automatically create when you draw objects on the screen but instead are special layers that can contain certain portions of your document. You can place one object or many objects on these special layers. This section describes layers and how you can use them to organize objects in your drawings. Organization can save you time and prevent accidental changes to your drawings.

Figure 13-2 illustrates the concept of layers. The three rectangles filled with a postscript fill of bubbles represent a cross-section of a page containing three separate layers. The three black rectangles in each layer represent three separate objects drawn on each layer. You learned in the preceding section that every object you draw on the page is placed above the last object drawn, including text.

When you create separate layers, you create a subset of layers that can be stacked in any order. All objects placed on a layer can be moved relative to each other within that layer. All of these separate layers and the objects placed on them make up the completed document. This ability to create separate

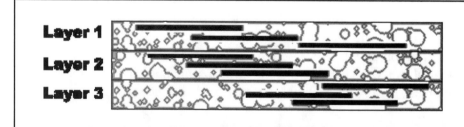

FIGURE 13-2   A cross-section of a page containing three layers

layers containing portions of the document provides the organizational flexibility referred to earlier.

Using the Object Manager to create multiple layers can be very confusing for many CorelDRAW users. If you take the time to learn how to work in a multiple-layer environment, however, you may find layers very useful. Keep in mind that you don't need to use multiple layers for most projects. This author has created hundreds of complex drawings using only a single layer (the default layer 1) with great success.

You can access the Object Manager either by choosing View | Dockers | Object Manager or by choosing Layout | Object Manager. Figure 13-3 shows the Object Manager Docker in the default configuration when two objects are on the page. The first time you access Object Manager it will display as a Docker window at the right side of the screen. Figure 13-3 shows the Object

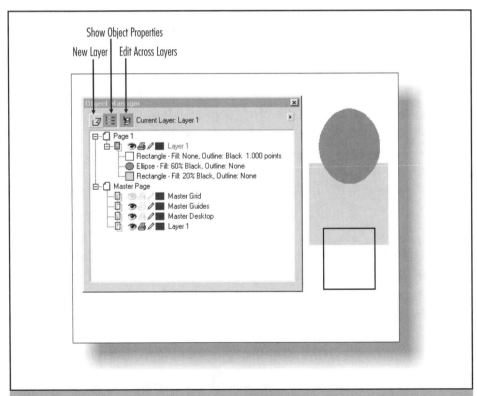

FIGURE 13-3   The Objects dialog box displayed in the default configuration with three objects selected

13

Manager in the undocked window mode so you can read it more easily. If you wish to display the Object Manager in a configuration, click the top of the Docker window and "tear it off" by dragging it out on to the desktop.

The area just below the Object Manager title bar contains three icons. From left to right they are New Layer, Show Object Properties, and Edit Across Layers. Click the New Layer icon to add a new layer to the document. Each new layer is named in sequential order after the default layer 1.

The second icon toggles on or off the description of each object's properties within a document. Notice in Figure 13-3 that the fill and outline properties of the ellipse and rectangles in the document are displayed. If you toggle the icon off, only the words "Ellipse" and "Rectangle" will appear.

The third icon toggles on and off the ability to edit across multiple layers. Toggling this function off prevents you from editing objects on a layer unless the layer is selected.

As mentioned, the Object Manager displays not only the objects in the document but the layers as well. If you only want to view the layers in the document shown in Figure 13-4, click the minus symbol next to the Page 1 folder. To view them again click the plus symbol that replaced the minus symbol.

Controlling The Layers In The Object Manager Dialog Box

The layers section of the Objects Manager dialog box first shows the Master Page icon and it is then divided into a tree of columns containing the various icons described next:

COLUMN 1   Right-click the overlapping rectangles icon to bring up the Layers pop-up menu shown in Figure 13-5. This menu lets you enable whether the layer is visible, printable, editable or whether it's a master layer. The remaining individual columns perform these same functions as well. You can also delete or rename a layer in this menu. Choosing Properties at the bottom of the menu brings up the Layer Properties dialog box discussed later in this chapter.

You cannot delete or rename a master layer.

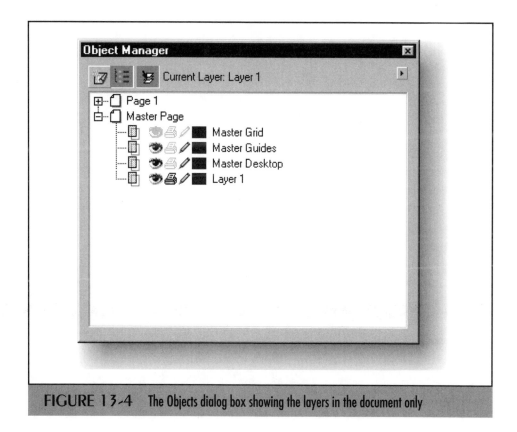

FIGURE 13-4   The Objects dialog box showing the layers in the document only

COLUMN 2   The second column, filled with eye icons, controls whether a layer is visible or invisible. Click the icons to toggle between the two options. If the icon is dimmed, the objects on that layer will be invisible. Making a layer invisible eliminates the sometimes lengthy redraw time for an object. Making a layer invisible can also help if a layer overlaps other objects in your document, making them hard to work on. It also comes in handy when you want to view only one layer at a time.

COLUMN 3   The Printer icons in column 3 can be toggled on and off to prevent or allow the printing of certain layers. The Printer icons that are dimmed by default can be turned on, allowing you to print the grid and guidelines in a document. Unless you are printing to a paper size larger than the page size, you shouldn't activate the Printer icon for the Desktop layer (because objects on the desktop should not normally print).

13

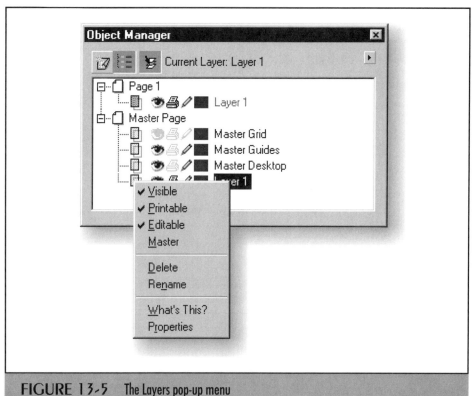

FIGURE 13-5   The Layers pop-up menu

COLUMN 4   The Pencil icons in the fourth column are used to lock specific layers. The purpose of locking a layer is to prevent the accidental editing or moving of objects on the locked layer. When objects are on a layer that has been locked, they cannot be selected or edited. This can confuse the new user who has not worked with layers before. If you cannot select an object, first check whether the object is on a locked layer. A layer is locked if the Pencil icon is dimmed. The Grid layer is locked by default and cannot be unlocked.

COLUMN 5   The icons in the fifth column represent layer colors. Double-clicking a color swatch lets you change the color assigned to the layer in the Object Manager dialog box. Using different colors for each layer can be helpful when viewing layers in a pseudo-Wireframe view while still in Preview mode. This technique is described later in this chapter.

COLUMN 6   The icons in the sixth column contain each layer's name. Master layers are repeating layers; therefore, any object placed on a master layer will appear on every page of a multiple-page document. The Grid, Guides, and Desktop layers are by default master layers and cannot be changed. This ability to place an object on a master layer allows you to use a masthead or any other object that you want to appear on every page without having to manually place it on each page. To make any layer a master layer, right-click a layer and choose Master from the pop-up menu.

Selecting A Layer To Work On

The gray area at the top of the dialog box (to the right of the three icons) tells you which layer is currently selected. It is similar to, yet different from, the Status Bar at the bottom of the screen. This is an extremely important piece of information because it can prevent you from placing an object on the wrong layer. If you are working with multiple layers, you must first select the layer you want to work on. You do so by clicking the name of the layer before drawing or placing an object. After you draw or place an object on that layer, the layer name will no longer be highlighted. Therefore, if you don't look at the top of the dialog box for the name of the currently selected layer, you could easily place your next object on the wrong layer. Looking at the Status Bar at the bottom of the screen merely tells you which layer the currently selected object is placed on, not the layer you're working on.

Using The Object Manager child Menu With Layers

You access the Object Manager child menu by clicking the arrow in the upper-right corner of the Object Manager dialog box. Figure 13-6 shows this menu. The child menu contains eight commands beginning with the New Layer command. Choosing the command adds a new layer, just as if you clicked on the upper-left icon on the Object Manager dialog box.

The second and third commands let you either move or copy selected objects to a different layer. If you select Move to Layer, the cursor changes to an arrow that you can use to click the name of the layer you wish to move the object to. If you select Copy to Layer, you're presented with the same arrow,

13

which you then use to place a duplicate copy of the selected objects on a different layer.

The next two commands, <u>H</u>ide Object Properties and <u>E</u>dit Across Layers, function the same as the second and third icons at the top on the Object Manager dialog box. Although the Show Object Properties icon sounds different, it functions the same in that it hides or shows the object properties in the Object dialog box.

The last three commands—Show Pages and Layers, Show <u>P</u>ages, and Show <u>L</u>ayers—control which of the selected items is displayed.

USING THE LAYER PROPERTIES DIALOG BOX

The Layers Properties dialog box shown in Figure 13-7 provides additional controls over the layers in a document. To access the Layers Properties dialog

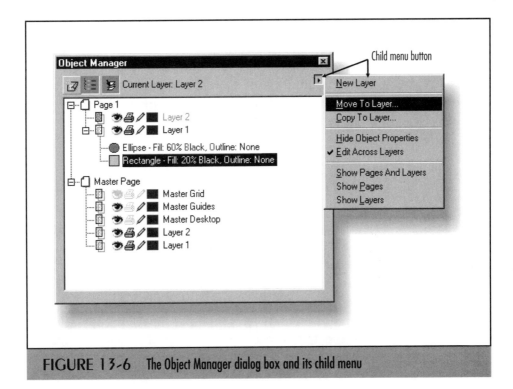

FIGURE 13-6   The Object Manager dialog box and its child menu

box, right-click a layer name. With the exception of the Override Full Color View and Apply Layer Changes to the Current Page Only commands, the remaining options are duplicates of options discussed earlier. The dialog box will also contains an extra Setup button when you choose either the Grid or Guides layer. Clicking this Setup button brings up their respective Setup dialog boxes, where you can control the Grid settings and Guideline placement.

The two options in the Layers Properties dialog box that are not found anywhere else in the Object Manager dialog box are described here:

▶ *Override Full Color View* When you put a check mark in the Override Full Color View check box, the object fills are hidden for all the objects on a layer except the outline. You can change the color of the outline for easy identification of the objects by clicking the Layer Color button, just as you could in the Object Properties dialog box. Using Override Full Color View is another way of hiding an object without making it completely invisible. This method reduces the redraw time for complicated objects while still letting you see their location on the page.

▶ *Apply Layer Changes to the Current Page Only* Placing a check mark in this check box applies all the settings you have changed in the Layer Properties dialog box to the selected layer on the page you are working on. You use this special setting only if your document contains multiple pages.

You can choose either Simple Wireframe or Wireframe view from the Property Bar to view all layers at once in with their assigned layer colors.

HIDING LAYERS

There are times when you want to hide layers, such as when you want a masthead to appear on only even-numbered pages, as shown in Figure 13-8. This figure shows a four-page booklet. A masthead appears on the two left-hand (even-numbered) pages, but it doesn't appear on the two right-hand (odd-numbered) pages. The masthead was placed only once on the first

13

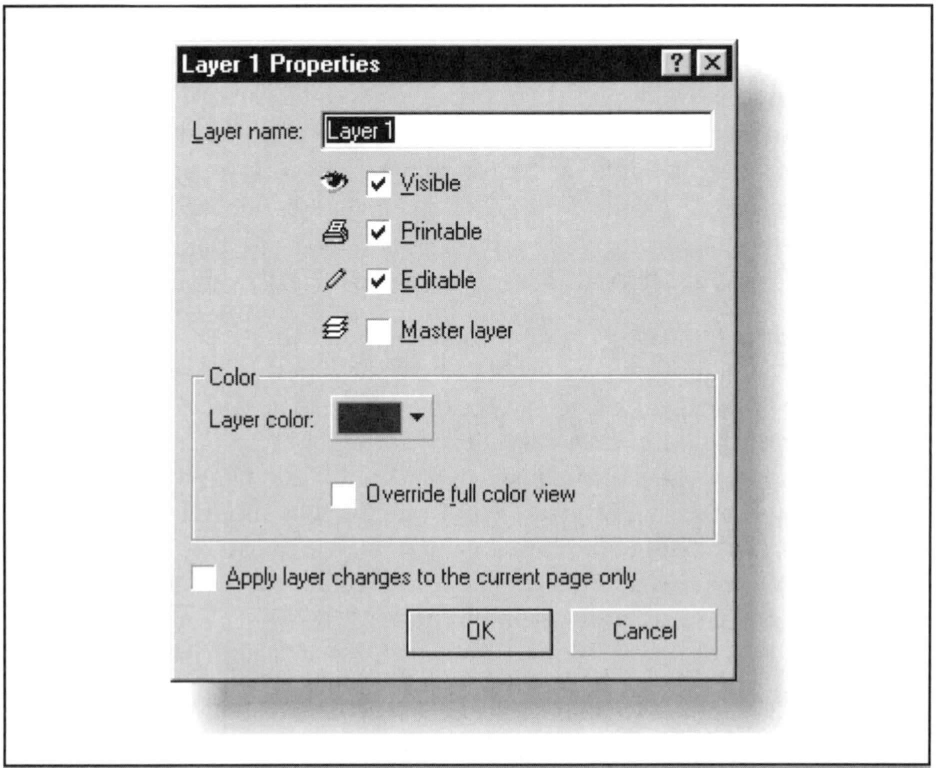

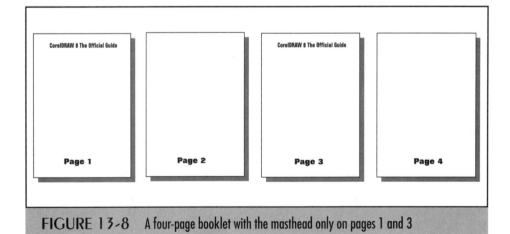

FIGURE 13-7   The Layer Properties dialog box indicating Layer 1 selected

FIGURE 13-8   A four-page booklet with the masthead only on pages 1 and 3

left-hand page. By changing the settings in the layers section of the Object Manager and Layer Properties dialog boxes, it was placed again on the second left-hand page without being placed in either of the right-hand pages.

Follow these steps to re-create the effect in Figure 13-8:

1. Open a new document.

2. Add three more pages by choosing Layout | Insert Page. When the Insert Page dialog box appears, type **3** in the Insert Page parameter box and then click the OK button. You can also add pages by clicking the + button in the navigation tools at the lower-left corner of the document window.

3. Open the Object Manager by choosing Layout | Object Manager.

4. Select Layer 1 at the bottom of the Object Manager in the Layers section.

5. Right-click the name Layer 1 to reveal the Layer pop-up menu and choose Master Layer. The layer name will change to Master Layer 1.

6. Select the Text tool from the toolbox and click the top of the page.

7. Type **CorelDRAW 8: The Official Guide** on page 1.

8. Click the page 2 tab in the lower-left corner of the document window to move to page 2.

9. Click the layer name (Master Layer 1) to highlight it.

10. Right-click to bring up the Layer pop-up menu and choose Properties.

11. Remove the check mark from the box next to the eye icon and put a check mark in the Apply Layer Changes to the Current Page Only box. Then click OK.

12. Click the page 4 tab at the bottom of the screen to move to page 4. Repeat steps 9 through 11.

Now click each page tab at the bottom of the screen. You will see that the masthead appears only on pages 1 and 3.

13

> **NOTE:** *If your projects can benefit from using layers, you should spend some time exploring the various settings and commands until you know them very well. If you will be using layers only occasionally, pay very careful attention to which layer you're working on. If you don't, you will find working with layers frustrating.*

> **TIP:** *You can click and drag on a Layer name to change the stacking order of layers within the layers section of object manage. You can also move objects you have drawn on the page to the Guides layer as a way to create custom guidelines.*

USING THE OBJECT MANAGER

The Object section of the Object Manager combines, to some degree, everything you learned at the beginning of this chapter in the discussions of object ordering and layers, plus more. So what is the Object Manager? The Object Manager section displays a complete visual representation of the active file you are working on. Because you can see every object in your document in a hierarchical structure, you can modify objects directly in the Object Manager. This hierarchical display shows the stacking order of each object and the individual layers on each page in the file. An icon is displayed next to each object in the list, followed by a brief description of the object's fill and outline properties. These icons are interactive. For example, if you select an icon in the list of objects, the corresponding object in the document will also be selected. Similarly, if you select an object in the document, the name of the object in the Object Manager will also be highlighted. When the object is selected in the Object Manager, you can modify the object within the document. In certain circumstances, you can edit the object right in the Object Manager itself—such as when changing the object's color. If you modify the object form within the Object Manager, the object in the document will automatically be updated.

The best way to learn how the Object Manager works is to practice using it. Follow these steps to learn some basic uses of the Object Manger:

1. Open a new document by choosing File | New.

2. Choose Layout | Object Manager.

3. Draw a rectangle on the page and give it a red fill.

4. Draw an ellipse on the page and give it a cyan blue fill.

5. Type **Corel** on the page. Use a nice bold font with a size of 72 points.

The Object Manager Docker should now look something like the one in Figure 13-9. Here the Object Manager is a dialog box rather than a Docker window so you can read it more easily. Notice that each of your objects is shown in its correct stacking order, and the object types are also named. The Artistic Text line shows the name of the font and font style. (If the window is not wide enough to display the rest of the Artistic Text information, you can enlarge it by dragging out on one of the corners.) The Ellipse line indicates that the fill color is cyan and that the outline is black with a hairline width. The Rectangle line indicates that the fill color is red and that this outline is also black with a hairline width.

 *If none of this information is displayed, click the + icon under the Page icon labeled Page 1.*

You can change the name of an object by clicking twice on (not double-clicking), the name and description line and then typing in the new name. You may want to give an object a name that is more descriptive than Ellipse, Curve, and so on. To make the name change take effect, press the ENTER key on the keyboard. Changing the name will only change the name of the object, it will not affect the description.

MODIFYING OBJECTS USING THE OBJECT MANAGER

One benefit of using the Object Manager is that you can modify objects by selecting them from within the Object Manager itself. Follow these steps to learn how to modify objects from within Object Manager:

1. Drag the color red from the color palette in the document window and place the colored square on the letter *A* icon in the Object Manager. Your text on the page will now change to red.

2. Drag the color green from the color palette in the document window and place the colored square on the Ellipse icon in the Object Manager. Your ellipse on the page will now change to green.

13

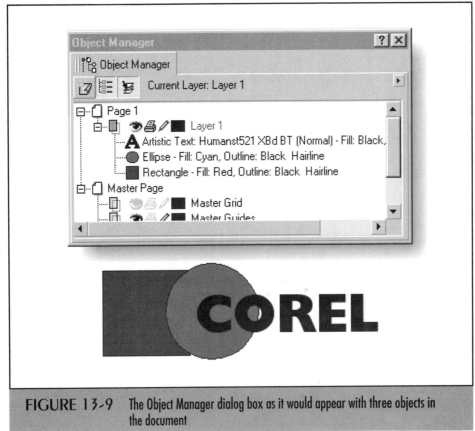

FIGURE 13-9   The Object Manager dialog box as it would appear with three objects in the document

As you can see, dragging colors from the palette directly onto the icon in the Object Manager changes the object's color on the page.

You may be wondering why you should learn how to change the color of objects using the Object Manager when you have been told throughout this book to color them in other ways. At times, certain objects in your document will be difficult to select because of their small size. When this situation occurs, locate the object in the object list in the Object Manager and select it from there. With the object selected, you can proceed to edit the object in any way you wish.

MOVING OBJECTS IN THEIR STACKING ORDER WITHIN THE OBJECT MANAGER

You can also move objects and layers in their stacking order within the Object Manager. Practice selecting and moving objects within the Object Manager by following these steps:

1. To emulate an object that would be hard to select, select the ellipse on the page and drag it so that it covers the rectangle. Notice that the ellipse is also selected in the Object Manager.

2. Click the rectangle in the Object Manager.

3. Drag upwards and the cursor will change to a solid black arrow pointing to the right. Place the arrow between the ellipse and the Artistic Text and release the left mouse button. The rectangle will now be placed above the ellipse and beneath the text.

Besides moving object within their stacking order, you can group objects by dragging the pointing arrow onto another object instead of in between objects. There are other advantages to the Object Manager, such as being able to drag and drop certain styles onto objects. Corel's Help menu can teach you some of these more unusual uses for the Object Manager.

Figure 13-10 shows a clipart image of a Mandarin duck with the Object Manager (shown in the Docker window mode) on the right. Notice that all the objects that make up the duck are listed in the order in which they appear on the page. You must be thinking we are nuts to think you can tell which object is which from the list of curve objects, and you are right. You can't tell which is which unless you select one of the name tags and change the color of the selected object to see which object changes. It soon becomes clear that using the Object Manager for drawings you have already completed and for clipart images is not really practical unless you have a strong desire to spend a lot of time figuring out which object is which.

Advanced users of CorelDRAW, however, may find a benefit in using the Object Manager when creating new drawings because they can name the objects in Object Manager as they create them, thereby eliminating any confusion as to which object is which. This ability to keep track of each object using a hierarchical display of the document can be important when you're dealing with hundreds of objects.

13

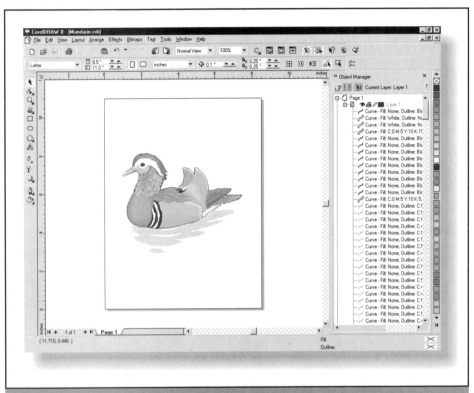

FIGURE 13-10   A clipart image with the various objects that make up the image listed in the Object Manager

You might ask if you are missing out if you don't use the Object Manager, but you probably are not. Although some may quibble with this viewpoint, in fact, the majority of users can work very efficiently by relying on the more traditional tools and effects, including object ordering and layering, as discussed earlier in this chapter.

14

RULERS, GUIDELINES, AND GRIDS

rtists sometimes feel that rulers, guidelines, and grids only get in the way—that these are the tools of technical illustrators, and artists don't need them. However, this is definitely not true, and enlightened artists will wonder how they lived without these extremely useful tools.

RULERS

The rulers appear above and to the right of the drawing window. If you're upgrading from CorelDRAW 6, you'll notice that the rulers are now smaller, but they retain all of their functionality.

MEASUREMENT SYSTEMS

Many different units of measurement are available with the rulers. The following sections describe the units of measurement available.

INCHES

Inches are the default unit of measurement. In versions shipped outside of the United States, the inch may not be the default unit, but it is still deeply ingrained in the product. The inch is the smallest unit in the measurement system used in the United States. It is equal to 2.54 centimeters.

MILLIMETERS

A millimeter is a very small unit of measurement in the metric system. It is equal to one tenth of a centimeter.

PICAS, POINTS

Picas and points are measures used in typography and design. Traditionally, there were just over 72 points to an inch, but this definition has been altered so that there are exactly 72 points in an inch. A pica is 12 points. Rather than a decimal point, a comma is used to mix these two measurements together.

Thus, the measurement 1,3 means 1 pica and 3 points, which is the same as 15 points.

Points

Usually, points are used alone only when measuring type size and line spacing, as the numbers can get rather large in other situations.

Pixels

The word "pixel" is short for picture element. Simply put, when you are zoomed in very close to a bitmap, a pixel is one of those itty-bitty squares you see. It is the basic unit of all bitmaps. Pixels are extremely useful for creating drawings that will eventually be converted into bitmaps, such as Web graphics.

Ciceros, Didots

One didot is equal to 1.07 points, and there are 67.567 didots in an inch. A cicero is 12 didots. This system is used by the French and is similar to the system of picas and points.

Didots

Didots are used alone, like points, to measure type size and line spacing. Each didot is equal to 1.07 points.

Feet

A foot is a larger unit of measurement in the measurement system used in the United States. One foot is equal to 12 inches.

Yards

There are 3 feet to a yard.

14

Miles

There are 5,280 feet to a mile.

Centimeters

A centimeter is a unit of measurement in the metric system. A centimeter is equal to 10 millimeters. It is also equal to .394 inches.

Meters

A meter is equal to 100 centimeters.

Kilometers

A kilometer is equal to 1,000 meters.

WORKING WITH THE RULERS

You should see the rulers on your screen when you first start CorelDRAW. If they are not visible, choose View | Rulers. The origin point of the rulers—the point where each ruler equals zero—is the lower-left corner of the page by default.

 *You can drag the rulers out into the drawing window by holding down the SHIFT key while pushing the ruler along. Hold down SHIFT while double-clicking the place where the rulers meet, and they will return to their docked positions.*

To make changes in the ruler defaults, you need to access the Ruler page in the Options dialog box, shown in Figure 14-1. Double-click the ruler itself. You can separately set the units of measurement used in the horizontal and vertical directions using any of the measurement units previous described. By default, the units will be the same since the Same Units for Horizontal and

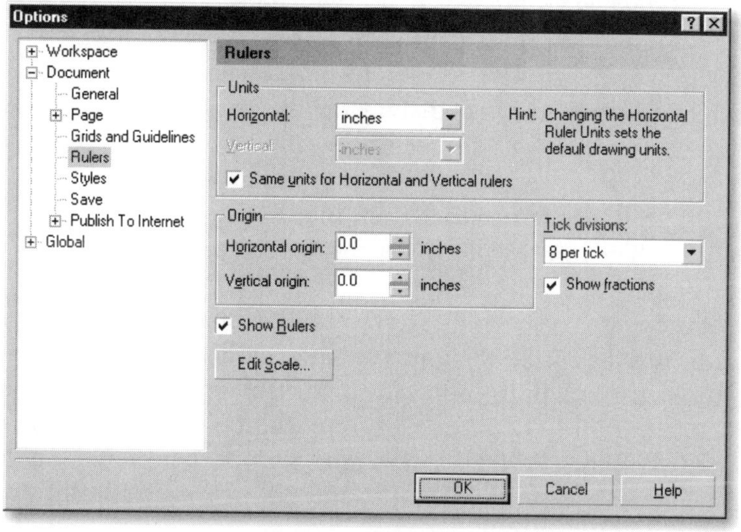

FIGURE 14-1   Ruler page in the Options dialog box

Vertical Rulers check box is checked. If you want to use different units, simply uncheck this box.

You can also set the origin of the ruler by typing the exact coordinates on the drawing page where you want the origin to be. A positive horizontal value will move the horizontal point to the right, and a positive vertical value will move the origin up.

Another way to change the origin is to click the little box where the rulers meet and drag the crosshairs that appear to the position where you want the origin to be. You'll notice that the rulers change as soon as you release the mouse button. Simply double-click the place where the rulers meet, and the origin will be reset to the default position.

The Rulers page in the Options dialog box also allows you to change the tick divisions on the ruler to 6, 8, or 10. The number of ticks you want displayed may depend on the measurement system you are using. Just below the Tick Divisions box is the Show Fractions check box, which is checked to show fractions instead of decimals on the ruler. When you're working in inches, seeing the fractions on the rulers can be quite handy. This setting is

14

especially useful when you're working with inches, as fractions such as "half an inch" or "quarter of an inch" are often used. With the metric system, the units all divide cleanly by 10 and therefore decimals make more sense.

Click the Edit Scale button to display the Drawing Scale dialog box shown in Figure 14-2.

The Typical Scales drop-down list provides drawing scales. For example, if you use the scale 1 inch equals 1 foot, the standard page of 8.5"×11" will equal 8.5'×11'. The rulers will display measurements according to this scale, as will any dimension lines you draw.

Some of the drawing scales just have numbers such as 1:1 or 1:2. The first number indicates the size of the unit you are creating and the second number indicates the size that will be indicated by the rulers. So with 1:1, a one-inch object is a one inch object. With 1:2, a one-inch object will be shown on the rulers to be two inches. In fact, a standard 8.5"×11" page will be displayed as 17"×22" if you choose the 1:2 scale. Other drawing scales follow this same formula.

If you can't find the scale you need in the Typical Scales drop-down list, choose Custom (at the bottom of the list) and create your own scale. In the

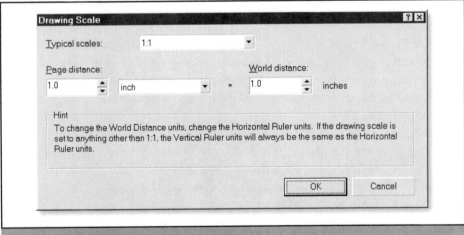

FIGURE 14-2   The Drawing Scale dialog box

Page Distance boxes, type the number of units and the type of units. In the World Distance box, type the value that you want the page distance to equal. Using the example where 1 inch equals 1 foot, you'd enter 1 inch as the page distance and 12 inches as the world distance. The world distance units are based on the units that are currently set for the rulers. If you're not happy with the units showing, simply change them on the Rulers page in the Options dialog box.

GRIDS

Each page has an underlying grid of invisible lines. By default, the grid is invisible and will not affect your work. However, you can put the grid to work for you. Select Tools | Options | Document | Grids and Guidelines. This will display the dialog box shown in Figure 14-3.

The frequency of the grid specifies the number of invisible lines in the grid between each ruler unit. For very small ruler units, you may want to enter a

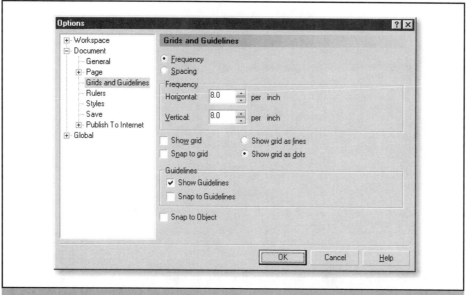

FIGURE 14-3   The Options Grids and Guidelines page in the Options dialog box with Frequency selected

14

fractional grid frequency. For example, if the ruler unit is a point, you might set the grid to 0.1 so that a gridline will appear at every tenth point.

A new option allows you to specify the spacing between grid dots. Selecting the Spacing radio button displays the spacing options shown in Figure 14-4.

As with gridlines, you can specify the distance between grid dots in both the horizontal and vertical directions.

The Sho<u>w</u> Grid check box displays the grid on the screen. By default, instead of seeing the actual gridlines you'll see a blue pixel at each place where the gridlines intersect one another. A new option in CorelDRAW 8, Show Grid as <u>L</u>ines, allows the grid to be shown as lines instead of dots, which makes the grid painfully obvious. At times, you'll not see the grid at every position, because the lines are limited to a certain density. For example, if the ruler unit were pixels and a gridline appeared at every pixel, the whole screen would be blue. As you zoom in, the gridlines will become increasingly dense until they

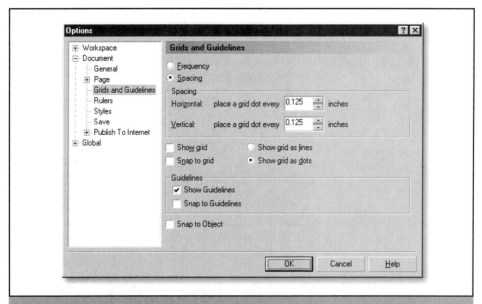

FIGURE 14-4   The Options Grids and Guidelines dialog box with Spacing selected

appear at every position as they are specified. Also, if you really hate blue, you can change the color in the Object Manager Docker window, described in Chapter 13.

Snap To Grid actually puts the grid to use. If you check this box, anything that you draw, distort, or drag will snap to the invisible gridlines. When you want to align things on the page or within an ad, for instance, the grid can be extremely useful, and it will certainly help you draw objects of precise sizes since the objects will snap to exact sizes.

In the Guidelines section of the page, you can specify whether guidelines are shown and if the snap will be enabled. And the last option allows you to enable Snap to Object.

You can also activate the Grid display by choosing View | Grid. You can turn on grid snapping with Layout | Snap To Grid (CTRL-Y). You'll also find icons on the Property Bar for Snap to Grid, Snap to Guideline, and Snap to Objects, as shown here.

GUIDELINES

Guidelines are very similar to the invisible gridlines. You can put them anywhere in either the vertical or horizontal orientation. They are used just like the grid except that they appear only where you place them instead of at a particular frequency.

Create a guideline by dragging either of the rulers onto the drawing window. A black dashed line will follow your cursor. When you release the mouse button, the guideline will be placed and the color will change to red. The ruler you drag from determines the orientation of the guideline. Thus, if you want a vertical guideline, drag from the vertical ruler.

14

Break the rules by holding down the ALT key while dragging out guidelines. This will create a guideline perpendicular to the ruler it came from.

To manually delete guidelines, select them and press the DEL key.

Guidelines have changed quite a bit in CorelDRAW 8. They work much more like any other object you've drawn on screen. If a guideline is currently selected, its color will change to red. You can drag guidelines to move them to a new location. If you click quickly, the handles will become rotation handles complete with a thumbtack. Use these handles and thumbtack to rotate the guideline to precisely the position you want.

Now, let's try something else. Make sure you have two guidelines on screen. Select the first one by clicking it. Now hold down the SHIFT key and click the second one. Yes, they are both selected. You can now nudge them, move them as one, delete them, rotate them, cut them, copy them, paste them or whatever you desire. You'll also notice that since they are both selected, they are both red. The key thing to remember is that selected guidelines are red and unselected guidelines are blue. With all of these new changes, it is very easy to create parallel slanted guidelines without doing any math!

There's also a new command that lets you select all of the guidelines. Choose Edit | Select All | Guidelines.

Usually, you'll want guidelines at an exact position or exact angle. Display the Guidelines Setup dialog box shown in Figure 14-5 by selecting Layout | Guidelines Setup or simply double-clicking any guideline.

The Horizontal and Vertical tabs of this dialog box are identical to each other. The left side lists the position of any existing guidelines. To add a guideline, type its position in the text box at the top of the list and click the Add button. To move an existing guideline, first select it from the list. Then type the desired position and click Move.

Slanted guidelines come in two flavors. Figure 14-6 shows the dialog box for Angle and 1 Point, and Figure 14-7 shows the dialog box for 2 Points.

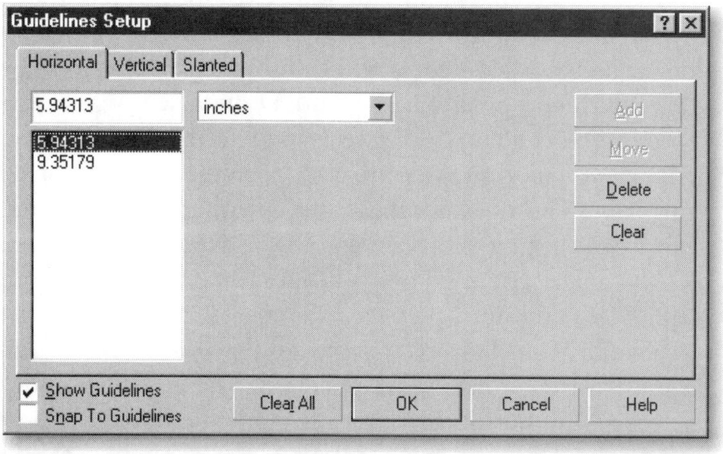

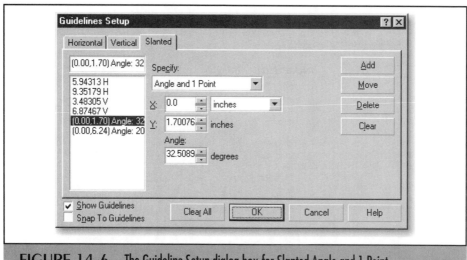

FIGURE 14-5   The Guidelines Setup dialog box with the Horizontal tab selected

FIGURE 14-6   The Guideline Setup dialog box for Slanted Angle and 1 Point

14

The list box at the left side of both dialog boxes shows all of the guidelines. Horizontal guidelines are followed by an *H* and vertical guidelines by a *V*. Once a guideline has been slanted, it will be listed with either a single position and an angle or with two positions, depending on how it was created.

Under Specify, you can choose between the two methods of slanting. With Angle and 1 Point, you need to enter the *x* and *y* points of a position on the edge of the drawing page. This does not mean a point where the guideline intersects the rulers, but where it intersects the edge of the specified page size. You also need to enter the angle. For 2 Points, you need to list the coordinates of two positions on the edge of the drawing page. After making changes to any guideline, you need to click the Move button to make the changes to take effect.

You can use the Delete button to delete only the selected guidelines, and you can use the Clear button to clear all guidelines of the type you have selected. Thus, if you are on the Slanted tab, Clear will clear all slanted

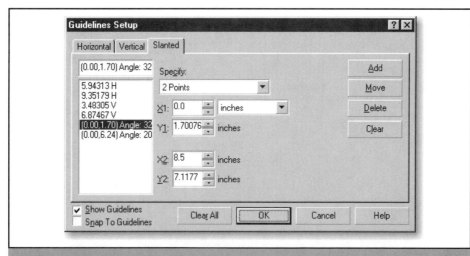

FIGURE 14-7   The Guideline Setup dialog box for Slanted 2 Points

guidelines. To clear all guidelines, use the Clear All button at the bottom of the dialog box.

The Show Guidelines check box controls whether the guidelines are visible on the page. Snap to Guidelines determines whether the guidelines will have an effect as you are drawing, moving, distorting, or doing anything else on the page.

Even though guidelines and grids are extremely useful, you will occasionally want to turn off snapping so you don't have to worry about objects jumping to the guidelines or grid.

USING OBJECTS AS GUIDES

Any object that can be drawn can be used as a guideline. You simply need to place it on the Guides layer. Chapter 13 discussed how to move objects to another layer and how to draw on the Master Guides layer. Keep in mind that objects drawn on the Guides layer do not work the same as guidelines. Snapping will only occur at the object's snap points (usually nodes) and not along the entire path of the object if you enable Snap to Object.

This same effect can be achieved without putting objects on the Guides layer. Just choose Layout | Snap to Objects. Again, other objects will snap only to the snap points of the snap object and not to the object itself.

GUIDELINE WIZARD

Placing guidelines manually is great for many projects. But there will be times when you know exactly where you want them and don't want to calculate the positions or even take the time to place them. That is where the Guideline Wizard can help you out. It came to be in CorelDRAW 7, but very few users found it since it was buried in the Script and Preset Manager roll-up. Well the roll-up has now morphed into a Docker and we'll show you how this wonderful tool works.

14

To open the Script and Preset Manager Docker, choose View | Dockers | Script and Preset Manager. When the Docker first appears, you'll see two folders in the Docker window, one labeled Scripts and one labeled Presets. Double-click the scripts folder. Now scroll through the list of scripts until you find one called guidewiz and double-click it. It should bring up the screen shown in Figure 14-8. For those who want to learn more about scripts, see Chapter 41.

This first screen really doesn't have any function other than to congratulate you for finding the Wizard and getting it started. So click Next to get to the good stuff.

The second Wizard screen, shown in Figure 14-9, presents two choices. You can either choose a Select a Customizable Guideline Type or Choose a

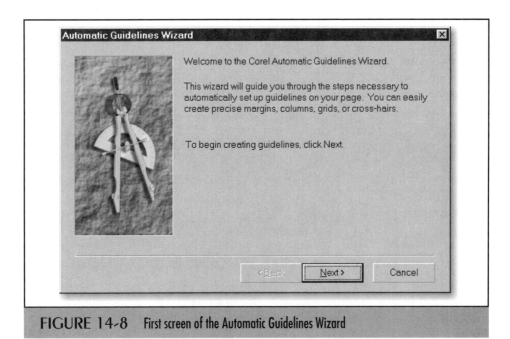

FIGURE 14-8   First screen of the Automatic Guidelines Wizard

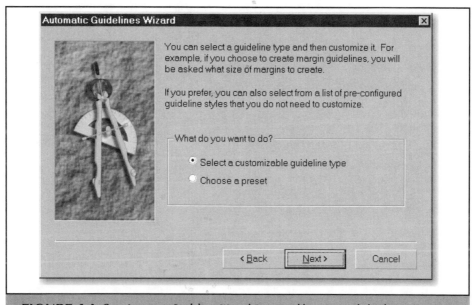

FIGURE 14-9 Automatic Guidelines Wizard Customizable or Preset dialog box

Preset. This first time, select the option Select a Customizable Guideline Type and click Next.

In the next Wizard screen, shown in Figure 14-10, you have a drop-down list of guideline types to choose from. They are Margins and Columns, Grid, and Cross-Hairs. For this exercise, choose Margins and Columns and click Next. You can explore the other types on your own later.

Now you will be asked to define the margins, as shown in Figure 14-11. By default, you only need to select the Top and Left margins as CorelDRAW will mirror the other two. But if you want the margins to be unbalanced, uncheck Mirror Margins and enter values for all four margins. When you've entered all the values, click Next.

Now you're asked if you would like columns, as shown in Figure 14-12. By default, the setting is No. So click the Yes radio button and change the

14

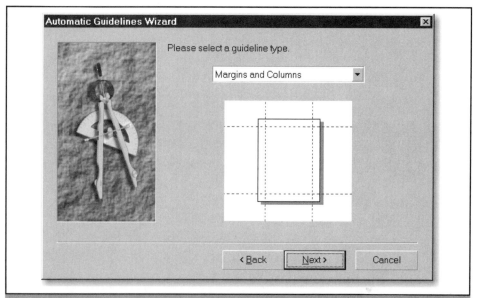

FIGURE 14-10 Automatic Guidelines Wizard Guideline Type dialog box

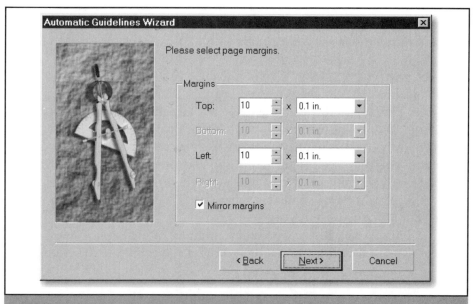

FIGURE 14-11 Automatic Guidelines Wizard Margins dialog box

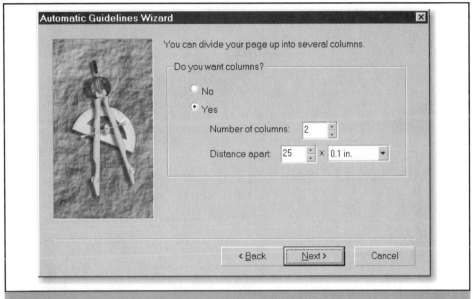

FIGURE 14-12   Automatic Guidelines Wizard Columns dialog box

number of columns to the number you desire. The last option is the distance between columns or the gutter measurement. Type in the distance you want and click Next.

OK, you've now defined where all of the guidelines will be placed. Next you've got to decide whether or not you want them locked, as shown in Figure 14-13. If you lock the guidelines, they cannot be accidentally moved. You can always unlock them by bringing up the Guideline Setup dialog box. So make your choice and click Next.

The last screen of the Wizard simply congratulates you for successfully pushing buttons and typing numbers. Click Finish and the guidelines you specified will appear on your document.

If you select Choose a Preset instead of Select a Customizable Guideline Type (see Figure 14-9), clicking Next displays the dialog box shown in Figure 14-14. In the preset drop-down list, you'll see seven choices of pre-made guidelines you can choose. So, if you were going to create a newsletter, the preset labeled Three Column Newsletter may be perfect for you. Make your selection and click Next.

14

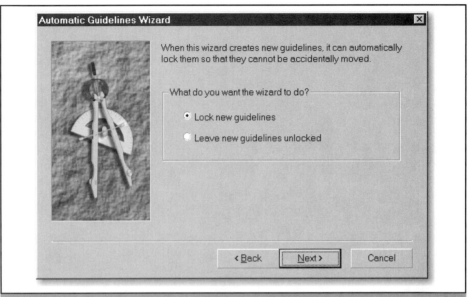

FIGURE 14-13   Automatic Guidelines Wizard Locked dialog box

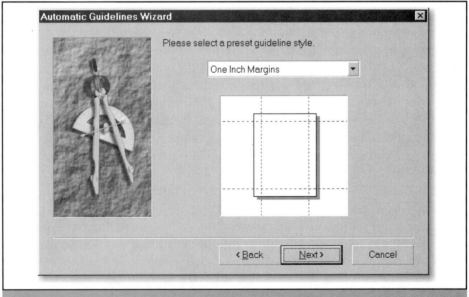

FIGURE 14-14   Automatic Guidelines Wizard Preset dialog box

Since the presets don't need to ask you any more questions, you'll get the dialog box shown in Figure 14-13 regarding the locking of guidelines.

You've seen how the Guideline Wizard can help you in precisely positioning guidelines. You've also seen how the scripting functionality can really automate CorelDRAW. So no longer will you struggle with your calculator to figure out exactly where the guidelines need to go for a four-column document!

Now that you understand how to use guidelines and grids, give them a try on your next project; we think that you'll see just how useful they can be.

15

COMBINING, BREAKING APART, GROUPING, UNGROUPING, SEPARATING, AND CONVERTING TO CURVES

The commands covered in this chapter share a common feature: They are all located in the Arrange menu and they all work with multiple objects. There may be some who question whether this statement applies to the Convert to Curves command, but often multiple objects are involved when converting to curves as well.

When you are instructed to select a command in this chapter, you will use the Property Bar whenever possible. If the command is not on the Property Bar, you will use the Arrange drop-down menu.

COMBINING

The Combine command, located on the Property Bar (CTRL-L), is active only when two or more individual objects are selected. It is perhaps the least understood of all the commands. The function of this command is to combine two or more objects into one. The Weld command also combines two or more objects into one, but in a different way. Differentiating between these two commands is important, but more important is understanding how the Combine command actually functions so you will know when to use it. Equally important is to recognize when objects have been combined.

KNOWING WHEN OBJECTS ARE COMBINED

Knowing when objects have been combined can be a great help when working with clipart. To see the effect of combining objects, draw a rectangle and an ellipse on the page. Now select both objects by marquee selection or by SHIFT-clicking. When the two objects are selected, look at the Status Bar at the bottom of the screen. The status line should indicate that you have two objects selected on layer 1. Click the Combine command on the Property Bar. Now look at the Status Bar again. This time it says that you have a curve selected on layer 1 with eight nodes. You no longer have an ellipse and a rectangle; instead, you have a single object, which is a curve.

Now use the Pick tool to move the objects to a different location on the page. They look like two distinctly separate objects, but CorelDRAW sees them as one—as the status line tells you. This seemingly confusing set of circumstances is why the Combine command can be difficult to understand.

 *If you are combining objects that are filled, the last object selected will determine the fill color. For example, if you select a yellow object and then a red object and combine the two, the resulting object will be red.*

BREAKING APART

The Break Apart command, Arrange | Break Apart (CTRL-K), works hand in hand with the Combine command. It too can be accessed from the Property Bar by clicking its icon. Its function is to undo the combining effect of the Combine command.

To see how Break Apart works, select the rectangle and ellipse you just combined and then click the Break Apart button on the Property Bar. Now select the rectangle. Notice that the selection handles surround only the rectangle and not the rectangle and ellipse. Look at the Status Bar again. It says that you have a curve selected, not a rectangle as you may have expected. This is because when you combine objects and then break them apart, the objects don't revert to what they were before they were combined; they become curve objects instead. With the rectangle now separated from the ellipse, the objects can be modified separately.

USING THE COMBINE AND BREAK APART COMMANDS TOGETHER

The fact that the Combine command works the way it does is what makes the command useful. One of the primary uses of the Combine command is to save disk space by combining objects that share the same attributes. Two combined objects will take up less disk space than the same two objects when they are not combined. Corel's clipart provides the best example of this attribute sharing. Figure 15-1 shows a horse in the clipart collection. If you want to follow along, the file name is Horse329.cdr and it's located in the Animals folder.

FIGURE 15-1   Original clipart image Horse329.cdr

When you first import clipart, you should check the status line to determine whether the objects are grouped. If they are, you will need to ungroup them before you can work on individual parts of the image (see "Grouping and Ungrouping" later in this chapter). With the horse image ungrouped, select the tail of the horse. The selection handles will surround more than just the tail (see Figure 15-2). The fact that the selection handles are surrounding an area larger than the tail area should alert you that the tail is combined with another part of the horse. To find out what other parts of the horse are combined with the tail, simply change the color of the tail. When you change the color of the tail, any other object that has been combined with the tail will also change color. In the case of Horse329.cdr, the mane of the horse was combined with the tail. They

FIGURE 15-2   The horse's tail is selected, with selection handles extending beyond the mane indicating that the two are combined

were combined because they shared the same color and outline attributes. If you want to change the color of the tail without changing the color of the mane, you will need to use the Break Apart command.

Remember, as demonstrated earlier with the ellipse and rectangle, the function of the Break Apart command is to uncombine the combined objects into separate objects again. When the objects are no longer combined, they can be handled like any other single objects.

To make the horse's tail a separate object, you need to select the tail and then select the Break Apart button on the Property Bar. This action will separate the tail from the mane. Interestingly, the mane is composed of two separate objects, so when you originally clicked the tail, you actually selected three objects combined together as one.

All this information sounds a little confusing at first. If you practice using the Combine and Break Apart commands on simple clipart objects, you will understand their functions more quickly.

USING THE COMBINE COMMAND TO CREATE BORDERS AND MASKS

One of the more common uses of the Combine command used to be to create borders and masks. When the Trim command was introduced in CorelDRAW 5 it took the place of the Combine command for this role (see Chapter 16). However, the Combine command will function differently than the Trim command if a object only partially overlaps another object or doesn't touch another selected object at all.

In the previous examples of the Combine command, the objects that were combined were separated from each other. If the objects being combined overlap, they behave in a completely different way. When objects overlap, a hole will be cut in the final combined object where the objects overlap.

The left side of Figure 15-3 shows an ellipse overlapping a rectangle. The ellipse and rectangle are both on top of a narrower rectangle in the background. On the right side of the figure, the ellipse and the top rectangle have been combined; you can see the hole created where the objects overlap, allowing the rectangle in the background to show through.

There aren't many times when this type of combining is particularly useful, but it can produce some very beautiful patterns, as shown in Figure 15-4. Follow these steps to create this design:

1. Draw an ellipse on the page approximately .5" wide by 2" tall.

2. Give the ellipse a light blue fill with a red outline.

3. With the ellipse selected, click a second time to reveal the rotation arrows.

4. Drag the center of rotation "thumbtack" to the bottom of the ellipse (see step (a) in Figure 15-4).

5. Choose <u>A</u>rrange | <u>T</u>ransform | <u>R</u>otate to bring up the Rotation dialog box.

6. Enter **15** in the Angle parameters box.

15

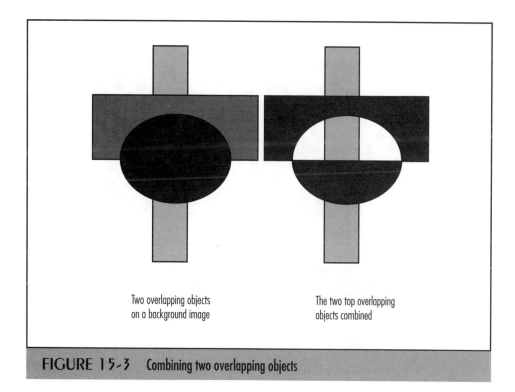

Two overlapping objects
on a background image

The two top overlapping
objects combined

FIGURE 15-3   Combining two overlapping objects

7. Click the Apply to Duplicate button 23 times. You should now have 24 ellipses in a circle, as shown in step (b) of the figure.

8. Marquee select all 24 ellipses and click the Combine button on the Property Bar. Your image should now look like the finished pattern in step (c) in Figure 15-4.

USING COMBINE TO CREATE A MASK WITH TEXT

Another interesting use of the Combine command is with text. Try putting text on top of an object and then combining the two to create a mask for an underlying object to show through. Figure 15-5 shows this effect. Text was combined with a rectangle, and a photo-CD image was placed underneath. Figure 15-6 looks different because the combined object was given a white fill

FIGURE 15-4   A pattern created using the Combine command

FIGURE 15-5   Text used to create a mask for the underlying photo-CD to show through

FIGURE 15-6 Filling the combined objects with the paper color to show only the photo-CD

to match the paper background, and the outlines were removed. This technique changes the look of the object so that the text appears to be filled with the Photo-CD image.

 *Although this masking method is a tried and true way to fool the eye into thinking you are looking through text into a background, this same effect can be created by applying PowerClip to the background image to the text. For information on PowerClip, see Chapter 21.*

GROUPING AND UNGROUPING

Grouping is a way to keep objects together as a unit. A good example of grouped objects is a clipart image. Usually a clipart image is made up of many individual objects. Grouping the objects prevents the accidental moving of a single object within the group. More important, it allows you to move a large number of objects at one time without adversely affecting the relationship of the objects within the group.

A group of objects can be blended from one group to another, and effects such as Perspective and Envelope can be applied to the group (see Chapter 18). Grouping several groups into a master group is also fairly common. The master group is not called a master group on the status line; it is merely a group composed of several groups. For example, if you select a group that contains three separate groups, the Status Bar will tell you have a group of three objects; CorelDRAW doesn't know the three objects are groups. Try to form the habit of grouping objects that share commonalties as a means of keeping order.

Figure 15-7 shows individual groups outlined with dotted lines within a master group.

The process of grouping is very straightforward. Simply select the objects you want to group and click the Group button on the Property Bar or use the shortcut (CTRL-G). Ungrouping is just as easy. To ungroup a group of objects, select the group and then click the Ungroup button on the Property Bar or use the shortcut (CTRL-U).

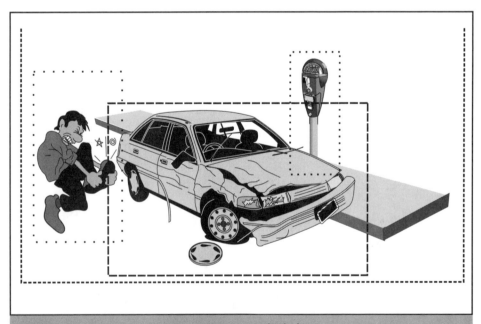

FIGURE 15-7   One master group containing individual groups

There is also an Ungroup All button on the Property Bar. The Ungroup All command literally ungroups all groups that are selected. If you select single groups, master groups, or a combination of both, all the objects within these groups will revert to single-object status when you choose Ungroup All.

SELECTING OBJECTS WITHIN A GROUP

It is not always necessary to ungroup a group of objects to edit an individual object within the group. For example, you can change the color of a particular object or adjust the size or shape of an object without ungrouping the group.

To edit an individual object within a group, hold down the CTRL key and select the object. Round selection handles will surround the object instead of the familiar square ones. Check the status line; it will tell you that you have selected a child object. A child object is a selected object within a group of objects. When a child object is selected, you can treat it just like any other object.

Figure 15-8 shows a group of objects on the left and a duplicate of this same group on the right. The duplicate group of objects on the right shows a child object (the body of the car) that has been selected and its original shape modified.

FIGURE 15-8   A child object selected and modified within the duplicate group

SEPARATING

The Separate command, Arrange | Separate, is used to take apart certain effects so that individual parts of the effect can be edited. Think of this process as an extra step that is required to edit individual objects within certain effects. The effects that you must separate prior to editing individual objects are Blend (including blends on a path), Clone, Contour, Extrude, Fit Text to Path, Dimension Lines, and Connector Lines. The Separate command separates the original object or objects from the objects created by these effects.

Consider two objects that are blended together (see Chapter 20 for information on blends). When the blend is created, it is made up of the two original control objects that were used to begin the blend and the blended steps created between the two objects. If you select the entire blend, the Status Bar will indicate that a blend group is selected. When you use the Separate command to separate the blend group, you are left with the original two control objects, which are now ordinary objects, and a single group of objects that had been the blend steps. This remaining group of objects can then be ungrouped.

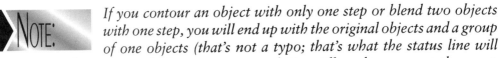

If you contour an object with only one step or blend two objects with one step, you will end up with the original objects and a group of one objects (that's not a typo; that's what the status line will say) when you use the Separate command. You still need to ungroup the group of one objects to have full editing control.

Figure 15-9 shows the transformation of a blend group using the Separate command.

CONVERTING TO CURVES

The primary function of the Convert to Curves command is to convert rectangles, ellipses, and text into fully editable shapes. You will use many different shapes when you create your projects in CorelDRAW, and most of them, with the exception of clipart, will start out as rectangles, ellipses, or freehand shapes. You will usually apply many CorelDRAW effects to these

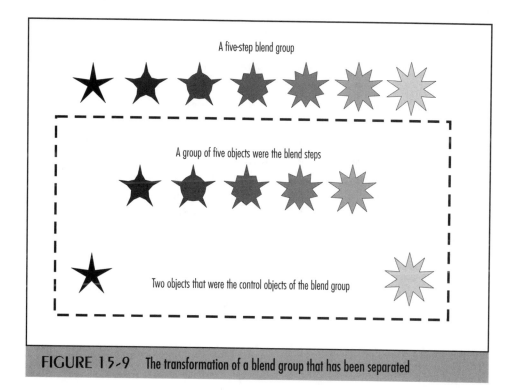

FIGURE 15-9   The transformation of a blend group that has been separated

objects to achieve your final image. In most cases, even though you use these effects, the original object will still retain its original identity. For example, if you extrude an ellipse, the control object is still an ellipse. If you apply an envelope to a rectangle, the new enveloped shape is still a rectangle. If you add perspective to a word you've typed, the word is still text.

You can have even greater control over all these objects if you convert them to curves. This is not to say you should convert every rectangle you draw or text you type to curves, but doing so gives you more artistic control over objects if you need it.

HOW TO CONVERT OBJECTS TO CURVES

To convert an object to curves, click the Convert to Curves icon on the Property Bar or use the shortcut (CTRL-Q). A basic ellipse has one node. When

the ellipse is converted to curves, it will have four nodes. A basic rectangle has a node at each corner. When it is converted to curves, the nodes become editable. Text has a node at the base of each letter for kerning purposes. When text is converted to curves, many additional nodes are added to form the shape of the text. It is these nodes that allow you to manipulate the text in a more artistic manner.

The right side of Figure 15-10 shows an ellipse that has been converted to curves. The figure shows where the four nodes will appear when the Shape tool is selected. The object on the right is the result of manipulating the four nodes into a different shape. A little more adjusting and it could fit on the shoes of a famous sports star. Just think: that logo could have been created with four nodes.

USING THE CONVERT TO CURVES COMMAND TO CREATE FREEHAND SHAPES

Converting an ellipse to curves is a way of creating freehand shapes without having to use the Pencil tool. Unless you have the steady hand of a diamond

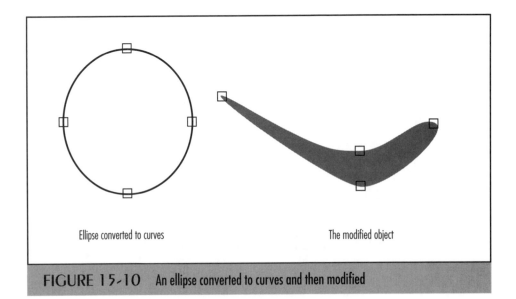

Ellipse converted to curves   The modified object

FIGURE 15-10   An ellipse converted to curves and then modified cutter, using a mouse to draw freehand shapes will produce jaggy perimeters. When you convert an ellipse to curves, you can maintain smooth lines as you manipulate the shape with the Shape tool.

The dolphin in Figure 15-11 also began life as an ellipse. After it was converted to curves, the Shape tool was used to manipulate it into the silhouette of a dolphin. Additional ellipses were added and converted to curves to make the various shapes required for the final image. Think of it as shaping a lump of clay. It's really quite simple when you get used to it. To learn about adding nodes and other Shape tool functions, see Chapter 8.

USING THE CONVERT TO CURVES COMMAND TO MODIFY TEXT

When you want to create really unusual looking text, the Convert to Curves command is the command to use. The top of Figure 15-12 shows the word "Dripping" using the font Cezanne. The bottom of the figure shows the text modified with the Shape tool after it was converted to curves. As you can see, there are many artistic possibilities when you convert text to curves.

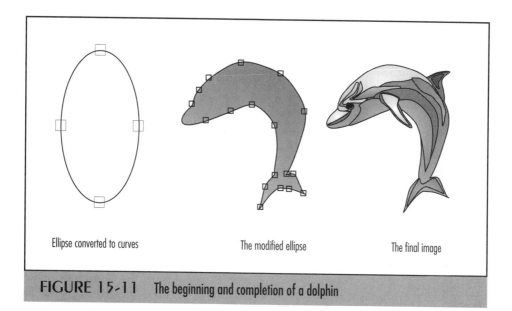

Ellipse converted to curves   The modified ellipse   The final image

FIGURE 15-11   The beginning and completion of a dolphin

The original text

Text converted to curves and modified

FIGURE 15-12   A word of text modified with the Shape tool after it was converted to curves

> *If you add either the Perspective or Envelope effect to an object and then decide to modify the object with the Shape tool, you must first use the Convert to Curves command again before you can further modify the object. See Chapter 18 for information on the Envelope and Perspective effects.*

Having read how to use the various commands covered in this chapter, you have also learned the relationship between the Combine and Break Apart commands as well as when to use the Separate command. Remember also that the Group command is an excellent way to keep together objects that share a commonality. Understanding these basic concepts will go a long way in helping you master CorelDRAW.

16

WELD, INTERSECTION, AND TRIM

his chapter covers three different commands, all of which will help you draw shapes more quickly and easily than drawing them freehand. They also share one thing in common. Before any of these commands will work correctly, each object must overlap at least one other object in some fashion.

This chapter discusses the use of the Weld, Intersection, and Trim commands using their respective roll-ups. You also have the option of selecting the Quick Weld, Intersection, or Trim commands from the Property Bar. As you learn how these commands work, you may find that using a Quick command on the Property Bar is faster than using the roll-ups. However, before you use these Quick commands, you should learn how these commands work using the roll-ups so that you completely understand each command's function. After you become a Weld, Intersection, and Trim expert, you can customize the Arrange menu so the Weld, Intersection, and Trim commands can perform as one-shot Quick commands. To find out how to make these commands function as one-shot Quick commands in the Arrange menu, refer to Chapter 40.

 *The Weld, Intersection, and Trim commands function differently when selected from the Property Bar. These differences are explained at the end of this chapter.*

THE WELD COMMAND

The function of the Weld command, Arrange | Weld, is to create custom shapes by combining two or more objects together to form a single shape. By default, the roll-up is grouped together with the Trim and Intersect roll-ups, as shown in Figure 16-1. This grouping of the roll-ups allows you to quickly switch among the three commands as you work.

Welding is an additive process requiring that objects overlap each other before they can be welded. What actually happens when you weld objects together is the areas that overlap are thrown away and the outside perimeter of the each object is welded together to form one single object. Figure 16-2 shows two objects before and after welding. On the left, two rectangles overlap each other to form the letter *T*. On the right is the result after the two rectangles are welded. Notice that the intersecting lines of the two rectangles have disappeared, and the two rectangles have become a single shape.

16

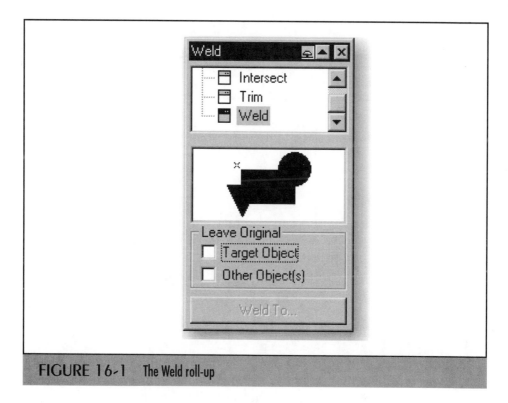

FIGURE 16-1   The Weld roll-up

USING THE WELD-TO BUTTON

Clicking the Weld To button at the bottom of the Weld roll-up is the default method for welding when you use the roll-up. To create the silhouette of the spray can shown in Figure 16-3, use the outline view on the left as a guide and follow these steps:

1. Draw a rectangle on the page for the body of the can.

2. Draw a circle and place it at the top of the rectangle, leaving about a fourth of the circle showing above the rectangle.

3. Draw two small rectangles like those shown in the figure and place them so they overlap each other and the circle.

4. Select all of the objects except the largest rectangle by SHIFT-clicking (these objects are called the Other Object(s); think of them as modifying objects) and then click the Weld To button.

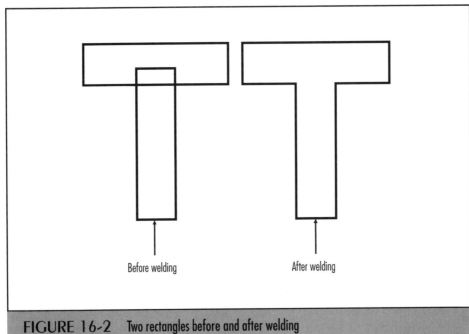

Before welding   After welding

FIGURE 16-2   Two rectangles before and after welding

5. A pointing arrow replaces the cursor. Use this arrow to select the large rectangle (this object is called the Target Object). When you select the second object with the arrow, all the objects will be welded together. You should have a silhouette of a spray can.

6. Color the silhouette with a fill of black. Your drawing should look like the right side of Figure 16-3.

This method of welding several objects together at once can be confusing when you are welding many objects. In the preceding example, instead of selecting all but the largest rectangle, you could select all the objects at once by marquee selecting. Then, when you click the Weld To button, you can use the arrow to select any of the selected objects. The weld function will work just as if you had selected the first three objects and pointed to the fourth.

The other options in the roll-up let you choose whether to leave the original of either the target objects or other objects after the weld function is executed.

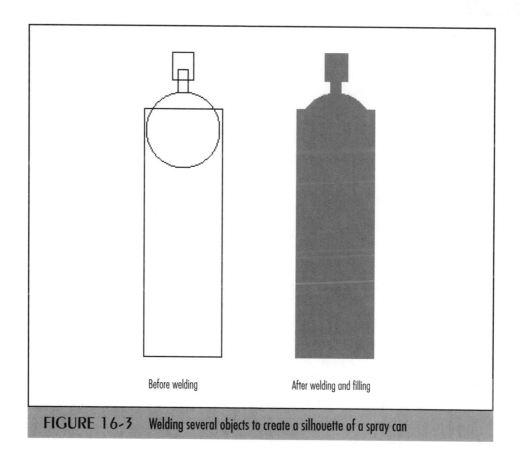

Before welding

After welding and filling

FIGURE 16-3   Welding several objects to create a silhouette of a spray can

Put a check mark in the appropriate boxes to retain either the original or target objects, or both. When you use the Weld command, you will rarely leave any of the original objects behind.

CREATING STREET MAPS WITH THE WELD COMMAND

Creating street maps can be frustrating without the use of the Weld command. Figure 16-4 shows a typical street map before and after the Weld command was used. To create street maps, you draw the streets using rectangles and then weld them together. If you need to add winding streets, try using the new

Natural Pen tool. You can vary the width by changing the settings on the Property Bar.

USING THE WELD COMMAND WITH GROUPS OF OBJECTS

An exciting new feature introduced in CorelDRAW 8 allows you to weld groups of objects. There are two ways that you can use these new feature. You can either weld all the objects within a single group of objects into one single curve object, or you can weld two different groups of objects together. Figure 16-5 illustrates the first method. A clipart image was selected from the Clipart library. The lamp contains 220 objects and takes up 52K of disk space. The group of objects was selected and the Weld button on the Property Bar was pressed. The result is a single curve object that can be used as a silhouette and a file size reduced to 18K.

The second method, shown in Figure 16-6, welds two separate groups of objects together. The table and tablecloth consisting of two objects was welded to the lamp containing three objects. The result is another silhouette of the two groups formed into a single curve object.

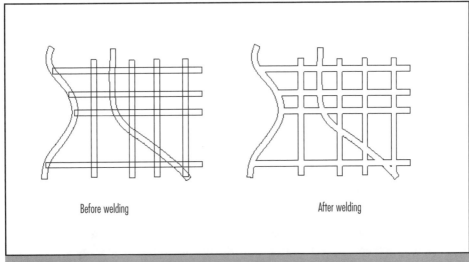

Before welding   After welding

FIGURE 16-4   Shapes drawn with the Natural Pen tool welded together with rectangles to create a street map

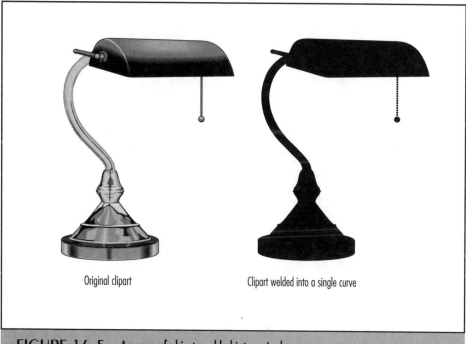

Original clipart   Clipart welded into a single curve

FIGURE 16-5   A group of objects welded into a single curve

THE INTERSECTION COMMAND

CAUTION: *The newly created shape caused when intersecting will be behind the object pointed to with the Intersecting Arrow. This will become evident as you follow the instructions throughout this section for using the Intersection command. The temporary work-around is to move the intersected object to the front, using the Order Command in the Arrange menu, after you complete the intersection.*

The function of the Intersection command, <u>A</u>rrange | <u>I</u>ntersection, is to create a new object in the shape of the area of the overlapping objects. By

Two groups of objects, one overlapping the other   Both groups welded into a single curve

FIGURE 16-6   Two different groups of objects welded together into one single curve

default, the roll-up is grouped together with the Weld and Trim commands; when selected, it looks like Figure 16-7.

If the way the Intersection command works seems puzzling, look at Figure 16-8. The image to the left of the arrow consists of an overlapping circle and rectangle. The shape outlined by the dotted line is the shape that will be created by applying the Intersection command. The object to the right of the arrow is the new object that was created. Notice that this new object is the shape formed by the overlapping objects. This example may seem unimaginative, but think how long it would take you to create this intersected shape without the Intersection command. Actually, this piece could be the start of a slice of watermelon or a lemon wedge. The point is that the Intersection command is a great way to create unusual shapes quickly.

16

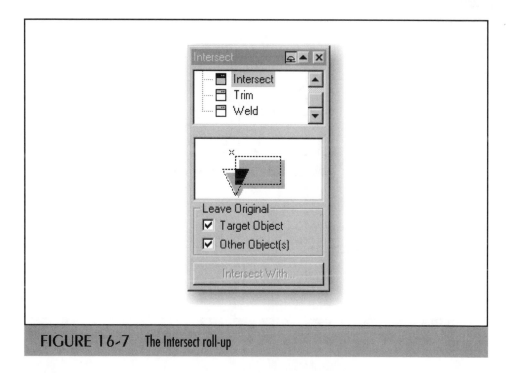

FIGURE 16-7 The Intersect roll-up

USING THE INTERSECTION COMMAND

Practice using the Intersection command by following these steps:

1. Draw two circles that overlap each other as shown at point (a) in Figure 16-9.

2. Click Intersect in the roll-up group to open the Intersect roll-up.

3. Put a check mark in both of the Leave Original boxes at the bottom of the roll-up.

4. Select one or both of the circles and click the Intersect With button.

5. Use the pointing arrow to select one of the circles. A third object will be created in the shape of the area created by your overlapping circles. Your two intersecting circles, along with the newly created intersected object, should look something like the ones at point (b) in the figure. If you want to end up with the new shape without the original objects, remove the check marks from the Leave Original boxes before you intersect the objects.

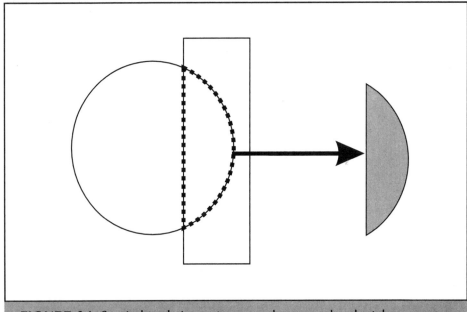

FIGURE 16-8   Applying the Intersection command to a rectangle and a circle

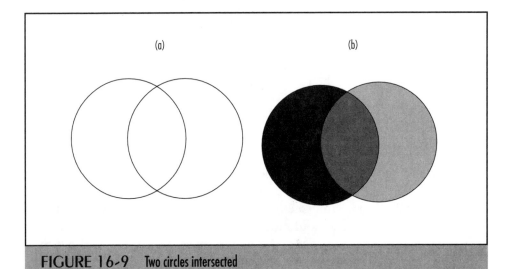

FIGURE 16-9   Two circles intersected

One of the more practical uses for the Intersection command is to color text with different fills in an irregular fashion, as in Figure 16-10. To create this example for yourself, open the Intersect roll-up and follow these steps:

1. Type the word **CHROME** using a large, bold font such as Bauhaus.

2. Click on the Treat as Filled button on the Property Bar to turn off the default setting of on.

3. Put a check mark in the Target Object and Other Objects(s) check boxes in the Leave Original section of the roll-up.

4. Draw a rectangle over the top half of the text, as shown at point (a) in the figure.

5. Press the SPACEBAR to select the rectangle. Then click the Intersect With button at the bottom of the roll-up.

6. Use the pointing arrow to select the text object. The intersection will be performed, and the newly created intersected object will be selected. Change its color by choosing a color from the color palette. The original rectangle and text will still be visible, as shown at point (b) in the figure.

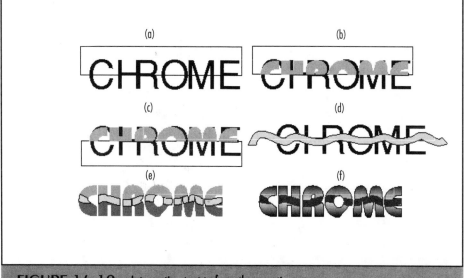

FIGURE 16-10   Intersecting text to form three sections

7. Remove the check mark from the Other Object(s) check box.

8. Select the rectangle you drew in step 4. Select the top-center selection handle and drag downward across the text so that the rectangle covers the lower half of the text, as shown at point (c) in the figure.

   With the rectangle still selected, click the Intersect With button and use the pointing arrow to select the text again. A second intersected object will be created, and the rectangle will disappear. Change the color of the second object to something different from the color of the first intersected object.

9. Select both of the newly created objects. With the cursor placed over the objects, right-click the objects. The Object menu will appear. Choose Order | To Back. This will place the intersected objects behind the original text.

10. Remove the check mark from the Target Object check box. There should not be check marks in either the Target Object or Other Object(s) check boxes at this point.

11. Select the Natural Pen tool and draw a waving line across and through the center of the text. Use a line width of approximately 0.1 inch. The line width can be set by selecting a size from the outline width drop down list on the Property Bar. The two halves of text and the wavy line should now look similar to the example at point (d) in the figure.

12. With the line still selected, click the Intersect With button and select the text with the pointing arrow. The text and the original line will disappear, leaving a third intersected wavy object over the top of the previously two intersected text objects, as shown at point (e) in the figure.

13. You can now color the three individual objects to complete the effect. The example shown at point (f) in the figure used opposing linear fountain fills for the top and bottom objects and a conical fill for the center object.

16

USING THE INTERSECTION COMMAND ON GROUPS OF OBJECTS

As with the Weld command, you can use the Intersection command on groups of objects. Frankly, there probably are not too many uses for this effect, but Figure 16-11 shows one possibility. A clipart image of the United States was used as a base image. A outline of the state of Nevada was drawn over the existing outline as part of the clipart group. The new outline and the group of 188 objects making up the map was selected and the Intersection button on the Property Bar was pressed. The resulting third shape was then enlarged and extruded to give the illusion of the state hovering above the map. This effect could just as easily been accomplished by ungrouping the map and making a duplicate of the state, and then proceeding with the extrusion. This is not the case if you want to use the Trim command with groups of objects. Read on to discover how to use this versatile command.

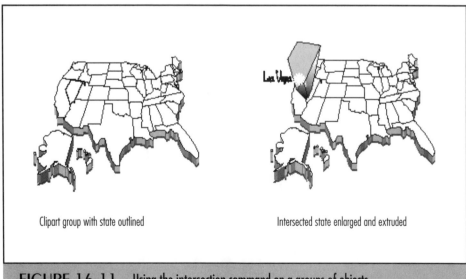

Clipart group with state outlined   Intersected state enlarged and extruded

FIGURE 16-11   Using the intersection command on a groups of objects

THE TRIM COMMAND

The Trim command, Arrange | Trim, is another command that lets you create unique shapes quickly and easily. Like the Weld and Intersection commands, it requires at least two overlapping objects. By default, the Trim roll-up is grouped together with the Weld and Intersection roll-ups; when selected, it looks like Figure 16-12.

USING THE TRIM COMMAND LIKE A COOKIE CUTTER

The Trim command works much like a cookie cutter. Instead of welding objects together like the Weld command or creating additional shapes like the Intersection command, the Trim command removes sections of an object. To trim two overlapping objects, you select the object you want to use as the

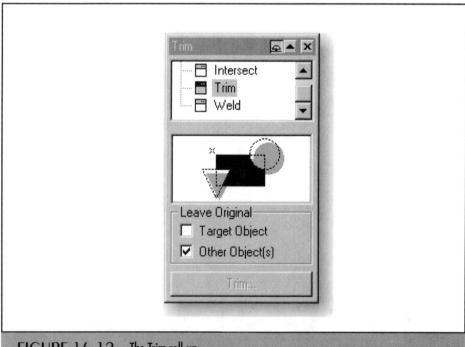

FIGURE 16-12   The Trim roll-up

trimming object and then click the Trim button at the bottom of the Trim roll-up. Use the pointing arrow to select the object you want to cut and then click the Trim button. The section removed from the last selected object is determined by the shape formed by the other overlapping object. Figure 16-13 shows an example of a basic trim. The overlapping objects on the left have not been trimmed. The half circle in the center is a result of selecting the square first and then the circle. This method uses the square to trim the circle. The square at the right is the result of selecting the circle first and then the square. This method uses the circle to trim the square. Can you see why Trim is described as the cookie cutter command?

By default, the Trim command leaves the original version of the other object on the screen. For instance, after the objects in Figure 16-13 were trimmed, the object used to trim will remain on the screen. If you don't want the trimming object to remain, remove the check mark from the Other Object(s) check box in the roll-up. If you forget to remove the check mark, simply delete the unwanted object after trimming.

Practice using the basic Trim command until you feel comfortable with the sequence of selection. Then try to duplicate the example in Figure 16-14 by following the steps outlined next:

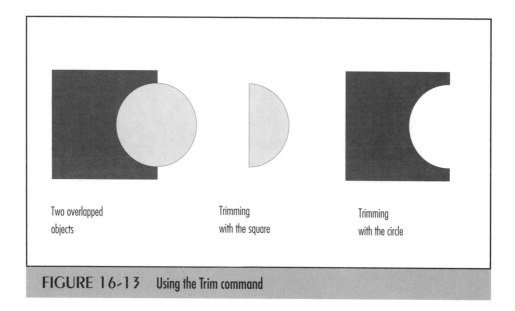

Two overlapped
objects

Trimming
with the square

Trimming
with the circle

FIGURE 16-13   Using the Trim command

1. Draw a circle and duplicate it six times.

2. Space the circles evenly apart in a straight line.

3. Draw a rectangle over the bottom half of the circles.

4. Remove any check marks from the Leave Original section of the roll-up.

5. Select the circles either by marquee selection or by SHIFT-clicking.

6. Click the Trim button and use the pointing arrow to select the rectangle.

7. Fill the remaining shape with a fill of your choice.

If you followed the steps correctly, your screen should look similar to Figure 16-14.

Many users think of the Trim command only as a way to trim closed objects by using other closed objects. Figure 16-15 shows that you can trim closed objects with open path lines as well.

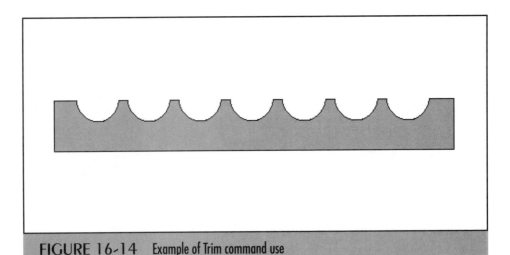

FIGURE 16-14   Example of Trim command use

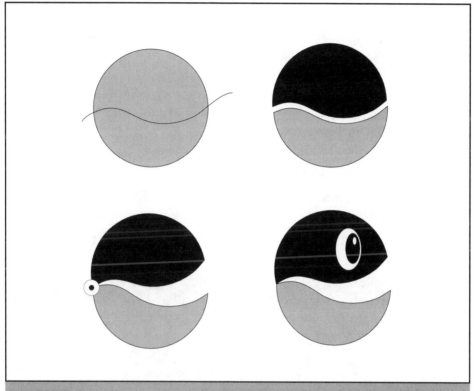

FIGURE 16-15   Trimming a circle with a single line and turning it into a fun image

If you would like to try this trim method, follow these steps:

1. Using the Ellipse tool, draw a circle on the page. Fill the circle with a light gray color.

2. Using the Freehand Pencil tool, draw a wavy line across the center of the circle like the one at the upper-left corner of Figure 16-15.

3. Remove any check marks from the Leave Original section of the Trim roll-up.

4. With the wavy line selected, click the Trim button.

5. Using the pointing arrow, select the circle.

6. Using the Pick tool, select the circle. Then click the Break Apart command on the <u>A</u>rrange | <u>B</u>reak Apart menu or click the Break Apart button on the Property Bar.

7. Select the top half of the circle and change its color to black. Your two halves of the circle should now look like the ones at the upper-right corner of the figure.

8. With the top half of the circle still selected, click a second time to reveal the rotation arrows.

9. Move the center-of-rotation thumb tack to the lower-left corner of the selected half, as shown at the lower-left corner of Figure 16-15.

10. Click the upper-right corner rotation arrow and rotate the top half of the circle to the left.

11. Add an ellipse for the eye, a second ellipse for the eyeball, and a third ellipse for the highlight in the eyeball and you're finished. The finished image should look like the one shown at the lower-right corner of the figure.

What is it, you ask? We don't know, but it's cute.

USING THE TRIM COMMAND WITH GROUPS OF OBJECTS

The ability to trim groups of objects has been on CorelDRAW users' wish lists for years, and now it is a reality. Figure 16-16 illustrates this great new feature. A clipart image of an elk containing 337 objects was opened and a freehand shape covering all but the head and neck of the elk was drawn. The freehand shape was selected first (the cookie cutter) and then the clipart group was selected. The Trim command was used and the result was a group of 197 objects making up just the head, antlers, and neck of the elk. This one new feature will save hours of image editing for anyone needing to modify clipart.

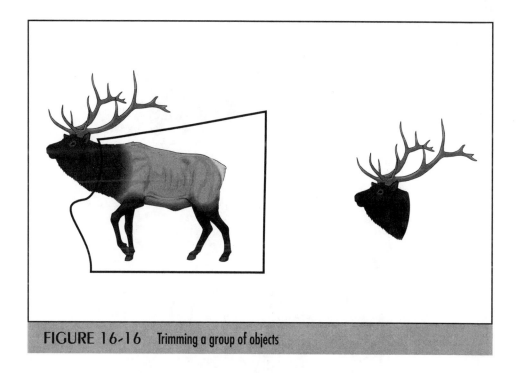

FIGURE 16-16   Trimming a group of objects

USING THE TRIM COMMAND IN PLACE OF THE COMBINE COMMAND

You learned at the beginning of this section that the Trim command is like a cookie cutter. You learned in Chapter 15 that the Combine command can be used to create holes in objects so they can be used as masks. The Trim command functions the same way if the trimming objects are completely inside of the object being trimmed. Figure 16-17 illustrates this quite well. The train in the figure is a Corel clipart image from the SYMB003 file located in the Transportation\Commercial folder. The background image of the painted desert is from Landscapes and Backgrounds in Corel's Professional Photo CD collection.

FIGURE 16-17 Using the Trim command to create a mask that allows the background image to show through

Here are the steps required to complete this image. You can use the same clipart as used in the figure or images of your own choice.

1. Open a background image of your choice.

2. Import any piece of clipart. Remember, you can not use clipart groups.

3. Place the clipart on top of the background image.

4. Draw an object large enough to surround both the background and the clipart.

5. Remove any check marks from the Leave Original section of the Trim roll-up.

6. Select the clipart object and then click the Trim button. Use the pointing arrow to select the object surrounding the background.

7. Fill the resulting object with an object fill of your choice. Figure 16-17 uses a conical fill from black to white.

USING THE WELD, INTERSECTION, AND TRIM BUTTONS ON THE PROPERTY BAR

The Weld, Intersection, and Trim buttons on the Property Bar function independently of their respective roll-ups. Note that changing the settings in the roll-ups does not change the commands on the Property Bar. That is, the commands on the Property Bar, shown here, always use the default settings.

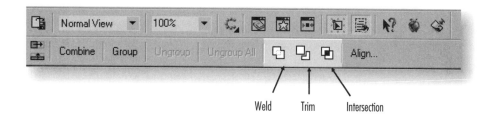

Weld   Trim   Intersection

The Weld, Intersection, and Trim commands located on the Property Bar work as follows:

► The Weld command welds all selected objects without leaving either the target object or other object(s) on the page.

► The Trim command trims the last selected object (the target object) and leaves all other objects on the page.

► The Intersection command leaves both the target and other object(s) on the page.

After having learned the different functions of the commands using the roll-ups, you may find it quicker to use the commands on the Property Bar for the majority of your work. If the default leaves an object on the page you don't want, simply delete it.

ALIGNING, DISTRIBUTING, COPYING AND PASTING, EFFECTS COPYING, DUPLICATING, AND CLONING

Some CorelDRAW users may have the eyes of an eagle and the steady hand of a diamond cutter, but if you weren't born with these gifts, the Align and Distribute commands are the answers to your problems. A great new feature lets you use single letter shortcut keys to align objects.

This chapter will also cover the new Smart Duplicate command and a special Copy From command, in addition to explaining the difference between pasting objects using object linking versus object embedding. Finally, you will learn how cloning objects can save you time.

ALIGNING OBJECTS

You access the Align command either by choosing <u>A</u>rrange | <u>A</u>lign and Distribute (CTRL-A) or by clicking the Align button on the Property Bar—by far the quickest way. The Align command allows you to precisely align two or more objects to either an edge of the page or the center of the page. You can also align objects to the center or edge of the last object selected. If you marquee select the objects, the lowest object in the stacking order is considered to be the last object selected (see Chapter 13).

Don't discount the importance of the last sentence of the previous paragraph. When you are aligning objects to other objects, the object to which all the other objects will be aligned is the object that is selected last.

A synonym for the word *align* is *put in line*. These words, in many ways, better describe the function of the Align command, which lets you line up objects with themselves or with the page.

The Align and Distribute dialog box is shown in Figure 17-1. By default, it appears on the drawing page with the Align tab selected.

At least one object must be selected before the Align and Distribute dialog box can be accessed from the <u>A</u>rrange | <u>A</u>lign and Distribute menu. Two objects must be selected before you can select the Align command from the Property Bar.

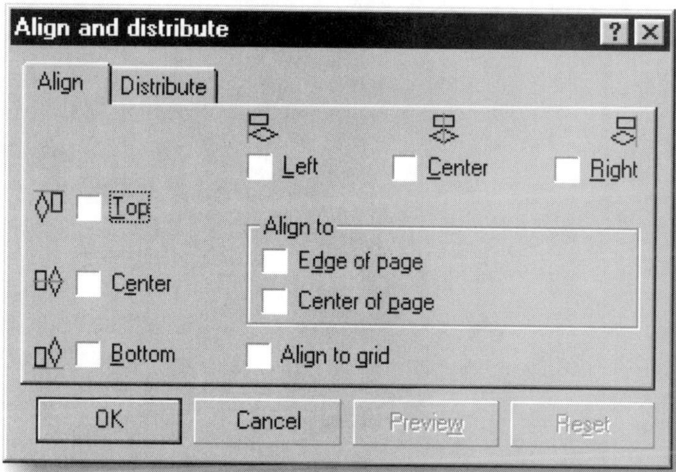

17

FIGURE 17-1   The Align and Distribute dialog box with the Align tab selected

LINING THINGS UP

Figure 17-2 shows a shark, an angelfish, and a clown fish randomly placed on a page. The stacking order of the three fish, starting at the back, is the shark, the angelfish, and then the clown fish.

You will now learn how to align objects to themselves and to the edges of the page. Figures 17-3 through 17-6 all began with the objects randomly placed like the ones shown in Figure 17-2.

Learning how the various settings affect the outcome is paramount in understanding how the Align command works. When aligning objects, you must always consider whether you want to align to the page or to another object. An easy way to keep track of what you are aligning to is this: If you don't enable any of the boxes in the Align To section of the Align tab, your objects will line up with the designated edge of the last selected object. If you do check one of the boxes in the Align To section, the selected objects will line up with the designated edge or center of the drawing page.

FIGURE 17-2   Three objects randomly placed on the page

The three check boxes spaced horizontally across the top of the dialog box are used to align objects horizontally to the left, center, or right of the page of the last selected object. The three check boxes spaced vertically down the left side of the dialog box are used to align objects vertically to the top, center, or bottom of the page or the last selected object.

Note the different underlined letters in the vertical Center check box and the horizontal Center check box. If you use the underlined

keys to enable the check boxes, the alignment will be determined by which underlined letter you use. Also, when following along with the examples in this chapter, you must be sure to choose the right option.

Figures 17-3 through 17-6 all use different settings from the Align dialog box. To see how these various alignments are achieved, place three objects on a page and follow along with the descriptions of the settings used for each figure. Remember that you can click the Preview button before you finalize

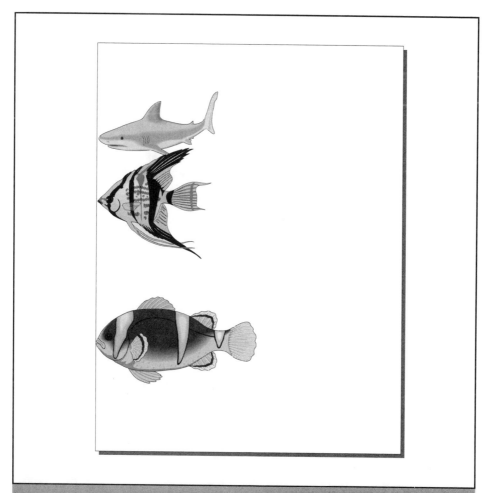

FIGURE 17-3   Aligning the left edge of objects to the left edge of the page by choosing Left | Edge of Page

any alignment. If you are not satisfied, click the Reset button and try a different setting.

Figure 17-3 shows the results of selecting all the objects and using the settings Left | Edge of Page. Notice how the left edge of each object aligns with the left edge of the page.

In Figure 17-4, the objects were individually selected using SHIFT-click, with the large clown fish selected last. Then the Right check box was enabled. This caused the right edges of the shark and the angelfish (the tails) to line

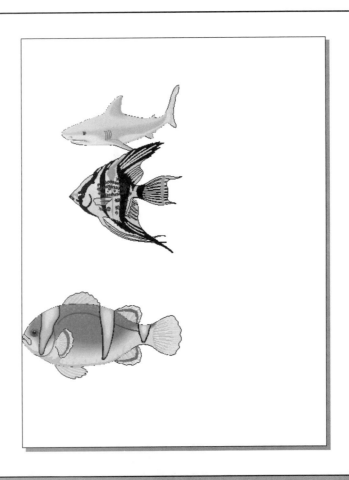

FIGURE 17-4   Aligning the right edge of objects to the right edge of the last selected object after enabling the Right check box

up with the right edge (the tail) of the clown fish. If you are following along, and your objects moved to an object other than the one you expected, you probably marquee selected the objects instead of selecting them one at a time. Marquee selection places the last selected object at the bottom of the stacking order.

Figure 17-5 uses the settings <u>T</u>op | <u>E</u>dge of Page to align all three objects to the top of the page. Vertical guidelines were placed at the front of each fish to show that although the objects have been moved to line up with the top of

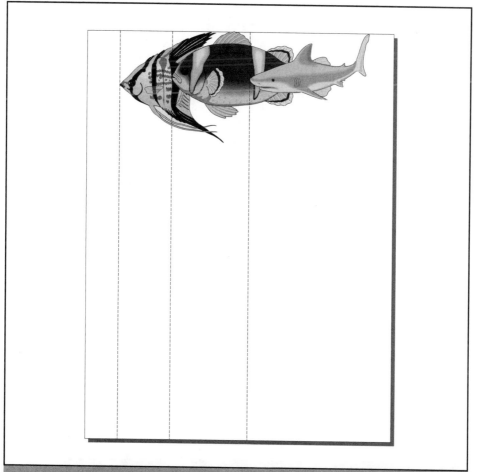

FIGURE 17-5   Aligning the top of objects to the top of the page by choosing <u>T</u>op | E<u>d</u>ge of Page

the page, they still maintain the same horizontal relationship to each other. We moved the fish in the stacking order for this exercise so that they would display better.

Figure 17-6 uses the settings Center | Center of Page to align all three vehicles to the center of the page while maintaining their vertical positions on the page.

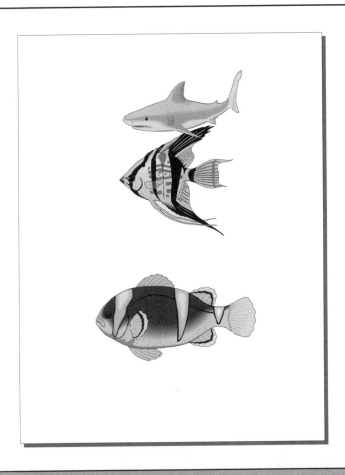

FIGURE 17-6   Aligning all three objects to the center of the page while maintaining their vertical positions on the page

CAUTION: *Enabling the Center of Page check box also enables both the vertical and horizontal Center check boxes. In the case of Figure 17-6, it was necessary to remove the check mark from the vertical Center box to achieve the alignment desired.*

TIP: *There is really no limit to the number of objects you can align at one time. However, don't overlook the benefit of aligning only one object to a specific place on the screen. For example, you may want to move an object to the center of the page by enabling the Center of Page check box. In addition, you can enable the Align to Grid check box if you want objects to snap to a grid when they are aligned.*

As you can see, there are many combinations of alignment settings you can use. You should practice using the different settings until you feel comfortable with them.

ALIGNING OBJECTS USING SHORTCUT KEYS

CorelDRAW 8 now lets you align objects using the following shortcut keys instead of the Align dialog box:

- ▶ T for top
- ▶ B for bottom
- ▶ R for right
- ▶ L for left
- ▶ C and E for center (vertically and horizontally)

Follow the same sequence rules as before for selecting objects that you want to align. Figure 17-7 shows a butterfly in each corner of a rectangle. Below each butterfly are the keystrokes used to place the butterfly in that position. Practice using these shortcut keys by drawing a rectangle and an ellipse on the page. Select the ellipse first and then SHIFT-click to select the rectangle. With the two objects selected, see how the ellipse goes to the edges of the rectangle as you press a shortcut key.

In the case of the Center short cut keys, when you press E the first object or objects align vertically to the middle of the last selected object, and when you press C the object or objects move to the center. In reality, it doesn't make any difference which letter you use first if our goal is to align the object in the center.

DISTRIBUTING OBJECTS

The Distribute command is used to evenly space objects on the page. It can take randomly spaced objects and distribute them in a predescribed manner evenly across the page. However, before you can use the Distribute command you must first use the Align command.

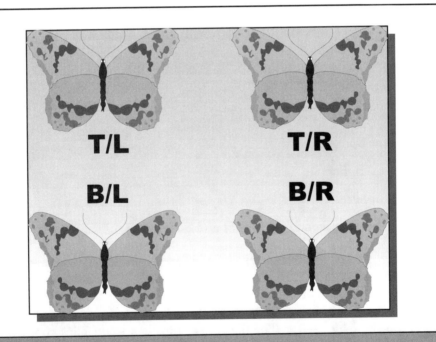

FIGURE 17-7   Aligning objects with shortcut keys

If you are currently working on a project and have skipped over the Align command because you need to distribute only a few objects, we have bad news for you. The Align command plays a part in using the Distribute command. Go to the beginning of this chapter and review the Align command settings before you try to use the Distribute command.

The Align and Distribute tabbed dialog box, shown in Figure 17-1, appears on the drawing page with the Align tab selected by default. Select the Distribute tab to display the Distribute page. The default Distribute page is shown in Figure 17-8.

The best way to become familiar with the Distribute command is to practice using it. The following sections provide examples for you to follow.

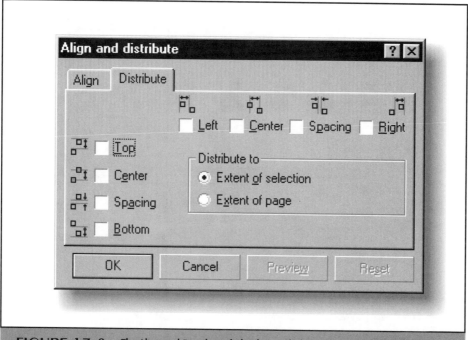

FIGURE 17-8   The Align and Distribute dialog box with the Distribute tab selected

BREAKING THE RULES: DISTRIBUTING OBJECTS WITHOUT USING ALIGN

The example in this section contradicts what was said earlier about having to use the Align command prior to using the Distribute command. This method is the exception and not the rule. Follow these steps to distribute objects without using the Align command:

1. Open the View | Dockers | Symbols Docker (CTRL-F11) and select the Food category. Scroll down the list of symbols until you find the coffee cup shown in Figure 17-9.

2. Drag the symbol onto the page, give it a black fill, and resize it to approximately 1 inch square.

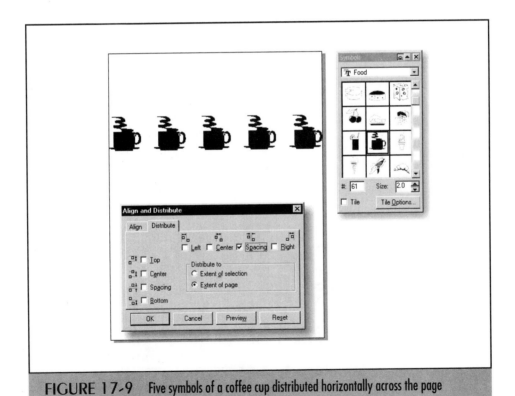

FIGURE 17-9   Five symbols of a coffee cup distributed horizontally across the page

3. With the symbol selected, press the + key on the numeric keypad four times. This will create four copies of the coffee cup on top of the original.

4. Click anywhere on the page to deselect the last duplicate object and then marquee select all five copies of the coffee cup.

5. Open the Align and Distribute dialog box and click the Distribute tab. Enable the Extent of Page radio button and the Spacing check box located in the horizontal row of check boxes.

6. Click the Preview button. Your coffee cups should be evenly distributed horizontally across the page, as shown in Figure 17-9.

7. Click the Reset button and enable the Extent of Page radio button again. Put a check mark in the Spacing check box in the vertical row of check boxes.

8. Click the Preview button. Your coffee cups should now be evenly distributed vertically up and down the page, as shown in Figure 17-10.

You may be wondering how the coffee cups would be distributed if any of the other horizontal or vertical check boxes were used with Extent of Page enabled. In fact, if any of the check boxes in the horizontal row are checked, the results will be the same as those in Figure 17-9, and if any of the check boxes in the vertical row are checked, the results will be the same as those in Figure 17-10. This is because all the objects were stacked on top of each other prior to using the Distribute command. If the objects were separated from each other, you would need to use the Align command prior to using the Distribute command.

USING THE ALIGN COMMAND BEFORE THE DISTRIBUTE COMMAND

For the example in this section, you need to use the Align command before performing the distribution.

1. Select the various food symbols shown in Figure 17-11 from the Food category in the Symbols Docker.

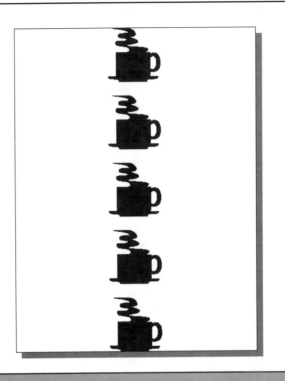

FIGURE 17-10 Five symbols of a coffee cup distributed vertically down the page

2. Drag the symbols onto the page and resize each symbol to approximately 1 inch square.

3. Select the Pick tool and drag each of the symbols to separate places on the page. (If you're wondering why you need to do this, it's because this example attempts to simulate a real-world project, where you may have several objects that were created at different times and that you now want to distribute across the page.) Your five symbols should be arranged something like those in Figure 17-11.

4. Marquee select all five symbols and open the Align and Distribute dialog box by clicking the Align button on the Property Bar.

FIGURE 17-11   Five different symbols randomly placed on the page

5. Enable the Center of Page box in the Align To section of the Align page and then click OK. All the symbols should now be stacked on top of each other.

6. With all five symbols still selected, move them to the lower-left corner of the page.

7. Make sure the symbols are still selected and open the Align and Distribute dialog box again. Select the Distribute tab and enable the Extent of Page radio button and the horizontal Spacing box.

8. Click the Preview button. Your symbols should now be evenly distributed across the bottom of the page.

17

9. Disable the horizontal Spacing box and enable the vertical Spacing box.

10. Click the Preview button again to see your food symbols evenly distributed vertically up and down on the left side of the page.

11. When you're satisfied with the results, click the OK button. Your symbols should be distributed as shown in Figure 17-12.

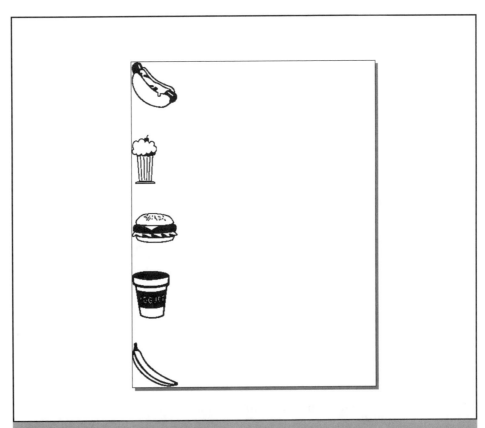

FIGURE 17-12   The five symbols evenly spaced vertically up and down the left side of the page

DISTRIBUTING LINES

A practical use of the Distribute command is to evenly space lines over the page. Imagine needing some ruled sheets of paper to take notes for a meeting and all you have is blank printer paper. Follow these steps to create a page with 20 evenly spaced lines on the paper and you're ready to take notes.

1. Draw a straight line horizontally across the page using the Freehand tool (hold down the CTRL key when dragging to constrain drawing to a straight line).

2. With the line still selected, press the + key on the numeric keypad 21 times to add 21 duplicates of the original line.

3. Deselect the last duplicate line and marquee select all 22 lines.

4. Open the Align and Distribute roll-up and click the Distribute tab.

5. Enable the Extent of Page radio button and the Top check box and click OK.

6. Remove the top and bottom lines, as they are aligned with the edges of the page and serve no purpose, and you're left with 20 evenly spaced lines on the page.

SMART DUPLICATING

Smart Duplicating is new to CorelDRAW 8. It could be considered in the same family as the Edit | Repeat command (CTRL-R) and the Distribute command. The Repeat command repeats the last transformation on an object, whereas the Smart Duplication remembers all transforms and properties edits and applies them to a duplicated object. Creating additional duplicates applies the same transforms/properties edits to the new duplicates.

In order to use Smart Duplicating you must first duplicate an object. You can do this either by selecting the object and then choosing Edit | Duplicate (CTRL-D) or by pressing the + key on the numeric keypad. Follow these steps to learn how to use Smart Duplication:

▶ Once the object is duplicated move the duplicate object to another position on the page.

► Choose Edit | Duplicate (CTRL-D) and a second duplicate object will be placed the same distance from the first duplicate that the first duplicate was moved from the original.

After reading this brief description of Smart Duplicating, you may wonder how you could use it in a real-world situation. Follow these steps:

1. Place an object at the upper-left corner of the page. Try using an object from the Symbols Docker.

2. Duplicate the object (CTRL-D).

3. Move the object one inch away horizontally from the original object.

4. With the duplicate object still selected, press CTRL-D again.

5. Continue pressing CTRL-D until the objects reach the right side of the page.

If you followed the steps correctly, you just equally distributed copies of the original object across the top of the page. Depending of the object you used, you have the beginnings of a decorative border.

The ability to use Smart Duplication will be lost once you deselect the object, select another object, or change tools. Smart Duplicating also retains the stretch, skew and rotation relative to the last duplicate.

COPYING AND PASTING

The Edit | Copy command (CTRL-C) is the same in CorelDRAW as it is in all Windows programs. It can be used in conjunction with the Edit | Paste command (CTRL-V) to copy and paste whole images or parts of images from one application or file to another.

THE PASTE SPECIAL COMMAND

The Edit | Paste Special command is a unique command that lets you copy an image from one application and paste it into CorelDRAW while at the same time enabling you to edit the image in CorelDRAW or link directly back to the source application for editing. For example, if you want to use a Corel PHOTO-PAINT image in a CorelDRAW file, you first open the image in Corel PHOTO-PAINT and then copy it to the clipboard. You then use one of the options in the Edit | Paste Special dialog box in CorelDRAW to paste it onto the CorelDRAW page.

This method of copying objects is called object linking and embedding, or OLE. When you select Edit | Paste Special, a Paste Special dialog box appears (see Figure 17-13) giving you a choice of pasting the image as an embedded object or a linked object. The default is Paste, which is the embedded method. There are three types of embedded files you can choose: Corel PHOTO-PAINT 8.0 image, Picture (Metafile), and Device Independent Bitmap. When you paste a file using the embedded method, you can edit the file by double-clicking on the pasted image. This action replaces the CorelDRAW menus and tools with those of the source application. You can then edit the embedded object using the menus and tools of the source application. The edited image does not affect the original image from which it was copied.

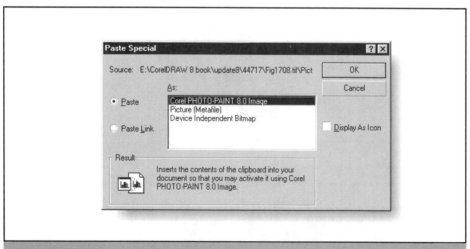

FIGURE 17-13   The Paste Special dialog box in its default configuration

Using the Paste method

Figure 17-14 shows an image that has been pasted using the <u>P</u>aste option with a Corel PHOTO-PAINT image as the source. Notice that the CorelDRAW page and page border are showing but all the tools and menus are Corel PHOTO-PAINT's. There will be scroll bars around the embedded image while you are in the editing mode. You can navigate around in the image just as you could in Corel PHOTO-PAINT itself. When you finish editing the image using the Corel PHOTO-PAINT tools, simply click anywhere on the page and the screen will return to the CorelDRAW menus and tools, leaving the image in its edited state.

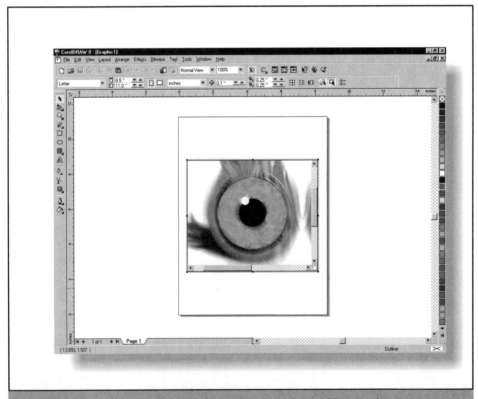

FIGURE 17-14   An embedded image in the edit mode pasted from Corel PHOTO-PAINT

 If you choose the Device Independent Bitmap option you cannot edit the pasted file in its source application. You can only edit the pasted image using the tools available in CorelDRAW.

Using the Linked Method

If you choose the Paste Link option in the Paste Special dialog box (see Figure 17-15) the pasted image is connected to the source application in a different way than when it's embedded. The pasted image is linked to the source file, which means that when a change in the source file is made, the change is reflected in the CorelDRAW file containing the pasted linked image. The benefit of choosing the linked option is that the size of the CorelDRAW file is kept to a minimum because the linked object still resides in the source application. This eliminates the need for two copies of the file on the hard drive. When you modify the file in the source application, the link is automatically updated in the CorelDRAW file. If you chose the Embed option, the object becomes part of the CorelDRAW file, and the file size will grow proportionally.

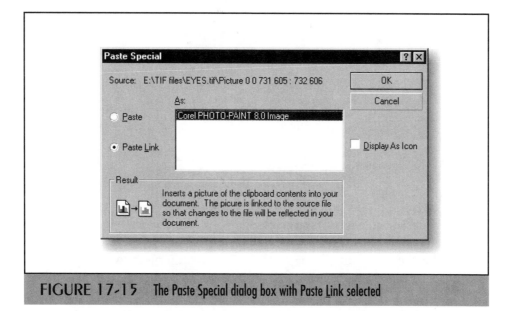

FIGURE 17-15   The Paste Special dialog box with Paste Link selected

When you double-click the pasted linked image the source application is opened (see Figure 17-14). This differs from when you double-click on an embedded image because the source application is actually independently opened. When you're finished editing, return to the CorelDRAW screen by saving your changes in the source application and exiting the application.

The disadvantage of using linked objects is that you have to modify the source image in the source application. This means you can't apply different effects to the pasted image without affecting the original image. There are a few exceptions to this statement: you can scale, mirror, and stretch linked images and you can apply PowerClips and Lenses to them.

EFFECTS COPY FROM COMMAND

Whereas the Edit | Copy command copies objects and places them on the Windows clipboard, CorelDRAW's Effects | Copy command is a Copy From command that allows you to copy an effect from one object and apply it to another object.

To copy an effect to another object, you select the object, or in some cases a group of objects, and then choose Effects | Copy to access the Copy child menu. From the child menu, select one of the Copy From commands. The cursor changes to an arrow, which you then use to select the object you want to copy.

CorelDRAW provides nine effects that can be copied to another object:

▶ *Perspective*   The Effects | Copy | Perspective From command copies the perspective from an object that has had perspective applied to it to another object or group of objects. Refer to Chapter 18 for more information on perspective.

▶ *Envelope*   The Effects | Copy | Envelope From command lets you copy the envelope of one object to another object or group of objects. Refer to Chapter 18 for more information on enveloping.

▶ *Blend*   The Effects | Copy | Blend From command allows you to select two objects and copy the blend attributes of another blend. This means the attributes of the two selected objects will stay the same, but the attributes of the blend will be used when the blend is copied. For example, if you select a red square and a blue square and then use the Effects | Copy | Blend From command on an existing blend, the red and blue squares will be blended with the same number of steps and accelerations as the blend you used to copy from. If the blend is a compound blend composed of different steps and accelerations, the section of the blend you point to will be the section copied. Refer to Chapter 20 for more information on blends.

▶ *Extrude* The Effects | Copy | Extrude From command copies all the extrude attributes from an existing extrusion and applies them to another single object. To see how this copying effect works, draw a rectangle on the page and apply an unconstrained envelope to it. Then extrude the enveloped rectangle. Now draw an ellipse on the page and use the Effects | Copy | Extrude From command to copy the enveloped rectangle. Refer to Chapter 19 for more information on extrusion.

▶ *Contour* The Effects | Copy | Contour From command copies the selected contour's attributes, including the outline and fill attributes of the contoured objects, while leaving the original fill and outline attributes of the original rectangle. For example, if you draw a rectangle on the page, fill it with yellow, give it a blue outline, and then copy a contour that uses a red fill with pink outlines for the control object and a green fill with orange outlines for the contoured objects, the attributes of the resulting new contour will be as follows: the control object will retain the original yellow fill and blue outline, and the contoured objects will blend from yellow to green fills, and their outlines will blend from blue to orange. Refer to Chapter 20 for more information on contours.

▶ *Lens* The Effects | Copy | Lens From command copies the selected lens and all its attributes to another object. This command is intended to copy a lens to a single object, although it is capable of copying a lens to a group of objects. If you were to do this, each object in the group would have the lens copied to it. Refer to Chapter 21 for more information on lenses.

▶ *PowerClip* The Effects | Copy | PowerClip From command copies the contents of a PowerClip to a new container object. The fill and outline of the new container object will not be affected. If the original PowerClip was created with the default option Auto-center

New PowerClip Contents disabled, the new container will not display the contents of the original PowerClip until you edit the new PowerClip container and move the contents inside the container. Refer to Chapter 21 for more information on PowerClips.

▶ *Drop Shadow*   The Effects | Copy | Drop Shadow From command copies the drop shadow from one object to another. This command will copy drop shadows from single objects or groups of objects. You can also copy a drop shadow from a group of objects to a single object. When you use this command, remember two things. You must click with the pointing arrow on the drop shadow, not the object that has the shadow. Secondly, the object you copy the drop shadow to must have a fill.

▶ *Distortion*   The Effects | Copy | Distortion From command copies the distortion attributes of one object to another. The results can sometimes produce effects unlike the distortion of the object that was copied. The shape of the second object (the copied to object) will vary if the two objects are not identical and contain a disproportionate number of nodes. However, happy accidents sometime produce some amazing results.

CLONING

Cloning objects can save you a lot of time on a project when you are working with duplicate objects. When an object is cloned, a duplicate is made of the selected object. The original object becomes the control object, and the duplicate object is called the clone object. For example, if you clone an ellipse, the Status Bar will call the clone a clone ellipse. Clones can be created from single objects, groups of objects, and three effect groups (Blend, Extrude, and Contour).

The benefit of using clones in your projects is that any attribute changes made to the control object are automatically made to the clone object. For example, if you used several duplicate objects in a project and they all needed to be equally resized, without the Clone command you would have to individually resize each object. If you had planned ahead and created clones of the first object, you would need to resize only the control object, and all the clones would be resized automatically.

The best way to learn a new command is to practice using it. Follow these steps to create a clone of a gorilla and modify the control object as shown in Figure 17-16:

1. Open the Symbols Docker and choose the Animals 1 category. Select the gorilla (the center symbol on the second row) and drag it onto the page. Give it a black fill.

2. With the gorilla selected, choose <u>E</u>dit | Clo<u>n</u>e to create a clone of the gorilla. If you have not changed the default Place Duplicates settings, a clone will be created offset from the original object by 0.25 inch both horizontally and vertically. Select the clone gorilla and move it away from the control gorilla.

FIGURE 17-16   Modifying a control object and its clone

3. Select the original object, which has now become a control curve and change its color to orange. Notice that the clone gorilla also changes to orange.

4. With the gorilla still selected, open the Envelope roll-up. Click the Add New button and use the cursor to move the side-middle nodes outward approximately 0.25 inch. See the gorillas gain weight.

5. Select the Shape tool and marquee select the nodes making up the gorilla's hand and upper arm. Drag the nodes upward approximately 2 inches and watch the arms of both gorillas grow longer.

As you can see from this short example, using the Clone command can be very useful and time saving.

USING CLONES IN CONJUNCTION WITH THE ALIGN AND DISTRIBUTE COMMANDS

You can also use clones in conjunction with the Align and Distribute commands described earlier in this chapter. Practice this cloning technique with the Santa Claus symbol shown in Figure 17-17:

1. Select the Santa Claus shown in Figure 17-17 from the Festive category in the Symbols Docker.

2. Drag the symbol onto the page, give it a black fill, and resize it to approximately 1 inch square.

3. Choose Edit | Clone four separate times to create four clones of the Santa Claus. Remember that each time you use the Clone command, you must re-select the control Santa Claus to create another clone.

4. Marquee select all five Santa Clauses and open the Align and Distribute dialog box by clicking the Align button on the Property Bar.

FIGURE 17-17   A control object and four clones spaced evenly down the page

5. Enable the Center of Page box in the Align To section on the Align page and then click the OK button. All the Santa Clauses should now be stacked on top of each other.

6. With all five Santa Clauses still selected, move them to the top-left corner of the page.

7. Make sure the Santa Clauses are still selected and open the Align and Distribute dialog box again. Select the Distribute tab and enable the Extent of Page radio button and the vertical Spacing box.

8. Click the Preview button. Your Santa Clauses should now be evenly distributed up and down the left side of the page.

9. Click the OK button. Your Santa Clauses should look like those in Figure 17-17.

10. Select the control object at the top of the page and resize it to approximately one half of its original size (if the top object is not the control object, see the Tip that follows). The four clones will take on the new attributes.

As you can see, the Clone command can be very useful.

If you use clones in a project and you want to find out which is the control object and which are the clone objects, right-click one of the objects that you know is either a clone or the control object. If you selected a clone object, the Object menu will display the Select Master command at the top of the menu. Select this command, and the control object will be automatically selected for you. If you got lucky and selected the control object the first time, the Object menu will display the Select Clones command. Select this command, and all the clones linked to the control object will automatically be selected together.

RULES GOVERNING CLONES

There are a few rules to keep in mind when working with clones:

▶ If you change any attributes of a single clone object, that attribute's link to the control object will be broken. For example, if you have a control object with four clones like those in Figure 17-17 and you change the color of one of the clones, you will break the color link between that clone and the control object. If you change the outline color of the same clone, you will break the outline link to the control object.

▶ If you change the size of the clone, you will break all links between the clone and the control object.

▶ The only effects that can be applied to a control object that will affect the clones are Envelope, Transparency, and Lens effects.

▶ If you delete a control object, all its clones will also be deleted.

CLONING OTHER EFFECTS

CorelDRAW's Effects | Clone command gives you the ability to clone effects and works much like the Copy From command discussed earlier. You can clone four effects: Blend, Extrude, Contour, and Drop Shadow.

To clone an effect for an object, or in some cases two objects, select the object and then select the Effects menu. From the drop-down menu, click one of the clone effects available from the Effects | Clone child menu. When you select one of the clone effects, the cursor changes into an arrow. Use this arrow to select the effect (Blend, Extrude, Contour, or Drop Shadow) you want to clone.

The use of each effect is described here:

▶ *Blend* To clone a blend, select two separate objects on the page. Marquee select both objects and choose Effects | Clone. From the child menu, choose Blend From. When the cursor changes to an arrow, select the blend group you want to clone. When you clone a blend, all the attributes of the control blend will be applied to the clone blend except the color attributes. For example, if you create two objects on the page, one colored red and the other colored green, and then create a clone from a 20-step blend group that went from purple to white, the resulting clone will contain 20 steps, including any accelerations or rotations contained in the control blend, but the colors will stay the same, blending from red to green. If you change the number of steps in the control blend the number will change in the clone blend.

▶ *Extrude* To clone an extrusion, select any single object (not a group) and choose Effects | Clone. From the child menu, choose Extrude From. When the cursor changes to an arrow, select the extrusion you want to clone. The selected object will be extruded with the same attributes as the control extrusion.

▶ *Contour* To clone a contour, select any single object (not a group) and choose Effects | Clone. From the child menu, choose Contour From. When the cursor changes to an arrow, select the contour you want to clone. The new clone will retain is original fill and outline color but will take on the attributes of the contour steps of the control contour.

► *Drop Shadow* To clone a Drop Shadow, select an object or group of objects and then choose Effects | Clone. From the child menu, choose Drop Shadow From. When the cursor changes to an arrow, use the arrow to click the drop shadow of the object you want to clone from. The new clone will be given a drop shadow like that of the original.

This chapter has covered features usually reserved for the advanced user. You could spend your entire life working in CorelDRAW and not be aware of your ability to do the things described here. For many users, this knowledge will be very useful. For the casual user, the information is here when you're ready for it.

PART
3

ADDING EFFECTS

18

ENVELOPING, DISTORTION, AND PERSPECTIVE

The effects discussed in this chapter share something in common: they each allow you to adjust the shape of an object or group of objects in a defined fashion. The Envelope effect allows you to force an image into a predefined shape or to warp the image into a freeform shape. The Distortion effect lets you unleash your creative powers or simply accept a happy accident or two. In either case, the results can be quite impressive. The Perspective effect lets you add perspective to portions of your drawings, giving the viewer a sense of depth when they view the image.

ENVELOPING

The Envelope effect lets you warp an object's form into an irregular shape. You can also apply this effect to groups of objects with the following exception: Before you can envelope a Blend, Contour, or Extrude group, you must first select a Blend, Contour, or Extrude group and click Arrange | Group to group the individual parts of these effect groups. After they have been grouped you can apply an Envelope effect to the new group.

In previous versions of CorelDRAW, the Envelope effect was contained in a roll-up and was accessed by choosing Effects | Envelope (CTRL-F7). Included in the roll-up were the Blend, Contour, Extrude, and Lens effects. If you wanted to apply an envelope to an object, you had to click the Add New button on the roll-up. The object was then surrounded with a bounding box with eight control nodes. You manipulated the nodes with the Shape tool, which was automatically selected for you when the envelope bounding box appeared.

CorelDRAW 8 has changed the way you envelope objects by creating an Interactive Envelope tool located on the Interactive Tools flyout. Its icon is the middle icon on the flyout and looks like a bent rectangle with a node on each side. We have circled it in Figure 18-1. When you select the icon with an object selected, a bounding box is automatically placed around the selected object. You can begin selecting and moving nodes while the Interactive Envelope tool is still selected. All the various setting that were on the Envelope roll-up now appear on the Property Bar when an object with an envelope is selected. The only envelope control missing from the Property Bar is the Create From eyedropper icon that was on the roll-up.

The Envelope roll-up is still available but works somewhat differently than before. For example, if you select an object and click the Add New button on the Envelope roll-up, the bounding box will appear around the object. Instead of the Shape tool being selected, as in previous versions, the new Interactive Envelope tool is selected and you proceed as if you had selected that tool first. Because of the change in how envelopes are applied, we will discuss the use of envelopes by solely using the interactive method. When it comes time to use the Create From command, we will use the roll-up. Figure 18-1 shows a star that has had an envelope applied to it. The image on the left shows the marching ants bounding box with its eight nodes. The image on the right has been filled to show the finished shape (it looks a little like a starfish). Figure 18-1 also shows the Property Bar when the enveloped object has been selected and the Envelope roll-up.

18

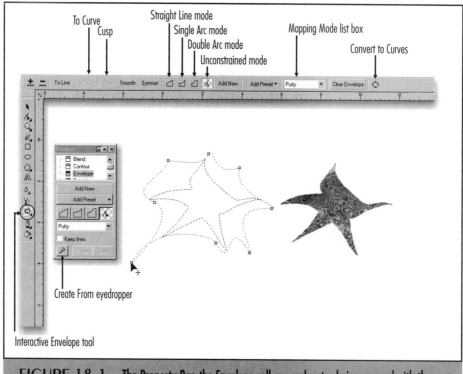

FIGURE 18-1 The Property Bar, the Envelope roll-up, and a star being warped with the Envelope effect

CHOOSING A MODE

Before you begin to envelope an object, you must click a mode button. Modes influence the way an envelope is shaped. The mode buttons are located in the middle of the Property Bar (see Figure 18-1). The modes are named by the way they function. They are, from left to right, the Straight Line mode, Single Arc mode, Double Arc mode, and Unconstrained mode.

Using the Interactive Envelope Tool

The steps required to envelope an object are:

► Select an object or a group of objects, and click the Interactive Envelope tool (a bounding box will automatically surround the object).

► Click a mode button on the Property Bar.

► Use the Interactive Envelope tool to select and move the nodes on the bounding box.

Practice this technique until you are comfortable manipulating the nodes. The nodes attached to the bounding box are unlike the nodes on normal curves unless you chose the Unconstrained mode. The nodes in the Straight Line, Single Arc, and Double Arc modes are constrained to create the shapes for which the modes are named. For example, when the Straight Line mode is selected, the bounding box lines remain straight between the nodes when a node is moved in any direction. Notice also that the dotted line indicating the object's shape is yellow and black while the dotted line indicating the envelope is red. If you use the Unconstrained mode, two blue handles will be attached to each node. When you move a node on the envelope, the red dotted lines indicate the intended new shape. The yellow and black lines representing the object indicate the actual shape that will be created. You can move only one node or node handle at a time, but the number of moves you can make is unrestricted. Each time you move a node the shape is updated in real time. When you are satisfied with the shape, press the SPACEBAR or click another tool in the toolbox.

The following illustration shows the Envelope effect applied to the word "Envelope" with the Straight Line mode in effect. The center node at the top of the bounding box was moved upward from the word to create the shape shown.

ENVELOPE

The four modes are divided into two different types: constrained and unconstrained. The behavior of the Envelope effect can be controlled by choosing the appropriate mode.

18

CONSTRAINED MODES

The Straight Line, Single Arc, and Double Arc modes—all of the modes except the Unconstrained mode—can be constrained to perform in a specified manner when you hold down the CTRL and SHIFT keys separately or together. An envelope will be constrained as follows when you hold down one or both keys:

► If you hold down the CTRL key and drag a node, the node on the opposite side of the bounding box will move in the same direction.

► If you hold down the SHIFT key and drag a node, the node on the opposite side of the bounding box will move in the opposite direction.

► If you hold down the CTRL and SHIFT keys together and drag a node, the four opposing nodes on the bounding box will move in opposite directions from each other. For example, if you drag a center node in the "Envelope" example discussed previously, the other three center nodes will move away from each other. If you drag any corner node, the other three corner nodes will also move away from each other, but because they are corner nodes, the result will be simply that the object is enlarged proportionally.

The following enveloped text shows the results of dragging the top center node on the bounding box upward away from the text using the three methods just described. In the examples, the Double Arc mode was used.

Using the CTRL key   Using the SHIFT key   Using the CTRL-SHIFT keys

Unconstrained Mode

When you use the Unconstrained mode, the nodes on the dotted bounding box behave just as they do on normal curve objects (see Chapter 8). This means that you can change a smooth node to a cusp node or even add or remove nodes. The ability to control the number of nodes or change the type of node lets you create some very interesting text shapes. Follow these steps to practice enveloping using the Unconstrained mode:

1. Type a word on the page using any font.

2. With the text selected, click the Interactive Envelope tool.

3. Click the Unconstrained mode button on the Property Bar.

4. Using the Interactive Envelope tool, select the top-middle node.

5. Move the node upward and away from the text. You should now be able to see the control handles (displayed as blue dotted lines) on the node more clearly.

6. Drag the control handles to curve the red dotted line.

7. Continue distorting the text by dragging other nodes.

8. Try adding a few nodes by double-clicking the red dotted line. To add several nodes at once, marquee select more than one node with the Interactive Envelope tool and click the + button on the Property Bar. This action will add a new node in between each node you selected.

9. Select a middle node and change it to a cusp node by clicking the Cusp button on the Property Bar. Drag one of the control handles to change one side of the dotted line.

10. Select a corner node and change it to a smooth node by clicking the Smooth button on the Property Bar. Move one of its control handles to move the lines on both sides of the node.

If you got carried away and ended up with a distorted mess, click the Clear Envelope button on the Property Bar to bring the text back to its original state.

Why did you select a middle node in step 9 and a corner node in step 10? The reason is that all middle nodes on an unconstrained envelope will, by default, be smooth nodes, and all corner nodes will be cusp nodes. Don't let this fact confuse you, because regardless of what the nodes are by default, you can always change them to accomplish the task at hand.

18

 *Most of the examples in this chapter use Artistic Text to show the Envelope effect. This is because the effect works best on Artistic Text. You can envelope shapes such as rectangles and ellipses, but for the most part, creating unusual shapes with rectangles and ellipses can be better accomplished by converting these shapes to curves and using the Shape tool to create a distorted shape. You can also use the Weld and Trim commands (see Chapter 16) to create unusual shapes. If you do decide to envelope shapes, the success or failure of getting what you expect is determined by how many nodes make up the shape. The more nodes, within reason, the better the envelope will shape the object based on the mode selected. For example, if you wanted to envelope a rectangle using the Straight Line mode, you would need to add nodes between each corner node for the effect not to end up as a pregnant rectangle.*

The following text objects are a result of applying an envelope using the Unconstrained mode.

> **NOTE:** *The Add New button on the Property Bar is used to apply a new envelope on top of the first envelope. This means that a new bounding box will surround the previous enveloped object just as if you were beginning to envelope a new object. Be careful using a new envelope as you can end up with a pretty distorted shape.*

Although text objects are generally the best objects to envelope, grouped objects can sometimes provide interesting results. Figure 18-2 shows clipart images of cars that have separately had unconstrained envelopes applied to them. As you can see, adding an envelope to a clipart image can provide that extra effect that would be difficult to achieve any other way. The added splotch effect was created using the new Interactive Distortion tool discussed later in this chapter.

APPLYING PRESET EFFECTS

The Add Preset button on the Property Bar lets you apply a predefined shape to an object. Preset effects are best suited to Artistic Text. When you click the

FIGURE 18-2   Two clipart images enveloped separately

Add Preset button, a drop-down list appears showing the available preset effects. To apply a preset effect, follow these steps:

1. Select the object to which you want the effect applied.

2. Click the Add Preset button and then select a preset effect from the drop-down list. A dotted line in the shape of the preset effect will surround your selected object.

3. Click the Apply button.

When you first use these preset effects, you will probably be disappointed because the effect will not be what you expected. The reason is that most of the shapes in the drop-down list are box-like in shape, and the text to which you are applying these shapes is quite narrow. The way to solve this problem is to stretch the text vertically—and horizontally, if necessary—until it appears to be about the height and width of the preset effect you are using. In the following illustration, the heart preset effect is applied to the word "Valentine" using the default font Arial Black. The squatty version is a result of leaving the text as it was typed. In the second, more pleasing version, the text was stretched to a height and width relative to the height and width of the heart prior to applying the preset effect.

VALENTINE   ⟪⟪⟪ℓENT⟫⟫⟫

Original text   Text with preset heart effect applied

Stretched text   Stretched text with preset heart effect applied

Preset effects really shouldn't be used on Paragraph Text because the same issues apply to Paragraph Text as to a single word: the height of the paragraph

affects the result of the preset envelope. The problem in applying a preset effect to Paragraph Text is that you can't stretch the characters within the paragraph to compensate for the height of the preset effect. The best way to place Paragraph Text inside a preset shape is to use the Interactive Text on a path method described in Chapter 22.

USING CREATE FROM

If you want to use the Create From command, you must choose Effects | Envelope to bring up the Envelope roll-up. This is the one use of the envelope effect that is not on the Property Bar. The Create From button (the button with the eyedropper on it) is located at the lower-left corner of the Envelope roll-up, next to the Reset and Apply buttons. The Create From effect lets you envelope a selected object in the shape of another object. The object you use as a target object must be a closed-path object and cannot be a combined object or an imported or grouped object. The Create From effect differs from the preset effects described previously in that, instead of shrinking the preset effect around the selected object, the Create From effect enlarges or shrinks the original object so that it equals the size and shape of the target object. Practice using the Create From effect by following these steps:

1. Using the Ellipse tool, draw a balloon-shaped ellipse on the page.
2. Type the word **BALLOON** using all caps.
3. Change the font to Bauhaus Hv BT or something similar.
4. With the text selected, click the Create From button.
5. Use the pointing arrow to click the outline of the circle. An envelope will appear around the text.
6. Click the Apply button.

If you followed the steps exactly, the word BALLOON should look like the example on the left in the illustration shown here. You may have expected the text to appear horizontally instead. The reason it didn't is because you used the default mapping mode, Putty. If you had used the Horizontal mapping mode, the text would look like the example in the middle. The example on the right uses the enveloped text placed on a radial filled ellipse. The text also was given a custom linear fill. You will learn more about mapping modes next.

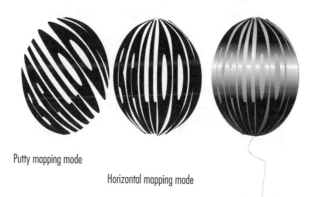

Putty mapping mode

Horizontal mapping mode

Enveloped text placed on a radial filled ellipse

CHOOSING A MAPPING MODE

You access the four available mapping modes by clicking the down arrow of the Mapping Mode list box on the Property Bar. Mapping modes are not the same as the modes found in the Constrained and Unconstrained mode boxes. When you choose a mapping mode, you define how the object fits inside the envelope. As you saw in the previous examples, the text will look very different depending on which mapping mode is selected. The Mapping Mode list box offers four mapping modes:

▶ *Putty* The Putty mode maps the corner selection handles of the original object to the envelope's corner nodes only. When a circle is used as a target object, the nodes on the resulting envelope are at twelve, three, six, and nine o'clock. When the envelope is applied, the node at the upper-right corner of the original object is aligned with the node at twelve o'clock on the circle (creating an effect like that shown on the left in the illustration of the word balloon being enveloped into a circle).

▶ *Original* The Original mode also maps the corner selection handles of the original object to the envelope's corner nodes, but it also maps the other nodes on the envelope to the edges of the original object's selection box. The Original mode will produce a more exaggerated distortion in some cases than the Putty mode.

▶ *Horizontal* The Horizontal mode stretches the original object to fit the size of the envelope and then compresses it horizontally to fit the envelope's shape.

▶ *Vertical* The Vertical mode stretches the original object to fit the size of the envelope and then compresses it vertically to fit the envelope's shape.

Copying the Envelope

The Copy Envelope From command copies the envelope from one object and applies it to another object or objects. Look again at the earlier example showing the word "Balloon" enveloped in a circle. If you had several words you wanted enveloped like the word "Balloon," you would select the words separately and then choose the Effects | Copy | Envelope From command.

The actual process of copying an Envelope effect is as follows:

1. Select the object to which you want to apply the Envelope effect.

2. Choose Effects | Copy | Envelope From and use the pointing arrow to click the object with the envelope you want to copy.

You cannot copy an envelope object if it has had another effect applied to it.

CLEARING THE ENVELOPE USING THE PROPERTY BAR

You can use the Clear Envelope button on the Property Bar to undo any and all changes made to the enveloped object. For example, if you were using the Unconstrained mode on an object and in the course of moving the nodes, the envelope became distorted to the point that you couldn't work with it anymore, you could click the Clear Envelope button to restore the object to either the last envelope applied (see "Using the Clear Envelope Command in the Effect Menu" next) or its original shape. You can use the Clear Envelope command anytime after an object has had an envelope applied to it.

Using the Clear Envelope Command in the Effect Menu

The Effects | Clear Effect command is context sensitive. If no object is selected, the command will read Clear Effect and be grayed out. If an object has an Envelope effect applied to it, the command will read Clear Envelope. Choosing the command with an enveloped object selected removes the Envelope effect from the object. If a single envelope was applied to a word or object, the Clear Envelope command will change the text back to its original state. If multiple envelopes were applied to an object, the Clear Envelope command can be repeated for each envelope applied to return to an earlier applied envelope.

 *If you have added more than one envelope to an object, you can quickly revert to the original object's shape by choosing Arrange | Clear Transformations.*

USING THE INTERACTIVE DISTORTION TOOL

The Interactive Distortion tool is new to CorelDRAW 8 and is found on the Interactive Tools flyout. The tool's icon resembles a wrinkled piece of paper. If you thought the Envelope tool distorted objects, you're in for an interesting and pleasant surprise. There are three different distortion modes that you can use with the tool: Push and Pull, Zipper, and Twister. Figure 18-3 shows an example of using each of these distortion modes on a circle object. The figure also shows the highlighted tool selected from the toolbox and the tool cursor applying the effect to the circle on the left.

The number and different kinds of distortions you can apply to objects are endless. The final result depends on the distortion tool you select, the placement and direction in which you drag the cursor, and the settings you make on the Property Bar. Draw an ellipse on the page and practice using the

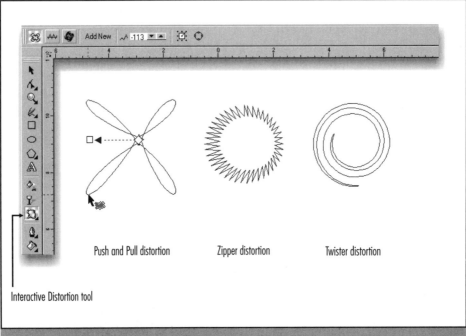

Interactive Distortion tool

FIGURE 18-3 Three circles after being distorted with the Distortion tool

Push and Pull distortion tool by clicking its button on the Property Bar. Use the cursor to drag the ellipse in different locations. The place that you first click and drag determines the outcome of the distortion. Figure 18-4 shows the Property Bar when the Push and Pull mode is selected.

▶ The word "Pull" was distorted by clicking the bottom center of the word and dragging to the left.

▶ The word "Push" was distorted by clicking the bottom center of the word and dragging to the right.

▶ The circle example shows the left placement handle at the top of the circle and the right handle dragged to the right.

▶ The eight-pointed star was created by clicking in the center of the star and dragging to the right.

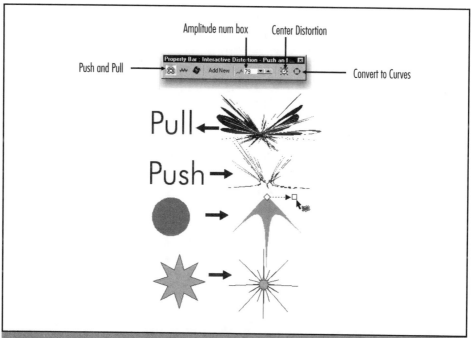

FIGURE 18-4   Four different objects distorted with the Push and Pull distortion tool

18

The other settings available with this tool are

▶ *Add New button* This button is not used to begin a distortion but instead is used to add a distortion on top of the existing one.

▶ *Amplitude num box* The number displayed in this box will change as you drag the object with the Distortion tool. You can enter different numbers and the shape of the object will automatically update the amount of distortion using the new setting.

▶ *Center Distortion button* When this button is enabled the left control handle is automatically placed in the center of the object.

▶ *Convert to Curves* This is the same Convert to Curves button that appears on the Property Bar when several other tool are selected. If you click this button when a distortion has been applied to an object, the distortion controls are removed and the object becomes a normal curve that can be further manipulated with the Shape tool.

Figure 18-5 shows examples of using the Zipper distortion tool. The same rules of cursor placement and direction of dragging apply here as well. Notice that the distortion effect on the spiral has zipper lines closer together than the star; this was caused by a change in the frequency setting described in a moment. Practice using this tool until you feel comfortable creating the effects.

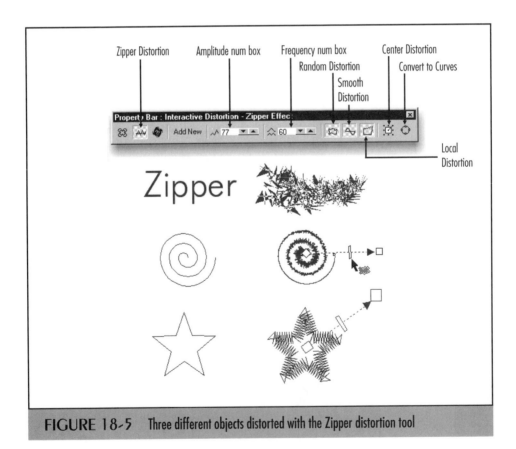

FIGURE 18-5   Three different objects distorted with the Zipper distortion tool

There are more settings available on the Property Bar when the Zipper tool is selected:

▶ *Add New button* As described earlier, this button is not used to begin a distortion but instead is used to add a distortion on top of the existing one.

▶ *Amplitude num box* The number displayed in this box will change as you drag the object with the Distortion tool. You can enter different numbers and the shape of the object will automatically update the amount of distortion using the new setting.

▶ *Frequency num box* The number displayed in this box will change when you drag the slider between the left and right control handles. You can also enter numbers directly in this box and the frequency of the zipper lines will automatically update.

▶ *Random Distortion* When you click this button the zipper lines will be distributed randomly around the object's shape.

▶ *Smooth Distortion* Clicking this button will round off the sharp corners of the zipper lines.

▶ *Local Distortion* Local distortion emphasizes the distortion over a particular area of the object, rather than randomly or from the center out.

▶ *Center Distortion button* If Center distortion is enabled, the object is distorted evenly around the distortion control handle. When the Center distortion is disabled, the object distortion "moves" toward the direction of the control pointer.

▶ *Convert to Curves* As described earlier, if you click this button when a distortion has been applied to an object, the distortion controls are removed and the object becomes a normal curve that can be further manipulated with the Shape tool.

You can enable any combination of the Random, Smooth, and Local buttons to increase the number of zipper variations.

Figure 18-6 shows examples of using the Twister distortion tool on three different objects. As before, the positioning of the cursor when you drag will determine the distortion results. The first example of using this tool on the word "Twister" demonstrates that text is not the best use of the tool; you will

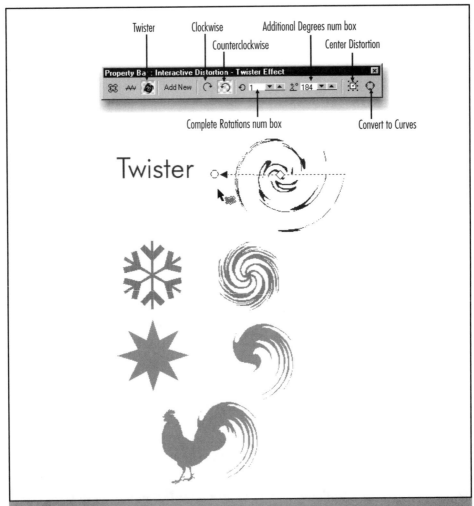

FIGURE 18-6   Three different objects distorted with the Twister distortion tool

get better results using objects other than text. The other two examples used a symbol from the Symbols Docker and an eight-pointed star drawn with the Polygon tool as the original shapes. The results obtained when the star was distorted with the Twister tool seemed like a perfect way to embellish the tail of a rooster taken from the Symbols Docker.

As with the other Distortion tools, there are other adjustment settings on the Property Bar when the Twister tool is selected:

18

▶ *Add New button* As with the first two distortion tools, this button is not used to begin a distortion but instead is used to add a distortion on top of the existing one.

▶ *Clockwise Rotation* Use this button to have your distortions travel in a clockwise direction.

▶ *Counterclockwise Rotation* Use this button to have your distortions travel in a counterclockwise direction.

▶ *Complete Rotations num box* Use this num box to enter the number of complete rotations you want your distortion to have.

▶ *Additional Degrees num box* This num box allows you to enter additional degrees to a complete rotation. For example, if you used one complete rotation, you could add 20 degrees more for a total of 380 degrees.

▶ *Center Distortion button* When this button is enabled, the left control handle is automatically placed in the center of the object and the distortion will flow outward from that center point.

▶ *Convert to Curves button* As described before, if you click this button when a distortion has been applied to an object, the distortion controls are removed and the object becomes a normal curve that can be further manipulated with the Shape tool.

Hopefully, you will find some unique uses for these amazing new tools. The next illustration shows how the Push and Pull distortion tool turned a seven-pointed star into some pretty daisies to which we added some stems and then planted in a pot.

PERSPECTIVE

Perspective adds a sense of depth and dimension to an object relative to the angle from which it is viewed. When you add perspective to an object in CorelDRAW, you create the illusion that an object is receding into the background. Almost everyone has stood in the middle of a road and observed the road narrowing as it gets farther away or has noticed that the telephone poles alongside the road look smaller as they get farther away. Most of us don't pay much attention to the fact that objects appear to become smaller as they get farther away because we live in a 3D world. The problem we face when working on a flat surface like a computer screen is there is no third dimension. We have to trick the viewer's eye into believing that a third dimension exists by using one or more of CorelDRAW's effects—in particular, the Perspective effect.

The Perspective effect can be used on single objects or groups of objects. It cannot be used on several objects at once; however, you can copy the perspective from one object to another (see the section "Copying Perspectives" later in this chapter).

CHOOSING ONE-POINT VERSUS TWO-POINT PERSPECTIVE

There are two types of perspective: one-point and two-point. The word "point" here refers to the vanishing point. Therefore, a one-point perspective uses one vanishing point, and a two-point perspective uses two vanishing points.

One-point perspective gives the illusion that an object is receding, and two-point perspective provides the added illusion that the object is leaning or twisted. The following illustration shows a one-point perspective and a two-point perspective below it.

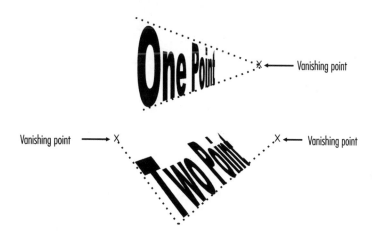

ADDING THE PERSPECTIVE EFFECT

To add perspective to an object, first select the object or group of objects to which you want to apply the effect. Then choose Effects | Add Perspective. After you have done this, the object or group will be surrounded with a rectangular selection box outlined with a dotted line with four nodes at each corner. Filling the entire selection box will be horizontal and vertical dotted gridlines. The Shape tool will automatically be selected for you. Use the Shape tool to apply perspective to the object by clicking a corner node and dragging.

Whether you apply a one-point or two-point perspective is determined by the direction you drag. As you drag the nodes, the vanishing points will appear on the page.

Here are the results you can expect when dragging any of the corner nodes or the vanishing points:

▶ If you hold down the CTRL key and drag any node horizontally or vertically, you will apply a one-point perspective. If you don't hold down the CTRL key to constrain the node as you drag so that it moves in a perfectly straight line either horizontally or vertically, you will create a two-point perspective.

▶ If you drag any node in a vertical direction after you have dragged a node in a horizontal direction, you will apply a two-point perspective.

▶ If you drag any node in a horizontal direction after you have dragged a node in a vertical direction, you will apply a two-point perspective.

▶ If you drag any node diagonally, you will apply a two-point perspective.

▶ When vanishing points becomes visible, you can move the vanishing points instead of the nodes to adjust the perspective, thereby retaining the overall size of the object.

 *If you can't see the vanishing points, zoom out on the page. It may be necessary to zoom out twice in certain situations.*

CREATING A TWO-POINT PERSPECTIVE

Two-point perspective involves the use of two vanishing points. The following illustration shows the use of two-point perspective on the words "Two Point." Dotted lines have been placed on the page to show how the horizontal and vertical sides of the words extend toward their respective vanishing points. Vanishing points were manually placed on the page to show the direction; you would really only see them if you zoomed out on the page.

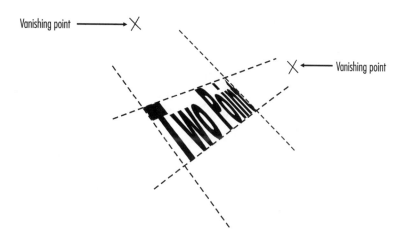

18

The next illustration has a similar two-point perspective applied to the word "Perspective." This time the word appears to be lying on its side slightly twisted. To illustrate the Perspective effect, dotted lines were drawn along the horizontal and vertical sides of the word to the point where they intersect with the vanishing points.

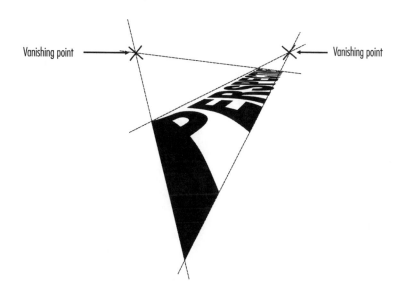

CREATING A SIMPLE
ONE-POINT PERSPECTIVE

Using Figure 18-7 as a guide, follow the steps to create a receding road with a one-point perspective. The following procedure includes a few extra steps so that your first lesson in using the Perspective effect will actually look like something when you are finished.

1. Draw a rectangle on the page and give it a linear fountain fill from light blue to white, as shown in section (a) of Figure 18-7.

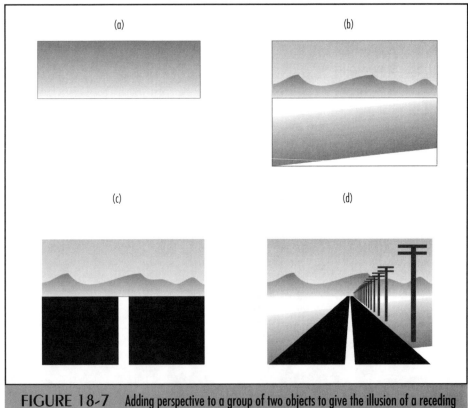

FIGURE 18-7   Adding perspective to a group of two objects to give the illusion of a receding road (shown in d)

2. With the rectangle selected, press the + key on the numeric keypad to place a duplicate on top of the first rectangle.

3. With the duplicate rectangle still selected, click the top-middle selection handle and drag downward over the first rectangle until the duplicate rectangle is below the first rectangle and approximately the same size. Give this second rectangle a linear fountain fill of white to brown.

4. Select the top rectangle again and repeat step 2.

5. With the duplicate rectangle still selected, click the top-middle selection handle and drag downward until the duplicate object is about a third the size of the original.

6. Convert this smaller rectangle to curves by clicking the Convert to Curves button on the Property Bar (CTRL-Q). Add the additional nodes to the shape and until you can manipulate the shape into a mountain range.

7. Fill this shape with a fountain fill of dark blue to white. Your drawing should now look like section (b) in Figure 18-7.

8. Select all three objects and remove their outlines.

9. Select the bottom rectangle filled with white and brown and press the + key on the numeric keypad to place a duplicate on top of this rectangle. Fill this rectangle with black.

10. With the black rectangle still selected, press the + key on the numeric keypad to place yet another duplicate on top of the black rectangle. Fill this rectangle with white.

11. With the white-filled rectangle selected, hold down the SHIFT key and drag a side selection handle inward toward the center until you have a narrow rectangle. Give this rectangle a white fill. Your drawing should now look like section (c) in Figure 18-7.

12. Select both the black and white rectangles by SHIFT-clicking and group them together by clicking the Group button on the Property Bar (CTRL-G).

13. With the group still selected, choose Effects | Add Perspective.

14. Using the Shape tool, click the upper-right node of the selection box.

18

15. Hold down the CTRL-SHIFT keys and drag the node inward toward the center. As you drag the right node, the left node will also move toward the center.

16. As you approach the center of the rectangle, the vanishing point will appear. Continue dragging inward until the vanishing point almost touches the two upper nodes. Then release the left mouse button. You can drag directly on the vanishing point if you wish.

17. Select the Pick tool to see the finished effect.

If you followed the directions correctly, your receding road should look something like section (d) in Figure 18-7. If your road doesn't have telephone poles on the side of the road, you didn't miss a step; we just thought the drawing looked more realistic with the poles. To find out how to add the telephone poles so they, too, are in perspective, turn to Chapter 20 and read the section on blends.

COPYING PERSPECTIVES

The Copy From command works by copying the perspective from one object and applying it to another object or objects. If this sounds familiar, it's because this command works just like the Copy Envelope command discussed earlier in this chapter. This command can be very useful when creating drawings that contain many objects with perspective. Once you add the correct perspective to the first object, you can apply the same perspective to all the other objects by using the Effects | Copy | Perspective From command.

On the left side of the illustration shown here is a clipart image of an English cottage with a castle in the background. We typed the words "To Castle" and included a symbol of a pointing hand in the text string (see Chapter 6 to find out how to put a symbol into a text string). The text was then stretched taller to ensure that the final perspective effect would fit correctly. The goal of the project is to copy the perspective of the side of the cottage onto the text. Once you have done this, you can place the text on the side of the cottage as if it were a sign pointing out the direction to castle.

The actual process of copying a Perspective effect is as follows:

1. Select the object to which you want to apply the Perspective effect.

2. Choose Effects | Copy | Perspective From and use the pointing arrow to click the object with the perspective you want to copy.

To copy the perspective from this particular piece of clipart, it was necessary to first create a new shape of the cottage wall with perspective applied to it. We couldn't use the pointing arrow to point at the original wall because a previous perspective effect had not been applied to it. The steps that were used are as follows:

1. A rectangle was drawn over the existing wall using the same width proportions (see the example on the left).

2. Perspective was then applied to the rectangle to match the shape of the original wall (see the dotted lines outlining the new shape in the example).

3. The text was then selected and the Effects | Copy | Perspective From command was used.

4. The pointing arrow was used to point at the newly created shape of the wall (the dotted outlined shape). The text now receives the perspective of the wall.

5. Finally, the text was scaled down and placed on the wall, as shown in the finished image on the right side of the illustration.

CLEARING PERSPECTIVES

Clearing a perspective completely removes the Perspective effect and returns the object to its state before the Perspective effect was applied. The Effects | Clear Effect command is context sensitive. If no object is selected, the command will read Clear Effect. If an object has a Perspective effect applied to it, the command will read Clear Perspective. Choosing the command with a perspective object selected removes the Perspective effect from the object.

Hopefully, this chapter has given you some knowledge that will help you improve your drawings. It is our belief that when you see how something works you can then use your own talents to implement what you have learned.

19

EXTRUDING

The Extrude effect lets you visually add a third dimension to two-dimensional objects. When an object is extruded, CorelDRAW creates projecting surfaces away from the original object in the direction of the vanishing point. In addition to extruding objects of various shapes and sizes, the Extrude effect can produce some very pleasant results when applied to text. CorelDRAW 8 now includes a 3D text module that lets you create true three-dimensional text, which may lessen the desire to use the Extrude effect. The difference between the 3D module and the Extrude effect is that the 3D module renders the object as a bitmap image while the Extrude effect creates the three-dimensional illusion as a vector object. If you are striving for crisp edges and lines, you should stay with the Extrude effect.

CorelDRAW 8 includes an Interactive Extrude tool that lets you create extrudes interactively in real time. The chapter begins by teaching you how to create extrudes by using the Extrude roll-up. Then you will move on to the interactive method. It is easier to learn how to use the Extrude effect and understand its complexities with the roll-up method, but once you've mastered that method you will probably find it quicker to use the interactive method.

The Extrude roll-up retains the last used settings even after you close the roll-up. This means that if the last extruded object you created was rotated, contained lighting effects, and used the new bevel effect, the next extrude you create will have these same properties. Of course, you can edit the properties after the extrude is drawn. If you want to return to the default settings, you need to use an existing extrude that you can edit to return the settings to their defaults. If there is no extrude on the page that you can use to edit, you have two choices: you can create a new extrude for the sole purpose of setting the defaults, or you can close CorelDRAW and open it again.

USING THE EXTRUDE ROLL-UP

To access the Extrude roll-up, choose Effects | Extrude (CTRL-E). When you open the roll-up, it will be grouped in an effects roll-up that includes the Blend, Contour, Envelope, and Lens effects.

When the Extrude roll-up is opened for the first time, it defaults to the Rotation page. The roll-up has five page tabs labeled with icons across the upper portion of the roll-up. When a page tab is selected, the roll-up changes to that specific page. Although the roll-up defaults to the Rotation page, you should select the Vanishing Point tab to begin a new Extrude effect, as shown in Figure 19-1. The five page tabs are, from left to right, Vanishing Point, Rotation, Lighting, Color, and Bevel.

The following paragraphs describe the elements that make up the Vanishing Point page.

VIEW WINDOW

The view window located just below the page tabs displays a representation of the shape and direction of the extrude type selected.

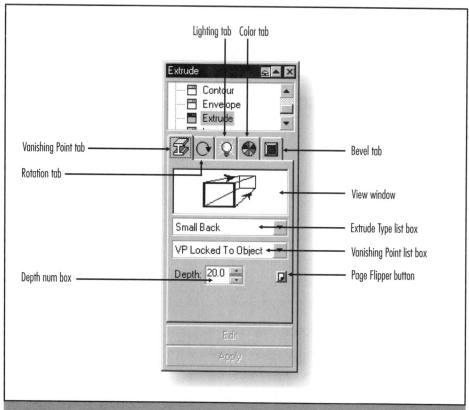

FIGURE 19-1   The Extrude roll-up with the Vanishing tab selected

EXTRUDE TYPE LIST BOX

The types of extrudes available are displayed in the list box underneath the view window. You can scroll the list box to choose one of six extrude types:

▶ *Small Back*   The lines of the extruded object recede backward toward the vanishing point and the back of the extrude is smaller than the control object.

▶ *Small Front*   The lines of the extruded object advance forward so the front of the extrude is smaller than the control object.

▶ *Big Back*   The lines of the extruded object recede backward toward the vanishing point and the back of the extrude is larger than the control object.

▶ *Big Front*   The lines of the extruded object advance forward so the front of the extrude is larger than the control object.

▶ *Back Parallel*   The lines of the extruded object recede backward and remain parallel to each other. The second object created by the Extrude effect is the same size as the control object.

▶ *Front Parallel*   The lines of the extruded object advance forward and remain parallel to each other. The second object created by the Extrude effect is the same size as the control object.

VANISHING POINT BOX

The Vanishing Point list box under the Extrude Type list box lets you choose whether the vanishing point is locked to the object or the page (the default setting is VP Locked to Object).

DEPTH BOX

The number you enter in the Depth num box determines the length of the extruded shape. If you enter the number 99, the extrude will extend all the way to the vanishing point.

PAGE FLIPPER BUTTON

The Page Flipper button, next to the Depth parameter box, changes the page to the absolute positioning page shown in Figure 19-2. On this page, you can set the vanishing point to a specific position on the page and lock the vanishing point relative to the page center or the center of the object.

When an extrude is created, it becomes a dynamically linked extrude group. A dynamically linked group consists of the original object, called the control object, and the newly created extruded objects. If the original object was a rectangle, it will be called the control rectangle when it is selected from within the extrude group. If the original object was text, it will be called

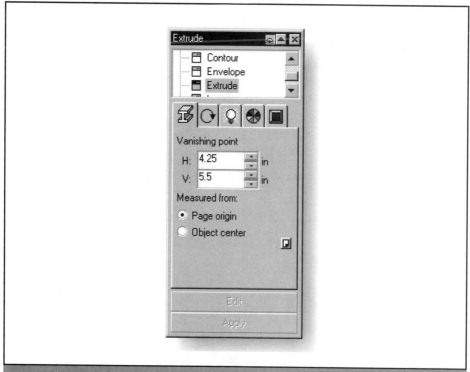

FIGURE 19-2   Vanishing Point page with the page changed with the Page Flipper button to show additional vanishing point settings

control text. When you change the properties of the control object, the changes are reflected in the extruded shape as well. For example, if you change the size of the control object, the extruded portion will be proportionally resized as well.

CREATING A BASIC EXTRUDE WITH VARIATIONS

Now that you know what's in the Extrude roll-up, it's time to practice creating extruded objects. If you have used the Extrude roll-up to create extruded objects prior to reading this chapter, close and reopen CorelDRAW to reset the Extrude roll-up defaults. Now follow the steps here to extrude a square.

CREATING AN EXTRUDED OBJECT

1. Open the Extrude roll-up by choosing Effects | Extrude. If you haven't yet used the Extrude roll-up in this session, the roll-up will open with the Rotation tab selected. Change to the Vanishing Point page by selecting the Vanishing Point tab.

2. Draw a perfect square in the upper left corner of the page (with the Rectangle tool selected, draw a rectangle while holding down the CTRL key) and give it a 20 percent black fill.

3. Use the default Small Back option from the Extrude Type list box.

4. Choose the Vanishing Point Locked to Object option from the Vanishing Point list box.

5. Leave the number 20 in the Depth parameter box.

6. Click the Edit button to activate the Apply button.

7. Click the Apply button and then click anywhere on the page to see the results.

8. Click on the Edit button to reveal an X on the page (this is the vanishing point.)

9. Click and drag the vanishing point down and to the right near the center of the page.

10. Click the Apply button again. Your extruded object should look something like the one shown here. You have just created and modified your first extruded object. But don't get too smug; it gets more complicated.

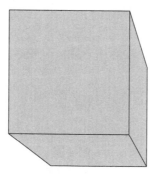

NOTE: *In previous versions of CorelDRAW you did not have to press the Edit button before pressing the Apply button as instructed in step 6. This added requirement will be eliminated when the first maintenance release is available.*

MOVING THE VANISHING POINT OF THE EXTRUDE

1. Deselect the extruded object you just created. Then re-select it and click the Edit button on the Extrude roll-up to make the extruded object active again (clicking the Edit button to make changes to an existing extrudes has always been a requirement in all version of CorelDRAW.) The vanishing point will be revealed near the center of the page.

2. Drag the vanishing point X to the lower-right corner of the page.

3. Click the Apply button and then click anywhere on the page to see the results. Your extruded object should now look something like the following illustration. Notice that the depth of the extrude became longer even though you didn't change the number in the Depth box. The reason for this is that the Depth setting is based on

a percentage of the distance between the control object and the vanishing point; it is not a fixed distance. When you moved the vanishing point you increased the distance between it and the extrude.

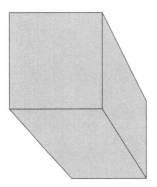

ADDING DUPLICATE EXTRUDES

1. Select the extrude group (not the control rectangle) and click the + key on the numeric keypad to create a duplicate of the extruded object directly on top of itself.

2. Move the duplicate extrude group to the lower-left corner of the page.

3. Repeat step 1 and move the duplicate extrude group to the lower-right corner of the page.

4. Repeat step 1 a third time and move the duplicate extrude to the upper-right corner of the page. The page should now look like Figure 19-3. Notice that all four extruded objects look the same because each extrude has its vanishing point locked to its own object.

CHANGING THE LOCK ON THE VANISHING POINT

1. Delete all but the original extruded object in the upper-left corner of the page.

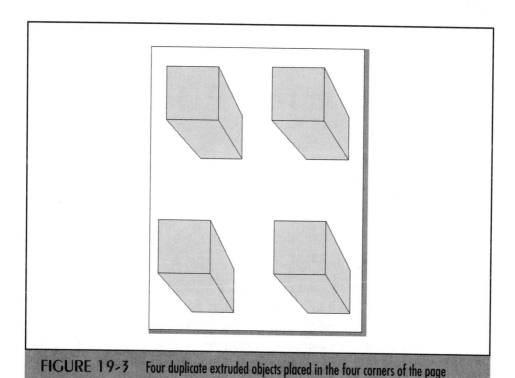

FIGURE 19-3   Four duplicate extruded objects placed in the four corners of the page

2. Select the original extruded object and click the Edit button on the Extrude roll-up to make the extruded object active. The vanishing point will be revealed on the page.

3. Place the cursor on the vanishing point X and drag it near the center of the page.

4. Select the down arrow in the Vanishing Point list box and select VP Locked To Page.

5. Change the number in the Depth parameters box to 50 and click the Apply button. The extruded object should now look like the one shown here.

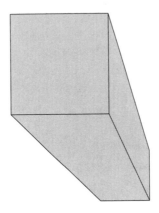

MAKING MORE DUPLICATES

Repeat steps 1 through 4 in the section titled "Adding Duplicate Extrudes."
The four extrude groups should now look like Figure 19-4. Notice that when
you changed the place to which the vanishing point was locked, the directions
of the extrudes changed as you moved them on the page. They all point near
the center of the page, where you moved the vanishing point. Now the
extruded objects appear to have perspective, as if you were looking down on
four tall buildings.

INCREASING THE DEPTH
OF AN EXTRUDE

1. Select the upper-left extrude group and click the Edit button. You
   are going to increase the depth of the extrude to its maximum value
   and change the location of the vanishing point by entering the
   coordinates manually.

2. Enter the number **99** in the Depth box. Click the Apply button. If
   the number reverts to the original number, you didn't click the Edit
   button in step 1.

3. Select the Page Flipper button next to the Depth box. The Vanishing
   Point page will be replaced by the Absolute Positioning page shown
   earlier in Figure 19-2.

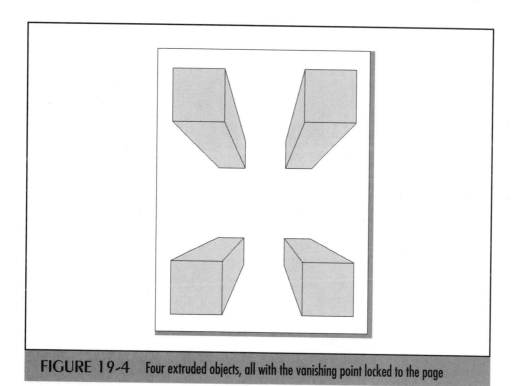

FIGURE 19-4 Four extruded objects, all with the vanishing point locked to the page

19

4. When you were told to move the cursor near the center of the page in step 3 in the section on "Changing the Lock on the Vanishing Point," you probably didn't get it in the exact center of the 8.5"x11" page, so enter the number **4.25** in the horizontal (H) box and **5.5** in the vertical (V) box.

5. Select the Page Origin Radio button in the Measured From section and click the Apply button. The extruded object in the upper-left side of the screen should appear as shown in Figure 19-5.

SHARING VANISHING POINTS

Sharing vanishing points means that you can change the vanishing point of one extrude to that of another extrude. It does not affect the depth settings of

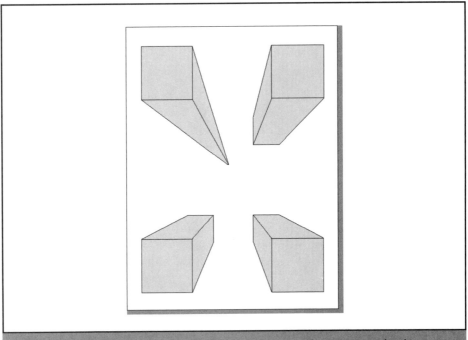

FIGURE 19-5   The upper-left extruded object with its vanishing point moved to the exact center of the page with a 99% Depth setting

the extrudes. So in this section you will also change the depth settings of three of the extrudes as you share the vanishing point of the fourth.

1. Select the Page Flipper button to return to the default vanishing point page.

2. Select the extrude group in the lower-left corner and then select Shared Vanishing Point from the Vanishing Point list box. The cursor will have a question mark next to it.

3. Use the cursor to select the extrude group in the upper-left corner. Do not click the Apply button yet.

4. Enter the number **99** in the Depth parameters box and click the Apply button. The extrude group will now share the vanishing point of the upper-left extrude group and the depth of the extrude will also match.

5. Select the extrude group in the lower-right corner and repeat steps 2 through 4.

6. Select the extrude group in the upper-right corner and repeat steps 2 through 4 a second time. Your page should now look like Figure 19-6. You have now created the illusion of the tallest buildings in the world.

If you want to see that the four extrudes do indeed share a single vanishing point, select one of the extrudes and click the Edit button on the Extrude roll-up. Move the vanishing point of the extrude to a different location on the page, click the Apply button and watch the other three extrudes magically follow the vanishing point.

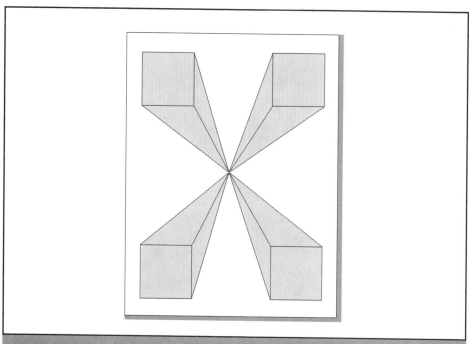

FIGURE 19-6   Four extruded objects with shared vanishing points

This exercise has taught you how to create extruded objects and change their vanishing points. It has also taught you the procedure for sharing the vanishing point of another extruded object. Now it's time to learn how to rotate an extruded object.

ROTATING EXTRUDED OBJECTS

Rotating extruded objects can add to the illusion of a third dimension. Our eyes sometimes get accustomed to seeing an extruded square that looks like a cube viewed straight on. When you rotate the cube, it gives a different dimension that we don't see as often. You can either manually rotate an extrude or, for the technically inclined, you can precisely rotate an extrude by changing the Angle, Phi, and Theta values.

 *Once an extruded object is rotated, the vanishing point can no longer be changed. To change the vanishing point of an extruded object that has been rotated, you must first edit the rotated extruded object (by clicking the Edit button) and remove the rotation by clicking the X button next to the Arc Ball on the Rotation property page. When the rotation has been removed, the vanishing point can be moved. If you want to return to the default setting of no rotation but there is no extruded object on the page that you can edit, you have two choices: you can create a new extruded object for the sole purpose of restoring the default setting of no rotation, or you can close the entire application and then open it again.*

MANUAL ROTATION

The Rotation tab is the second tab from the left on the Extrude roll-up. The icon is a full circle ending with an arrow. When the tab is selected the Extrude roll-up looks like the one shown in Figure 19-7.

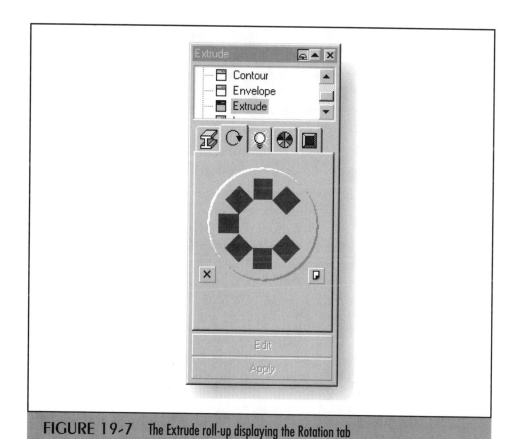

FIGURE 19-7   The Extrude roll-up displaying the Rotation tab

Often you will want to rotate an extruded object to change its perspective. Practice rotating an extruded object by following these steps:

1. With the Vanishing Point tab selected, draw a perfect square on the page and give it a fill of white.

2. Place the square in the upper-left portion of the page and extrude it by clicking Edit and then the Apply button. The extrude will be drawn with a depth of 99 because that is the last vanishing point setting you used if you just completed the steps in the preceding section, "Creating a Basic Extrude with Variations."

3. With the new extruded object still selected, change the Depth setting to 20 and click Apply.

4. Select the extrude group (not the control rectangle) and click the + key on the numeric keypad to create a duplicate of the extruded object directly on top of itself. Move the duplicate extruded object to the center of the page.

5. Select the Rotation icon to change to the Rotation page and then click the Edit button.

6. Place the cursor in the middle of the Arc Ball (the cursor will change to a hand) and drag to the right so the Arc Ball is at approximately a 45 degree angle. For your first rotation, move the cursor only a little to the right; later you can go crazy and rotate the object in any direction you want. Notice that the Arc Ball rotates in three-dimensional space with dotted lines surrounding the extrude object to indicate the change in rotation.

7. When you are happy with the indicated change, click the Apply button. Your rotated extruded object should look something like the extruded object with the dotted lines in Figure 19-8. Notice that the extrude depth becomes longer, and the extruded object no longer looks like a cube.

8. With the center extruded object selected, change the Depth setting on the Vanishing Point page to 10 and click the Apply button. The extruded object should now look more like the cube shown in Figure 19-9.

You've just rotated your first extrude. Now you will learn how to extrude objects where the angles of rotation are precisely controlled.

PRECISE ROTATION

Follow these steps to precisely rotate an extruded object:

1. Draw a perfect square on the page and fill it with 20 percent black. Then click the Edit button and then the Apply button.

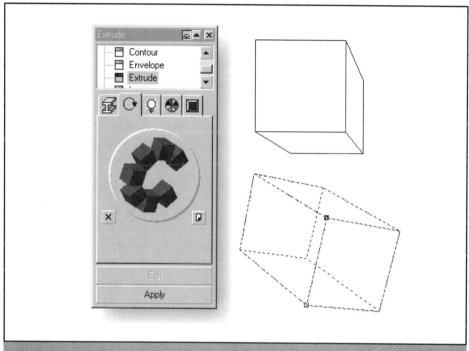

FIGURE 19-8   A basic rotated extruded object

2. The extruded object will be rotated with a depth of 10 because that is the last setting you used if you just completed the section "Manual Rotation." Change the settings on the Vanishing Point page to the default values of Small Back, VP Locked To Object, and a Depth value of 20.

3. Select the Rotate tab to display the Rotation page. Click the X at the lower-left area of the Arc Ball to remove the previous rotation setting.

4. Click the Apply button to extrude the square using the default settings.

5. Select the Page Flipper button at the lower-right corner of the Arc Ball. The Rotation values page will be displayed. You enter the angle, phi, and theta values, respectively, in the boxes numbered 1, 2, and 3. These values closely relate to those of the x, y, and z axes when using a 3D program.

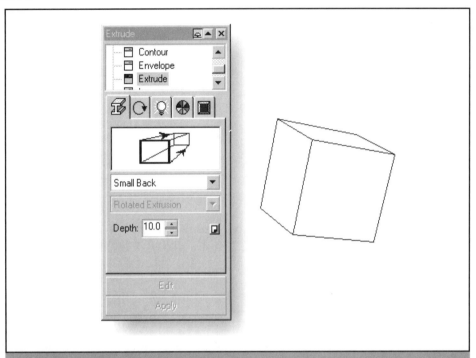

FIGURE 19-9   The basic rotated extruded object with the depth setting reduced to 10

6. Click the Edit button to activate the extruded object. If you have not deselected the Extrude group, the dotted line selection box will be displayed to indicate the Extrude is active. If the dotted line selection box is not displayed, select the Extrude group and click Edit. If the Extrude group is not active, the rotation will not work.

7. Place the cursor in box number 1 and enter 30. Enter **15** in box number 2 and enter **20** in box number 3. Each time you enter a new number, the position of the extrude dotted lines will be updated on the screen. Click the Apply button to make the changes take effect. Your extruded object should now look something like the one at the bottom in Figure 19-10.

Congratulate yourself: you have again created another extrude.

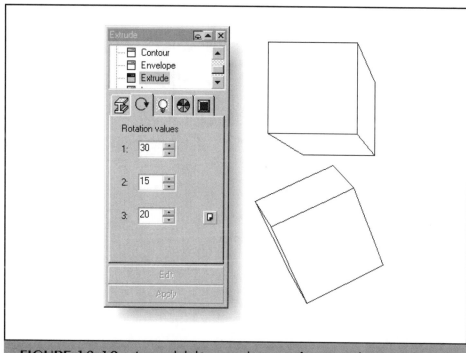

FIGURE 19-10   An extruded object rotated using specific rotation values

ADDING LIGHTING EFFECTS

Many users like to shade the extruded objects they create using the lighting feature in the Extrude roll-up. To change to the Lighting page, click the Lighting page icon: the light bulb. The default Lighting page is shown in Figure 19-11.

The Lighting page consists of three light icons numbered 1 through 3 next to a window with a grid representing a cube. An Intensity slider is located in the center of the roll-up, and below that is a check box that lets you use the full color range when applying lighting to an extrude group.

Practice using the lighting feature by following these steps:

1. Draw a perfect square; remember to change back to your default settings. Fill the square with baby blue. Place the square in the upper-right corner of the page.

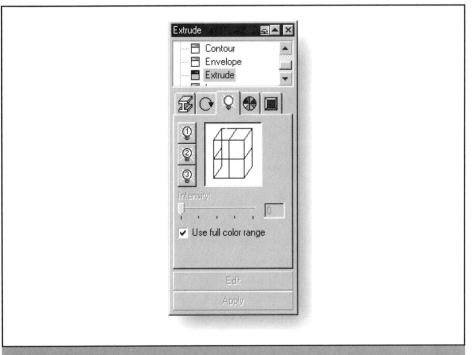

FIGURE 19-11 The default Lighting page

2. Extrude the square using the default values of Small Back, VP Locked To Object, and a Depth setting of 20.

3. Rotate the extruded object until you can easily see its three sides. Use Figure 19-12 as a guide.

4. Select the Lighting property tab.

5. With the extrude group selected, click the number 1 light. A circle with the number 1 is placed in the front upper-right position on the grid. Notice that a three-dimensional ball now appears inside the grid. If you look closely, the ball is lighted as if the light were indeed coming from the upper-right corner. If you look even closer, you will see a shadow cast by the ball on the imaginary floor.

6. Leave the number 1 light set to its default intensity of 100 percent and leave the Use Full Color Range box checked.

7. Click the Apply button. Your extruded cube should now be shaded similar to the one in Figure 19-12.

8. Select the extrude group again and click the number 2 light. The light will be placed on top of the number 1 light. Select the number 2 circle and drag it to the back left of the cube (use Figure 19-13 as a guide). Leave the check mark in the Use Full Color Range box and the Intensity slider at 100 percent.

9. Click the Apply button. Your shaded extruded object should look like the one shown in Figure 19-13. Notice that the extruded object is now shaded in a more natural way. If your extruded object doesn't look like the one in Figure 19-13, it probably was not rotated exactly like the one in the figure.

19

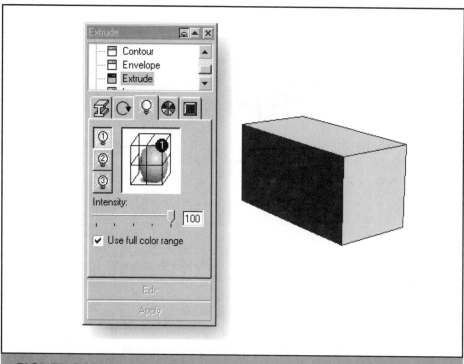

FIGURE 19-12 An extruded object with a single light coming from the top right

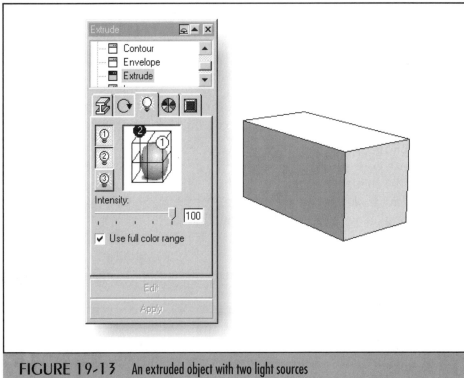

FIGURE 19-13 An extruded object with two light sources

There are a total of three lights available to light your objects. Practice using different light placements and intensity settings until you feel comfortable using the lighting controls.

 *Lights can be toggled on and off by selecting the respective icon number in the icon row.*

FILLING EXTRUDED OBJECTS

The Extrude roll-up contains a Color page that allows you to control the manner in which an extrude is filled. By choosing the different options, you can fill the control object with one color scheme and the extruded portion with a different color scheme. To change to the Color page, choose the Color property tab (using the icon with the color wheel). The default Color page looks like the roll-up shown in Figure 19-14.

You can choose among three fill options: Use Object Fill, Solid Fill, and Shade. These fill options are described here:

▶ *Use Object Fill* This option applies the fill used for the control object (the original object) to the extruded portion. When this option is selected, the Drape Fills option becomes available. If the Drape Fills box is checked, the entire extrude is filled as if the extrude were a single object. For example, suppose you used a bitmap fill containing a portrait of a lady. The filled extrude would contain one image of the lady's face and it would appear as if it were taking up the entire area making up the extrude. If Drape Fills is not checked, each of the pieces of the extrude together with the control object would contain a separate portrait of the lady's face; when you viewed the extrude you would see all or part of the lady's face (depending on the size of the extrude) in each separate object making up the extrude.

FIGURE 19-14   The default Color page

▶ *Solid Fill* This option enables you to select a solid fill from the drop-down palette on the roll-up and use it to fill the extruded portion. You can select a different fill, using any of CorelDRAW's fill options, for the control object. For example, you can fill the extruded portion with a solid color and then fill the control object with a texture or fountain fill. Figure 19-15 shows the Extrude roll-up with the Solid Fill radio button selected. Notice the drop-down palette displayed by clicking the Using button in the center of the roll-up.

▶ *Shade* The Shade option is a variation of the Solid Fill option. It allows you to shade the extruded portion using two different colors selected from the From and To drop-down palettes. Figure 19-16 shows the Extrude roll-up with the Shade radio button selected. The drop-down palettes for each color are displayed by clicking the From and To buttons.

EXTRUDING TEXT

Now that you are familiar with the process of extruding, rotating, and lighting rectangles, it's time to spice up your work by learning how to extrude and fill text. Follow these steps to learn how to use the fill options:

1. Type the word **Extrude** on the page using a nice bold font at a size of approximately 120 points (we used the font Impact).

2. Fill the text with a vertical fountain fill from black to 10 percent black and give the text a white outline.

3. With the text selected, extrude the text using the default values of Small Back, Locked to Object, and a Depth setting of 20. Then click Apply.

4. When the text is extruded, place the cursor on the vanishing point and move the cursor so the vanishing point is in the center, approximately 1 inch above the text. If you deselected the extrude, click the Edit button to make it active. Click Apply to make the change take effect.

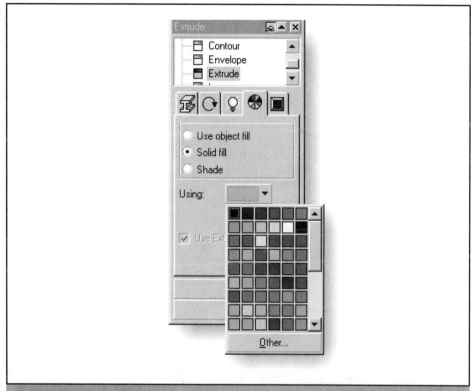

FIGURE 19-15   The Color page with the Solid Fill button selected and the color palette displayed

5. Select the Color page tab to change to the Color page. Select the Use Object Fill radio button and click Apply again. If a check mark appears in the Drape Fills box, remove it. Your extruded text should look like the text at the top of the illustration shown here.

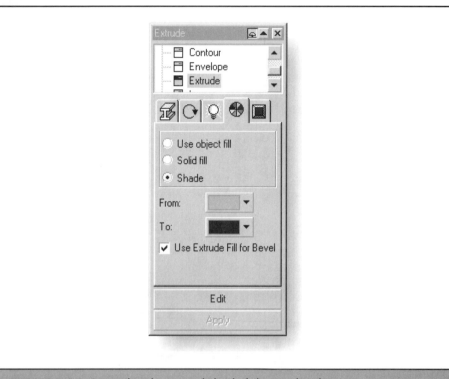

FIGURE 19-16　The Color page with the Shade button selected

6. With the extruded text still selected, put a check mark in the Drape Fills check box and click the Apply button. Your text should now look like the text at the bottom of the illustration. Notice the difference in how the two text objects were filled. The extruded portion in the first illustration was filled as if each part of the extrude were a separate object, whereas the text object in the second illustration was filled as if it were a single object.

7. With the extruded text still selected, click the Solid Fill radio button. The Using box should show the color black. Select the Color button and choose Cyan from the drop-down palette. Then click the Apply button. Your extruded text should now look something like the following illustration, which shows the fountain fill you used in step 2 filling the control object, and the color cyan filling the objects that make up the extruded portion.

8. With the extruded text still selected, put a check mark in the Shade box.

9. Select the From button and choose Cyan from the drop-down palette.

10. Select the To button and choose Red from the drop-down palette.

11. Click the Apply button to see the results. Your object should now be filled like the text shown here. The control object should be filled with a horizontal linear fill from black to 20 percent black. The extruded portion should be filled with a vertical linear fill of red to cyan.

You should be expert at filling extruded objects by now, so it's time to use the new Bevel feature.

USING THE BEVEL FEATURE

When a bevel is applied to an object, four beveled edges are added to the control object of the extrude. You can control both the bevel depth and beveled angle. You even have the option of showing only the beveled object. When you choose Show Bevel Only, the extruded portion disappears, and you're left with only the beveled object. If you create a bevel-only object and it is selected, the status line will report a bevel group. This ability to create a beveled object further expands the numerous uses of the Extrude effect.

The Bevel page tab is selected by choosing the far right icon in the Extrude roll-up. Figure 19-17 shows the Extrude roll-up with the Bevel page displayed.

FIGURE 19-17   The Bevel page

Follow these steps to familiarize yourself with the Bevel feature:

1. Draw a square approximately 4 inches square in the upper-right corner of the page (the size is important). Give it a fill of 20 percent black. Extrude the rectangle using the default values of Small Back, Locked to Object, and a Depth setting of 20.

2. With the extruded object still selected, click the Bevel page tab and select the Use Bevel check box.

3. Enter 0.333 in the Bevel Depth box and leave the default setting of 45 in the Bevel Angle box.

4. Click the Apply button to see the results. Your beveled square should look similar to the extruded object shown here.

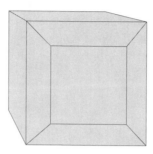

5. With the beveled square still selected (remember that if you deselect an extruded object, you must click the Edit button after you reselect it to make it active), select the Show Bevel Only check box and click the Apply button.

6. You should now see the beveled portion only, as in the following illustration.

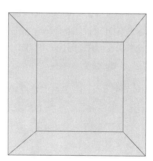

7. Remove the check mark from the Show Bevel Only check box and click the Apply button. The original extrude will reappear with the bevel still attached.

8. Remove the check mark from the Use Bevel box and click the Apply button again to see the bevel disappear, leaving you with the original extruded object.

Try repeating these steps, but this time use an ellipse instead of a square as the original object. When you get to step 3, click the spin button next to

19

the Bevel Depth box and use the up and down arrows to experiment with different settings. Do the same with the settings in the Bevel Angle box.

> *The depth of a bevel should be measured in relation to the size of the control object. If your control object (which could be text) is small, use smaller numbers in the Bevel Depth box.*

CREATING 3D TEXT

Now try using the bevel effect on text. Follow these steps to create 3D text:

1. Type the word **GLASS** on the page using a bold font at approximately 120 points (we used the font Impact). Use all caps.

2. Fill the text with black and give it a white outline.

3. With the text selected, extrude the text using the default values of Small Back, VP Locked to Object, and a Depth setting of 20. Then click Apply.

4. When the text is extruded, place the cursor on the vanishing point and move the cursor so the vanishing point is in the center, approximately 2 inches above the text. If you deselected the extruded object, click the Edit button to make it active. Click Apply to make the change take effect.

5. Select the Color page icon to change to the Color page. Select the Shade radio button and choose 20 percent black from the From drop-down palette and choose magenta from the To drop-down palette. Then click Apply again.

6. Select the Bevel page tab and put a check mark in the Use Bevel box. Enter **0.04** in the Depth box (note that a small value is used because the text is relatively small) and **45.0** in the Bevel Angle box.

7. Put a check mark in the Show Bevel Only box and then click the Apply button. Your bevel-only text should look like the following illustration.

8. Now remove the check mark from the Show Bevel Only check box and select the Color page tab again.

9. Remove the check mark from the Use Extrude Fill for Bevel check box. The Bevel color button will be revealed when you disable the check box.

10. Select the Shade radio button and choose 20 percent black from the From drop-down palette and choose magenta from the To drop-down palette. Then click Apply again.

11. Click the Bevel color button and choose a powder blue fill from the drop-down palette. This extra option lets you fill the bevel with a different color than that used for the extruded portion of the extruded object.

12. Click the Apply button to see the results. Your extruded text showing the powder blue bevel should look something like the following illustration.

USING THE INTERACTIVE EXTRUDE TOOL

Now that you've learned how to create extrudes using the roll-up method, it's time to advanced too the new Interactive Extrude tool. This tool, in conjunction with the Property Bar, lets you do everything you can do using the roll-up method. The best way to learn this tool is to jump right in and practice using it. Follow these steps to learn how this fascinating tool works:

1. Draw a rectangle on the page approximately 4 inches square. Fill the object with 50 percent black.

2. Select the Interactive Extrude tool from the Interactive tool flyout shown in Figure 19-18.

3. Click the rectangle and drag up and to the right. Notice that a white square is placed in the center of the rectangle with a dotted line pointing in the direction in which you dragged. The X at the end of the dotted line is the vanishing point. This means you can interactively place the vanishing point in any position when creating the extrude. Your extruded rectangle should look similar to the one shown in Figure 19-19.

4. With the Interactive Extrude tool still selected, click the Depth slider (the white bar on the dotted line) and drag it toward the vanishing point. Use Figure 19-20 as a guide. Sliding this bar along the dotted line allows you to control the depth of the extrude. Your extrude should now look similar to Figure 19-20.

5. Now comes the fun part. Click on the extrude (not the slider) to reveal the rotate cursor controls. Place the cursor inside the dotted circle. The cursor will change to the one shown in Figure 19-21. This cursor lets you move the object in the *x*, *y*, and *z* axes. Practice rotating the extrude in all three axes by dragging the cursor until it looks similar to Figure 19-21.

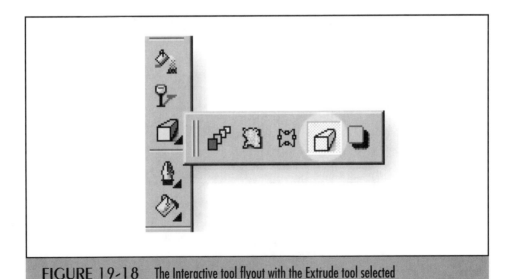

FIGURE 19-18   The Interactive tool flyout with the Extrude tool selected

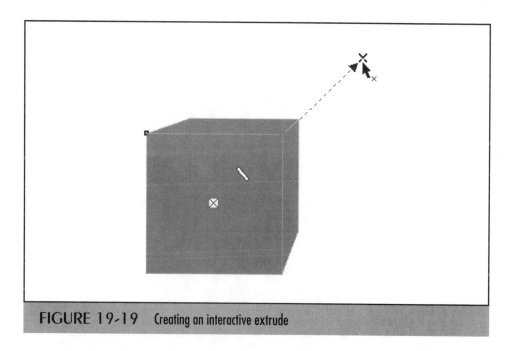

FIGURE 19-19   Creating an interactive extrude

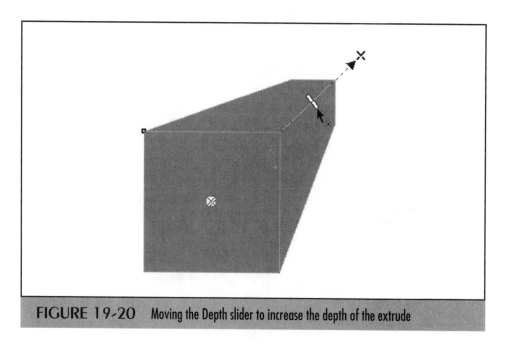

FIGURE 19-20   Moving the Depth slider to increase the depth of the extrude

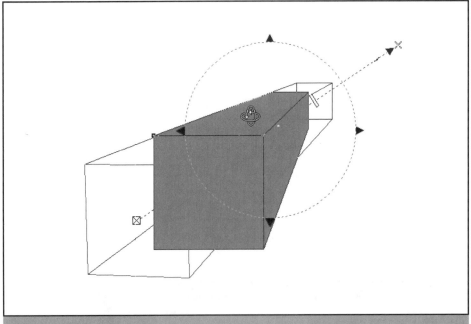

FIGURE 19-21   Rotating an extrude in the *x, y,* and *z* axes

6. Place the cursor on the outside of the dotted circle and the cursor changes to the one shown in Figure 19-22. This cursor lets you rotate the object in the *z* axis. Again, practice rotating the object until it looks similar to the one in Figure 19-22.

7. Place the cursor inside the dotted circle again and rotate the object until it looks similar to Figure 19-23. As you drag, try to end up with the object reduced in size and the vanishing point located in the position shown in the figure. Moving the cursor is a trial and error process so don't get discouraged. Just keep dragging the cursor in different directions until your object resembles the one in figure. You may need to undo some of your steps and try again. It is not as important to replicate the figure as it is to learn the process of rotating.

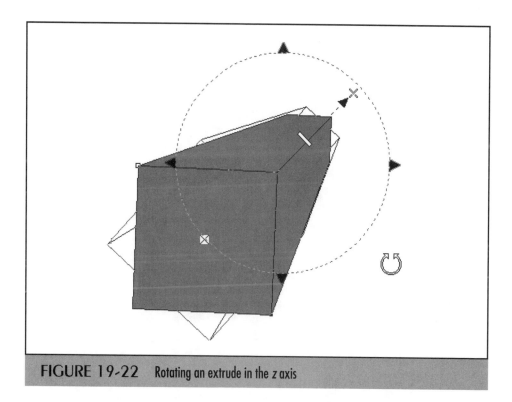

FIGURE 19-22 Rotating an extrude in the *z* axis

8. With your rotated object still selected with the Interactive Extrude tool, click the Lighting button on the Property Bar (see Figure 19-24).

9. Click the arrow on the Extrude lighting icon next to the Lighting button (see Figure 19-24) to display the lighting controls.

10. Click light number 1 to place the light in the default position on the grid. Move the Intensity slider all the way to the right. Click off the lighting controls in the Desktop area to see the results. Your extruded object should now look similar to the one in Figure 19-24. If it doesn't, don't despair; at the very least you have learned how to use the Interactive Extrude tool.

Figure 19-25 shows the Property Bar when the Interactive Extrude tool is selected. Also displayed are the Extrusion Type drop-down box, the Rotation Values box, and the Shade to Extrude Color palette. As you can see from this figure, all the controls that are available in the Extrude roll-up are available

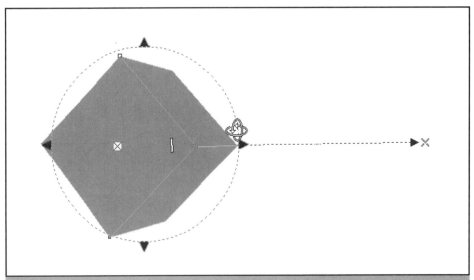

FIGURE 19-23   Changing the size and rotation of an extruded object

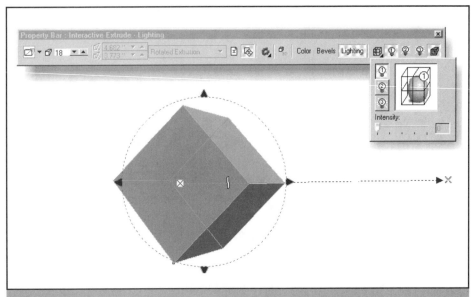

FIGURE 19-24   Applying interactive lighting effects to an extrude

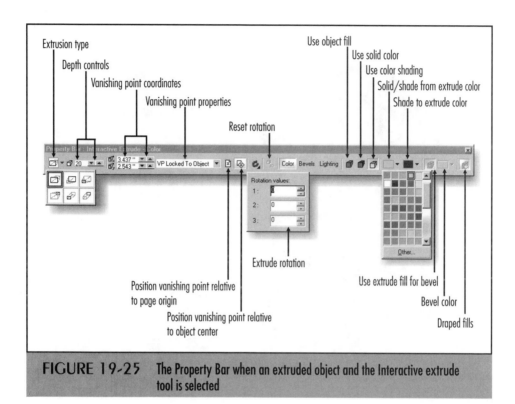

FIGURE 19-25 The Property Bar when an extruded object and the Interactive extrude tool is selected

on the Property Bar when an extruded object and the Interactive Extrude tool are selected.

A THIRD-PARTY EXTRUSION SCRIPT

You have learned a great deal about extrudes in this chapter, but a chapter on extrudes would not be complete without telling you a secret. The secret we are talking about is called TEKit™ by Foothills Graphics. As a Corel Solutions partner, Foothills Graphics has created a script that runs in CorelDRAW and turns an ORTHO view into an ISO view in a matter of seconds. Figure 19-26 shows the TEKit script dialog box with a .cdr file of a control panel on the left. We have used a lens to magnify the front of the panel to show the extruded dials, knobs, and nuts on the panel. We can attest to the fact that something like this, which would takes hours to extrude in CorelDRAW, takes but a few

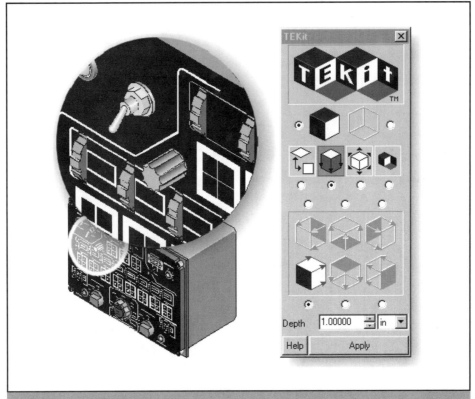

FIGURE 19-26   Using the TEKit script to extrude items on control panel

minutes using TEKit. For information on obtaining this script for CorelDRAW 8, go to Foothill's Web site at www.foothillsgraphics.com.

Creating extrudes can give your work a three-dimensional look, but don't overdo it. Simpler can often be better when trying to get your message across. Sometimes just adding perspective (see Chapter 18) to an object can give the viewer the sense of depth you're trying to convey.

20

BLENDING AND CONTOURING

The Blend and Contour effects share what appear to be common attributes. For example, the group of objects on the left here is a Blend group, and the group of objects on the right is a Contour group. As you can see, they look identical. However, except in this one particular use of the two effects, they are completely different. The Blend effect is used to morph one object into another, using a series of intermediate steps. The Contour effect creates duplicates of the original object on either the inside or outside of the original object. The difference between the two effects will become obvious as you learn more about them.

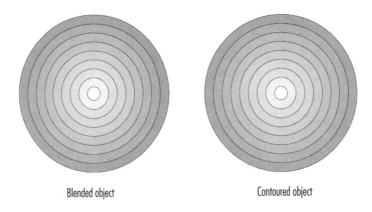

Blended object   Contoured object

THE BLEND EFFECT

The Blend effect can be used in a number of different ways and it all begins with two objects. These objects can be as simple as a rectangle or an ellipse or as complicated as a clipart group containing hundreds of objects. Blends can be used to create the illusion of perspective or mimic the look of neon. Blends can also be used for practical purposes such as spacing objects around another object or just on the page itself.

Before you jump right in and start creating blends, it is important to understand the parts of a blend. To begin, a blend is called a blend group, not just a blend. The blend group consists of three parts: two control objects (the start and end objects) and a group of objects containing the objects created when the Blend effect is applied. The following illustration shows a five-step blend starting with a swimming goose and blending to a flying goose. (This illustration is intended only to show the parts of a blend and is not meant to be a work of art.) The swimming goose is one control object, and the flying goose is the second control object. The objects in between the control objects are a group of five objects created by the Blend effect.

All objects in a blend group are dynamically linked. This means that if you move one of the control objects to a different location on the page, the blend will automatically be updated according to the new control object position. The next illustration shows the same geese as before, but this time the flying goose has been moved upward to give the illusion that the goose is actually taking off. When the flying goose was moved, the blend was updated to the new location. Notice also that the spacing between the geese has increased in the second illustration. This is because the blend effect, by default, always spaces the intermediate steps equally between the two control objects. You control the distance between the intermediate steps by accelerating or decelerating the steps discussed in the section on the Acceleration page.

CREATING A BLEND

Although you can create a blend using the new Interactive Blend tool and choosing the settings from the Property Bar, for your first blend, you should use the Blend roll-up. Open the roll-up by choosing Effects | Blend (CTRL-B). The roll-up first appears on the screen in the default configuration shown in Figure 20-1. The Steps tab is selected, and the number 20 appears in the num box. Without changing the defaults, create a blend by following these steps:

1. Open the Blend roll-up by Choosing Effects | Blend.

2. Draw two rectangles on the page. Color one red and the other blue.

3. Select both the rectangles and click the Apply button.

4. Select the red rectangle and change its color to yellow.

5. Select the blue rectangle and move it to a different location on the page.

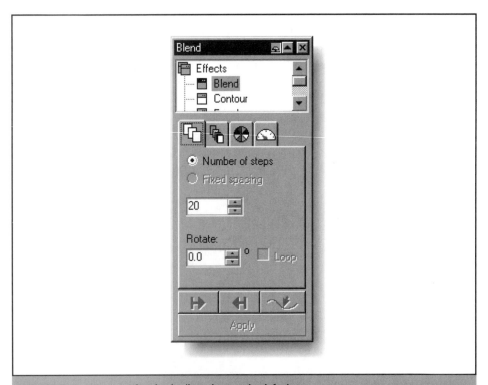

FIGURE 20-1   The Blend roll-up showing the default Steps page

In the first four steps, you created a basic blend and modified it by changing the color of one of the control objects. In the fifth step, you changed the direction of the blend and spacing between the intermediate steps. Not bad for your first blend.

USING THE BLEND ROLL-UP TO CONTROL THE LOOK OF BLENDS

Now that you have learned how to create a basic blend, it's time to explore the various ways you can change a blend to make it look and act differently. The Blend roll-up provides the necessary controls to let you do such things as placing a blend on a path and even looping a blend. The roll-up contains four tabbed pages. Each page contains the settings and controls for changing various attributes of the blend. At the bottom of the roll-up, directly above the Apply button, are three buttons. These buttons control the start and end of a blend and allow you to place a blend on a path. Each of the tabbed pages is described here. You will learn how to use all of the settings later in the chapter.

THE STEPS PAGE

The Steps page options allow you to control the number of intermediate objects within a blend in addition to spacing and movement attributes of the blend. The Steps page is the default page and was shown in Figure 20-1. It offers the following options:

▶ *Number of Steps* Enabling this radio button lets you enter the desired number of intermediate blend steps in the num box. You can enter any number between 1 and 999. The default is 20.

▶ *Fixed Spacing* This button is dimmed unless you are working with a blend on a path. When this radio button is enabled, the num box changes from numbers of steps to the current unit of measure. If you are using the default unit, inches, the num box will reflect the current distance in inches between each intermediate blend step.

▶ *Rotate* Enter the desired number of degrees of rotation in the Rotate num box. The maximum number you can enter is 360.

▶ *Loop* Enabling the Loop check box will curve the blend in the middle based on the number of degrees of rotation entered. If you enter 360 degrees of rotation with the Loop box checked, the blend will actually travel in a 360-degree bend in the center of the blend. The check box becomes active when a number is entered in the Rotate num box.

THE ACCELERATION PAGE

A basic blend evenly distributes the colors and the intermediate steps between the two control objects in the blend. The controls and options on the Acceleration page allow you to deviate from the basic blend by controlling the way the fill and outline colors, as well as the intermediate steps, interact with each other. The Acceleration page is shown in Figure 20-2.

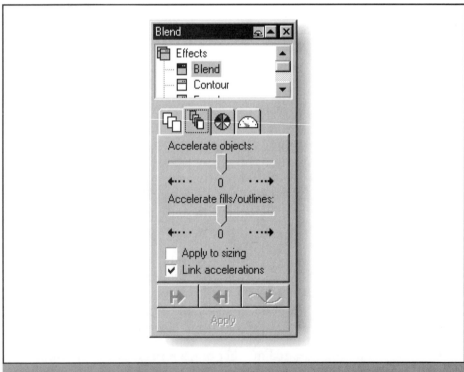

FIGURE 20-2   The Acceleration page of the Blend roll-up

Each of the controls and options is described here:

▶ *Accelerate Objects* Moving the slider to the left accelerates the intermediate objects toward the start of the blend. Moving the slider to the right accelerates the intermediate objects toward the end of the blend.

▶ *Accelerate Fills/Outlines* Moving the slider to the left accelerates the fill and outline colors toward the start of the blend. Moving the slider to the right accelerates the fill and outline colors toward the end of the blend.

▶ *Apply to Sizing* When you enable this check box, the acceleration between the size of the starting object and ending object is increased or decreased relative to the position of the Accelerate Objects slider.

▶ *Link Accelerations* If you enable this check box (it is on by default), the slider position of the Accelerate Fills/Outlines will move to the same relative position as the Accelerate Objects slider.

20

THE COLOR DIRECTION PAGE

The colors of the intermediate objects in a basic blend are dictated by the colors of the blend's control objects. If you create a basic blend from red to blue, the intermediate objects of the blend will be filled with various shades of red, purple, and blue. By using the three direction buttons on the Color Direction page, you can control the sequence of colors that will appear in the blend. A color wheel is adjacent to the direction buttons. The Color Direction page is shown in Figure 20-3.

The three options on this page starting at the top are as follows:

▶ *Straight Linear Blend* When you choose this button, the colors of the two intermediate objects change in a straight line, blending the starting color with the ending color as it passes through the color spectrum. The color wheel will display a straight line moving across the color wheel.

▶ *Clockwise Blend* When you enable this button, the colors of the intermediate objects blend, beginning with the starting color, with the ending color as it passes around the color spectrum in a clockwise direction. The color wheel will display an elliptical line moving around the color wheel in a clockwise direction.

FIGURE 20-3   The Color Direction page of the Blend roll-up

▶ *Counterclockwise Blend*   When you enable this button, the colors of the intermediate objects blend, beginning with the starting color, with the ending color as it passes around the color spectrum in a counterclockwise direction. The color wheel will display an elliptical line moving around the color wheel in a counterclockwise direction.

Using either the Clockwise or Counterclockwise Blend option can create rainbow-like color blends.

THE MISCELLANEOUS OPTIONS PAGE

The last page on the Blend roll-up displays four buttons that perform miscellaneous blend functions. The Miscellaneous Options page is shown in Figure 20-4.

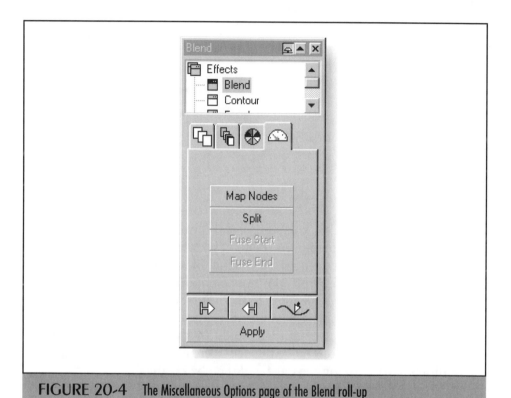

FIGURE 20-4   The Miscellaneous Options page of the Blend roll-up

These are the options on this page:

▶ *Map Nodes* When you blend two objects together, CorelDRAW uses the first node on both the start and end objects and creates the intermediate objects based on their relative locations. If you are blending two completely different shapes, the intermediate shapes created may not give you the results you expected. When you click the Map Nodes button, you can use the pointing arrow to select matching nodes on the two control objects. By experimenting with different nodes, you can alter the way the intermediate shapes look. The following illustration shows the geese blended earlier in this chapter blended again after using the Map Nodes option. A node at the front of the beak of the swimming goose was mapped to the node at the front of the beak of the flying goose. As you can see, a more pleasing morphing effect was achieved.

▶ *Split* This option lets you add a new control object to a blend by converting one of the intermediate objects into a third control object. This action changes the original blend into a compound blend. The compound blend is now composed of the starting object of the original blend blending to the newly added control object. The newly added object then blends to the ending object of the original blend. Remember that blends are dynamically linked objects; thus, you can move the newly created control object to a different location on the page and thereby create a bend on the blend. An example of a split blend is shown here.

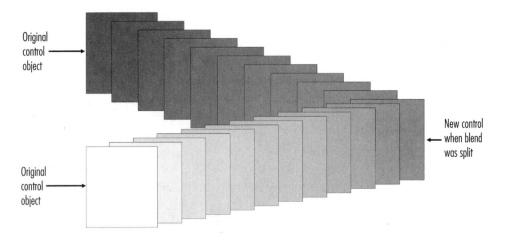

▶ *Fuse Start* This option removes any additional control objects from a compound blend and converts it back to a single blend.

ORVIETO - UMBRIA

Hans Joachim Kardinal

*This 12-layer image shows a part of the beautiful old city of
Orvieto in Umbria, Italy and is based on a photograph taken by the artist.*

GYONGYI KATONA

*This image, which suggests the sovereignty, elegance,
and sensuality of the superdiva, Marlene Dietreich, was created
using basic drawing tools, various fills, blends, transformations and effects.*

William J. Barbosa

The Alien Princess was created over a 6-month period by the artist. The inspiration for the image came from an encyclopedia of photographic images.

SIMONE PAMPADO

Many of DRAW's tools were used to create this reproduction of a watch.

SIMONE PAMPADO

This classic timepiece, created by the same artist as the previous image,
takes advantage of the versatility of CorelDRAW.

HUAN LE TRAN

This poster design is a composite of different
elements created by the artist using CorelDRAW's blend, linear
transparency, fountain fill, and duplicate and PowerClip tools, among others.

MARK ROSE

This poster resulted from brainstorming in which the author used himself
as a model and studied personal photos of hot-air balloons. First, the figure and balloon
were created as rough pen drawings, then they were scanned and imported together.

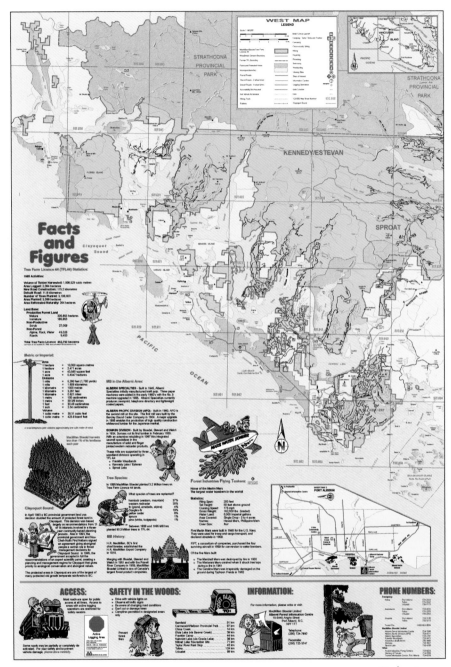

CARLOS ACOSTA

This "Recreational & Logging Map" was the winner of the
Technical category of Corel's World Design Contest for August, 1997.

Frits Godin

Several original, hand-drawn images from the author were
combined and reshaped in CorelDRAW to create this final image.

Theodor Ushev

This menu cover contains elements from a geographic map from the 16th century and was created as different layers that were combined with various multiple settings.

This corporate identification for the SUN EMPIRE company consists of design elements which are all curves, except for the name of the company, which was originally made of fonts converted to curves.

Tomasz Wawzyczek

Tomasz Wawrzyczek

Simple techniques were used to create this logo including freehand drawing for the shapes of the kids, mono-color fills, and adding text to images.

This wine label incorporates a scanned photo which had the rows of grapevines drawn in. Various DRAW features, including weld, transform mirror, combine and node edit were used to produce the final image.

Doug Forsythe

This image was created by applying various DRAW features including trim, blend, fountain fills, contour, weld, transparency and PowerClip, to an image scanned from a motorbike magazine.

Ng Chia Choon

This vector illustration represents the system of connecting rods for the movement of an actual locomotive from the 1880s in Modena, Italy.

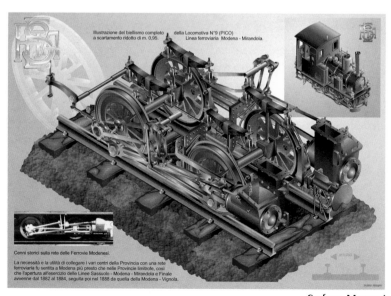

Stefano Maugeri

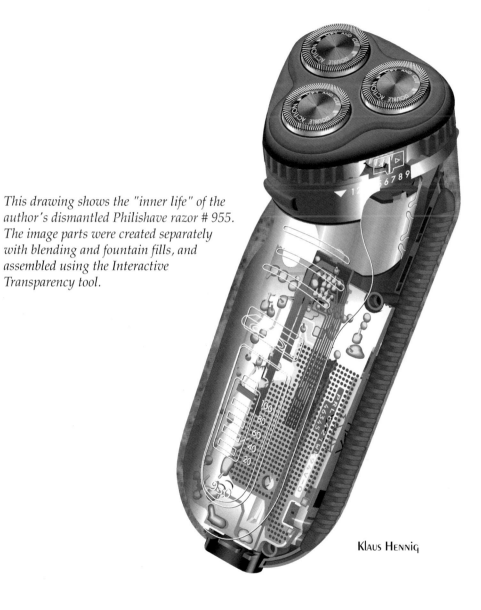

This drawing shows the "inner life" of the author's dismantled Philishave razor # 955. The image parts were created separately with blending and fountain fills, and assembled using the Interactive Transparency tool.

Klaus Hennig

Shown here is the illustration of applying transparency to circles to create the illusion of three dimensions. This exercise is documented step-by-step in Chapter 21.

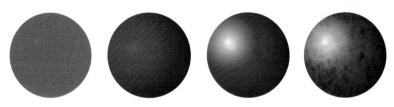

FOSTER D. COBURN III

Shown here is the illustration of applying transparency to a bitmap so that it merges with the background image. Two different variations are shown. This exercise is documented step-by-step in Chapter 21.

FOSTER D. COBURN III

FOSTER D. COBURN III

A Tinted Grayscale lens was placed over the whole photograph except the lips. The shape of the lips was created with the Shape tool and then cut out of a rectangle covering the entire image using the Combine command. This way the lips are not affected by the lens and therefore stand out from the rest of the image. Using a Tinted Grayscale lens is further described in Chapter 21.

A grid of CMYK color swatches. Each swatch lists its C, M, Y, K percentage values:

Row 1:
- C 0 / M 0 / Y 0 / K 100
- C 0 / M 0 / Y 0 / K 90
- C 0 / M 0 / Y 0 / K 80
- C 0 / M 0 / Y 0 / K 70
- C 0 / M 0 / Y 0 / K 60
- C 0 / M 0 / Y 0 / K 50
- C 0 / M 0 / Y 0 / K 40
- C 0 / M 0 / Y 0 / K 30
- C 0 / M 0 / Y 0 / K 20
- C 0 / M 0 / Y 0 / K 10

Row 2:
- C 100 / M 100 / Y 0 / K 0
- C 100 / M 0 / Y 0 / K 0
- C 100 / M 0 / Y 100 / K 0
- C 0 / M 0 / Y 100 / K 0
- C 0 / M 100 / Y 100 / K 0
- C 0 / M 100 / Y 0 / K 0
- C 20 / M 80 / Y 0 / K 20
- C 0 / M 60 / Y 100 / K 0
- C 0 / M 40 / Y 20 / K 0
- C 0 / M 20 / Y 20 / K 60

Row 3:
- C 20 / M 20 / Y 0 / K 0
- C 40 / M 40 / Y 0 / K 0
- C 60 / M 40 / Y 0 / K 0
- C 60 / M 60 / Y 0 / K 20
- C 40 / M 40 / Y 0 / K 20
- C 60 / M 40 / Y 0 / K 40
- C 40 / M 40 / Y 0 / K 60
- C 40 / M 20 / Y 0 / K 40
- C 100 / M 20 / Y 0 / K 0
- C 40 / M 0 / Y 0 / K 0

Row 4:
- C 20 / M 0 / Y 0 / K 20
- C 20 / M 0 / Y 0 / K 40
- C 20 / M 0 / Y 0 / K 60
- C 20 / M 0 / Y 0 / K 80
- C 40 / M 0 / Y 20 / K 60
- C 60 / M 0 / Y 40 / K 40
- C 40 / M 0 / Y 20 / K 40
- C 60 / M 0 / Y 20 / K 40
- C 60 / M 0 / Y 60 / K 0
- C 60 / M 0 / Y 20 / K 0

Row 5:
- C 60 / M 0 / Y 20 / K 20
- C 20 / M 0 / Y 20 / K 20
- C 20 / M 0 / Y 20 / K 0
- C 40 / M 0 / Y 40 / K 0
- C 20 / M 0 / Y 40 / K 40
- C 20 / M 0 / Y 40 / K 40
- C 20 / M 0 / Y 60 / K 20
- C 20 / M 0 / Y 40 / K 20
- C 40 / M 0 / Y 100 / K 0
- C 20 / M 0 / Y 60 / K 0

Row 6:
- C 0 / M 0 / Y 20 / K 80
- C 0 / M 0 / Y 20 / K 60
- C 0 / M 0 / Y 20 / K 40
- C 0 / M 0 / Y 40 / K 40
- C 0 / M 0 / Y 60 / K 20
- C 0 / M 0 / Y 60 / K 0
- C 0 / M 0 / Y 40 / K 0
- C 0 / M 0 / Y 20 / K 0
- C 0 / M 20 / Y 40 / K 40
- C 0 / M 40 / Y 60 / K 20

Row 7:
- C 0 / M 20 / Y 60 / K 20
- C 0 / M 60 / Y 80 / K 0
- C 0 / M 40 / Y 80 / K 0
- C 0 / M 40 / Y 60 / K 0
- C 0 / M 20 / Y 100 / K 0
- C 0 / M 20 / Y 40 / K 0
- C 0 / M 20 / Y 40 / K 60
- C 0 / M 60 / Y 60 / K 40
- C 0 / M 60 / Y 80 / K 20
- C 0 / M 60 / Y 60 / K 0

Row 8:
- C 0 / M 40 / Y 40 / K 0
- C 0 / M 20 / Y 20 / K 0
- C 0 / M 40 / Y 20 / K 40
- C 0 / M 60 / Y 20 / K 20
- C 0 / M 60 / Y 20 / K 20
- C 0 / M 100 / Y 60 / K 0
- C 0 / M 60 / Y 40 / K 0
- C 0 / M 80 / Y 40 / K 0
- C 0 / M 40 / Y 20 / K 0
- C 0 / M 40 / Y 0 / K 60

Row 9:
- C 0 / M 60 / Y 0 / K 40
- C 0 / M 40 / Y 0 / K 0
- C 0 / M 40 / Y 0 / K 20
- C 0 / M 20 / Y 0 / K 40
- C 0 / M 20 / Y 0 / K 20
- C 20 / M 60 / Y 0 / K 20
- C 20 / M 80 / Y 0 / K 0
- C 20 / M 60 / Y 0 / K 0
- C 20 / M 40 / Y 0 / K 20
- C 20 / M 40 / Y 0 / K 0

Row 10:
- C 20 / M 40 / Y 0 / K 60
- C 20 / M 40 / Y 0 / K 40
- C 40 / M 60 / Y 0 / K 0
- C 20 / M 100 / Y 0 / K 0
- C 40 / M 80 / Y 0 / K 0
- C 60 / M 80 / Y 0 / K 0
- C 40 / M 60 / Y 0 / K 40
- C 60 / M 80 / Y 0 / K 20
- C 100 / M 100 / Y 100 / K 100

PETER McCORMICK

A printed version of Corel's default Custom Color Palette with the percentages of each color value. Refer to Chapter 9 for more information.

▶ *Fuse End*   This option removes any additional control objects from a compound blend and converts it back to a single blend.

To fuse a blend, click the compound blend while holding down the CTRL key. Either the Fuse Start or Fuse End button will become active, depending on which half of the blend you clicked. If there are several control objects as a result of splitting a blend more than once, you have to click the Fuse End button once for every extra control object before the blend completely reverts to the original blend.

The last three buttons at the bottom of the roll-up, just above the Apply button, appear on all pages in the roll-up. They are the Start, End, and Path buttons.

▶ *Start*   When you click the Start button, a drop-down menu offers two options. The first option is New Start. This option lets you define a new control object to blend to. For example, suppose there are three objects on the page: one orange, one blue, and one green. If you blend the orange object to the blue object and then decide you should have blended the orange object to the green object, you would do the following: Select the blend containing the orange and blue control objects. Click the Start button and select New Start. Use the arrow that will replace your cursor to select the green object. Click the Apply button to make the change take effect. The blue object will now be blended to the green object.

CAUTION: *If you get a message saying "The start object must be behind the end object," select the new object you want to blend to and put it behind the first control object in the original blend by right-clicking on the new object and Choosing Order | Behind in the Object menu. Use the arrow to click on the first control object.*

The second option displayed by the Start button is Show Start. When you select this option, the first control object in the blend is selected, and the selection handles appear.

▶ *End*   The End button works like the Start button, but offers the New End and Show End options. (Note that the Caution also pertains to the New End option, but instead of putting the new object to the back, you need to place it in the front by right-clicking the new object and Choosing Order | In Front Of from the Object menu.)

► *Path* When you click the Path button, a drop-down menu appears with three options. The first option is New Path. This option lets you point to the path where you want to place the blend. The second option is Show Path. This option selects the path of a selected blend so you can identify or edit the path. The Detach From Path option lets you detach the blend from the path. Detaching the blend from the path returns the blend group to its original state.

CREATING BLENDS

You created a basic blend earlier in this chapter and learned how the various settings on the pages of the blend roll-up can affect a blend. Now it is time to apply what you've learned. Before you begin, be sure the Blend roll-up is displayed with the Steps page selected.

CREATING A BLENDED STAR

A simple yet interesting blend effect involves blending two copies of the same object together. The technique involves placing one scaled-down object inside a larger object. To create a blend using this technique, follow these steps:

1. Click the Symbols button on the Toolbar (CTRL-F11) shown here, to bring up the symbols Docker window.

2. Scroll down through the category lists until you reach Stars1.

3. Select the star at the upper-left corner of the list box and drag it onto the page. Give it a fill of 20 to 30 percent black.

4. Scale the symbol to approximately 3 inches square by dragging outward on a corner selection handle.

5. With the star selected, press the + key on the numeric keypad to create a duplicate of the star.

6. Select a corner selection handle and drag inward while holding down the SHIFT key. Continue dragging inward until the duplicate star is approximately half the size of the original.

7. Fill the smaller duplicate star with the color white. Your two stars should look like the ones shown here.

8. Marquee select both stars and remove their outlines.

9. Enter **20** in the Steps num box in the Fill roll-up and click Apply.

Your star should look like the one shown here.

Another interesting effect involves a similar technique with a completely different result. Follow these steps to create this unusual flare effect. Use Figure 20-5 as a reference as you create this effect. The final results will be more apparent when seen in color.

1. Right-click the Polygon tool in the Toolbox and choose Properties from the pop-up menu. Click the down arrow in the num box and change the setting to 4 sides.

20

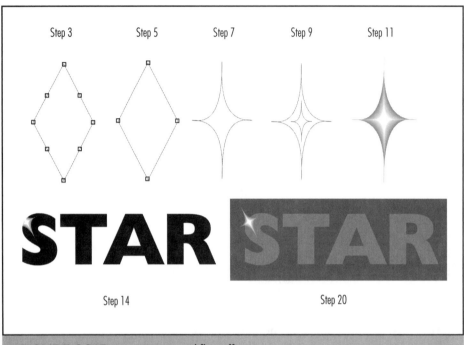

FIGURE 20-5   Creating a special flare effect

2. Draw a diamond shape on the page. You could also use the Freehand tool but we thought it would be fun to demonstrate how you can draw a simple diamond shape with the Polygon tool.

3. If you used the Polygon tool, your shape will look like the one shown in step 3 in Figure 20-5.

4. With the shape selected, choose Arrange | Convert to Curves (CTRL-Q) or click the Convert to Curves button on the Property Bar.

5. Click the Shape tool and delete the four nodes in-between the four corners of the diamond. Your shape should now look like the one in step 5.

6. With the Shape tool still selected, marquee select the remaining four corner nodes and click the To Curve button on the Property Bar. Click anywhere on the page to deselect the nodes or press the ESC key.

7. Using the Shape tool, click the lines between each corner node and drag inward to create the shape shown in step 7.

8. Click the Pick tool to select the shape and press the + key on the numeric keypad. This will place a duplicate shape directly on top of the original shape.

9. With the duplicate still selected, click a corner selection handle and drag inward while holding down the SHIFT key until the duplicate shape is about the size shown in step 9 in the figure.

10. Fill the outer shape with a light blue fill and the inner shape with a white fill and remove the outlines from both objects.

11. Blend the two shapes together using 20 steps to create the flare. Your flare should now look similar to the one in step 11 in the figure.

12. Type the word **STAR** on the page. Use a bold font similar to the one shown in Figure 20-5. We used Humanst 521 XBt BT with a size of 150 points. Fill the text with the same light blue fill you used in step 10 earlier.

13. Place the flare at the upper-right corner of the letter S. You will need to right-click on the flare to reveal the Object Properties menu and choose <u>O</u>rder | To <u>F</u>ront. This action will place the flare on top of the text.

14. Click twice on the flare to reveal the rotation arrows. Rotate the flare counterclockwise approximately 30 degrees. Your text and flare should now look similar the one in step 14 in the figure.

15. With the flare still selected, Press CTRL-C to place a copy of the flare on the clipboard. This is one of the most important steps. If you don't make this copy the effect won't work.

16. With the flare still selected, choose Effe<u>c</u>ts | Po<u>w</u>erClip | Place Inside Container. Use the pointing arrow to select the text. The flare will now appear inside the letter S and that portion outside the letter will be gone.

20

> **NOTE:** *If the flare appears in the center of the text, undo the effect and follow these steps: Choose Tools | Options, expand the Workspace folder, and click Edit. Look for the entry Auto-center new PowerClip contents. Remove any check marks to disable it. Click the OK button. Now repeat step 16 and the flare will appear inside the letter S correctly.*

17. Draw a rectangle larger than the text and place it behind the text. Fill the rectangle with a color of your choice. We used red (see step 19).

18. Now it's time to use the flare you copied to the clipboard. Press CTRL-V to paste the flare on top of the original.

19. Select the outer control object on the blended flare and change its color to the color you used for the rectangle (remember, we used red). You may need to zoom in on the flare to select the outer control object or select Show Start from the Blend roll-up.

20. Now comes the final step that make all the others worthwhile. Select the text with the PowerClipped flare and bring it to the front by right-clicking it and choosing Order | To Front from the Object menu.

That's all there is to it. Twenty quick steps and you have this great-looking flare effect. Your finished flare effect should look as good or better than the one in step 20 in Figure 20-5.

ROTATING AND LOOPING BLENDS

You should be ready to try something more difficult. Rotating and looping blends can provide some interesting effects. Follow these steps to create a rotated blend. Use the blends shown in Figure 20-6 as a guide.

1. Open the Blend roll-up and draw three small circles on the page. Separate two of them by about 4 inches.

2. Fill the circles with a radial fountain fill. A fountain fill of black to white was used in the example (see Chapter 10 for information on filling objects).

3. Select the two separate circles and enter **20** in the Steps num box.

4. Enter minus (-) **360** in the Rotate num box and click the Loop check box.

5. Select the two circles and click the Apply button.

6. Move the third circle below the rotated blend using the example inside the dotted box in Figure 20-6.

7. Select the left control ellipse on the rotated blend and the third circle and then enter 360 in the Rotate num box.

8. Click the Loop check box.

9. Click the Apply button. Your two blends should look like the example in the lower-left section of Figure 20-6. The arrows in the figure represent which two objects are being blended together.

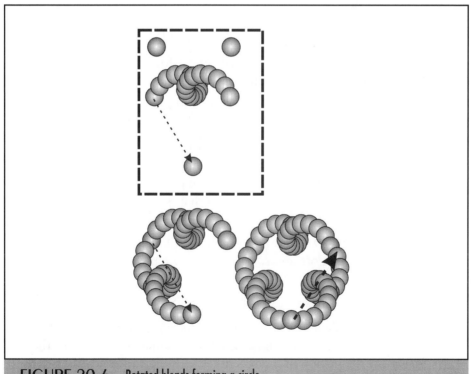

FIGURE 20-6 Rotated blends forming a circle

10. Select the right control ellipse on the second blend and the right control ellipse of the first blend.

11. Enter 360 in the Rotate num box and click the Loop check box again.

12. Click the Apply button. Your finished circle of rotated blends should look like the one in Figure 20-6.

USING BLENDS TO CREATE A PERSPECTIVE EFFECT

When you look down a road, things that are farther away appear smaller. Trying to duplicate this effect in CorelDRAW has been made easier by the addition of the Acceleration controls in the Blend roll-up. Follow these steps to create a Perspective effect using the accelerated blending technique:

1. Draw a rectangle that covers the top half of the page.

2. Fill the rectangle with a 90 percent linear fountain fill, using blue at the top and white at the bottom.

3. With the rectangle selected, press the + key on the numeric keypad to create a duplicate rectangle.

4. With the rectangle selected, click the top center selection handle and drag down across the upper rectangle until you reach the bottom of the page. You should now have a rectangle covering the bottom half of the page filled with a fountain fill that is the reverse of the top rectangle's fountain fill.

5. Fill this rectangle with a linear fountain fill, using brown at the top and white at the bottom. You should now have what appears to be the sky meeting the horizon line.

6. Remove the outlines from both of the rectangles.

7. Draw a rectangle approximately 6 inches wide in the center of the bottom rectangle, beginning at the horizon line and ending at the bottom of the page. Fill the rectangle with black. This will be the road. Your image should now look like the one shown here.

8. Select the rectangle you just drew and choose Effe<u>c</u>ts | <u>A</u>dd Perspective.

9. Select the upper-right selection handle with the crosshair cursor and drag to the left until your road looks like the one shown here. Hold down the CTRL key to constrain the top of the rectangle to the horizon.

20

You have now created a basic scene. The next step is to add some trees along the road.

1. Choose <u>T</u>ools | Sym<u>b</u>ols (CTRL-F11) to display the Symbols roll-up.

2. Scroll down through the category list until you find the Plants category.

3. Click the top-middle symbol in the list box and drag it onto the page.

4. Scale the symbol down to the size shown here and place it near the end of the road. Remove the outline from the tree and give it a fill of 20 percent gray.

5. Make a duplicate of the tree and place it in the foreground on the right side of the road. Give it a fill of black.

6. Select the top-left corner selection handle of the foreground tree and drag upward to the left until the tree reaches the height of the horizon line.

7. Select the top-middle selection handle and stretch the tree upward until it almost reaches the top of the page. Your image should now look something like this.

8. Select both trees and enter 8 in the Steps parameter box of the Blend roll-up.

9. Click the Acceleration page tab and move the Accelerate Objects slider halfway to the left. Leave the Link Accelerations box checked.

10. Click the Apply to Sizing check box.

11. Click the Apply button.

12. Draw a 2-inch diameter circle in the sky, remove the outline, and give it a radial fill of light yellow to white.

You should now see something like the image shown here. You could call it "Moon over Miami."

USING ACCELERATED BLENDS TO CREATE SHADOWS

Blends have long been used for shadow effects, but they lacked the effect of a true shadow. Now that it's possible to adjust the acceleration of blends, you can create a lifelike cast shadow. Follow the steps here to create a ball with an accelerated cast shadow:

1. Create a ball by drawing a circle on the page. Remove the outline and give it a radial fill with the highlight near the upper-left corner (see Chapter 10 for information on filling objects). We made the ball in the example a pool ball by adding an extra white circle and the number 9.

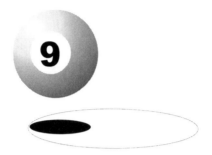

2. Draw a large ellipse under the ball, similar to the one shown here. Fill the ellipse with the background color (white).

3. Make a duplicate of the first ellipse and scale it down in size to approximate the one shown here. Fill this ellipse with the color black.

4. Select both ellipses and remove the outlines.

5. With both ellipses still selected, enter a number higher than 50 in the Steps parameter box to create a smooth blend effect.

6. Click the Acceleration tab and move the Accelerate Objects slider halfway to the right. Leave the Link Accelerations box checked.

7. Click the Apply to Sizing check box.

8. Click the Apply button.

9. Select the ball you made in step 1 and then right-click to bring up the Object menu. Choose <u>O</u>rder | To <u>F</u>ront to place the ball in front of the blend you just created.

10. Move the ball down over the blend so that it looks like the one shown here.

ATTACHING A BLEND TO A PATH

Making a blend follow a specific path can produce some interesting effects. One example of this is shown in Figure 20-7. We have blended ellipses and placed them around another ellipse to create the illusion of a makeup mirror.
    To create this effect, follow these steps:

1. Create an ellipse approximately 5 inches tall. Fill it with a linear fountain fill of 20 percent black to white and remove the outline.

2. Draw two small circles and fill them with a radial fill of 30percent black to white and remove their outlines.

3. Select both circles and blend them together using 15 steps.

4. With the blend group selected, click the Path button and select <u>N</u>ew Path at the lower-right corner of the roll-up, seen here highlighted on the roll-up. Your cursor will change to the funny looking cursor shown in Figure 20-7. Use this cursor to click the ellipse.

5. Click the Blend Along Full Path check box and click Apply. Presto, the light bulbs are surrounding the mirror. If you want fewer light bulbs, simply reduce the number of steps in the blend.

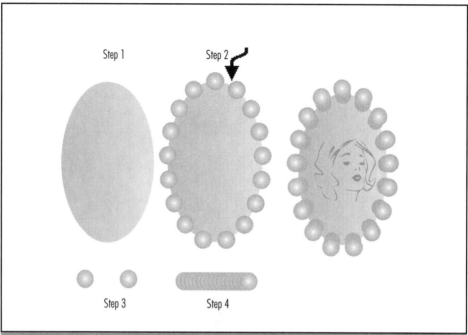

FIGURE 20-7   Placing a blend on a path to create a makeup mirror

We decided to create a 3D effect so we made duplicates of the light bulbs, colored them darker gray, and placed them behind the original bulbs to create shadows on the mirror. Follow the remaining steps to create this 3D effect.

6. Duplicate the blended bulbs on the path.

7. With the new set of bulbs on the path, choose <u>A</u>rrange | <u>S</u>eparate. This action separates the blend on a path. You end up with the original 5-inch high ellipse, two small circles (the old control circles), and a group of 15 circles (the 15 steps you selected in the Blend roll-up).

8. Click the original 5-inch high ellipse and delete it.

9. Marquee select the remaining circles (the two control circles and the 15-step group) and group them by clicking the Group button on the Property Bar.

10. Select a corner selection handle and drag inward to shrink the circles approximately 10 percent.

11. Place the circles you shrunk on top of the original light bulbs.

12. With the circles still selected, right-click and choose Order from the Object menu. Choose Behind. Use the arrow to click on the original light bulbs. The shadow bulbs will be placed beneath original bulbs.

13. Align the smaller bulbs until they give the illusion of shadows. Stretch or shrink them until they look correct.

It only took five steps to create the basic effect and eight more to add shadows. Taking the time to add the shadows can make the difference between an acceptable drawing and one that stands out from the norm. We added one more touch by placing a outline image of a woman on the mirror.

There are many different effects that can be created by attaching blends to paths; this is only one of them. Paths can be open or closed. Use your imagination, and you will be able to find many uses for this interesting Blend effect.

CREATING PATTERNS WITH THE BLEND EFFECT

You can create many geometric patterns using the Blend effect. Let's begin by creating two geometric shapes, and then blending them together to create a beautiful pattern. Follow the steps below using the steps in Figure 20-8 as a guide.

1. Draw an ellipse approximately .5 inches wide by 2 inches tall.

2. Give the ellipse a blue to white linear fill with a red outline.

3. With the ellipse selected, click two times to reveal the rotation arrows.

4. Click and drag the center of rotation thumbtack to the bottom of the ellipse (see step 3 in Figure 20-8). If you hold down the CTRL key while dragging you can place the thumbtack at the exact bottom of the ellipse.

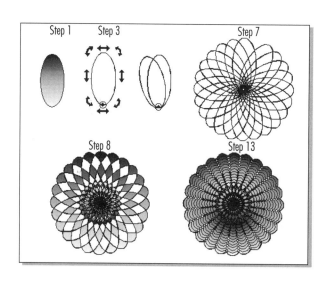

FIGURE 20-8   Creating a geometric pattern by combining and blending shapes

5. Choose Arrange | Transform | Rotate to bring up the Rotation dialog box.

6. Enter the number 15 in the Angle num box.

7. Click the Apply to Duplicate button 23 times. You should now have 24 ellipses in a circle as shown in step 7.

8. Marquee select all 24 ellipses and click the Combine button on the Property Bar. Your image should now look like step 8 in Figure 20-8.

9. With the new combined shape selected, press the + key on the numeric keypad to place a duplicate of the shape on top of itself. Fill this shape with a linear fill of white to blue (180 degrees opposite from the original).

10. Scale the duplicate shape to approximately one quarter the size of the original shape.

11. Select both shapes and press C and then E on the keyboard to center-align them.

12. With the two shapes still selected, blend them together using a 10-step blend. Your finished image should look like step 12 in Figure 20-8. Wouldn't this image fit well in a Southwestern theme?

As we often do, we decided to use the pattern in a different way. The image shown here is a result of using a clipart image and our blended pattern. The peacock's tail in the original clipart was rather ho-hum so we used our pattern to create a new tail. Remember that blends are dynamically linked. Therefore we simply placed the blended pattern to the right of the bird, selected the smaller (middle) control object, and dragged it over to the peacock's body. The blend was updated in its new configuration, becoming the beautiful tail shown here.

20

SEPARATING BLENDS

There will be times when you need to separate a blend group, as you experienced earlier when you learned how to add shadows to the blend on a

path. For example, you may want to take apart a blend to use one of the intermediate objects in the blend group. As a review, create a blend, click the blend group (not one of the control objects) and choose Arrange | Separate. Once a blend group is separated, you will be left with the original control objects and the group of objects containing the intermediate steps created by the blend. To ungroup the group containing the intermediate objects, click the Ungroup button on the Property Bar.

BLENDING LINES TO LINES

When most users think of the Blend effect they think of blending shapes to other shapes. Sometimes you can get some interesting effects by blending outlines to outlines. Figure 20-9 shows an example of blending two spirals to one another. Follow these steps to re-create this effect:

1. Select the Spiral tool and drag out an elliptical-shaped spiral similar to the one shown in Figure 20-9. We use five revolutions in the spiral shown here. Give the spiral an outline width of 16 points.

2. Press the + key on the numeric keypad to place a duplicate spiral on top of the first spiral. Change the duplicate spiral's outline to white.

3. With the duplicate selected, drag it upwards approximately .5 inches.

4. Change the outline width of the duplicate to 1 point. The two spirals should look like those at the top of Figure 20-9.

5. Select the two spirals and blend them together using a 40-step blend.

Your finished blend should look similar to the one at the bottom of Figure 20-9.

USING THE INTERACTIVE BLEND TOOL

Now that you know how the Blend effect works, it's time to learn about the Interactive Blend tool and some of its new capabilities. The best way to learn

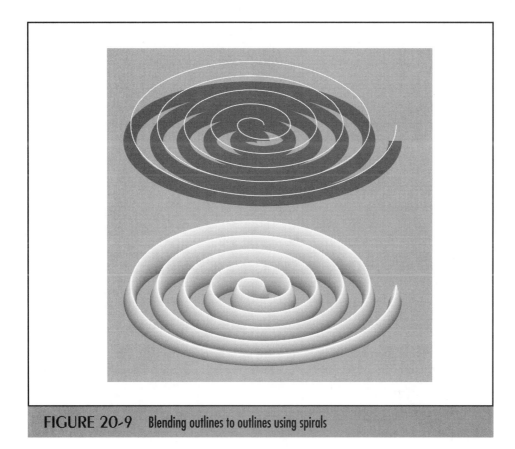

FIGURE 20-9   Blending outlines to outlines using spirals

20

how to use this tool is to jump right in and try it. Follow the steps here to create a simple blend:

1. Draw one large circle and one small circle on the page. Refer to Figure 20-10 for the placement of the circles.

2. Click the Interactive tool flyout in the toolbox and select the Interactive Blend tool shown here.

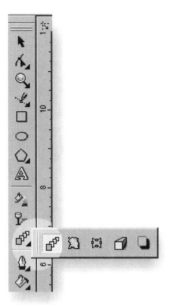

3. Using the Interactive Blend tool, click and drag from the large circle to the small circle. You will create a dotted line with a square at the beginning and end as you drag.

4. Release the mouse button to see the results of your first interactive blend as shown in Figure 20-10.

Now let's try one of the new features of this tool. Create two more circles, as you did in step 1 of the last exercise, and select the Interactive Blend tool again. This time hold down the ALT key and draw an irregular-shaped path from one circle to the next. End on the second circle and release the ALT key and mouse button. Your blend should look similar to the one shown here. This shape has possibilities, perhaps an elephant's trunk?

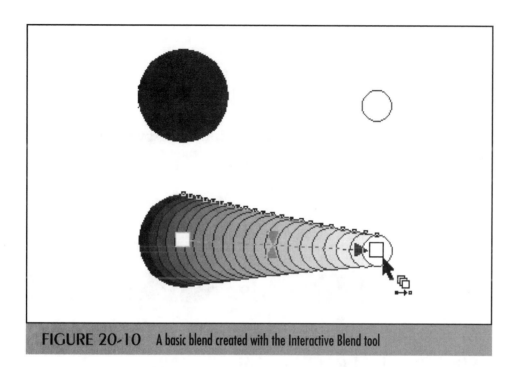

FIGURE 20-10   A basic blend created with the Interactive Blend tool

20

Once a blend is created and is selected like any other object, the Property Bar displays most of the controls that are found in the Blend roll-up. Figure 20-11 shows the Property Bar when a blend is selected. After practicing with the Interactive Blend tool and the controls on the Property Bar, you may feel more comfortable using this combination than using the Blend roll-up.

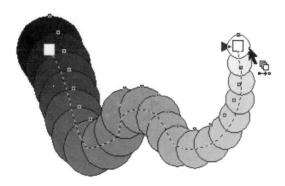

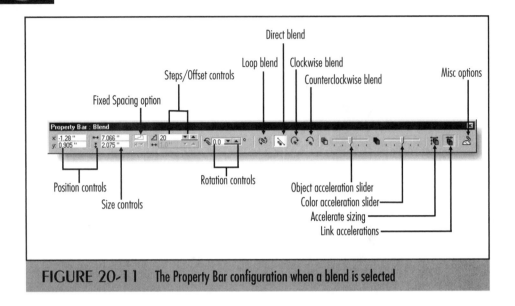

FIGURE 20-11   The Property Bar configuration when a blend is selected

USING THE INTERACTIVE OBJECT AND COLOR ACCELERATION SLIDERS

A new feature of the Interactive Blend tool lets you control the acceleration of both objects and colors of a blend using sliders attached to the dotted line of the interactive blend.

The blend at the top of Figure 20-12 shows a blend in the process of being created with the Interactive Blend tool. You can see the triangle-shaped slider controls moved to the left of center. The slider controls are linked by default, so when you move one the other goes with it.

Moving the sliders to the left, as in Figure 20-12, forces the color of the control object on the right to remain in effect for a longer period than the color of the control object on the left. Because the sliders are linked, the numbers of objects within the blend are spaced closer together at the left of the blend as well.

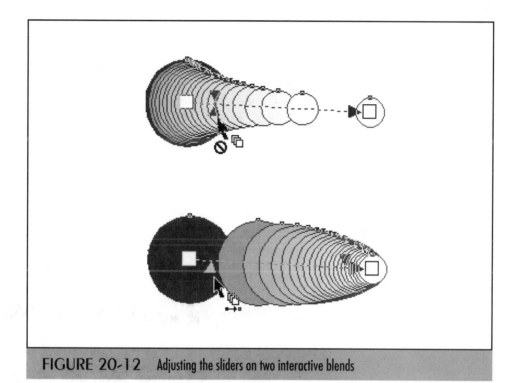

FIGURE 20-12   Adjusting the sliders on two interactive blends

20

An easy way to remember what happens when you move sliders to the left or right on the dotted line is the following: Moving a slider toward one end or the other affects a majority of objects in favor of the attributes (color and size) of the control object at the opposite end. In other words, you are dragging the attributes of one control object toward the other and those attributes are dominant over the attributes of the control object you are dragging toward. That's simple isn't it?

The blend at the bottom of Figure 20-12 is different because the sliders are no longer linked. This was accomplished by clicking the Link Acceleration button on the Property Bar to disable it (this button can be toggled on or off).You can also enable or disable the slider linking by double-clicking on a slider handle.

The bottom slider controls the color and the top slider controls the object spacing. As you can see, the Color slider on the bottom has been moved to

the right and the Object slider on the top has been move to the right. Visually, it goes against what we just said. This is because the color dominance of the white control object is opposing the object dominance of the black control objects. What does all this tell you? It tells you, forget most of the rules and make whatever adjustments to your interactive blends are necessary to end up with results that please you.

BLENDING OBJECTS FILLED WITH SPOT COLORS

We can't end the blend section without sharing the news that you can finally blend spot colors together without the intermediate steps turning into process colors. Users asked for this feature and it is finally available. Follow these steps to see how it works:

1. Draw two rectangles on the page.

2. Fill one with a spot color from the Pantone Matching System color palette (see Chapter 9).

3. Fill the second rectangle with a different Spot color from the same palette.

4. Remove the outlines from both rectangles, or, if you want outlines, make sure you use a spot color for the outlines as well.

5. Blend the two rectangles together

6. Choose File | Print and click the Separations tab. As you can see in Figure 20-13, the only colors listed are the spot colors you selected. The intermediate steps of the blend are tints of the original two spot colors.

USING THE CONTOUR EFFECT

The Contour effect adds concentric duplicates of the selected object that are either smaller and inside the original object or larger and outside the original object. The fill and outline colors assigned to the duplicate objects blend into the fill and outline colors of the original object. You can control the number

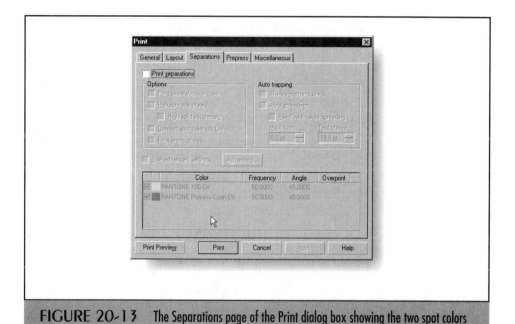

FIGURE 20-13   The Separations page of the Print dialog box showing the two spot colors used in the blend

of duplicate objects created and the distance between the objects. The number of concentric duplicate objects is determined by the number entered in the Steps num box. The distance is determined by the number entered in the Offset num box. A good example of this effect is shown in the following illustration of what could be the elevation lines on a golf course fairway.

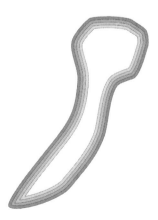

 *Contours can be applied only to single objects and Artistic Text. Single objects can include objects that have been combined.*

The Contour roll-up is shown in Figure 20-14 along with the Property Bar. You open the roll-up by choosing Effects | Contour (CTRL-F9). Both the roll-up and Property Bar offer several ways to control the look of a contour. As with all the effects, if you use the roll-ups, you must click the Apply button to make the changes take effect. If you're using the Property Bar, the changes take effect immediately.

Here are the options on the Contour roll-up and the Property Bar:

► *To Center* This setting ignores the Steps value and adds as many concentric duplicate objects as possible inside the original object based on the Offset value entered. For example, if you contoured a

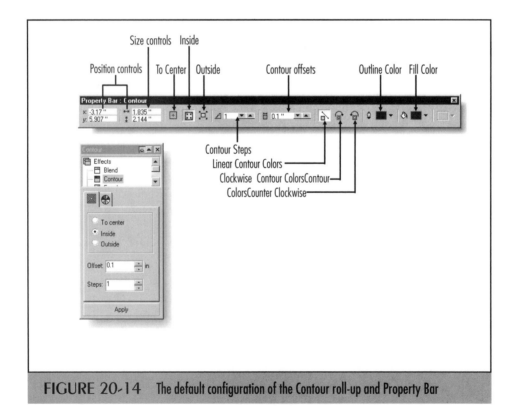

FIGURE 20-14   The default configuration of the Contour roll-up and Property Bar

2-inch diameter circle using the To Center option using a 0.1-inch offset, 10 additional concentric circles would be placed inside the original circle. Remember that the distance between each object is being reduced both horizontally and vertically, so you end up with 10 circles instead of 20. The example shown here is a 2-inch diameter circle that has been contoured using To Center with a 0.1-inch offset.

► *Inside* This setting also adds concentric duplicate objects inside the original object, but instead of adding as many duplicates as possible, it lets you control the offset and the number of steps. The total number of steps is limited by the size of the original object and the size of the offset distance you use. If you try to enter too many steps for the offset, the steps value will change to the maximum steps allowed for the size of the offset. The contour shown here is a 2-inch diameter circle contoured using Inside with a 0.1-inch offset using four steps.

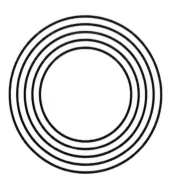

20

▶ *Outside*   This setting adds concentric duplicate objects outside the original object, but unlike with the first two options, you are not limited by the number of steps or the offset distance. The outside contour expands the duplicate objects as opposed to contracting them as the Inside option did. Keep in mind that the numbers you enter in the Steps and Offset num boxes greatly affect the look of the contour. The example here shows an irregularly shaped object contoured to the outside using an offset of 0.2 inch and five steps.

For your first Contour effect, you will create a button for a Web site:

1. Draw a circle that is about 2 inches in diameter.

2. Contour the circle to the outside, with an offset of 0.25 inch and one step.

3. Click Apply.

4. Choose Arrange | Separate.

5. Fill each of the objects with gradient fills to simulate the look of 3D. Try using a conical fill on the outer ring and a linear fill on the face of the button itself.

6. Remove the outlines or color them with a complementary color.

7. Add artwork or text to the front of the button to complete the effect.

Your button should look similar to the one shown here.

USING THE COLOR SETTINGS IN THE CONTOUR ROLL-UP

The Color page of the Contour roll-up (see Figure 20-15) lets you choose the fill and outline colors for the last object created by the Contour effect. These colors will then blend with the fill and outline colors of the original object. The color controls are just as easily accessed on the Property Bar.

To see how the colors blend together, follow these steps:

1. Draw a circle on the page approximately 2 inches in diameter and give it a red fill. Leave the default black outline on the circle.

2. Open the Contour roll-up and enable the Outside radio button.

3. Enter **0.1** in the Offset num box.

4. Enter **7** in the Steps num box.

5. Click the Color Wheel tab to change to the Color page.

6. Click the Fill icon (the paint bucket) and select one of the blues in the drop-down palette.

7. Click the top Direction icon on the left side of the large color wheel. It's the one depicting a diagonal straight line with a small square at the lower-left side.

8. Click the Apply button to see the results.

20

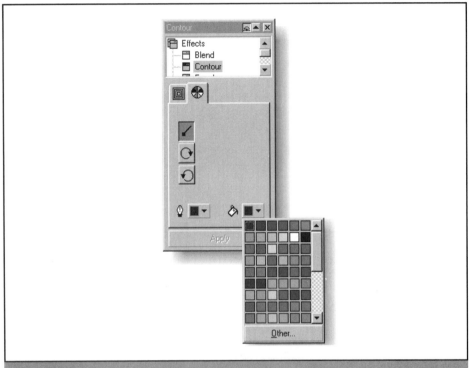

FIGURE 20-15   The Color page of the Contour roll-up

Notice that the last outside object created by the Contour effect is filled with the color blue you selected in step 6. This object then blends with the original red object, thereby creating the colors seen in the middle six offset steps.

If you select the Counterclockwise Direction icon in the roll-up, the blended colors will be colors made up of greens and yellows, as these are the colors in the color wheel when you travel in a clockwise direction between blue and red in the color spectrum.

If you select the Clockwise Direction icon, the blended colors will be made up of purples and pinks, as these are the colors in the color wheel when you travel in a counterclockwise direction between blue and red in the color spectrum.

Creating a Fillable Outline

You cannot fill an outline with any of CorelDRAW's custom fills. This is a problem for vinyl cutters who would like to create letters with fillable outlines. The Contour effect comes to the rescue for the vinyl cutters, and it can create interesting artistic effects as well.

To create a fillable outline, you need to create two separate contours. When contouring text, you have to contour each letter separately to get the proper effect. This means typing the first letter of the word and contouring it both inside and outside, and then typing the second letter and contouring it inside and outside. Continue contouring one letter at a time until you are finished. Try this technique using the word "FUN." Remember to work on one letter at a time.

1. Type the letter **F** in a fairly heavyweight font such as Arial Black and make it 144 points in size.

2. Enter **0.028** inch (2 points) in the Offset num box.

3. Click the Inside radio button.

4. Enter **1** in the Steps num box.

5. Click the Color page tab and choose the color red from the fill color picker drop-down palette. Doing this will distinguish the contour object from the text object.

6. Click the Apply button to create the contour.

7. With the contour group still selected, use the <u>A</u>rrange I <u>S</u>eparate command on the contour group. You will be left with a "group of 1 objects."

8. Click the Ungroup command on the Property Bar to ungroup the "group of 1 objects."

9. Select the original *F* again.

10. This time, contour the *F* to the outside by 0.028 inch using one step.

11. Repeat steps 5 and 6, but in step 5 choose blue for the fill color.

12. Now select the red inner contour and the blue outer contour and combine them together. Combining the two contours creates the

20

fillable outline of the letter *F*. Remove the original text, and you should end up with an object like the one shown here.

If you are creating vinyl, you have everything you need to cut the outline. If you are creating artwork for print, you can continue with the project by leaving the original text and filling the newly created outline object and the original text with fills of your choice. The newly contoured outline object in the text shown here has been filled with a linear fill, and the original text uses an opposing linear fill.

Creating a Fillable Outline Using a Script

You learned how to create a fillable outline by yourself, but you can also create one by using the Fillout script provided in the Script and Preset Manager Docker window (displayed in roll-up mode in Figure 20-16). This script automatically creates a single offset contour from the selected outline. The contour is also automatically filled with a fountain fill of your choice. To create a fillable outline using the Fillout script, follow these steps:

1. Draw a three-revolution spiral on the page (if you don't know how to draw a spiral, see Chapter 4).

2. Choose Tools | Scripts | Script and Preset Manager.

3. Double-click the Scripts folder to display the available scripts.

4. Click and drag the Fillout icon from the roll-up and drop it on the spiral. The Filled Outline Maker dialog box will appear (see Figure 20-16).

5. Click the down arrow in the list box to the right of the Fountain-Filled Outline Width num box and select Points as the measurement method. Leave the width setting at 10 points.

20

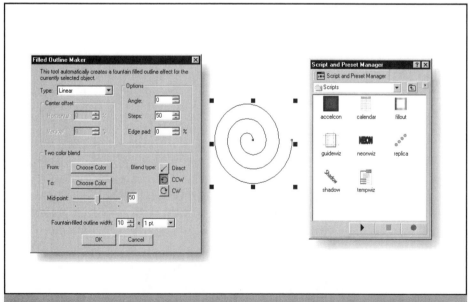

FIGURE 20-16   The Filled Outline Maker dialog box with the spiral and the scripts in the Scripts roll-up window

6. Click each of the Choose Color buttons and choose red from the upper palette and orange from the lower palette.

7. Click the counterclockwise button (CCW) for the Blend Type. This will create a rainbow fill.

8. Use the default value, Linear, in the Type list box.

9. Click the OK button to see the Contour effect applied to the spiral. The Filled Outline Maker message box will appear, telling you that the filled outline has been applied (see Figure 20-17).

10. If you are satisfied with the results, click the OK button in the message box. If you are not satisfied, click the Try Again button and readjust the settings in the Filled Outline Maker dialog box.

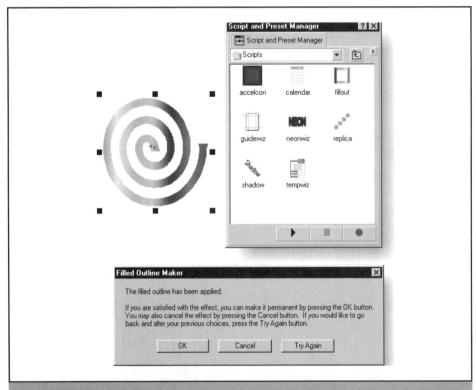

FIGURE 20-17   The Spiral after applying the fillable outline and the Filled Outline Maker message box

CONTOURING TEXT

There are uses for contouring text other than creating fillable outlines. One important use of the Contour effect is to create a font that is either a bolder or lighter weight than what is available from your font list. You can contour a word to the inside to create a lighter weight font or to the outside to create a bolder weight font. When you are through contouring, simply delete the original text, and you'll be left with your new font. Technically, this is not really a font, but instead is a curve object.

The examples shown here use the Britannic Bold font. The *A* on the left shows a lighter weight version of the font created by contouring to the inside. The *A* on the right is a bolder weight version created by contouring to the outside.

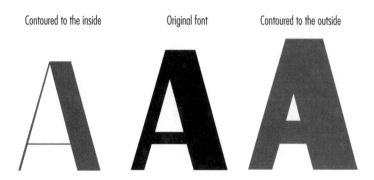

Contoured to the inside   Original font   Contoured to the outside

This chapter has taught you how to create blends using both the Blend roll-up and the Property Bar. Blends can be used to create dozens of special effects. Experienced CorelDRAW users continually find new ways to use this fascinating feature. You have also learned how to use the Contour effect to create concentric objects from a source object to create everything from fillable outlines to lighter or bolder weight fonts. Experimenting with these effects can produce some very interesting results.

21

LENS, TRANSPARENCY, AND POWERCLIP

he effects in this chapter produce radically different effects, yet they also have many similarities. One of the biggest problems you'll find with any of these effects is that they can cause serious printing problems. You may need to convert the resulting effect into a bitmap for it to print properly. The whys and wherefores of these problems will be detailed as each effect is described.

LENS

The Lens effect should be thought of not by the object it is applied to, but rather the objects behind it. Objects that have a lens applied are important only for their shape and their positioning. When you apply a lens, the fill that was in the object will no longer be present, but the outline will remain. Each object can have only one lens, but you can duplicate the object on top of itself and apply another type of lens to the duplicate. A lens can be applied only to a closed path.

 *Although you can place a lens over anything, beware of how lenses are placed. We heard from a user who had scanned a map and then placed 118 lenses over the top of the map to indicate various businesses. When it came time to print, the print file created was well over 1 gigabyte. This was because each lens required that the whole bitmap be printed again—and if any of the lenses had been stacked on top of each other, the problem would have been even worse. In these situations, it may be better to open the .cdr file you created in Corel PHOTO-PAINT, which compresses all of the lenses into a single bitmap again, which will print much more easily. Or select all of the objects and convert them to a bitmap within CorelDRAW.*

To bring up the Lens roll-up, choose Effects | Lens or use the ALT-F3 shortcut key. Originally, it is part of the Effects grouped roll-up. The following illustration shows it separated from the group; the Brighten lens is selected. Simply click Lens in the list at the top of the roll-up and drag its page onto the desktop if you prefer to work with the Lens roll-up separately.

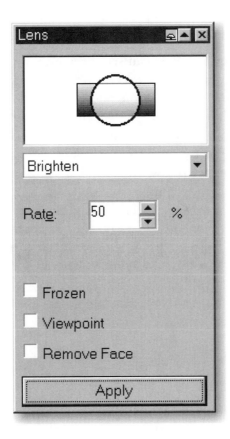

21

At the top of the roll-up is a crude depiction of what the Lens will create. The objects will always be a rectangle and a square rather than the real objects in your drawing. Once you learn how each of the lenses works, you'll probably not use the preview very often.

Three other options—the Frozen, Viewpoint, and Remove Face check boxes—are available to all lenses. Each of these options will be demonstrated later in this chapter.

The following types of lenses can be selected from the Lens roll-up: Transparency, Magnify, Brighten, Invert, Color Limit, Color Add, Tinted Grayscale, Heat Map, Custom Color Map, Wireframe, and fisheye.

TRANSPARENCY

With the Transparency lens, you can select the rate of transparency and the color or shade of the object. If the selected object has already been filled, the color will be the same as that fill. If the rate is set to 0%, nothing will happen since the object will have no transparency. If the object is set to 100%, the resulting effect will be the same as giving the object no fill at all. With any percentage between the two extremes, the object will become uniformly transparent. If the number is low, you will be able to see the objects behind the transparency object only faintly.

Traditionally, this roll-up selection has been the only way to add transparency to an object. Now it can be done in another way, through the use of the Interactive Transparency tool described later in this chapter. You'll find that this way provides many more options and will be the preferred method in almost all situations.

MAGNIFY

With the Magnify lens, only one parameter is available, and that is the amount of magnification. Any value from .1 to 100 can be used. Using .1 will actually shrink the objects behind the lens rather than magnify them as the name of the lens suggests. Setting the magnification all the way to 100 will enlarge the object by 100 times, to a gigantic size. Most of the time, you'll use a much smaller number, probably between 2 and 10.

One of the most interesting uses for this lens is in working with maps. Suppose you have a map of an entire area or city and you want to magnify the area directly surrounding a particular landmark. If you just place an ellipse or rectangle above the area you wish to magnify, it will also cover up part of the map, which can cause problems, as shown in Figure 21-1. Luckily, the Frozen and Viewpoint options can help correct this problem.

THE FROZEN OPTION

With the map, the problem is that you can't see the area near the magnified area because it is covered by the lens. You might think that the obvious solution is just to move the lens out of the way. Go ahead and try it. Notice that the lens changes as it is moved. Remember that a lens does nothing more

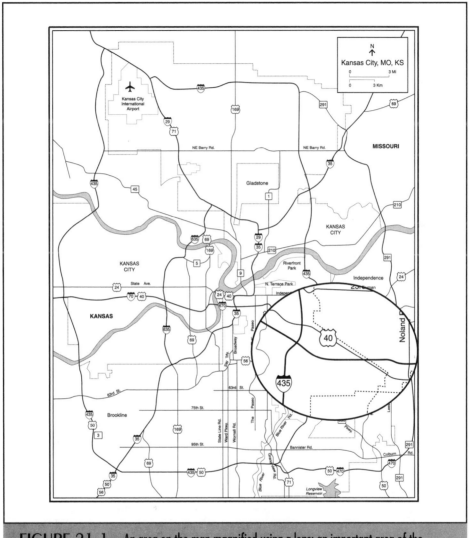

FIGURE 21-1   An area on the map magnified using a lens; an important area of the map is covered

21

than affect the objects behind it. When you move the lens, the objects behind it change.

If you check Frozen in the roll-up and then click Apply, the lens will become a snapshot of what is behind it. Then you can move it anywhere you like, and it will not change. So this is one way to solve the problem with the map: simply freeze the lens and move it someplace where it isn't covering anything important. But there is another solution.

The Viewpoint Option

Another way to solve the problem is to use the Viewpoint option. Normally, a lens affects what is directly behind it, so the viewpoint is directly behind it as well. If you check the Viewpoint check box in the Lens roll-up, however, you can move the viewpoint. As soon as you check this box, an Edit button will appear. Click the Edit button, and an X will appear at the center of the lens object. Drag the X anywhere in your drawing. Wherever it is placed will become the reference point for the lens. To finish the effect, click the End button (it used to be the Edit button) in the roll-up. Then click Apply, and the lens will be complete.

So with both the Frozen and Viewpoint options available, which one should you use? This really depends on the drawing. If you expect the objects that the lens affects to change, you'll probably want to use the Viewpoint option because it will be updated automatically. Using Frozen gives you a static view that will change only if you update the lens.

 *It must be stressed once again that a lens affects what is behind it, so if you create new objects that are above the lens object in the stacking order, they will not be affected by the lens. This applies to the Viewpoint option as well. If you draw a new object and the lens doesn't change, make sure to move the new object down in the stacking order until it is below the lens object. A great way to do this is by using the Object Manager because it gives you a visual representation of the stacking order.*

Now that you've seen how the Frozen and Viewpoint options can help you, take a look at Figure 21-2 to see the same map using the Viewpoint option to move the highlighted area off to the side. Note that we've added a light gray transparency over the area that is magnified so that the viewer can easily see what the magnified portion is taken from.

BRIGHTEN

Have you ever played with the Brighten knob on your monitor or television? Of course you have, because you wanted to adjust the picture so that it was

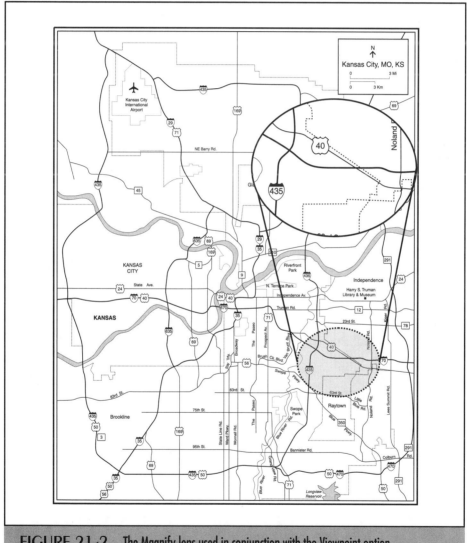

FIGURE 21-2   The Magnify lens used in conjunction with the Viewpoint option

21

just right. The Brighten lens works in a similar matter except the changes apply only to the object to which the lens is applied.

When you select Brighten from the drop-down list in the roll-up, you'll also see that the parameter box is now labeled Rate. Whatever percentage you type, from 0 to 100, will increase the brightness of the objects behind the lens object. If you set the percentage to 100 percent, everything will become white, so this value is not really desirable. Clearly, the higher the number, the brighter the lens.

You can also type a negative percentage, and the lens will behave as a Darken lens. Using a value of 100 percent will make the lens black. Figure 21-3 shows the effects of using both the Brighten and Darken lenses.

FIGURE 21-3   The Brighten and Darken lenes used on a photograph to create a simple ad

INVERT

Look through those old photos you hid in a shoebox, but instead of looking at the prints, look at the negatives. Some of them are quite bizarre, yet graphically appealing. We don't expect you to want a negative of Uncle Harry in your projects, but some of the textures can be fascinating.

This effect is quite easy to create within CorelDRAW using the Invert lens. When applied, it will display the objects behind it in their complementary CMYK colors—basically it is very similar to a photographic negative.

To create an inversion lens, choose Invert from the drop-down list and click the Apply button. Unlike the other lenses, the Invert lens has no other parameters to set.

One interesting side effect that you should be aware of is that when the lens object is over the drawing page, it will invert the background as well. This usually means that you get black since the page is most often white.

THE REMOVE FACE OPTION

You just saw that the Invert lens can create a problem when placed over a blank page since it also inverts the page. CorelDRAW 7 added an extra feature to solve this problem. If you check the Remove Face check box, the lens will be applied only to areas with "stuff" behind them. This means that the Invert lens won't try to invert a naked page. Figure 21-4 shows an example of the Invert lens used with and without the Remove Face option checked. The difference is quite noticeable.

COLOR LIMIT

If you've ever done photographic work, you are familiar with the various color filters you can use. The Color Limit lens is similar to a camera filter. It allows only the color you select and black to show through the lens.

When you select Color Limit from the drop-down list in the roll-up, you'll be presented with two other choices. You can select the rate and the color that will be limited. The rate can be anything from 0 to 100 percent. The higher the rate, the less color that is allowed through the lens. If the rate is 100, only black and the color selected will remain.

Suppose you have several objects on the page that are solid red and solid green:

21

Remove Face option not checked

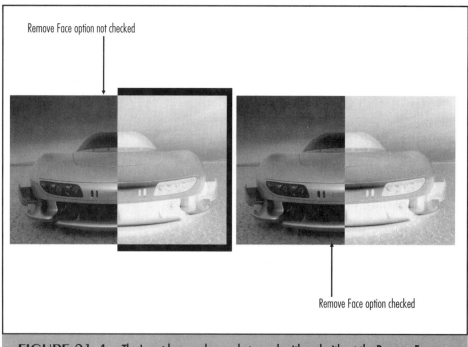

Remove Face option checked

FIGURE 21-4   The Invert lens used on a photograph with and without the Remove Face option checked

1. Draw another objects that surrounds all of the existing objects.

2. Apply a Color Limit lens of 50 percent strength and the color red. You'll see that the red objects were unchanged, but the green objects are now closer to a forest green. If any areas of the white page were showing, they should be pink. You might say that this is like looking at the world through rose-colored glasses.

3. Change the rate to 80 percent and click Apply. Now the green objects are a very dark green that is nearly black. The page will be almost red, and the red objects themselves are still unchanged.

Remember that if you don't want the lens to affect the blank parts of the page, check the Remove Face check box.

COLOR ADD

The Color Add lens is probably the most difficult to understand. It is based on the additive light model, where the more color you have, the closer you get to white. The best way to understand what is happening is to create the effect manually:

1. Create two objects, coloring one red and one green.

2. Create another object off to the side and leave it unfilled for now.

3. Draw another object that covers the red and green objects.

4. Apply a Color Add lens with a rate of 50 percent red to the last object you created. The object that was originally red should be unchanged. Because the background is white, adding light will not change its color at all, but you'll see that the formerly green object is now a yellowish green.

5. Fill the object that was created off to the side with an RGB fill of 128 red, 255 green, and 0 blue. That fill simulates a green object that has been covered by a 50 percent red Color Add lens. Notice that the color is the same as in the lens you created earlier.

6. Change the lens so that its rate is 100 percent. The green object should now be completely yellow, and if you left a black outline on the object, you'll notice that it has changed to red. Black is no light, and you have added red light to it; thus, the result is red.

7. To see this effect in the object off to the side, change the RGB fill to 255 red, 255 green, and 0 blue. That is the exact formula for creating yellow, and so this object should look the same as the "green" object under the lens.

TINTED GRAYSCALE

How many times have you wanted to convert something from color to grayscale? This is exactly what the Tinted Grayscale lens will do. Place an object around some clipart or a photograph and apply a Tinted Grayscale lens. Instantly, the original image will be converted. Normally, when you visualize this scenario, you think about black and white, but the "grayscale" can be any color you like.

Select Tinted Grayscale from the drop-down list in the roll-up. Choose the color you desire for the darkest shade and click Apply. Everything in the original image will be a shade of the color you chose.

One of the best ways to use this lens is with a photograph, but remember that you don't have to apply the lens to the whole photograph. Create smaller objects that will highlight a certain part of a black-and-white photograph in color, or use the Combine command to cut the shape out of a larger rectangle to leave only a small portion of the photograph in color and convert the rest to grayscale.

An example of a Tinted Grayscale lens is shown on the color pages at the center of this book since it doesn't reproduce well in black and white.

HEAT MAP

Heat Map is just another name for Infrared. Using this lens allows you to measure the level of "heat" in an image. A very limited palette of white, yellow, orange, red, blue, violet, and cyan is used to indicate the various levels of heat. The "hot" colors in an image are mapped to red and orange, and the "cool" colors are mapped to violet and cyan.

When you select Heat Map from the drop-down list in the roll-up, you'll also get the chance to choose a value for the palette rotation. With the rotation set to 0 percent, the effect is exactly as just described, but if you change it to 50 percent, the cool colors are represented as hot and vice versa.

Using the Heat Map lens is a great way to get a very abstract image from a photograph. Most of the time, you can't even recognize the original image.

CUSTOM COLOR MAP

The Custom Color Map lens is similar to the Tinted Grayscale lens except that you choose the colors and their order. Everything within the lens will become a shade of the two colors you select. For truly colorful effects, you can even use the rainbow options.

When you select Custom Color Map from the drop-down list in the roll-up, you are presented with three other choices. The colors can be mapped in a direct palette, forward rainbow, and reverse rainbow. You can also choose two colors for the beginning and end of the lens. A Direct Palette maps directly from one color to the other. Each of the rainbow options defines the direction of the rainbow as it moves around the color wheel.

Two separate color pickers are provided. They work like all the other color pickers in CorelDRAW. Between them is a small button. Click it, and the colors reverse their order. There is nothing more frustrating than picking the colors and finding that they are at the wrong ends of the fill. This little button solves that problem in a heartbeat.

In areas behind the fill where nothing appears, the To color will be used. The possibilities with this fill are really awesome.

WIREFRAME

Since the beginning of CorelDRAW, there has always been a Wireframe view, but to get the wireframe look on a particular area of the drawing was difficult. Using the Wireframe lens, it is easy to get the look with the colors of your choice for the outline and fill. All objects behind the lens will take on the fill and outline colors that you specify.

Select Wireframe from the drop-down list in the roll-up. Again, two color selectors will appear. Next to each color selector is a check box. If you want to change only one of the colors and leave the other untouched, simply uncheck the appropriate check box. Note that objects behind the lens that have no fill will now be filled with the color you choose. Figure 21-5 shows an example of a Wireframe lens.

Applying a Wireframe lens over a bitmap will treat the bitmap as a rectangle.

FISHEYE

You've seen a fisheye lens in action before. Through a fisheye lens, the whole world seems to exist in a spheroid. This same effect can be applied to objects in CorelDRAW. Note that the Fisheye lens works only on vector objects and has no effect on bitmaps. Similar effects are possible in Corel PHOTO-PAINT if you need to work with bitmaps.

The best way to envision this lens is to imagine that you are going to place the objects behind the lens on a ball. If you use a positive value for the rate,

FIGURE 21-5   The Wireframe lens in action

the objects will appear to be on the front curved surface of the ball. Negative values will make the objects look as if they are on the back side of the ball. The smaller the number, the smaller the area of the ball you will be working with; if you use a large value for the rate, the objects can wrap all the way around the ball. Rates can be anything from -1,000 to 1,000, with a value of zero having no effect at all.

To see the Fisheye lens in action, try the following example:

1. Draw some graph paper with five cells in either direction.

2. Ungroup the rectangles and fill every other one with black.

3. Regroup the rectangles.

4. Draw a circle that is about one and a half times larger than the rectangles and perfectly centered around them.

5. Apply a Fisheye lens with various rates to see exactly how they affect the objects.

Figure 21-6 shows two examples of this experiment.

INTERACTIVE TRANSPARENCY TOOL

The Interactive Transparency tool is found in the toolbox. To use it, you must apply the transparency to an existing object or group of objects.

We'll walk you through several small projects so that you can see how the tool works. Suffice it to say that once you understand what is happening, it is much easier to use the tool properly.

The Interactive Transparency tool creates a grayscale bitmap that acts as a transparency mask on an object. If you have used Corel PHOTO-PAINT extensively, this concept will make perfect sense. The rest of you should read on.

In a grayscale bitmap, you can have up to 256 shades of gray, ranging from solid white to solid black. Where the bitmap is solid black, the object will have

21

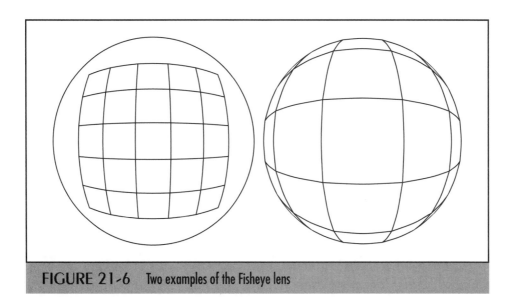

FIGURE 21-6   Two examples of the Fisheye lens

full transparency. The white areas provide no transparency. The gray levels in between provide transparency relative to their shade of gray.

When you use the Interactive Transparency tool, you are doing nothing more than creating this grayscale bitmap using the same fill types and methods that are used with the Interactive Fill tool that was described in Chapter 10. Now that you understand the basics of how this tool works, let's try a few examples. For a quick look at how transparency works, we'll create a Red ball.

1. Draw a simple Red circle. It looks very flat, but with some shading it can look three-dimensional.

2. Make a copy of the circle using CTRL-C.

3. Paste the copy on top of the original using CTRL-V.

4. Change the color of the copy to Black.

5. Select the Interactive Transparency tool and choose Fountain from the Property Bar.

6. Click the Radial Fill icon.

7. Move the center of the fill towards the upper-left part of the circle.

8. Adjust the size of the transparency circle until the ball looks real to you.

What we did was take the red circle and add black shading through the use of the Interactive Transparency tool. To make the ball look more realistic, we'll make it look like a bright light is shining on the ball.

1. Select the top ball with the transparency and copy it to the clipboard with CTRL-C.

2. Paste in another copy with CTRL-V.

3. Change the fill color of this new transparent object to White.

4. Select the Interactive Transparency tool so that you can edit the transparency.

5. Drag the color White from the color palette and drop it on the black square of the transparent object.

6. Drag Black onto the original white square of the transparent object.

7. Adjust the outside edge of the transparency until you feel it looks good.

Now you've seen a quick example of how to use transparency to create shadows and highlighting so that the red ball looks more realistic. You could have done this by creating a custom fountain fill, but it probably would have taken a little longer. One benefit to this method is that it works with any type of fill and not just a solid color. So you've got one more step to finalize this little project.

1. Select the original red circle. A quick way to do this is by using the TAB key until the red object is selected. Watch the Status Bar until it shows that the selected object has a red fill.

2. Use the Interactive Fill tool to fill the circle with the Wood17m.cpt bitmap fill found in the /Tiles/Wood/Medium directory of the third CD from your CorelDRAW 8 package.

Now you should see a beautiful wooden ball. Figure 21-7 shows the progression of these steps from the original red circle through our wooden ball.

This first example showed you how transparency could be used to add highlights and shadows to objects. There certainly was nothing fancy about how it worked. You just need to observe how light affects objects and re-create that with transparent objects.

21

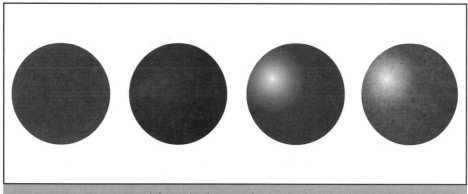

FIGURE 21-7   From left to right, the original red circle, the red circle with shadow applied, the red circle with shadow and highlight, and the wooden ball

Now we're going to merge two photographs together. This technique is very useful if you find two pictures that each contain an element that you would like to use. Getting this effect has traditionally been something that you would do in an image editing package like Corel PHOTO-PAINT. Now you have a choice.

1. Import the files 771017.wi and 771012.wi from the \Photos\Petsii folder on third CD that came with CorelDRAW 8.

2. Select the picture of the kitty, right-click, and choose <u>O</u>rder | To <u>F</u>ront from the pop-up menu.

3. Place the two pictures so that they sit on top of each other and the right third of the kitty picture overlaps the left third of the puppy picture.

4. Select the Interactive Transparency tool, click the kitty's face, and drag to the right edge of the image.

You should now see that the two images seem to merge together. You may need to adjust the transparency somewhat until the picture looks just right. The finished image looks similar to the one shown in Figure 21-8.

Remember that you must have the Interactive Transparency tool selected to see the tools on the Property Bar.

Our last project will introduce you to some of the other settings on the Property Bar. Let's first discuss some of these settings.

The Property Bar shown here is the initial Property Bar shown when the Fountain Transparency type is selected. Clicking the Edit Transparency button will bring up the familiar Fountain Fill dialog box that was discussed in Chapter 10. Remember that when you create transparency, you are creating

21

FIGURE 21-8   On the top are pictures of the kitty and puppy before they are merged to create the finished image on the bottom

a grayscale transparency mask. With the Fountain Transparency, you are using the Fountain Fill to create a gradient from black to white.

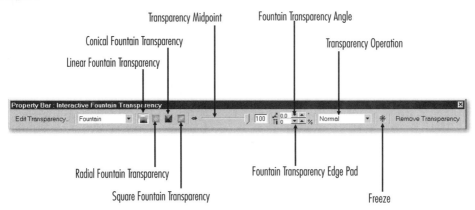

In the case of Fountain Transparency, the Property Bar will have a series of four buttons: for linear, radial, conical, and square fills. These can be changed right on the Property Bar or within the Fountain Fill dialog box.

To the right of the four buttons is a slider control which controls the transparency level at the selected point. It is initially set to 100 percent.

When you are editing the fill, you can choose any colors you want. The darker the color, the more transparency, regardless of what appears on the slider. Unfortunately, the sliders and dialog boxes do not change to reflect each other in this regard. All of the colors will be converted to grayscale for the final transparency.

The next series of settings controls the angle of the fill and the edge padding. These settings are set to change with the Fountain Fill dialog box. You can also make the changes manually. Click the object that has the transparent fill, and you'll see two rectangles with a dotted line between them. The angle on the Property Bar is the angle of this line. Click and drag either of the rectangles to change the angle. The farther the rectangles are inside the edge of the object, the larger the value for the edge pad. If the rectangles are outside the object, there will be no edge pad, and this option will be reset to zero on the Property Bar. If you manually type in a value, the start/end indicators will move back inside of the object.

Another drop-down list just to the right of the text boxes for the angle and edge pad provides all of the different Transparency Operations that are available. These are the same modes that have been available in Corel PHOTO-PAINT. The best way to understand these operations is to simply experiment. While they always work in the same manner, the results are very dependent on the objects beneath the object you have selected, so describing them is like trying to hit a moving target. The modes include Normal, Add, Subtract, Difference, Multiply, Divide, If Lighter, If Darker, Texturize, Hue, Saturation, Lightness, Invert, And, Or, Xor, Red, Green, and Blue. We'll show you an example of using a Transparency Operation in our next project.

If you've finished creating and want to convert your objects into something permanent, click the Freeze icon. This will freeze the transparent object exactly as shown when the Freeze button is selected, and any objects that were showing through will show in the result as well. However, if you move the object, you'll notice that things look strange, since the transparency will not change. Thus, this option is certainly something you should do after everything else is finished. If you need to get back to editing the transparency, you can try using the Undo (CTRL-Z) command. Since Undo is now saved with the document, you can Undo this step even after saving. If you click on the Freeze button a second time, it will toggle back to an unfrozen state and you can continue to edit the object.

 *The resolution of the bitmaps created by the transparency tool is dependent on the resolution of the page. Select Tools | Options | Document | Page | Size to change the resolution.*

The last option on the Property Bar is the Remove Transparency button. This button is pretty self-explanatory. You may also notice that the Status Bar reports that the objects with transparency have a lens applied; after all, consider that Transparency is just a special form of a lens.

So far, we've only discussed adding a Fountain Fill transparency. You can also add several other kinds of transparencies. The Uniform transparency gives the same level to the whole object; this is very similar to what the Transparency lens traditionally offered. You can also use Pattern and Texture transparencies.

Pattern transparencies allow you to choose any of the two-color bitmaps, full-color vectors, or color bitmaps for your transparencies. You can then create some really awesome effects. The Texture transparencies allow you to use any of the many texture fills that were described in Chapter 10.

21

Our next project will paint graffiti onto a brick wall.

1. Draw a rectangle that is approximately 4 inches by 2 inches.

2. Using the Full Color Bitmap Pattern fill, fill the rectangle with the Stone15m.cpt fill found in the \Tiles\Stone\Medium directory of the third CorelDRAW CD.

3. Enter **www.unleash.com** as Artistic Text. Select the font Staccato 555 BT at 48 points and move the text so that it is approximately centered in the "brick wall."

4. Rotate the text 10 to 15 degrees so that it is angled up and to the right. And give it a fill of green.

5. Convert the text to a bitmap. Choose Bitmap | Convert to Bitmap and choose 24-bit RGB, Transparent Background with a resolution of 200 dpi.

6. Now blur the text by choosing Bitmap | Blur | Gaussian Blur. We used a radius of 5 for the blur, but feel free to adjust it until you are happy.

> **NOTE:** *Make sure that you have "Auto inflate bitmaps for bitmap effects" enabled in Tools | Options | Document | General for this effect to work properly.*

Already the text is starting to look as if it were spray painted onto the wall. But we want to take the texture of the bricks into consideration. So let's apply some transparency to the text.

1. With the Interactive Transparency Tool selected, choose a Uniform Transparency and adjust the Starting Transparency slider to 0.

2. Now select Multiply from the Transparency Operation drop-down box and you'll see the brick pattern emerge from the text; it is starting to look very real.

3. Change the Transparency Operation to Difference. The text will change to purple and there will be very little paint in the area between bricks. There's quite a difference just from changing this one option.

Figure 21-9 shows the last two versions of our brick wall. You'll also find this image on the color pages so that you can see the colors.

POWERCLIP

A PowerClip sounds like a heavy-duty hedge trimmer or the latest style in hair styling, but the name is just a fancy marketing term for the ability to paste an object inside of another object. Anything you create in CorelDRAW can be pasted inside any other object or group of objects.

FIGURE 21-9   The top brick wall has the Transparency Operation of Multiply on the text while the bottom version uses Difference

21

When using a PowerClip, you need to become familiar with two basic terms: artwork that will be pasted inside of another object is called the *contents*, and the object in which the contents are placed is called the *container*. The container does not have to be a closed path, but the contents will not be displayed until the container path is closed. The container can be a group, but in that case, separate copies of the contents will be pasted inside each object within the container group.

A PowerClip can create a complex clipping path, and complex clipping paths can generate problems when printing. Therefore, attempt to keep the path of the container object fairly simple. If problems arise, you may have to convert the whole object to a bitmap or use the instructions described at the end of this lesson to export and reimport the PowerClip objects.

CREATING A POWERCLIP

Before you begin creating a PowerClip, there is an option you need to set. Choose Tools | Options | Workspace | Miscellaneous and find the Auto-center New Powerclip contents check box. Make sure that there is *not* a check in this box. Checking this box can cause a tremendous amount of confusion.

> **NOTE:** *The main reason that the Auto-center new Powerclip Contents option is checked by default is so a PowerClip will always result in a visible object within the container object. However, when you create a PowerClip, you will usually place the container in the exact position that you need. Therefore, this option does not need to be checked for these situations.*

Now you need your content object and your container object. Place the container in relation to the contents, knowing that any part of the contents outside of the container will be clipped—it will still exist, but it won't be visible. Once you have everything placed correctly, choose Effects | PowerClip | Place Inside Container. This tells CorelDRAW that you want to put anything that is selected inside a container, but the program has no idea what to use for a container. Therefore, you'll see a large arrow on the screen. Use the arrow to point and click the container object.

Work through a simple example so you'll understand a little better how PowerClip works:

1. Draw a large rectangle and fill it with "cheese." We just used yellow, although it isn't too realistic.

2. Draw a much smaller circle and fill it with "pepperoni." If you don't like pepperoni, substitute your favorite ingredient or ingredients.

3. Duplicate the pepperoni and scatter it all over the cheese until you have a good-looking pizza.

4. Group all of the pizza objects together.

5. Off to the side, draw a triangular slice. You can create a triangle with the Polygon tool and then use the Shape tool to round the outside edge.

6. Drag the slice shape over the top of the rectangle.

7. Select the pizza object and choose E<u>ff</u>ects I P<u>o</u>werClip I <u>P</u>lace Inside Container.

8. Now use the big arrow to point at the slice.

Your result should be a slice of pepperoni pizza, as shown here.

TIP: *If you right-click and drag the "pizza" and drop it onto the "slice," you will receive a pop-up menu when you release the mouse button. That menu contains the option PowerClip <u>I</u>nside. Select that option and you get an interactive method for PowerClipping.*

If you had tried to draw this same object freehand, you would have had to worry about trimming each piece of pepperoni to line up perfectly with the edge of the slice. You can certainly do that, but it's not nearly as easy as using PowerClip.

Now that you have an idea of what PowerClip does, use your imagination to think of the many ways it can be used. One of the more popular uses is for cropping bitmaps. We've been asked thousands of times how to get rid of those stupid white squares around bitmaps. This is something that can be done with the Bitmap Color Mask quite easily if the background is a single solid color that isn't used elsewhere, but it can be quite difficult with a busy background. Using PowerClip, however, it is as simple as drawing an outline around the part of the photograph that you wish to cut out. Sometimes drawing that shape will be time consuming, but it is not a difficult process.

EDITING POWERCLIPS

You've just finished PowerClipping something and it didn't turn out the way you expected. Maybe something was left out, or maybe the positioning was out of whack. No need to undo the PowerClip and start over—you can edit the existing PowerClip.

Select the PowerClip object and choose the Effects | PowerClip | Edit Contents command. The contents will now appear in their entirety, and the container will be displayed as a blue outline. At this point, you can make any changes that you desire. Move things around, recolor them, draw new objects, or do whatever you need to do to make things just right. When you've made all the necessary changes, choose Effects | PowerClip | Finish Editing This Level. This will put the PowerClip back together for you with all of the changes.

The other option you have is to just take the PowerClip completely apart. Simply choose Effects | PowerClip | Extract Contents, and the PowerClip will be broken into the contents and the container object.

WORKING WITH COMPLEX POWERCLIPS

If you find that a PowerClip you've created is causing you problems, you can simplify it by exporting and reimporting the pieces:

1. Select the PowerClip objects.

2. Choose <u>F</u>ile | <u>E</u>xport.

3. Select Encapsulated PostScript (EPS) from the Save As <u>T</u>ype drop-down list.

4. Check the Selected <u>o</u>nly check box and click the Export button.

5. In the EPS Export dialog box, just click OK.

6. Choose <u>F</u>ile | <u>I</u>mport.

7. Find the file you just created and highlight it.

8. Select the PostScript Interpreted (PS, PRN, EPS) file type and click Import. You'll get an Import PostScript dialog box. Just click OK and the file will be imported.

 To get information on the File Export dialog box, see Chapter 27.

Now you should have the original PowerClipped objects back in your drawing. However, the container object no longer hides objects; it actually trimmed them. Now there is no longer a clipping path, and the file should be much easier to print.

Lens, Transparency, and PowerClips are some of the most "flashy" features in CorelDRAW. They also can present the most difficulties in printing. All of these features should be used carefully, not only because of their complexity but also from a design standpoint. And if you're creating the images for the Internet, you're going to convert them into bitmaps anyway.

21

22

FITTING TEXT TO A PATH

The Fit Text to Path effect is probably one of the least understood features in CorelDRAW. Like most of CorelDRAW's features, understanding it boils down to understanding what takes place when you apply the effect to an object or group of objects. When you understand how it works, using it becomes easy. If you want to unravel the mystery of the Fit Text to Path feature, take the time to read this chapter from beginning to end. The last section of the chapter describes how to use the interactive method with the Fit Text to Path controls on the Property Bar. First, though, you will learn how the Fit Text to Path effect works using the Fit Text to Path roll-up.

FITTING TEXT TO A PATH

Fitting text to a path dynamically links the text to the path so that the text flows along the path. "Dynamically linked" means that the text is affixed to the path, and the relationship between the text and the path will remain the same even if you modify the text or the path.

For example, if you use the Fit Text to Path feature to place a word or a string of words on a path, you can change the words or you can change the path, and the words and the path still stay together. CorelDRAW recognizes two types of paths: closed paths and open paths. The Fit Text to Path roll-up automatically adjusts for the type of path you select. So you see, it isn't as complicated as you may have thought.

THE FIT TEXT TO PATH ROLL-UP

The Fit Text to Path roll-up provides the controls for placing the text in the correct location and orientation on the path. The Fit Text to Path roll-up is accessed by choosing View | Roll-ups | Fit Text to Path. When text and a path are selected together, the roll-up configuration will change depending on whether a closed or open path is selected. Figure 22-1 shows the roll-up with text and an open path selected. Figure 22-2 shows the roll-up with text and a closed path selected.

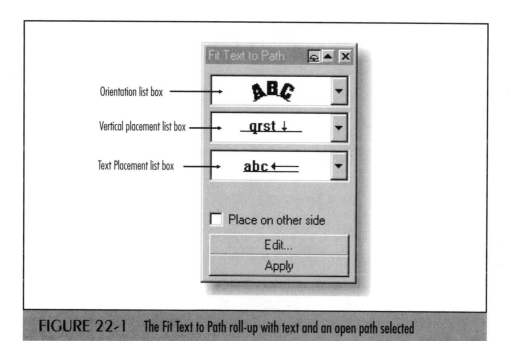

Orientation list box

Vertical placement list box

Text Placement list box

FIGURE 22-1   The Fit Text to Path roll-up with text and an open path selected

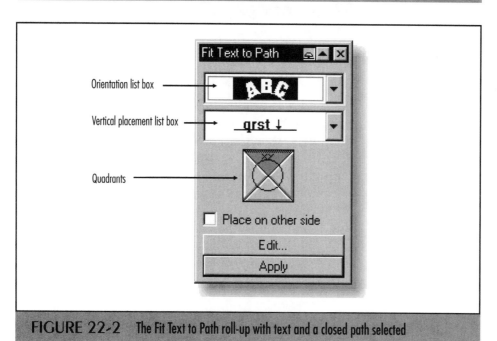

Orientation list box

Vertical placement list box

Quadrants

FIGURE 22-2   The Fit Text to Path roll-up with text and a closed path selected

22

FITTING TEXT TO AN OPEN PATH

Fitting text to an open path is the easier of the two methods of fitting text to paths. To begin, choose View | Roll-ups | Fit Text to Path to open the roll-up. Follow these steps to place text on an open path:

1. Draw a curved line on the page using the Freehand tool. Use the example shown here below.

2. Type the words **This isn't as hard as I thought** on the page. Use a nice bold font of 24 points.

3. Select the text and the curved line together.

4. Click the Apply button. Your text should now look similar to the example shown here.

Now that you're an expert at putting text on a path, let's see what else you can do once the text is on the path. For starters, you can change the way the letters lie on the path by changing the orientation of the letters. Select the text on the path you just created and then scroll in the Orientation list box (refer to Figure 22-1) and select the second style from the top. Click Apply again.

Your text should now appear to be leaning along with the shape of the curve, as in the example shown here:

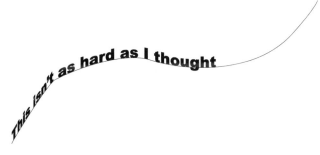

With your text on the path still selected, go back to the default options by selecting the top style in the Orientation list box. Now scroll in the Text Placement list box and choose the middle option (this and the other two options are the justification options for the text). After you have selected the text placement, click the Apply button again. Your text on a path should now be placed in the center of the path and should look like the example shown here:

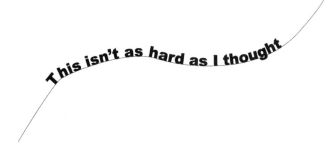

With the text on the path still selected, select the third option in the Text Placement list box to use right justification. Select the second option in the Vertical Placement list box to display the text under the path. Now click the Apply button to see the results. Your text on a path should look like the example shown here. The text should be right-justified and below the path instead of on top of the path.

ADJUSTING THE TEXT ON AN OPEN PATH

You can change the position of the text string or individual letters along the path using the two methods described next.

Using the Fit Text to Path Offsets Dialog Box

To use the first method, click the Edit button on the roll-up. This will bring up the Fit Text to Path Offsets dialog box. Enter the amount in inches that you want to move the text along the path. For example, if you want to move the text to the left 1 inch, you would enter –1.0. To move it to the right, you would enter 1.0.

Using the Shape Tool to Edit Text on an Open Path

To use the second method, the one you may find the easiest, use the interactive method. Practice using the interactive method by drawing a line on the page and then typing the words **This is easy** on the page. Select the text and the line and click the Apply button on the roll-up. Follow these instructions to move the text along the path:

1. Select the Shape tool in the toolbox and use it to select the text on the path.

2. When the text is selected, marquee select all the nodes attached to the individual letters.

3. Click any one of the nodes with the Shape tool and drag the string of text manually along the path. When you are satisfied with the placement, release the left mouse button and select the Pick tool. Practice dragging the text left and right on the path. Your text should look like this when you have the text selected with the Shape tool.

In addition to moving the entire text string, you can adjust the spacing of individual letters by selecting their respective nodes and dragging them along the path. A good example of this is shown here. The upper string of text has been placed on a wavy line. Notice that certain letters crawl on top of each other. In the bottom string of text, individual letters have been dragged along the path so all the letters appear evenly spaced.

You can also adjust the word spacing along the path by using the Shape tool while holding down the CTRL key and then dragging the right handle (the horizontal chevron arrow beneath the path) to the right. Practice this technique by placing five or six words on a path. Here is an example of the results of this technique:

No chapter on fitting text to a path would be complete without placing a text string on a spiral. Follow the steps here to place a string of text on a spiral:

1. Draw a three-revolution spiral on the page (if you don't know how to draw a spiral, see Chapter 4).

2. Type the words **Going down the drain** on the page using a bold font.

3. Select the text and the spiral.

4. Use the default options in both the Orientation and Vertical Placement list boxes.

5. Select the right justification setting in the Text Placement list box.

6. Click the Apply button.

7. Select the Shape tool and use it to drag the right spacing handle to the right while holding down the CTRL key until the text is approximately in the configuration shown here:

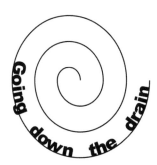

MOVING THE PATH

Up until now you have learned how to place and move words and letters along the path. Now you will discover that you can also move the path. You can move the path to either dramatically change the shape of the path or just subtlety change the path for alignment purposes. The example here shows the path before and after it is moved. Remember that the path is dynamically linked to the text, so when the path is changed, the text follows.

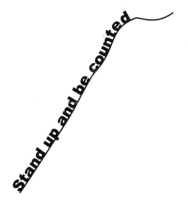

To move the path, you select the Shape tool just as you did when you moved the text on the path. However, this time, instead of selecting the text with the Shape tool, select the path. When the path is selected, the nodes on the path will be revealed. Then it's simply a matter of clicking and dragging the nodes and moving the node control handles until you're satisfied with the shape of the path.

If you are not familiar with the use of the node control handles, see Chapter 8.

> **CAUTION:** *As a rule, do not enable the Place on Other Side check box when placing text on an open path because the text will be placed backwards. If you want to place the text on the other side of the path, use the options provided in the Vertical Placement list box. This does not mean you should never use the Place on Other Side option. It can be used for a special effect.*

FITTING TEXT TO A CLOSED PATH

When you fit text to a closed path, CorelDRAW senses you have selected a closed path and changes the roll-up display to the configuration shown in Figure 22-2 at the beginning of this chapter.

Fitting text to ellipses is commonly used when creating logos. For example, a Little League team may have its insignia inside a circle with the team name flowing around the circle. Other artistic uses include flowing text around an object.

The process of fitting text to a closed path is almost as simple as placing text on a open path, yet many users have difficulty when it comes to adding a second word or string of text to the ellipse. The secret lies in using the very feature you were just cautioned not to use: the Place on Other Side option.

FITTING TEXT TO A CIRCLE

The best way to learn how to place text on a closed path is to jump right in and do it. Follow these steps to place two separate words on an ellipse:

1. Select the Ellipse tool from the toolbox and draw a perfect circle on the page by holding down the CTRL key as you drag out the ellipse. Make the circle approximately 5 inches in diameter.

2. Type **ARIZONA** on the page using all caps and a bold font of 36 points.

3. Select the text and the circle. Leave the options in the roll-up set to their defaults.

4. Click the Apply button.

5. The word ARIZONA should now be placed on the top of the circle, as shown here.

The first part was as easy as placing text on an open path. Now place the second word at the bottom of the circle.

6. Type **SIDEWINDERS.**

7. Select the new word and then select the circle.

8. Leave the default setting in the Orientation list box.

9. Choose the second option in the Vertical Placement list box, which shows the text just underneath the line.

10. Click the bottom quadrant.

11. Check the Place on Other Side check box.

12. Click the Apply button.

Your circle should now look like the one shown here. We added a special touch by placing the text on the path onto a clipart image of a baseball. We removed the outline so only the text appears. We also added the clipart image of a rattlesnake. Before you think we don't know our sports teams—we do realize that the real baseball team in Arizona is called by another name.

22

You have just learned the secret of placing two separate words on a closed path. The key to your success was the fact that you enabled the Place on Other Side option. If you want to see what would happen if you didn't enable this option, select the text on a path, remove the check mark, and click the Apply button again. The text will be upside down and backward.

Editing Text on the Circle

Now you will change the words on the circle. While you're at it, you'll change the font and point size as well. Follow these steps:

1. With the Pick tool selected, click the word ARIZONA to select the text on the path. The Status Bar will indicate that you have selected a compound object of three elements.

2. Hold down the CTRL key and click the word ARIZONA two more times (this does not mean to double-click). After you have clicked the word a second time, it should have eight selection handles surrounding it. This means you have isolated the text from the path. The Status Bar will confirm this fact by telling you that you have selected Artistic Text and by displaying the name of the font you used.

3. Choose Te<u>x</u>t | E<u>d</u>it Text (CTRL-SHIFT-T) to bring up the Edit Text dialog box.

4. Replace the word ARIZONA by highlighting the word and typing in the name of your favorite state or city.

5. While still in the Edit Text dialog box, scroll in the Font list box and pick another font.

6. Still in the Edit Text dialog box, click the down arrow in the Size list box and choose a new point size.

7. Click the OK button to see your changes take effect. Notice that even if your replacement word had more or fewer letters, the text still remained centered at the top of the circle.

8. Click the word SIDEWINDERS and repeat steps 2 and 3.

9. Change SIDEWINDERS to the name of your favorite sports team—perhaps a team based in the city or state you used at the top of the circle.

10. Use the same font and point size that you used for the name you used at the top of the circle. Make sure the text is highlighted in the Edit Text dialog box when making the changes.

11. Click the OK button again to view the finished product.

 *Editing text on an open path is done the same way as on an ellipse. Click the text while holding down the CTRL key to isolate the text and then change the text in the Edit Text dialog box.*

PLACING TEXT ON THE INSIDE OF A CIRCLE

Now that you learned how to place text on the outside of a circle, follow the steps here to place t ext on the inside of a circle:

1. Draw a perfect circle on the page approximately 5 inches in diameter.

2. Type the words **I'm going around** using a bold font of 36 points.

3. Select both the words and the ellipse.

4. Leave the default setting in the Orientation list box.

5. Choose the second option in the Vertical Placement list box, which shows the text underneath the line.

6. Use the default Quadrant setting, and then click the Apply button.

Your text should now look like the example shown here:

1. Now put some more text inside and at the bottom of the circle. Type **in circles** on the page.

2. Select the new words and the ellipse together.

3. Leave the default options set in the Orientation list box.

4. Choose the first option in the Vertical Placement list box, which shows the text resting on the line with the descenders below the line (the default setting).

5. Click the bottom quadrant.

6. Check the Place on Other Side check box.

7. Click the Apply button to see the results.

Your circle and text should now look like the example shown here:

Now that you know the secret of placing and editing two separate words on a circle, you shouldn't hesitate to use this effect in your projects.

Adjusting Text on a Closed Path

There's more to learn about working with text on a closed path. You can move the text along the path of the ellipse just as you did when you moved the text on an open path. This time you will also learn how to move the text away from the path. Follow these steps:

1. Draw a 5-inch-diameter circle on the page as you did in the previous exercises.

2. Type the words **I'm going around in circles** on the page using a bold font of 36 points.

3. Select the text and the ellipse and click the Apply button.

4. With the text on a path still selected, click the Edit button to bring up the Fit Text to Path Offsets dialog box.

5. Enter **0.16** in the Distance from Path parameter box and click OK.

6. Click the Apply button again.

The text and the circle should look like the example shown here:

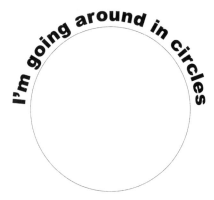

7. Select the Shape tool from the toolbox and click the text.

8. Marquee select the entire text string.

9. Click one of the nodes on the text string and drag the entire string of text to the right about a quarter of the way around the circle. Release the left mouse button when you're satisfied with the placement.

The text and the circle should look something like the example shown here:

USING THE INTERACTIVE FIT TEXT TO PATH METHOD

Now that you know how to place text on a path using the Fit Text to Path roll-up, it's time to learn the quicker interactive method. The interactive method uses the Text tool in combination with the Property Bar, speeding up the process of placing text on a path. Figure 22-3 shows the Property Bar when text on an open path is selected. Figure 22-4 shows the Property Bar when text on a closed path is selected.

As you can see by the options on the Property Bar, everything you can do using the roll-up, you can do using the Property Bar. The only difference is that the sequence of certain steps is different when using the Property Bar rather than the roll-up.

PLACING TEXT ON AN OPEN PATH

Practice using the interactive method in combination with the Property Bar by following the steps here. When you are told to click on a list box, spin box, or button, use the one on the Property Bar.

22

1. Draw a curved line on the page using the Freehand tool.
2. Click the Text tool in the toolbox.

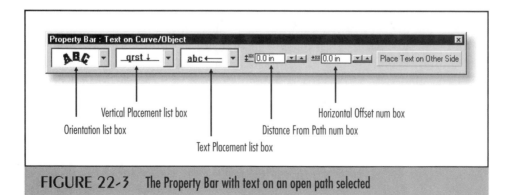

FIGURE 22-3 The Property Bar with text on an open path selected

3. Place the text cursor directly on the line. When the text cursor changes to the I-beam cursor, click to place a text insertion point at the beginning of the line.

4. Type **CorelDRAW Version 8 is Great!** The text will automatically be placed on the path.

5. Click the desktop area to deselect the text.

6. Click the text again to select the text on the path.

7. Click the down arrow of the Text Placement list box and select the Center Justification option from the drop-down list. Your text on a path should look similar to the text on a path shown here.

8. With the text on the path selected, click and hold the up arrow of the Distance from Path num box until you reach 0.2 inch. Your text should move upward away from the line by 0.2 inch as shown here.

As you have now learned, the options on the Property Bar affect text placed on an open path just as they do when you use the roll-up. The difference is that you don't have to click the Apply button or open and make changes in the Offsets dialog box to make the changes take effect. Practice using the other options; you will discover that they, too, work like the options on the roll-up and in the Fit Text to Path Offsets dialog box.

Editing Text on an Open Path Using the Interactive Method

To change fonts using the Property Bar, select the text while holding down the CTRL key. This action isolates the font from the path, allowing you to change the font or the font size in the respective list boxes on the Property Bar. Additionally, you can use the Shape tool to edit text on an open path just as you can text placed on the path using the Fit Text to Path roll-up.

PLACING TEXT ON A CLOSED PATH

Placing text on a closed path is not quite the same with the interactive method as with the Fit Text to Path roll-up. You will have to learn an extra step to place text on the top and bottom of a closed path such as an ellipse if you use the controls on the Property Bar. Figure 22-4 shows the Property Bar when text on a Closed path is selected.

Follow the steps here to place two strings of text on an ellipse using the options on the Property Bar. You will examine the differences between this method and the roll-up method after you finish the exercise.

22

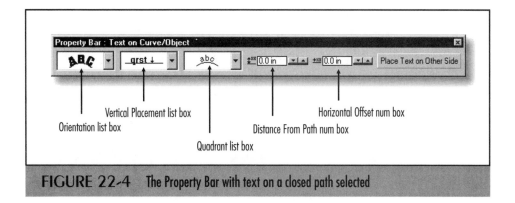

FIGURE 22-4   The Property Bar with text on a closed path selected

1. Draw an ellipse on the page. Give it a radial fill if you wish.

2. Click the Text tool and place the crosshair of the text cursor on the outline at the top of the ellipse (the text cursor will change into an I-beam).

3. Type the words **Sat on a wall**. As you type, the text will automatically be center-justified on the top of the ellipse.

4. When you're finished typing, click the Pick tool and the text will be selected. If you accidentally deselect the text, hold down the CTRL key and click the text to reselect it. While the text is selected, change to a nice bold font by choosing one from the Font list box on the Property Bar.

5. Change the font size to 36 points by selecting this point size from the Font Size list on the Property Bar.

6. Click anywhere on the page or desktop to deselect the text.

7. Click the text again to select the text and the a path. The Property Bar will now change to the Fit Text to Path options.

8. Click the down arrow of the Vertical Placement list box and choose the second option down, which shows the text beneath the line. Notice that the text immediately moves inside the ellipse, following the contour of the inside of the ellipse.

9. Click the down arrow of the Text Placement list box and choose the third option down, which shows the text underneath an arc. Notice that the text immediately moves to the inside bottom of the ellipse and the text is backward.

10. Click the Place on Other Side button. The text is moved from the inside of the ellipse to the outside bottom of the ellipse and is no longer backward. The text and ellipse should look something like this illustration.

11. Now you are ready to place the next string of text on the top of the ellipse. Select the Text tool and place the crosshair of the text cursor on the outline at the top of the ellipse (the text cursor will change into an I-beam).

12. Type the words **Humpty Dumpty**. As you type, the text will automatically be center-justified at the top of the ellipse again.

13. When you're finished typing, click the Pick tool and the text will be selected. With the text still selected, change the font to the same font you used before by choosing it from the Font list box on the Property Bar.

14. Change the font size to 36 points by selecting the point size from the Font Size list on the Property Bar.

15. Click the desktop to deselect the text.

Your text and ellipse should now look like the example shown here. We added a little extra touch to show what happened when Humpty Dumpty fell off the wall.

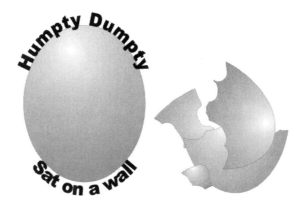

Congratulate yourself on placing two strings of text on an ellipse using the interactive method. When you get used to this new way of working, it will be faster than using the roll-up method.

 *There is an alternate method to begin the process of interactively placing text on a path. If the text is already on the page and you want it placed on a path, select the text and the path and choose Text | Fit Text to Path. The text will automatically be placed on the path. Once the text is on the path, use the controls on the Property Bar to make any additional changes*

PLACING TEXT WITHIN A CLOSED PATH

One of the more interesting uses of the new interactive method is typing text directly inside a closed path. This method differs from placing text inside a closed path where the text is dynamically linked to the path. Typing text directly inside a closed path actually wraps paragraph text within a shape you select, much as if you had used the Copy From command in the Envelope roll-up (see Chapter 18). However, the interactive method is far superior to using the envelope method because it is not dependent on the physical size and shape of the text.

Practice using this new tool by following these steps:

1. Draw an ellipse on the page.
2. Select the Text tool from the toolbox.

3. Hold down the SHIFT key and place the crosshairs of the text cursor on the outline at the top of the ellipse (the text cursor will change to an I-beam with the letters AB in a box next to it). Your ellipse should now look like this:

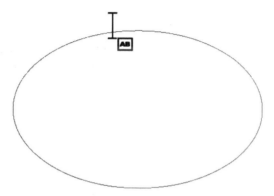

4. With the I-beam still displayed, click once with the left mouse button. A text insertion point will be placed at the top middle portion of the ellipse and a dotted line will flow around the inside of the ellipse, as shown here.

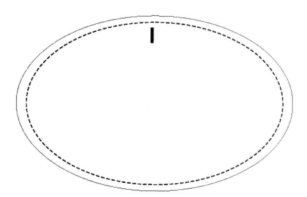

22

5. Begin typing inside the ellipse and your text will automatically flow from one side of the ellipse to the other. Fill the entire ellipse with text.

6. When you're finished typing, click the Pick tool to complete the task. You will now see your text inside the ellipse, as shown here. You can fill the ellipse with any of CorelDRAW's fills as a background to the text.

Notice
we can now type in the
oval and the text is contained
within the boundaries of the ellipse.
We have actually created an oval-shaped
Paragraph Text bounding box containing
the text. Once the text is placed inside
the ellipse, the ellipse could be
removed leaving the Paragraph
Text in the shape of an
oval

7. You may want to remove the ellipse so that only the text is visible in the shape of the ellipse. To do this, hold down the CTRL key and select the Paragraph Text (this will isolate the text from the ellipse). Press the TAB key and the ellipse will be selected. Now press the DELETE key to delete the ellipse. Check the status line first to make sure you are deleting the Control Ellipse and not the Paragraph Text Inside a Path. Do this now and your text should look similar to the text shown here.

Notice
we can now type in the
oval and the text is contained
within the boundaries of the ellipse.
We have actually created an oval-shaped
Paragraph Text bounding box containing
the text. Once the text is placed inside
the ellipse, the ellipse could be
removed leaving the Paragraph
Text in the shape of an
oval

8. Now select the text again and the status line will indicate you have selected only Paragraph Text (see Figure 22-5). Notice the window shade handles attached to the top and bottom of the ellipse. By clicking and dragging on these handles you can resize the shape of the paragraph text.

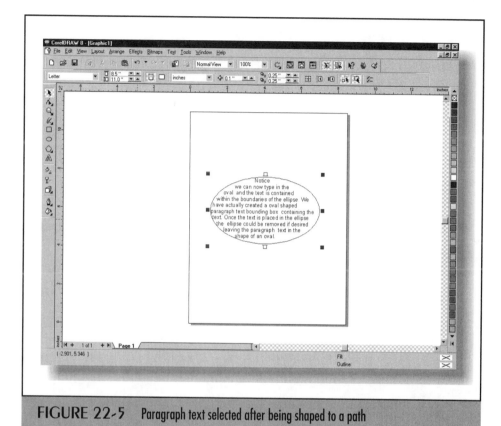

FIGURE 22-5   Paragraph text selected after being shaped to a path

If you try to place more text inside a shape than it will physically handle it will get cut off. To solve this problem you would need to either change the point size of the text so that all the text fits or make the shape larger.

A real-world example of interactively typing text inside a shape is shown in the following illustrations. A symbols clipart image of a plaque was used as the shape. This type of shape posed a small problem in that the text flowed straight across the plaque correctly but lower than expected. The bounding box controlling the placement of the text prevented the text from being placed higher. To solve the problem, we added a small symbol at the top.

22

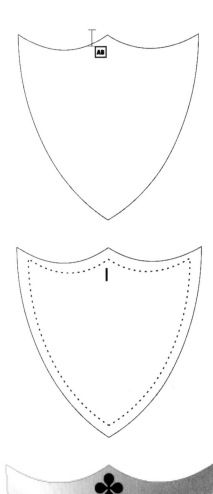

FITTING PARAGRAPH TEXT TO A PATH

Fitting paragraph text to paths can provide some very interesting results. When we interactively typed text into a shape, new paragraph text was created. Flowing existing paragraph text into a shape is done differently. This unique manipulation of Paragraph Text is described in Chapter 6, "Creating and Manipulating Text."

COMPARING THE ROLL-UP AND INTERACTIVE METHODS

The difference between the roll-up method and the interactive method when placing two separate text objects on a closed path (such as an ellipse or rectangle) is that you must work backward if you have always used the roll-up method. Remember, in the roll-up method you placed the first text object on top of the circle and then placed the second text object on the bottom of the circle. The interactive method requires you to work in a specific order because any additional text added to a closed path is automatically placed at the top of the closed path. This means you have to move any previously placed text to a different location on the path to make room for the newly added text.

> *Technically, you can place a second text object on the top of a closed path if another text object is already there. The problem is, the second text object will be hard to select because it will be obscured by the first text object. It is best to follow the steps outlined earlier.*

This chapter has taught you several different ways to place text on a path using both the Fit Text to Path roll-up and the interactive method. You may be wondering which method is best to use. Based on our experience, we recommend using the new interactive method with the Property Bar. We didn't begin the chapter with the interactive method because we felt you would get a better understanding of the Fit Text to Path effect by first learning the roll-up method and then adapting to the interactive method.

23

COLOR ADJUSTMENTS
AND BITMAP EFFECTS

CorelDRAW 8 offers color adjustment capabilities on vector and bitmap objects plus the ability to apply bitmap effects to bitmaps right in CorelDRAW itself. These new features eliminate the need to open Corel PHOTO-PAINT to use many of its effects.

The ability to make global color adjustments to the entire drawing or individual parts of a drawing can greatly improve the look of the final image. The ability to apply bitmap effects to imported bitmap images, or vector images that have been converted to bitmaps, can lessen the need to use an image editing program like Corel PHOTO-PAINT.

The color adjustment controls are located in the Effects drop-down menu, and the Bitmap effects are located in the Bitmaps drop-down menu.

COLOR ADJUSTMENTS

There are six color adjustments available in the Effects | Color Adjustments child menu, shown in Figure 23-1.

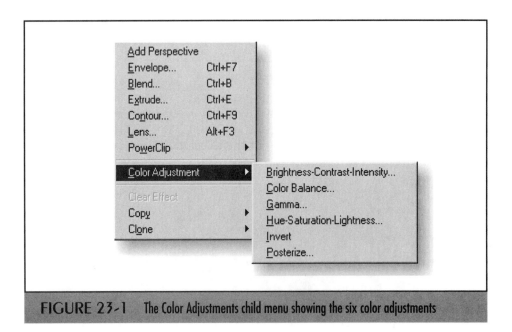

FIGURE 23-1   The Color Adjustments child menu showing the six color adjustments

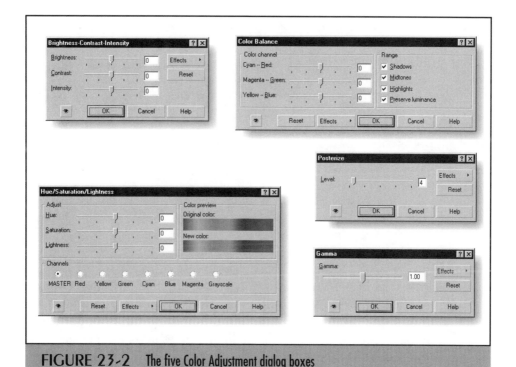

FIGURE 23-2 The five Color Adjustment dialog boxes

Each of these color adjustments can be applied to either bitmap images or vector images. Figure 23-2 shows each of the color adjustment dialog boxes that you would see if you selected the various options from the Color Adjustment child menu. The Invert command (not shown in Figure 23-2) does not have a dialog box because its function simply inverts (uses the complementary colors of) the colors of the selected objects.

The color adjustments are described here.

Brightness-Contrast-Intensity	Allows you to make individual adjustments to the brightness, contrast, and intensity of the selected objects or the entire image.
Color Balance	Allows you to make adjustments to the color values in the image. The controls are arranged in complementary pairs of the primary (RGB) and secondary (CMY) colors. Notice that the RGB values are on the right and the CMY values are on the left. Basically, these controls allow you to replace certain colors with their complements in varying degrees.

Gamma	Enhances the detail in low contrast images without greatly affecting the shadows or highlights. The slider control darkens or lightens a normal image while maintaining the contrast relationship between colors in the image.
Hue, Saturation & Lightness	Allows you to individually control the hue, saturation, and lightness of an object or the entire image. Use the slider controls or enter values directly in the parameter boxes.
Posterize	Allows you to reduce the number of colors in an image by moving the Level slider. The lower the number, the fewer the color ranges used until finally the colors are reduced to solid blocks of color. Negative values of the colors are also used, producing abstract-like images. Use the slider control to determine the number of colors in the image.

Figure 23-3 shows a CorelDRAW vector image of a calendar on the left and a duplicate calendar on the right. The cartoon image of the donkey sweeping leaves has been lightened by moving the Lightness slider to a setting of 70 in the Hue, Saturation & Lightness dialog box. The Master radio button was left checked (the default mode), therefore lightening the Cyan, Magenta, and blue in the image. Making the image lighter gives a watermark effect to the image and makes the calendar more readable where it overlays the cartoon.

FIGURE 23-3   Using the lightness slider on a portion of the duplicate calendar

Using this lightness control on your images can produce some very pleasing results. The ability to control which colors are affected adds greatly to the effectiveness of this filter.

Figure 23-4 shows the effects of using the hue adjustments on duplicate clipart images of a Bachelor flower. Changing the hue allows you to change the overall color of the flower from the original blue to pinks, purples, and yellows by entering positive and negative numbers using the slider control. With this simple control, you can change the colors of your images to fit the overall look and feel of the project. Think about it; what easier way is there to change a simple blue flower into a beautiful bouquet of different colored flowers?

Figure 23-5 shows two identical images of a small child reading a book to her friend. The top image is the original, and the bottom image uses the

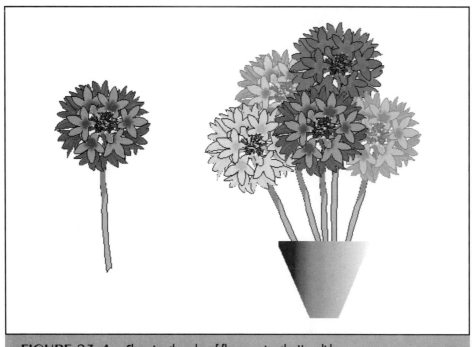

FIGURE 23-4   Changing the color of flowers using the Hue slider

FIGURE 23-5   Using the Posterize color adjustment on a photo

Posterize color adjustment with a Level setting of 3. You can still see what the overall image is after the posterizing effect has been applied, but it now looks more abstract. If you would like to use this image, it is on CD3, Photos. The path to the file is Photos/children/513053.

BITMAP EFFECTS

The Bitmaps drop-down menu, shown in Figure 23-6, contains five bitmap editing controls, seven bitmap effects categories, and five plug-in filters.

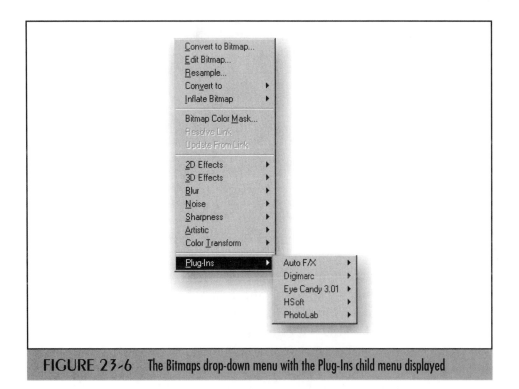

FIGURE 23-6 The Bitmaps drop-down menu with the Plug-Ins child menu displayed

The first four entries in the drop-down menu are described here. The other options are described a bit later.

23

Convert to Bitmap	Use this command to convert a vector image to a bitmap image. You must use this command on vector images before you can use any of the bitmap effects.
Edit Bitmap	Use this command to edit bitmaps in CorelDRAW that can't be edited using the effects available in the Bitmaps drop-down menu. For example, if you want to paint the image with Corel PHOTO-PAINT's Airbrush tool, you have to do it in Corel PHOTO-PAINT, not in CorelDRAW. When you choose this command, Corel PHOTO-PAINT is opened with your bitmap displayed. After making the necessary changes, click Save in Corel PHOTO-PAINT's File menu and then exit PHOTO-PAINT. The CorelDRAW screen will reappear, showing your modified bitmap image.

Resample	Choose the Resample command to change the size or resolution of the bitmap image using the Resample dialog box.
Convert To	The Convert To command lets you change the bitmap image from one type to another. For example, you can convert an RGB 24-bit image to a grayscale 8-bit image (you can convert a color image to grayscale. More important, if you are incorporating bitmap images into your CorelDRAW files and those files will be output with process colors, you should always convert color bitmaps to CMYK 32-bit images so they will print correctly.

USING THE BITMAP COLOR MASK

When you choose Bitmaps | Bitmap Color Mask, the Bitmap Color Mask dialog box appears (see Figure 23-7). The bitmap color mask is most frequently used to make certain colors in a bitmap transparent. For example, when you import bitmaps, they often appear using a rectangular background filled with white. Making the white background transparent so the underlying image shows through is the job of the bitmap color mask. Figure 23-7 is a good example of how the color mask works. The image on the left has been imported from CD3 (using Photos\Images\Cartoon\ Alien15.tif). You can see the white background of the bitmap image against the gray background of the page. The image on the right has been adjusted using the bitmap color mask. The background color has been made transparent, allowing the gray background of the page to show through.

The actual process of making a color transparent in a bitmap is as follows:

1. Select the imported bitmap image.

2. Open the Bitmap Color Mask dialog box (choose Bitmaps | Bitmap Color Mask).

3. Click the top color bar.

4. Click the Eyedropper tool. The cursor will change into an eyedropper.

5. Use the eyedropper to sample the color you want to make transparent (in this case, the white background). A check mark will be placed next to the color bar, and the color you sampled will appear in the color bar.

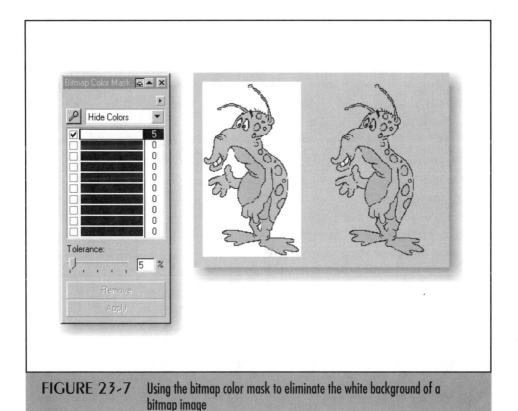

FIGURE 23-7   Using the bitmap color mask to eliminate the white background of a bitmap image

23

6. Move the Tolerance slider to the right until you reach 5%. The Tolerance slider controls the range of color hues that will be made transparent. In the case of white, setting the slider to 5% simply allows for any slight variation or imperfection in the color white.

7. Click the Apply button to see the results.

The bitmap color mask works great on most bitmap images with solid background colors, but it is not the answer to all your masking needs. For the best results, you should import bitmap images that require the backgrounds to be removed as CPT images, with the image made into a floating object. For information on how to create floating objects, refer to *Corel PHOTO-PAINT 8: The Official Guide* by David Huss (Osborne/McGraw-Hill, 1997).

IMPORTING BITMAPS WITHOUT BACKGROUNDS

In the past, you couldn't get rid of that pesky white background when you imported a bitmap image. This problem has now been solved. The answer lies in one of two methods used to create the bitmap file. The first method is to open PHOTO-PAINT, mask the portion of the bitmap image you want to isolate, and save the file with a .tif extension. It is important that the mask be present when the file is saved as a .tif. The second method is to convert the mask you created into a floating object. Use the Edit |Copy to File command and save the file with a .cpt extension. You can now import the bitmap images into CorelDRAW. If you used the mask only method, the bitmap will appear with only the masked area displayed. The entire bitmap image will be there, but just the masked portion will be visible.

If you used the second method, the floating object will appear without a background. This ability to import masks and floating objects virtually eliminates the need to use the bitmap color mask. It is often easier and more accurate to open a normal bitmap in Corel PHOTO-PAINT and create a mask or floating object, then copied and saved as a .cpt file and imported into CorelDRAW. For a comprehensive discussion of creating floating objects in Corel PHOTO-PAINT, refer to *Corel PHOTO-PAINT 8: The Official Guide*.

There are a number of floating objects already available on CD3. The image at the bottom of Figure 23-8 shows one of these floating objects correctly placed on top of an image of a seascape. Importing this type of bitmap image is no different than importing any other image. Choose Import from the File menu and change to the CD drive where the image is stored. Locate the file using the Import dialog box. When you find the file you want, click the Import button to bring the file onto the CorelDRAW page.

If you want to re-create the image shown at the bottom of Figure 23-8, begin by importing the background image of the seascape from CD3. The path to the file is Photos\Coasts\380000.wi. When this particular image is imported, it will be about twice the size of the page (assuming that your page size is 8.5"x11"). Drag one of the corner selection handles of the image inward to reduce the image's size to fit the page. Now it's time to import the floating

FIGURE 23-8   Importing a Bitmap image containing a Floating Object

23

object image of the eagle. The path to the eagle is Objects\Animals\Eagle2.cpt. When this particular object is imported, it will be smaller than what you will want. Increase its size by dragging one of the corner selection handles outward until the image reaches the desired size.

When you import a floating object like the eagle, although it looks similar to any imported bitmap, it is actually made of a group of two bitmaps: the eagle itself and a white background. To remove the white background from the object, click the Ungroup button on the Property Bar. When the two bitmaps are ungrouped, delete the white background. Your image should now look similar to the image at the bottom of Figure 23-8.

CONVERTING TO BITMAPS AND THE BITMAP EFFECTS FILTERS

The remaining entries in the Bitmaps drop-down menu are bitmap effects filters. The ability to use these effects within CorelDRAW lets you work more efficiently because you don't need to open Corel PHOTO-PAINT to apply an effect to an imported or converted bitmap.

Basically, all the bitmap effects in Corel PHOTO-PAINT are available in CorelDRAW, with the exception of those effects that require the bitmap image to be masked before the effect can be applied. Masking is a Corel PHOTO-PAINT procedure and cannot be done in CorelDRAW.

You notice we mentioned converted bitmaps in the first paragraph. Yes, you can convert an existing vector image into a bitmap right in CorelDRAW itself. Simply select the vector object or group of objects and choose Bitmaps | Convert to Bitmap. The Convert to Bitmap dialog box shown here will appear.

The options available in the dialog box are

▶ *Color* Click the down arrow and choose the color depth that fits the way the image will be used. The default is 32-Bit CMYK because generally you will be outputting to a printer that supports CMYK.

► *Dithered*   Choose this option if you are using a color depth of 256 or less.

► *Transparent Background*   Choose this option to eliminate the white box around the image.

► *Use Color Profile*   Choose this option if you are using a color profile for the rest of the document.

► *Resolution*   Click the down arrow in the num box and select the appropriate resolution for the document.

► *Anti-aliasing*   Choose the appropriate setting for the type of bitmap you are creating. If you choose Normal or Super-sampling, additional colors will be added to the edges of objects in the image that have contrast to each other. This gives these edges the illusion of smoothness. These colors are a combination of each adjacent color. For example, if a red color is adjacent to a green color, anti-aliasing would add pixels containing tints of red and green where the two colors come together. When a color is adjacent to the background color, which would often be white when converting a vector to a bitmap, anti-aliasing would add shades of gray and tints of the color next to the white background. As a rule of thumb, choose Anti-aliasing when converting a vector object to a bitmap. To get the best anti-aliasing, choose Super-sampling.

This chapter can't cover all the effects available; however, the following sections point out a few of the more spectacular effects that you may want to use. The only thing you need to remember is that the bitmap must be selected before you can apply the effect.

PAGE CURL

Page Curl is one of the most popular effects. The Page Curl dialog box with an image that has the effect applied is shown in Figure 23-9.

To use the Page Curl effect, follow these steps:

1. Select the bitmap.

2. Choose <u>B</u>itmaps I <u>3</u>D Effects I Page <u>C</u>url.

23

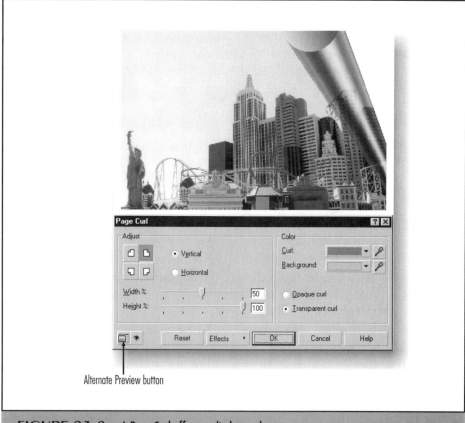

Alternate Preview button

FIGURE 23-9 A Page Curl effect applied to a photo

3. Select the corner that you want to curl.

4. Use the slider controls for both the Width and Height of the curl.

5. Choose either Vertical or Horizontal orientation.

6. Choose either Opaque or Transparent for the curl.

7. Click a color button for both the curl and the background. If you want to use a color from the image, use the Eyedropper tool to sample a color in the image.

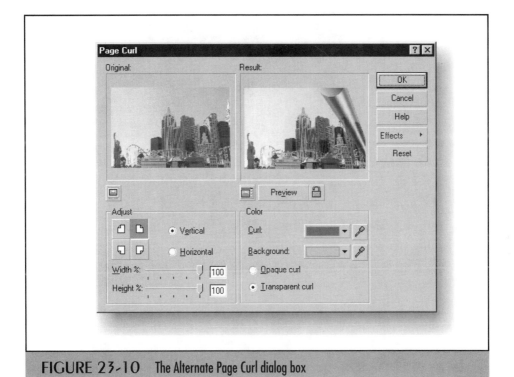

FIGURE 23-10 The Alternate Page Curl dialog box

23

8. Click the Preview button (the eye) to see the effect. If you are not satisfied, continue to change settings. If you prefer to use the alternate Page Curl dialog box (see Figure 23-10), click the Alternate Preview button to the left of the Preview button, the one located at the lower-left corner of the default Page Curl dialog box. The benefit of using this dialog box is that the preview is faster.

9. When you are satisfied with the results in either of the dialog boxes, click the OK button.

VIGNETTE

The Vignette effect is popular for use on portraits. Figure 23-11 shows this effect applied to a photo of a girl on her way to a rodeo. To use the Vignette filter, choose Bitmaps | Artistic | Vignette.

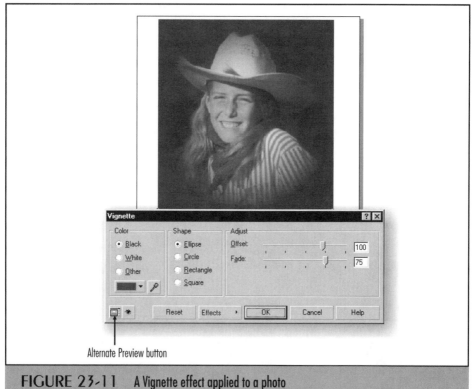

Alternate Preview button

FIGURE 23-11   A Vignette effect applied to a photo

Three vignette color modes are available: Black, White, and Other Color. If you choose the Other Color button, a palette is displayed. Choose a color from the palette. You can also click the Eyedropper tool and sample a color from the image. The color you choose from either of the modes or with the Eyedropper tool will be the color that is used to fade into the image.

Use the Adjust sliders to control the amount of offset and fade applied to the vignette. As always, you can preview the results before clicking the OK button. You can also use the alternate Vignette dialog box by clicking the Alternate Preview button in the lower-left corner of the default Vignette dialog box.

USING PLUG-IN FILTERS

CorelDRAW 8 supports plug-in filters, including many third-party filters. You must load the filters by choosing Tools | Options | Workspace | Plug-ins (see Figure 23-12) before you can use them. To load a plug-in filter, follow these steps:

1. With the Plug-ins dialog box displayed, click the Add button. The Select a Plug-in Folder dialog box will appear. Change to the folder where the plug-in filter is stored, select it, and click OK. The filter will now be added.

2. Click the OK button in the Plug-ins dialog box to finish loading the filter.

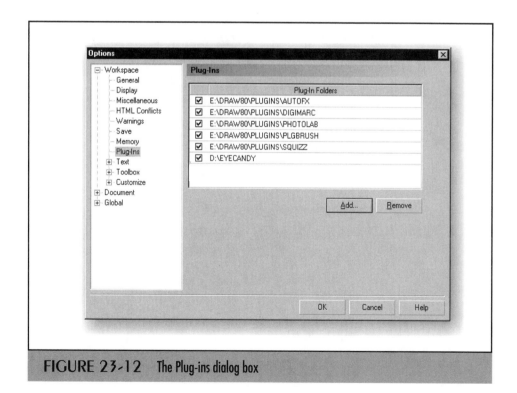

FIGURE 23-12   The Plug-ins dialog box

Now that the filters are loaded, choose Bitmaps | Plug-ins to access the Plug-ins child menu (refer back to Figure 23-6). CorelDRAW 8 supplies five plug-ins; they are shown as loaded in Figure 23-12. Some of these filters can be very useful bitmap editing tools.

The Eye Candy filter at the bottom of the list is not supplied with CorelDRAW 8 but is one of the more popular third-party filters. Eye Candy is a collection of several filters. Figure 23-13 shows Eye Candy's Water Drop filter being applied to a beach scene.

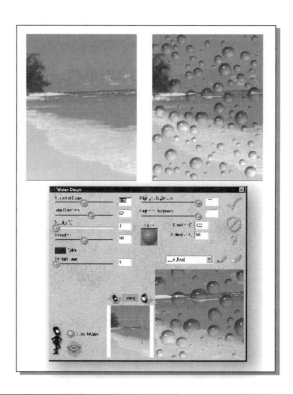

FIGURE 23-13   Applying Eye Candy's Water Drop filter to a beach scene

REATING DUOTONES

Many designers use duotones in place of CMYK images. The advantage of duotones is that there are only two separations to be made instead of the usual four when working in CMYK colors. Two plates mean lower cost to the client. Using only two colors can sometimes improve what otherwise would be a mediocre image. You can also select certain colors to create a mood in the image. In Figure 23-14, a duotone has been applied to the image on the right.

To create a duotone, follow these steps:

1. Import a bitmap image.

2. Choose <u>B</u>itmaps | Con<u>v</u>ert To | <u>D</u>uotone.

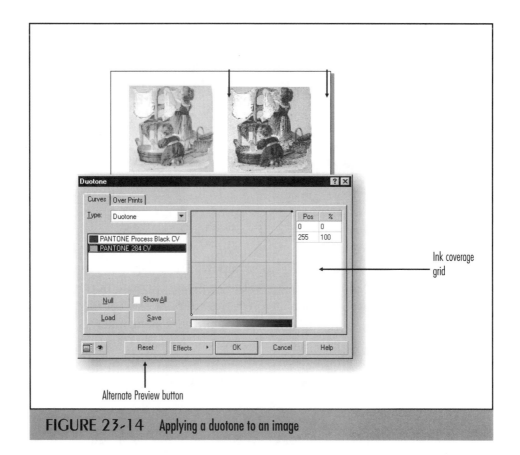

FIGURE 23-14   Applying a duotone to an image

3. When the Duotone dialog box appears, choose Duotone from the Type list box.

4. Double-click the Pantone process yellow color button to reveal the Select Color dialog box.

5. Choose the Pantone color you want to use. If you wish to use another spot color system, select it from the Type list box in the Select Color dialog box.

6. Don't change the Pantone Process Black CV color for a standard duotone. Black is commonly used to enhance the shadows in the image. You could use another color to create a special effect.

7. Adjust the ink coverage on each color by first clicking on each color button dragging the curve in the grid at the right of the dialog box.

8. Click the Preview button (the eye in the lower-left corner) to see the results. This would be a good time to use the alternate Duotone dialog box to preview the ink coverage adjustments. To use this alternate dialog box, click the Alternate Preview button in the lower-left corner of the dialog box.When you satisfied with the results, click the OK button in the Duotone dialog box.

LINKING BITMAP IMAGES

A new feature in CorelDRAW 8 enables you to link bitmaps when importing them into CorelDRAW. This feature lets you add bitmaps to your drawing while reducing the size of your file. This is what actually takes place: The bitmap file you import into your .cdr file remains in the folder where it was originally stored. Instead of the file being imported, a low-resolution preview header file is used for placement only in the .cdr file. The real image stays in the folder where it is stored. When it comes time to print the .cdr file with the image, the real file is retrieved for printing. The Bitmaps menu includes options on updating the bitmap and resolving the link to a bitmap. These options are discussed after you learn how to link a bitmap image.

To link a bitmap to your drawing, follow these steps:

1. Choose File | Import to bring up the Import dialog box.

2. Change to the drive and folder where your bitmap is stored.

3. Enable the Link Bitmap Externally box at the bottom of the Import dialog box.

4. Click the Import button at the top of the dialog box.

5. Position the import placement cursor on the page where you want to display the image.

6. Click once to place the bitmap in its original size. You can also use the placement cursor and drag to define a custom size for the image. If you hold down the ALT key while dragging, the image will be distorted.

You cannot use any effects on a Linked bitmap.

Updating a Linked Bitmap

When you update a linked bitmap, you're telling CorelDRAW to go back and re-import the file. This is done if you know changes have been made to the file since it was originally imported as a linked file. Because the linked file displayed on the page is merely pointing to the original file, it is simple to update the link. The changed preview header is now displayed in place of the old one. The actual process of updating a linked bitmap is as follows:

▶ Select the linked bitmap with the Pick tool.

▶ Choose Bitmaps | Update From Link.

Resolving a Linked Bitmap

Resolving a linked bitmap removes the link between the bitmap header file and the original bitmap. When you resolve the bitmap, the low-resolution header is replaced with the actual high-resolution file. The bitmap is no longer linked and behaves like any other bitmap file.

To resolve a linked bitmap do the following:

▶ Select the linked bitmap with the Pick tool.

▶ Choose Bitmaps | Resolve Link.

23

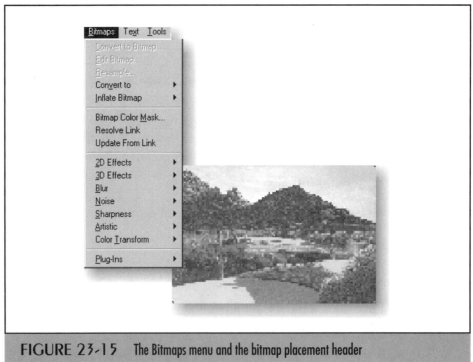

FIGURE 23-15   The Bitmaps menu and the bitmap placement header

Figure 23-15 shows the Bitmaps menu with the imported linked bitmap placement header. We then added a figure to the original bitmap image and updated it using the Update From Link command. After it was updated we used the Resolve Link command to bring the file in permanently. Figure 23-16 shows the header after it has been updated and resolved.

CREATING TRANSPARENT DROP SHADOWS

CorelDRAW 8 now lets you create transparent drop shadows. These drop shadows are bitmap images that can be applied to another bitmap image or vector image. Follow these steps to learn how to create this great effect:

1. Click the Text tool and type the word **Drop Shadows** on the page. We used the font Brochure at 72 points.

FIGURE 23-16   The updated linked file after the link was resolved

2. Click the Interactive Drop Shadow tool on the Interactive Tool
   flyout shown here.

3. Click and drag on the text object to create the shadow, as shown in Figure 23-17. The farther you drag away from the object, the longer the drop shadow.

Congratulate yourself; you just created your first drop shadow. The Property Bar lets you control the look of the drop shadow even more than you can with the interactive tool. The illustration shown here shows another drop shadow effect with each setting controlling it identified on the Property Bar (if you use Average in the Direction List box the Shadow Edges option is dimmed).

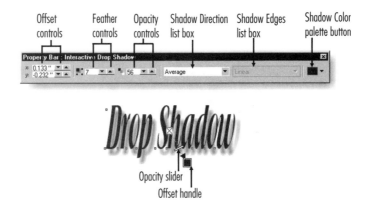

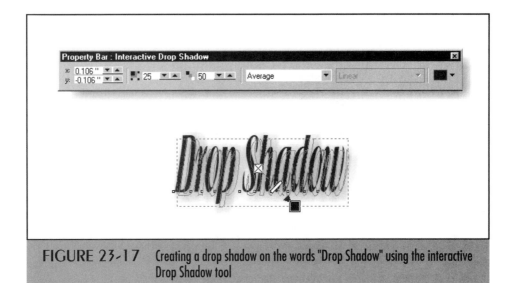

FIGURE 23-17   Creating a drop shadow on the words "Drop Shadow" using the interactive Drop Shadow tool

Practice using this tool to discover the many different types of drop shadows you can create, even changing the color of the shadow. Try dragging the Offset handle and the Opacity slider with the interactive tool to see the change in the shadow. Then try the various controls on the Property Bar. The illustration shown here use a setting of Outside in the Direction list box and Inverse Squared from the Shadow Edges list box.

The last illustration shows a drop shadow being applied to an imported bitmap image. You can even apply a drop shadow to a group of objects.

23

This chapter has covered several of the new bitmap capabilities available in CorelDRAW 8. Take advantage of this ability to use these bitmap effects directly in CorelDRAW, and eliminate the need to take the extra time to open and use PHOTO-PAINT.

PART
4

INPUT AND OUTPUT

24

COREL COLOR PROFILE WIZARD

The Corel Color Profile Wizard is a graphics utility that can be run as a stand-alone application or from within CorelDRAW itself. To run the Color Profile Wizard from within CorelDRAW, see the next section. To run the Corel Color Profile Wizard separately, select it from Corel's Graphic Utilities section in the Start menu programs.

The purpose of the Color Profile Wizard is to calibrate your monitor, printers, and scanner so you can reach that elusive goal of "what you see is what you get." Corel knows that color management is difficult for the average user, so they have provided the Color Profile Wizard to take you through the steps of making sure your devices work properly together and with consistency. The Corel development team has created profiles for dozens of different monitors, scanners, and printers, making it easy for most users to calibrate their systems. It's simply a matter of choosing your particular monitor, printer, and scanner from a list of profiles.

USING THE COLOR PROFILE WIZARD FROM WITHIN CORELDRAW

To run the Color Profile Wizard from within CorelDRAW, choose Tools | Options. Then click the + symbol next to the word "Global" on the left side of the Options dialog box. Now click on the + symbol next to the word Color Management to expand the Color Management tree. Now click the word "Profiles" and the dialog box shown in Figure 24-1 will appear.

The Color Profile Wizard runs automatically when you click the Color Profile Wizard button in the Profiles dialog box shown in figure 24-1. The first screen you will see lists each device with a generic profile selected.

Follow these steps to calibrate your system using the Color Profile Wizard:

1. Click each list box and use the down arrow to scroll through the drop-down lists until you find the name and model for each of your devices. The Separations Printer list contains the names of printers and image setters that are used for producing color separations. This list is usually used to select the name of the image setter your service bureau uses, but it can be used for any printer that outputs CMYK color. Figure 24-2 shows the same screen with devices that have been selected.

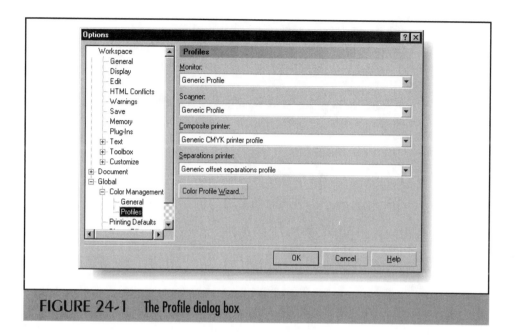

FIGURE 24-1   The Profile dialog box

If your devices are not listed in the Profile drop-down lists, you have three options. The first option would be to choose to use a Generic Profile. The second option would be to choose "Get profile from disk" if you didn't install the profiles during the initial installation. If you choose this option the Browse For Folder dialog box shown here appears.

24

Change to the drive and folder where CorelDRAW 8 is installed and click the + icon to expand the folder. Choose the Color folder and click the OK button. The Install from disk dialog box shown here will appear.

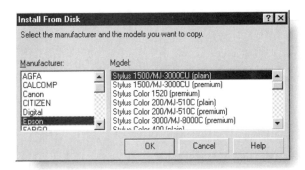

Choose the device you want to install and click OK.

You really only have a third option if the manufacturer of your device has provided you with a color profile they have created. If you have such a profile, simply choose the "Get profile from disk" option and change to the folder where you have the profile stored. Select the profile and it will be installed.

 *Generic profiles are selected by default. The fact that profiles are already selected, even though they are generic, means that Color correction is turned on.*

When you're done making your selections, click the OK button. That's all there is to it; you have just selected the color profiles for your system devices. If you change any of the devices, simply go to this dialog box again to select different profiles.

HOW TO USE A COLOR PROFILE

You've learned how to select a color profile for your system; now you need to know how to use it. Remember, you select a color profile for your system so you can view the colors in your images as they will be printed.

To ensure the color profile you selected is functioning, you must choose Tools Options | Global | Color Management. Enable the Calibrate Colors for Display check box. You will be presented with three entries that you can check: Simulate Composite Printer, Simulate Separations Printer, and Highlight Colors Out of Printer Gamut. To get the most benefit from the color management system, you should check one of the printer options and the color

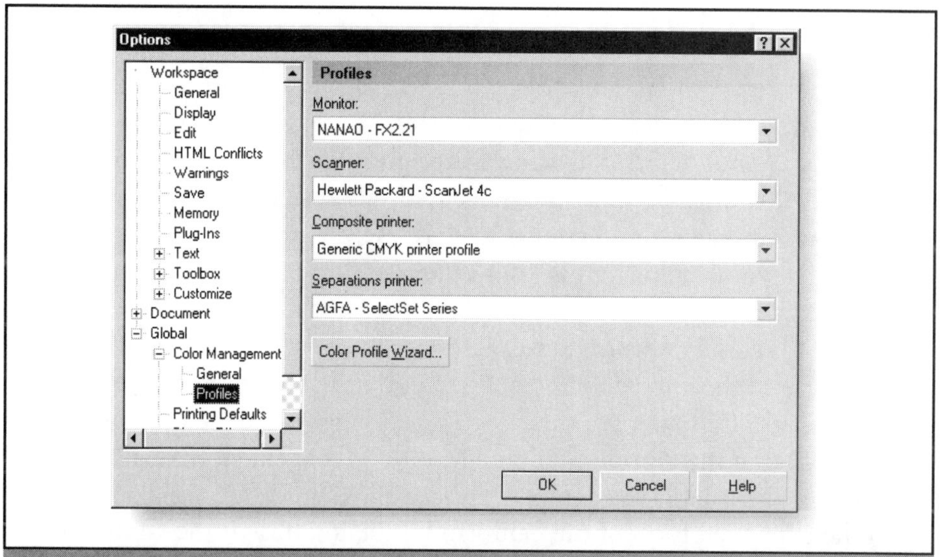

FIGURE 24-2   The Profiles dialog box after selecting device profiles

gamut option. The Simulate Composite Printer option should be checked because that's the primary purpose for using a color profile. The Highlight Colors Out of Printer Gamut option allows you to check that colors you have used in your drawing will indeed print (see the following section, "Color Gamut"). The Color Management dialog box is shown here.

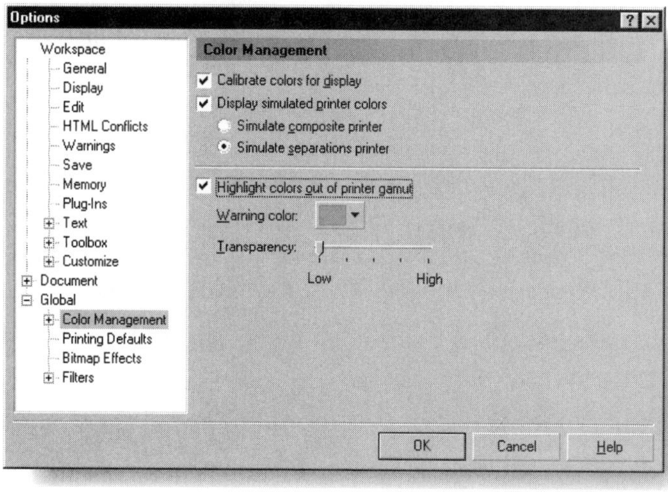

24

COLOR GAMUT

Gamut color refers to the range of color that a device can produce. The color management system uses the Gamut Color feature to warn you if you are using a color that cannot be printed using the printer named in your color profile. In practice, this warning most often occurs if you use colors from any of the RGB models or palettes and your printer is a CMY or CMYK printer. If you fill an object with a color that is "out of gamut," the object will display with the default gamut color (neon green). This does not mean it will print with a green fill, it is simply a warning to you that the color you have used will not print exactly as the one you chose. When you are creating images for screen display using RGB palettes, turn off the Highlight Colors Out of Printer Gamut option in the Options | Global | Color Management dialog box.

You can also enable the gamut alarm by clicking the Options drop-down list in the expanded form of the Uniform Fill dialog box or the Color roll-up and choosing Gamut Color from the flyout. Before you set the gamut alarm, select the appropriate device profiles in the Color Management Option.

CUSTOM CALIBRATIONS

Corel provides profiles for most of the popular monitors. If your monitor is not shown in the drop-down list, you can choose a generic monitor or calibrate your monitor using the calibration controls in the Color Profile Wizard. You may want to calibrate your monitor even if it's on the list if the monitor is a few years old or the lighting conditions in your room are unusual. This will ensure that the monitor's output is accurate and consistent. We recommend calibrating your monitor only if you are an experienced user.

To calibrate your monitor, follow these steps:

1. Run the Color Profile Wizard from within CorelDRAW (see "Using the Color Profile Wizard from within CorelDRAW" at the beginning of the chapter). The dialog box will look like the one shown in Figure 24-2 but with your devices selected.

2. Highlight the Monitor list box showing the currently installed monitor profile.

3. Click the Color Profile Wizard button to reveal the Color Profile welcome screen shown in Figure 24-3.

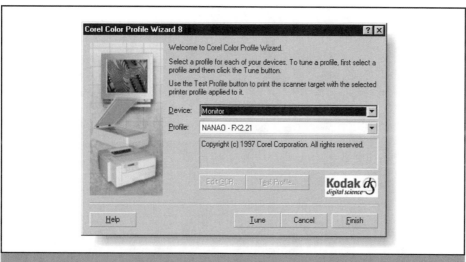

FIGURE 24-3 The Color Profile Welcome screen

4. Choose monitor from the Device drop-down list.

5. Choose the model name of your monitor from the Profile drop-down list. If your model isn't listed, Choose Generic from the bottom portion of the drop down list.

 *If your monitor is not listed in the list of profiles, the manufacturer of your monitor did not supply a profile. Corel has created profiles for the major manufacturers, which fit 99 percent of the market. You can create your own profile, as described in the following steps.*

6. Click the Tune button.

7. The next screen you will see (see Figure 24-4) asks you to enter the name of the manufacturer of your monitor and the model name. If you chose your monitor and model from the previous screen, the same information will appear here. If you chose a generic monitor, enter the name and model of your monitor in the space provided.

8. Click the Next button.

9. The next screen, shown in Figure 24-5, asks if you have a colorimeter. This is a mechanical device used to calibrate monitors.

24

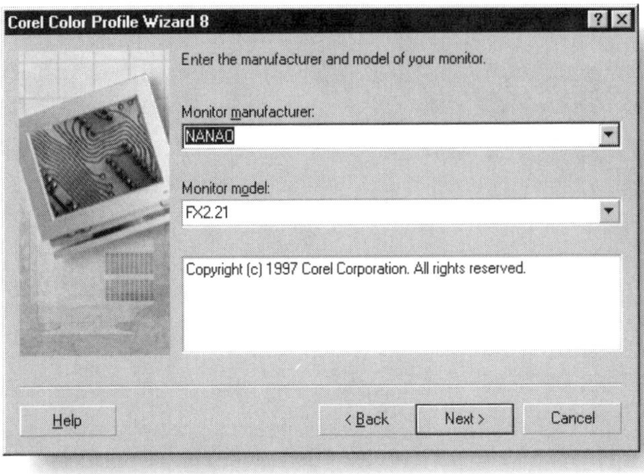

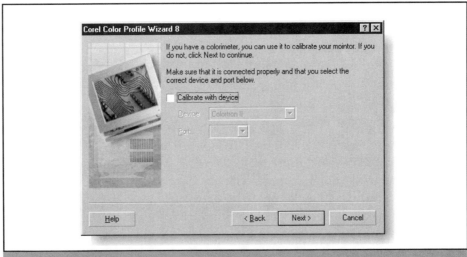

FIGURE 24-4   The monitor manufacturer and model information screen

FIGURE 24-5   The Colorimeter screen

If you have one, check the appropriate boxes and calibrate the monitor with the device. If you don't have a colorimeter, click the Next button.

10. The next screen you will see (see Figure 24-6) contains the controls to calibrate your monitor chromatically. The idea is to use the controls to adjust the reds, greens, and blues so that the target image in the upper-left corner of the screen matches the printed target that comes in the CorelDRAW box.

   The way it's done is to remove the check mark from the Identical RGB Values box and adjust the red, green, and blue colors one at a time. To adjust a color, enable the radio button next to the color's name. Click either the up or down arrow in the num box next to the color you're adjusting. Watch the colors in the colors displayed in the lower-left area of the screen. Try to match the color on the right half with the colors in the left half. A good way of seeing if they match is to squint your eyes or, if you wear glasses, remove them so

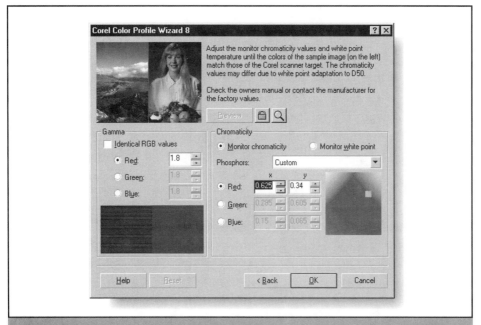

FIGURE 24-6   The Chromatic control screen

you're looking at the colors out of focus. These methods will help you match the colors more easily. When the colors match, move on to the next color and repeat the steps.

11. You may need to adjust the white point temperature settings before the colors match the target image. To adjust the white point temperature, click the Monitor White Point radio button (see Figure 24-7). Move the slider control to the left or right through the temperature range until the brightness of the screen image matches the printed target image.

Make sure your monitor has been on for at least one hour before calibrating it. Adjust the monitor brightness to what you would normally use for the room lighting conditions.

FIGURE 24-7   The White Point Temperature control screen

When you are satisfied with the results, click the OK button to return to the Welcome to Corel Color Profile Wizard screen. After calibrating your monitor, you can calibrate your scanner and printer if a profile is not listed among the many scanners and printers in the list boxes. If you do not need to calibrate either your scanner or printer, click the Finish button in the lower-right of the Welcome dialog box.

Unless your devices are not listed in the drop-down lists or you feel they may not be performing at their proper levels, you do not have to manually calibrate your devices. Using the profiles provided in conjunction with the Color Profile Wizard will do a better job than manual calibration.

This chapter has introduced you to the new Color Profile Wizard. You have learned how easy it is to create a color profile for your system if your devices are listed in the device drop-down lists. You have also learned how to calibrate your monitor manually if you feel it's necessary because of the age of the monitor or unusual lighting conditions. Whichever method you use—calibrating manually or by using the Wizard—it's important to calibrate your system by creating a color profile to ensure accurate color output.

24

25

SCANNING AND CORELSCAN

It is becoming more commonplace to find a scanner on the average user's desktop as the cost of scanners keeps going down. Now that you can apply effects to bitmap images within CorelDRAW 8 itself, many users will discover the benefits of using scanned images in their projects.

TYPES OF SCANNERS

Scanners are available in three types: hand-held, flatbed, and drum. The most commonly used scanner type is the flatbed. Hand-held scanners are very inexpensive, but they require a steady hand to operate. They do have their place in the world of scanning, even though they're not used that often. One important use of a hand-held scanner is to scan a fragile document that can't be removed from its binding. Drum scanners are very expensive and therefore reserved for high-end users such as service bureaus and companies such as Corel Corporation.

A flatbed scanner is much like an office copy machine. A traveling light bar illuminates the work placed on the glass plate. The reflected light from the image is passed through a lens onto the charged couple device (CCD) sensors. The amount of red, green, and blue light information is collected from the sensors and sent to the computer.

Unlike a photographer, who spends a great deal of time in the dark room developing and enlarging film, a person using scanning software can process an image in minutes and can adjust the size, resolution, contrast, brightness, tonal control, and saturation of the image.

Professional photographers go to great pains to get the lighting and exposure just right so they spend less time in the darkroom. Similarly, you should spend the extra time to make the necessary software settings and adjustments prior to committing to the final scan. You must first determine the correct resolution to scan your image. The resolution is determined by the quality you are seeking and the requirements of the printer. (The printer may mean the physical printer that sits on your desktop or the person who will print the job.) A good rule of thumb is to scan your image at one and one half times the line screen of your printer.

THE BASICS OF SCANNING

You can scan many kinds of things on a flatbed scanner, ranging from images on paper to a pair of pants. You can scan small three-dimensional objects or even art work that exceeds the size of the scanner surface. If you think we are joking about the pants reference, we're not. We once needed a denim texture fill so we scanned the pocket of a pair of Levi's. Candy wrapped in cellophane looks great when scanned. The reflections off the cellophane really sparkle.

Before you scan an image, you should determine how you will be using the image. If the image will be used only for screen display, you can scan at a relatively low resolution such as 100dpi. However, if you plan on using the image for a display ad as well, then you should scan the image at a higher resolution and lower the resolution for the screen image in an application such as Corel PHOTO-PAINT. If your scanned image will be printed in grayscale, you may decide to scan it in color as well for future use. Once you discard original information (the color values in a grayscale scan, for example), they are lost to the file forever.

The images you can scan are grouped into three basic categories: line art, halftones, and continuous-tone (full-color and black-and-white photographs) images.

SCANNING LINE ART

Line art is considered to be a black-and-white image. If you are planning on converting the scanned black-and-white bitmap image into a vector image using either CorelDRAW's AutoTrace feature or the stand-alone application Corel OCR-TRACE, you should scan the image at a minimum of 300 dpi (dots per inch) for best results. If the line art image contains very fine lines, scan the image as a grayscale image instead of as a black-and-white image.

If you are planning to leave scanned lineart as a bitmap image for printing on commercial presses, you should scan at the output resolution (dpi) of the press, but not exceeding the maximum optical resolution of the scanner.

SCANNING HALFTONES

When discussing halftones, you need to differentiate between scanning an image using the Halftone setting in your scanner software and scanning an image that has been previously printed as a halftone (pictures in magazines, for example).

You should avoid scanning images using the Halftone setting in the software in most cases. Only use this setting if you are planning to print on a printer that cannot generate its own halftone dots, such as a dot-matrix printer.

25

The second form of halftone is a grayscale or color image that has been previously printed in a magazine or book. Scanning this type of halftone presents a problem because its image is made up of tiny halftone dots created by the printing process. Before you even attempt to scan an image that has been previously printed, make sure you have the right to do so. Copyright laws are very specific on this subject.

The best way to ensure good results when scanning an image that has been printed before is to scan the image at the proper resolution (see Table 25-1 later in this chapter) and then to open the scanned image in a paint program such as Corel PHOTO-PAINT to remove the moiré pattern that results from scanning the halftone dots. The best filter to use to eliminate the moiré pattern is the Effects | Noise | Remove Moire filter in Corel PHOTO-PAINT. When the moiré pattern has been removed, use the Effects | Sharpen | Unsharp Mask filter to return the image to its original sharpness.

SCANNING CONTINUOUS TONE IMAGES

Continuous tone images can be either grayscale or color. The images that fall in this category are black-and-white or color photographs and original artwork such as oil paintings. It is imperative to select the proper settings in the scanning software prior to the final scan if you want good results. Although some books on the market recommend that you work on improving the image after it has been scanned, you should make every effort to adjust the scanner software settings so your final scan produces the best-quality image possible. The rationale behind this advice is the very old saying that goes something like this: "You can't make a silk purse out of a sow's ear"—that is, you can't expect to improve an image if the data is not present. Other than adjusting for hue and saturation, you should treat a grayscale image like a color image.

SCANNING ISSUES

It is extremely important to scan at the proper resolution. If you scan an image at too low a resolution, the image will become pixelated. If you scan using a resolution that is too high, the scanner has to throw away information that it can't use. The effect of this on the final image is a loss of subtle detail.

To produce the best-quality prints or film, use the rule of thumb for scanning an image by using a dpi setting of one and a half times the line screen (screen frequency).

There are two methods for determining the correct scanning resolution. The first measures in pixels, and the second measures in inches. Before you begin scanning using either of these methods, you must determine the optimum resolution by asking your printer what line screen will be used to create the film. This is extremely important if you want a high-quality scan.

USING PIXELS AS THE MEASUREMENT UNIT

Measuring in pixels can be less complicated than using inches. For example, if your printer tells you that he or she will be using a line screen of 133 on your project, which is a common line screen in commercial printing, multiply that number by 1.5 and round up to the nearest value divisible by 25. In this case, 1.5x133 equals 189.5, so you would round up to 200 dpi.

The next thing you need to determine is the final output size. If the size of the output image will be the same as the original, use the resolution that the formula calls for (in this case 200 dpi) and enter that number in your scanning software and proceed to scan the image. If the output image will be smaller or larger than the original, use the scaling adjustment in your scanning software to scale the image to the desired size. For example, if you are scanning an image that is 5x7 inches and you have determined that the correct scanning resolution is 200 dpi, the image will measure 1000x1400 pixels. If you decide to output the image at twice the original size, at 10x14 inches, you will need to use the scaling adjustments in the scanning software to increase the size of the image by 200 percent, making the final scanned image 2000x2800 pixels.

Remember that once you know the correct resolution at which to scan your image, it's simply a matter of multiplying that number by the size of the final output image.

25

USING INCHES AS THE MEASUREMENT UNIT

The second method is to determine the size of the output image using inches as the unit of measure. You can use the formula ((LDOxLS)x1.5) divided by LDI = OSR, where

- ► LDO = Longest dimension of the output image
- ► LS = Line screen to be used in the final output
- ► LDI = Longest dimension of the input image
- ► OSR = Optimum scanning resolution in DPI

For example, suppose you are scanning a photo that is 8x10 inches, and you want to output your image at a size of 4x5 inches with a 150-line screen. Use these values: LDO=5, LS=150, and LDI=10. Plug these numbers into the following formula:

((5x150)x1.5) divided by 10 = 112.5 dpi (round up to 125 dpi)

Here is another example. Suppose you are scanning a photo that is 5x7 inches, and you want to output your image at a size of 10x14 inches with a 100-line screen. Use these values: LDO=14, LS=100, LDI=7. Plug these numbers into the following formula:

((14x100)x1.5) divided by 7 = 300 dpi

Table 25-1 shows the default line screen of output devices rated by dpi. (For example, a 300 dpi laser printer produces a default line screen of 60.) This table will help you determine the correct resolution for scanning.

CORELSCAN

CorelSCAN is a separate graphics utility that provides a Wizard to guide you through the scanning process. CorelSCAN is installed by default if you use the Typical installation method. If you used the Custom method and didn't

Maximum dpi of the Printer	Default Line Screen
300	60
600	80
1000	100
1200	133
1270	133
1693	150
3386	200

TABLE 25-1   Various Line Screen Resolutions of Printers

install CorelSCAN the first time you installed CorelDRAW 8, run Setup again to install the utility (see Chapter 1).

The CorelSCAN Wizard can help in outputting a quality scan if you are new to scanning. The Wizard takes you through the process of scanning various types of images, from photographs to pictures in newspapers. The best way to learn how to use the CorelSCAN 8 Wizard is to jump right in and get started.

USING CORELSCAN 8

The following steps correspond to the different stages you go through as you scan a photograph with CorelSCAN.

1. Run the CorelSCAN utility by double-clicking its icon in the Graphics Utilities folder. You can access CorelSCAN from within CorelDRAW by choosing File | Acquire From CorelSCAN but we recommend using the utility separately until you familiarize yourself with its use.

2. The first screen you will see is the Welcome to CorelSCAN screen shown in Figure 25-1. Select your scanner from the Scanner Configuration list box and click the Configure Scanner button. We are using the DeskScan II 2.5 (driver UI) that ships with most Hewlett Packard scanners for this session.

25

FIGURE 25-1   The CorelSCAN Welcome screen

Do not enable the Use Advanced Interface check box or you will be taken directly to your scanner's interface instead of CorelSCAN's interface.

The second screen to appear is the Scanner Configuration screen, as shown in Figure 25-2. Click the down arrow on the Device Color Profile list box and choose the name of your scanner. If your scanner does not appear in the list, either you did not select it during the installation process or a profile doesn't exist for your scanner. If you didn't install your scanner's color profile during installation, you can install the scanner profile by running the Color Profile Wizard discussed in Chapter 24. If your scanner is not listed in either the Color

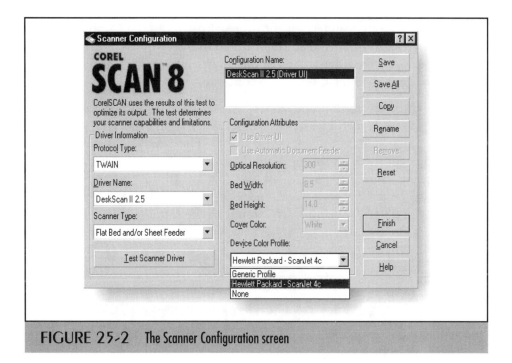

FIGURE 25-2   The Scanner Configuration screen

Profile Wizard or during the installation process, choose Generic Profile from the list.

If your scanner has its own color correction which cannot be disabled (newer HP and Umax scanners, for example), check None for the Profile.

3. After you have selected a color profile, remove anything that is currently on the scanner glass and click the Test Scanner Driver button to allow CorelSCAN to test the capabilities of your scanner. When the driver test is completed, the name of your scanner and the driver number with the words "Flat Bed" will appear below the first

25

listing of your scanner. Click this new listing and the Configuration Attributes information section located in the center of the Wizard will display the information about your scanner (see Figure 25-3). Now click the Finish button to continue.

The third screen that appears brings you back to the Welcome screen (see Figure 25-4). Select the new configuration you just created in step 3 (it displays the words "Flat Bed"). It is very important to select this new configuration and not the default configuration displaying the words "Driver UI." If you chose the latter, the interface of the scanner driver would display in place of the CorelSCAN Wizard. This would be the same as if you had

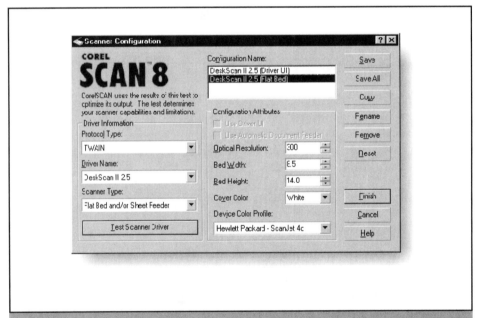

FIGURE 25-3   The Scanner Configuration screen after the scanner test has been completed

FIGURE 25-4 The Welcome screen shown for the second time

the Use Advanced Interface button at the bottom of the Welcome
screen. It streamlines the CorelSCAN options into one dialog box
list where you can double-click each setting to make changes, and
then save the settings into a Custom setting.

4. With the correct configuration selected, click the Next button to
   begin the actual scanning process.

5. Figure 25-5 shows the fourth screen to appear. This is the point at
   which you will perform the actual scan. Place a photograph on the
   scanner glass and close the scanner cover. Click the word "Prescan"
   near the bottom of the screen. The image of your scanned photo
   will appear in the preview window with selection handles

25

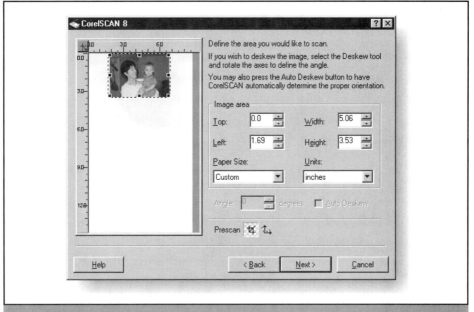

FIGURE 25-5   Defining the area of the image to scan

surrounding it. The Crop tool next to the word "Prescan" will automatically be selected. Using the Crop tool, click the selection handles to crop the image. You can control the area you wish to scan by entering the values in the Width and Height num boxes in the Image Area section of the screen. This will change the size of the selection box. You then use the Crop tool to place the selection area on the portion of the image you wish to scan.

If the image is skewed, you can adjust the skew with the Skew tool next to the Crop tool. You can either enable the Auto Deskew box or manually deskew the image using the Deskew tool. You can also deskew the image by entering a skew angle in the Angle num box when the Deskew tool is selected. When you're satisfied with the dimensions of the image click on the Next button.

NOTE: *If the scan preview image is black or otherwise distorted, you probably have your scanner's own color calibration enabled or another setting in the scanner UI is interfering with the CorelSCAN utility. Go back to the beginning screen of CorelSCAN and this time choose the driver UI to scan. It is possible that you can change some of the settings in the driver UI to produce a good preview, and then return to the "Flat Bed" driver setting, but if not, scan with your scanner's UI from within CorelSCAN and then follow along with the remainder of this chapter.*

6. The next screen (shown in Figure 25-6) asks what type of image you are scanning. Choose the description that best fits the image and click the Next button.

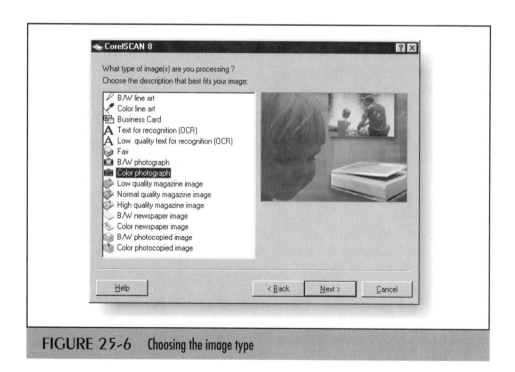

FIGURE 25-6 Choosing the image type

25

7. The screen shown in Figure 25-7 lets you choose the destination of the scanned image, as it pertains to what you are going to do with the image, from a drop-down list. In most cases, you should choose High Quality Art. The quality can be limited by the type of the original image. For example, if you're scanning a black-and-white newspaper image, the High Quality Art option is not available. You are also given a choice of the final color for the image. This example uses RGB 24 bits, which will produce an image in the full-color range with 16.7 million colors. If you choose the Direct to Color Printer destination you can choose the 32-bit CMYK color option. After choosing the color quality, click the Next button.

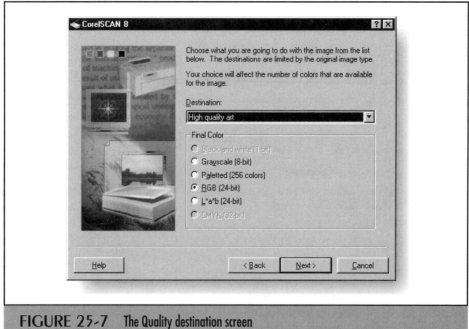

FIGURE 25-7   The Quality destination screen

8. The next screen, shown in Figure 25-8, lets you choose the resolution for your scanned image. Here a recommended resolution is shown at 300 dpi. The recommended resolution is not based on anything more than what is commonly used for the type of image you're scanning. Refer to the information earlier in this chapter to determine what resolution will be correct and then enter the value in the Use Custom Resolution parameter box. In this example, we entered 200 dpi. When you are done, click the Next button.

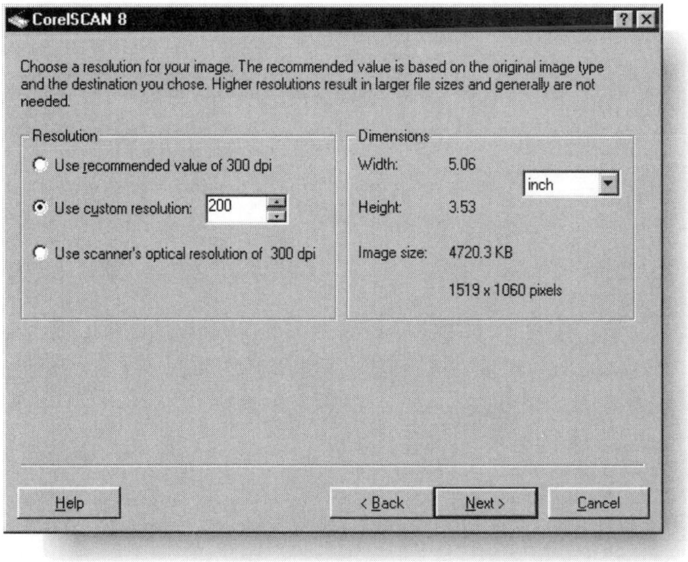

FIGURE 25-8   Choosing a resolution

25

9. Figure 25-9 shows the Image Enhancement screen. You can choose the Automatic mode, or you can use the adjustment sliders to manually control the image appearance. To preview the results of any changes, click the Preview button (the middle button under the Before window). If you're not satisfied with the changes, click the Back button next to the Preview button to revert to the unedited version. When you are satisfied with the results, click the Next button. The example in Figure 25-9 uses the Automatic mode.

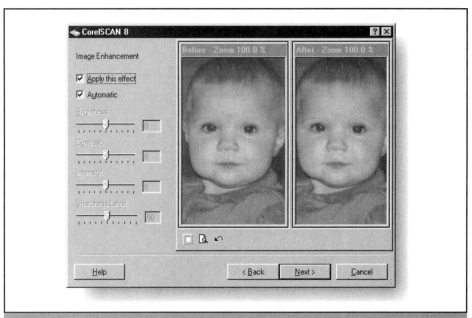

FIGURE 25-9   The Image Enhancement screen

10. The following screen is the Red-Eye Removal screen. Figure 25-10 simulates the use of the Red-Eye Removal. The only time you would use the Red-Eye Removal filter is when the eyes of the subject have changed from their natural color, a problem often caused by flash photography. If there is a change in the subject's eye color, click the Eye icon under the Before screen and use the Magic wand cursor to click in the eye. Adjusting the tolerance slider controls the amount of area that is masked. Next click the Eye Color button and select a color from the drop-down palette to replace the color in the selected

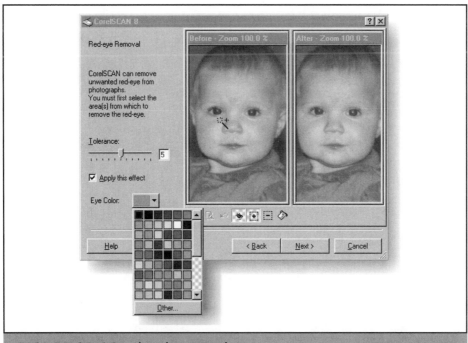

FIGURE 25-10   The Red-Eye Removal screen

25

area. If you can't find a suitable color, click the Other button at the bottom of the palette and choose a color from one of the color models. Whether or not you use the Red-Eye Removal filter, click the <u>N</u>ext button.

11. The screen shown in Figure 25-11 lets you choose whether you want to use the Dust and Scratch removal filter. Generally, you should use this filter. It will remove little specks as small as dust particles from the scanned image. Click the Preview button at the bottom of the screen under the Before image to see the effect of the filter in the After image. When you are satisfied with the results, click the <u>N</u>ext button.

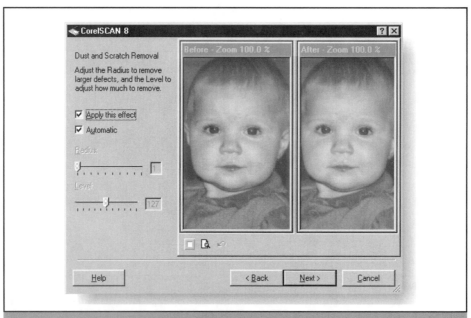

FIGURE 25-11   The Dust and Scratch Removal screen

12. The next screen is the Destination screen, shown in Figure 25-12. Enter a name for the scanned image and choose a folder in which to store it. You will also be asked to choose a file type. We recommend saving your images either as .cpt or .tif images. You are also given the opportunity to save the unprocessed scanner data so you can edit the image later without rescanning it. When the information is correct, click the Next button.

13. The final check screen (see Figure 25-13) lists all the information about the image being scanned, including the settings you chose via the Wizard. If any of this information is incorrect, click the Back button to back up to the screen that needs correction. When you are satisfied, click the Finish button. You can now access your scanned image from the folder where it was saved.

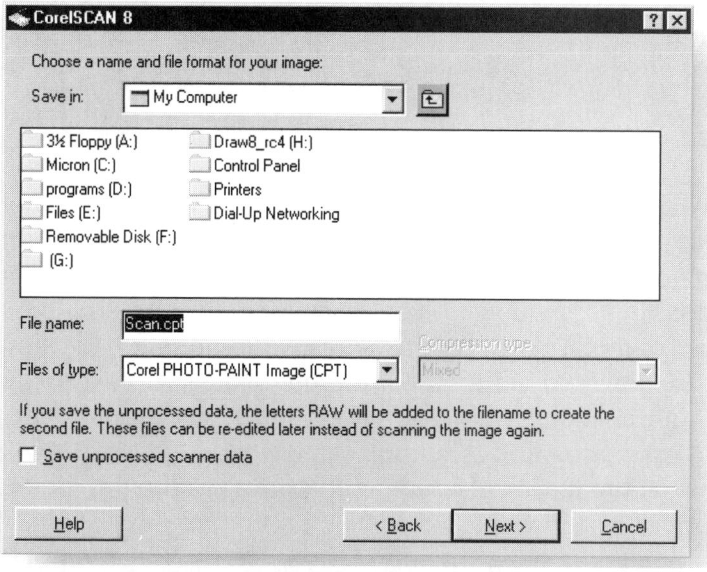

FIGURE 25-12 The file destination screen

25

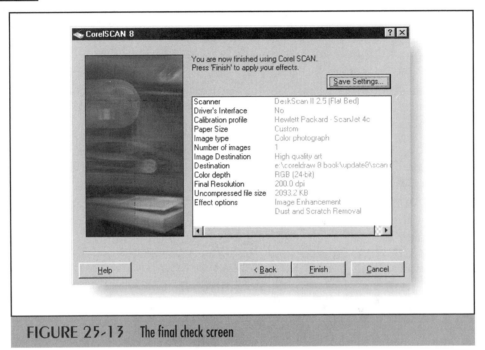

FIGURE 25-13　The final check screen

Every image presents a different set of circumstances. The only way to learn how to correctly scan images is to practice, practice, practice.

Unless you are completely new to scanning or don't feel comfortable making decisions regarding color, sharpness, and resolution, the authors recommend using the software that ships with your scanner as the primary means of scanning your work. If you use your scanner's software coupled with the earlier information in this chapter you should get excellent results.

As you have discovered, scanning is a complex subject. There are books written just on the subject of scanning. We have tried to provide you with as much information as possible to help you understand the scanning process so that your scans result in high quality images. The CorelSCAN utility can help make this possible.

26

IMPORTING AND
OPENING FILES

With most software, opening files is very straightforward and the import options are very limited. CorelDRAW is just the opposite. With most projects, you'll need to use many different files. Text will come from a word processor, bitmaps will come from your favorite bitmap editing program (such as Corel PHOTO-PAINT), and some elements may come from other CorelDRAW files or even from a Macintosh user. With each type of file that you open or import, the procedures may be slightly different. This chapter explores the many aspects of opening and importing files so that you'll know exactly how to work with the files you need.

THE OPEN/IMPORT DIALOG BOX

You use the same dialog box to both open and import files. However, the list of file types is much more extensive when you are importing files. This dialog box is what is called a common dialog box, as it is used throughout most Windows programs. An example is shown in Figure 26-1.

You may see a similarity here with Windows Explorer, which makes sense because this dialog box works just like Windows Explorer in many ways. The main part of the dialog box lists the files by name, with a small icon to their left. You can change this view with the buttons above the main window. The rightmost button changes the view to Details, which shows the file size, type, and date to the right of the file name. If you choose Details, you will see only a single column of file names rather than the multiple columns you see in the default List view. You can change back to List view with the List button just to the left of the Details button.

In the upper-left corner of the dialog box is the Look In drop-down list box, which lets you choose the computer, drive, and folder for which information will be displayed. To change to a folder lower than the one currently displayed, double-click the folder in the main window. To move one folder up in the hierarchy, click the button just to the right of the drop-down list. The next button to the right automatically creates a new folder. Of course, you can also create a new folder by right-clicking in the main window and choosing New | Folder from the pop-up menu. On that same menu you'll find numerous other options just like those in Windows Explorer.

Several years ago, someone asked how to delete a file in CorelDRAW. We all got this weird look on our faces since that was not something you'd even think of trying to do in CorelDRAW. Wasn't that the purpose of Window's

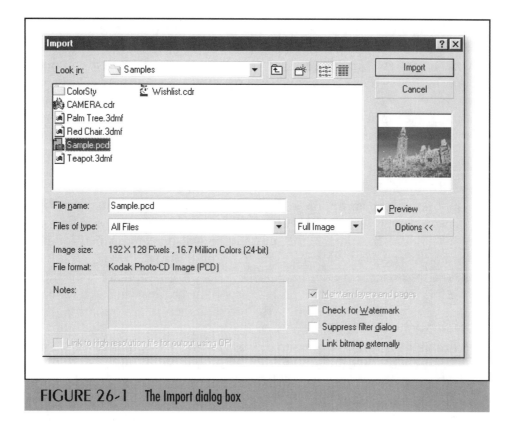

FIGURE 26-1   The Import dialog box

File Manager? Now you can do this by simply clicking the file name and pressing the DEL key. You can even rename a file by clicking the name twice, just as in Explorer. These small enhancements are one of the main productivity benefits provided by the Windows 9x interface.

The name of the selected file is shown in the File Name list box just below the main window. If you want to see only files of a certain format, select that format from the Files of Type drop-down list. For some file formats, that is the only way to reliably open or import files. If you've selected a bitmap to import, another drop-down list is available that allows you to choose which part of the image to import. This process will be discussed later in this chapter.

26

You can select multiple files for opening or importing by holding down the CTRL key while clicking on each file name.

To the right of the main display window, a preview of the selected file will be displayed if the Preview check box is checked. Some file formats do not provide a preview, and those that do can sometimes be saved without a preview header. In those cases, you'll just see a large X in the preview window.

If you've chosen not to see all options, there is nothing in the dialog box other than the Open or Import and Cancel buttons. However, if the Options button shows two arrows pointed inward (<<), the dialog box contains the maximum amount of information and clicking the Options button will decrease the amount of information shown. If the arrows are instead pointing outward (>>), click the Options button to expand the dialog box.

The first additional option is the Image Size information box. Any time you have a bitmap selected, this area will show you the image size in pixels and the color depth. Note that this information will appear only in the Import dialog box as you cannot open a bitmap in CorelDRAW.

Below the image size information is another information area that shows the file format. This information can be especially helpful when you have not specified a particular file format. If the format contains subformats that can be identified, they will be shown as well.

Some file formats allow notes to be stored with the file. If a file with stored notes is selected, they will be displayed in the large Notes text box.

At the lower-left corner of the dialog box is a check box labeled Link to High Resolution File for Output Using OPI. OPI stands for Open PrePress Interface. This feature will commonly be used when you have a service bureau scan files for you at a high resolution. The bureau will give you a low-resolution version of the file for placement within your document. If you import with this option checked, the larger file can be substituted by the service bureau when they output your file.

Several other options are available. When you are importing files that contain multiple layers or pages, you have the option of retaining those layers and pages. This is turned on by default. Note that it is grayed out for files where it wouldn't apply. Bitmaps can have a watermark stored within their data so that the creator of the image can be identified. When you've selected a bitmap for import, the Check for Watermark option is available. If you would like CorelDRAW to look inside the bitmap for a watermark, select this option.

A few filters will bring up another dialog box after the original Open/Import dialog box. If you find that all you are doing is accepting the default settings, you may want to avoid this extra dialog box. Simply check the Suppress Filter Dialog check box, and the file will be imported using the default settings.

The last option gives you the ability to import a bitmap but leave it linked to an external file. If the external file changes, so will the image inside of CorelDRAW. And since CorelDRAW saves only a small proxy image, your CorelDRAW files will be much smaller than if you imported the bitmap without linking. On bitmap formats and files where linking is available, the Link Bitmap Externally check box will be available. Chapter 23 supplies more information on working with externally linked bitmaps.

PLACING IMPORTED FILES

Prior to CorelDRAW 8, an imported file would automatically be placed on the page. Now you'll get a special cursor with an attached file name that allows you to precisely place the file. It works much like the Rectangle tool in that you draw from one corner to another. By default, the image will be constrained to its original aspect ratio. Holding down the ALT key will allow you to distort the image.

 *A good way to import a file and retain its placement on the page is to right-click on the file name in either the Import dialog box or the Scrapbook and select Import from the pop-up menu.*

If you have chosen to import multiple files, the process of placing files will continue until all files have been imported. For those who would rather just see the images, a double-click will import the file in its original size, as in previous versions. Dragging the file from the Scrapbook with the left mouse button will place the file in the position in which you drop it.

SPECIAL CONSIDERATIONS FOR PARTICULAR FORMATS

Many of the file formats are straightforward. Others require special attention when you import them. This section describes the most commonly used

26

formats that require special handling. The other formats are described in the help files should you require further information.

CORELDRAW CDR AND CDX FORMATS

The CDR format is CorelDRAW's native format, but each version of CorelDRAW that has been released includes a new format. CorelDRAW 8 can read only files created in version 3 and higher. If you need to access older files, you'll need CorelDRAW 5 or earlier. Occasionally, a CDR file will become corrupted and cause errors during opening or importing. If CorelDRAW 8 encounters a corrupt object, it will try to skip that object and continue opening the file. Most of the time this will allow you to open a file that previously could not be opened. Then you'll just need to find out which object was skipped and re-create it.

CDX files are simply compressed CDR files. Files in this format are used on some of Corel's Artshow CDs.

COREL CMX AND CPX FORMATS

The CMX format was used for the clipart that was supplied with CorelDRAW in past versions. You can also save files in this format, but it does have some limitations. Effects are not kept live. This means that if you have a Blend effect in your file, it will be saved as a group of objects rather than as a blend. Clipart that was originally created with blends can then be difficult to edit since those blends become just a group of objects. Since CorelDRAW 8 provides clipart in CDR format, this should be less of a issue than in the past.

CPX is just a compressed version of CMX.

ADOBE ILLUSTRATOR, POSTSCRIPT INTERPRETED, AND EPS FORMATS

You'll come across files in EPS format quite often. How you handle them can vary greatly, however, because there are several variations of EPS, and each is quite different from the next.

Adobe Illustrator files are sometimes given the .eps extension, and sometimes they're given the .ai extension. However, the contents are the same. The Illustrator format is actually a small subset of EPS.

Since Illustrator has been one of the most popular design packages on the Macintosh, the AI format has been one of the best ways to share files across platforms. Earlier versions of CorelDRAW have done a poor job of accurately importing AI files, but much has been done to improve the filter in CorelDRAW 8, so you should be able to import AI files with few problems. You must make sure, however, to select the AI format so the files don't get confused with the other variations of EPS.

The worst problem you'll now find in working with AI files is the differences in font names. Panose should help you solve the problem, but it still won't always choose the right font for you. As long as you haven't chosen the Suppress Filter Dialog box, you'll have the opportunity to choose the fonts that are substituted.

True EPS files are normally treated like a black box. When they are imported by a program, the data is basically just stored, and a low-resolution header is displayed on the screen. Then when the document is printed, the actual EPS data is sent to the printer. If you don't print to a PostScript printer, the low-resolution header is printed instead. This is how CorelDRAW handles an EPS file if you choose Encapsulated PostScript (EPS). But there is another way.

The PostScript Interpreted filter will actually convert the contents of the file into editable objects. Most of the time, this process works fairly well. The main problem is that a large number of objects can be created. This is not a bug in CorelDRAW, but rather is the result of the way the data is stored in the EPS file. You'll also notice that the PostScript Interpreted filter is very resource intensive. If your system is low on memory, it could crash. The more complex the information in the EPS file, the harder it is to interpret the file and the longer it takes to interpret, so if it seems to be taking a long time to import a file, just wait. If something goes wrong, you'll definitely know it.

CorelDRAW 8 enables the PostScript Interpreted filter to handle multiple page files including color separations.

BITMAP FORMATS

Bitmaps work differently from vector files. They are always rectangular, even though they may seem not to be. Areas that are white in the bitmap really consist of white pixels, and they will cover up objects behind them. There are

ways to make bitmaps into odd shapes. PowerClips are discussed in Chapter 21, and the bitmap color mask is discussed in Chapter 23. With these effects, you can eliminate parts of a bitmap you don't want. You can also use the Shape tool to crop a bitmap into an odd shape, as described in Chapter 8. The best way to get an odd-shaped bitmap is to work with the image in PHOTO-PAINT and save the file in CPT format with a mask or as floating objects.

When you import a bitmap, CorelDRAW looks at the size of the bitmap in pixels and the resolution in dots per inch. It then sizes the bitmap based on those numbers. So if you have a bitmap that is 600 pixels by 400 pixels at 200 dpi, it will be sized to 3 inches by 2 inches in CorelDRAW. You can easily enlarge or reduce the bitmap by grabbing the handles as with any other object, but remember that the exact number of pixels will not change. Therefore, if you make the object larger, it may look very pixelated, and if you make it smaller, extra data will be stored unnecessarily, so the best thing to do is to size the bitmap appropriately in Corel PHOTO-PAINT before importing it into CorelDRAW.

If you will be outputting the file to a CMYK printer, you'll want to convert it to CMYK in Corel PHOTO-PAINT. If the destination is a grayscale device, convert the file into a grayscale bitmap. The important thing is that you will most likely need to prepare the file in Corel PHOTO-PAINT before using it in CorelDRAW. Although CorelDRAW 8 has capabilities for working with bitmaps (see Chapter 23), this editing is still best done in Corel PHOTO-PAINT.

Cropping Bitmaps

At times, you'll want to import a bitmap, but you'll want only a certain area of it instead of the whole thing. In this case, you'll want to crop the image. You can do this prior to importing in Corel PHOTO-PAINT, but you can also crop the image when it is imported. After you select the bitmap you wish to import, select Crop from the drop-down list to the right of the file name. After you click the Import button, you'll be presented with another dialog box, shown in Figure 26-2.

There are two ways to crop an image. You can grab the handles surrounding the image and drag them so they surround the area you wish to keep. You can also specify the size to keep by entering the Top, Left, Width,

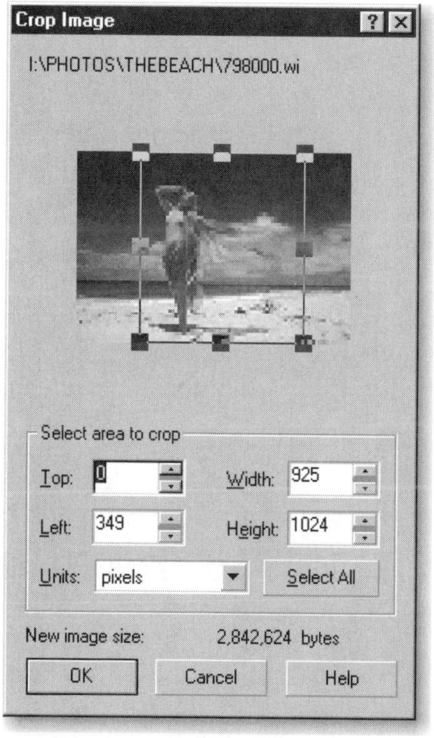

Crop Image   ? ✕

I:\PHOTOS\THEBEACH\798000.wi

Select area to crop

Top: 0   Width: 925

Left: 349   Height: 1024

Units: pixels   Select All

New image size: 2,842,624 bytes

OK   Cancel   Help

FIGURE 26-2   The Crop Image dialog box

and Height values for the image. By default, the Units value will be pixels, but you can change to any measurement system that CorelDRAW supports. If you want to bring in the whole image, simply click the Select All button. Near the bottom of the dialog box, the new size of the image in bytes is listed. Note that this is the uncompressed size.

26

 *Cropping an image during import will reduce the size of the file, while cropping an image with the Shape tool only hides portions of the image.*

Resampling Bitmaps

Sometimes the bitmap you wish to import may not be the correct size. If it is too small, you may want to find a way to get a larger original without resampling, since resampling may degrade the quality of the image. You can use resampling to reduce the size and still retain a good-quality image, at least to a point.

When you select a bitmap to import, choose Resample from the drop-down list to the right of the file name. Once you click Import, you'll be presented with a dialog box similar to that shown in Figure 26-3.

The first section allows you to change the width or height of the image either using the specified units or specifying a percentage of the current size.

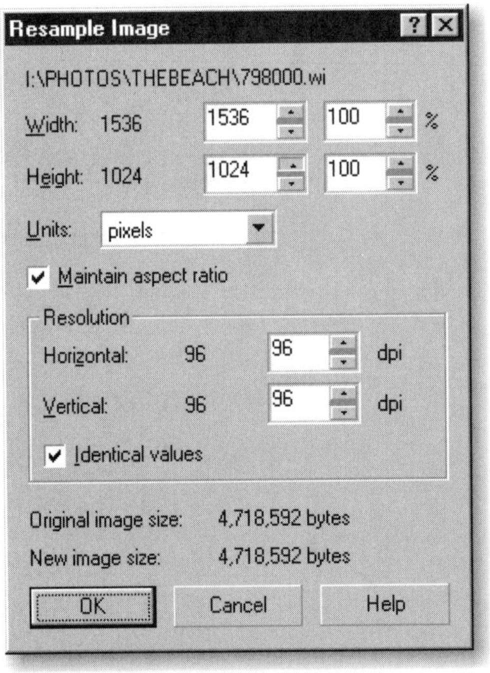

FIGURE 26-3   The Resample Image dialog box

If you check the Maintain Aspect Ratio check box, any changes made to one of the values will also affect the other value.

The next section lets you set the resolution of the image. You learned in Chapter 25 that the resolution of an image is, for the most part, a meaningless number. Changing the resolution does not necessarily change the size of the bitmap. This setting is meaningful only when you know the output resolution that will be used to print the image. If you do wish to change the resolution, you can do so in both the horizontal and vertical directions. If you want both values to be the same—and rarely would you not want this—then check the Identical Values check box.

At the bottom of the dialog box, you are informed of the original and new sizes of the image in bytes. Note that these are uncompressed values, and so the saved file may be much smaller.

COREL PHOTO-PAINT CPT FORMAT

In earlier versions, Corel PHOTO-PAINT files worked very much like other bitmap files. However, files that contained floating objects were not imported correctly; these objects disappeared when imported. Now the problem has been solved. When you import a .cpt file containing floating objects, you'll notice that you have a group of objects on the page. The floating objects remain floating and cut out in CorelDRAW. This provides a fantastic way to touch up artwork with the precision of CorelDRAW. It is also a great way to delete an unwanted background from a photograph.

Embedding Watermarks

A new technology has emerged recently that allows digital photographs to have a watermark embedded in them that contains copyright information. If you'd like to learn more about the technology that is used in both CorelDRAW and Corel PHOTO-PAINT, visit the home page of Digimarc at http://www.digimarc.com.

When you check the Check for Watermark check box in the Import dialog box, CorelDRAW will look at the bitmap you are importing and extract any copyright information that may be present. This information will then be displayed as part of the object's properties in the Status Bar. Note that checking for this information will make the import process take a little longer.

26

> **Tip:** *For those of you who wish to include watermarks on your own images, a plug-in filter has been included that works in both CorelDRAW and Corel PHOTO-PAINT. Note that you'll need to contact Digimarc to purchase a serial number to embed.*

PHOTOCD (PCD) FORMAT

Kodak created the PhotoCD format for storing 35mm photographs on a compact disc that could then be viewed on television. The consumer market never really caught on to PhotoCDs, but the graphics market soon found that this was a great way to store photographs. The problem with the files is that since they were developed for viewing on television screens, they are not really optimized for a printing press. With the controls provided by CorelDRAW, this limitation can be overcome.

After you select a PhotoCD file for import, you'll see a dialog box similar to the one in Figure 26-4. A sample PhotoCD image in stored in the \Draw\Samples folder on CD1.

You'll see a large preview of the image in the middle of the dialog box. Above the preview, at the left, is a drop-down list for selecting the size of the image you want to import. PhotoCD files can store up to six resolutions of the image within a single file, from the tiny Wallet size (192×128 pixels) to the huge Billboard size (6,144×4,096 pixels). Most files contain only five sizes, with the largest being the Poster size (3,072×2,048 pixels). As you change the size of the image you desire, the estimated image size will be displayed below the preview.

Another drop-down list at the upper-right corner of the dialog box lets you choose the color depth of the file, from 16.7 million colors to 256 colors to 256 grayscale. Sometimes it is best to choose 16.7 million colors even if you will be using fewer colors in the final image. This way all manipulations you make to the file will be performed using the highest quality.

Once you've selected the size and color depth of the image, click the Enhancement tab. Although making color corrections to the image is not required, it is highly recommended. There are two methods: GamutCD and Kodak Color Correction. In most circumstances, the GamutCD method will produce the best results. The dialog box for GamutCD correction is shown in Figure 26-5.

Most PhotoCD files contain a black border around the actual image. You must be careful when performing color correction that the black border does

FIGURE 26-4   The PhotoCD Image dialog box

not influence the image. In the lower-left corner of the dialog box is the Set
active area radio button. Select this radio button and then marquee select the
actual image area you wish to adjust. Then select the Set neutral colors radio
button. Use your mouse to select the lightest area of the image where you can
still distinguish details. You may want to use the RGB values on the right side
of the dialog box to help you distinguish which color is beneath your cursor.
Click the image where you find the lightest color. Repeat this process for the
darkest color.

   At any time, you can preview the results of the color correction by clicking
the Preview button in the upper-right corner of the dialog box. Two types of
previews are available: Fast Preview and Best Preview (which is slower). If
you wish to return the image to its original state, click the Reset button.

26

FIGURE 26-5   The PhotoCD Image dialog box for GamutCD enhancement

Many images do not have a true white or true black in them, so you can select Adjust white in image or Adjust black in image. Simply check the appropriate check box. Both of these options are activated by default, so if your image contains no black, you may want to deselect the Adjust black in image check box, or you can adjust the Absolute black value to a value that is appropriate for the colors in your image. The same procedure is available for Absolute white.

When you are making color corrections to your image, you may need to make several adjustments before getting everything just right—so make the changes, preview them, and then make more adjustments if necessary.

When Kodak Color Correction is selected, the dialog box changes as shown in Figure 26-6.

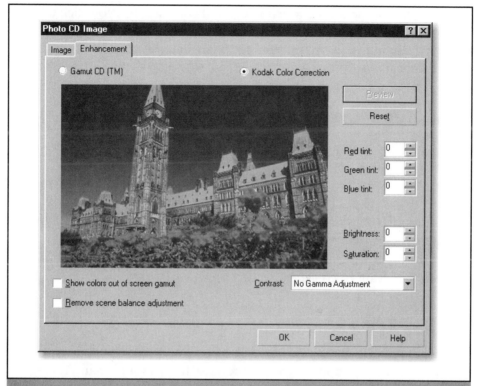

FIGURE 26-6 The PhotoCD Image dialog box for Kodak Color Correction

The controls you have using this method are much less automated. You can adjust the red, green, and blue tints in the image as well as the brightness, saturation, and contrast. All of these changes require you to enter a number except for Contrast, which provides ten different levels of contrast from which you can choose.

When the image was originally scanned, the scanner operator included information to balance the scene. By checking the Remove scene balance adjustment check box, you can remove this information. Check the Show colors out of screen gamut check box to make sure that the adjustments you've made are valid. When you click Preview, any colors that are out of gamut (can't be displayed correctly on your screen) will change to blue or red. Continue to make adjustments until there are no colors out of gamut.

26

Regardless of the color correction method you use, once you click OK, the image will be brought into CorelDRAW with all adjustments made. Since some of these adjustments are very processor intensive, it may take a little while for the import process to complete on slower systems.

Creating Your Own PhotoCDs

Recently we had a project where we needed to scan 30 images for a brochure. We were given slides, negatives, and transparencies. Because we don't have a slide or transparency scanner, we chose to create a PhotoCD instead. This was a great solution to the problem, since the cost was less than three dollars an image and we now have a permanent copy of each scan in five different resolutions. Our time alone for a scan would easily exceed the three dollar cost of the PhotoCD scans. So next time you're faced with a project such as this, you may want to consider creating a PhotoCD.

WORD PROCESSOR FORMATS

The Import dialog box lists a number of text and word processing filters, including all of the modern word processor formats and many long-gone formats as well. When you import the text from these formats, very little of the original formatting is retained. In fact, the person who creates the word processor file should not do any formatting, as the time spent doing so will most likely be wasted.

When the file is imported, it will be placed on the page so that it fills the page size. If the text won't fit on the current page, more pages will be created until there are enough to hold all of the text. These text boxes will be automatically linked to flow from one frame to the next. Unfortunately, there is no way to tell CorelDRAW not to create these extra pages, and often you will need to delete the extra frames and then re-create them where you need them using a different size.

A way around this problem is to first create a paragraph text frame and then import the text from the Edit Text dialog box. If you use this method, the text will be placed into the frame you drew, and no other frames or pages will be created. This new method makes page layout in CorelDRAW 8 much easier than in past versions.

We've explained each of the common types of import filters. The individual filters may have specific limitations. Check the Help | Technical Support section of the help files to get detailed information on any of the filters.

26

27

EXPORTING AND
SAVING FILES

Once you've spent lots of time working on an image, you don't want to throw it away—so you save the file for future use. This used to be a fairly straightforward operation, but now there are many useful options to choose from. Also, a .cdr file isn't always what you want, so you need to know about the various handy export filters that are available. This chapter doesn't cover all of them, but it explains the most important ones.

SAVING FILES

When you choose File | Save (CTRL-S), the Save Drawing dialog box you see will be nearly identical to the Open/Import dialog box you explored in the preceding chapter. All of the features of the Windows Explorer are just as applicable here as in the Open/Import dialog box. An example of the Save Drawing dialog box is shown in Figure 27-1.

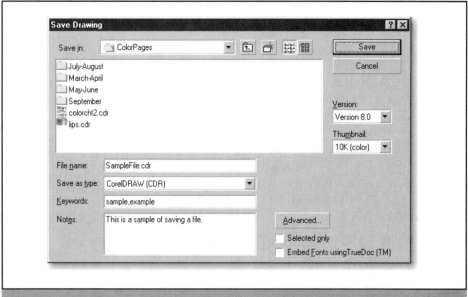

FIGURE 27-1 The Save Drawing dialog box

Below the main window is the File Name text box. Type in a name for your file and feel free to make it as long as 255 characters. You can either add the .cdr extension yourself, or leave it blank and let CorelDRAW do it for you.

If you want to give a file a name that doesn't include a .cdr extension or that includes another extension, place the entire name in double quotation marks.

By default, the file will be saved as a CorelDRAW (.cdr) file, but you can choose other types from the Save as type drop-down list. Note that in previous versions you had to export files if you wanted a format other than .cdr. That is no longer necessary.

The Keywords and Notes sections allow you to specify information about the files. Keywords are words that you can search for a particular topic. Thus, if you had a picture of a German Shepherd, you might want to enter **German Shepherd, Dog,** and **Animal** as keywords. In the Notes box, you can enter a more detailed description of the image. These notes will be displayed in the Open Drawing dialog box and can be especially helpful when you have a number of files with similar names or when you want to pass a file to another user.

At the right side of the dialog box are two drop-down lists for choosing which version of the CorelDRAW file format to use and how big of a thumbnail to include. Only versions 5, 6, 7, and 8 of CorelDRAW are supported. If you need to save to an older format, you'll need a copy of CorelDRAW 5. Thumbnails are small bitmaps of the file that can help you to identify the file in the File Open dialog box or the Scrapbook. They are not required, and leaving them out makes the file slightly smaller.

Two other options are available in this main dialog box. You can save only those objects that are currently selected by checking the Selected only check box. This can be handy if you have a certain element in your drawing that you wish to save for future use. Just make sure to change the name so you don't overwrite the file containing the whole drawing. And you need to have the objects selected before attempting to save the file or the Selected only check box will not be available. CorelDRAW 7 introduced the ability to embed the fonts you've used in the .cdr file itself using the TrueDoc technology discussed in Chapter 38. Just check the Embed Fonts using TrueDoc check box.

There are more options that are considered advanced functions; click the Advanced button to access these additional features. Note that all of the

27

features apply to CorelDRAW 8 files, but not necessarily to older formats. The Options Save box is shown in Figure 27-2.

The first option in this dialog box is Save Presentation Exchange (CMX). You'll learn more about the CMX format a little later, but for now note that having this extra data is useful if you plan to use the .cdr file in other Corel products such as Corel PHOTO-PAINT, Corel VENTURA, or CorelDREAM 3D. Otherwise, it just enlarges the file by a factor of 1.5 or 2.

If the Use current thumbnail option is checked, CorelDRAW will not generate a new thumbnail each time you save a file. By default, this option is turned off.

With each release of CorelDRAW, the file format has produced files that were larger than those in the previous version. This expansion was especially noticeable in the move from CorelDRAW 5 to CorelDRAW 6. Going from a 16-bit file format to a 32-bit file format nearly doubled the file sizes. CorelDRAW 6 included an option that seemed like a way to compress files, but it only affected texture fills. Now there are many ways to compress files.

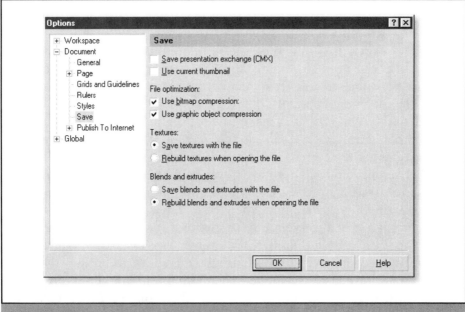

FIGURE 27-2   The Options Save dialog box

Both bitmaps and vector objects can be compressed using LZW technology. This is the same compression format that is used by the PKZIP program and .tif files. With only this type of compression, you should see a significant reduction in file size. Texture fills are nothing more than bitmaps. You can have them saved as bitmaps in the file or have them regenerated when the file is opened. Obviously, regenerating them can take some time, but it can save a significant amount of space on your hard drive. Similarly, blends and extrudes can create a large number of new objects. Now you can save just the original objects with the information to rebuild the effect when you open the file. Again, this is a great way to save space if you have the extra time.

EXPORTING FILES

If every program could work with native CorelDRAW files, exporting wouldn't be necessary. However, Corel does not disclose its file format, and, in addition, in some applications the Corel format would not be appropriate. Therefore, Corel enables you to save or export files in a wide variety of formats. This section describes the formats that you will probably use most often and explains how to best optimize the files. For those formats not discussed here, check the help files for information.

AI FORMAT

Adobe Illustrator is currently the leading graphics package on the Macintosh (but Corel is now chasing close behind). The AI format is also used in many other applications, especially in sign-cutting and graphics software. Corel's Export filter for AI has been poor in past versions, but they've taken great pains to rewrite the filter for maximum compatibility.

When you select exporting to AI, you'll see the dialog box shown in Figure 26-3.

The Compatibility drop-down list shows each version of Adobe Illustrator that was released prior to CorelDRAW 8. By default, it selects Adobe Illustrator 4.x, but if you are creating files for users with a later version, simply select that version from the list. You can also select whether the destination is the PC or Macintosh platform.

You can leave text as text or have it converted to curves when you export. Remember that font compatibility may be a problem if the file is opened on

27

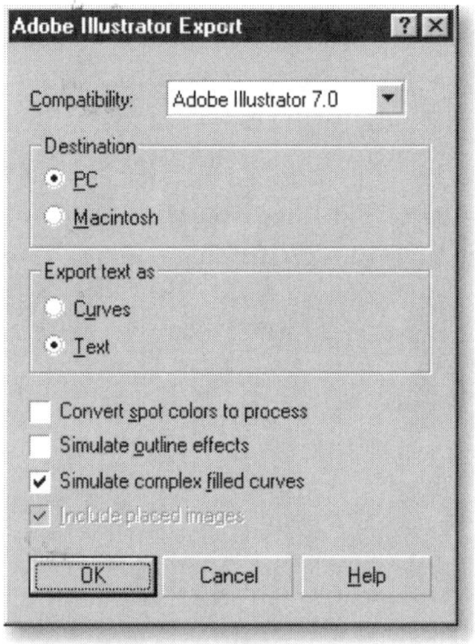

FIGURE 27-3   The Adobe Illustrator Export dialog box

the Macintosh. Spot colors can be automatically converted to their process equivalents. Remember that these colors will be quite different than they would be if they were printed with the true spot color inks. If effects, such as dotted lines, have been used on outlines, you can select Simulate outline effects to get a close approximation. Similarly, there are some types of fills that do not have an equivalent feature in Illustrator. So checking Simulate complex filled curves will try to match the fills as closely as possible. If you have included bitmap images in your file, they can be included in the Illustrator file, but note that this is only supported in newer versions of Illustrator.

EPS FORMAT

Encapsulated PostScript, or EPS, is the best file format to use for maximum compatibility with all of the features contained in CorelDRAW. It can be used by almost all programs on the PC and the Macintosh, but it does require a PostScript printer to print correctly.

Many Macintosh-biased service bureaus may ask you to convert your .cdr files to EPS format for output. This is not a good idea because it means that the service bureau is going to place the file in another program to print them. In fact, Quark Express contains some limitations that will affect the proper printing of Corel EPS files. Note that these are limitations in Quark Express and not in Corel's export filters.

When you choose EPS, you'll see the dialog box shown in Figure 27-4.

Just as with the Adobe Illustrator filter, you can convert text to curves or leave it as text. If you choose Text, the fonts can be embedded within the file so that the recipient doesn't need them, but this does increase file size. In most instances, it is best to leave the text as text, but if you have very short blocks of text and numerous fonts, converting to curves would be a good idea.

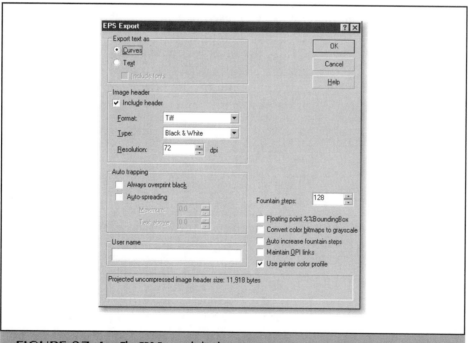

FIGURE 27-4   The EPS Export dialog box

27

Since most operating systems cannot display PostScript files on the screen, EPS files can contain a header for display purposes. By default, the Include header check box is checked. The header can be either a .tif or .wmf file. .tif files provide maximum compatibility. When you use them, you can specify the type (color depth) and resolution. The bitmap display can be quite good if you choose 8-bit color and a high resolution, although doing so is not always a good idea.

We've had very bad luck with some so-called graphics professionals who assume that all EPS files should be opened in Photoshop. When this is done, all they get is the bitmap header which is a much lower quality than the embedded PostScript data. They blame Corel instead of learning how to correctly use their software. We've also experienced this same problem with magazines for which we've written. If we are the "experts" and these so-called professionals aren't willing to listen, we can only imagine the problems experienced by the average users. We just can't stress enough that the header is only supposed to be used for a low-resolution screen preview.

The header you include is also used when the file is printed to a non-PostScript printer. Because the TIF header may look very crude, you can also specify a WMF header. This approach provides the best onscreen display and printing since WMF is a vector format, but since it is a Windows-only format, these files have limited compatibility with layout software and should be used with caution. Also, the WMF format cannot display bitmaps, so it may provide a poor rendition of a file if it contains bitmaps.

Trapping information can be included within the EPS file. It is applied in two different ways. Choosing the Always overprint black option prints black ink on top of any other color rather than trying to cut out the text. Since adding black does not change the color much, this is the best way to trap small black text on a colored background. Spread traps are also supported, through the Auto-spreading option. You can specify the maximum width of the trap and the point at which text will begin to be trapped. Any manual traps you create will always be present in the EPS file. For more information on trapping options, see Chapter 29.

The size of the .eps file is stored in the first few lines of data as the bounding box. Typically this is an integer, but by checking Floating point %%BoundingBox, you can have it stored as a floating-point value. There are several other options that are also available in the Print dialog box, as described in Chapter 29. Since printing to a PostScript printer and printing EPS files are very similar, it is no surprise that these options are in both places. See Chapter 29 for a full discussion on these features.

CMX FORMAT

Earlier you saw how .cmx files can be embedded within a .cdr file. You can also save them as stand-alone files. The thing to remember about .cmx files is that any effects in the file will not be saved as live effects. Thus, Blend effects will still look the same when a .cmx file is opened, but they will be difficult to change. Ditto for Extrude, Fit Text to Path, and other effects—so whenever you save a file in .cmx, you should make sure you have a .cdr file as well.

PDF FORMAT

PDF is the native file format for Adobe's Acrobat line of products. If you need to create Acrobat files with all of the features possible in Acrobat, you should get a copy of Acrobat 3.0, as CorelDRAW 8 supports only a subset of the features in the PDF format.

To have the page size you specify in CorelDRAW respected by the export filter, you must create an object that covers the whole page. Otherwise, the page created will be scaled to hold all objects in the drawing. Another benefit of Acrobat is the font fidelity it provides. Fonts can be embedded or imitated. CorelDRAW 8 does not embed fonts in an Acrobat file, so font fidelity can be lost. The font name in the exported file will not be the same as that used in CorelDRAW. Note that this is not an Acrobat bug since CorelDRAW never gave it the proper font name to work with.

Using the Acrobat Distiller to create .pdf files allows various levels of control over the way bitmaps are stored. However, when exporting from CorelDRAW, none of these options are available. This can create files that are larger than they need to be, since compression is not applied.

If you need to create an Acrobat file quickly, this filter will do the job, but users who require more will want to get a copy of Acrobat.

27

COREL IMAGE MAP, COREL BARISTA, AND HTML FORMATS

These filters are used to create special items for inclusion on a Web page. They will be covered in depth in Chapter 39.

TTF AND PFB FORMATS

CorelDRAW is a great program for font creation, although this feature is hidden from obvious view. CorelDRAW doesn't contain many of the high-end features found in programs such as Macromedia's Fontographer, but it is great at creating the font characters. The help files contain extensive information on how to prepare a proper character for export. Search the Index tab for "font conventions, becoming familiar with."

Once you've created a character (you can create only one at a time), select either the PFB (PostScript) or TTF (TrueType) export filter. When you click Export, you'll see the Options dialog box shown in Figure 27-5.

The Family name entry is the main name of the font, without any weight attributes. If the font contains symbol characters rather than alphabetical characters, check the Symbol Font check box. Only four styles are available in the Style drop-down list.

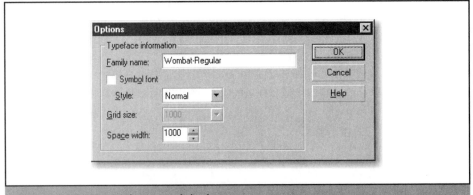

FIGURE 27-5   The Options dialog box

This dialog box also provides Grid size and Space width settings. These values will differ between the PostScript (1000) and TrueType (2048) formats. Only in very rare circumstances will you want to change these values.

Click OK, and a second dialog box appears, as shown in Figure 27-6.

The left side of the dialog box displays the character and three lines. The two vertical lines represent the left and right sidebearings of the character. You cannot move the left sidebearing, but you can adjust the right one numerically. To do so, uncheck the Auto check box and modify the Character width value. You'll notice that the right sidebearing moves to the left when you enter lower numbers and to the right when you enter higher numbers.

You also need to assign the character a position in the font. You can do this either through the scrolling list of characters or by entering the ASCII code in the Character number box.

Last, you need to specify a design size. The default value is to 720 points, and if you've followed the instructions provided in the help file, you should leave this value unchanged. Click OK to write the changes to the font file.

You'll need to repeat this process for each character of the font, making sure to use the same names each time. Also ensure that you place every new character in a different ASCII position so one doesn't overwrite an existing character. When you are finished, install the font using the processes described in Chapter 38 and then start using your new font.

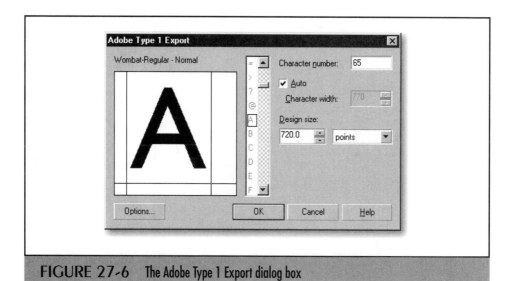

FIGURE 27-6   The Adobe Type 1 Export dialog box

27

BITMAP FORMAT

Quite often, you'll want to export your artwork to a bitmap format. You can do this in two ways. Using CorelDRAW, you can simply export to that format; this method will be discussed here in detail. However, the best way is to open a .cdr (or .cmx) file directly in Corel PHOTO-PAINT. The dialog boxes in both instances are very similar, but the results are not always the same.

When you select one of the bitmap formats, you may be presented with the Compression Type drop-down list if it is applicable to that flavor of bitmap. If you want the file compressed, choose the compression format from that list. The compression types will vary from format to format, and some formats, such as JPEG, will present a second dialog box with compression information.

For all bitmap formats, the dialog box shown in Figure 27-7 appears.

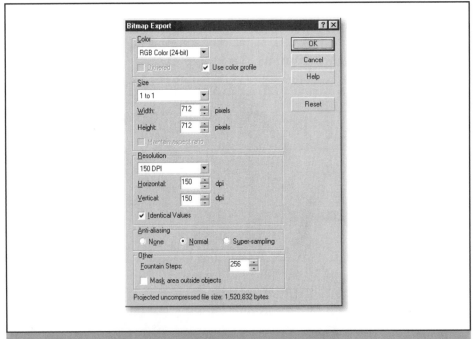

FIGURE 27-7   The Bitmap Export dialog box

Your first choice is the color depth of the file. Select the appropriate choice from the drop-down list. Remember that your choice should reflect the palette you have used. Therefore, if you want to export to RGB, you should use an RGB palette to select your colors in CorelDRAW. For color depths other than 16 million or CMYK, the Dithered option is available. This helps to retain the look of the original image in the lower color formats. However, this option is not always desirable, such as when creating a GIF of the smallest size. You also have the option of using the color profile to convert RGB colors to CMYK or vice versa.

You can also choose the size of the image from a drop-down list. Several popular monitor resolutions are in the list, as are 1 to 1 and Custom. Most of the time, you'll want to use 1 to 1. The fixed monitor sizes are of little use unless you want your images to fit that aspect ratio. Also, you really need to design your images with exporting in mind so that you used the correct aspect ratio in CorelDRAW. When using the Custom option, make sure that you keep the Maintain aspect ratio check box checked so the image does not become distorted. If ever this distortion is required, uncheck this check box. If you select Maintain aspect ratio, entering a value in either the Width or Height box will automatically change the value in both boxes.

Resolution rears its ugly head again in this dialog box. We can't stress often enough that this value is quite often very deceptive. Several of the popular resolutions are listed in the drop-down list, and Custom can be found at the bottom. With Custom, you can type any resolution you like, down to 60 dpi. For some applications, a smaller value may be required, so you'll have to reset the resolution in the other application.

Below Resolution is the Anti-aliasing section. If you don't want to introduce any more colors into your image, make sure to choose None. Adding anti-aliasing can improve the look of line art, but it can hamper the creation of transparent GIF files. Two types of anti-aliasing are provided. Normal uses the image size you choose, and Super-sampling creates a bitmap four times the size you choose and then resamples it down to the size you specified. Thus, Super-sampling produces a much higher-quality image but exacts a severe time penalty for larger images.

Specifying a number of Fountain Steps can help to eliminate banding. But slight color changes over a large area will always have problems. A really great new option is Mask area outside objects. If you are exporting to a format that can store masks (especially CPT), having the mask created automatically can save you a tremendous amount of work later.

27

As you are making changes, you'll notice that the projected size of the file is shown at the bottom of the dialog box. Note that this size is for uncompressed files, so if you compress your bitmap, the actual file size should be much smaller.

GIF, JPEG, AND PNG FORMATS

The GIF, JPEG, and PNG formats are all variations on bitmaps. Since they are mainly used when creating artwork for the Internet, they are discussed fully in Chapter 39.

Exporting files properly is the key to using your CorelDRAW artwork in other applications. If the file isn't exported properly, the looks may be changed or it may not be able to be imported into the application of your choice.

28

PAGE SETUP

CorelDRAW offers a wide variety of paper sizes, including foreign paper sizes. It also includes sizes for envelopes and labels. With the exception of labels, all of the paper sizes can be selected directly from the Property Bar, which is quicker than selecting them from the Options dialog box.

USING THE PROPERTY BAR TO SET UP THE PAGE

The default page setup is Letter 8.5" × 11" Portrait mode. The paper size and orientation can be selected directly from the Property Bar. The page setup options are available on the Property Bar only if nothing is selected on the page and either the Pick or Shape tool is selected from the toolbox. The Paper Size list box is at the far left end of the Property Bar, next to the Paper Width and Height boxes. Next to these are the Portrait and Landscape Orientation buttons. To select a paper size, select the down arrow and choose a type from the drop-down list. Figure 28-1 shows the Property Bar in its default mode. If you prefer to measure your page in units other than inches, click the down arrow on the Drawing units list box and pick a unit of measurement.

The only paper sizes missing from the drop-down list on the Property Bar are those for labels. These are not included in this list because of the vast number of label styles available. You can select labels from an Options dialog box discussed later in this chapter.

USING THE OPTIONS DIALOG BOX TO SET UP THE PAGE

In previous versions of CorelDRAW, you changed the page settings in a single Page Setup dialog box. Version 8 uses four separate dialog boxes, including page layout styles such as Booklet and Tent Cards, numerous label styles, and a new category called Backgrounds. There are two ways to access these new dialog boxes: The easiest method is to double-click the open document's page border. Figure 28-2 shows the default dialog box as it appears when you double-click the border. The second method involves choosing Tools | Options to bring up the default Options dialog box and then expanding the tree

Paper Size drop-down list
Paper Width and Height boxes
Portrait Orientation button
Landscape Orientation button
Drawing Units drop-down list

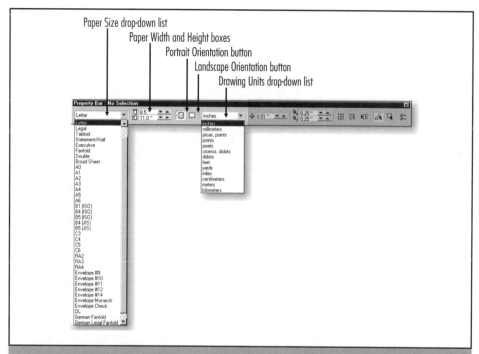

FIGURE 28-1   The default Property Bar with nothing selected and the Paper Size and Drawing Units drop-down lists displayed

structure to get to the size dialog box shown in Figure 28-2. Use Figure 28-2 as a guide to expanding the tree structure. The actual steps are: Tool | Options | Document | Page | Size.

USING THE PAGE/SIZE DIALOG BOX

Figure 28-2 shows the Page/Size dialog box selected. Keep in mind that several of the settings in this dialog box are also on the Property Bar. The page options for size are as follows:

▶ *Normal Paper/Labels*   The default is Normal Paper. Selecting Labels will take you to the Options/Label dialog box.

▶ *Portrait/Landscape*   Enable either of the radio buttons to select the orientation of the page. The preview window at the right displays the orientation selected.

28

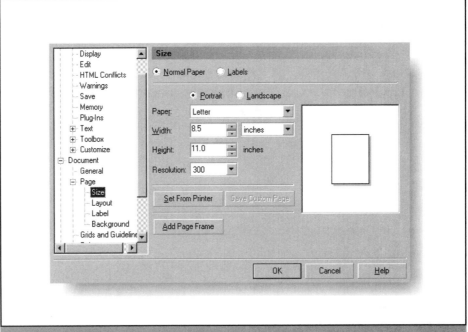

FIGURE 28-2　The Options dialog box with Page | Size selected

▶ *Paper* Select the down arrow on the list box to scroll through the list of paper sizes.

▶ *Width/Height* The Width and Height boxes are automatically updated to reflect the paper size selected. If you select Custom at the top of the list, you can enter values directly in the num boxes. By default, measurements are shown in inches. You can change to various other measurement systems by selecting them from the drop-down list.

▶ *Resolution* Clicking the down arrow lets you choose a resolution from a drop-down list. If you need a resolution other than those in the list, click Other at the bottom of the list and enter your custom resolutions.

▶ *Set From Printer* This button sets the paper size to the default setting of your default printer.

▶ *Add Page Frame* Click this button to place a rectangle on the page the size of the paper. This rectangle is an object just like any other object and will be filled with the default fill and outline colors. Remember, it will print just like any other object; therefore, if you are printing on colored paper, you would not use the page frame to represent the paper.

USING THE PAGE/LAYOUT DIALOG BOX

Six different layout styles are available in the Page / Layout dialog box. The default style is Full Page. When you select the down arrow on the list box, you'll get a choice of five additional styles. Do not confuse these styles with CorelDRAW's Graphic and Text styles and the new Color styles. These are layout styles, and as the name implies they allow you to design your projects so the images print in the proper orientation on the sheet. When you select a particular style, the preview window shows a graphical representation of the style. Below the list box are two context-sensitive description lines that change whenever you select a new style. These descriptive lines tell you the number of pages per sheet required (see "Adding More Pages" later in this chapter) and the size of each page. Each available style is listed here:

▶ *Full Page* This is the default style. One full page is printed per sheet.

▶ *Book* Two pages per sheet are printed so the document can be cut in the middle.

▶ *Booklet* Two pages per sheet are printed so the document can be folded vertically in the middle.

▶ *Tent Card* Two pages per sheet are printed so the document can be folded horizontally for a top fold.

▶ *Side-Fold Card* Four pages per sheet are printed so the document can be folded horizontally for the top fold and vertically for the side fold.

▶ *Top-Fold Card* Four pages per sheet are printed so the document can be folded vertically for the side fold and horizontally for the top fold.

28

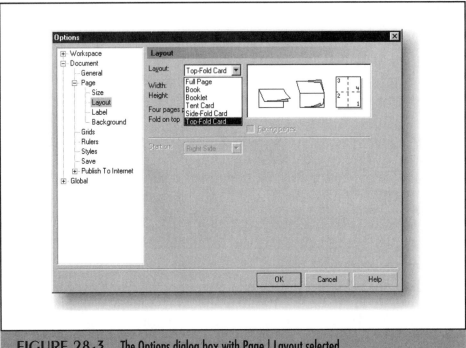

FIGURE 28-3 The Options dialog box with Page | Layout selected

Figure 28-3 shows the preview window with a graphical representation of the Top-Fold Card option.

The remaining options in the Layout section are

► *Facing Pages*   Enabling this option allows you to see facing pages if your document contains multiple pages.

► *Start On*   This list box lets you choose which page to start with if your document has multiple pages and you have enabled the Facing Pages check box.

If either of these options are grayed out it means they are not available for the style selected.

USING THE PAGE/LABEL DIALOG BOX

Labels are handled differently than the other layout styles. They are not included in the Paper Size drop-down list on the Property Bar because an additional list box is required to show all the various styles. You instead select a label style from the Label Types list box in the Page/Label dialog box. After you select a label from the dialog box, the word "Label" will appear on the Property Bar to let you know what label style is currently being used.

The Label list box contains folders for all the popular brands (and brand styles) of labels. When you expand a folder by selecting the + button next to the folder, a list of all the labels available for that particular brand's styles appears. Figure 28-4 shows the Avery Laser 5095-2.3x3.3 Badge style selected. Notice that the preview window displays the labels as they would actually appear on a real sheet of labels.

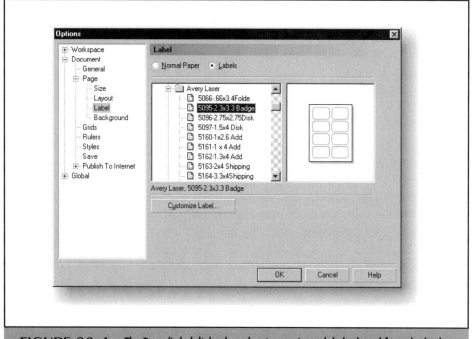

FIGURE 28-4   The Page/Label dialog box showing an Avery label selected from the list box

28

 *If you don't see the labels shown in Figure 28-4, click on the Labels radio button at the top of the Page/Label dialog box.*

After you select the label style and click OK, the first label with a page border the size of the label will be displayed. For example, suppose you select the Badge labels shown in Figure 28-4, which are set up with eight labels per page. If you need to enter different information for each label, you can enter the information on page 1 and then click the + button in the navigation tools at the bottom of the drawing window to add a second page. When the second page is displayed, you can enter the new information. You can continue adding pages until you reach the total number of labels required for the project. Figure 28-5 shows an Avery Laser 5095-2.3×3.3 Badge label on page 8. Notice the page tabs on the navigation toolbar. To switch between pages, simply click the appropriate page tab.

FIGURE 28-5   The eighth page of a set of Avery labels

If you want to print labels with the same information on each label, you use a different process. Follow these steps to place the same information on every label:

1. Select a label style from the Label Type list box.

2. Choose Layout | Insert Page to bring up the Insert Page dialog box. Enter the number of extra pages required for the number of labels you will be printing. For example, if you want to print 50 labels, enter 49 in the Insert Page num box and click on OK.

3. Choose View | Dockers | Object Manager to bring up the Object Manager dialog box.

4. Right-click Layer 1 and click Master Layer in the pop-up menu shown here. This action will place the information from the first page on every page (label) in the document.

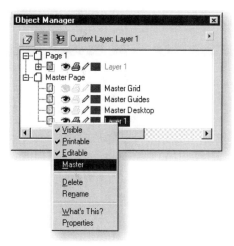

That's all there is to it. When it comes time to print the labels, CorelDRAW knows you're printing labels and will automatically add the number of label sheets required for the number of labels (pages) created, regardless of whether you are printing the same or different information on the labels.

28

CREATING CUSTOM LABELS

CorelDRAW 8 lets you create custom labels. From the Page/Label dialog box click the Customize Label button to bring up the Customize Label dialog box shown in Figure 28-6. To create custom labels, simply enter your coordinates in the various num boxes.

USING THE PAGE/BACKGROUND DIALOG BOX

CorelDRAW 8 now lets you control the fill properties of the backgrounds. This is like creating a Page Frame discussed earlier except in this case you define the fill properties here in this dialog box. Click Background at the bottom of the Page tree to display the Page/Background dialog box shown in Figure 28-7. Across the top of the dialog box are three radio buttons: No

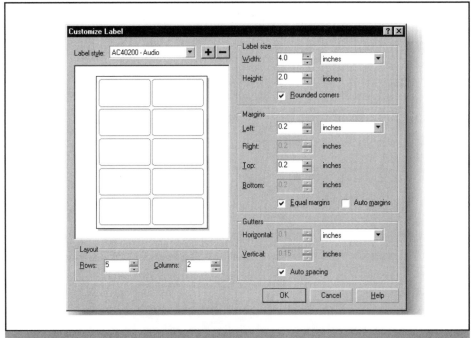

FIGURE 28-6   The Customize Label dialog box

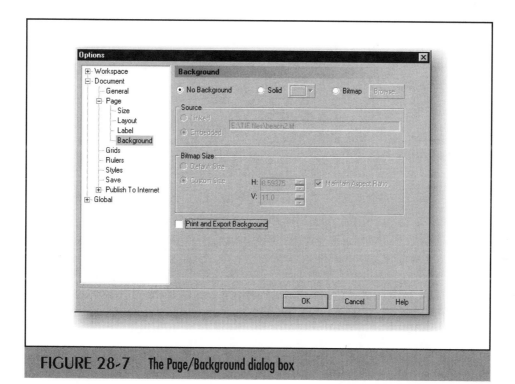

FIGURE 28-7 The Page/Background dialog box

Background (the default), Solid, and Bitmap. To fill the background with a solid color, enable the Solid radio button and the drop-down palette box is activated. Click the down arrow and select a color from the palette.

When you enable the Bitmap radio button, as shown in Figure 28-8, the Browse button is activated. Clicking this button allows you to select a bitmap image from anywhere on your hard drive. When you use a bitmap as a background, the dialog box reveals other options. The first is the Source option; it lets you choose whether the bitmap file is linked to the file or embedded in the file. (For more on object linking and embedding, see the section "Linking Bitmap Images" in Chapter 23.)

The second option is Bitmap Size. Enabling the Default Size radio button uses the actual size of the selected bitmap image. If the image is smaller than the paper size, it will be tiled into the background. If it is larger than the paper size, only a portion of the image will display. When you enable the Custom Size radio button, enter custom horizontal and vertical dimensions for the selected bitmap image in the num boxes. When you use a custom setting, the

28

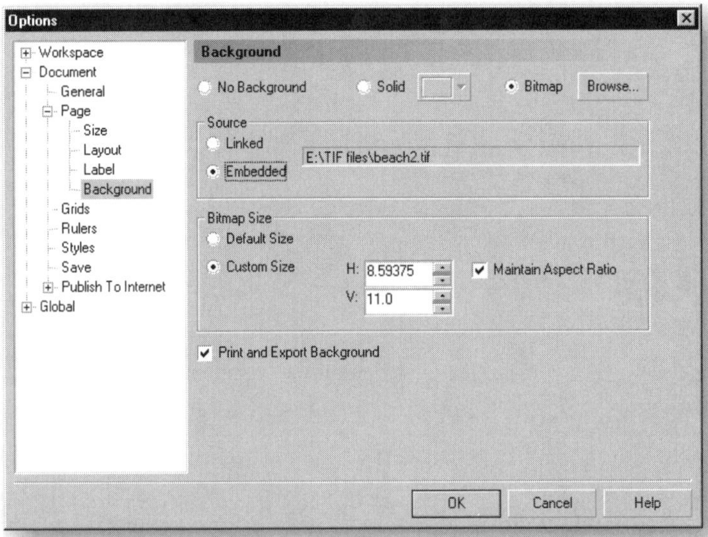

FIGURE 28-8   The Page/Background dialog box when a Bitmap image has been used

selected bitmap will be resized to fit the dimensions. Figure 28-9 shows a bitmap image used as a Background fill.

The third option in the Page/Background dialog box is the Print and Export Background check box. If you do enable this check box, the background fill will print. If you export the document to another format, the background fill will be exported as part of the document.

ADDING MORE PAGES

There are two ways to add more pages to your documents: You can add pages one at a time, or you can add several pages all at once. To add pages one at a time, click the + button on the navigation toolbar at the bottom of the drawing window. To add several pages at once, choose Layout | Insert Page and enter the number of pages in the Insert Page dialog box. You have the option of adding the pages before or after the currently selected page.

FIGURE 28-9   Using a bitmap image as a background fill

MOVING BETWEEN PAGES

When are you working with multiple-page documents, you often want to work on a specific page or simply move to the previous or next page. There are two ways to move between pages one page at a time. The first method is to click either the left or right arrowhead on the navigation toolbar at the bottom of the drawing window. The second method is to click the PGUP or PGDN key to move forward or backward one page.

To go directly to the first or last page, move to the navigation toolbar again and click the left icon with arrowhead pointing at a line to go to the first page or click the right icon with arrowhead pointing at a line to go to the last page.

If you want to go to a specific page, choose Layout | Go To Page. Enter the page number in the num box in the Go To Page dialog box, shown here.

28

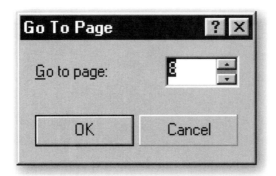

If you're an experienced CorelDRAW user, you have just learned the newest way to control your page setup. If you liked the old way better, you can still use the old Page Setup dialog box. See "Customizing the User Interface" in Chapter 40.

In summary, you have learned that there can be more to setting up a page than you may have thought. You have also learned how to add more than one page to your documents and how to create labels.

29

PRINTING

Printing is probably the most important topic of all when you're working with CorelDRAW. Unfortunately, it is also one of the most difficult to master. This chapter discusses everything from printing the simplest drawing to producing a color separation. The interesting thing about a color separation is that the techniques used are essentially the same as those for creating a high-quality black-and-white image, with one or two extra steps. Thus, even if you don't work with color, you can still gain valuable information from this chapter that you can use to improve the quality of your output.

Many of the printing problems that people experience are actually design problems. It is very easy to create artwork that just won't print or causes great difficulty in printing. In almost every case, there's a workaround to solve the problem. Throughout this book, you'll find information on printing problems and how to solve them. Just remember: if it doesn't print, it's just a video game!

 *Some of the printing problems that you encounter are problems with your printer driver. Check with your hardware vendor to make sure you have the latest driver.*

SERVICE BUREAUS

For those of you who are not familiar with service bureaus, we'll describe them briefly. Most users can't afford, or have no desire to work with, the equipment needed to produce the film for color separations, color slides, posters, and various other projects. A service bureau purchases and maintains this expensive equipment and lets you pay only for the services you need. If you need film for color separations, you pay the service bureau for each set of film they output. The main problem you'll find is that not all service bureaus will work with DRAW files. This usually results from a heavy bias toward the Macintosh, for which DRAW only became recently available.

Finding a good service bureau can be really tough. When you do find a good one, be sure to work with it, because it can be a valuable partner in many of your projects. It can also be a good source of information. And you can help the people who work with you by keeping them informed as to the status of your project and anything that they may need to know before outputting the job.

Corel provides a list of its authorized service bureaus on its Web site. This is a good starting point, but you should still do more research to make sure you choose someone who is willing to really work with you. Ask other DRAW users in your area what service bureau they are using and whether they know anything about the ones you've located. Ask the people at the service bureau for the names of its clients who use DRAW. If they hesitate, you may want to look elsewhere.

You certainly shouldn't start this search process on the eve of an important project. If you wait until the last minute, you may make a hasty (and costly) decision. Before sending that important rush project to a service bureau, test the firm by sending a simple file with no time constraints. You may need to spend a little money up front to test several service bureaus, but in the long run, this experimenting will pay you back many times over.

THE PRINT DIALOG BOX

All previous versions of CorelDRAW always displayed the Print dialog box before anything was printed. Now there are ways to avoid this dialog box, but it contains too much important information for you to skip it completely.

To bring up the Print dialog box, shown in Figure 29-1, choose File | Print (CTRL-P) from any view of the document, including Print Preview. This dialog box is divided into four major sections: Printer, Print range, Copies, and Print style.

If you are already in the Print Preview screen, selecting File | Print (CTRL-P) will automatically print the document. Click the Options button to bring up the dialog box in Figure 29-1.

PRINTER

The Printer section of the Print dialog box is where you choose the printer to which the file will be sent. At the top is a drop-down list of all of the printers currently installed. Note that these names are not the names of the printer models, but rather the names they were given by whoever installed the printers. This means that sometimes you won't know your printer by the name displayed here.

After you select a printer, information about it will be listed just below its name. Status indicates the current status of the printer: it may be unavailable,

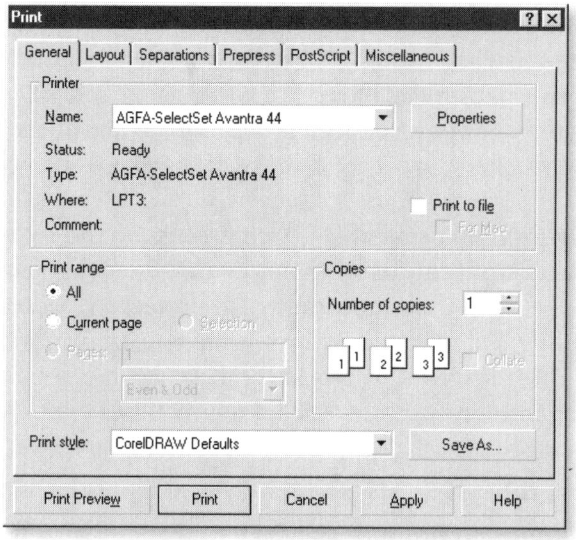

FIGURE 29-1   The Print dialog box

busy, or ready to go. Type tells you exactly what model of printer you are working with, since the name can be misleading. Where tells you how the printer is connected to your computer: via a network, a local port, or even a file. The Comment field may contain a comment about the printer; the comment would be supplied by the printer driver, but this field is rarely used.

In the lower-right corner of the Printer section are two check boxes. The top check box enables printing to a file. If you'll be preparing a file for a service bureau or for Adobe Acrobat, this feature is extremely important. It allows you to print using the features of a printer at a distant location, then supply the finished print file to that location. If you plan to use Print to file, it is a good idea not to connect the printer to the file port, because doing so can create conflicts. Instead, connect the printer to a "phantom port," such as LPT2 or LPT3, then check the Print to file check box. Check this box only if you will be preparing a PostScript file for a service bureau or for Acrobat. Otherwise, you can just print directly to the printer.

Just below the Print to file check box is the For Mac check box. This option becomes available only when Print to file is checked. When For Mac is checked, the CTRL-D characters normally included at the beginning and end of the print stream are replaced by spaces. This function is extremely important if the file will be output on a Macintosh computer, since Macintosh computers interpret CTRL-D as the end-of-file character. Even though this feature is specifically designed to help in outputting files on a Macintosh, it doesn't do any harm if the file is output on a PC. Therefore, it is a good idea to check For Mac whenever you are creating a file for service bureau output.

In the upper right of the Print dialog box is the Properties button. Click it and you'll be presented with all the options available on the printer you've selected. The dialog boxes that follow are completely dependent on the printer selected and the operating system you use. The dialog boxes are supplied by the operating system itself and not by CorelDRAW. Thus, this section discusses what you can, in general, expect to find in these dialog boxes, but it does not go into specific details.

Figure 29-2 shows the Properties dialog box for an AGFA Avantra imagesetter under Windows NT 4. Figure 29-3 shows a similar dialog box for use under Windows 95.

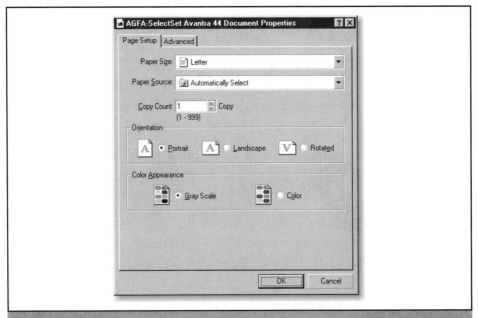

FIGURE 29-2 Printer Properties dialog box for an imagesetter operating under

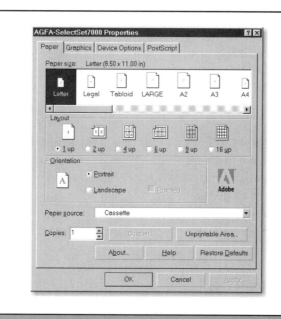

FIGURE 29-3   Printer Properties dialog box for an imagesetter operating under the Adobe Windows 95 driver

The most important settings to verify are the paper size, number of copies, and page orientation. Paper size is especially important when you're printing to film. Make sure you select a paper size larger than the document you've created if you need to print the various printer's marks, such as crop marks, registration marks, color bars, or densitometer scales. The number of copies can be set either in this dialog box or in the Print dialog box itself; it makes no difference which one you use. Note that changing the number of copies in the driver will be reflected in all applications, not just CorelDRAW. If you specify a large number of copies, make sure you reset the copy count before printing another file for which you want only one copy. Most of the time, the orientation is automatically adjusted by CorelDRAW after it displays a message asking you if it is all right to make the change. In most cases, you'll want to allow DRAW to change the orientation for you, but in some situations you won't. However, you can change the orientation to whatever you need.

For example, many times we need to print the dialog boxes you see in this book. If these files are wider than they are tall, Draw will ask to change the page orientation to Landscape. However, since we want all screen shots to be

29

oriented the same way, we choose to leave the page in Portrait orientation. If we didn't do this, we'd frequently have to rotate pages to read the text in the dialog boxes.

 *When you're printing files for Adobe Acrobat, you'll almost always want to print in Portrait orientation, even though the paper is wider than it is tall. If you don't print the pages in Portrait mode, Acrobat will rotate them on your screen so that you have to tip your head sideways to read anything. Suffice it to say that this is a pain in the neck.*

PRINT RANGE

The Print range section of the Print dialog box allows you to choose exactly the pages or objects you wish to print. By default, it is set to print all the pages in the document and everything on those pages. You have the option of printing only the current page or the current selection. The Selection option is dimmed if nothing is selected in your file.

 *If you select Tools | Options | Global | Printing Defaults, there is a checkbox for printing the current page only by default.*

You can also print only certain pages if your document contains more than one page. Type the page numbers you want to print in the text box to the right of the Pages radio button. If you want to print nonconsecutive pages, place commas between the page numbers. To print a range of consecutive pages, type the beginning number following by a hyphen and the ending number. These two methods can also be mixed together.

Below the page numbers is a drop-down list containing three choices: Odd Pages, Even Pages, and Even & Odd. You can use this list to select those selections of pages without having to type the page numbers manually.

COPIES

As we've already discussed, you can specify the printing of multiple copies in the Printer Properties dialog box. (You can also do this in the Copies section of the Print dialog box.) You can also specify whether the copies should be collated. If you choose Collate, printing will take much longer, because each

copy of the document will be sent to the printer separately, rather than all of them at once with the instruction to print each page multiple times. This means that the complete set of data will be sent for each copy that you request. If you don't collate the pages, the data is sent once with an instruction to print multiple copies of each page.

PRINT STYLES

At the bottom of the Print dialog box, you can select a set of printing defaults from the Print style drop-down list. When you first install DRAW, the only style available will be CorelDRAW Defaults, but you can add more yourself. This process is described later in this chapter.

If Print Preview is not already displayed, a Print Preview button will be shown at the lower left of the Print dialog box. If you already have Print Preview displayed in the background, it won't be there.

To start printing using the current options, click the OK button. Clicking Cancel will return you to the view you had before you entered the Print dialog box. If Print Preview is displayed, the Apply button will apply the changes you've made to the Print Options.

PRINT LAYOUT

The Layout tab of the Print Options dialog box controls the location of the image on the page. Figure 29-4 shows the Print Options Layout dialog box.

IMAGE POSITION WITHIN PAGE

At the top of the dialog box are options for sizing and positioning the image on the page. The default setting is As in document. This means simply that everything will be sized and positioned based on your document. Next is Fit to page, which will resize the original image so that it fits the page size exactly. Your third option is Reposition images to, which gives you a drop-down list of nine different positions around the edge of the page and the exact center. If you elect to reposition the image, you can also resize the image. By default, you can change only the Width. Since Maintain aspect ratio is also checked by default, the Height value is calculated automatically. However, you can

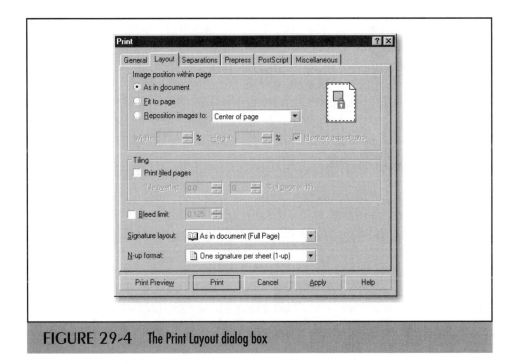

FIGURE 29-4   The Print Layout dialog box

uncheck the Maintain aspect ratio check box and enter values for both Width and Height. Note that this practice will distort the image and thus should be used cautiously.

Tiling

If your artwork extends beyond one page, you can have it tiled across as many pages as you need. Check the Print tiled pages check box; the dialog box will change slightly so that you can define a tile overlap. The overlap can be specified as either a measurement or a percentage of the page width.

Other

The last few options span various categories. First, there is a check box that allows you to limit the bleed. Bleed allows your artwork to extend beyond the

drawing page when it is printed. Bleed is extremely important for offset printing because it allows your artwork to extend all the way to the edge of the page in the finished piece. If you check Bleed limit, you can type in a maximum amount of bleed that will be printed. Normally, this won't be necessary, since most artists create the bleed objects to the exact size their printers require.

Signature Layout

Signature layout is a form of imposition. Imposition is a method used in offset printing so that you can print several document pages on a single large sheet of paper. If you carefully arrange the document pages, the larger sheet of paper can be folded or cut so that the pages will be in the exact positions where they are needed. Typically, this has been done by the "stripper" (these strippers do wear clothes), but the age of electronic publishing allows you to impose the pages before they are printed. This saves money on film and labor, not to mention time.

Several Signature Layout styles have been predefined for you and can be selected from the drop-down list. For example, you can select Side Fold-Card, which is a style set up to work with a four-page DRAW document. Each of the pages will be arranged on a single sheet of paper so that when the paper is folded, it will create a greeting card that opens from the side. Page 1 in your DRAW document will be the front of the card, pages 2 and 3 will be the inside portion, and page 4 will be the back. The first time you use this feature, you may find it a little frustrating, but once you see how it automatically arranges and rotates the pages to create the proper layout, you'll be using it quite often.

The real power of layout styles lies in the capability they afford you for creating your own styles. This can be done visually in the Print Preview screen; it will be described later in this chapter.

N-up Format

Whereas the Signature Layout options provide a way to print multiple pages on a single sheet with very powerful control over how the image will appear, the N-up format options enable you to print the same page multiple times on a single sheet or just to print multiple pages on a sheet. Select the format you want from the drop-down list.

29

If you've chosen a particular type of label in <u>T</u>ools | <u>O</u>ptions | Document | Labels, the name of that label style will appear in the drop-down list. Just as with the Signature Layouts, you can create your own N-up formats in the Print Preview window. This will be discussed in more detail later in this chapter.

SEPARATIONS

If you will be printing large quantities of a document in color, color separations will be necessary. Color separations are nothing more than black-and-white images of each of the spot, or process, colors used in your document. But getting these black and white images correct is something of an art form. By following the instructions described below, you'll be able to step into the world of color printing in no time.

The first option on the Separations tab, shown in Figure 29-5, is Print <u>s</u>eparations. If you are creating a separation, this box should be checked.

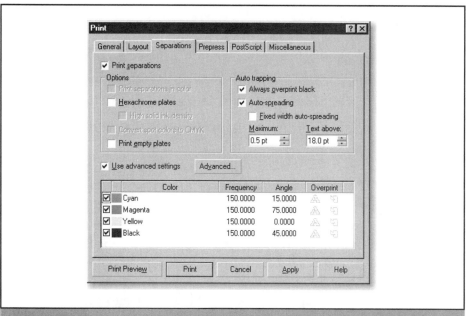

FIGURE 29-5   The Print Separations dialog box

Options

In the Options section, you have the option of printing separations in their own colors rather than in black, but you will rarely want to do this, because the majority of color separations are printed in black. Note that this option is available only when you've selected a color printer for the output device. The actual color is added when the paper is on the printing press. You might, however, use this option to print each separation in color on a sheet of film, or overlay. When all the overlays are stacked together, they will show you an approximation of the final output.

A new feature in DRAW 7 was the ability to print hexachrome plates, a type of separation that uses six colors instead of four to provide more accurate color. Of course, when six colors are being used, you need more than the normal four sheets of separations. Before using this technology, you should discuss it in detail with your printer and service bureau. Some devices use a high solid ink density. If that is the case with the device you will be printing on, you should check the High solid ink density check box. Your service bureau should be able to tell you whether this is necessary.

Spot colors can be converted to process colors when you are creating a separation, but this is not ordinarily a good idea. If you are expecting an exact color that you have chosen from a swatch book of spot colors, you will be very disappointed. Spot colors are meant to be printed with an ink that has been premixed. Trying to re-create that color with process colors can lead to disastrous results.

The last option is Print empty plates. If you want to pay for a blank piece of film, check this box—though this is almost never a good idea.

Auto Trapping

When you're printing colors that touch, quite often there will be problems in getting the two colors to register (line up) correctly. This is because of the mechanical limitations of the printing press. To compensate for these limitations, it is sometimes necessary to trap the artwork so that the colors will overlap slightly.

To create a manual trap, you need to add an outline to the object that is to be trapped. Change the color of the outline either to the color of the selected

29

object or to the color that the object touches. If you make it the color of the selected object, you are creating a spread trap. If you make it the color of the outside object, you are creating a choke trap. The last step is to right-click on the object and make sure that Overprint Outline is checked in the pop-up menu. If it is not checked, click on it.

 *Printing an overprinted outline will work only on a PostScript printer.*

CorelDRAW 8 provides two tools for automatically trapping a document. The Always overprint black check box makes any black fill or outline overprint any color hidden beneath it. The idea is that black on top of another color is still black. Be aware, though, that black printed this way will actually be a bit shinier and darker than plain black.

Check Auto-spreading to use artificial intelligence to add spread traps wherever CorelDRAW deems them necessary. The maximum amount of the trap is controlled by the number in the Maximum text box. You can also specify trapping for text only if it is above a specified point size. By default, trapping is performed only on text that is larger than 18 points. You should either leave this default setting alone or make it applicable to even larger text. When trapping is performed, outlines are added to the letters. This can destroy the look of small text.

The last option is Fixed width auto-spreading. When this check box is selected, the Maximum parameter box changes to the Width parameter box. Normally the spread is a variable amount not exceeding the value specified in the Maximum box; with this box checked, it is a fixed amount, as specified in the Width box.

 *Do not use the Auto-spreading function if you have created manual traps in your document. If you do, DRAW will try to create traps of the traps you've created.*

By using the various auto-spreading methods in the Print Options Separations dialog box, you can spare yourself the trouble of creating the traps manually. But to get the very best results, you will want to create the traps manually, because this gives you much more control.

Advanced Settings

Custom halftone angles and screens can be controlled by checking the Use advanced settings box and then clicking the Advanced button. This control is especially important if you want to change the screen angles of spot colors. The Advanced Separations Settings dialog box will be discussed a little later in this chapter.

 *The Use advanced settings checkbox is only available if you are printing to a PostScript device. There are other settings that also require a PostScript device, so if something is currently unavailable to you, that is probably why.*

The Advanced Separations Settings dialog box, shown in Figure 29-6, allows you to choose from several predefined screening technologies or to enter your

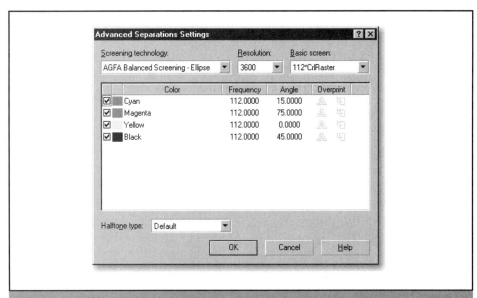

FIGURE 29-6 The Advanced Separations Settings dialog box

own custom frequencies and angles. Most frequently, an imagesetter will automatically change the frequencies and angles from the generic settings shown here to those appropriate for that imagesetter. That means this box is usually not necessary. Ask your service bureau if you are in doubt.

For each screening technology listed, several different resolutions and screens are available. When you're changing these values, you should be in close contact with both your service bureau and your printer to make sure that you choose the correct settings.

With some screening technologies, you will see CrlRaster listed in the Basic screen box. These listings indicate AGFA's Cristal Raster technology, which produces stochastic, or frequency-modulated, screens. The results that Cristal Raster creates can be incredible, but you should use this technology carefully, and you should contact your printer and service bureau before using it. A major problem is that the service bureau may not be able to provide you with matchprints. This will force you to go to press without a proof. Another problem is that sometimes an excess amount of ink will be laid down. Thus, if you do choose to use stochastic screening, make sure you choose a service bureau and printer that are familiar with the pitfalls you may encounter.

The middle of the dialog box shows each of the colors used in the document. You can change the screen frequency, angle, and overprinting of any color individually. Simply select the color you wish to change and use the Frequency and Angle text boxes to enter new values. If you check the Overprint color check box, you can also specify whether this option applies to graphics, text, or both. Note that changing any of these values can create severe problems if it is not done carefully.

At the bottom of the dialog box is a drop-down list of halftone types. The default halftone type is usually a dot or an ellipse, depending on the technology chosen. A number of specialty dots are shown in this list. The results of using an alternative halftone type can be quite interesting, but problems can occur if the printer or service bureau is not prepared to work with these alternative types.

When you exit the Advanced Settings dialog box, the changes you have made will be reflected at the bottom of the Print Options Separations dialog box. If you chose not to use Advanced Settings, you can see the colors used in the document, along with the settings for their frequencies, angles, and overprints. The only change you can make here is to select the colors that you wish to print. By default, the colors used in the document will be selected.

PREPRESS

The Prepress tab brings you to the Print Options Prepress dialog box, shown in Figure 29-7. This contains many important settings that you need when you're outputting film for offset printing.

PAPER/FILM SETTINGS

The first two settings can usually be left turned off (not checked). The first setting (Invert) controls whether the image is printed as a positive or a negative, and the second (Mirror) controls whether the job is printed with the emulsion side of the film up or down. You will need to ask your printer what type of film is desired. Then ask your service bureau what type of file it needs to give your printer the correct film.

Here is why it is often best to leave these two settings unchecked: Suppose your printer asks for negative film and that you therefore check the Invert

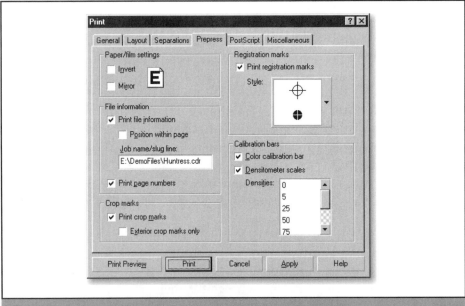

FIGURE 29-7   The Print Prepress dialog box

check box. Your service bureau may change this same setting in the imagesetter, and it is common for service bureaus to make everything a negative. In this case, however, your file will then be output as a positive. The same sort of problem can occur if you choose the Mirror option. Therefore, speak with both your printer and your service bureau before setting either of these options.

Here is a specific example of the situation we have just described: The printer of this book wants to receive right-reading emulsion-down negative film. This would mean that both of these options would need to be checked to get the file correct in the preview window. However, our service bureau prefers that we send it a file without these settings activated. Thus, we just output our file as if we were printing a plain positive image on paper, and the service bureau does the rest for us.

File Information

The next setting turns on Print file information. Any job output from an imagesetter should have this setting activated. You can print the information within the document by checking the Position within page check box. This is very handy for stamping a printout with the file name, time and date printed, and more. You can also add a page number to the bottom of each page if you like. Note that this information is outside the page, and therefore will not affect the look of your document, unless you check Position within page. Another option in CorelDRAW 8 allows you to specify the job name or slugline that will be printed. This setting defaults to the name of the current file, but you can type any name you wish.

Crop Marks

The next two settings are related to crop marks. Crop marks should always be present when you are outputting a job for a service bureau. They show the service bureau the page boundaries. If you check Exterior crop marks only, any crop marks within the page boundaries will not be printed. This option is especially useful when you've created impositions. Most important, crop marks are used by the printer to determine where to crop (cut) the page.

Registration Marks

Registration marks are just as important as crop marks when you're creating a color separation. Turn them on by placing a check in the Print registration marks checkbox. Registration marks give your printer a way to line up the multiple sheets of film accurately. The style of registration marks can be chosen graphically by clicking the sample shown and selecting your choice from the graphical drop-down list.

Calibration Bars

The next two settings are related to the calibration bar and the densitometer scale. These allow your printer and service bureau to make sure their equipment is working properly. Both of these should be activated for service bureau output. To turn them on, place checks in both the Color calibration bar and Densitometer scales check boxes. When you select Densitometer scales, a list of the densities that will be printed appears. You can change these values by double-clicking any of the numbers. The number will then be editable, and you can change it to anything you wish. However, before doing so, contact your service bureau, because the defaults are the standard densities that the service bureau will likely expect.

POSTSCRIPT

If you are outputting to a PostScript printer, setting various options in the Print PostScript dialog box, shown in Figure 29-8, is a virtual necessity. It is accessed by clicking on the PostScript Preferences button in the Options dialog box.

Compatibility

Select the version of PostScript used in your printer from the drop-down list. If you use an older version than those your printer supports, it can make your files larger and slower than necessary. However, it is only helpful if you are truly using a PostScript device that supports the new features. Most PostScript printers released in the past few years use PostScript Level 2, and PostScript

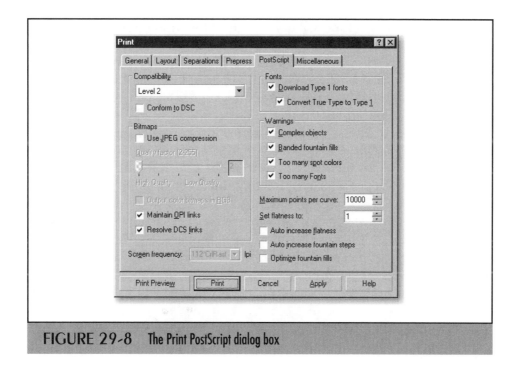

FIGURE 29-8   The Print PostScript dialog box

3 printers have just started to appear. Check the user manual for your printer to find out what it supports.

Bitmaps

If you selected PostScript Level 2 or PostScript 3, you can use JPEG compression on any included bitmaps. Remember that JPEG is a lossy compression (see Chapter 39 for a more complete description of JPEG) and that it may decrease the quality of your output. The slider lets you choose the level of the quality. The lower the quality, the more compression you get. Be sure to use this option with great caution.

Next is a check box for outputting color bitmaps in RGB instead of the default CMYK. You may want to choose this option when you're outputting to slides or to an Adobe Acrobat file. Another check box lets you maintain OPI links—OPI stands for Open Prepress Interface. If you receive files scanned at your service bureau, they will quite often be low-resolution copies for you to place in your document. The service bureau keeps the high-resolution files and swaps them for the low-resolution copies when the files are output. The most common format used is OPI, so this option is needed if you want your service bureau to be able to swap in the correct image for you. Another related option is Resolve DCS links. You should check with your service bureau to find out whether it wants you to resolve the links or whether it will do that for you.

Below the bitmaps section is the setting for Screen frequency. If you are outputting separations, you have probably already changed this setting in the Separations tab. Otherwise, you'll want to set it here. To set an appropriate screen frequency, you'll want to ask your printer (the person) what is required for the job. If the job will not be printed on a printing press, the limits of your desktop printer (the machine) should be considered. The value depends on many factors, such as the printing press, the paper (or fabric) type, and the quality you desire. Higher frequencies are great if they will work with all the other factors.

Fonts

If you are using a PostScript printer, which you obviously are or this option wouldn't be available, make sure you check both the Download Type 1 fonts and Convert True Type to Type 1 check boxes. This will ensure that any needed fonts (other than the fonts stored within the printer) will be downloaded to the printer or output file. More information on each of these font formats is given in Chapter 38.

Warnings

You can turn on warning dialog boxes for Complex objects, Banded fountain fills, Too many spot colors, or Too many Fonts. These warnings will pop up as the file is being printed. If you are new to color separations and high-resolution output, the warnings will help you understand where problems may be occurring. For those who have advanced knowledge of output, these options are not necessary.

Other

The flatness setting controls how smoothly each curve is drawn. The best setting is always 1, but complex jobs may not be able to print with this setting. Your best bet is to leave the setting at 1 and check the Auto increase flatness check box. This will cause CorelDRAW to try the flatness at 1, then 2, then 3, and so on until it reaches 11 (assuming that 1 is specified in the Set flatness to box). CorelDRAW will try values up to 10 plus the number you type in. Anything higher than 11 will probably cause changes that will be visible to the naked eye, and may cause problems. One way to avoid changing the flatness is to change the number of points in the curve from the default value to a lower value, such as 400. This is necessary only if you have a PostScript Level 1 device. Lower numbers are allowed, but they can cause printing to take much longer. If a file will not print, you can attempt a maximum number of curves as low as 20.

Several check boxes help you optimize the fountain steps and fountain fills. It can be helpful to check these in case you made a mistake elsewhere when you were setting the number of fountain steps. These boxes will correct those mistakes.

MISCELLANEOUS

The Print Miscellaneous dialog box, shown in Figure 29-9, contains all the settings that don't belong into any of the other tabs.

At the top of the dialog box is a check box for using a Color Profile for output. It is available only if you are outputting to a color device or are printing color separations. If you wish to change the settings for your color profile, click the Set Profiles button. Now you can select profiles for your monitor, scanner, composite printer, and/or separations printer. For more information on choosing and using color profiles, see Chapter 24.

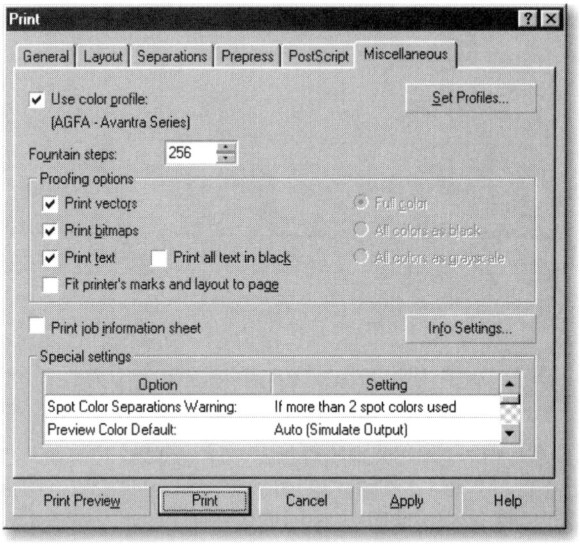

FIGURE 29-9 The Print Miscellaneous dialog box

For the highest quality output, set Fountain steps to 256. This is the maximum allowed in PostScript Level 1 and 2 devices. If you are using a PostScript 3 device, it supports up to 1024 levels, but that is certainly an extreme value. The number of fountain steps (levels of gray that can be printed) that are possible on any given printer at any given line screen can be calculated with the following formula:

Fountain steps = $[(DPI)/(LPI)]^2$

DPI (dots per inch) refers to the printer resolution. LPI (lines per inch) refers to the screen frequency.

Proofing Options

In the Proofing options section of the dialog box, you'll find many options that can assist you in printing quick proofs of your design. The first three options allow you to choose whether vectors, bitmaps, or text is printed. If you know that a large bitmap is correct, simply uncheck Print bitmaps to save the time it would take to print the bitmap. If you choose to print text, you can print it entirely in black, which can be helpful if you have a very light-colored text that may be difficult to proof if it is printed on white paper.

On the right side of this section, you can choose whether the document is printed in color, with all colors converted to black, or with all colors as levels of grayscale.

The last option in this section is Fit printer's marks and layout to page. Proofing a job that contains crop and registration marks on your local printer can sometimes be difficult, since these marks often are outside of an 8.5"x11" page. Availability of these options is dependent on custom page positioning and the separations options chosen.

Job Information Sheet

If you want to make your service bureau operator happy, be sure to check the Print job information sheet check box. To see what will be printed, click the Info Settings button. It will bring up the dialog box shown in Figure 29-10.

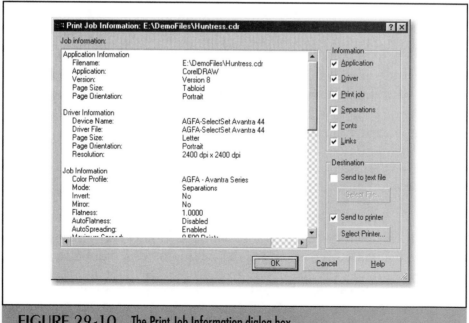

FIGURE 29-10   The Print Job Information dialog box

The figure shows some of the details of the job information dialog box. You can choose the options that will be printed by checking the appropriate check boxes on the right side of the dialog box. By default, they are all checked. You can also choose whether the information will be output as a file or to a specific printer. This information is printed immediately after you print the main file.

Make sure that you don't select the imagesetter as your output destination for the job information sheet, because it would be very expensive to print this information to film. The whole idea behind printing this information sheet is to show the service bureau what is contained in the PostScript PRN file you are providing for output.

Special Settings

At the bottom of the dialog box is the Special Settings section. Here you will find a number of options that can solve very specific printing problems. Each of the options is documented in the Help file that comes with DRAW. Search the index for "Special settings" to find this valuable information.

PRINT PREVIEW

Print Preview was added in CorelDRAW 7. It can be accessed by clicking the Print Preview button at the bottom of the Print dialog box. This allows you to see the file exactly as it will print, including the various printer's marks. The Print Preview main screen is shown in Figure 29-11.

The default preview shows you exactly how your image will look when it is printed on the selected printer. If the printer is not a color printer, of course the preview will not be in color. Color separations will not be previewed in color either, since they are output as grayscale, as shown in Figure 29-11. The default preview can be changed with the View | Preview Color | Color command. You'll also see several other options that can be set for the preview.

Unlike the preview screens of old, this one allows you to zoom to any level you wish, with either the Zoom tool or the drop-down list of zoom levels. The bottom of the screen contains tabs for each page to be printed, including separations. You can also use the navigation buttons to move between pages.

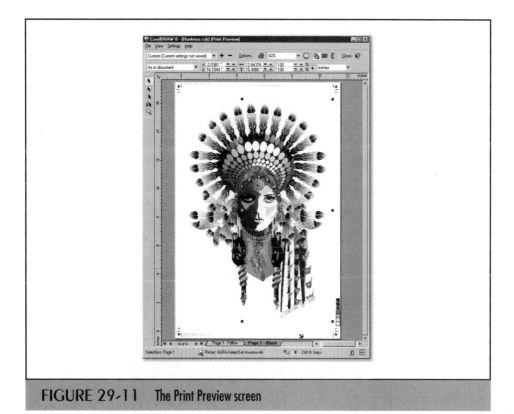

FIGURE 29-11   The Print Preview screen

You can use the Options button to activate the dialog boxes discussed previously to make further changes. You'll also notice that many of the dialog boxes discussed in this chapter can be accessed directly from the Settings menu.

CREATING SIGNATURE LAYOUTS

When a printed piece is created, often multiple pages of the document will be output on the same sheet of film. After printing, the paper is carefully folded and cut to produce the finished multiple-page document. Each of these large sheets of film is called a signature; creating them in CorelDRAW 8 is accomplished in the Print Preview screen. When you select the second tool down in the Print Preview toolbox, your screen will show how the pages will be laid out. The controls for changing the signature are located on the Property Bar, as shown in Figure 29-12.

Controls on the Property Bar allow you to set the number of rows and columns of pages to be included on the sheet, gutter spacing, whether it should be designed as double-sided, and how the pages are to be ordered. This ordering can be page order, saddle order, or stacking order. If you click directly on the pages represented in the signature, you can change the page number assigned and the amount of rotation for each.

At the far left of the Property Bar is the name of the Signature Layout style. If you have customized the layout, it will probably be represented as Custom.

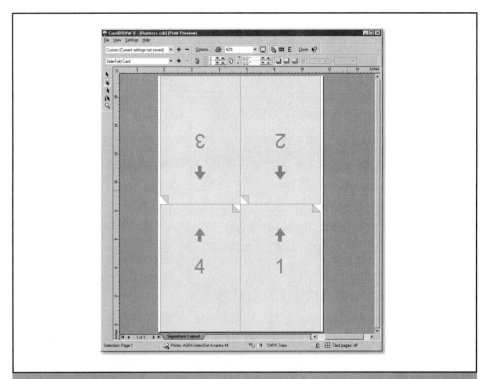

FIGURE 29-12 Print Preview screen for previewing a Signature Layout

29

Clicking on the + icon will allow you to save this new style so that it can easily be recalled later.

CREATING N-UP FORMATS

Similar to the Signature Layout is the ability to create formats for N-up printing. Select the third tool down in the toolbox and the screen and Property Bar will be changed, as shown in Figure 29-13.

Many of the controls on the Property Bar are the same as those for Signature Layout. You can again control the number of rows and columns. Next to this setting is a button that will clone one page onto each of the pages

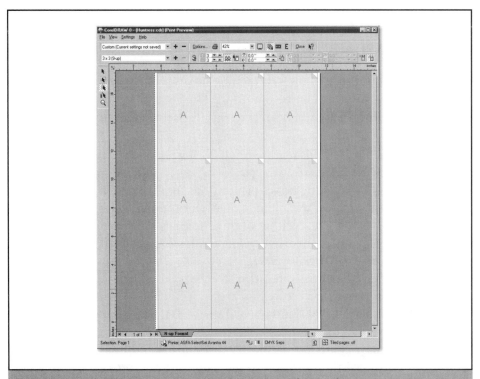

FIGURE 29-13   Print Preview screen for previewing the N-up format

represented in the preview. This is especially useful if you are creating a set of labels, for example. And each of the label templates provided with CorelDRAW will automatically set up this screen for you. The rest of the settings on the Property Bar are for setting the gutters and margins. However, if you are creating labels using a predefined template, you will not want to change these settings.

ADDING PREPRESS MARKS

The fourth button down in the Print Preview toolbox allows you to set the Prepress marks visually. For the most part, the Property Bar simply allows you to select icons, as opposed to selecting check boxes in the Print Prepress dialog box we discussed earlier.

SAVING PRINT STYLES

With the myriad settings in the Print dialog boxes, remembering which check box and buttons to press can be daunting. The great thing is that if you can get through it just once, you'll be able to save the settings for future use at any time.

For example, we used this feature often during the production of this book. We are required to print any images to be used and supply them to the publisher. Some of the dialog boxes print rather small, so we want them fitted to the page. We also want the file information on the page so that the name of the file is on every image. Neither of these settings is difficult to specify, but it can be a nuisance to set them every single time you need to print. Thus, we created a print style for this purpose.

Select File | Save Print Style (CTRL-S) to overwrite the default style or File | Save Print Style As (F12) to create a new one. You can also select the Save As button in the Print General dialog box. Either way, you'll be presented with the dialog box shown in Figure 29-14.

If there is a particular setting that you don't want to include in the print style, simply uncheck the box next to the name. At the top of the dialog box is the name of the print style itself. Choose a name that is descriptive, such as

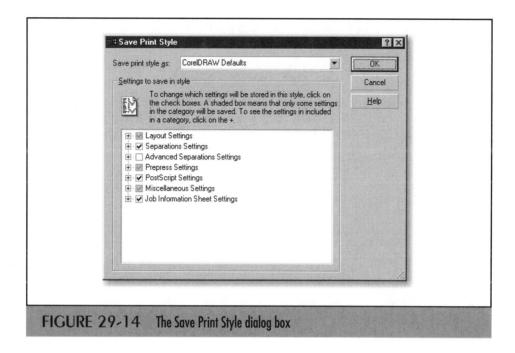

FIGURE 29-14   The Save Print Style dialog box

"Screen Shots" or "150 line-screen color seps." In the future, these styles will be listed in the main Print dialog box. Choose them from the drop-down list and print. You can also share these styles with other users who don't fully understand the print dialog boxes.

USING THE DUPLEXING SETUP WIZARD

Most users have a good reliable printer for printing on one side of the page. Often, however, you'll need to print something on both sides of the page. By using the Duplexing Setup Wizard, you can print on both sides of the paper with ease.

To begin the process, select Settings | Duplexing Setup Wizard (CTRL-D) while you're at the Print Preview screen. You'll see a series of dialog boxes that walk you through the printing of sample pages. At the end, you'll be presented with instructions on how to accurately print double-sided pages from CorelDRAW.

Armed with the knowledge learned in this chapter, you should now be ready to tackle almost any type of printing job, from the simplest flyer to a full-color brochure. Just keep in mind, when you feel that some of this information is unnecessary, that "if it doesn't print, it's just a video game." And when you think that color printing seems difficult, just remember that it's nothing more than printing several sheets of black-and-white.

PREPARE FOR SERVICE BUREAU WIZARD

As a CorelDRAW user, one of your most difficult tasks can be dealing with service bureaus. This is largely because service bureaus have a bias towards the Macintosh platform. Each new release of CorelDRAW has added features to make this task a little bit easier. And with CorelDRAW 7 Revision B (Build 7.467) came a huge surprise, the Prepare for Service Bureau menu item. In this chapter we'll walk you through the Service Bureau Profiler to create a profile for a service bureau and then use that profile to output a CorelDRAW file.

The Service Bureau Profiler is a separate utility that will create a profile for the equipment used by a service bureau. It is not installed with a default installation and so you must do a custom install and make sure to select it. When installed, it will appear in the Productivity Tools subgroup of your CorelDRAW 8 group.

CREATING A SERVICE BUREAU PROFILE

First you'll create a profile for a service bureau. This is really something that only service bureaus should do. But, in a pinch, you may need to create one yourself, especially if you know CorelDRAW better than your service bureau. If you already have the appropriate profile from your service bureau, the first section of the chapter will help you to understand the information that it contains. In the second section, you'll learn how to use the profile.

The Profiler works as a Wizard and walks you through the process of describing a particular type of equipment and how you would prefer to receive files. Figure 30-1 is the first screen you will encounter. It is asking if you wish to create a new profile or to edit one that already exists. For now, select Create a New Profile and click Next.

On the next screen, Figure 30-2, you need to enter some descriptive information about your service bureau. For the description, make sure to include the output device name and anything else that distinguishes this particular profile from others. This is the information that will be presented to the end user in CorelDRAW. Fill out the rest of the information, should the

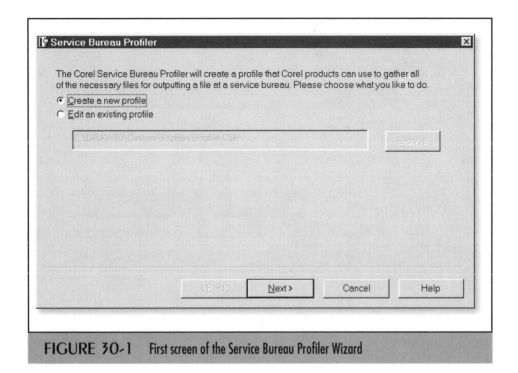

FIGURE 30-1   First screen of the Service Bureau Profiler Wizard

customer need further contact information. When you've finished filling out this section, click Next.

In the next dialog box, shown in Figure 30-3, you will be asked what you would like the customer to supply. This can include native CorelDRAW files in several different versions, PostScript print files, and hard copy, as shown in the figure. Setting up the profile correctly can greatly ease the burden of the service bureau by having the end user automatically create usable .PRN files. When you've made your selections, click Next.

Next you will be asked for information on the printer driver that the end user should have installed, as shown in Figure 30-4. Be very specific and, if the end user will not have this driver readily available, make sure that it is

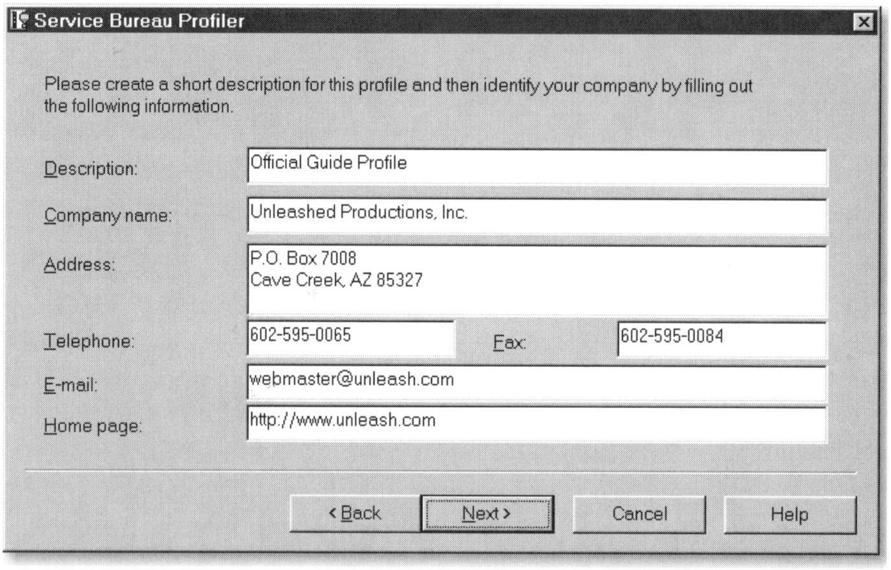

FIGURE 30-2 Service Bureau Profiler Description dialog box

easy for him or her to get a copy of it. Under the Paper Size option, you can specify either an exact paper size or the maximum size that the device can handle. Unless you have a specific need for exact paper sizes, we recommend that you specify the maximum size. The last entry allows for printer's marks. By default, it is set to half an inch. This should be adequate for most service bureaus, but it is easy to change if you need more room. When you are finished, click Next.

The Wizard will now ask you about color management, as shown in Figure 30-5. You can specify whether or not color management is used. If in doubt, you should probably learn more about the color management system built into CorelDRAW, as described in Chapter 24. If you choose to use a color

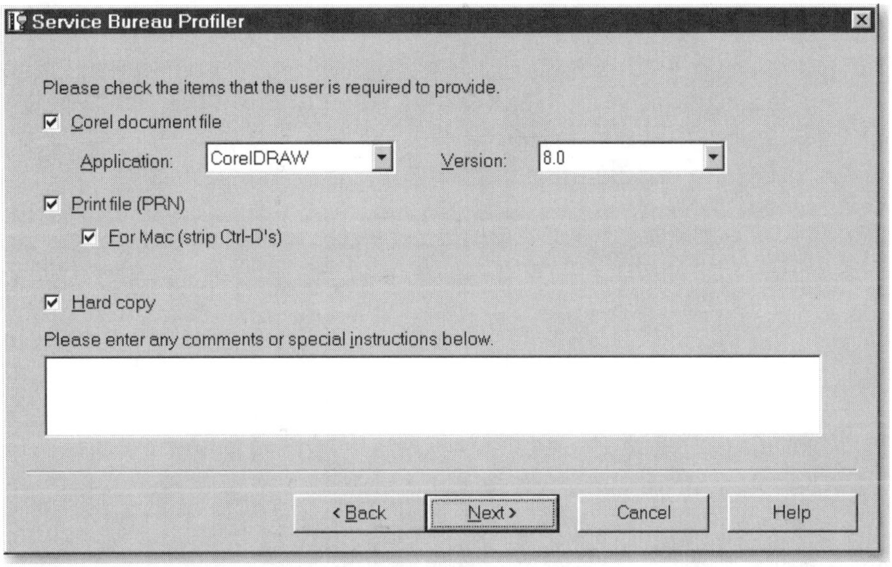

FIGURE 30-3   Service Bureau Profiler Files to Provide dialog box

management profile, you'll need to select the exact profile that should be used. Note that the default install for CorelDRAW 8 will not install most of the profiles from the CD-ROM. Only if you do a custom install or manually install profiles will they be copied to the hard drive. So many of the users will not have these profiles installed. It may be a good idea to supply the color profile with your service bureau profile and the printer driver. When you are finished, click Next.

The dialog box shown in Figure 30-6 contains many different settings taken from throughout the Print dialog box. Each of these settings is described in detail in Chapter 29. The first choice is whether or not separations will be printed. For output to slides or other composite devices, separations would not be wanted. The next few settings all deal with whether various printers

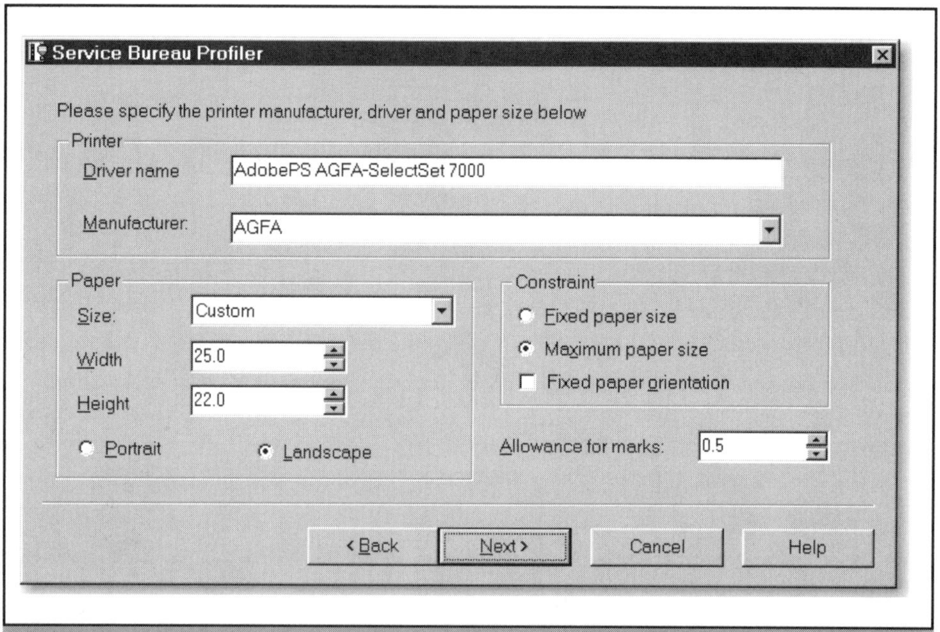

FIGURE 30-4 Service Bureau Profiler Printer Driver Information dialog box

marks should be printed. If you are printing separations, you will probably want all of them selected. The number of fountain steps is dependent on the line screen chosen and the resolution of the output device. The optimum setting is 256 for PostScript Level 1 and 2 devices. If you are lucky enough to have a PostScript Level 3 device, you'll want to set this at the highest number of steps supported at the output resolution and line screen. Registration marks are very important if you are printing separations and you have a choice of several different types from the drop-down list. Lastly, you can choose whether you want a negative and which side the emulsion faces. Part of this is dependent on what the printer desires. But most service bureaus can change this directly on the imagesetter. When you are finished, click Next.

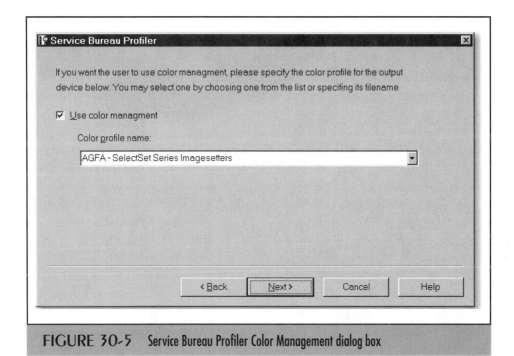

FIGURE 30-5   Service Bureau Profiler Color Management dialog box

If you have chosen to print separations, you will be presented with the dialog box shown in Figure 30-7. Again, each of these settings is described in more detail in Chapter 29. The first option is to print the separations using Hexachrome colors. This setting produces some incredible colors, but is not widely supported and is very difficult to proof. Certainly it wouldn't be used in most profiles. The same goes for converting spot colors to CMYK. This setting can produce some very bad color shifting and should not be used unless absolutely necessary. There is also an option to print plates that are empty. This means that it will print blank film. Use this option with great caution, since it is a good way to waste money. Trapping is very important and not well understood by the average CorelDRAW user. There are ways to manually

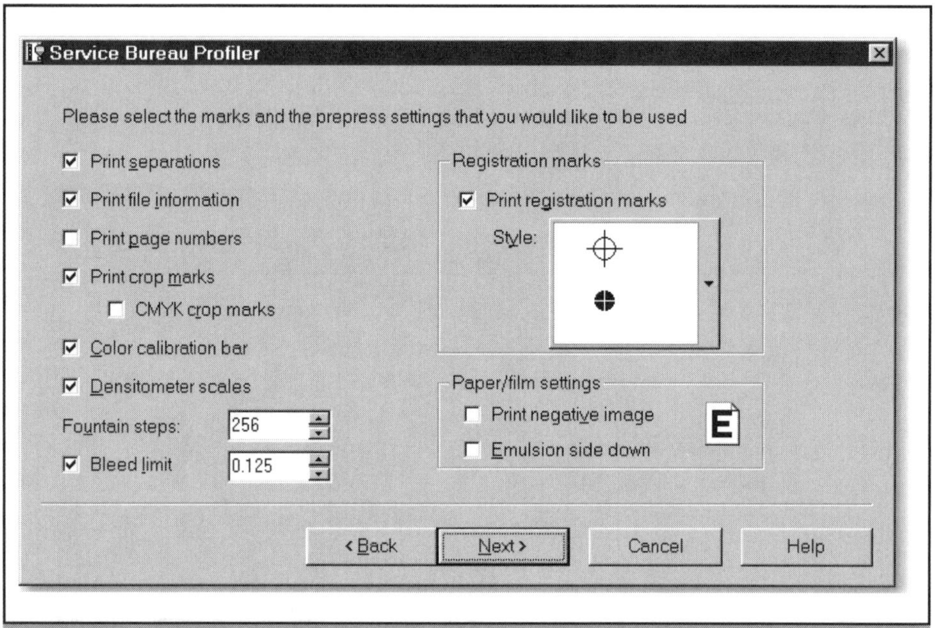

FIGURE 30-6   Service Bureau Profiler Marks and Prepress dialog box

trap, but only the most advanced users use them. So the auto-trapping option can help to solve this problem. Overprinting black will rarely cause a great change of colors. Black printed on top of another color will still be black, albeit a glossier black. Auto-spreading will apply a spread trap where CorelDRAW feels it is appropriate. The main problem with this option is that it will trap any manual traps that were created in the file. If you select auto-trapping, you can specify whether it is a fixed width or variable and the amount of trapping. You can also set the smallest size of text to which a trap will be applied. This is important, since a trap can dramatically change the look of small text. When you are finished, click Next.

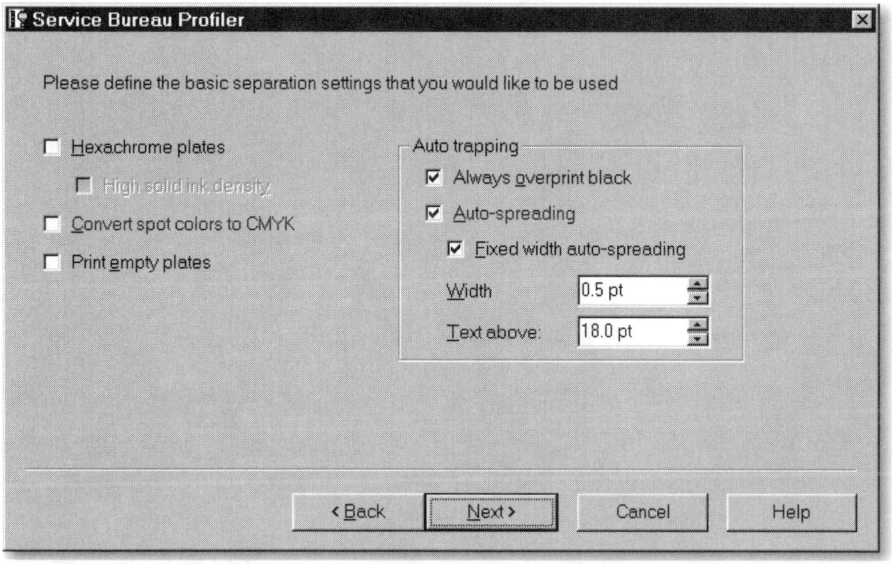

FIGURE 30-7 Service Bureau Profiler Separations Settings dialog box

The dialog box shown in Figure 30-8 allows you to specify screen frequencies and angles. The first setting is for the shape of the halftone dots used. Each of the colors—cyan, magenta, yellow, black, and generic spot colors—can be chosen in order. Once you choose a color, you can specify a particular screen frequency and angle for that color by clicking directly on the number. When you are finished, click Next.

The dialog box in Figure 30-9 contains more of the information from CorelDRAW's Print dialog box. If you are using a PostScript Level 2 device, you definitely want this option checked. This will optimize the file created. One of the additional options available in Level 2 is JPEG bitmap compression.

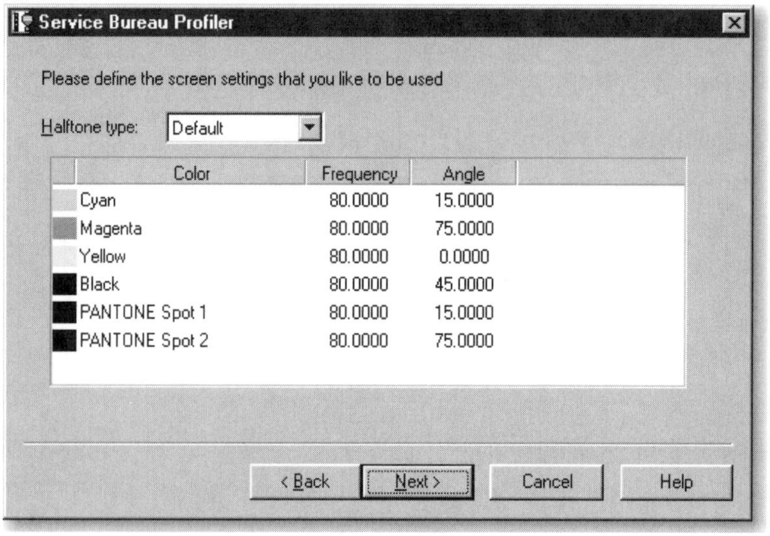

Service Bureau Profiler   ✕

Please define the screen settings that you like to be used

Halftone type: | Default   ▾ |

Color	Frequency	Angle
Cyan	80.0000	15.0000
Magenta	80.0000	75.0000
Yellow	80.0000	0.0000
Black	80.0000	45.0000
PANTONE Spot 1	80.0000	15.0000
PANTONE Spot 2	80.0000	75.0000

   < Back   Next >   Cancel   Help

FIGURE 30-8   Service Bureau Profiler Screen Settings dialog box

This is a lossy compression format and can cause problems on some devices, so use this option with caution. Outputting bitmaps in RGB is a good idea for slide output as well as for creating Acrobat files for Internet use. OPI links are used when a customer is given a low-resolution file that will be linked with a high-resolution scan during the film creation process. If in doubt, go ahead and check this option as it won't hurt anything. Conform to DSC and Resolve DCS Links are also both helpful in making sure that you get accurate files, because enabling the Conform to DSC option will conform the PostScript file to the DSC (Document Structuring Convention). DSC is the standard used when processing PostScript files through third-party applications for trapping, imposition, etc. Enabling the Resolve DSC links option automatically resolves file links when the PRN file is created.

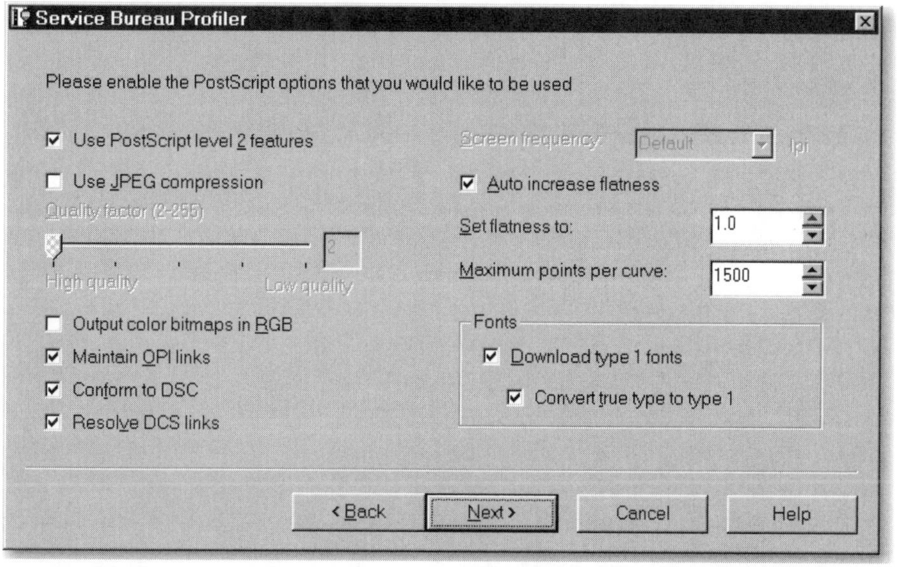

FIGURE 30-9   Service Bureau Profiler PostScript Options dialog box

In our example, you'll see that the screen frequency is dimmed. This is because we specified the values in the previous screen of the Wizard. Auto Increase Flatness is very useful for helping complex jobs to output. It will automatically increase the flatness value in steps of 2 until it reaches 10 plus the value you enter. If the job will not output that particular object then move on to the next one. Flatness should be left at the default of 1 as the Auto Increase Flatness option will take care of higher values. The Maximum Points Per Curve option is also used to decrease the complexity of a print job. Here the default should probably be lowered quite a bit to 200 if you are using a PostScript Level 1 device. This will increase the print time, but most jobs should process without any problems. Lastly is the Fonts section. If you want

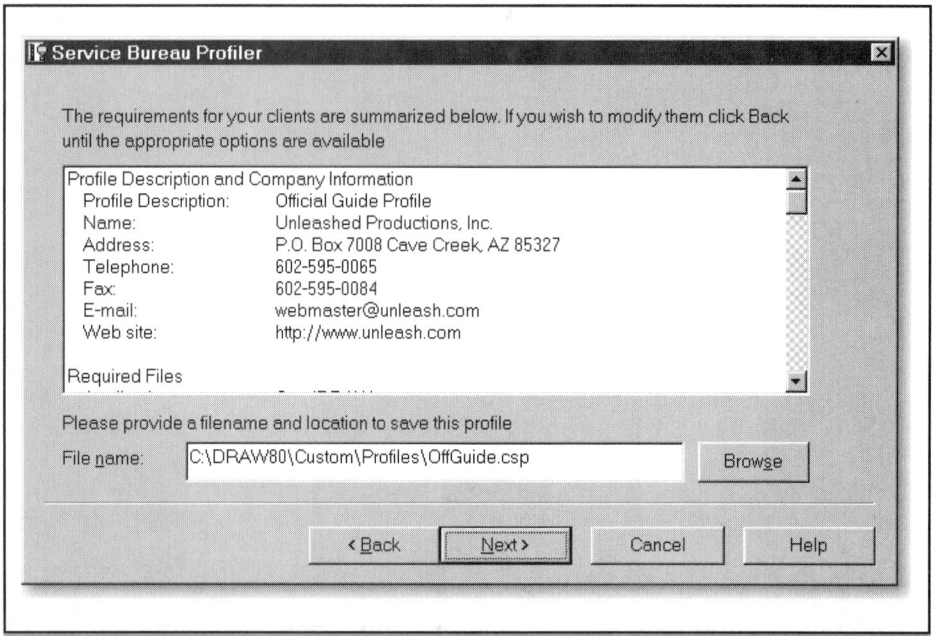

FIGURE 30-10   Service Bureau Profiler Summary dialog box

fonts to be embedded within a print file, you'll definitely want to check both of these items. If you do not enable font downloading, they will be output as graphics. When you are finished, click Next.

The last information screen will provide a summary of all of the information you've entered so far, as shown in Figure 30-10. Go over all of this information carefully to see if you've made any mistakes. If you need to make changes, press the Back button until you reach the appropriate screen. If everything is correct, give your profile a file name and click Next.

You've successfully created a profile. Now you'll be given the option of having the file automatically uploaded to Corel's Web site, as shown in Figure 30-11. Service bureaus that want to increase their share of the CorelDRAW market should definitely take advantage of this service as there are a number of frustrated CorelDRAW users looking for a good service bureau. And the price is right for this exposure—*free*!

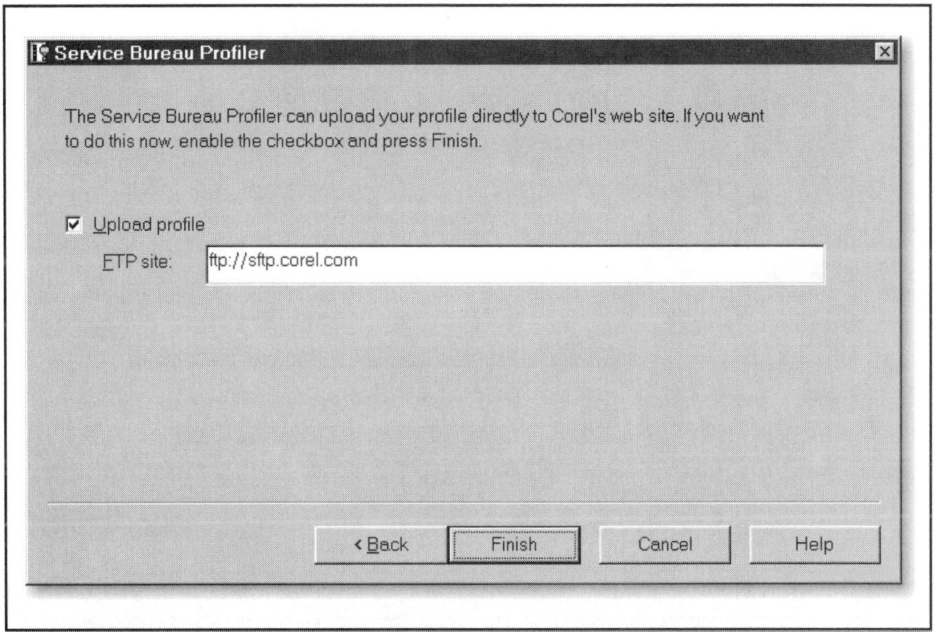

FIGURE 30-11   Service Bureau Profiler Upload dialog box

PREPARE FOR SERVICE BUREAU WIZARD

Now that we've shown you how to create a service bureau profile, we'll show you how to use that profile or one that has been supplied with CorelDRAW to give your service bureau exactly what they need to accurately output your documents.

In order to use the Wizard, you must have an open document containing at least one object. Although the Wizard will help you to create a file for the service bureau, it is still a good idea to consult with both your printer and service bureau in advance to meet their desired specifications for the file.

To start the Prepare for Service Bureau Wizard, choose File | Prepare for Service Bureau. The first screen of the Wizard is shown in Figure 30-12. It presents a list of all of the profiles that are found on your system, including the profile you created in the first part of this chapter. You also have the option

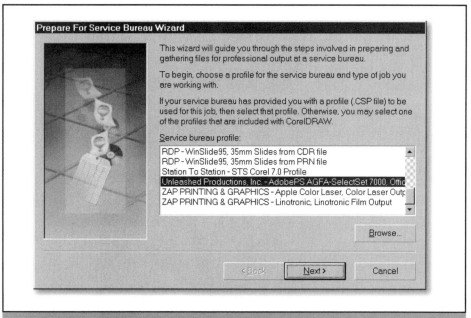

FIGURE 30-12   Prepare for Service Bureau Profile Selection dialog box

of browsing your system for other profiles that are not in the default directory. The last option in the list is to download a profile from the Internet. This will take you to Corel's Web site (assuming you are connected, of course), where new profiles are located.

Once you've found an appropriate profile and clicked Next, you may be presented with a screen showing any notes included in the profile. You'll obviously want to read them carefully and proceed accordingly. Click Next after reading the Notes. If you don't receive this screen, there are no notes to read.

Next, you'll be presented with the screen shown in Figure 30-13 if the service bureau has specified that a certain driver is needed. Otherwise, the next dialog box you see will be Figure 30-18. Here you are told the name of the printer driver that the profile requires and a list of the drivers installed on

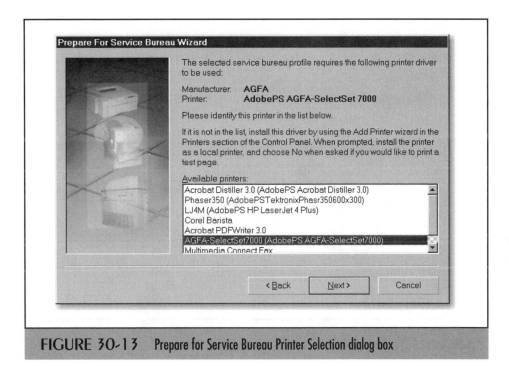

FIGURE 30-13   Prepare for Service Bureau Printer Selection dialog box

your system. If the required driver is not installed on your system, you'll need to exit the Wizard and install the correct driver. Most of these drivers are supplied with Windows 95 or NT. Another source is Adobe's PostScript driver, which is provided with Adobe Type Manager for Windows 95. If those don't provide the correct driver, you may want to check the Web site of the printer vendor or ask the service bureau to provide the driver for you. Once the correct driver is installed, select it from the Available Printers list in the Wizard and click Next.

The next Wizard dialog box, shown in Figure 30-14, is for choosing the size of the paper that your file needs. You are told the actual size of the .cdr file and the maximum paper size supported by the service bureau. The currently selected page size is shown in bold. To change the current size, click the Printer Properties button. This will bring up a dialog box similar to the

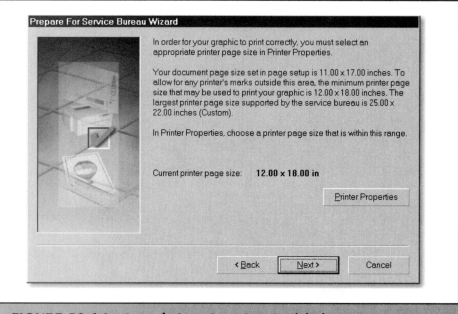

FIGURE 30-14   Prepare for Service Bureau Paper Size dialog box

one in Figure 30-15. Note that we are using the Adobe PostScript driver so the dialog box can look quite different from the same dialog box in Windows 95 or Windows NT. The important thing is to find the Paper Size selections and choose an appropriate size for your print job. Remember that if you wish to print crop marks, registration marks, and others prepress items, you'll need a paper size larger than your actual file. If your paper size is too large or small for the driver settings, you'll get another dialog box with this warning.

Click OK after choosing the correct paper size and then Next to get to the next screen of the Wizard, which is shown in Figure 30-16. Here you are told the name of the color profile requested in the service bureau profile and the profile that is currently selected. If there is not a match, you can click the Set Profiles button to bring up Corel's Color Manager. You'll need to find the correct profile in the Separations drop-down list. For those of you who are not familiar with color profiles, refer to Corel's online help or Chapter 24. When you have the correct profile, click Next.

30

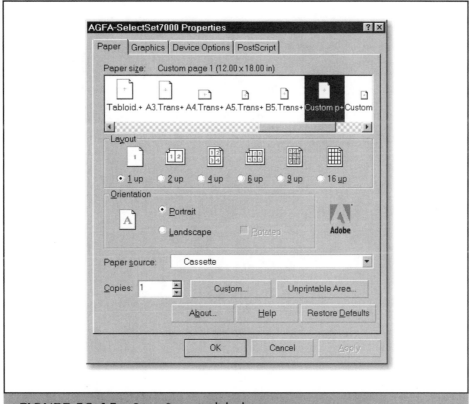

FIGURE 30-15   Printer Properties dialog box

Now it is time to work with fonts, as shown in Figure 30-17. You are presented with a list of the Font Names and their corresponding filenames if the document requires fonts. There are several options for getting the correct fonts to the service bureau. The first is to check the Embed Fonts Using TrueDoc check box. This will save a copy of the .cdr file with the fonts embedded. Our experience has been that this method of embedding fonts is not reliable enough for a tight deadline. So if your hide is on the line if the job doesn't get printed, you shouldn't rely on embedding the fonts. Another option is to collect the font files and supply them to the service bureau. But this will most likely be a severe violation of the license agreement for the

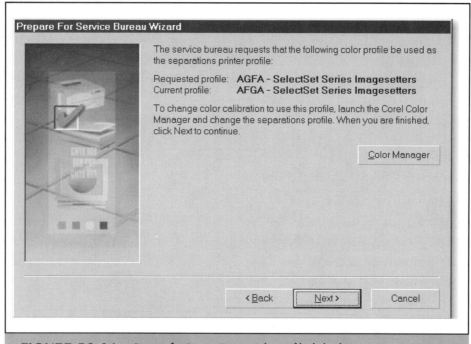

Prepare For Service Bureau Wizard

The service bureau requests that the following color profile be used as the separations printer profile:

Requested profile: **AGFA - SelectSet Series Imagesetters**
Current profile: **AFGA - SelectSet Series Imagesetters**

To change color calibration to use this profile, launch the Corel Color Manager and change the separations profile. When you are finished, click Next to continue.

Color Manager

< Back   Next >   Cancel

FIGURE 30-16   Prepare for Service Bureau Color Profile dialog box

fonts and is not recommended even though many service bureaus request the files. The last option is to ask the service bureau if they have the fonts. If you've used fonts supplied with CorelDRAW and the service bureau has CorelDRAW, this should not be a problem. If you've used other fonts, the service bureau may have to purchase their own copy of the fonts. Once you have the fonts straightened out, click Next.

The next dialog box asks for information about you, as shown in Figure 30-18. Simply fill in all of the information and click Next.

Now you'll be asked for the name of the folder where all files created by the Wizard will be placed, as shown in Figure 30-19. The default name will be the folder that currently contains the file with a subfolder named the same

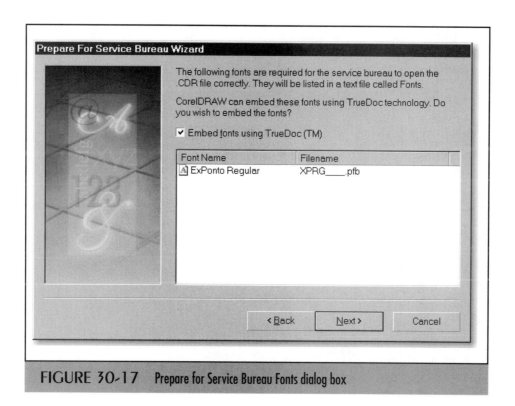

FIGURE 30-17   Prepare for Service Bureau Fonts dialog box

as the current file name. Since the files can be quite large, make sure that you specify a location that will have enough room. It is not uncommon for print files to exceed 50MB or higher, especially if you have a file containing high-resolution bitmaps. And whatever you do, do not point to a folder on a removable disk as this will dramatically slow down the creation of the files. You can easily copy the whole folder to a removable disk after the Wizard is finished. When you've entered an appropriate folder name, click Next.

Now it is time to look at the Print Preview to make sure everything is correct before proceeding. Figure 30-20 shows the next screen of the Wizard, which includes a Print Preview button. Chapter 29 describes how the Print

Prepare For Service Bureau Wizard

To allow your service bureau to easily identify the files that you send them, the following information will be included in the print job information file. After you have made any necessary revisions to this information, click Next to continue.

Your name: Foster D. Coburn III

Company: Unleashed Productions, Inc.

Address: P.O. Box 7008

Phone: 602-595-0065   Fax: 602-595-0084

Email: foster@unleash.com

Job name: OfficialGuideColorPage1

Comments:

< Back   Next >   Cancel

FIGURE 30-18   Prepare for Service Bureau Customer Information dialog box

Preview screen works, for those who are not familiar with it. After you are satisfied that the preview looks the way you want, click the Next button.

If you do notice something wrong in the Print Preview, you'll either need to Cancel the Prepare for Service Bureau Wizard and return to CorelDRAW to correct the problem or click the Back button in the Wizard to return to the screen that controls the problem area. If in doubt, contact the service bureau that is to receive the file and discuss the problem with them. It is much better to discuss the problem now rather than after some film has been ruined.

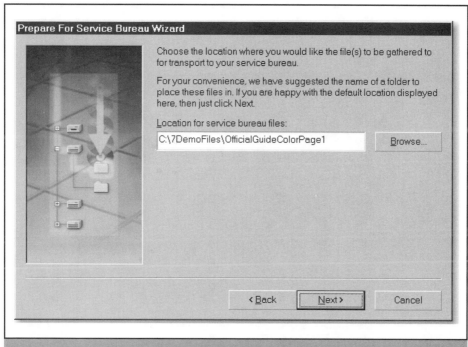

FIGURE 30-19   Prepare for Service Bureau File Destination dialog box

The next screen shows a progress meter for your file as shown in Figure 30-21. The larger and more complex your document file, the longer it will take to process. This is usually a good time to fetch another cup of coffee or take a lunch break. Most files should finish in less than five minutes, but it wouldn't be uncommon for a file to take half an hour or more especially if you have a slow computer.

The last screen, shown in Figure 30-22, will appear automatically when the file has finished processing. Each of the files that was created will be listed.

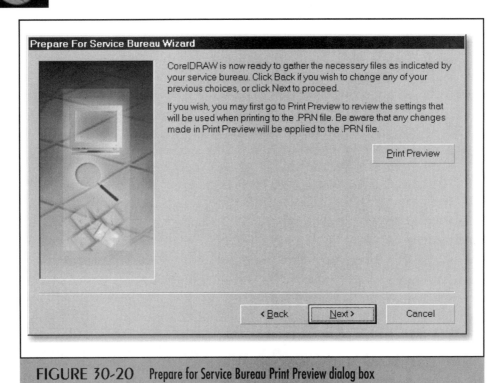

Prepare For Service Bureau Wizard

CorelDRAW is now ready to gather the necessary files as indicated by your service bureau. Click Back if you wish to change any of your previous choices, or click Next to proceed.

If you wish, you may first go to Print Preview to review the settings that will be used when printing to the .PRN file. Be aware that any changes made in Print Preview will be applied to the .PRN file.

[Print Preview]

[< Back] [Next >] [Cancel]

FIGURE 30-20   Prepare for Service Bureau Print Preview dialog box

In this example, there were four files, including the CorelDRAW (.cdr) file with the fonts embedded, a PostScript Print file (.prn), and two text files. Fonts.txt lists each of the fonts used in the job and should be supplied to the service bureau so they know which fonts to load. JobInfo.txt provides the service bureau with a great deal of information on how the .prn file was created and also should be supplied to them. Lastly is a note at the bottom of the dialog box asks you to print a sample of the file for the service bureau so that they know what to expect.

If one or more of the job files were not created, a dialog box listing those files will be displayed instead. This is your signal that something went wrong and that it's time to click the Back button and begin troubleshooting.

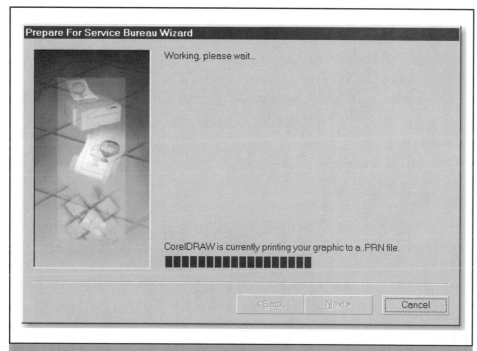

FIGURE 30-21   Prepare for Service Bureau File Preparation dialog box

Now you simply have to click the Finish button and get the files to the service bureau for output. You should consult with them to find out what type of removable media they support since the files more than likely will not fit on a floppy disk. And don't forget to supply the printout so that they can compare their output with yours.

With this Wizard, creating files for a service bureau has been greatly simplified. Unfortunately, there are few profiles available and so you may not find one for your favorite service bureau. Talk to that service bureau and see if they can create one for you and definitely suggest that they buy this book to learn how it works!

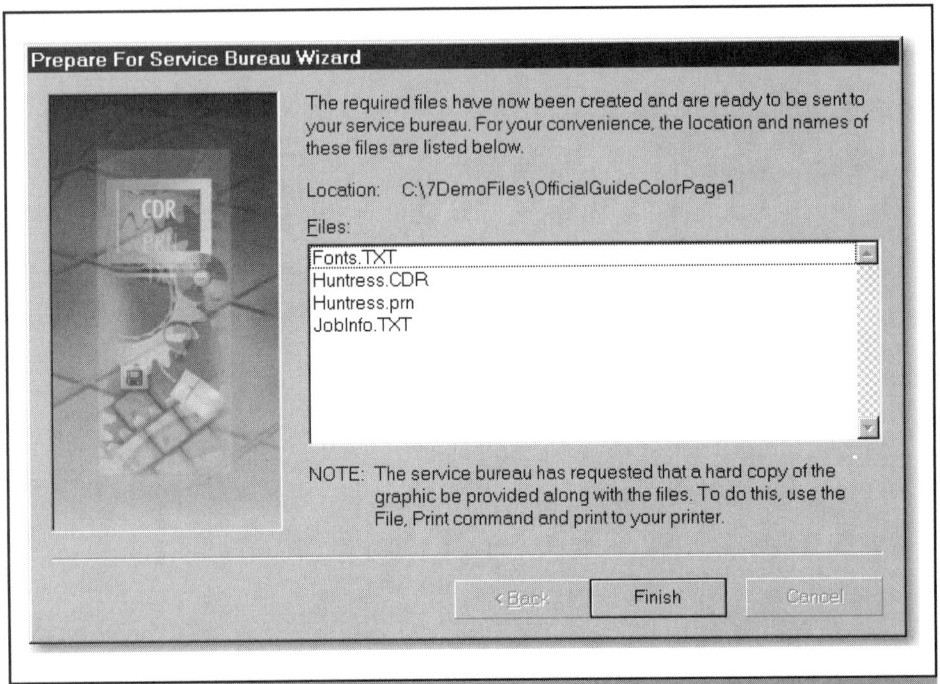

Prepare For Service Bureau Wizard

The required files have now been created and are ready to be sent to your service bureau. For your convenience, the location and names of these files are listed below.

Location: C:\7DemoFiles\OfficialGuideColorPage1

Files:

Fonts.TXT
Huntress.CDR
Huntress.prn
JobInfo.TXT

NOTE: The service bureau has requested that a hard copy of the graphic be provided along with the files. To do this, use the File, Print command and print to your printer.

< Back   Finish   Cancel

FIGURE 30-22   Prepare for Service Bureau File Listing dialog box

PART
5

ADVANCED TOPICS

31

WRITING TOOLS

orelDRAW is by no means a word processor, but there are many times when you need the functions of a word processing program. For example, nothing is more embarrassing than misspelling a word in an ad, and using inch marks for quotations is a sure sign of someone who hasn't been in the business for long. With the writing tools included with CorelDRAW 8, these problems can be minimized.

FIND AND REPLACE

CorelDRAW 8 has two types of Find and Replace command. The first type is for graphical objects and is described in Chapter 34. This chapter is concerned with finding and replacing text. Either of these commands will find all occurrences of text within your drawing, even if the text is on multiple pages.

Bring up the Find Text dialog box with the Edit | Find and Replace | Find Text command. The dialog box is shown here.

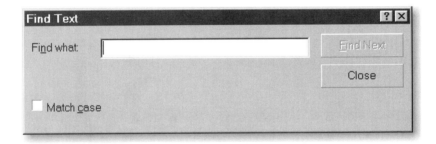

Type the text you want to find in the Find what text box. If you want the search to be case sensitive, check the Match case check box. This means that if the word you typed has a capital letter, the search will match the desired word only if it has the same capital letter. When you're ready, click the Find Next button. This will highlight the next text block that contains the desired text. It will not highlight the word within that text block, however, so if the text is contained within a full page of Paragraph Text, you will have to manually search for it.

Clicking the Find Next button again will move forward in the document to the next text block containing the desired text. If multiple instances of the desired text are within one Paragraph Text block, the search feature will highlight the block only once and then move on to the next block. If the text cannot be found, a message will appear telling you that the text can't be found.

To take the search one step further, use the Edit | Find and Replace | Replace Text command. It will present the Replace Text dialog box shown here:

31

Now after the desired text is found, it can be replaced. Type the replacement text in the Replace with text box. To replace the text in only the first text block encountered, use the Replace button. Note that this option replaces every occurrence within the highlighted text block, so if you replace "the" within a large block of Paragraph Text, there will undoubtedly be lots of changes. The Replace All button replaces every occurrence of the specified text within every text block in the document.

When using the Replace Text dialog box, you must be very careful how you search for text. Remember that it will also find the characters you specify within other words. In those cases, you may want to type the desired word followed by a space and possibly preceded by a space so that only whole words will be found.

One of the most common mistakes of typists new to word processing is to add extra spaces between sentences. Use Find and Replace to replace all occurrences of two spaces with a single space. Repeat this process until all extra spaces have been eliminated. If you are using fixed-width fonts, this process should not be used.

TYPE ASSIST

If you've used any modern word processor, Type Assist should look very familiar. It made its debut in CorelDRAW 5, but most users are unaware that it exists. It can be quite useful, and in CorelDRAW 8, all of its features are set by default to work without any user intervention.

To access the Type Assist dialog box, choose Text | Writing Tools | Type Assist. The Type Assist Options dialog box shown in Figure 31-1 will appear.

The first option is Capitalize first letter of sentences. This works very similarly to the Sentence Case option of the Change Case command discussed in Chapter 6. The first letter following sentence punctuation will automatically be capitalized. Sentence punctuation includes the period (.), exclamation point (!), question mark (?), and the Spanish-language symbols

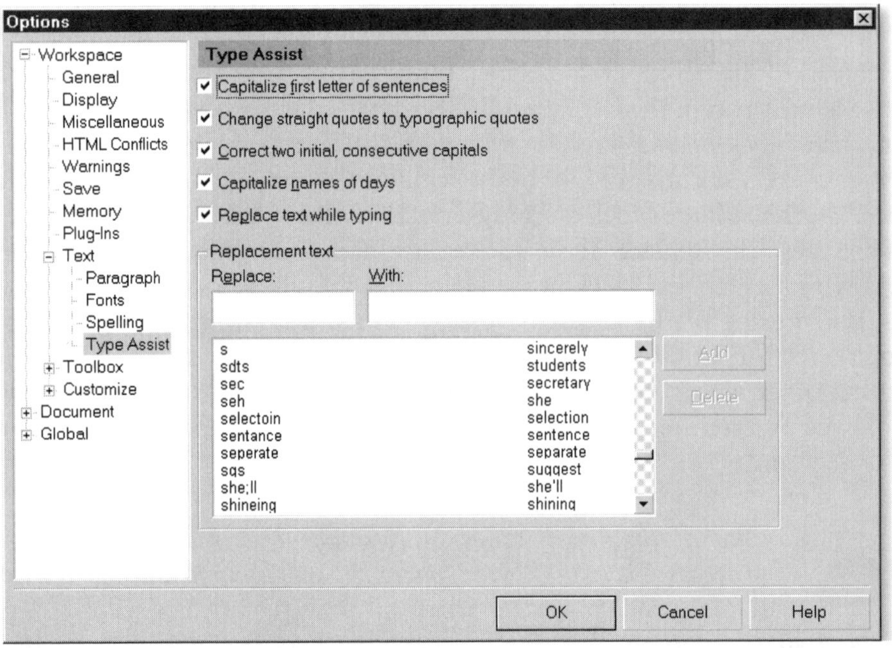

FIGURE 31-1   The Type Assist Options dialog box

¿ and ¡. Other marks such as the colon (:), semicolon (;), and comma (,) will not be affected.

One of the most common mistakes made by desktop publishing rookies—and many veterans—is using the inch and feet marks as quotation marks. With Type Assist, there is no need to remember weird ASCII codes to type the correct quotation marks. Simply check the Change straight quotes to typographic quotes check box. Now you just type the "wrong" quotation marks, and Type Assist will convert them to curly quotation marks for you.

The curly quotation marks feature will also convert marks following numbers that are meant to be inch and feet marks. In this situation, you must turn off the feature.

When you are typing really fast and use the SHIFT key, you sometimes may hold it down a little bit too long. Then you may end up with more than one capital letter at the beginning of a word. Check the Correct two initial, consecutive capitals check box, and the extra capital letters will be changed back to lowercase.

Do you need to type abbreviations like PC, CD, and DTP often? If so, they will be converted to Pc, Cd, and Dtp. In this situation, you'll need to disable the Type Assist feature for converting initial consecutive capitals.

Proper grammar says that the names of the days of the week need to be capitalized. We all forget to do this from time to time, but Type Assist can be set to remember for you. Check the Capitalize names of days check box.

The last option is Replace text while typing. When this option is checked, the replacement table at the bottom of the dialog box is used. The left side of the table shows what you type, and the right side of the table displays the text that will appear on the screen. For example, you can type (c) to get the © symbol. You'll also notice that quite a few commonly misspelled and mistyped words are in the table with their wrong and correct spellings.

Another great use for the Replacement text table is for abbreviations. Since we're talking about CorelDRAW 8, wouldn't it be great to type CD8 and have CorelDRAW 8 appear? Click the cursor in the Replace text box and type **CD8**. Now TAB to the With text box and type **CorelDRAW 8**. Click the Add button.

Now every time you type CD8 using Artistic or Paragraph Text, it will automatically be converted to CorelDRAW 8.

If you would like to remove a particular entry from the table, highlight it and click the Delete button. A good example of this would be the entries for *s* and *j*. How often have you typed the letter *s* followed by a space only to see the word "sincerely" appear. Or you type the letter *j* followed by a space and the word "gentlemen" appears. This is Type Assist in action. So rather than turn it off, simply scroll down through the list until you find *j*, highlight it and press the Delete button. Repeat the process for *s*. Now that troublesome twosome won't bother you again.

SPELL CHECKER

When Corel purchased WordPerfect a couple of years ago, many users wondered what was going to happen. One immediate result is that CorelDRAW now includes the spell checker, grammar checker, and thesaurus that WordPerfect developed. This strengthens the effectiveness of CorelDRAW's other tools.

To spell check text, choose Text | Writing Tools | Spell Check or simply use the CTRL-F12 shortcut key. If you have text selected when you bring up the spell checker, the selected text will be checked; otherwise, the whole document is checked.

When a misspelled word is found, you'll be presented with the dialog box shown in Figure 31-2.

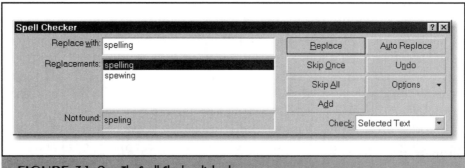

FIGURE 31-2   The Spell Checker dialog box

The top box will display the word that the spell checker doesn't understand. Just below it will be the best suggestion for a replacement and below that will be a list of other possible replacements. On the drawing page, you'll notice that the work is highlighted so you can see it in context with the rest of the text. If none of the words suggested are correct, type the correct text in the Replace with text box and then click the Replace or Auto Replace button. If you don't want any changes made to the word, use the Skip Once or Skip All button, depending on how many more times the word may appear. If the word is a frequent thorn in your side or a word that you use often, use the Add button to add it to the list. If you make a mistake, simply click the Undo button.

Many more options are available when spell checking. Click the Options button to display the menu shown here:

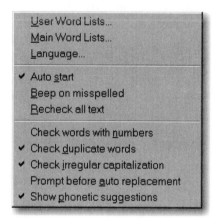

With these options, you can customize the spell checker so that it works exactly as you want. For more information on these functions, click the ? button in the title bar of the Spell Checker dialog box.

AUTOMATIC SPELL CHECKING

All of the latest word processors have a great feature that puts a red squiggly line under any misspelled words. Since Corel is now in the word processing business, that functionality has been added to CorelDRAW as well. By default, this feature is turned on, but if it's off, you can access it by choosing Tools | Options | Text | Spelling. This will bring up the dialog box shown in Figure 31-3.

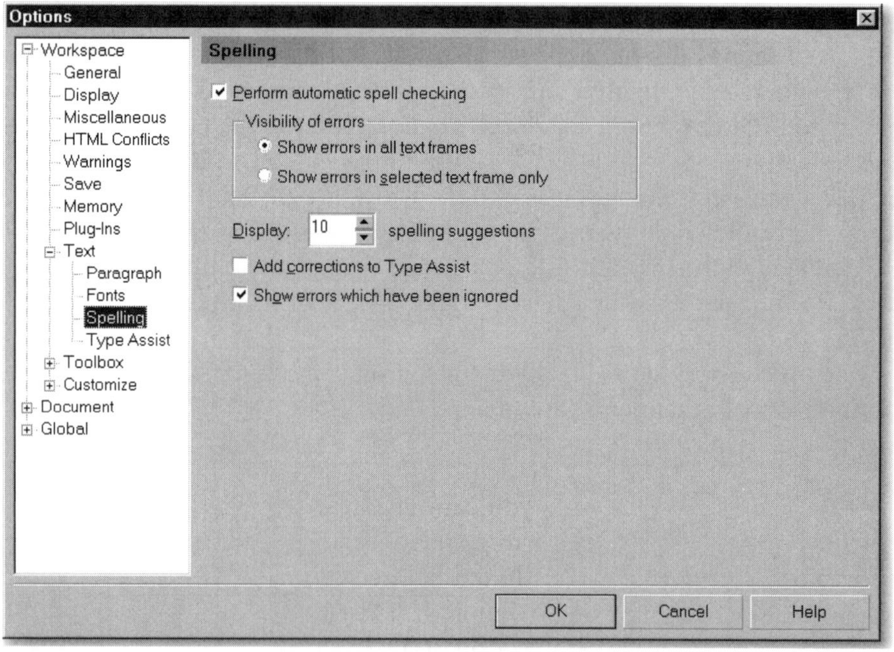

FIGURE 31-3   The Spelling Options dialog box

Checking the Perform automatic spell checking check box will activate the new spell checking feature. You can also choose to show errors in all text frames or in only the selected text frame. The latter provides the fastest performance if you have large quantities of text on screen.

When a word is highlighted, simply right-click it with the Text tool, and you will be presented with a pop-up menu like the one shown here. This menu lists proposed correct words. The number of words depends on how many corrections are found in the spell checker word list and the number you specify in the Options dialog box.

```
boozer
bizarre
bezoar
Beazer
Bazar
bazar
bazaar
baser
Béziers
Bezier

Ignore All

Spelling...        Ctrl F12
Thesaurus...
```

When you correct a word, you can have it automatically added to Type Assist if you check the Add Corrections to Type Assist check box. Note that this may add many words and should be used carefully. You can also specify Show errors which have been ignored. This option can be useful if you accidentally skip making a correction of a particular word. Having the error still shown will remind you that the word may be a problem or that you may want to add it to your user word list.

GRAMMAR CHECKER

Grammar checking was also brought in to CorelDRAW from WordPerfect's Grammatik program. You can now check your text on many different levels for errors in spelling and grammar. To access the grammar checker, choose Text | Writing Tools | Grammatik. This will bring up a dialog box like the one shown in Figure 31-4.

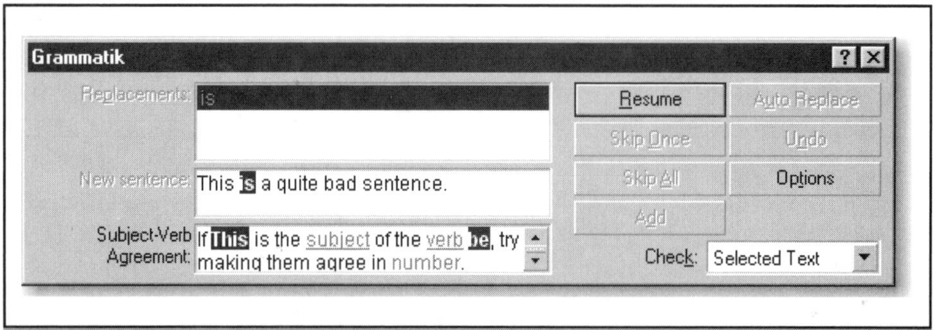

FIGURE 31-4   The Grammatik dialog box

You'll notice that the right side of the dialog box is very similar to the Spell Checker dialog box. The dialog box describes the error and suggests how best to correct the problem. If there are replacements to suggest, these will be shown in the Replacements box, and the corrected sentence that Grammatik suggests will be shown in the New sentence box. You can either use the correction or ignore it, but there is no way that you can edit the change to be made.

There are quite a few other things that you can check by clicking the Options button and selecting an item from the drop-down list. For more information on each of these items, please see the Help file that came with CorelDRAW.

THESAURUS

Suppose you're working (or is that puttering?) really hard on a document, and you want to find a way to say something with a different word. Choose Text | Writing Tools | Thesaurus, and you'll be presented with a blank dialog box similar to the one shown in Figure 31-5. Note that we've already proceeded with the next step so that the image shown is not empty.

Type a word in the Insert text box and click the Look Up button. The lower-left box will fill with suggested words or phrases, and the lower-right

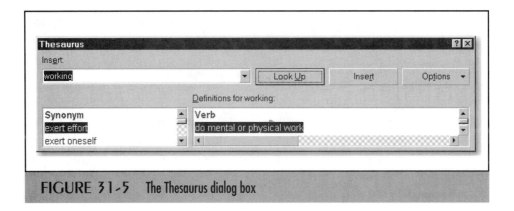

FIGURE 31-5   The Thesaurus dialog box

box will provide definitions of the word. The results of the search depend on the choices you make in the Options drop-down menu shown here. If you don't understand any of these choices, click the ? on the title bar of the dialog box, and it will provide you with information to help you understand.

You can have the Thesaurus find many different types of words or phrases related to the word you specify. From the Options menu, you can decide which of these types will be shown in the lower-right and lower-left list boxes.

If you highlight a word in your document before bringing up the Thesaurus, you can automatically replace it with a new word or phrase. Select the new word or phrase in the lower-left list box and click the Insert button. Your original word or phrase will now be gone, and the new one will be in its place.

 *Make sure that you only select the word and not the spaces surrounding the word, as it may affect the results.*

TEXT STATISTICS

As you work on a document, you will often find it handy to know certain information about the text within the document. The Text | Text Statistics command will give you information about either the selected text block or all the text in the document (if no text is selected). An example of the Statistics dialog box is shown in Figure 31-6.

This dialog box lists the types of objects and the number of each object. The types of objects that may be listed include Paragraph Text frames, Paragraphs, Artistic Text objects, Lines, Words, Characters, and Fonts.

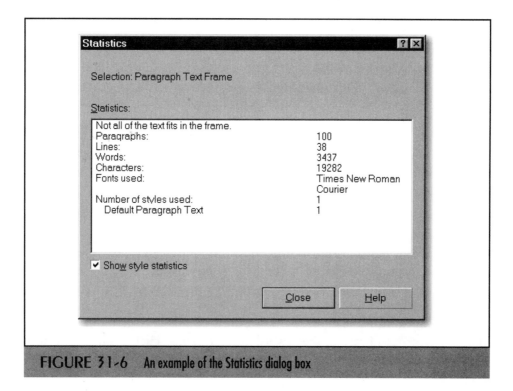

FIGURE 31-6 An example of the Statistics dialog box

Knowing the fonts used in a document can be extremely important when it comes time to share the document with another user or a service bureau.

If you check the Sho<u>w</u> style statistics check box, more information related to text styles will be displayed. This information includes the number of styles used, a list of the styles, and the number of times each style was used.

With the various word processing tools that are provided, CorelDRAW has the capability to work with all of the text in your ad, flyer, or newsletter. And since these tools are common to many Corel applications, the learning curve for using each application is much smaller. Just keep in mind that longer text-intensive projects are best handled in a true page layout package such as Corel Ventura.

31

32

EXTRACTING AND MERGING TEXT

S omewhere in the world, there is a user of CorelDRAW who thinks this program is a word processor. Well, it isn't, and you will sometimes find it easier to edit text with a word processor than with CorelDRAW. To do this, you will need to get the text out of CorelDRAW and into a format your word processor can read (extract it), and then to get the edited text back into CorelDRAW (merge it back).

The methods for doing this are the same for both Artistic and Paragraph Text. Just create your drawing with all the text you want. Then when it comes time to edit the text outside of CorelDRAW, follow the instructions in this chapter.

As CorelDRAW has grown, it has added more and more features that were once the domain of word processors. Now it can spell check, grammar check, and much more. So there is less need to use the Extract and Merge Back commands, and Corel has removed the commands from the default menus that come with CorelDRAW 8. But all is not lost. You can fully customize the menus to do exactly what you need. And the commands do still exist. In Chapter 40, we describe how to customize CorelDRAW. So when we get to the section on customizing menus, we'll show how to add these two commands since it is a somewhat lengthy explanation. So for those who aren't familiar with this process, turn to Chapter 40. The rest of you, continue on.

EXTRACTING TEXT

When you extract text, first save your CorelDRAW file. Otherwise, a message asking you to save the file will be displayed. You don't need to select the text, since all text within the document will be extracted. You next just choose the Text | Extract command, if you've customized your menus as explained earlier, and you will be prompted for a file name and location. The text will be converted to an ASCII file with your text and various markers so that CorelDRAW can accurately re-merge the file.

Open the text file in your favorite word processor and make the necessary changes. You'll notice the symbols @PTXT prefacing any Paragraph text and @ATXT prefacing any Artistic text. Many of the other markers will be contained with angle brackets (< and >). Make sure that you edit only the text and that these markers remain unchanged; otherwise, the file will not re-merge correctly, if at all.

When you are done editing the file, save the file as plain ASCII text. If you save the file in the format of the word processor, CorelDRAW will not be able to use it.

 *Another great use for this feature is to just extract all of the text so that you can use it elsewhere—maybe for page layout or even a Web page.*

MERGING TEXT

To bring the text back into your CorelDRAW document, you'll need to have the document loaded. Select Text | Merge Back, assuming that you've customized your menus as described earlier, and choose the text file that you edited. Your edited text will be brought into your document so that it replaces the existing text. Some attributes such as font, font size, character spacing, and alignment will be retained. Attributes that affect individual characters such as the character angle, baseline shift, and font style will not be maintained since the text they refer to may have changed. If an effect has been applied to the text, you may notice that there will be alterations. You can reapply the effect to the text to correct any problems.

The ability to extract and merge text is more important when you are working with large blocks of Paragraph Text. In that case, you might want to explore a different method. Create the text in your favorite word processor and perform any editing in the word processor. When the text has your final approval, import it into CorelDRAW. This will eliminate the need to worry about the markup codes within the text and the need to reapply attributes.

USING PRINT MERGE

If you've used a word processor for any length of time, you've probably performed a mail merge operation. Mail merge is great for producing plain old form letters, but suppose you want to create a really great-looking document that can be merged with a set of data? You can do this with CorelDRAW if you carefully prepare your CorelDRAW document and the data that is to be merged.

PREPARING THE DRAWING

When preparing a drawing to be merged, you must observe several restrictions. You can create anything you want in the document, but any text that is to be replaced must be Artistic Text. Within that Artistic Text string, you can enter any text you want, but it must be unique from other strings. For example, you can use the text "Name," where a person's name would be substituted. Just keep in mind that the name being substituted may be substantially longer than the four characters in the word "Name." Any of the attributes applied to the original text string, such as font, size, and alignment, will also be applied to the substituted text. The only effects that will not be applied to the merged data are Blend and Extrude.

Once you've designed the drawing to your liking, simply save it as a .cdr file just like any other file.

Now it is time to prepare the data that will be merged with your drawing.

PREPARING THE TEXT

The hardest part to the whole merging process is creating a data file, since this is a very exacting process. You can create the file in your favorite word processor, but it may be easier to just use Windows Notepad. Advanced users may want to use the Database Publisher utility that comes with Corel Ventura to automate the process.

The first item in the file should be the number of text blocks that will be merged. For example, if there are three items that are going to be replaced, insert the number 3.

Next, you need to list each of the text blocks that will be replaced. The text must be preceded and followed by the backslash (\) character. Make sure that the text is typed exactly as it appears in the CorelDRAW document, including its spelling and punctuation. The last character must not be a space, or the process will not work. Each of the data elements can appear on a separate line, or all of the elements can be grouped together on a single line.

Now you need to enter the data that will be merged into your document. Again, it must be preceded and followed by the \ character. Here are two examples of the data file, one with each set of data on a single line and the other with the data on separate lines.

```
Data on one line:3
\Name\\Class\\Date\
\Joe Q. User\\CorelDRAW 8 Boot Camp\\March 19-21, 1998\
\Jane Artist\\CorelDRAW 8 Boot Camp\\April 2-4, 1998\
```

Data on separate lines:

```
3
\Name\
\Class\
\Date\
\Joe Q. User\
\CorelDRAW 8 Boot Camp\
\March 19-21, 1998\
\Jane Artist\
\CorelDRAW 8 Boot Camp\
\April 2-4, 1998\
```

32

Once the data has been entered properly, save it in plain ASCII format.

MERGING THE DOCUMENT WITH THE TEXT

When you execute the merge operation, the text file cannot be open, so make sure you've closed the file in your text editor. You will not see any of the pages on the screen before they are printed, so take a second to look at the data file to make sure it is correct before you precede.

 *A common problem that users may encounter is that the original text in CorelDRAW may contain invisible characters such as a space or a carriage return. So if you're having problems, check the text carefully!*

Print Merge is yet another command that has been removed from the default menu structure. So you'll also have to customize your menus to add it to the File menu where it used to be located. Once you've done that and opened your drawing, simply select File | Print Merge. You will be prompted to select the text file containing the merge data. Click OK, and your merged documents will soon come out of your printer. If things don't look right on the document, the data file probably contains errors that need to be corrected.

Figure 32-1 shows a sample certificate before the data file is merged. Figure 32-2 shows an example of what the certificate looks like after the Print Merge operation.

The ability to merge a data file into CorelDRAW lets you create some really awesome documents that just aren't possible in your word processor or database. Getting the syntax of the data correct can be daunting at first, but once you master that the process is quite simple.

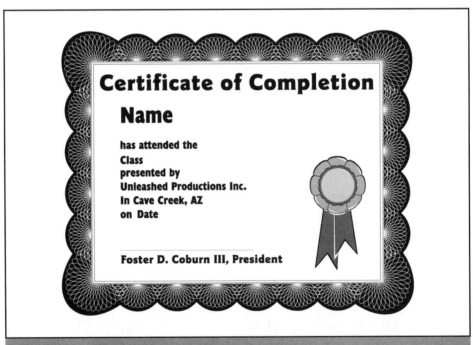

FIGURE 32-1   Certificate template to be merged with a data file

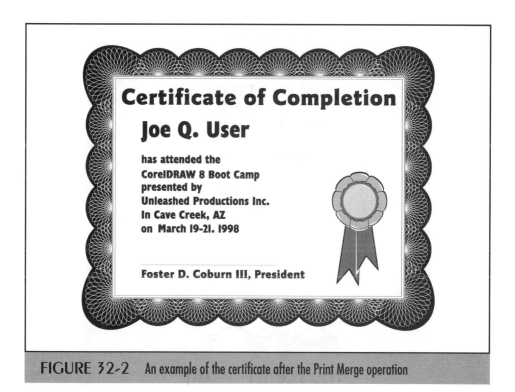

FIGURE 32-2   An example of the certificate after the Print Merge operation

LIMITATIONS OF PRINT MERGE

Let's look at a common task that CorelDRAW users may want to perform. Suppose you want to create a set of name tags for an event. You've gone down to your office supply store and purchased some premade tags that you can run through your laser printer. They come eight to a sheet and CorelDRAW even has a label template that works perfectly. So far, so good. The problem is that the Print Merge operation only works on one document at a time rather than the multiple pages within the same document that would be required to print the name tag labels. There is a workaround, but it is extremely tedious. You will need to create variables titled "Name1," "Name2," "Name3," and so on and more variables if other data such as their company name needs to appear on the label. Suffice it to say that this process is not very smooth.

33

STYLES, TEMPLATES, AND SCRAPBOOKS

One of the best ways to improve your productivity is to take advantage of the features described in this chapter. Styles come in many flavors, and they allow you to easily create reusable elements. With Color Styles, radical color changes are extremely simple to make. Templates give you a good starting point for creating standard types of documents. Scrapbooks make it extremely easy to manage the plethora of clipart and stock photos that are included with CorelDRAW.

GRAPHIC AND TEXT STYLES

Graphic and Text styles have been available in CorelDRAW since version 4, but many users know of their existence only through the dialog box that warns you that the styles in the file being opened don't match the default styles. By understanding how styles work, you'll be able to produce work faster. (You'll also avoid receiving the messages that sometimes appear telling you that you are missing fonts even though your file contains no text.)

When you first load CorelDRAW, you will be working with the default template, called CORELDRW.CDT. As you'll see later, some templates contain actual objects. However, the default template contains only the default styles. To see the styles in the current document, select Layout | Graphic and Text Styles (CTRL-F5). By default, they will be displayed as a Docker. If you drag the Docker onto the desktop, it will look similar to the one shown here.

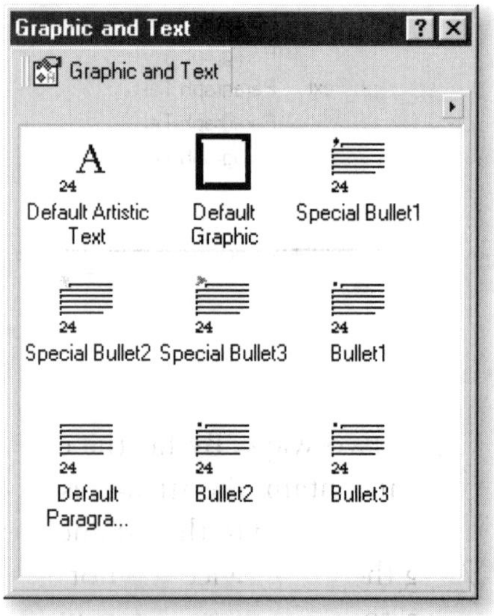

You'll notice that there are three types of styles: Artistic Text, Graphics, and Paragraph Text. The default template includes several styles for Paragraph Text, including many with bullets, but there is only one style each for Artistic Text and Graphics.

Applying any of these styles to an object is simple. Select the style you wish to apply and drag it onto the object to which you want it applied. The cursor will change to indicate that you can drop the style. The other way to apply a style is to right-click any object and choose the appropriate style from the pop-up menu that appears.

When you first see the roll-up, the icons will all be rather large. You have the option of changing the view so that it is in list format instead. Right-click the white area inside the display area and select <u>V</u>iew | <u>D</u>etails from the pop-up menu. This will change the list of styles so that they look similar to the ones shown here.

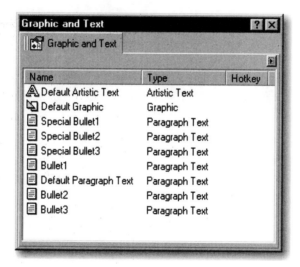

CREATING STYLES

You can create new styles in two ways. By far the easiest method is to drag an object (text or graphic) that contains the attributes you want onto the Styles window. It will be automatically added to the list and named. You can change the name simply by clicking the name twice (do not double-click) and typing the new name. If you wish to make more extensive changes, highlight the name, right-click it, and choose Properties from the pop-up menu. The dialog box shown here will be displayed.

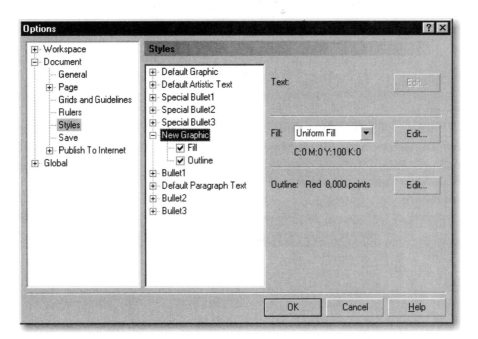

By navigating through the tree structure of the style you wish to change, you can edit all attributes of the style. Each of the major attributes has an Edit button; when you click this button, you will be taken to the appropriate dialog box for changing the attribute. If you don't want a certain attribute to be part of the style, just deselect that option.

The other way to create a new style (or modify an existing style) is to right-click an object (text or graphic) that contains the attributes you want in your style. Choose Styles | Save Style Properties from the pop-up menu and you will be presented with the dialog box shown here.

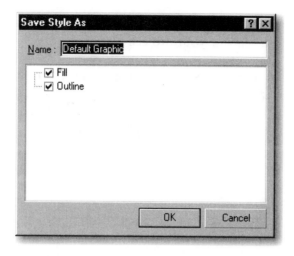

Give the style a new name if you don't want to override the attributes of the selection's current style. Note that if you don't change the style name, all other objects with the selected style will be affected by your changes—which can be desirable. If you don't want certain attributes to be part of the style, deselect them in this dialog box before you click OK.

COLOR STYLES

Have you ever created a really intricate design based on a single color or two colors and then decided that you would really prefer the design to be a different color? Changing every single object would be very time consuming, so you just leave things as they are. With the new Color Styles, such a change can be made nearly instantly.

First you will start with an existing design to see how color styles can be created automatically. You'll use the file CAR104.CDR, located in the

\Clipart\Transpor\Cars folder. The car in the image is a red color, but let's say you really need a blue car for your project.

1. Choose Layout | Color Styles to bring up the Color Styles Docker. We dragged it out onto the page so that it is floating as shown here.

2. You'll see five buttons in the window. Choose the one on the far right, Auto Create Color Styles. If it is dimmed, remember that you must have the objects selected that are to become your new color styles.

3. The following dialog box will appear. Just to make sure that everything will work properly for this image, click the Preview button and the right window of the dialog box will show the color styles.

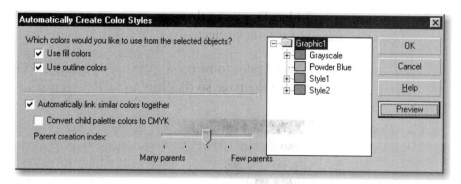

4. Nothing will seem to happen, but you should now see a + sign next to Graphic1 in the right side of the dialog box. Click it.

5. It looks as if most of the car's colors have changed to Style 1, which is a kind of orange color. Click the + sign next to this label to see all the colors. Unfortunately, this style contains not only the car color but also the color of the orange headlights. Therefore, we'll need to adjust the Parent Creation index slider so that more parent colors will be created. Move it to the left one notch and click Preview again.

6. Now you'll see that there are two reddish-orange styles and one that is orange. The body of the car is divided between two styles and the headlights have their own separate style. Just click OK.

7. You'll now see the same hierarchy of colors in the Color Styles Docker. We want to edit the car color, so select Style 1 and click the middle button with the color wheel on it at the top of the dialog box.

8. In the color palette, find the shade of blue that you want to use for the car. Select it and click OK. You should now see that most of the car has changed to blue.

9. Repeat this process with Style 2, changing it to a slightly darker blue. Unfortunately, this style also contains some of the colors in the headlight. It is probably best to start the process over again, adding even more parents, so that none of the headlights are grouped with the body of the car. But for now, we'll move on.

Voilà! You now have a blue car with some really wild-looking headlights. Now let's take a closer look at the dialog box you just used.

The first choice you can make is whether to create the styles from fill colors or from outline colors. In the example, you didn't need to worry about outline colors, since they were all black and you didn't want to change them. You can also choose not to create duplicate color styles. This option is useful if the same style could be created from outlines and fills; instead of having a separate style for each, you would find them combined.

Be sure to choose the Automatically Link Similar Colors Together option. If this is not chosen, you'll get many more styles, and therefore changing the color of a whole drawing won't be nearly so easy. You can also choose to convert any child color from its current color scheme to CMYK as the styles are created.

The last option is a slider that controls the number of parent colors created. If you slide the pointer to the far left, there will be little tolerance between color shades. Sliding it to the right provides a wide range of tolerance. Your best bet is to leave the slider at the default (middle) position for most drawings. By clicking the Preview button, you can see exactly what styles will be created and you can adjust the slider accordingly to get exactly the styles you need.

That is the automated way to create color styles; in our opinion, it is the best way. Create your drawing, then have the styles created from the drawing. However, there is another way that lets you create your own styles.

NOTE: *There is a bug when you use Auto Create Color Styles using spot colors in a new drawing. If you have saved the file and reopened it, then it will work just fine. If not, the color styles created will not be correct. This is a fantastic way to change spot colors and their tints on the fly!*

The button at the far left of the Colors Docker will create a new color style. It brings up the New Color Style dialog box, just like the Uniform Fill dialog box discussed in Chapter 10. Whatever color you choose will become your new parent color. While you're in the New Color Style dialog box, you can give your new style a name, or you can click the name twice (don't double-click) in the roll-up and then change the name. If you have a parent color selected, you can create a child for that parent by clicking the next button in the Docker. It will provide you with the dialog box shown here.

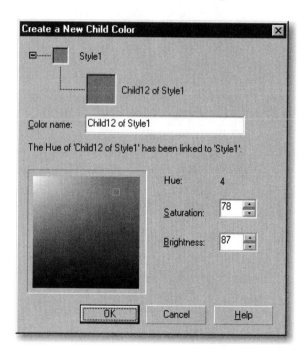

33

In the Create a New Child Color dialog box, you can enter a name for the child color. Most of the time, it is best to leave the name alone so that it shows the link to the parent. You can change only the Saturation and Brightness values for the child color, because changing the Hue value would make it a distant cousin instead of a child!

Instead of manually creating child colors, click the fourth button in the Styles roll-up. This will automatically generate shades of the parent color, as shown in the following dialog box.

Up to 20 different shades can be created. With the radio button, you can specify whether the shades should be lighter, darker, or both in relation to the parent. You can also control the similarity of the new colors to the original ones with the slider control.

Another way to get to the commands is to right-click any of the color styles. This will bring up the menu shown here.

TEMPLATES

In essence, a template is nothing more than a CorelDRAW file with a different extension. Templates can be repositories for predesigned work; they can store styles you've created as well as content.

A number of templates are provided with CorelDRAW; examples of each are shown in the clipart manual. These templates are divided into CorelDRAW templates and Paper Direct templates, which are meant to be used with paper supplied by Paper Direct.

To bring up a template, choose File | New From Template and you'll be presented with the Template Wizard, shown here. Select the set of templates you want to choose from. You can choose from CorelDRAW templates, Paper Direct templates (text and paper samples), and Paper Direct templates (text only). Then click Next.

33

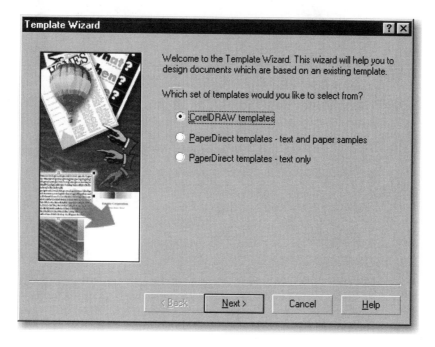

Now you'll be presented with a list of template types. Make a selection, then click Next.

You can now choose a subtype of a template based on your previous selection. Again, make your choice, then click Next.

The next screen lists individual templates, as shown here.

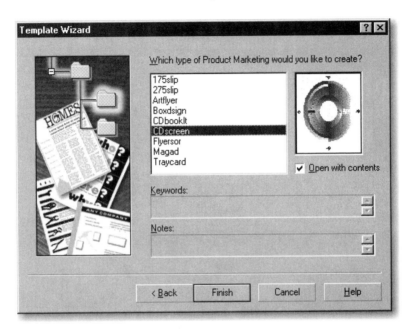

In the upper right, you'll see a small preview of the template, just as in CorelDRAW's File Open dialog box. You'll also see the option Open with contents. You can either bring in only the styles from the template or include any text and graphics that may be in the file.

Once you've made all your selections, click Finish. The file will be opened in CorelDRAW.

You'll soon see that templates are very similar to clipart, but instead of being just one graphic, a template contains a whole document.

You must select the Open with Contents option if you want guidelines to be loaded from a template file.

CREATING YOUR OWN TEMPLATES

Any documents that you regularly create are good candidates for templates. To create your own template, choose the CorelDRAW Template (CDT) File Type in the Save As dialog box. Since all of the templates are normally stored in the \Draw\Template folder below the main folder where CorelDRAW was installed, you can even add your own templates to the Wizard by putting them in that folder.

If you don't want to go through the Wizard each time you want to use a template, select File | Open and select the CDT file for the template that you want to open. You will be presented with a dialog box where you can choose whether to open the template for editing the template itself or to use it as a template for a new document, and with or without contents.

33

To learn more about how to create your own templates, you may want to open one of the Paper Direct templates and dissect it using the Object Manager.

SCRAPBOOKS

Scrapbooks provide ways of looking at your Clipart, Photos, Favorite Fills and Outlines, 3D Models, Ftp sites, and other files that you may want to use in CorelDRAW. The Scrapbook Docker is very similar to the Mosaic roll-up that was featured in older versions of CorelDRAW, but it has much more functionality.

Each of the sections of the Scrapbook can be opened from the View | Scrapbook drop-down child menu, or you can just click the appropriate icon on the Library toolbar. Unfortunately, the easy method of switching between scrapbooks by clicking similar icons within the Scrapbook window was removed. If you want this capability back, you'll need to open each of the Scrapbooks and their icons will be part of the Docker window.

Let's begin with the Clipart Scrapbook by selecting View | Scrapbook | Clipart. The only thing it contains is a folder labeled Clipart. If you don't already have the clipart CD in your CD-ROM drive, this page will ask for it. Double-click the folder (just as in Explorer), and you'll see a list of all the folders on the Clipart CD. Africa will be the first item listed. Double-click it to see the contents. Again, you'll see a long list of folders. Double-click Art. Now you should see a number of files shown as small icons with the filename below each. The icons are rather small, but you can enlarge them. Right-click the white space in the roll-up and choose View | Thumbnail Size from the pop-up menu. This brings up the following dialog box.

Change the Size value to Large and click OK. All the icons should be much larger and easier to interpret, as shown here.

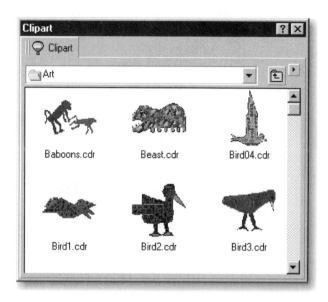

Now you simply need to locate the file you wish to add to your drawing. Drag it onto the drawing page. This will automatically import the file at the point where you release your mouse button.

Many times you'll have a few pieces of your own "clipart" that is reused quite often in a project. A quick way to create such files is to simply drag the object or objects that you wish to save directly into the Browse window. This will save the image as a "Scrap." You can rename the file after dropping it in the Scrapbook, but it will not generate a thumbnail. A better idea would be to create a folder on your hard drive where all such files will be located. Save each of the "clipart" images in this folder and then use the Scrapbook to access the files. This way they will all have a thumbnail associated with them.

At first, the features discussed in this chapter may not seem to be as impressive as some others. But templates can help increase your productivity by giving you a starting point for a project; moreover, once you have experienced the need to make drastic changes in a project very late in the design cycle, you'll learn to appreciate the use of styles.

34

FIND AND REPLACE
WIZARDS

Y ou've just imported some clipart, you resize it, and all of the outlines go crazy; or it comes time to print, and there is an extra spot color somewhere in your drawing. These are some of the common situations that make you wish that there was an easy way to globally change attributes of objects.

Early versions of CorelDRAW required you to step through a drawing object by object until you found what you were looking for and then change the setting. Now with the Find and Replace Wizards, this task is much simpler.

FIND WIZARD

If you choose Edit | Find and Replace | Find Objects, you'll be presented with the Find Wizard's initial screen, shown in Figure 34-1.

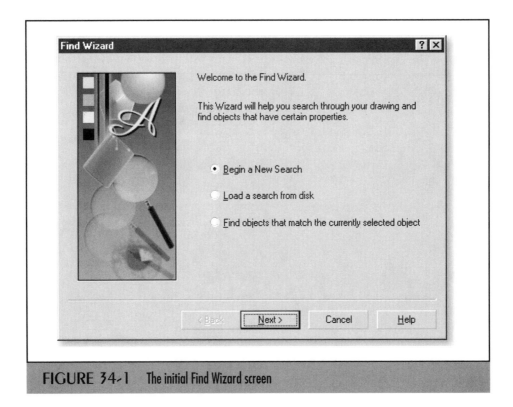

FIGURE 34-1   The initial Find Wizard screen

Notice that there are three options. The simplest option for most operations is <u>F</u>ind objects that match the currently selected object. Create an object containing the attributes you wish to find and then use this option. Just remember that it will find objects exactly like the one you created. However, the nice thing is that you can edit the attributes before the search begins, so this option is a great way to make sure all of the relevant attributes are included.

USING PRESET FINDS

Because the Find Wizard can be somewhat overwhelming to the first-time user, Corel provides preset options for several of the most common attributes you may want to find. These include PANTONE fills, PANTONE outlines, overprinted outlines, scale with image off, and text with RGB fills.

Choosing <u>L</u>oad a search from disk displays a standard File Open dialog box, where you can select any searches you previously saved. The five types of searches previously mentioned will always be listed in this dialog box. Since each of these searches is a separate file, you can share your favorites with other users.

Once you've made your choice, the first object of that type will be found and selected. If no such object exists, a message will let you know. If such an object is found, the following dialog box appears.

The controls here are similar to those in a spell checker. Find <u>N</u>ext finds and selects the next object, if there is one, and Find <u>P</u>revious finds and selects the previous object, if there is one. Find <u>A</u>ll finds and selects all objects that match your specification. The <u>E</u>dit Search button takes you back to the Find Wizard so you can specify different attributes.

Whenever an object is selected, you can make any changes you desire. With this particular option, there is no way to easily replace the attributes you find with different attributes. However, a few search and replace functions are included, as discussed later in this chapter.

CONDUCTING NEW SEARCHES

The real power of the Find feature lies in the Begin a New Search option. If you choose this option and click Next, you'll be presented with the dialog box shown in Figure 34-2.

Here, each type of object is listed individually as well as by general type, such as Text. Place a check mark next to each type of object that you want to find. Sometimes the type of object is not important because you want to find every object with a certain property. In that case, make sure to check Find any type of object at the top of the dialog box. For now, just select Ellipses for a sample search.

Three other tabs in this dialog box allow you to choose specific types of fills, outlines, and special effects for inclusion in your search criteria. These tabs each provide a list similar to that shown for the Object Types tab. For a

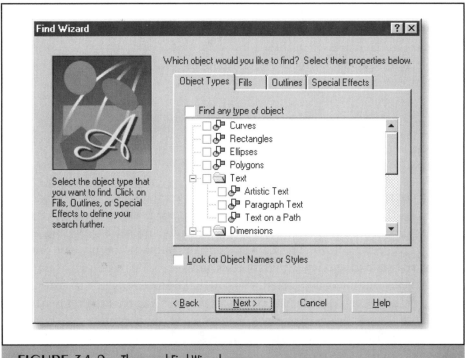

FIGURE 34-2   The second Find Wizard screen

sample search, go to the Fills tab and select Uniform Color. Then go to the Outlines tab and select Outline properties. Finally, go to the Special Effects tab and select Blend. At the bottom of a dialog box is a check box labeled Look for Object Names or Styles. If this is checked, all other parts of the dialog box will be dimmed. If you choose this option and click Next, you'll see the dialog box shown in Figure 34-3.

In the Object Manager, you can name each of your objects. If you have named objects and want to search on those names, check the Object name check box and type the name you wish to find. If you can't remember whether you used names with uppercase or lowercase letters, make sure to not check the Match case check box.

When searching for styles, you have the choice of searching for a specific style name or a style type. You can even search for both an object name and a style if you so desire.

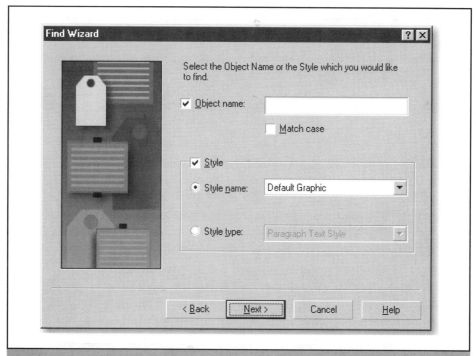

FIGURE 34-3 Find Wizard screen for selecting an object by name or style name

Clicking Next now displays a dialog that summarizes all of your search criteria and allows you to begin finding objects. This dialog box will be discussed later in this chapter after the rest of the Find options have been discussed.

As long as you haven't chosen Look for Object Names or Styles, clicking the Next button will display a series of dialog boxes asking for more information on the options you have selected. The first dialog box you will see is shown in Figure 34-4.

The example selection criteria only looked for ellipses. In the upper-left corner of the dialog box, all of the types of objects you've selected are listed. At the bottom of the dialog box is a complete description of the search criteria. This information is provided just to show you your choices and cannot be changed directly.

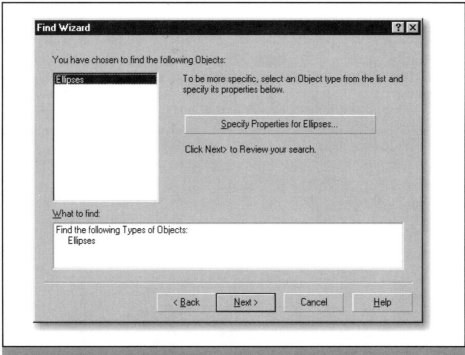

FIGURE 34-4   Find Wizard dialog box for more detailed information on ellipses

This example searches for ellipses, so you can choose Specify Properties for Ellipses. This brings up the dialog box shown in Figure 34-5.

This dialog box includes all of the parameters that can be set for ellipses. If there are any specific parameters that you don't understand, refer to Chapter 4 for more information. Note that you can also search for ellipses of a specific width and height. Doing this will narrow the search considerably; you should use these criteria with caution. Click the OK button to return to the previous dialog box.

If you choose to find other types of objects, you will be able to specify properties for those types individually. When you've finished specifying properties for all the object types selected, click the Next button to display the dialog box shown in Figure 34-6.

This example searches for objects with a uniform fill. In this dialog box, you can specify that you want to find any objects with a uniform color fill or only those objects with a specific uniform color fill. If you want to find a specific color, click the color picker and find the exact color you need. Another

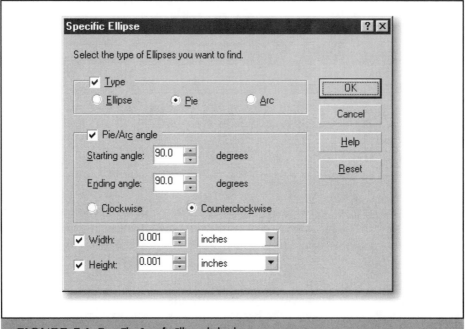

FIGURE 34-5   The Specific Ellipse dialog box

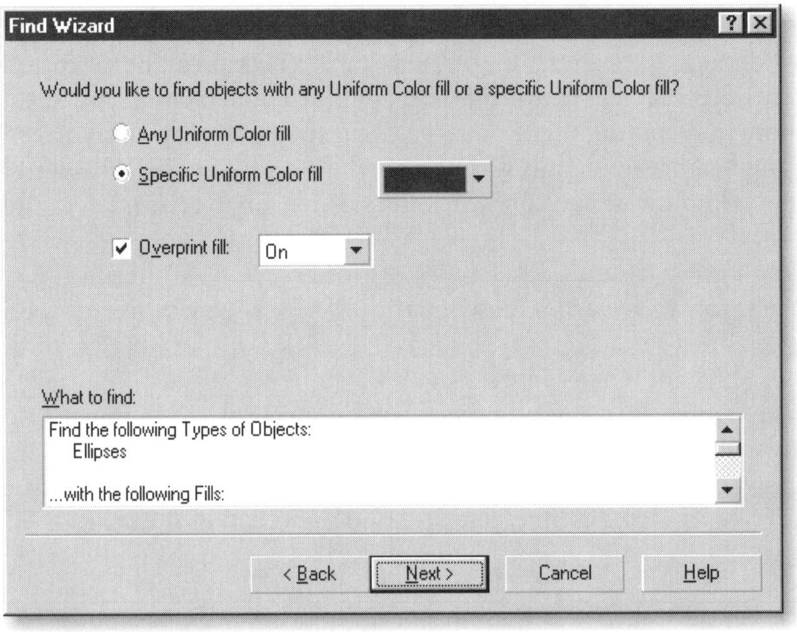

FIGURE 34-6   Find Wizard screen for finding objects with a uniform fill

check box lets you specify whether the overprint attribute of the fill is important. If you check Overprint fill, you can specify whether the attribute should be turned on or off. Again you'll see a complete description of your search criteria at the bottom of the dialog box.

Click Next to go to the dialog box shown in Figure 34-7. Now come all of the specific properties of outlines you wish to find. The first option lets you choose the width of the outline. If you don't want to find a specific width, make sure that the Width check box is not checked. Just as with the fills, you can specify a color or the overprint attribute. You can also specify whether the outline is behind fill, whether the scale with image attribute is set, and the type of line cap on the line. All of these options were described in Chapter 11. Remember that if you don't care about a particular attribute, just uncheck the check box next to it. As with the previous dialog boxes, the complete search criteria are shown at the bottom of the dialog.

Click Next to display the dialog box shown in Figure 34-8.

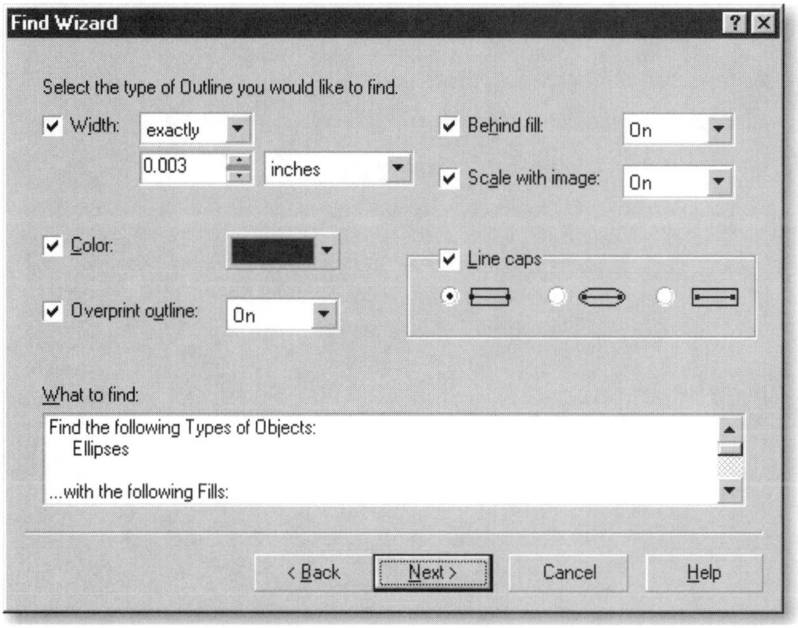

FIGURE 34-7   Find Wizard screen for specific outline properties

Just as with the types of objects, if you have chosen a particular effect, it will be indicated in the upper-left list box of this dialog box. This example searches for objects with a blend. Therefore, you can choose Specify Properties for Blend to see the following dialog box.

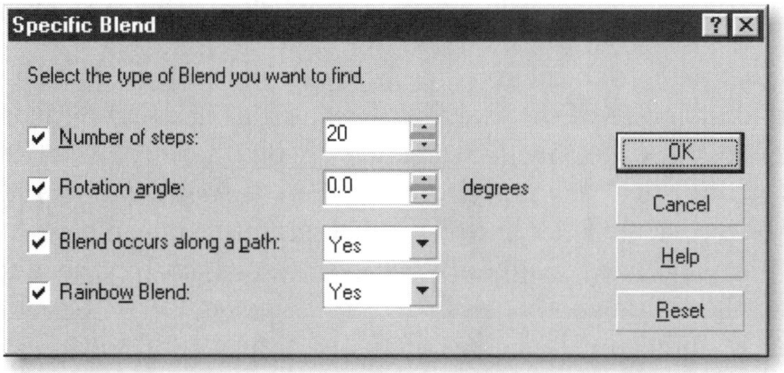

Find Wizard

You have chosen to find the following Special Effects:

Blend

To be more specific, select an Effect from the list and specify its properties below.

Specify Properties for Blend...

Click Next> to Review your search.

What to find:

Find the following Types of Objects:
  Ellipses

...with the following Fills:

< Back | Next > | Cancel | Help

FIGURE 34-8 Find Wizard screen for special effects

For blends, you can specify only the number of steps, rotation angle, whether the blend occurs along a path, and whether the blend is a rainbow blend. Once you've specified all of the attributes for blends and other effects you may have chosen, click the OK button to return to the previous dialog box. As before, a complete description of the search criteria is shown at the bottom of the dialog box.

Click Next to go to the next dialog box, shown in Figure 34-9. It provides a complete description of the search criteria. If this is a search that you will perform again, click the Save button so you won't have to specify all of the attributes again. Check the criteria, and if there is something you left out or wish to change, use the Back button until you return to the dialog box where you can make the desired changes. When everything is correct, click the Finish button, and the search will begin. From this point on, the search will behave exactly like the predefined searches discussed earlier in this chapter.

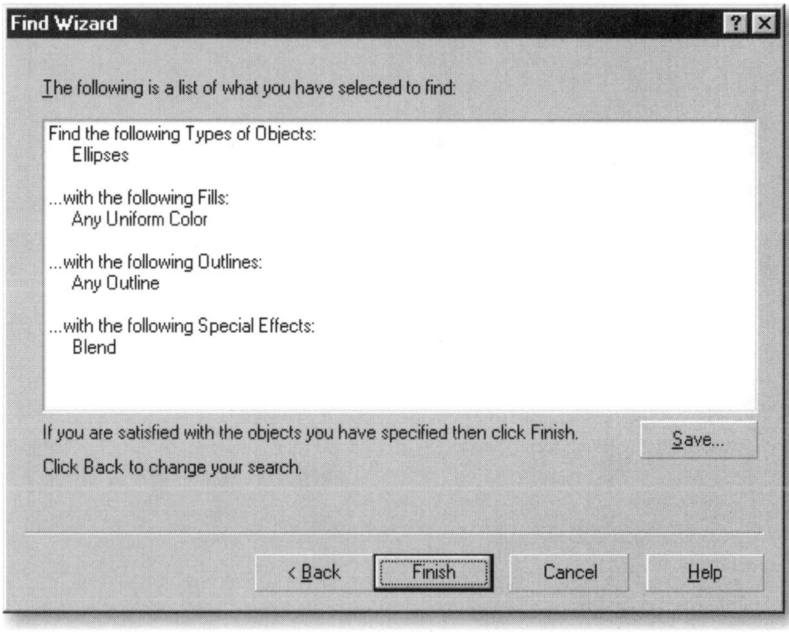

FIGURE 34-9   Final Find Wizard screen

REPLACE WIZARD

The Replace Wizard lets you search for a limited set of attributes and replace them with something else. Access the Replace Wizard by choosing Edit | Find and Replace | Replace Objects. You'll be presented with the initial Replace Wizard dialog box, shown in Figure 34-10.

Normally the Replace Wizard will search through all the objects in your drawing, but if you specify Apply to currently selected objects only, it will search only the selected objects.

REPLACE A COLOR

If you select Replace a color and click the Next button on the initial screen of the Replace Wizard, you'll see the dialog box shown in Figure 34-11.

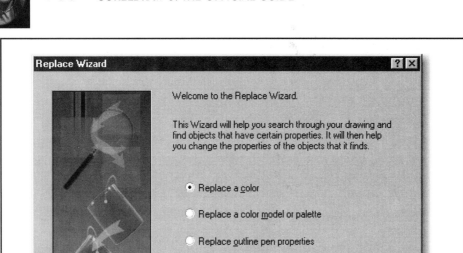

FIGURE 34-10   The initial Replace Wizard screen

Two color pickers appear at the top of the dialog box. The top one specifies the color that you want to find, and the bottom one specifies the replacement color. These color pickers show the default palette in a drop-down box. But by clicking other, you can access the Uniform Fill dialog box discussed in Chapter 9 to select any color from any palette. You can choose whether to replace the colors in outlines or fills, but you cannot do both at the same time.

The standard way of searching for colors is to look only at objects that have a uniform fill. However, you can also choose three other fill types by checking their check boxes: Apply to fountain fills, Apply to 2-color pattern fills, and Apply to monochrome bitmaps. These options don't cover all of the fill types, but they cover the ones used most often.

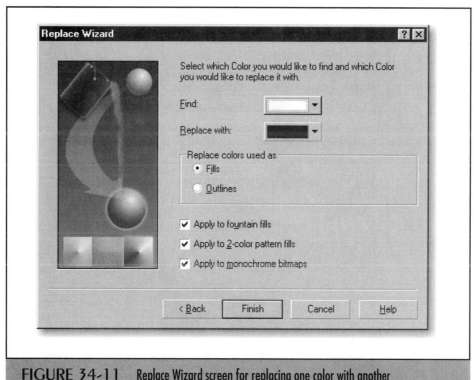

FIGURE 34-11   Replace Wizard screen for replacing one color with another

REPLACE A COLOR MODEL OR PALETTE

If you select Replace a color model or palette and click the Next button on the initial Replace Wizard screen, the dialog box shown in Figure 34-12 will appear.

You have three choices for the search. You can find any color model or palette, find a color model, or find a color palette. If you choose to find a specific color model or palette, you can choose which of the models or palettes to find. Then you need to choose which color model to use for the replace operation. Note that you can't choose a palette here since there is no way to map colors into a palette. For that, you'll need to use the Replace Color Wizard shown earlier and replace each color one by one.

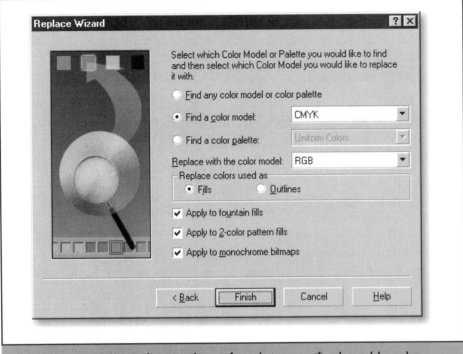

FIGURE 34-12 Replace Wizard screen for replacing a specific color model or palette

As with the Replace Colors Wizard, you have the option of replacing fills or outlines, but not both at the same time. You can also replace the colors within fountain fills, 2-color pattern fills, and monochrome bitmaps.

REPLACE OUTLINE PEN PROPERTIES

If you select Replace outline pen properties and click the Next button on the initial Replace Wizard screen, you'll see the dialog box shown in Figure 34-13.

You can search for and replace three properties of outlines: Outline width, Scale outline with image, and Outline Overprint. Searching for objects that have the Scale outline with image feature turned off and then turning it on again can be very useful when editing the clipart supplied with CorelDRAW. The appearance of art in the clipart library can change dramatically since the scale outline attribute is not turned on in most of the clipart. Changing the

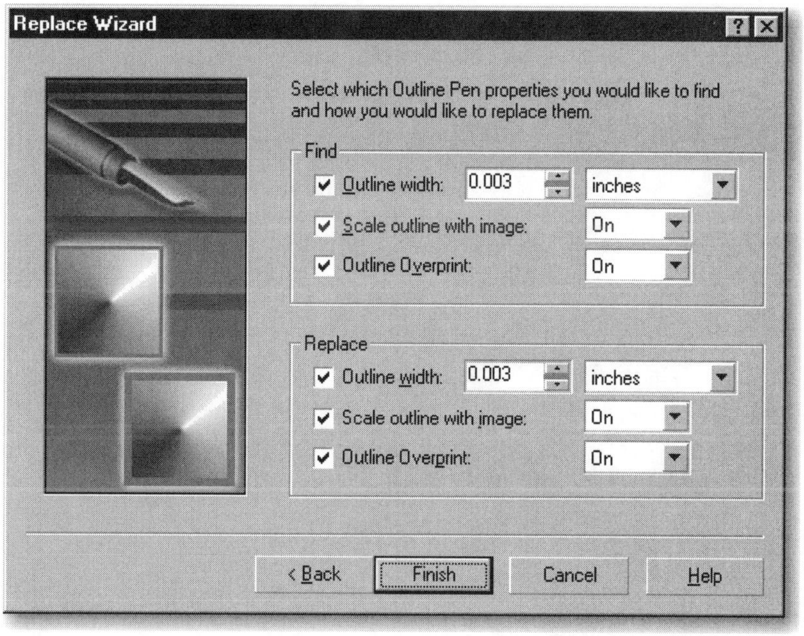

FIGURE 34-13   Replace Wizard screen for replacing outline properties

outline width could come in handy if you've used the default of hairline for your outlines. This is extremely small, especially when outputting at very high resolutions. For this reason, you may want to globally replace the outlines with a thicker outline. Making changes to the overprint setting will only affect the output to a PostScript device and should be used carefully. This option is discussed in more detail in Chapter 29.

REPLACE TEXT PROPERTIES

You can select Replace text properties and click the Next button on the Replace Wizard initial to display the dialog box shown in Figure 34-14.

Text has three properties that can be searched for and replaced: the font name, weight, and size. The Replace Wizard lists only the currently installed

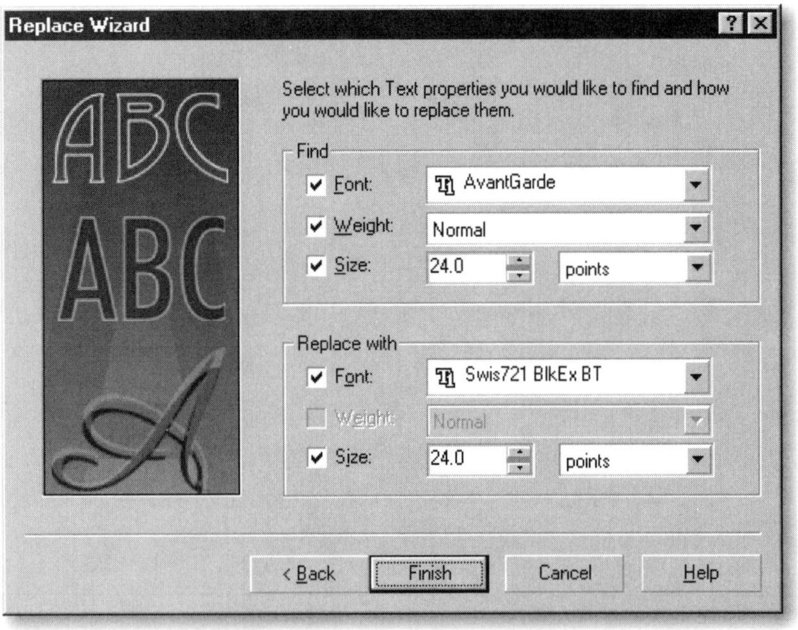

FIGURE 34-14   Replace Wizard screen for replacing text properties

weights in the Weight drop-down list. This way, you can't choose any weights that do not exist.

We remember the many times that we've had to change the outline properties of an object so that they were all set to scale with image, or the last-minute color changes when a picky client couldn't stand our choice, or even the times when there was a single spot color object in a drawing that we just couldn't find. Now with the Find and Replace Wizards, all of these tasks are extremely simple. Just don't tell your clients (or your boss) how easy these changes can be!

35

BARCODE WIZARD

Twenty years ago, it was rare to see a bar code on a product and even more rare for a store to be able to use that bar code. Nowadays, there are very few products without a bar code and few stores without a bar code driven cash register and inventory system. As designers, you will be called upon to create a bar code at some point. So this chapter introduces the different types of bar codes available in CorelDRAW 8 and explains how to create them using the Barcode Wizard.

BAR CODE SYMBOLOGIES

Although we generally speak of a bar code as a singular item, there are actually many different types of bar codes. Most types are used for a specific purpose or industry. The following bar code symbologies are available in CorelDRAW 8:

- ▶ *Codabar* This code is used for retail labeling. It is mostly numeric, but also includes six special characters (- : $ / + .). It is widely accepted in libraries and the medical industry and has become a standard as a way to label blood bags. But there is one place that you've probably all seen it and that is on Federal Express envelopes and also on photo-finishing envelopes.

- ▶ *Code 25* This code is also know as Code 2 of 5, but is not to be confused with Interleaved 2 of 5. The numbers refer to the fact that each character is represented by five bars, two of which are thick bars. It is a very old code that is not widely used today. Uses include warehouse inventory handling, photo-finishing envelopes, airline ticketing, baggage handling, and cargo handling.

- ▶ *Code 39* This code is very similar to the Interleaved 2 of 5 code. As with Code 25, the name comes from the fact that there are three thick bars and spaces within the nine bars that represent each character. Code 39 is one of the most popular symbologies since it can encode the full ASCII character set and is very tolerant of printing errors. It is commonly used by the auto parts industry and the military.

- ▶ *Code 128* This code uses the full ASCII character set. Its use is mainly in the health care industry.

▶ *EAN-13 & EAN-8* These stand for European Article Number (or International Article Number) and are used outside of North America instead of UPC codes on all general merchandise retail products. EAN is the most widely used symbology in the world. EAN numbers are assigned by the ICOF in Brussels, Belgium (011-32-2218-7674). The first two digits are used to indicate the country, with the U.S. and Canada being assigned the numbers 00 through 09. Since the first number was always 0, it was dropped. This subset is the UPC code, which will be discussed in a moment. They are also used quite commonly on books. In this case, the first three numbers are always 978. The next nine digits are the first nine numbers in the book's ISBN number. The last digit is a computed check digit. The EAN-8 uses compression to get longer numbers into fewer digits for products that have a limited space on their packaging. This works unless the last digit of the book or product number is a zero.

▶ *ISBN* Technically speaking, ISBN (International Standard Book Number) is not a bar code since it simply prints numbers using the OCR-A font. Typically, it is used with the EAN-13 bar code, which is known as a Bookland bar code. The ISBN part of the code consists of the letters ISBN followed by ten numbers.

35

▶ *ISSN* This code is very similar to ISBN. It stands for International Standard Serial Number. Again, it is just printed in the OCR-A font. But it can have the EAN-13 code attached to it just as with ISBN. ISSN will accept seven characters and will add a check digit for a total of eight characters.

▶ *ITF & ITF-14* ITF stands for Interleaved 2 of 5. It should not be confused with Code 25. Code 25 only stores information in the bars themselves while ITF stores information in the bars and the spaces between them. So it is a much more compact code. It is commonly used in warehouses and heavy industrial applications. ITF-14 is limited to 14 characters and includes "Bearer Bars." These are nothing more than a thick border around the bar code. It is quite often used on corrugated cartons.

▶ *JAN-8 & JAN-13* These two codes are nearly identical to the EAN codes described earlier. All JAN codes begin with either 45 or 49, which are the two number prefixes for Japan.

▶ *MSI/Plessey* The Plessey code was originated in England. It was modified slightly with the addition of two check digits for accuracy and readability by the MSI Data Corporation.

▶ *Pharmacode* Pharmacode was invented by the Weber company for use in the pharmaceutical industry. It is used on labels, leaflets, cartons, and other packaging materials.

▶ *POSTNET & FIM* POSTNET is used by the United States Postal Service to code ZIP codes for easier sorting of mail. With this code, you can use either 5-, 9-, or 11-digit ZIP codes. FIM (Face Identification Marking) is another bar code used by the Postal Service. There are four variations to the code which indicate whether the postage is paid and whether a POSTNET bar code exists.

▶ *UPC-A & UPC-E* These stand for the Universal Product Code. This is the code you find on most items sold at retail in North America. The UPC-A code contains 12 numbers total. The first 6 numbers are assigned to companies by the Uniform Code Council (513-435-3870) and the next 5 are numbers created by the manufacturer of the product. The last number is generated automatically as a check digit. UPC-E only contains 7 numbers and is used on packaging that requires a smaller label, such as soda cans and candy bars.

USING COREL'S BARCODE WIZARD

Many of you will attempt to follow the instructions for using the Barcode Wizard and find that you don't have it installed. By default, it is not installed. See Chapter 1 for more information on how to do a custom install and install the Barcode Wizard.

1. To begin using the Barcode Wizard, select Edit | Insert Bar Code. You will be presented with the dialog box shown in Figure 35-1.

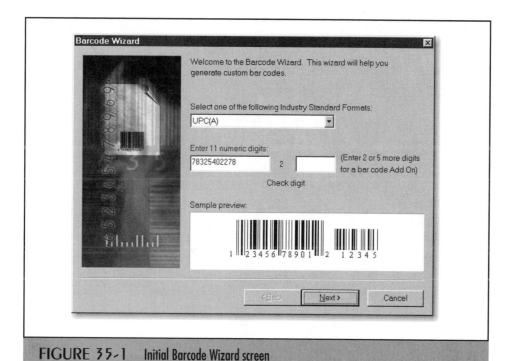

FIGURE 35-1   Initial Barcode Wizard screen

2. First, you must select the "Industry Standard Format" you wish to use. We've been referring to these as symbologies. Depending on which symbology you choose, you will be asked to enter a series of numbers and/or alpha characters. For this exercise, we're going to create a UPC-A bar code. For this code you need to enter 11 numbers. A twelfth number will be created as a check digit. You can also enter either 2 or 5 digits as an add-on. We've chosen not to add one is this example. When you're finished, click Next to get the dialog box shown in Figure 35-2.

3. This dialog presents you with a number of properties specific to the bar code. By default, they are set to the standard values for the code you have chosen and should only be changed if you have specific values that must be met and are still valid for the chosen code. The most important value to change is the resolution of the printer. This must be accurate for the device that will output the bar code or the

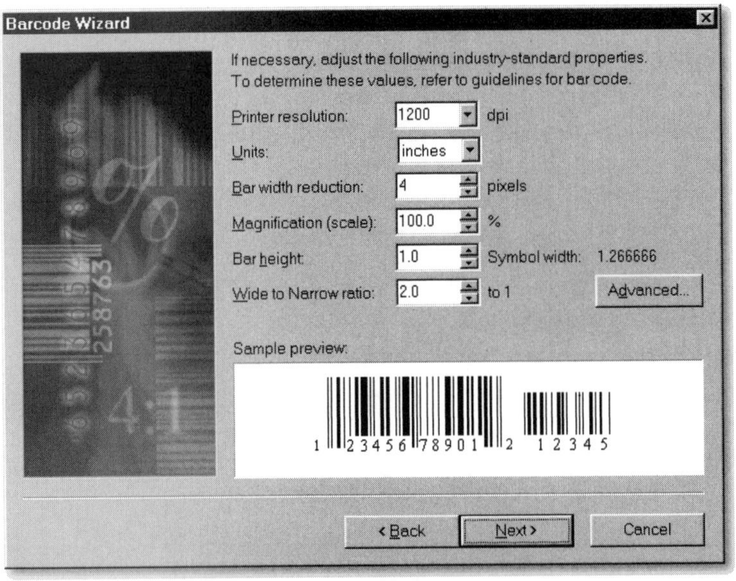

FIGURE 35-2 Barcode Wizard Industry Standard Properties dialog box

code may not be readable. If in doubt, do not guess! When you are finished, click Next to get the dialog box shown in Figure 35-3.

4. The first set of selections is related to the font used by the bar code. Most of the time, these options will be dimmed because there is either no font or the text must follow certain specifications for the code you are creating. Center sys/check determines whether the check digit is centered vertically beside the symbol. Show add-on text will display the text characters above the add-on part of the bar code if it exists. Add-on text at bottom places the add-on text below the symbol instead of above it. Show Quiet Zone marks will add the carat symbol at the edge of the code so that it is not cropped too closely. Place text above will place the text above the symbol rather than the default of below. It is dimmed in our example as UPC must have the text below it. Show FACT data only applies to Code 39 and it supplies extra data that is typically hidden. Show asterisks is also used with Code 39 to show the start and stop characters. Show

Barcode Wizard   ☒

Adjust the following properties for the text in your bar code.

Font: Ͳ OCR-B-10 BT   ▼   Size: 10 ⬍ pts

Weight: Normal   ▼

Alignment: Center   ▼

☐ Center sys/check   ☐ Place text above
☑ Show add-on text   ☐ Show FACT data
☑ Add-on text at bottom   ☐ Show asterisks
☐ Show Quite Zone marks   ☐ Show start/stop

☑ Make this bar code Human Readable (show text)

Sample preview:

1 ‖23456‖78901‖2 12345

< Back   Finish   Cancel

FIGURE 35-3   Barcode Wizard Properties dialog box

start/stop applies to showing the start and stop characters for
Codabar. Lastly, there is Make this bar code Human Readable.
"Human readable" simply means that text is shown in addition to
the symbol. When you have made all of your selections, click Finish
or click Back if you need to make any changes.

Once you've clicked Finish, the bar code symbol will appear as part of
your CorelDRAW document. The sample we created is shown here:

It is embedded into your document as an OLE object. So if what you created isn't quite right, you can always go back in and edit it. When you have the bar code selected, you can select Edit | Corel BARCODE 8.0 Object. This will give you a child menu with three options: Open, Edit, and Convert. Edit and Open both do the same thing. They will bring up the Barcode Wizard screen that we discussed earlier. So if you need to make a change to any of the values, this is the best way to do it. Convert will display a dialog box that lets you convert the bar code into another format. This is useful if you open a file that has a bar code created in an earlier version that needs to be converted.

Just as with any other object, you can rotate and size the bar code symbol. But it would be a very bad idea to resize the code since this may render it unreadable. You should make any sizing changes by editing the code in the Barcode Wizard.

There may come a time that you wish to work with individual parts of the bar code graphic. When it is created, it is a single OLE object. To convert it to a graphic, cut it to the clipboard using the CTRL-X shortcut key. Then choose Edit | Paste Special, which will bring up the dialog box shown in Figure 35-4.

You should have the choice of at least two different formats. One is the Corel BARCODE 8.0 format that we started with. The other is Picture (Metafile). If you choose Picture, each of the bars and the text will be pasted

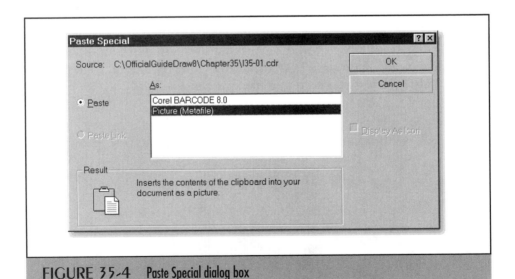

FIGURE 35-4   Paste Special dialog box

as separate editable objects. By default, they will be placed at the very center of your page, rather than the original location of the bar code.

PRINTING THE CODE

Bar codes must be printed properly or the bar code readers may not be able to decipher the code. It is quite common to print a POSTNET bar code straight through a laser printer and have no problems with the post office, but that wouldn't always be the case with a UPC code. For the codes that will be appearing on any type of retail product, you should print them to film at no lower than 2400 dpi. And before you issue a long print run for labels, make sure that the label can be scanned accurately by a bar code reader or you may face a very expensive mistake.

35

36

CREATING AN OBJECT DATABASE

You've seen it listed in the menu and you've probably even selected it once or twice. "It" brought up the Object Data Docker. We've dragged it onto the drawing page to show it as a roll-up here. At this point, you probably are still scratching your head and wondering just what this thing actually does.

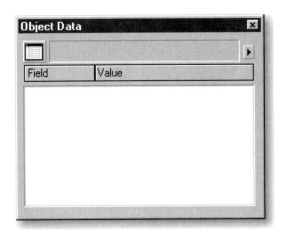

The Object Data feature has been around for several versions now. Each year when writing this book, we've tried to figure out exactly how and why someone could use the feature. Recently a project came up that was an obvious use for this feature. So we'll document how we used it and propose several other ideas for how it might fit into your projects.

A SIMPLE EXAMPLE

In this situation, we were selecting new furniture for our office. We knew the exact dimensions of the various pieces of furniture and drew them to scale in CorelDRAW. This was fairly easy since CorelDRAW can support a page size as large as 150 feet square. We also drew a diagram of each office to scale. So now we can move the various pieces of furniture around in the office before buying anything. None of this is really interesting yet.

So once we got all this furniture placed in our model office, as shown in Figure 36-1, there were some questions that we wanted answered. Most important is how much all this new furniture will cost. And knowing the total

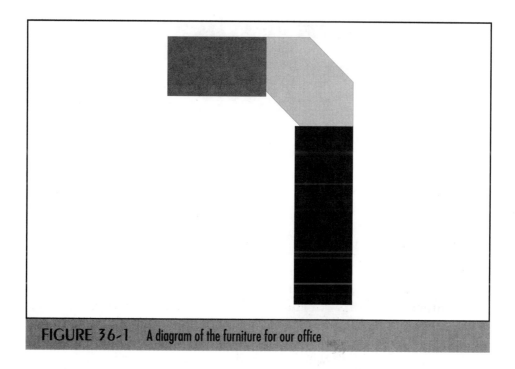

FIGURE 36-1   A diagram of the furniture for our office

36

weight could be useful for figuring the shipping cost. We could always print the diagram, write the price and weight of each object on the printout, and then get out the calculator. Nothing too difficult there, but why not let CorelDRAW do this grunt work for you?

So if CorelDRAW is going to do the calculations, it will need to know the cost and weight of each item. This is where the Object Data function steps in. Our first step is to add the appropriate fields to our database. The three fields that we need are Name, Cost, and Weight. We haven't discussed Name previously, but it would be nice to have a way to identify which piece is which.

To add these fields, click the flyout arrow and choose Field Editor from the flyout menu. This will bring up the dialog box shown here. When this dialog first appears, four fields will be listed. Name and Cost, the first two, are fields that we already planned on using. The Comments field could be used to enter a longer description for each object. The last field, CDRStaticID, can be very confusing. As CorelDRAW creates objects, each of them is assigned an ID number so that it can be tracked. This is the only field that cannot be edited or deleted. All of the others can be changed or removed as you please.

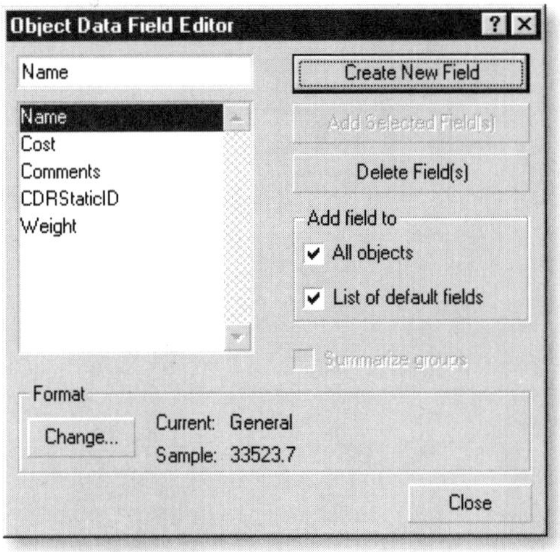

We still need a field to hold the weight values. So click the Create New Field button; CorelDRAW will add a field by the name of Field0. While it is selected, you can type in a new name at the top of the dialog box.

By default, any new field will be assigned the formatting type of General. We know that the weight will be entered as a number, so click the Change button in the Format section of the dialog box. This will bring up the Format Definition dialog box shown here.

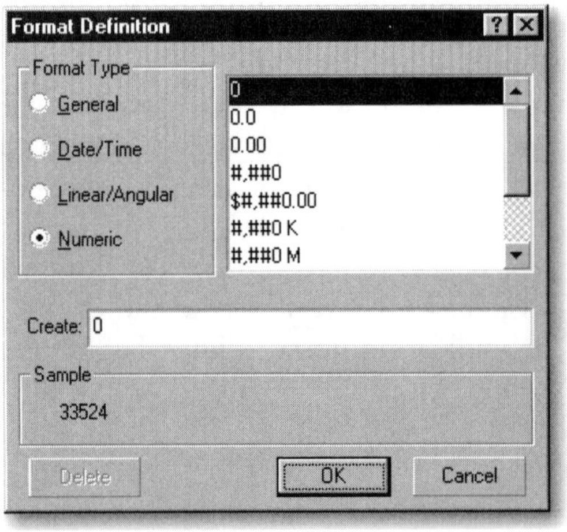

Along the left side of the dialog box are the four major types of formats that are available. You want Numeric for the weight field. Once you've selected Numeric, a number of different formats appear in the list on the right side of the dialog box. You want the one at the top of the list, just a plain zero. In reality, it would be nice to append the abbreviation for pounds, lbs, but there is no way to do this.

Click OK to finish changing the formatting and return to the Object Data Field Editor. You're all finished there, so click the Close button. Now we need to put in the data for each of the objects. In Figure 36-1, we color coded each of the pieces of furniture. So we need to select each piece and type in the data associated with it. First, we'll select the green rectangle. In the Object Data roll-up click Name. Now enter an appropriate name in the text box at the top of the roll-up. Next, select Cost and enter the cost. Repeat the process again for Weight and Comments. When finished, the roll-up should look like this:

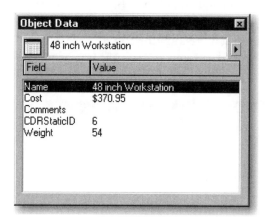

36

Once you've entered all of the data, you'll probably be curious how to use it all. In order to get a total of all objects, you need to select all of them. You can do this easily by double-clicking the Pick tool. Now click the spreadsheet icon in the upper-left corner of the Object Data roll-up. This will bring up the dialog box shown here. We've expanded it so that all of the data is displayed at once.

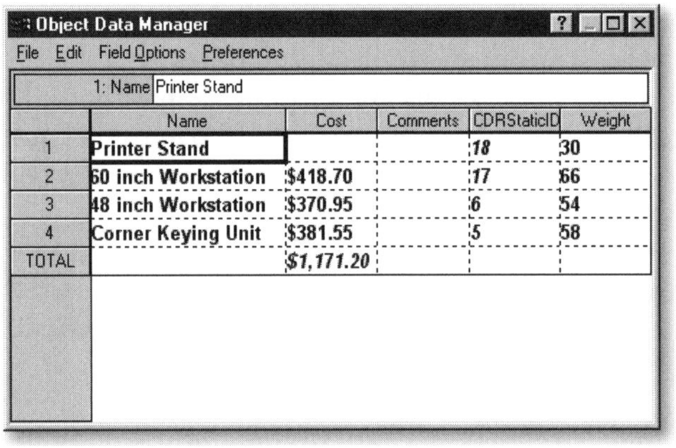

Object Data Manager ? _ □ ✕

File Edit Field Options Preferences

1: Name Printer Stand

	Name	Cost	Comments	CDRStaticID	Weight
1	Printer Stand			18	30
2	60 inch Workstation	$418.70		17	66
3	48 inch Workstation	$370.95		6	54
4	Corner Keying Unit	$381.55		5	58
TOTAL		$1,171.20			

As you can see, each of the objects is listed by name along with the cost, weight, and other information. Below all of this information is the total. Some of the fields may have a total calculated, but not all of them. For example, the weight is not being totaled. Click the word "Weight" at the top of the column and the whole column will become highlighted. Next choose Field Options | Show Totals. Now you'll see that the weight has been totaled as shown here.

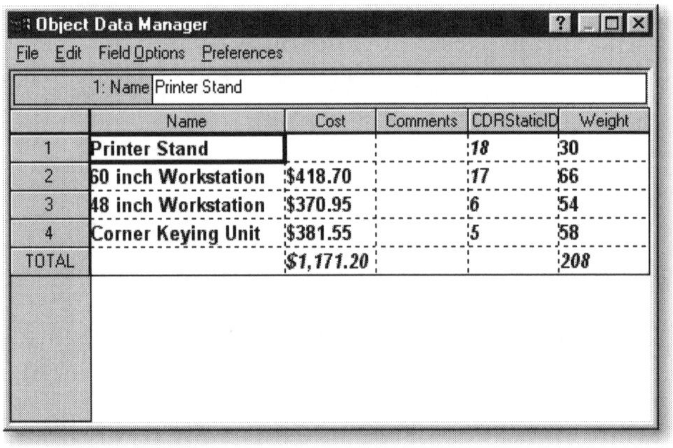

Object Data Manager ? _ □ ✕

File Edit Field Options Preferences

1: Name Printer Stand

	Name	Cost	Comments	CDRStaticID	Weight
1	Printer Stand			18	30
2	60 inch Workstation	$418.70		17	66
3	48 inch Workstation	$370.95		6	54
4	Corner Keying Unit	$381.55		5	58
TOTAL		$1,171.20			208

The mini-spreadsheet we have created can be printed for future reference. You can also select the data and paste it into a spreadsheet such as Quattro Pro or Excel. But only the data will be pasted and not the formulas, column headings, or row headings. It would be nice to be able to link this information to a spreadsheet or database, especially for much larger uses than our simple project.

OTHER USES

Let's look at a more extensive project where using the Object Data roll-up could come in handy. Suppose you decide that it sure would be nice to have a deck in the backyard. Using CorelDRAW, you can diagram every single board you'd need to complete the job. And many of the boards would be identical. So if you draw one of each type of board and assign Object Data to it, you could easily have a list of necessary materials and cost totals before you take a trip to Home Depot.

But this project would expose a few more limitations. Let's say that there are 100 of a particular type of board. But instead of telling us that we need 100 pieces, the Object Data Manager lists the piece 100 times. So we'd have to manually count how many boards are needed. Heck, that is as bad as watching paint dry!

Let's say that this particular board costs $2.49. But as you're reading the Sunday newspaper, you see that the board is on sale for only $1.99. That means that you would have to change the price manually on every single board. Changing one board will not affect the others even if you've cloned (Edit | Clone) all of the boards. So having the ability to tie the data to an external data source such as a database or spreadsheet could come in very handy for large projects.

Now let's say that this particular board, when cut in half, is also quite plentiful in our project. We could create a quantity field that only applied to this type of board and enter .5 for the half boards. This would also solve the problem of totaling the number of boards needed. But if we use ten different types of boards, it would be quite redundant to create ten different quantity fields.

So we can accomplish our deck using this feature, but not without several workarounds. Instead of home improvement, think in terms of designing a

36

telephone system for an office of over 100 people. This would require deciding where various phone terminals and other equipment are located. CorelDRAW is certainly capable of doing the drawing, but it may fall short in doing the cost calculations. For example, how would you calculate the cost of wire? There is no way to multiply a cost per foot times the length of the line.

Now you know what the Object Data feature is all about. We've shown you two different examples of how it can be used and the various limitations it imposes. So start using it in your projects and if you have an interesting use for it, please let us know by sending e-mail to idea@unleash.com. Who knows, maybe CorelDRAW will integrate this feature with Quattro Pro or Paradox in future revisions. Only time (and customer demand) will tell.

37

CREATING CUSTOM ARROWHEADS, PATTERNS, SYMBOLS, AND LINE STYLES

CorelDRAW provides the tools to create custom arrowheads, symbols, patterns, and line styles. When you see the word "custom," you may think, "Here we go again; another learning curve to conquer." However, the good news is that creating custom arrowheads, symbols, patterns, and line styles is really quite easy.

CREATING CUSTOM ARROWHEADS

Although there are dozens of arrowheads to choose from, there never seems to be the one you need for that special project. When you find yourself in this situation, it's time to create your own. If you follow three simple rules, you will be creating arrowheads with the best of them. First, the object used to create the arrowhead must be a single object; this can include objects that have been combined. Second, the object you create should fill an area approximately 6 inches in either direction and be in a left-to-right or right-to-left orientation. This means if the shape of the object naturally points to a specific orientation such as a flying bird, it should point to either the left or right. Third, you are limited to a total of 200 arrowheads in the drop-down list at any given time.

To create a custom arrowhead, follow these steps:

1. Either draw an object on the page or use any of CorelDRAW's symbols. These can include the Symbols clipart found on the CD. Remember that the object must be a single object; you can't use groups, for example. The example here uses a flying goose found in the Animals category of the CorelDRAW Symbols Docker window.

2. Scale the object so that the longest dimension is approximately 6 inches.

3. Choose Tools | Create. When the flyout appears, choose Arrow.

4. You will see a message that asks if you want to create an arrowhead from the selected object. Click the OK button.

In the wink of an eye, you have just created your first custom arrowhead. To see if you did indeed create an arrowhead, draw a line on the page and click the left or right End Arrowhead selector on the Property Bar. When the drop-down list appears, scroll down the list of arrowheads. When you reach the bottom, your new custom arrowhead will magically appear. Figure 37-1 shows the Arrowhead drop-down list from the Property Bar with the flying goose arrowhead at the bottom of the list. This figure also shows the line drawn on the page with the new arrowhead placed on the right end.

To remove an arrowhead that has been applied to a line, click the upper-left thumbnail image in the Arrowhead drop-down list.

EDITING ARROWHEADS

To edit an existing arrowhead, select the line and open the Outline Pen dialog box shown in Figure 37-2 by clicking the Outline Pen button on the Outline

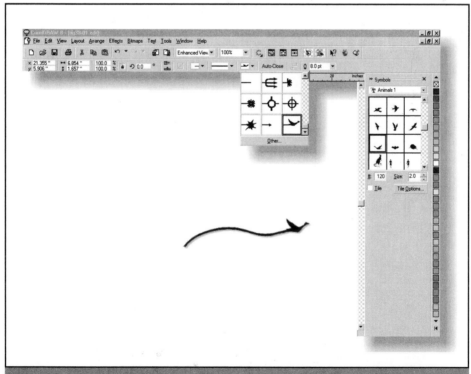

FIGURE 37-1   A custom arrowhead created by using a symbol from the Symbols roll-up

37

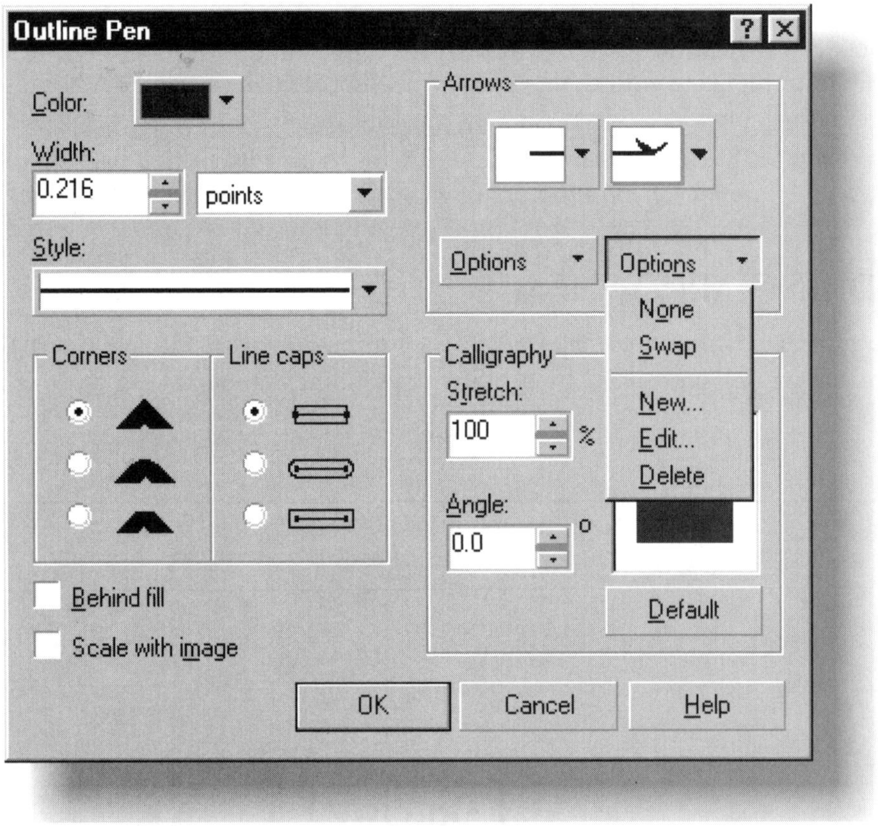

FIGURE 37-2 The Outline Pen dialog box with the Options drop-down menu selected

Tool flyout. Choose any of the five options by clicking the Options button and choosing from the drop-down menu.

 *Even though there is an Options button for both ends of the line, if you make a change to the right end of an arrowhead, the left end will be modified as well.*

The five options on the menu are None, Swap, New, Edit, and Delete.

▶ *None* Select this option to remove any exiting arrowhead from the selected line.

▶ *Swap* Select this option to move the existing arrowhead to the opposite end of the line.

▶ *New* Select this option to modify and save a new arrowhead without affecting the original arrowhead. This can now be done using the Edit Arrowhead dialog box accessed from the Arrowhead drop-down list on the Property Bar (see the next section).

▶ *Edit* Select this option to permanently modify an existing arrowhead. When you modify an arrowhead using this option, the modified arrowhead will permanently replace the original arrowhead.

▶ *Delete* Select this option to permanently delete an arrowhead from the drop-down list. Because there's a limit of 200, you may want to delete certain arrowheads you will never use.

MODIFYING EXISTING ARROWHEADS

CorelDRAW lets you modify existing arrowheads by changing their placement in relation to the end of the line. You can also scale them horizontally, vertically, or proportionally. You can even create mirror images either horizontally or vertically. If you use the New option in the Option drop down list you can modify an existing arrowhead and save it as a new arrowhead. This new arrowhead will appear at the bottom of the arrowhead drop down list. If you want to permanently change the arrowhead, choose the Edit option. Either option brings up the Edit Arrowhead dialog box shown in Figure 37-3.

37

> **CAUTION:** *The Edit Arrowhead dialog box selected from the Options drop-down list in the Outline Pen dialog box saves arrowheads differently than the Edit Arrowhead dialog box accessed by clicking the Other button at the bottom of the Arrowhead drop-down list on the Property Bar. When modifying an existing arrowhead through the Outline Pen dialog box, always select New from the Options drop-down list. If you select Edit, the changed arrowhead will permanently replace the original arrowhead. However, if you modify an arrowhead using the Edit Arrowhead dialog box accessed by clicking Other at the bottom of the arrowhead drop-down list on the Property Bar, the original arrowhead will remain unchanged, and a new one will be created and displayed at the bottom of the drop-down list.*

To modify an arrowhead, first select an arrowhead by choosing it from the Arrowhead drop-down list. Now click the Options button beneath the selected arrowhead. From the Options drop-down menu, select New. When the Edit Arrowhead dialog box (shown in Figure 37-3) appears, the selected arrowhead will appear in the edit window with eight selection handles surrounding it.

Here are the editing tools available in the Edit Arrowhead dialog box:

► *Selection Handles* The selection handles surrounding the arrowhead are used to change its size or shape. Using one of the corner selection handles will proportionally resize the arrowhead. Using a middle selection handle will stretch the arrowhead inward toward the center or outward away from the center.

► *Nodes* There are nodes at various points along the outline of the arrowhead. If you select any of these nodes, you can move the arrowhead in any direction. This ability to move the arrowhead allows you to position the arrowhead above or below the line. It even lets you move the arrowhead horizontally away from the line. There is also a node at the end of the line that appears in the Edit Arrowhead dialog box. It can be difficult to see because the arrowhead sometimes conceals it. However, if you place the cursor at the very end of the line and drag to the left, you should see the line getting shorter. Making the line shorter is another way of separating the arrowhead from the line.

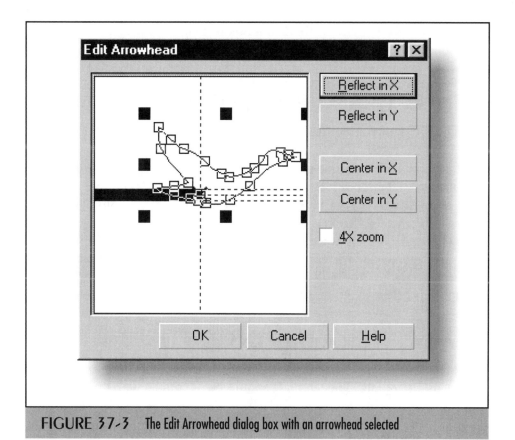

FIGURE 37-3   The Edit Arrowhead dialog box with an arrowhead selected

37

► *Reflect in X* This button mirrors the arrowhead horizontally. This can be useful when you want the arrowhead to follow the line rather than point away from the line.

► *Reflect in Y* This button mirrors the arrowhead vertically.

► *Center in X* This button centers the arrowhead vertically relative to the center X in the middle of the edit window.

► *Center in Y* This button centers the arrowhead horizontally relative to the center X in the middle of the edit window. To position the center of your arrowhead directly in the middle of the edit window, you select both the Center in X and Center in Y buttons.

► *4X Zoom* Check the 4X Zoom box to magnify the edit window by the power of 4.

CREATING CUSTOM PATTERNS

CorelDRAW gives you the ability to create custom pattern fills from vector or bitmap images. Pattern fills are image tiles that are repeated over and over as they fill the selected object. A good pattern fill is one that tiles seamlessly. This means the viewer should not be able to see where the individual tiles begin or end.

There are two types of pattern fills: two color and full color. Full-color pattern fills are also broken into two categories: vector and bitmap. The bitmap category is considered to be anything other than two-color bitmaps, which are monotones. The easiest of these fills to create are the two-color and vector pattern fills. You will see later in this section that you don't create bitmap fills in the way you create the two-color and vector fills.

CREATING VECTOR PATTERNS

To create a custom vector pattern, you must first define an area on the page to serve as a template. The template should be of equal length on all sides.

Creating a Template

Follow these steps to create a template:

1. Click the top ruler and drag down two horizontal guidelines, placing one at 8 inches and the other at 4 inches vertically.

2. Click the vertical ruler and drag out two vertical guidelines, placing one at 2 inches and the other at 6 inches horizontally. The guidelines should now form an area 4 inches square inside the lines.

3. It is usually difficult to place the guidelines at exactly the right place. To avoid creating a template that is not square, double-click each guideline and manually set the position of both the horizontal and vertical guidelines in the Guideline Setup dialog box. (Even though we recommend a 4-inch-square area, you can make your area any size you wish as long as the sides are all of equal length.)

 *Remember that when you change the position designation in the Guideline Setup dialog box, you must click the Move button prior to clicking the OK button for the change to take effect. Refer to Chapter 14 if you need to brush-up on guidelines.*

4. You will be creating a polka-dot pattern. Turn on Layout I Snap to Guidelines in the Guideline Setup dialog box.

5. Click the Rectangle tool and draw a square the size of the 4-inch template (when Snap to Guidelines is turned on, the rectangle will snap to the corners of the template).

6. Fill the rectangle with a color of your choice and remove the outline.

7. Click the Ellipse tool and draw a circle on the page while pressing CTRL-SHIFT to create a perfect circle (use the circles in Figure 37-4 as a guide to the size of the circle). Fill the circle with a color that contrasts with that of the rectangle.

8. Now it's time to accurately place this circle and four others at specific locations on the rectangle. Open the Position roll-up by choosing Arrange I Transform I Position (ALT-F7).

9. Remove the check mark from the Relative Position check box.

10. With the ellipse selected, type the coordinates of the upper-left intersecting guidelines in the Horizontal and Vertical parameter boxes located in the Position roll-up. The correct numbers using the example shown here are 2.0 inches (Horizontal) and 8.0 inches (Vertical).

11. Click the Apply button to move the ellipse to the designated coordinates.

12. With the ellipse still selected, press CTRL-D to create a duplicate.

13. With the duplicate ellipse selected, enter the coordinates for the upper-right intersecting guidelines, just as you did in step 10. The correct numbers for these coordinates are 6.0 (Horizontal) and 8.0 (Vertical).

14. Click Apply to move the ellipse to the designated coordinates.

15. Make a duplicate of the second ellipse just as you did in step 12.

37

16. With this duplicate selected, repeat step 10 using new coordinates of 6.0 (Horizontal) and 4.0 (Vertical). These coordinates will position the third ellipse at the lower-right intersecting guidelines.

17. Now make a duplicate of the third ellipse and use the coordinates 2.0 (Horizontal) and 4.0 (Vertical) to place the fourth ellipse at the lower-left intersecting guidelines. As before, click the Apply button to make the move take effect.

18. Make a duplicate of the fourth ellipse and set the coordinates at 4.0 (Horizontal) and 6.0 (Vertical). These coordinates will place the fifth ellipse in the center of the template. Click Apply to complete the move.

If your template looks like the one in Figure 37-4, you followed the instructions correctly.

Creating the Pattern

Be patient; you are almost finished. You have finally reached the stage where you can actually create the pattern.

1. Choose Tools | Create | Pattern. The Create Pattern dialog box will appear. Click the Full Color radio button.

2. Click the OK button. The cursor will change to a crosshair extending the full length and breadth of the screen.

3. Use the point of the intersecting crosshairs to click and drag a bounding box beginning at the upper-left corner of the template and ending at the lower-right corner. With Snap to Guidelines still turned on, it should be easy to create a bounding box in the shape of the square. If you're not sure whether you have accurately delineated the square, watch the color of the guidelines as you drag out the square. When you are exactly over the edges of the rectangle, the guideline will change from blue to yellow, and you can release the mouse button.

4. When you have finished dragging out the bounding box, the Create Pattern message box will be displayed on top of your pattern, asking if you want to create a pattern from the selected area. Click the OK button to bring up the Save Vector Pattern dialog box.

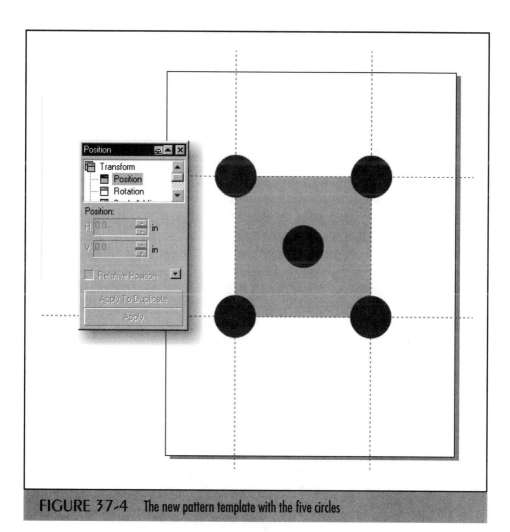

FIGURE 37-4   The new pattern template with the five circles

5. Give your custom pattern a name with a .pat extension. You should store your custom patterns in a folder you have created expressly for custom patterns. If you store them in the default folder, Corel80\Custom\Patterns, they will appear in the Pattern drop-down list when you choose it.

Congratulate yourself. You have created your first custom pattern.

Using Your New Pattern

Now it's time to see if the pattern you created will indeed create a polka-dot pattern. Follow these steps to fill an object with your new pattern:

1. Draw a large rectangle on the page.

2. Select the Pattern fill button on the Fill flyout.

3. When the Pattern dialog box appears, click the Full Color radio button.

4. Click the Load button. The Import dialog box will appear. Change to the folder where you stored you custom pattern and select it from the folder.

5. When you have selected your custom pattern from within the Import dialog box, click the Import button. Your custom pattern will appear in the preview window shown in Figure 37-5.

6. Enter 2.0 in the <u>W</u>idth and <u>H</u>eight num boxes in the Size section of the roll-up.

7. Click the OK button to see the results.

If you followed all the steps, you should see the pattern shown here.

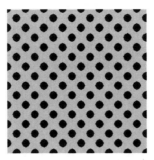

You may wonder why you placed the four outside ellipses so they were centered on the point of the intersecting guidelines. The reason for this unusual placement is to ensure that the pattern will tile seamlessly. Had you placed the ellipses in the corners of the rectangle as shown here, the resulting pattern would not have been a polka-dot pattern.

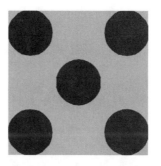

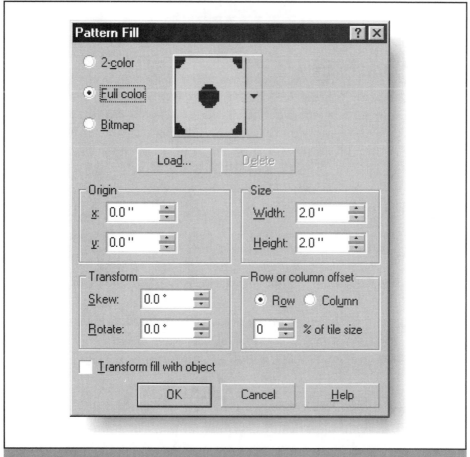

FIGURE 37-5   The Pattern dialog box selected from the Fill flyout with the custom pattern loaded

Rather, the pattern would have resembled clustered dots, as shown here.

EDITING PATTERNS

You can change the color schemes of vector patterns by editing the .pat file. Suppose you like a particular default pattern or even a custom pattern you have created, but the colors don't work with the project you are working on. When you are faced with this situation, you can simply open the pattern file with the .pat extension, make the necessary color changes, and then save the modified file with a new name. You don't have to draw a bounding box prior to saving the modified file.

When saving a modified .pat file, you cannot move the pattern from the place on the page where it first appears on opening, and you must save the file with the Selected Only box enabled.

If you are filling an object with a pattern fill that requires trapping, simply trap the objects in the pattern file. Then when you fill the object, the entire pattern fill will be trapped.

CREATING TWO-COLOR PATTERN FILLS

You create two-color pattern fills using the same steps you used to create a vector pattern. The difference is, after you have created the images you want to use as a pattern, you select the Two-Color radio button instead of the Full Color radio button from the Create Pattern dialog box that appears when you select <u>T</u>ools | Cre<u>a</u>te | <u>P</u>attern. Your images used for the pattern area will automatically be converted to a monochrome bitmap image and will appear at the bottom of the Two-Color drop-down list in the Pattern Fill dialog box when accessed from the Fill flyout. Your new pattern will also be available from the Two-Color drop-down list on the Property Bar when the Interactive Fill tool is selected.

Technically, you don't have to create a perfect square when beginning to create two-color and vector pattern fills. You can delineate any area you wish of your image and a tile will be created. The caveat is that it probably will not tile seamlessly.

CREATING BITMAP PATTERN FILLS

You don't create bitmap pattern fills the same way that you create two-color and vector pattern fills. You create them by using an existing bitmap image. This bitmap image could be a photograph or simply an abstract bitmap background.

The way to fill an object with a bitmap fill is to click the pattern fill icon on the Fill flyout to reveal the Pattern Fill dialog box, choose Bitmap, and click the Load button. The Import dialog box will appear with Patterns listed in the Look <u>I</u>n drop-down list. Click the folder icon (with the arrow) next to the Look <u>I</u>n drop-down list. The word "Custom" will appear in the Look <u>I</u>n drop-down list. Double-click the Tiles folder below the Look <u>I</u>n drop-down list and choose a bitmap fill from the available fills. Creating new bitmap fills is fully covered in Chapter 10.

When you use bitmap images as a fill, you have virtually no control over how the edges of the images will tile together, unlike with two-color and vector fills. As a result, bitmap pattern fills often shown the telltale lines where the sides don't match on all four corners of the tiles when the object is filled.

37

CREATING CUSTOM SYMBOLS

The are hundreds of symbols available in the Symbols roll-up, but invariably the symbol you need is not in the roll-up. Corel's development team knew they couldn't make a symbol for every situation, so they made it possible for you to create your own. Creating symbols is even easier than creating arrowheads because you don't have to be concerned with how big to make the original object.

You can create a custom symbol from any single curve object, including objects that are combined or welded into one object. This means you could make your company's logo into a symbol as long as it has been combined or welded into a single curve object. For information on combining objects see Chapter 15.

Follow these steps to create the symbol shown in Figure 37-6.

1. Open the Symbols Docker window by clicking its icon on the Property Bar.

2. Select the Animals 1 category and drag the mountain goat shown in Figure 37-6 on to the page.

3. Using the rectangle tool, draw a rectangle over the body of the goat.

4. Convert the rectangle to curves by selecting the Convert to Curves button on the Property bar.

5. Use the Shape tool to modify the rectangle until the box covers all but the head and neck of the goat.

6. Select the box and then the goat (the sequence is important) and click on the Trim tool on the Property Bar.

7. Delete the box; you will be left with just the head and neck of the goat.

8. Select the newly created symbol and choose <u>T</u>ools | Cre<u>a</u>te | <u>S</u>ymbol.

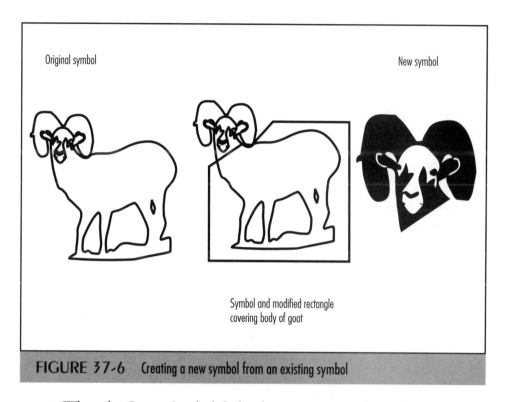

Original symbol

New symbol

Symbol and modified rectangle
covering body of goat

FIGURE 37-6   Creating a new symbol from an existing symbol

9. When the Create Symbol dialog box appears, as shown here,

37

Create Symbol   ? X

Symbol category:

My Symbols   OK

TT Animals 1
TT Animals 2   Cancel
TT Arial Alternative
TT Arial Alternative Symbol
TT Arial Special G2
TT Arrows1
TT Arrows2

choose a category from the list. You may want to type a custom name in the <u>S</u>ymbol category box so all your custom symbols will be together.

That's all there is to it. You just created a symbol. Now close the Symbols Docker window and re-open it. Select the category where you saved your new symbol and drag it onto the page. If you created a new category for your new symbol, as was done here, all the preview boxes in the Docker window will display the new symbol, as shown in Figure 37-7. As you create new symbols and add them to your custom category, the preview boxes will update accordingly. You can add up to 255 symbols in each new category.

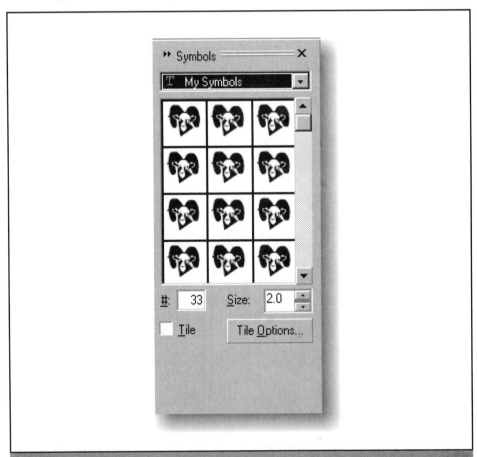

FIGURE 37-7   The Symbols Docker window displaying the custom category and symbol created in the previous steps

CREATING CUSTOM LINE STYLES

Creating custom line styles in CorelDRAW is as easy as pointing to and clicking a style bar. Follow the steps here to create a custom line style:

1. Select the Pencil tool from the toolbox and draw a line on the page.

2. With the line still selected, click the Outline Style Selector on the Property Bar. The Line Style drop-down list will appear, as shown here.

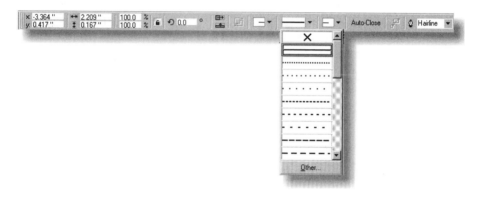

3. Click the Other button at the bottom of the list.

4. The Edit Line Style dialog box shown here will appear in its default configuration, as shown here.

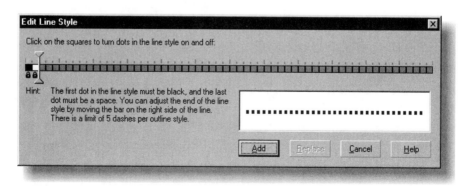

37

The instructions in this dialog box are very good. Refer to them in the future if you are not certain what to do.

5. The slider bar is positioned so that only two squares are visible. The first square must always be turned on. The second square is blank. This combination of the first square highlighted and the second square left blank produces the pattern shown in the preview window at the lower-right corner of the dialog box.

6. Drag the slider bar to the right until ten squares are revealed.

7. Turn on the second through seventh squares by clicking the squares (to turn off a square that has been turned on, click it a second time). Skip a square and turn on the ninth square, leaving the tenth square blank (turned off). Your outline style should now look like the one shown in Figure 37-8. Notice that the squares that are turned on next to each other form a dash, and the single highlighted square forms a dot.

8. Move the slider until 35 squares are revealed.

9. Turn on the first seven squares. Leave the eighth and ninth squares blank and turn on the tenth.

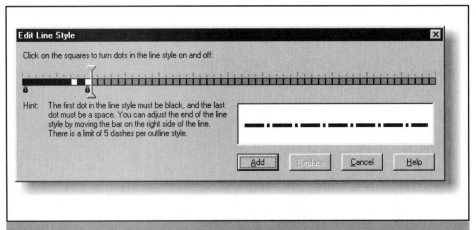

FIGURE 37-8   A custom line style using dashes and dots in a repeating pattern

10. Leave the remaining 25 squares blank. Your line style should now look like the one shown in Figure 37-9.

   If you want to save your custom line styles, click the Add button. Your custom outline style will be added to the bottom of the drop-down on the Property Bar.

Now that you're at to the end of the chapter, you can see that it's not as difficult to create custom effects as you may have thought. Having this ability to create custom effects can give you that edge over your peers that makes your work stand out from theirs.

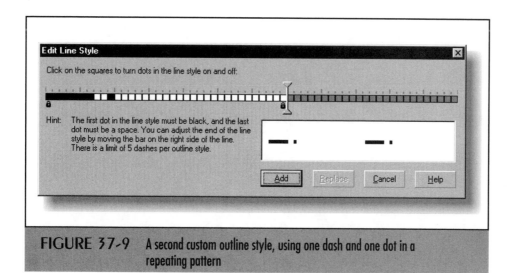

FIGURE 37-9 A second custom outline style, using one dash and one dot in a repeating pattern

37

FONTS, FONT FORMATS, PANOSE, AND FONT MANAGEMENT

W hen Corel first started as a company, it introduced a product called Corel Headline. Headline had the ability to apply numerous special effects to one of the many fonts that were included with the Corel program. Back in 1988, "many" fonts meant less than 50. Corel Headline later became known as CorelDRAW, and the number of fonts included in the product is now well over 1,000. Working with a large amount of fonts provides great freedom for a designer, but managing the fonts can be tricky.

We find that most users don't understand the various formats of fonts that currently exist in the marketplace. So, we'll explain each of the formats and give you some guidelines on how each format is best used. With the plethora of fonts available, the problem of font substitution crops up quite often. CorelDRAW includes Panose, which is a semi-intelligent method of substitution. We'll explain how it works and how to put it to use. And for those who aren't familiar with installing and managing fonts, we'll explain how this works.

WHAT IS A FONT?

The definition of a font has changed since type became available on computers. A font used to be a specific size and weight of a specific font family. For example, Times Roman 12 point was a single font, Times Roman 14 point was another font, and Times Bold 12 point was yet another font.

Now a font is a specific weight of a specific font family. The point size isn't part of the definition because digital fonts are fully scaleable to any point size. No longer are fonts metal blocks of a specific size. Now fonts are stored as mathematical equations that can be reproduced on the screen and in print.

FONT FORMATS

When you purchase a computer, you choose which operating system to install. There are several popular operating systems to choose from, each with its pros and cons. Likewise, you can choose among fonts. There are two major formats in the world of fonts—PostScript and TrueType—and a third format is being introduced soon to replace the existing two. A few other fonts and technologies are available as well. Most people are aware that these different formats are available, but they don't understand the benefits of each and how to make an intelligent choice between the two. The result is that most users choose a font format to use without considering the consequences of that choice. Many times this misinformed choice will cause future problems that can get very expensive.

WFN

The WFN format is a proprietary format created by Corel for use with early versions of CorelDRAW. It became unnecessary in CorelDRAW 3 when support for PostScript and TrueType fonts was added, and it was eliminated completely in CorelDRAW 6. If you still have WFN fonts that you'd like to use in your work, you'll either have to use an older version of CorelDRAW or convert them using Ares FontMonger, which is now very hard to find.

POSTSCRIPT TYPE 1

The PostScript Type 1 font format was invented by Adobe Systems in the 1980s and became the worldwide standard for digital type software. Although it is the font format used in the PostScript page description language, it does not require a PostScript printer to be used. When used with a PostScript printer, the font is directly downloaded to the printer rather than being rasterized (converted to a bitmap) and then sent to the printer.

Characters in a PostScript font are constructed using bézier curves, which just happens to be the same method CorelDRAW uses to create curves. This approach is especially beneficial when you convert a font to curves, as fewer nodes are needed to accurately describe the shape. For example, Figure 38-1 shows two versions of the same letter Q from Adobe's ExPonto font. Each has been converted to curves, and the nodes are indicated with boxes on the characters. The character on the left is from the PostScript version of the font and contains 127 nodes. The version on the right is the TrueType character, and it contains 163 nodes. This is a very significant difference for just a single character. Note that the difference may not always be as great in number, but will be similar in percentage.

If you were only dealing with a single character, this problem would be minimal. But multiply that difference by a word or sentence of text and you can see that the difference becomes quite significant. Remember that each

38

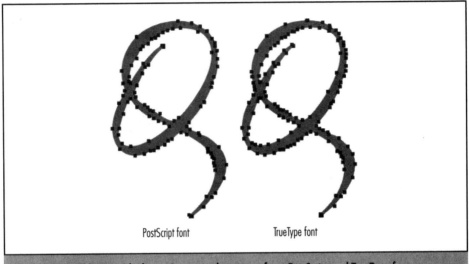

PostScript font   TrueType font

FIGURE 38-1   The letter *Q* converted to curves from PostScript and TrueType fonts

node increases the complexity of the object and makes the file a little bit bigger. In this case, the extra nodes provide no benefits.

To display PostScript fonts on the screen (and print them on non-PostScript printers), the Adobe Type Manager (ATM) utility is required for Windows 95. This is an inexpensive utility program that is frequently included with software and new fonts. A limited version of ATM 4.0 is included with Corel Ventura 7. Windows NT directly supports PostScript fonts, although a version of ATM was made available in May 1997 that provides a much more reliable screen display. The direct support of PostScript fonts by Windows NT 4 is very poor as it simply converts the fonts to TrueType as they are installed, and there can be numerous errors in the conversion process. This problem should be eliminated in Windows NT 5, which will include the ATM technology.

PostScript fonts are supported across many different operating systems, and more than 30,000 different fonts are available. Some of these fonts are what are called "expert sets" that include extra characters such as old-style figures, small caps, ligatures, and other variations. Expert sets are extremely useful for professional typography.

A subset of PostScript fonts are multiple master fonts. These fonts contain at least two design axes such as weight, width, style, and optical size. From the base font, many different variations can be created to assist in copy fitting and the creation of special effects without compromising the type by artificially squeezing and stretching.

TRUETYPE

TrueType was invented by Apple Computer to compete with the PostScript technology. For historians, the original name was Royal Type. It was less expensive for Apple to create its own font format than to license the PostScript technology from Adobe. TrueType was later licensed by Microsoft to include in Microsoft's operating systems. Unlike PostScript fonts, TrueType fonts have no corresponding page description language.

TrueType characters are created using quadratic B-splines. Thus, when a TrueType character is converted to curves in CorelDRAW, it has more nodes than the same character in a PostScript font, as you saw in Figure 38-1.

TrueType support is built in to Windows 3.1, Windows 95, Windows NT, and the Macintosh OS. It has become the default standard on Windows platforms because of Microsoft's influence but has been very poorly received on the Macintosh.

TrueType fonts are rasterized by the operating system except when they are printed on a PostScript printer. In that case, they are converted to a PostScript font and then downloaded. This conversion process causes a degradation in quality and a slight delay in printing. Windows NT uses a TrueType font to display PostScript fonts on the screen; however, it downloads the actual PostScript data when printing on a PostScript printer.

When TrueType fonts were released, the market was flooded with new fonts. Many of these fonts were of extremely low quality and bundled in large quantities. While the temptation to purchase these font packages is very high, be very careful as they can cause problems when you use them. This is true of any of the font formats bundled in large quantities for a very low price. Remember that the cost of a font for a major project is minimal compared to the cost of having to reprint film.

OPENTYPE

After years of battling over font formats, Microsoft and Adobe called a truce in the spring of 1996. The result of the truce is the OpenType font format. In essence, it combines the PostScript and TrueType formats into one single format. This means that either font format will be fully supported by future versions of Windows.

This new format is really an extension of TrueType called TrueType Open v2. Fonts designed for TrueType Open will support much larger character sets, and applications will be able to perform great typographical tricks with them. Strangely, it does not include typographic characters such as ligatures in the thousands of characters it supports. Note that while the technical name is TrueType Open, the more common name is OpenType. This is mainly to avoid the bad reputation that TrueType has earned among graphics professionals. OpenType may be the solution to many of the type problems that users currently face. But OpenType support is not included in any currently released operating system and no fonts are expected to be released until mid-1998 at the earliest. Since there is no operating system support and no fonts, the level of support within CorelDRAW 8 is relatively unknown.

TRUEDOC

TrueDoc is not so much a font format as a technology. It works with the other formats to create a synthetic variation on the font that can be embedded in your CorelDRAW file.

When you embed a font in your file, the character shape recorder (CSR) is invoked, and it creates a synthetic glyph for each character necessary. This synthetic font is called a portable font resource (PFR). The recipient of your file can load it, and the character shape player (CSP) will re-create the font data from the PFR. It can be re-created as either a bitmap or a vector. When sent to the printer, it can even be sent in PostScript format so there are no printing problems associated with it. In addition, you should see no degradation in quality, although, because of the conversions, the conversion may not be exact.

Font embedding using TrueDoc is available in the File Save dialog box of CorelDRAW, as described in Chapter 27. It is also an integral technology for Corel's Barista product, which is built in to Corel Ventura 7 and Corel WordPerfect 8. Strangely, the ability to embed fonts in a Barista document does not apply to CorelDRAW 8. Instead, all text is converted to curves and can look awful.

 *The initial release of Barista does not work correctly in Netscape Navigator 3.x if fonts have been embedded using TrueDoc. This is because TrueDoc does not conform properly to the Netscape plug-in architecture. It does work correctly with Netscape Navigator 2.x and Netscape Communicator 4.x, which has built-in TrueDoc support. Note that this only affects Barista documents with embedded fonts and shouldn't affect documents created by CorelDRAW 8.*

CHOOSING WHICH FORMAT TO USE

Most users do not make a conscious decision regarding which format to use. Instead they just use the format that is forced upon them. As you are installing CorelDRAW, you will be offered the option to install fonts—in this case, TrueType fonts, even though both formats are supplied on the CorelDRAW CD.

Before deciding which format to use, keep the following points in mind: Both TrueType and PostScript are just as easy to install and use when you use the Adobe Type Manager Deluxe or Font Navigator utility programs described a little later in this chapter. All of the fonts included with CorelDRAW are supplied in both TrueType and PostScript format. There is no extra cost to use either format. You can even use both formats at the same time and in the same document. Or you can begin a document with one format and finish it with the other just by loading the other font format—the fonts have exactly the same internal names.

If you will be using a PostScript printer at any time, either in your own office or at a service bureau, you really should use PostScript fonts. Many service bureaus will refuse jobs that use TrueType—and for good reason. Files that use only a single TrueType font can cause output errors and can even cause the imagesetter to crash in rare instances.

If you will be using Adobe Acrobat Distiller to create online documents, this program will behave much better if you use PostScript fonts. TrueType fonts generally become embedded under a really obscure font name that will not always be recognized by other machines.

If you have other software that supports only TrueType, you may need to use TrueType. An example of this is fax software and 3D rendering programs. Many of these do support both formats, but there are exceptions.

38

Even after considering these issues, many users may still be tempted to use TrueType no matter what since it is endorsed by Microsoft and it just seems easier. We've worked with several clients in the sign cutting industry who complained about the quality of the lettering in the signs they generated with CorelDRAW. The problem was more noticeable to sign cutters as they commonly output letters that are several feet high. After researching the problem, we realized that it was TrueType that was causing the awful output. The clients switched immediately to PostScript and saw a dramatic change in the quality of their signs.

 *We've noticed that PostScript fonts redraw significantly faster than TrueType fonts. This is especially evident if you are using large blocks of Paragraph Text.*

STORING THE FONTS

A few years ago, it was quite easy to keep track of the 100 to 200 fonts that most users owned. Now with CorelDRAW supplying over 1,000 fonts and users typically having many more, it can be very important to manage them properly. The first step in font management is learning how to properly store them on your system.

Some users prefer to keep their fonts on the CorelDRAW CD-ROM. This is a really bad idea because at some point you'll remove the CD and therefore you'll remove all of the fonts. We suggest that you copy the fonts to your hard drive. This will take approximately 50MB of space, but with the current low prices for huge hard drives, that is a minimal amount. If you are using a FAT partition table on your hard drive, you'll want to copy the fonts to a small partition since the files are typically fairly small and would waste unnecessary space on drives with a large cluster size. Follow these instructions to copy the files:

1. Create a folder entitled TT, PS, or both in the root of the drive to which you will copy the files. It is very important that the names be as short as possible.

2. On the CorelDRAW CD, locate the Fonts folder. This folder contains several other folders entitled Symbols, Ttf, Type1, and

Windows95. Go into either the Ttf or Type1 folder, depending on which type of font you wish to use.

3. Copy all of the folders from within the Ttf to your newly created TT folder or from the Type1 folder to your PS folder. This may take a few minutes.

4. Now change to the Symbols folder on the CorelDRAW CD-ROM. In it you will find both Ttf and Type1 folders. Copy the contents of your desired font type to a Symbols folder within your TT or PS folder.

5. Lastly, copy the Windows95 folder to your hard drive. All of these fonts are TrueType and so for clarity's sake should go into a TT folder.

You've now copied all of the fonts to your hard drive. Unfortunately, there are a couple of steps remaining. All of the files you copied from the CD-ROM are still marked as Read Only. So you need to remove the Read Only attribute. This will take a few minutes, but you only have to do it once. The main reason for turning off the Read Only attribute is so that you will have the ability to completely manage the fonts within Font Navigator. Without doing this, you will not be able to delete the files.

1. Go into one of the folders that you copied. For example, the first folder inside of TT or PS should be A. Select all of the files inside of that folder by clicking on the first one, scrolling to the end of the list and SHIFT-clicking on the last one.

2. Press ALT-ENTER to bring up the Properties dialog box shown in Figure 38-2. You'll probably notice a check mark in the Read-Only check box in Figure 38-2. If it isn't there, great. But if so, click on it and remove it.

You'll have to repeat these last two steps for each folder that was copied. It isn't really fun, but it should only take five to ten minutes. The last step is only necessary if you chose to copy the PostScript fonts and only if you wish to save some hard disk space. Along with the fonts, an AFM file was copied for each font. This is not necessary for use with CorelDRAW or most other Windows applications. So go into each of the folders one last time and delete all of the AFM files. Again, this is a bit of a hassle, but should only take a few minutes.

38

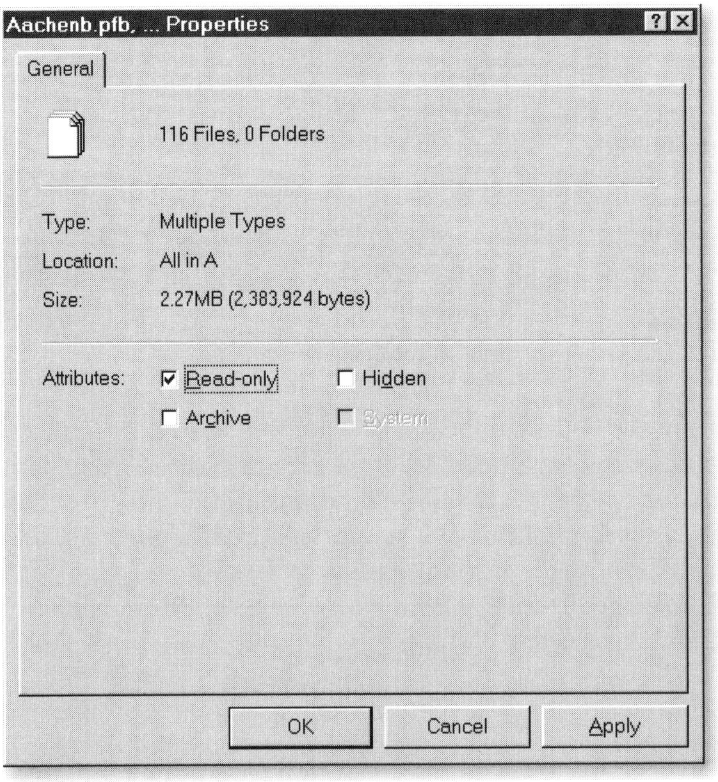

Aachenb.pfb, ... Properties   ? ✕

General

                    116 Files, 0 Folders

Type: Multiple Types
Location: All in A
Size: 2.27MB (2,383,924 bytes)

Attributes: ☑ Read-only   ☐ Hidden
             ☐ Archive   ☐ System

                    OK   Cancel   Apply

FIGURE 38-2   Properties dialog box for font files

You've now got all of the fonts on your hard drive and available for use. Note that they are not installed and will not drain your system resources other than the small amount of hard drive space that they occupy. And if you ever need the font files, you'll know exactly where to find them.

If other programs provide fonts, just follow these same steps so that you can keep all of your fonts under control.

INSTALLING FONTS

The standard way of installing fonts can be difficult and certainly does not allow you to easily manage the large number of fonts that are included with CorelDRAW. Thus, this section briefly describes two utility programs that can assist you in dealing with your fonts.

USING THE CONTROL PANEL

To install fonts in either Windows 95 or Windows NT, you can use the built-in Control Panel applet. In Windows 95, it will only allow you to install TrueType fonts, and in Windows NT, it will support both TrueType and PostScript to a certain extent. Here are a set of instructions for installing a new font on your system:

1. Open the Start menu and choose Settings | Control Panel.

2. From the Control Panel, double-click the Fonts icon. You'll see a folder similar to that shown in Figure 38-3. Note that this screen is from Windows 95, so it will not list PostScript fonts. These fonts would appear in Windows NT.

3. Choose File | Install New Font. You'll see a dialog box similar to the one in Figure 38-4. The figure shows a folder that contains several fonts.

4. If you are using Windows 95, simply select the font or fonts you wish to install and click the OK button. Windows NT users have the option of selecting PostScript fonts. If you do this, an extra dialog box will appear. This extra dialog box lets you specify several options regarding how the fonts are installed.

 *If you want your PostScript fonts to be downloaded accurately, make sure that you allow them to be copied to the Windows folder. This is not a problem if you are using ATM for Windows NT.*

38

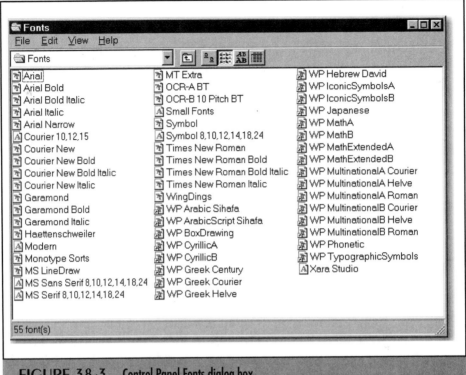

FIGURE 38-3   Control Panel Fonts dialog box

USING ADOBE TYPE MANAGER DELUXE

Adobe Type Manager Deluxe (ATM) has two functions. The first is to rasterize PostScript fonts for screen display and for printing on non-PostScript printers. The second function, new to this version, is to perform basic font management. You need ATM if you wish to use PostScript fonts in Windows 95; it should be available for around 50 dollars from your favorite software vendor. It is also highly recommended for Windows NT users as it will alleviate many problems of using PostScript fonts with just the built-in support.

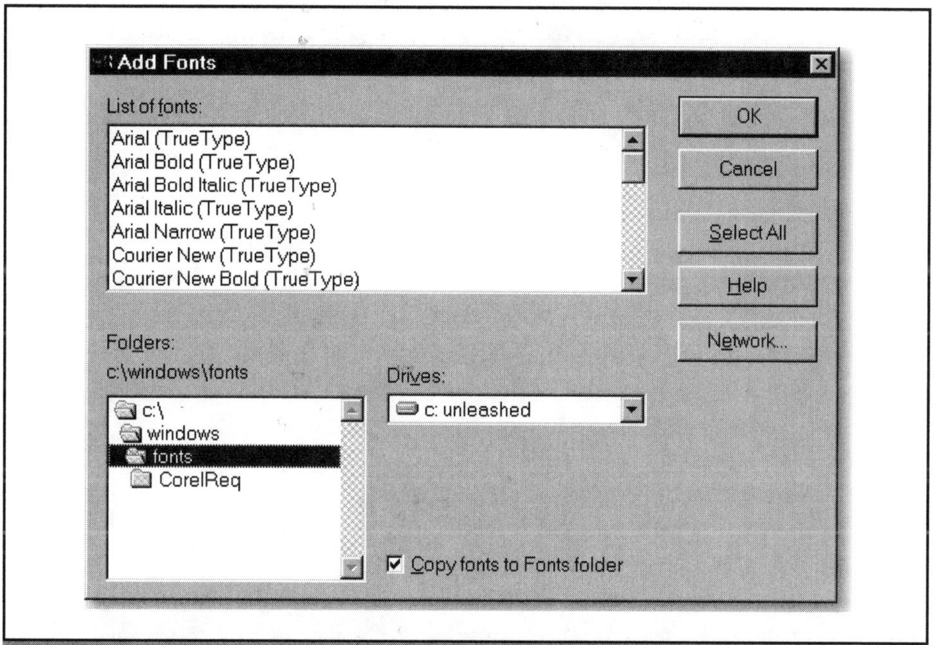

FIGURE 38-4 The Add Fonts dialog box

Ventura 7 provides a "lite" version of ATM that will rasterize the fonts, but it doesn't provide font management. This isn't a problem since Font Navigator (described a bit later) is supplied with CorelDRAW 8.

When you use this program, the first dialog box that you'll encounter displays a list of font sets, as shown in Figure 38-5. Here you can select the sets or groups of fonts you wish to have activated. The Starter Set is created automatically when you first install ATM. It will contain all fonts that were installed on your system when you added ATM.

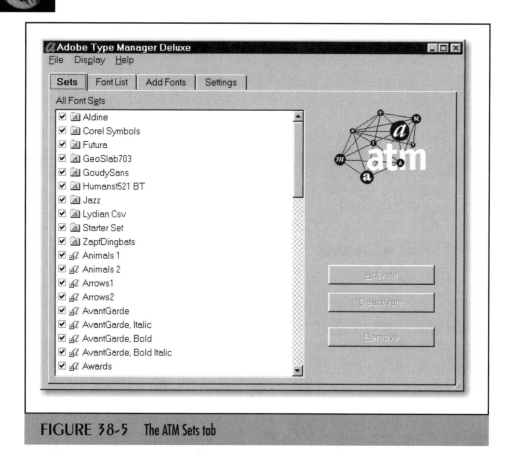

FIGURE 38-5   The ATM Sets tab

You can also view all of your fonts on the Font List tab, shown in Figure
38-6. Here the fonts are all shown individually. You can control what is
displayed by choosing All Installed Fonts or Only Active Fonts. You can select
a font in the list and click the Remove button to delete it from the list if it is
no longer necessary. Note that this list only shows the fonts that ATM knows
about and not every font on your system. There is no easy way to have it
search for all the fonts, as there is in Font Navigator.

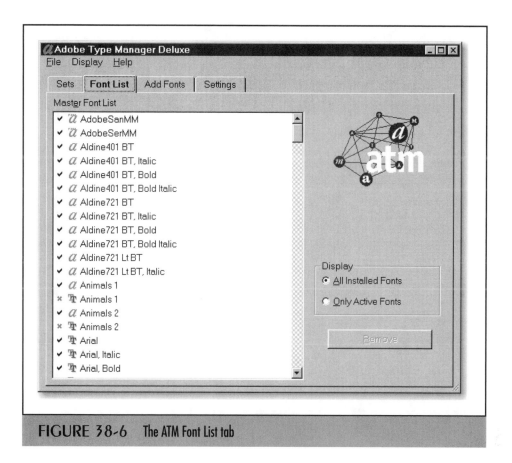

FIGURE 38-6   The ATM Font List tab

You can add fonts using the Add Fonts tab, shown in Figure 38-7. Again, the currently installed fonts are shown on the left, and the folder where the new fonts are located is displayed on the right.

You can use the Settings tab, shown in Figure 38-8, to turn ATM off or on. You can also assign a certain amount of memory to a font cache. This memory will then save the prebuilt font glyphs so they do not need to be re-created each time you use the font. The default setting of 256K is normally

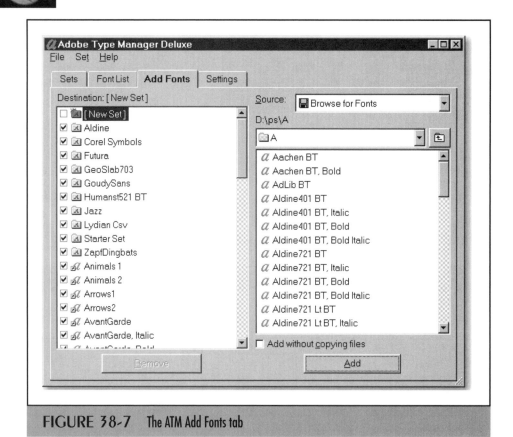

FIGURE 38-7 The ATM Add Fonts tab

adequate unless you use a large number of fonts in a single project. You can specify a particular directory where new fonts will be stored. Such directories can quickly become filled, so you may want to do some planning before arbitrarily placing all your fonts in a single directory.

ATM also provides a number of settings related to font display, font substitution, and sample sheets, as shown in Figure 38-9. You access these settings by clicking Advanced on the Settings tab. These settings are explained in detail in the ATM manual.

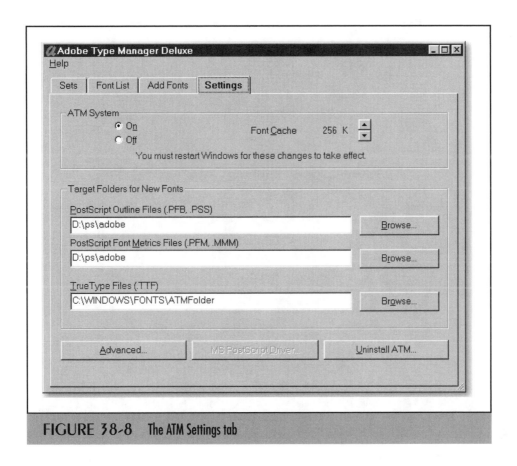

FIGURE 38-8   The ATM Settings tab

USING FONT NAVIGATOR

Font Navigator is to fonts what slices are to bread. This program makes it extremely easy to manage large numbers of fonts. It is included with CorelDRAW 8, but is not installed if you choose the default install. You must do a Custom installation and specifically ask that it be installed. For more information on the installation process, see Chapter 1.

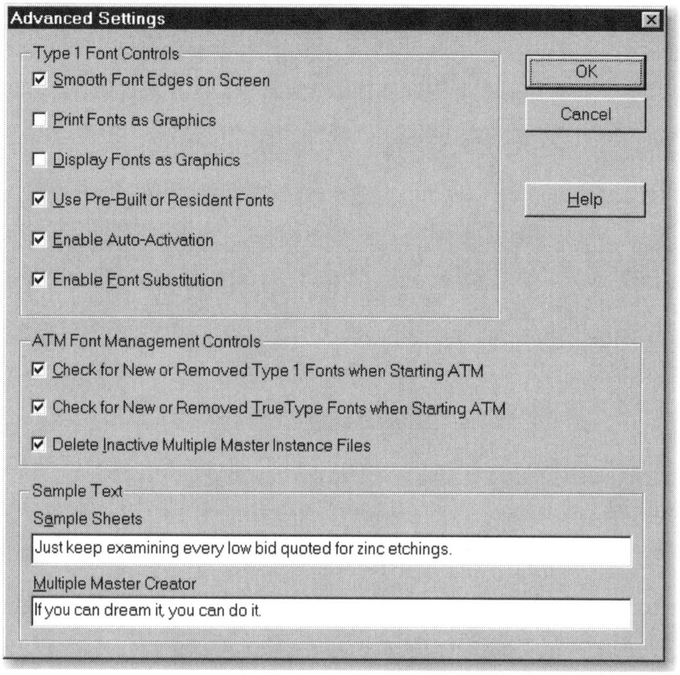

Advanced Settings   ✕

Type 1 Font Controls
☑ Smooth Font Edges on Screen   ⬜ OK

☐ Print Fonts as Graphics   Cancel

☐ Display Fonts as Graphics

☑ Use Pre-Built or Resident Fonts   Help

☑ Enable Auto-Activation

☑ Enable Font Substitution

ATM Font Management Controls
☑ Check for New or Removed Type 1 Fonts when Starting ATM

☑ Check for New or Removed TrueType Fonts when Starting ATM

☑ Delete Inactive Multiple Master Instance Files

Sample Text
Sample Sheets

    Just keep examining every low bid quoted for zinc etchings.

Multiple Master Creator

    If you can dream it, you can do it.

FIGURE 38-9   The ATM Advanced Settings dialog box

Font Navigator will automatically find all of the fonts on your system. So before you run it, you might as well get all the fonts copied to your hard drive as described earlier in this chapter. Once you have the fonts copied, run Font Navigator. Note that it is found in the Productivity Tools subfolder of the CorelDRAW 8 folder in the Start menu. The first time that you run the program, it will automatically bring up the Font Navigator Wizard shown in Figure 38-10. This first dialog box is just an introduction, so read the information and click Next.

The Font Navigator Wizard will search each of your hard drives you specify for fonts and can also search a CD-ROM drive, as shown in Figure 38-11. But finding fonts on a CD is only useful if the CD is *always* in the drive.

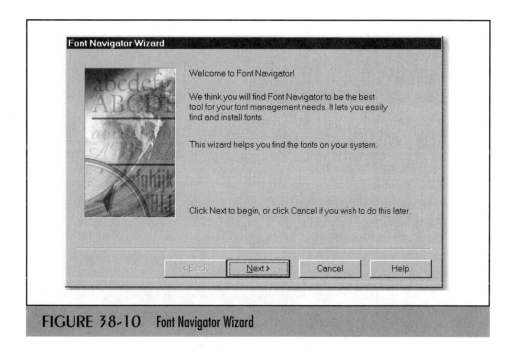

FIGURE 38-10   Font Navigator Wizard

This Wizard will create a font catalog for you automatically. Note that it does not install any fonts, but rather locates them so that they can be installed later.

As Font Navigator searches your drives, it will give you a running progress report, as shown in Figure 38-12.

Once it has finished searching your drives, you'll see the main Font Navigator window shown in Figure 38-13. There are four major windows here. The upper-left window contains the contents of the Font Catalog. Fonts that have a TT are TrueType fonts and T1 indicates a PostScript font. A check mark indicates that the font is currently installed.

The upper-right window are the currently installed fonts and font groups. To install a font, you simply drag it from the Font Catalog window into the Installed Fonts window. And to uninstall, you simply drag the font from the Installed Fonts window back into the Font Catalog window or right-click and select Uninstall Fonts from the pop-up menu. It just doesn't get any easier than that.

38

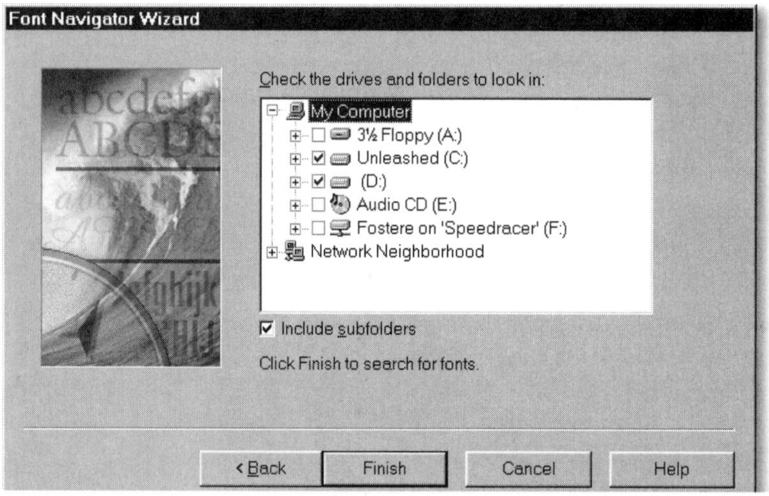

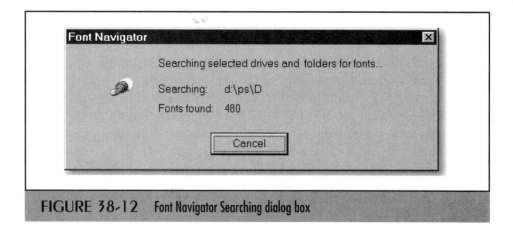

FIGURE 38-11   Font Navigator Wizard Font Location dialog box

The lower-right window is the Font Sample window. Drag any font into this window to see a quick sample. If the font contains more than one weight, the preview will show each one of them. And as with installed fonts, dragging a font out will remove its display.

FIGURE 38-12   Font Navigator Searching dialog box

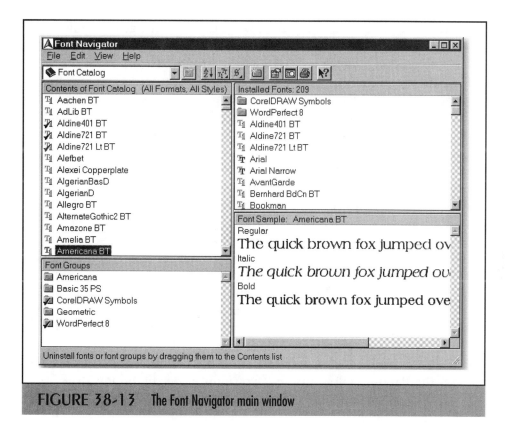

FIGURE 38-13 The Font Navigator main window

The real power of the application lies in the lower-left window, where the font groups are shown. You can create as many groups as you like. So creating groups for a particular job or client will help you to work with any related jobs in the future. When the current job is finished, uninstall the font group until it is needed again.

To create a new group, right-click the Font Groups window and choose New Group from the pop-up menu. If you wish to rename the group, just type in a new name as soon as the folder is displayed. Or to rename it later, right-click the group and choose Rename from the pop-up menu.

Now you need to add some fonts. Drag all of the fonts you want from the Font Catalog and drop them directly onto the group folder that you just created. They will automatically be added to the group.

38

Once you've created a font group, you can install the group by dragging the group into the Installed Fonts window and uninstall the group by dragging it out of the Installed Fonts window. So font groups are just as easy to work with as individual fonts.

Some of the font groups that we'll create are for the symbols supplied with CorelDRAW and for the WordPerfect symbols. Creating groups for the symbols makes it easy to uninstall them when you no longer need them. Then we'll create groups based upon a particular client or project. This way we can install the fonts when needed and take them out when a project is done. You can even share your group files with other users.

This discussion only scratches the surface of Font Navigator's power. To fully understand how this program works, look at its online help file, which includes detailed descriptions of how everything works.

OK, so Font Navigator is a great way to manage your fonts. But it gets even better now that Corel has integrated it into CorelDRAW 8. After Font Navigator has cataloged the fonts on your hard drive, select Tools | Options | Workspace | Text | Fonts and click the radio button to Use Font Navigator Catalog on Open. Then click the Panose Font Matching button and be sure that the Allow font matching box is checked. Now when you open a CorelDRAW document that uses fonts that are not currently installed, you will see the Panose dialog box, but you now have the option to let Font Navigator install the missing fonts permanently or temporarily for use only in the current CorelDRAW session. The font list within CorelDRAW 8 displays permanently installed fonts in black type and temporarily installed fonts in gray type as shown in Figure 38-14.

Panose substitution is still available as used in previous versions. Details on Panose substitution are covered later in this chapter.

 *This will not work properly unless Font Navigator is closed.*

How many times have you gotten a Panose message warning that a particular font was needed, but not currently installed? Panose is discussed in the next section.

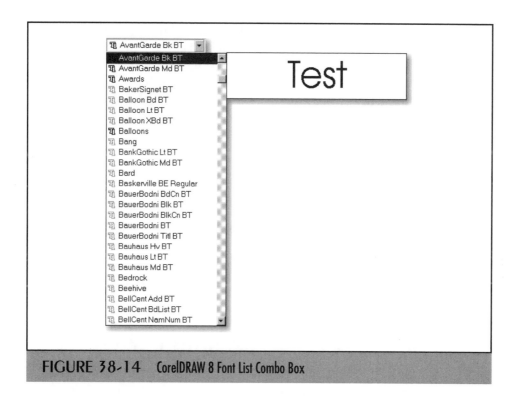

FIGURE 38-14   CorelDRAW 8 Font List Combo Box

FONT SUBSTITUTION

You've spent hours on a project using just the right font to get your message across, and at the last minute someone changes the font and prints the project without your knowledge. You'd probably be pretty upset if this were to happen. Guess what—it happens all the time, and most users aren't aware of it. This operation is called font substitution, and it is built into CorelDRAW and Windows.

Font substitution can be harmless if all you need to do is read a document. When it alters your design, changes line or page breaks, and causes text to overlap, however, it is evil.

A classic example of font substitution may occur quite often when you print. The default font in CorelDRAW is Avant Garde Bk BT. This font is very

38

similar to the Avant Garde font that is built in to PostScript printers. The characters are nearly the same, but the spacing and kerning are not even close. Thus, often the Avant Garde in the printer will be used to print when Avant Garde Bk BT was used on screen, and what you get out of the printer will not look the same as what you see on screen. This sort of substitution happens quite often with Arial and Helvetica as well. Windows has a built-in font substitution list in the PostScript print drivers. Make sure that you disable all substitution. You might even want to ask your service bureau to do the same to avoid any problems.

> **NOTE:** *We mentioned earlier how often the two variations on Avant Garde get substituted. We've seen many documents that were identifiable as something done in CorelDRAW simply because of this substitution, which is so obvious when printed. It can not be stressed enough that substitution should be avoided at all costs if a document is to be printed.*

USING PANOSE FOR FONT SUBSTITUTION

The Panose system tries to substitute fonts according to font attributes rather than using a random approach. It was developed by ElseWhere and has been incorporated into Windows as well as CorelDRAW.

Panose can substitute fonts in several ways. Because of the way trademarks apply to fonts, some fonts are nearly identical except for their names. A font may basically have been copied and assigned a different name that was not trademarked. Thus, you'll find that CG Omega, Optima, and Zapf Humanist have characters that look alike. Panose can help you to substitute fonts in cases like this. Remember, though, that even if the characters are identical (and they won't be), the spacing and kerning can be quite different.

> **TIP:** *Font Navigator will allow you to see the names of fonts that are very similar to a particular font. Right-click any font name within Font Navigator and choose Properties. In the Properties dialog box, select Analog Names and you'll see a list of names of all other fonts similar to the one you've chosen. If the Analog Names tab isn't visible, there are no other names stored with the font.*

Another common situation when Panose is useful is when files are being shared between Macintosh computers and PCs. PC font names often contain spaces, whereas their Macintosh counterparts do not. Panose keeps a database of font names to spot these differences across platforms. In most cases, the font substituted will be identical as it will be from the same font foundry.

The most interesting feature of Panose is its ability to assign a number to fonts based upon characteristics of the characters. This substitution uses a font that is similar in characteristics rather than just a font with the same name but different spacing in the name. It uses x-height, midline, letter form, arm style, stroke variation, contrast, proportion, weight, serif style, and family type to determine the ten-digit number assigned. Panose will find a font with a similar classification number to substitute for a missing font.

SETTING PANOSE PREFERENCES

To change the Panose preferences, you must dig deep to find them. Choose Tools | Options (CTRL-J) | Workspace | Text | Fonts and then click the Panose Font Matching button to display the dialog box shown in Figure 38-15.

If you want font matching turned off completely, simply make sure that Allow Font Matching is unchecked. Since there will then be no "intelligent" way to substitute for missing fonts, the default font will be used for all missing fonts.

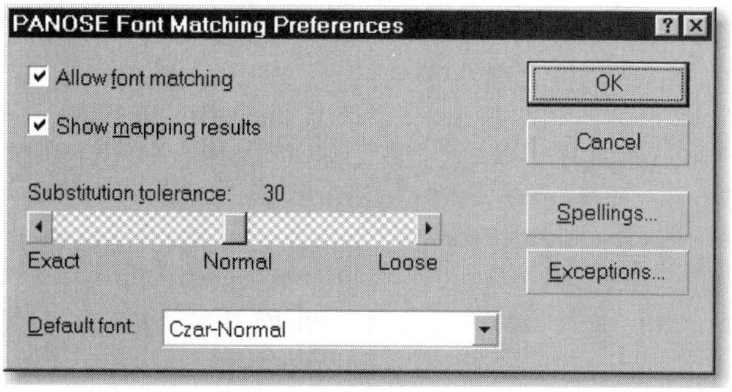

FIGURE 38-15   Panose Font Matching Preferences dialog box

If you check the Show Mapping Results check box, you will see a list of any substitutions made when you open a file that is missing fonts. The Panose Font Matching Results dialog box will be discussed later in this chapter.

 *You can not disable Font Matching if you are using Font Navigator to automatically install missing fonts.*

Earlier you learned how Panose assigns a ten-digit number to a font. This number is used with the Substitution Tolerance slider. This slider controls how close a font's number must be to the missing font. If it doesn't fall within that range, the default font is substituted instead. If you move the slider all of the way to the left, only an exact match will be made for the font. If you slide it all of the way to the right, the substituted font may not be very close to the original font. By default, the slider is left in the middle to provide a chance for "similar" fonts to be substituted.

If no match is found, the font in the Default Font box at the bottom of the dialog box is used. This defaults to AvantGarde Bk BT-Normal, one of the fonts supplied with CorelDRAW 8. However, you may want to use a symbol font of some sort instead. Then when substitution occurs, you'll be able to spot it instantly so you can make any appropriate changes.

 *The Alefbet and Czar fonts that come with CorelDRAW are a great choice for the default font as most users have no need for these alternative alphabets.*

If you click the Spellings button, the Alternate Spellings dialog box shown in Figure 38-16 appears.

You'll see two columns of font names. The left column contains the common Windows name of a font, and the right column contains the Macintosh name. Notice that the Macintosh names contain spaces and the Windows names do not. If a particular name is not on the list, you can add it by clicking the Add button. If you want to change a listing, select the font name in the list and click the Edit button.

You can also specify certain font matching exceptions that will be used. Back in the Panose Font Matching Preferences dialog box, click the Exceptions button. It will bring up the dialog box shown in Figure 38-17.

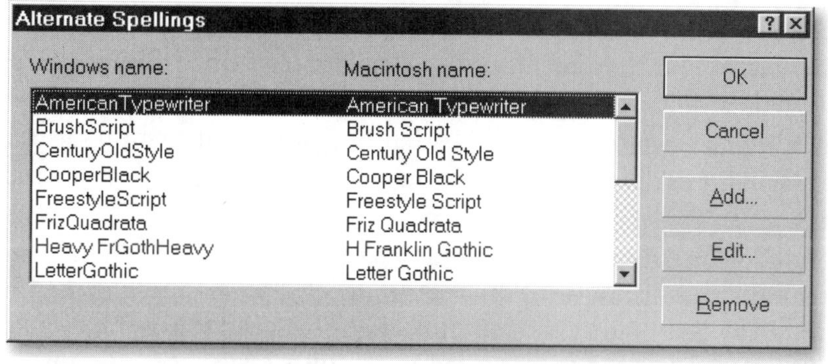

FIGURE 38-16   The Panose Alternate Spellings dialog box

Initially, the dialog box will be blank since no exceptions have been made. You can modify this list directly by clicking the Add button and entering a new exception. You can also add fonts to the list when a file is opened that is missing fonts. If you change the suggested font substitution to another font, you'll be asked if you want to save the change as a permanent exception.

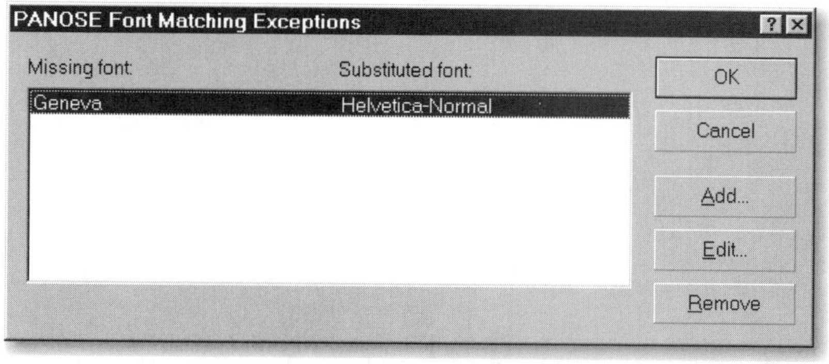

FIGURE 38-17   The Panose Font Matching Exceptions dialog box

PANOSE IN ACTION

So now that you understand all of this Panose stuff, what does it do? Hope-fully, it won't do anything because font substitution won't be necessary. However, if you open or import a file that is missing fonts, you'll see a dialog box that will list each font that is missing and allow you to substitute the font of your choice.

The dialog box displays three columns of text. The first column lists any fonts that are missing. Some of the fonts in this list are not used in the file and are listed here simply to drive you nuts. The list doesn't show the fonts *used* in the file, but rather the fonts stored in the file's style sheet. Because of the way CorelDRAW manages styles, you'll frequently have lots of extra fonts in the style sheet that are never actually used in a file. It is a good idea to create a style sheet that is devoid of extra fonts. Style sheets are described in Chapter 33.

In the middle column is the font that will be substituted for the missing font. The last column states whether the substitution will make a permanent change in the file or will apply only to this drawing session.

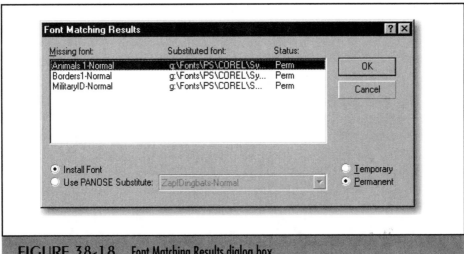

FIGURE 38-18   Font Matching Results dialog box

To change any of the proposed substitutions, select the missing font listing and select the font you'd like substituted from the <u>S</u>ubstituted Font drop-down list. Again, if you think the missing font warning is bogus, make sure to substitute some weird-looking symbol font. If the font is truly missing, you'll find it really quickly. To change the status of a font substitution from temporary to permanent or vice versa, simply select the <u>T</u>emporary or <u>P</u>ermanent radio button.

When you're done, click OK, cross your fingers, and clutch your voodoo doll tightly! Hopefully everything will come out to your liking.

Quite often fonts are taken for granted. Hopefully, now that you understand the many pitfalls that you may encounter, you'll spend a little bit more time making sure that they are used correctly. In the long run, your documents will thank you and so will your clients.

38

39

CORELDRAW AND THE INTERNET

I n the past three years, we've taught thousands of people how to use CorelDRAW and Corel PHOTO-PAINT at our seminars. Two of the most frequent complaints we've heard are that what appears on the screen doesn't look anything like what prints on the printer, and that the files required to create professional-quality work are huge. So what if we were to tell you that we can solve both of these problems, and that you can use this knowledge to make a quite comfortable living in creating graphics? Welcome to the World Wide Web!

Because the Web is viewed on the screen, just like the tools you use for design, the final product looks exactly as you expected, and because the graphics must pass through a slow communication device, such as a modem, files must be small or their transmission won't succeed. In addition, every company is madly rushing to have its own presence in cyberspace—which creates a tremendous demand for designers of Web graphics.

WEB DESIGN BASICS

Designing for the Web means putting everything you possibly can into a very small area. Figure 39-1 shows the Netscape Navigator browser in its standard configuration on a 640×480 monitor. You must assume a screen this small since the average user works at that resolution, and you must cater to the lowest common denominator. The shaded area is the area where the Web page will be displayed, and you can see that there is a space of only 638×361 pixels for content. To get an idea of how small that actually is, consider that the icons on your Windows desktop are 32×32 pixels.

SIZING YOUR IMAGE

When you create graphics, you must keep in mind the small area you have to work with. No graphic should exceed 600 pixels in width and 300 pixels in height, and even that size can create a file that takes too long to download. Also note that many users can see only 256 colors on their monitor. Therefore, designing everything in 24-bit color (16.7 million colors) makes no sense for the majority of people. Not only can people not see all these colors, but the display may be worse and the file will take longer to download.

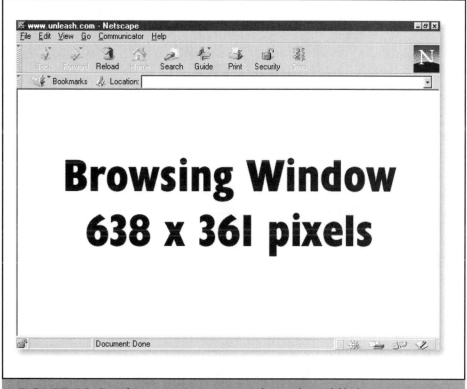

COLORING YOUR IMAGE

Using the right colors is extremely important in all types of design. For jobs that go to print, you should use CMYK colors, which can look quite different on screen than in print. For Web graphics, you should use RGB colors. Since the final output device is the screen, when you design for the Web, what you see is generally what you get. Note that everyone's monitor is slightly different, and that is why we say "generally."

CorelDRAW includes two special palettes that each contain 216 colors designed specifically for Netscape Navigator and Microsoft's Internet Explorer. Each of these palettes contains exactly the same colors, with the

39

difference being in the order of the colors. If you design with these colors, you should not see any dithering on a 256-color screen.

DETERMINING THE RIGHT FILE SIZE

One of the most common questions asked by budding Web designers is "How big should my files be?" We've heard this question answered in many different ways, but we don't feel it has an exact answer. Instead, you need to learn how to determine for yourself the file size that is appropriate for the Web site you are designing.

Again, you need to assume that visitors to a Web site have 14.4 baud modems, even though these are becoming outdated; you must assume the lowest common denominator. On a 14.4 baud modem, it takes about 1 second to download 1K of data, so if you have a 30K graphic, it will take 30 seconds to download. The real question thus becomes, "How long will the visitors to the Web site be willing to wait?" Once you've answered that question, you can decide on the maximum size of all files on a particular Web page. A common answer will be a file size that takes no more than one minute to download, thus limiting all content to under 60K.

WEB FILE FORMATS

There are several different file formats that are widely used on the Internet, each with its pros and cons. This section discusses how to decide which format is best for you.

GIF AND GIF ANIMATION FORMATS

The GIF format is especially useful for line-art images rather than photographs. It is easy to create this type of graphic in CorelDRAW because of the geometric shapes that are usually involved. For example, suppose you have a Corel clipart image. It started out as Erthfon.cdr in the \Communic\ Telephne section of the CorelDRAW 8 clipart library.

Now you need to decide how big you want the image to be on your Web page. This sizing information should be in pixels as that is the only way to truly measure an image on the Web. You want to use this image as a button, so a width of 150 pixels would be about right. A good way to figure the size in CorelDRAW is to set your rulers to use pixels. Another way is to treat each inch as 100 pixels; thus, if you want the image to be 150 pixels, you can just make it 1.5 inches wide. You can resize it easily by changing the width value on the Property Bar, making sure that the Maintain Proportional Sizing or Aspect Ratio button is depressed.

At some point, the image must be converted into a bitmap. This can be done either within CorelDRAW or during the export process. Here you will do both so you can see how both approaches work.

1. Choose <u>B</u>itmaps | <u>C</u>onvert to Bitmap to display the dialog box shown in Figure 39-2.

2. In the Color section, you can choose either 24 Bit - 16 Million Colors or Paletted (8 bit). The GIF format can save only up to 256 colors, so you may as well choose Paletted now.

3. Although checking Dithered will give you an image that is closer to the original, it will also create a larger GIF file since dithering is difficult to compress. We suggest that you don't use dithering, especially on line art.

4. Checking Transparent Background will have no effect when you export the file. Check this option only if you want to use the file within CorelDRAW for other purposes.

5. Make sure that Use Color Profile is not selected. Otherwise, you will see a terrible color shift in the image. Note that you also have to turn off Calibrate colors for display in the <u>T</u>ools | <u>O</u>ptions | Global | Color Management dialog box.

6. Set the Resolution value to 100 dpi. You'll have to type in the value since it is not available in the drop-down list. Remember that earlier you decided that 1 inch would equal 100 pixels.

7. Under Anti-aliasing, you should select None. The other settings will provide a prettier picture, but at the expense of file size. If the quality you get from the conversion is not what you want, try using the Super-sampling method.

8. Click OK.

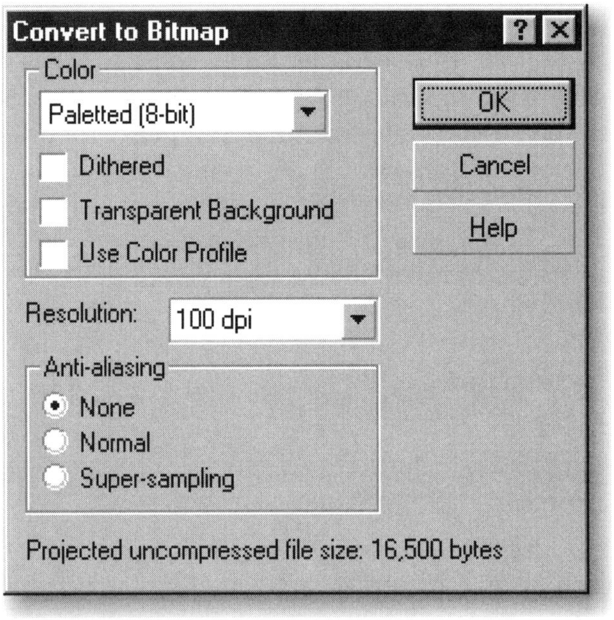

Convert to Bitmap

Color
Paletted (8-bit)

☐ Dithered
☐ Transparent Background
☐ Use Color Profile

Resolution: 100 dpi

Anti-aliasing
⦿ None
◯ Normal
◯ Super-sampling

Projected uncompressed file size: 16,500 bytes

OK   Cancel   Help

FIGURE 39-2   The Convert to Bitmap dialog box

Now your image will be a bitmap stored in the CorelDRAW file. Just to make sure that you've done everything correctly, select the bitmap and press ALT-ENTER to bring up the bitmap's properties. You should see a dialog box similar to the one shown in Figure 39-3.

If the pixel size of the bitmap does not seem correct, you should start the whole process over again. Carefully check each step to make sure that you followed all of the instructions. Unfortunately, one little mistake can really throw off everything in this exercise.

You've now seen one way to convert vector artwork into a bitmap, but there is another way. There is no reason that you can't do both, but one of them is definitely required.

1. Choose File | Export (CTRL-H) to display the Export dialog box discussed in Chapter 27.

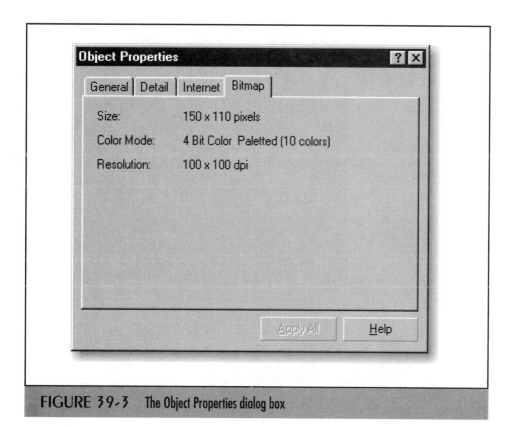

FIGURE 39-3   The Object Properties dialog box

2. Give your file a name, such as worldphone.gif. Although it may
   seem unimportant at first, the case of the name is extremely
   important. Windows does not differentiate between uppercase and
   lowercase letters, but UNIX does. Since most of the Internet is based
   on UNIX computers, you must be careful to always spell a file name
   correctly, including the case of the letters. A good rule is to always
   name files in all lowercase to avoid any confusion.

3. In the Save as type drop-down list, choose CompuServe Bitmap
   (GIF).

4. Check the Selected only checkbox.

5. Click the Export button, and you'll be presented with the Bitmap
   Export dialog box shown in Figure 39-4.

39

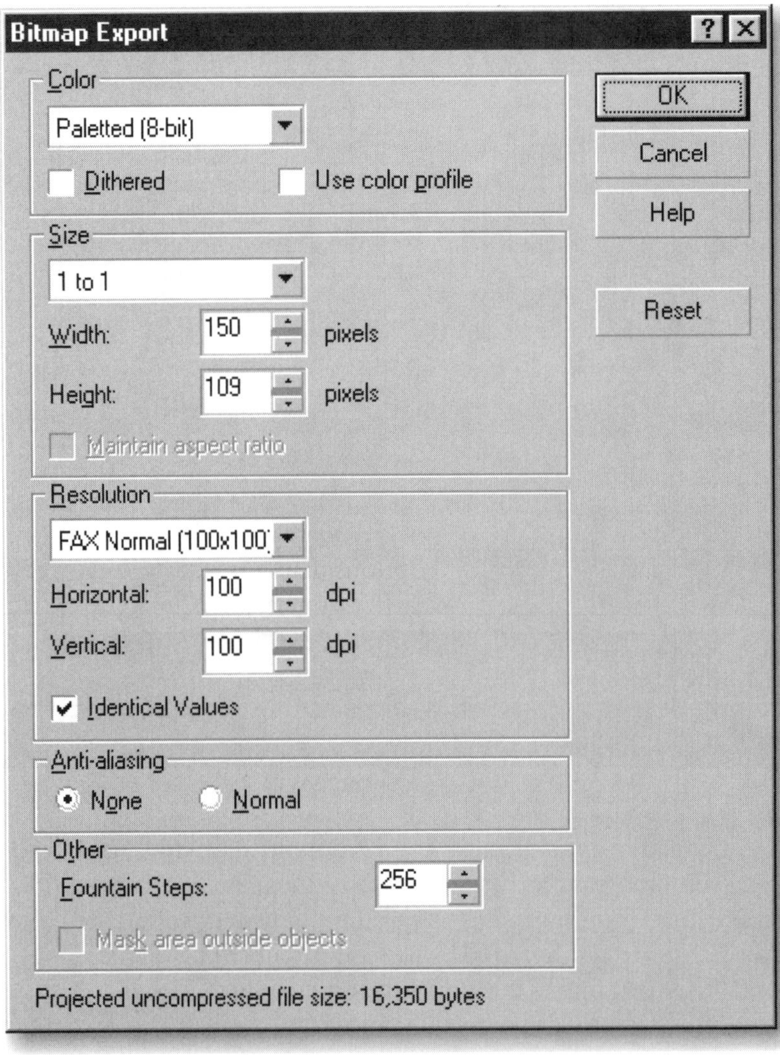

Bitmap Export   ? X

Color

Paletted (8-bit) ▼

☐ Dithered   ☐ Use color profile

Size

1 to 1 ▼

Width: 150 ▲▼ pixels

Height: 109 ▲▼ pixels

☐ Maintain aspect ratio

Resolution

FAX Normal (100x100) ▼

Horizontal: 100 ▲▼ dpi

Vertical: 100 ▲▼ dpi

☑ Identical Values

Anti-aliasing

◉ None   ○ Normal

Other

Fountain Steps: 256 ▲▼

☐ Mask area outside objects

Projected uncompressed file size: 16,350 bytes

OK

Cancel

Help

Reset

FIGURE 39-4   The Bitmap Export dialog box

6. In the Color section, select Paletted (8-bit) and make sure that Dithered is not checked. Dithering may produce a more attractive graphic, but at the expense of size. Again, make sure that Use color profile is not checked.

7. In the Size section, choose 1 to 1 from the drop-down list. The Width and Height values will change automatically.

8. In the Resolution section, select FAX Normal (100x100) from the drop-down list.

9. In the Anti-aliasing section, select None.

10. In the Other section, leave the Fountain Steps at the default of 256.

11. Click OK.

One way or another, your graphic has now been converted to a bitmap. The GIF file format contains several special options that you may want to use. These options are presented in the GIF89a Options dialog box shown in Figure 39-5.

The GIF89a Options dialog box will automatically be displayed just after the Bitmap Export dialog box when you are exporting to GIF format. In the upper-left corner of the dialog box is the original image and the upper-right corner contains a preview of your graphic.

You now need to determine whether you want to interlace the file. If you choose Interlace, a crude version of the image will initially appear on the Web page, and then this image will gradually improve as more data is downloaded. The overall download time is not any quicker; it just appears to be quicker since the crude image appears first. If your image is very small, you probably should not use interlacing, but on larger images you should.

One of the benefits of the GIF format is that it offers transparency. That means you can select a color that will be hidden when placed on a Web page. Since most graphics aren't rectangular, this can be very useful. When exporting from CorelDRAW, the only options available are None and Image color. You'll notice that there are other options, but they are available only when exporting from Corel PHOTO-PAINT.

If you want transparency, select Image color. You can select the color you wish to be transparent from the palette, but it may be difficult to distinguish

39

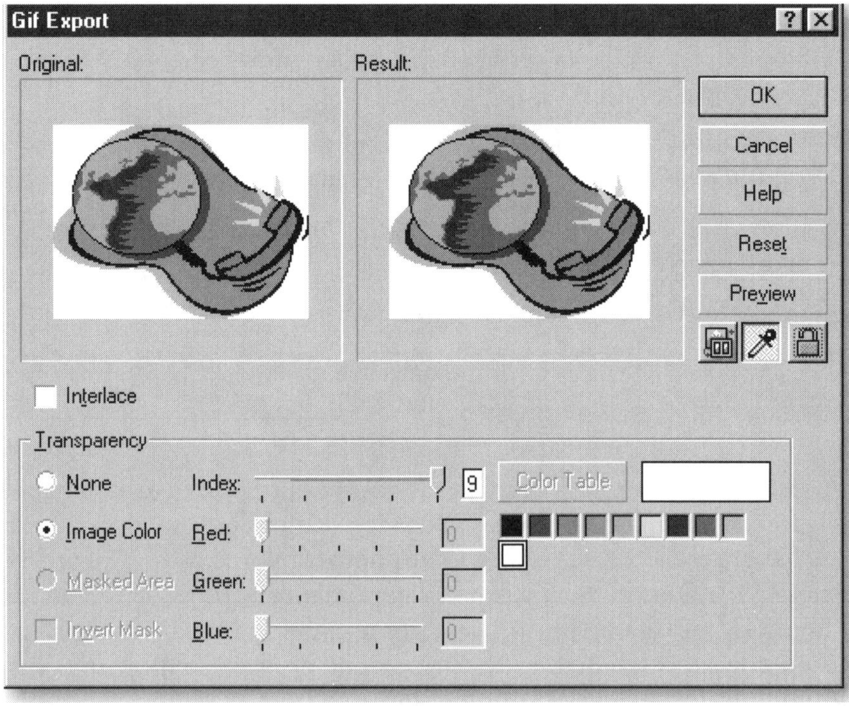

FIGURE 39-5   The GIF89a Options dialog box

the exact color you want. A better way is to click the eyedropper in the preview window of the original image on the color you wish to be transparent. In the clipart example, a white box appears around the image. Click with the eyedropper on the white box, and white will be selected in the palette and in the Transparency section of the dialog box. Now you just need to specify the GIF file in your Web page, and you'll be all set.

Here you have worked through the process of creating a GIF file completely within CorelDRAW. In reality, you should use Corel-PHOTO-PAINT to do much of the conversion work. It provides options to decrease the color depth to fewer than 256 colors and provides several options for choosing those colors. It can create smaller files that are superior in quality.

PORTABLE NETWORK GRAPHICS (PNG) FORMAT

The PNG file format is a new format that is supposed to supplant the GIF format. It can support 24-bit graphics and interlacing. It provides much better support for transparency, but you must use PHOTO-PAINT as the transparency requires that a mask be created.

JPEG FORMAT

JPEG was developed to store 24-bit images in a small file. It accomplishes this by using lossy (note that this is not "lousy" misspelled) compression. Each time you open and then resave a JPEG image, it degrades in quality. The amount of degradation is directly related to the amount of compression, so the greater the amount of compression, the worse it will look. Nevertheless, this format provides a great way to put photographs on the Internet in full color. Be sure to keep a copy of the original file before JPEG compression, however, just in case the quality drops too much.

JPEG does not support transparency and works only on 24-bit images. A new variation on JPEG allows it to save a "progressive" image, which is basically the same as interlacing. However, these progressive JPEG files cannot be viewed in older Web browsers.

To export to JPEG format, marquee select the graphic, go to File | Export, and choose JPEG Bitmaps (JPG) from the Save as type drop-down list. Check Selected only. Give the file an appropriate name and location and then click the Export button. Next you will see the Bitmap Export dialog box that we discussed in the GIF Export section. Make sure to select RGB Color (24-bit) in addition to setting the resolution and other options before clicking OK.

The JPEG Export dialog box, shown in Figure 39-6, provides several more options. This dialog has been significantly upgraded in CorelDRAW 8. As with the GIF Export filter, there are two previews showing you a before and after view of the image. On the left side of the dialog box are the Enhancement controls. Compression is the main control that will shrink the size of the file. Leaving the slider all the way to the left will produce a file that most resembles the original, but with less compression. If you move the slider to the far right, the file will be very small, but may be of very low quality. Remember that JPEG is a lossy format, and so when the file is reopened, it may lose some or

39

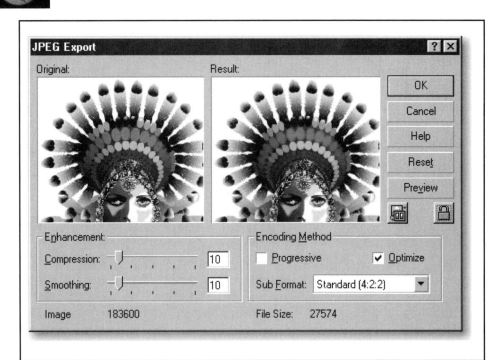

FIGURE 39-6 The JPEG Export dialog box

all of its detail. At any time you can click the Preview button to see exactly how the compression is affecting the quality of the image. And at the very bottom of the dialog box are two numbers showing the size of the image and the resulting file.

Below compression is the Smoothing slider. By using smoothing, you can sometimes squeeze the files a little bit more. It should always be used when you are working with a paletted image, but is much less necessary when you are working with 24-bit images. It is helpful if there is a large area of plain background. Smoothing should be decreased when the file includes text and it will become very hard to read.

You also have several options for the Encoding Method. The first option, Progressive, performs a function very much like interlacing. It is supported by Netscape Navigator 3.*x* and higher and Microsoft Internet Explorer 3.*x* and higher. Selecting Optimize will generally decrease the file size. Under Sub

Format, there are two choices: Standard (4:2:2) and Optional (4:4:4). Experiment with these settings until you get the right amount of quality and compression. Once everything looks good, click the OK button.

WAVELET (WI) FORMAT

You may have noticed that the photos supplied with CorelDRAW 8 are all stored in Wavelet (WI) format. This is a fairly new format that can compress files even smaller than JPEG with a higher quality. However, although the JPEG format slowly degrades with greater compression, the WI format will simply disintegrate if you apply too much compression.

Wavelet files are not supported in the current Web browsers as of this writing, but they are scheduled to be supported in future releases of both Microsoft Internet Explorer and Netscape Communicator. Thus, this format may be popular on the Web by the time you read this book.

To export to WI format, marquee select the graphic, go to File | Export, and choose Wavelet Compressed Bitmap (WI) from the Save as type drop-down list. Check Selected only. Give the file an appropriate name and location and then click the Export button. Again, you'll get the Bitmap Export dialog box where you should choose RGB Color (24-bit) among other options before clicking OK. You'll see the Wavelet Export dialog box, as shown in Figure 39-7.

In the Enhancement section of the dialog box, you have several options for compressing the image. First is the Compression slider. It works almost identically to the one in the JPEG Export dialog box. The higher the compression, the smaller the file will get. But this will also cause a loss of quality. Adjusting the Contrast and Edge sliders can also affect the amount of compression and the quality. You should experiment with these sliders and then click Preview until you have a file of the optimum size and quality. Again, note that the image size and file size are shown at the lower-right corner of the dialog box.

You also have two options for the Encoding Method. Speed can be set to either Normal or Fast. Normal will create the smaller file, but at the expense of speed. On a fast machine, the difference is not noticeable. Path can be set to either One, Two, or Three. Try different settings to see which provides the smallest file. Note that it doesn't go in any particular order. So choosing One is not necessarily better or worse than Three. When satisfied with the size and quality, press OK to finish exporting the file.

39

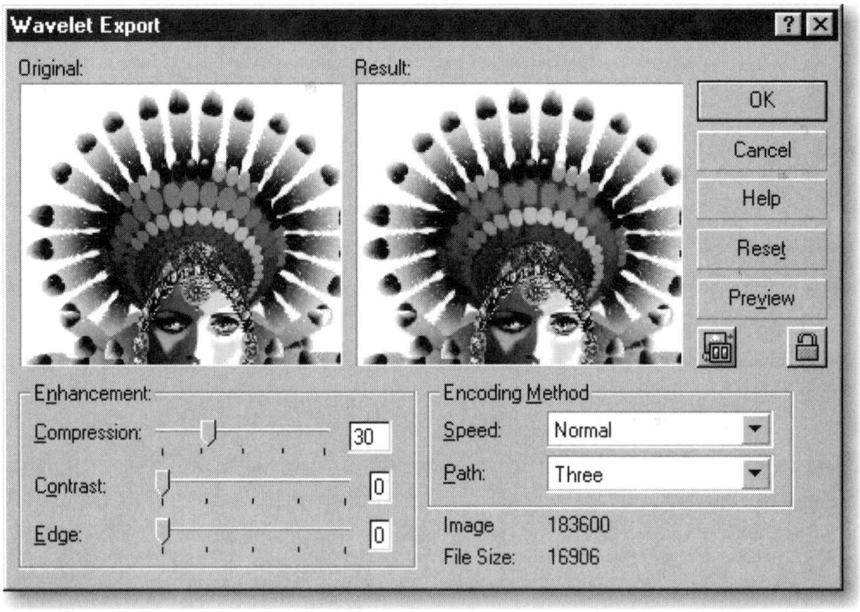

FIGURE 39-7   The Wavelet Export dialog box

CREATING A WEB PAGE

Image maps are large graphics that have areas defined within them that correspond to hyperlinks. Commonly, there will be button-like images on the image map that can be clicked as if they were individual buttons, but they really are just parts of one large image in which various areas are defined in HTML code.

The coding of an image map depends on whether the mapping is done on the client or the server computer, but you really don't need to know much about the coding other than the type that you will need. For now, you just need to worry about creating an image with the defined hotlinks.

ASSIGNING URLS

Any object you create in CorelDRAW can have a URL assigned to it. To do this, you'll need to activate the Internet Objects toolbar, shown here.

To activate this toolbar, right-click the gray area immediately surrounding the buttons on any of the toolbars currently on the screen. From the pop-up menu, select the Internet Objects toolbar. Another method for assigning URLs is to use the Object Properties Docker, which you can access by using the ALT-ENTER shortcut key with an object selected. It is shown here in an undocked state.

The following instructions are for the Internet Objects toolbar, but they should work equally well in the Object Properties Docker.

1. Select the object to which you wish to assign a URL.

2. On the Internet Objects toolbar, type the full URL in the Internet Address box or choose an existing URL from the drop-down list.

3. If you wish to assign a bookmark to the object, type it in the Internet Bookmark box.

4. Click the Show Internet Objects button. (It is the button just to the right of the Internet Bookmark box.) Objects that have been assigned a URL can be clearly identified by a color and hatch pattern if this button is depressed.

5. The next two buttons specify whether the object's hotspot is defined by its shape or by its bounding box. Choose one of these buttons. If the shape is a complex shape, it is best to choose the bounding box button.

6. The next button lets you assign a foreground color to the object. This color will be displayed as crosshatching on the screen. It will not be used in the final rendering of the object when it is exported to a bitmap or when it is printed. Select a foreground color from the drop-down color palette.

7. Another drop-down color palette is found at the far right end of the toolbar. This specifies the background color of the selected object. Select a background color from the palette.

Note that the foreground and background colors are used only to call your attention to any objects that have been tagged with a URL. If you change these colors with no objects selected, the colors you choose will apply to all objects that have a URL assigned. If you change the colors with an object selected, they will apply only to the selected object.

CREATING WEB FORMS

CorelDRAW 8 has added numerous new features for creating Web pages in addition to graphics. The biggest addition has been in the area of elements for

Web forms. When you choose Edit | Insert Internet Object, you are presented with a child menu containing each of the various elements that you can create, as shown here.

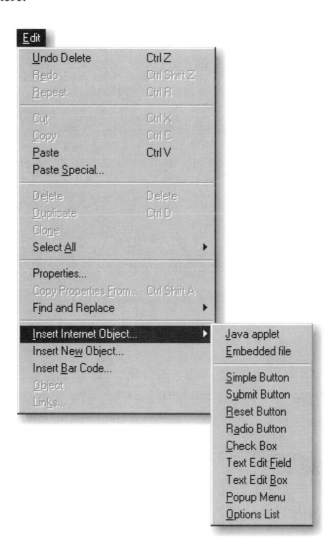

To fully understand how each of these elements works, you'll need to have some knowledge of HTML and its syntax. We'll show you how to edit the properties of one of the elements and then you can explore the other types on your own, since they all work alike.

With the child menu displayed, select Options List and the object will be attached to your cursor. Click the page where you would like it displayed and it will be inserted. Although it seems as though it can be resized, resizing won't have any effect. The Property Bar will allow you to assign a name to the element which will be used when the form is processed by a CGI script.

For this particular element, you'll need to populate the list with data. Select the object and press ALT-ENTER to bring up the Object Properties dialog box. We need to work with the List tab of the dialog, as shown here.

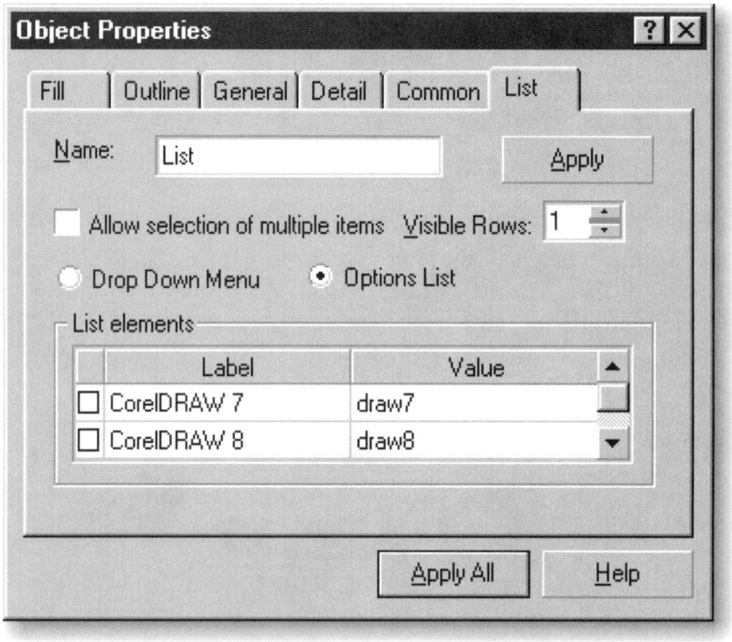

In this case, there are several changes that can be made. By default, you can select multiple items from the list when it is displayed in a Web browser, but you can disable this feature if you want. Visible Rows specifies how many items will initially be visible. If the items don't all fit, scroll bars would be provided automatically in the browser. The list can either drop-down or not, based on whether you select Drop Down Menu or Options List.

The last, and most important, part is for the entry of the data. Anything you place in the Label column will be displayed in the browser. The value is what is sent to the CGI script. To the left of each label element is a check box. If it is checked, this item will be selected by default.

 *If you are creating forms and don't understand the options, it is probably a good idea to pick up a good reference book on HTML.*

For the form to work properly, you'll need to define the method in which it is to be processed. With nothing selected, right-click the page and choose Properties from the pop-up menu. This will bring up the Object Properties window shown here.

The first item you must enter is the URL of the CGI Script that will be used to process the script. This script will be different for each user as it is supplied by the company that hosts the Web page. The Method and Target entries will also be specified to you by the Web host so you should discuss the appropriate values with them.

 *If you do not enter values for how to process the form, you will receive error messages upon exporting the file.*

As you are designing a Web page, it is extremely important to try and line up each element in some sort of grid. When you export the page to HTML, the most common file will be created as a table. The easier the elements fit within a grid, the less complex the table will be.

PREPARING FOR EXPORT

Before you export the file for the Web, you should check to see if there are any potential problems. Choose <u>V</u>iew I <u>D</u>ockers I <u>H</u>TML Object Conflict to bring up the HTML Conflict Analyzer Docker window shown here. Note that we've undocked it.

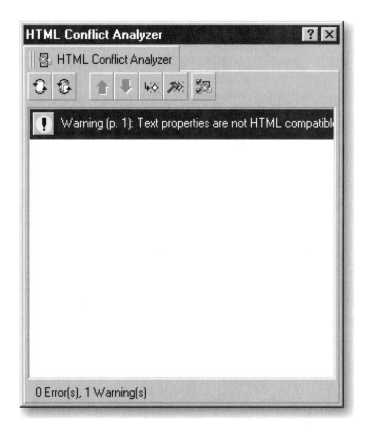

Click the far left button to analyze the current document. As you can see in the image shown here, there is one warning that has been brought to our attention. This particular error is warning us that some text is not HTML compatible. This just means that the text will be converted to a bitmap and not regular text. Fix this problem by selecting the text and choosing Text | Make Text HTML Compatible and the warning will disappear from the HTML Conflict Analyzer. But there are elements supported in regular text that will not be supported in HTML text.

To get a full list of the errors that are being checked, press the button on the far right side of the HTML Conflict Analyzer and you'll get the dialog box shown in Figure 39-8.

HTML Conflicts are just another part of your Workspace (see Chapter 40), so if there are particular warnings that you want checked on one type of project and not on another you can save them to a custom workspace. Each of the warnings is self explanatory.

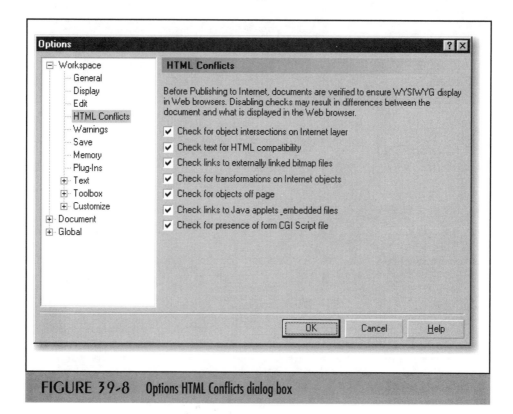

FIGURE 39-8   Options HTML Conflicts dialog box

39

EXPORTING TO HTML

When you have your page all finished, it becomes time to export it to HTML. Choose File | Publish to Internet to get the dialog box shown in Figure 39-9.

This initial screen gives you three options for export. We've already discussed how to directly export single images earlier in this chapter. Barista is a method of creating a bloated Java application and should not be used. So we'll just discuss how to create HTML. You can continue using the Wizard or click the Use Internet Dialog button, which takes all of the elements in the Wizard and places them in a single dialog box. We'll use the Wizard. Click Next to get the next screen, as shown in Figure 39-10.

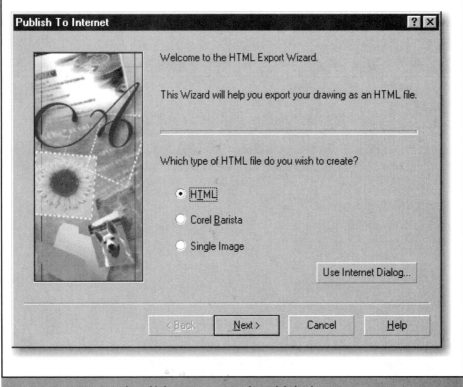

FIGURE 39-9   The Publish To Internet Wizard initial dialog box

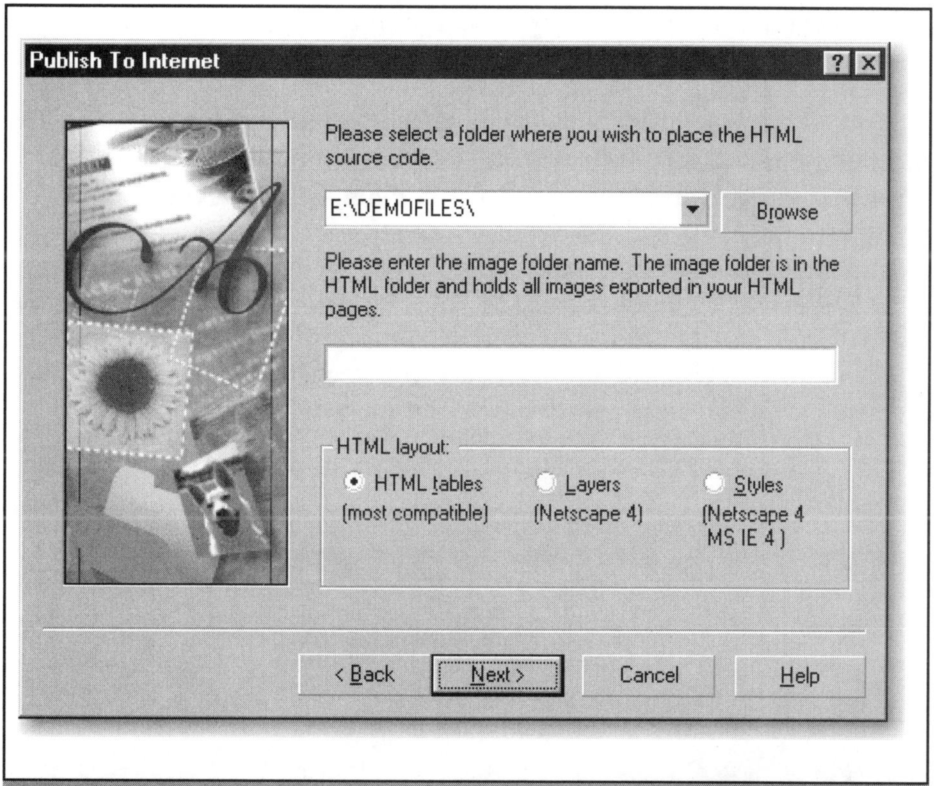

FIGURE 39-10   The Publish To Internet Wizard screen for selecting destination files and browser

Your first choice is the folder in which the resulting HTML file will be stored. If there are images to be created, you can also specify another subfolder where they will be stored. A great way to create a Web page in CorelDRAW is to import each graphic as a linked bitmap. Then you can optimize the graphics and not have CorelDRAW export them. The last choice in this screen is for the destination browser. Unless you are specifically targeting only Netscape 4 users or Internet Explorer 4 users you should leave this at the default of HTML tables. This is the most compatible option, but it does create very complex tables to retain positioning of the various elements on the page. Once you are finished, click Next.

39

The next screen gives you several options for images. These options were described earlier in the sections on JPEG and GIF files. Clicking Next again will bring you to Figure 39-11.

Each of the pages in your CorelDRAW file will be listed. You can place a check mark next to each page that you wish to export or press the Export All Pages button. Next to the page number is room to enter a title. The title is taken from the name that has been assigned to each page tab in your file. If you would like to change it, do so here and the tabs will also be updated. You can also specify the name of the HTML file that will be created for each page. In theory, a single CDR file could contain an entire Web site, which could then be exported to HTML all at once. Once you've made any needed changes, click the Finish button and the file will be exported.

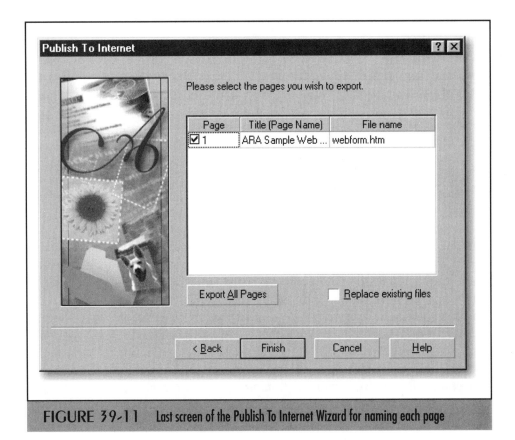

FIGURE 39-11   Last screen of the Publish To Internet Wizard for naming each page

40

SETTING OPTIONS
AND CUSTOMIZING
THE USER INTERFACE

W e all work in different ways, and the options and interface of CorelDRAW are not optimal for everyone's style of working. Luckily, you can change almost everything in CorelDRAW to make it more to your liking. This chapter walks you through the many settings found in the Options dialog box and discusses the customization that you can do.

When you first install CorelDRAW, a number of options are already set for you. Corel tries to set default values that are appropriate for the majority of people. Nevertheless, you will want to change many of these settings to get the most benefit from the options. All of the options described here can be accessed with the Tools | Options (CTRL-J) command. The Options dialog box provides more than sixty dialog boxes full of information. This section describes each of these dialog boxes and their settings.

Along the left side of the dialog box is a tree structure of all the types of settings that you can adjust. If there is a plus (+) sign next to a category, there are subcategories available. Just click the + and they will be revealed. To hide them again, click the minus (-) sign that replaces the + sign. This will collapse the tree.

WORKSPACE

The concept of workspaces is new to CorelDRAW 8. Now several users may use the same installation of CorelDRAW and each one can work with a different environment. And you may want different settings based upon the type of project you're working on. Workspaces allow you to save the user interface settings for each person or project so that you can easily return to those settings as needed. Figure 40-1 shows the Workspace section of the Options dialog box.

At the top of the dialog box, you can see which workspace is currently loaded. Unless you have changed it, it should read _default. Just below that is a list of all the available workspaces. Initially there is the _default workspace and several other workspaces that mimic CorelDRAW 7, Adobe Illustrator, Macromedia Freehand, and others.

To create a new workspace, simply click the New button. This will bring up the dialog box shown in Figure 40-2.

First, you'll need to enter a new name for the workspace. Make sure to give it a descriptive name so that you can remember its purpose. Next you

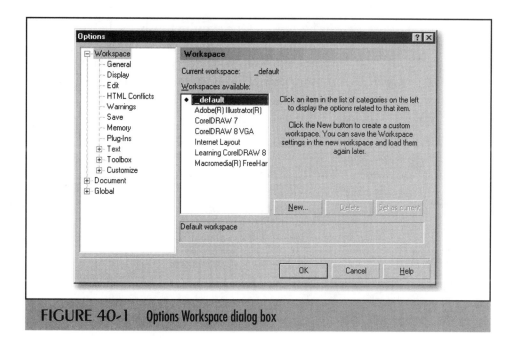

FIGURE 40-1   Options Workspace dialog box

need to choose the existing workspace to base it on. Choose the one that is most similar to what you want in the new workspace so you'll have fewer changes to make. Last, you need to enter a description of the new workspace. Make sure to expand on the name you gave it so that there is no question

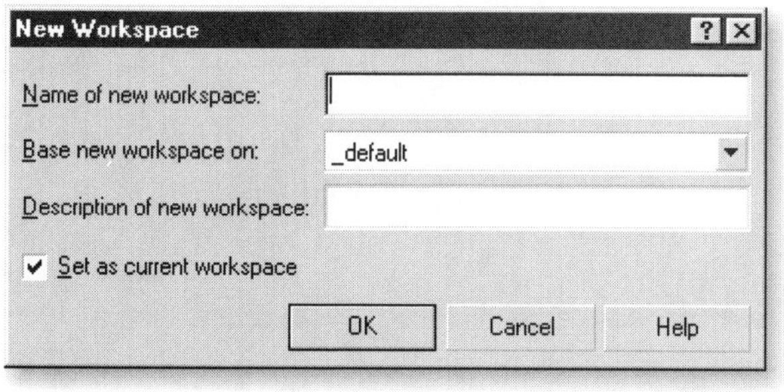

FIGURE 40-2   New Workspace dialog box

40

about how this workspace is best used. Once you're finished, click OK to get back to the main Workspace dialog box.

If you wish to delete a workspace, simply select it from the list on the left and click the <u>D</u>elete button. But the most important thing to do is to select a workspace that you want to use. Once selected, click the <u>S</u>et as current button. This will put the workspace into use. And as you'll see in the next few pages, there are a number of settings that can be controlled by a workspace.

> TIP: *Copy the _default to a new Workspace name instead of making changes to the actual default. This way, you'll always have the default in case you need to go back.*

GENERAL

Bring up the General dialog box shown in Figure 40-3 by clicking the word General under Workspace in the Options tree structure.

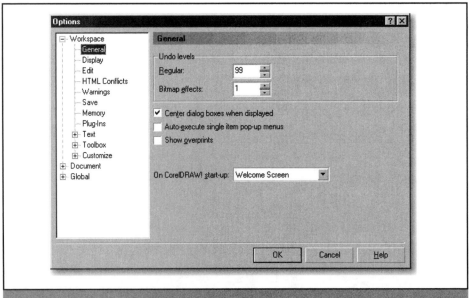

FIGURE 40-3   Options General dialog box

Undo Levels

It happens all the time. You do something such as deleting an object that you think you no longer need, and then you realize that it is needed after all. No problem; simply use the Edit | Undo (CTRL-Z) command. In the good old days of CorelDRAW, you could undo only the last action. CorelDRAW 5 increased this limit to 99. The limit is now 99,999, which is way too many for any user. Every action that can be undone will be stored in memory, so setting this high a number can quickly drain your system's resources. A nice compromise is to set Regular undo to 10. Note that the default setting is 99 and this can cause your system resources to drain rather quickly and cause instability. It is best to reduce this setting to a lower number like 10.

There is now a separate undo setting labeled Bitmap effects, which relates to the effects that you apply using the Bitmap menu. Since these effects are usually even more memory intensive than regular operations, you'll want to keep this setting much lower. The maximum value here is 99, and the default is 1. You may want to change this value to 2 or 3 just so you can undo more than one effect, but keep in mind that these are very memory intensive.

Center Dialog Boxes

Do you ever find yourself moving a dialog box to a certain position on the screen only to find that it doesn't appear there the next time it is used? By default, Center dialog boxes when displayed is checked. This means that all dialog boxes will be automatically centered. If you uncheck this option, the dialog boxes will remember their last position and not automatically center themselves.

Auto-Execute Single Item Pop-Up Menus

Some of the pop-up menus that appear when you right-click have a single item. In those cases, you can have that function automatically executed by checking Auto-execute single item pop-up menus. You'll see later that you can customize the right-click pop-up menus so that they only contain one item. In this case, auto-execution is quite helpful.

40

Show Overprints

When the Show overprints option is checked, you will see a hatching pattern on any objects for which there is an overprinted fill or outline. Three types of hatching are used: one for an overprinted fill, another for an overprinted outline, and yet another for both overprints. By default this option is turned off.

On CorelDRAW! Start-Up

When you started CorelDRAW for the first time, you were presented with a dialog box that asked you what task you wanted to perform. You may have just selected something to get rid of this box. If you want to change the setting to one of the other options, choose it from the On CorelDRAW! start-up drop-down list.

DISPLAY

Click the word Display under Workspace in the tree structure of the Options dialog box to see the dialog box shown in Figure 40-4. Here you will find the many options that affect the way your drawing is displayed.

Preview Colors

The colors used to display a drawing on screen can be dithered from either the Windows palette or Corel's own 256-color palette. If you are using a video adapter that displays only 256 colors, it is best to use Corel's palette. If your system can display 16-bit or 24-bit color, you'll want to use Windows dithering. With the high number of colors, there usually isn't any dithering at all.

Another option available to users with only 256 colors is to use a palette optimized to the best 256 colors in an image. This palette created may alter the display of other running applications, but it will provide the best possible image in CorelDRAW. This option is not shown since our system is displaying more than 256 colors.

Refresh

Any time you make changes to your drawing, CorelDRAW will attempt to redraw the screen. Sometimes this can take quite a long while. However, the

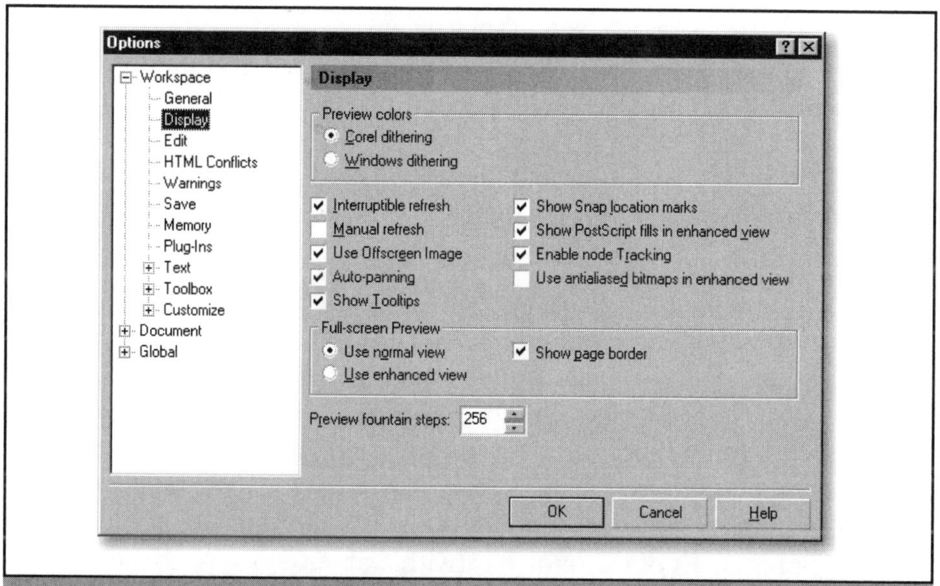

FIGURE 40-4   The Display Options dialog box

part you want to see may have been the first thing drawn, or you may not even need to see a redrawn screen to continue your work. If you check the Interruptible refresh check box, you can stop screen redrawing by clicking anywhere on the screen or pressing any key. For example, suppose you've finished a drawing and are ready to print, but the drawing will take two minutes to redraw. With this option checked, you can just use the CTRL-P shortcut and start printing right away.

If you don't want CorelDRAW to redraw the screen until you specifically tell it to, check the Manual refresh check box instead.

Offscreen Image

CorelDRAW 8 can handle the redraw of images quite differently than previous versions. It builds a bitmap version of your display off of the screen and then draws it all at once. So when you make changes to your drawing, only the parts that have changed will be redrawn. It will also instantly redraw after you've had

40

a dialog box or roll-up on screen above the image. By default this method is active because Use Offscreen image is checked. But if you want to return to the redraw methods used in CorelDRAW 7, just uncheck this selection.

Auto-panning

Suppose you're right in the middle of moving an object and realize that it needs to end up just off the edge of your screen. If you have Auto-panning checked, the screen will scroll automatically when you near the edge of the drawing window. If you go too far and place your cursor above the scroll bars, the cursor will change to the international No symbol, indicating that you can't drag and drop to that location. However, if you stop just short of the scroll bars, the screen will scroll in the direction that you are moving. There are quite a few situations in which auto-panning will help you. The key is to move your cursor just short of the scroll bar (within about 7 pixels) so the screen is panned correctly.

Show ToolTips, Snaps, and PostScript Fills

A graphical user interface forces icons upon us. Sometimes icons are very easy to understand, but some icons just can't be deciphered. Tool Tips can help solve this problem. If your cursor hovers over an icon, a little yellow text box will pop up, providing the name of the icon's function. As long as the Show Tooltips check box is checked, this help will be provided. Note that a longer description of the command is also provided on the Status Bar no matter how the Tool Tips option is set.

When you are using Snap to Objects, Guidelines, or Grid, a blue marker will appear at the point where the snap occurs. By default, Show Snap location marks is activated, but you can eliminate these marks by unchecking this option.

A new feature to CorelDRAW 7 was the ability to display PostScript fills on the main screen when working in the Enhanced view. This provides great functionality, but the display can be very slow. By default, the Show PostScript fills in enhanced view option is activated, but those with slower systems may want to turn it off. Note that this option has an effect only when you use PostScript fills.

Node Tracking

One of the nice new features in CorelDRAW 8 is the ability to manipulate objects and nodes when you have a drawing tool selected. If you do not want the ability to edit nodes with drawing tools, remove the check mark from the Enable Node Tracking check box.

Antialiased Bitmaps

When you are using Enhanced view, you can have all bitmaps shown with antialiasing. Your bitmaps will have smoother edges and will generally look better this way. But they may look a tad blurry and will take longer to display. Check Use antialiased bitmaps in enhanced view to enable this feature.

Full-Screen Preview

In Full-Screen Preview mode, only your document will be displayed. You have the choice of using Normal view or Enhanced view when you are in this mode. By default, the Normal view is used. Checking the Show page border check box will display the border of the page in this preview screen. This feature can be helpful when you want to know where objects are located in relation to the edge of the page.

Preview Fountain Steps

You want everything displayed on the screen with the maximum quality, but you also want it to get there as fast as possible. Gradient fills are one of the slowest fills to redraw. Their quality is controlled by the value in the Preview fountain steps box. The default in CorelDRAW 8 is the maximum value, 256 steps. Even at this maximum setting, the redraw speed is still much faster than in previous versions. However, if you want to speed it up even more, lower the setting to 50, which provides good quality, although it leaves gradient fills visibly banded.

40

> **NOTE:** *The value specified for the number of preview fountain steps is also used when you export to many different file formats. For the best exports, make sure to change this value to 256 before exporting. If you are converting to a bitmap, it is usually easier to just open a .cdr file in Corel PHOTO-PAINT, as the file will then always be created at the highest quality.*

EDIT

Click the word Edit under Workspace in the tree structure of the Options dialog box to get the dialog box shown in Figure 40-5.

Duplicate Placement

When you create a duplicate (CTRL-D) or a clone, it will be offset from the original object by the values you enter as the Horizontal and Vertical values. Many users like to change these values to 0 so that duplicates are placed

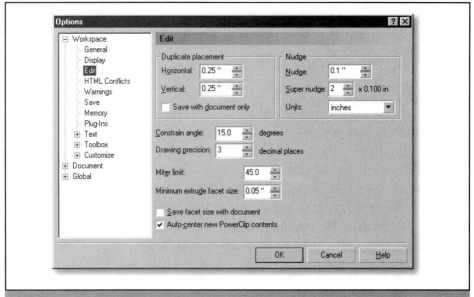

FIGURE 40-5   The Options Edit dialog box

directly on top of the original object. Remember that you can also quickly create a duplicate on top of the original object by pressing the + key on the numeric keypad. The values set here will not have an effect when the + key is used. Checking the Save with document only box will restrict this change to the current document only rather than changing all future documents.

Nudge

Nudging objects and nodes is a great way to get them exactly where you want them. The arrow keys on the keyboard will move an object by the amount specified here. Super nudge is the Nudge function on steroids. Hold down the SHIFT key when you click the arrow keys, and the nudge amount will be multiplied by the Super nudge value. This simple shortcut key provides an easy way to move objects by a small or a large amount. You can also select the type of Units you wish to use for your Nudge value. By default it is inches, but many users prefer to change it to another system of units.

Constrain Angle

As you work within CorelDRAW, you can use the CTRL key to constrain a number of functions. The angle used to constrain is a multiple of what is entered here. This value will affect rotating, skewing, adjusting control points, drawing straight lines, and adjusting fountain fills.

The default value of 15 degrees is sufficient for most users, but you may find that for a particular project, a different value works better.

Drawing Precision

CorelDRAW 6 and its 32-bit architecture achieved nearly unlimited precision. The level of precision also meant that every number was displayed with extra significant digits—which were usually zeros. The drawing precision is the maximum number of digits that will appear after a decimal point. The default is 3 and will be more than sufficient for most artists. Those who create technical drawings may wish to increase this value slightly, but the days of flaunting precision are over!

40

Note that trailing zeros are no longer displayed at any time. Only significant digits are displayed to the precision you specify. The number displayed will be rounded if significant digits are not displayed.

Miter Limit

The Miter limit value determines the angle size below which miter joints will not be created at the corners of objects. If you draw an object with angles below the specified limit, the joints will be beveled. This feature eliminates the problem of corner joints extending far beyond the actual corners at small angles.

Minimum Extrude Facet Size

When you are extruding objects, sometimes a series of objects will be created to simulate the shading necessary to make the object look realistic. The number of objects created is controlled by the Minimum extrude facet size value. The higher the value, the fewer the number of objects. For most uses, the default is just fine. Since this value will rarely need to be changed, you can select Save facet size with document to save the size with a particular document.

Auto-Center New PowerClip Contents

When you PowerClip an object inside of a container, you can check Auto-center new PowerClip contents to automatically center the object being PowerClipped within the container. This option is on by default. In most situations, you will find it easier to manually place the objects relative to one another, and therefore you'll want this option turned off.

HTML CONFLICTS

Select HTML Conflicts under Workspace in the tree structure of the Options dialog box to get the dialog box shown in Figure 40-6.

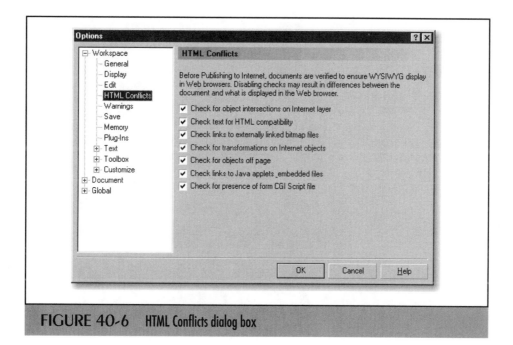

FIGURE 40-6   HTML Conflicts dialog box

When you are creating a file that will be exported to HTML, it is a great idea to check the document for objects that may cause a problem. You can do this with the HTML Object Conflict Docker. In the Options dialog box you specify the types of problems that you want to be found. Each of the warnings is fairly self-explanatory and should all be checked unless there is a specific option that you do not feel would cause a problem. The HTML Object Conflict Docker is discussed in Chapter 39.

WARNINGS

Select Warnings under Workspace in the tree structure of the Options dialog box to get the dialog box shown in Figure 40-7.

There are various functions in CorelDRAW that may not perform as you originally expected. For example, Texture Fills will only support RGB colors

40

Options

□ Workspace
　General
　Display
　Edit
　HTML Conflicts
　Warnings
　Save
　Memory
　Plug-Ins
　⊞ Text
　⊞ Toolbox
　⊞ Customize
⊞ Document
⊞ Global

Warnings

☑ Show Dialog when converting to CMYK
☑ Show Dialog when Spot Color Lens and/or Lens over Spot Color
☑ Show Dialog when texture fill is not RGB
☑ Show Dialog when converting to duotone
☑ Show Dialog when applying lens effects to duotones
☑ Show Dialog when distortion is too complex
☑ Show Dialog when replacing a softmask with a color mask
☑ Show Dialog when effects applied to text with embedded graphics
☑ Show Dialog when importing file into a document with facing pages

OK　　Cancel　　Help

FIGURE 40-7　Warnings dialog box

even though you can select colors in other models. These colors will then be converted back to RGB. Now there is a warning dialog box that will tell you that your colors will be converted. Here is an example of this warning:

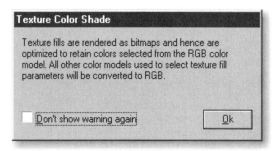

Texture Color Shade

Texture fills are rendered as bitmaps and hence are optimized to retain colors selected from the RGB color model. All other color models used to select texture fill parameters will be converted to RGB.

☐ Don't show warning again　　　　Ok

All of the other warnings are for problems that can affect you in a way that you might not expect. Unless there is a specific problem that does not concern you, you should leave them all checked.

SAVE

Select Save under Workspace in the tree structure of the Options dialog box to get the dialog box shown in Figure 40-8.

Auto-Backup

As a safety net, you can have the current file automatically back up your work at specified time intervals. By default, Auto-backup is set to 10 minutes. You should set this value according to the amount of work that you are willing to re-create should you lose your file. Remember that each time the file is backed up, the computer will take some time for saving, so you don't want to be interrupted too often. By default, your file is saved in the same folder as the .cdr file itself, but if you select Always back-up to and specify a folder, all files

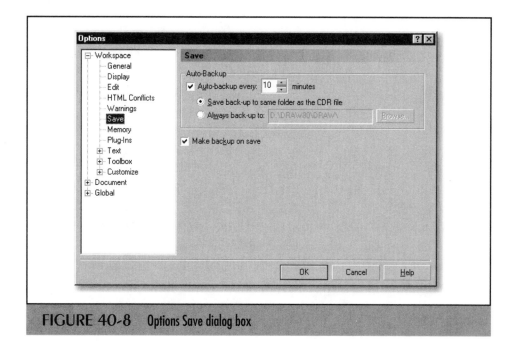

FIGURE 40-8   Options Save dialog box

will be sent to the folder you specify. To avoid auto-backup altogether, simply uncheck the Auto-backup check box.

Any file saved by the auto-backup feature will be clearly labeled as a file that has been automatically backed up. It will be labeled with the file name "Autobackup of *filename*" so you can easily find it. If you exit CorelDRAW gracefully (that is, the program doesn't crash), the file will be deleted. Therefore, the only time this file will remain is if you have run into a problem.

Make Backup on Save

As you save a file, you can have the previous version of the file saved with a .bak extension by checking the Make backup on save check box. This is yet another safety net so you don't lose any important data. Since this feature will keep two copies of files on your hard drive, you may want to turn it off. If you leave this option activated, you may want to clean up your files on a regular basis so your hard drive does not fill up.

MEMORY

Select Memory under Workspace in the tree structure of the Options dialog box to get the dialog box shown in Figure 40-9.

Swap Disks

In the Swap Disks section, you can specify a Primary disk and Secondary disk. Should CorelDRAW need more memory than you have in your system, it can use hard disk space as temporary memory. Most programs use the Windows swap file, but CorelDRAW uses its own file so that it doesn't overload the normal Windows swap file. From either drop-down list, select the drive where you wish the swap file to be placed. It will indicate to you how much space is free on that drive. If there isn't at least 100MB free, it is probably not a good idea to use that drive.

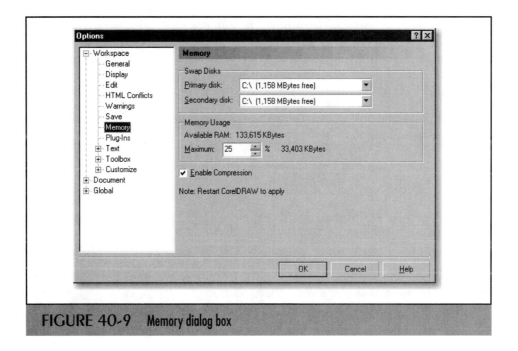

FIGURE 40-9   Memory dialog box

MEMORY USAGE

Memory usage will first report to you exactly how much RAM you have available to programs. You can specify a Maximum percentage of that memory that CorelDRAW can use. In Figure 40-9, we have specified 25%, which provides 33,403KB of memory on our system. If you have a high number of bitmap undos or plan to use a lot of bitmap effects, you should increase this to 50%.

COMPRESSION

Selecting the Enable Compression check box will automatically compress the bitmap data in the swap file. There is no advantage to turning this option off.

40

 *For the memory options to take effect, you have to restart CorelDRAW, as mentioned in the dialog box.*

PLUG-INS

Select Plug-Ins under Workspace in the tree structure of the Options dialog box to get the dialog box shown in Figure 40-10.

Plug-In Folders

You can now use PhotoShop-compatible plug-in filters within CorelDRAW. If you have purchased additional filters, you can add them to the Bitmaps menu in CorelDRAW by clicking the Add button and choosing the folder that contains the filters. Similarly, you can delete filters by selecting the appropriate folder in the list and clicking the Delete button.

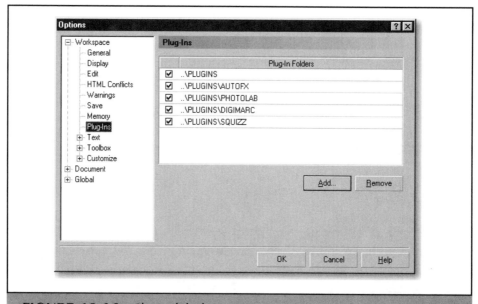

FIGURE 40-10   Plug-Ins dialog box

While most plug-ins will work fine within CorelDRAW, those that require a mask or layers will not work since CorelDRAW doesn't support those features.

TEXT

Select Text under Workspace in the tree structure of the Options dialog box to get the dialog box shown in Figure 40-11.

Edit Text on Screen

You can enter text in two different ways when you click the text cursor in the drawing window. By default, you can type the text directly in the drawing window, but if you deselect Edit text on screen, you'll immediately go to the Edit Text dialog box.

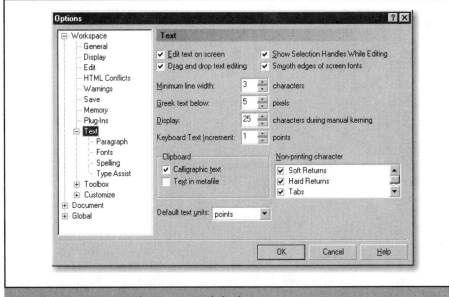

FIGURE 40-11   The Options Text dialog box

Drag and Drop Text Editing

When text is selected, you can drag it and drop it into a new location when editing text on the screen. This feature is supported only when Drag and drop text editing is checked. This feature can be very sensitive and therefore somewhat difficult to use. This means that you may occasionally move text that you didn't intend to move, and at other times you won't move the text that you do want to move.

Show Selection Handles While Editing

When you are editing text, you can choose to have the object handles and the X in the middle of the object continue to display after a brief pause in editing. By default the Show Selection Handles While Editing check box is checked. But if you find the handles distracting or unnecessary, you can deselect this option.

Smooth Edges of Screen Fonts

The ability to antialias the edges of fonts was added in CorelDRAW 7. Checking the Smooth edges of screen fonts check box will activate this feature. By default, it is checked. If your display uses less than 65,000 colors, you will not be able to use this feature.

Minimum Line Width

When working with small blocks of Paragraph Text, you may find it difficult to fit many text characters in the frame's width. The Minimum line width setting specifies the minimum number of characters allowed on a line.

Greek Text Below

When text becomes too small to accurately display on the screen, it is greeked. Greeked text appears as a gray line instead of as individual text characters.

The Greek text below value specifies the minimum number of pixels high that a character must be; otherwise, it will be greeked. Text that is greeked will display much faster than the text itself.

Display During Kerning

As you manually kern text, the screen will display the number of characters specified in the Display parameter box.

Keyboard Text Increment

The Keyboard Text Increment box lets you specify the amount of change in text when you use the CTRL-8 or CTRL-2 shortcut key. By default, this option is set to 1 point. Note that this does not affect the CTRL-4 and CTRL-6 shortcut keys, which select the next size in the font size drop-down list.

Clipboard

When you copy text to the clipboard, you can choose to have the text retain any calligraphic effects. You can also specify whether the metafile format retains the text as text or converts it to a graphic. By default, text is converted to a graphic.

Default Text Units

When working with text in CorelDRAW, the units used are points. You can change these units by selecting another unit from the Default text units drop-down list.

Nonprinting Characters

If you choose Text I Show Non-Printing Characters, the types of nonprinting characters checked here will be displayed. By default, all types of characters are selected.

40

PARAGRAPH

Select Paragraph under Text in the tree structure of the Options dialog box to get the dialog box shown in Figure 40-12.

SHOW LINKING OF TEXT FRAME

CorelDRAW 8 lets you see which text frames are linked to others. When one frame is selected, a small line will be shown between the frames. You will also see the page number if the linked frame is on a different page. Check Show linking of text frame to activate this feature. By default, it is checked.

SHOW TEXT FRAMES

By default, paragraph text frames are displayed on screen when you are editing the text within them. But if you deselect the Show text frames check box, you will only see the text.

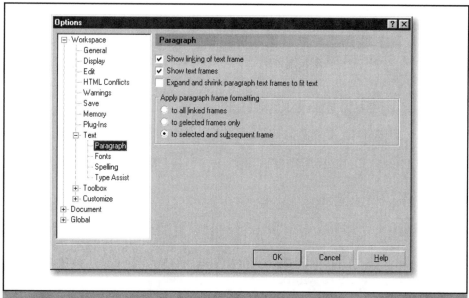

FIGURE 40-12 Options Paragraph dialog box

Expand and Shrink Paragraph Text Frames

As you are typing Paragraph Text on screen, the paragraph text frame can be automatically resized to fit the amount of text if you check Expand and shrink paragraph text frames to fit text.

Paragraph Frame Formatting

When you make changes to the formatting of a paragraph frame, such as in the number of columns, you can have the changes apply to all linked frames, to selected frames only, or to selected and subsequent frames.

FONT

Select Fonts under Text in the tree structure of the Options dialog box to get the dialog box shown in Figure 40-13.

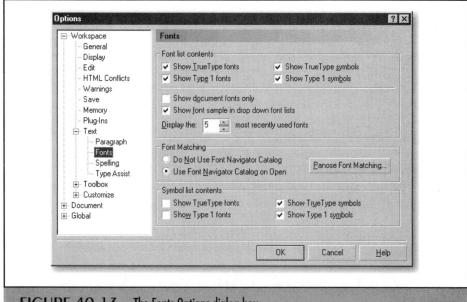

FIGURE 40-13   The Fonts Options dialog box

Font List Contents

Often, your font list may have extra fonts that you don't wish to have in the list. You can obviously uninstall those fonts, but if they all come from the same type of font, you can turn them off within CorelDRAW. You have the option of displaying TrueType or Type 1 fonts and symbols, so if you don't want to see symbol fonts, simply uncheck those options. If you work in a PostScript-only environment, turn off the display of TrueType fonts.

 *A quick way to change the fonts displayed is to right-click the Font drop-down list on the Property Bar.*

Show Document Fonts Only

Another way to really shorten the font list is to display only the fonts used within the current document. To activate this option, simply check Show document fonts only. Note that with this option activated, you will not be able to choose any new fonts.

Show Font Samples

As you scroll through the font list, a sample of the font will be shown. If you would rather not see this sample, uncheck Show font sample in drop down font lists. Having this feature turned on can slow down the display of the list.

Most Recently Used Fonts

The names of the fonts that you've used most recently appear at the top of the Font drop-down list. By default, the most recent 5 fonts are listed. You can change this value to display up to 20 font names.

Font Matching

CorelDRAW 8 includes the Font Navigator utility, which helps you to manage the fonts on your system. It is described in Chapter 38. CorelDRAW can include the fonts in the Font Navigator font catalog when opening files. Any needed fonts will be automatically installed if the Use Font Navigator Catalog on Open option is selected. If you would prefer for this not to affect opening files, select Do Not Use Font Navigator Catalog. The Panose Font Matching information is discussed in Chapter 38.

Symbol List Contents

Just as you can control which fonts appear in the drop-down list, you can control which types of fonts appear in the Symbols roll-up. By default, only symbol fonts in both formats are shown.

 *A quick way to change the symbol fonts that are displayed is to right-click the Symbols drop-down list.*

SPELLING

The Spelling options were discussed in Chapter 31.

TYPE ASSIST

Type Assist is a fantastic tool for helping to correct typographical errors. The Type Assist options are described in detail in Chapter 31.

TOOLBOX

When you select the plus sign next to Toolbox, CorelDRAW displays a list of the tools in the tree structure of the Options dialog box. Click the tool that you want to change, and the dialog box will show you all of the applicable options for that tool.

40

PICK TOOL

Select Pick Tool from the tree structure of the Options dialog box to get the dialog box shown in Figure 40-14.

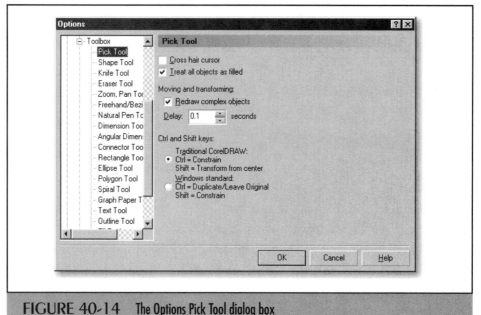

FIGURE 40-14   The Options Pick Tool dialog box

People used to using CAD programs may want to check the Cross hair cursor box to use this option. The small cursor will be replaced by a cursor with crosshairs that extend completely across the drawing window. By default, the crosshair cursor is turned off.

Selecting Treat all objects as filled allows you to select objects by clicking anywhere inside the object instead of just on the outline. This option is activated by default, unlike in some previous versions. If this option is checked, you may find it difficult to select an object behind the front object.

As you move or transform objects, you can display the changes by checking Redraw complex objects. The changes are displayed only when you stop moving your cursor for a period of time longer than that set in the Delay parameter box. By default, this option is turned on with a delay of 0.1 second.

Traditionally, the CTRL key has been used to constrain objects, and the SHIFT key to transform objects from the center. Now you have the option of using the Windows standard, where the CTRL key duplicates objects and the SHIFT key constrains objects. If you choose the Windows standard, the ALT key transforms objects from the center.

Note that if you are using CorelDRAW on a Macintosh, these keys work according the standard Macintosh conventions. The SHIFT key is used to constrain objects and the COMMAND key will transform objects from the center.

SHAPE TOOL

Select Shape Tool from the tree structure of the Options dialog box to get the dialog box shown in Figure 40-15.

When you are auto-reducing nodes, the number of nodes that are deleted is based on whether or not a node falls within the standard deviation from the line. This standard deviation is set in the Auto-reduce parameter box. The higher the number, the more nodes are removed. When more nodes are removed, however, the shape of the curve may be altered more than you like. You will find the default setting appropriate in almost all situations.

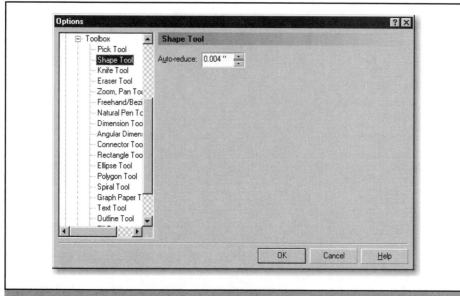

FIGURE 40-15 The Options Shape Tool dialog box

KNIFE TOOL

Select Knife Tool from the tree structure of the Options dialog box to get the dialog box shown in Figure 40-16.

You can select two options to be applied when you use the Knife tool to cut an object. You can leave the pieces combined into a single object by checking the Leave as one object check box. By default, the objects will not remain combined. Checking Automatically close object will automatically create a closed path from objects that have been cut using the Knife tool, so they can be filled. By default, the objects will be closed.

ERASER TOOL

Select Eraser Tool from the tree structure of the Options dialog box to get the dialog box shown in Figure 40-17.

The eraser thickness determines how much of an object is erased as you drag your cursor over it. By default, Thickness is set to 0.25 inch. You can

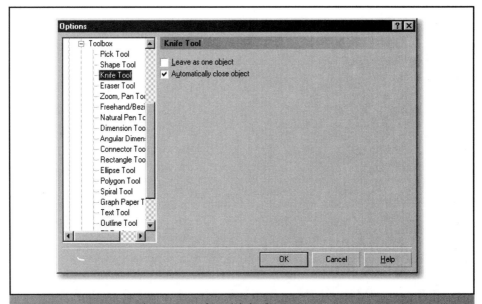

FIGURE 40-16   The Options Knife Tool dialog box

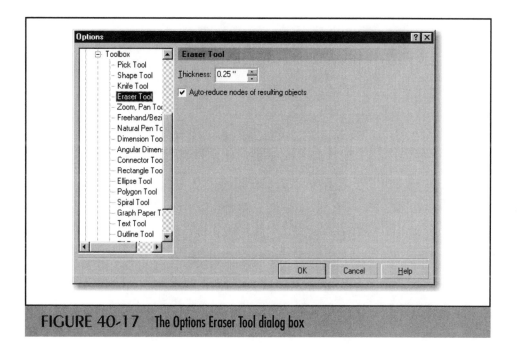

FIGURE 40-17   The Options Eraser Tool dialog box

choose to clean up the extra nodes when all erasing is finished by selecting Auto-reduce nodes of resulting objects. By default, this option is checked.

ZOOM AND PAN TOOLS

All of the options for the Zoom and Pan tools are described in Chapter 12.

FREEHAND AND BÉZIER TOOLS

Select Freehand/Bezier Tool from the tree structure of the Options dialog box to get the dialog box shown in Figure 40-18.

Freehand tracking determines how closely CorelDRAW tracks your freehand drawing when it calculates the nodes used in the object you are drawing. The lower the number, the higher the number of nodes that will be created as CorelDRAW tries to re-create the line to match your drawing as closely as possible. This number can be any value between 1 and 10, with the default being 5.

40

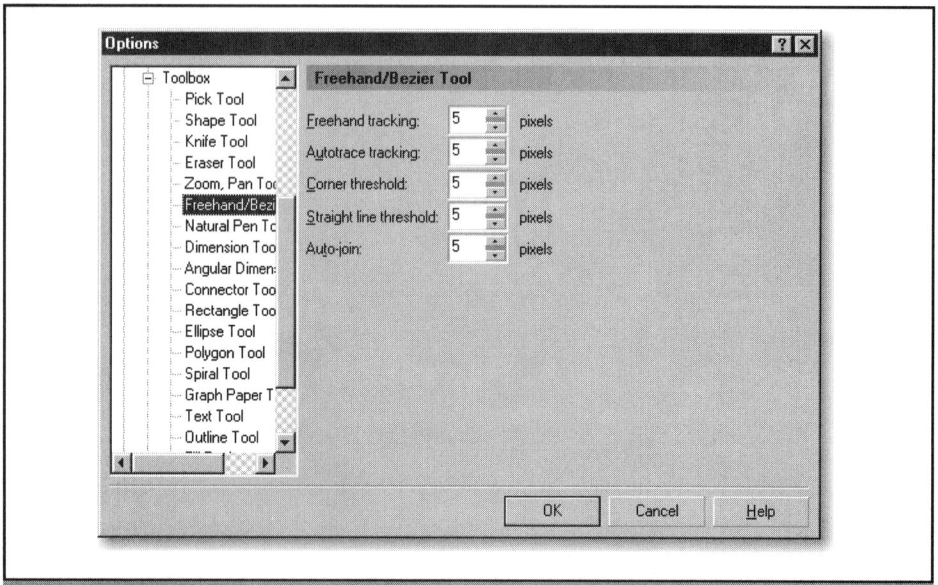

FIGURE 40-18   The Options Freehand/Beziér Tool dialog box

The Autotrace tracking option works much like Freehand tracking except that it is used when you use the Autotrace tool to trace bitmaps.

The Corner threshold option determines whether smooth nodes or cusps are used when you draw a freehand or autotraced line. Lower numbers produce more cusp nodes, and higher numbers produce more smooth nodes. This number can be any value between 1 and 10, with the default being 5.

The Straight line threshold option works similarly to the Corner threshold option. A smaller number produces more curve segments when you are drawing a line, and a larger number produces more straight-line segments.

The Auto-join option determines how close in pixels the two end nodes of an object must be before they are joined. If you enter a low number, you will have to be more accurate in your drawing.

NATURAL PEN TOOL

Select Natural Pen Tool from the tree structure of the Options dialog box to get the dialog box shown in Figure 40-19.

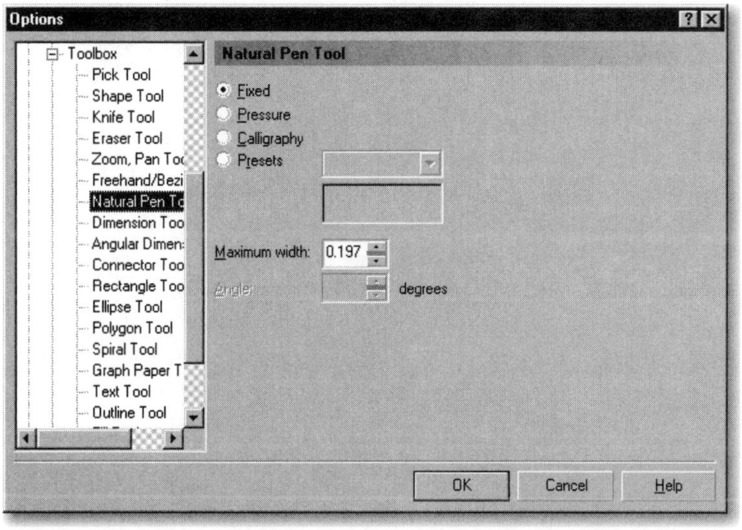

FIGURE 40-19   The Options Natural Pen Tool dialog box

The options specified for the Natural Pen tool are simply the default values that will be used when the Natural Pen tool is selected. These are the same options that appear on the Property Bar, as described in Chapter 5.

DIMENSION TOOL

Select Dimension Tool from the tree structure of the Options dialog box to get the dialog box shown in Figure 40-20.

Again, the values entered for the Dimension tool are simply the default values that will appear on the Property Bar when drawing dimension lines. All of the options for dimension lines are discussed in Chapter 5.

ANGULAR DIMENSION TOOL

Select Angular Dimension Tool from the tree structure of the Options dialog box to get the dialog box shown in Figure 40-21.

40

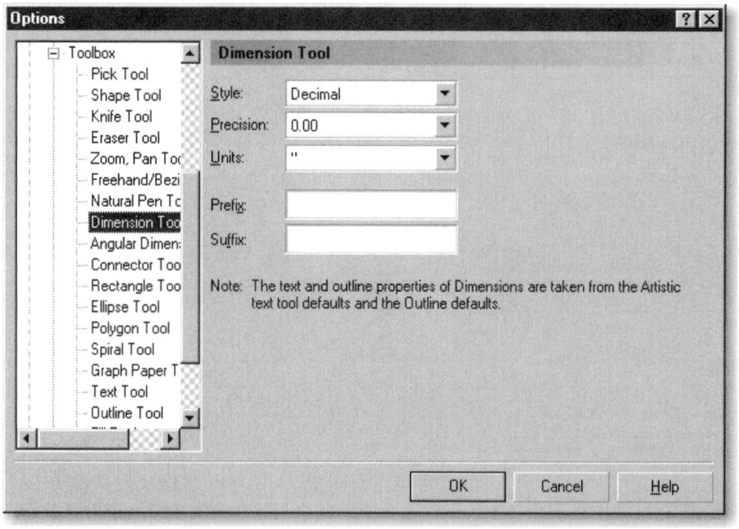

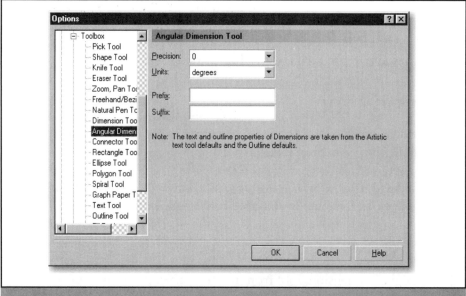

FIGURE 40-20   The Options Dimension Tool dialog box

FIGURE 40-21   The Options Angular Dimension Tool dialog box

Just as with the Dimension Tool, the values entered for the Angular Dimension tool are simply the default values that will appear on the Property Bar when drawing angular dimension lines. All of the options are discussed in Chapter 5.

CONNECTOR TOOL

Select Connector Tool from the tree structure of the Options dialog box to get the dialog box shown in Figure 40-22.

Connector lines can be set to either Snap to closest node or Lock to connector node. These defaults will be reflected in the Property Bar as you draw connector lines. All of the options for connector lines are discussed in Chapter 5.

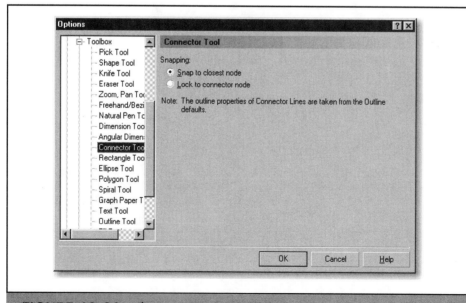

FIGURE 40-22   The Options Connector Tool dialog box

40

RECTANGLE TOOL

Select Rectangle Tool from the tree structure of the Options dialog box to get the dialog box shown in Figure 40-23.

Chapter 4 discussed the corner roundness for rectangles. The value set here will be the default roundness for any new rectangles. By default, the roundness is zero—that is, the corners of rectangles will not be rounded at all.

ELLIPSE TOOL

Select Ellipse Tool from the tree structure of the Options dialog box to get the dialog box shown in Figure 40-24.

The options shown for the Ellipse tool were discussed in Chapter 4. The values set here will be the defaults for any new ellipses you draw.

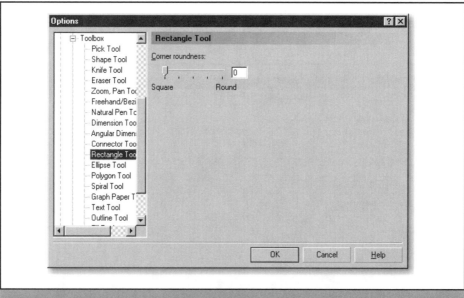

FIGURE 40-23   The Options Rectangle Tool dialog box

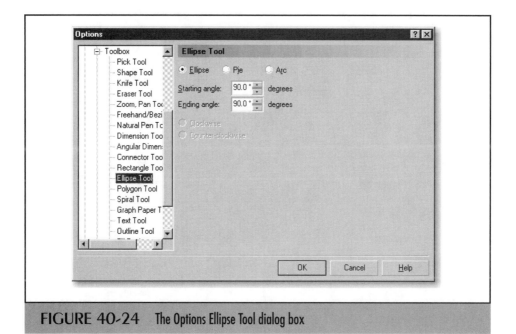

FIGURE 40-24   The Options Ellipse Tool dialog box

POLYGON TOOL

Select Polygon Tool from the tree structure of the Options dialog box to get the dialog box shown in Figure 40-25.

The options shown for the Polygon tool were discussed in Chapter 4. The values set here will be the defaults for any new polygons you draw.

SPIRAL TOOL

Select Spiral Tool from the tree structure of the Options dialog box to get the dialog box shown in Figure 40-26.

The options shown for the Spiral tool were discussed in Chapter 4. The values set here will be the defaults for any new spirals you draw.

40

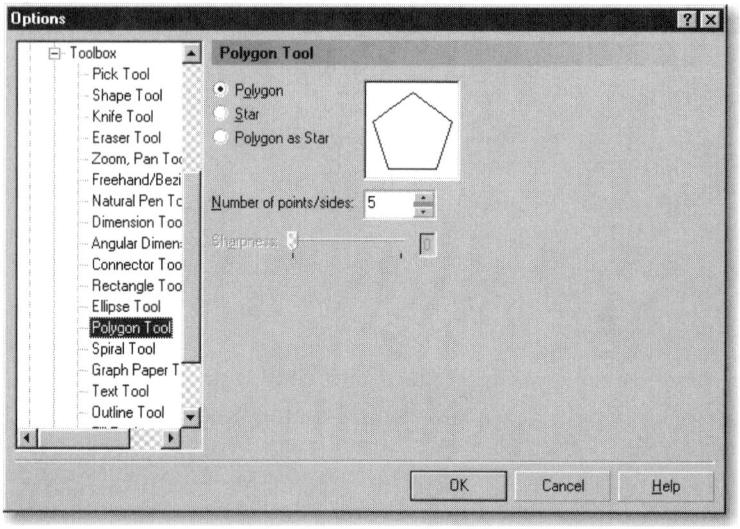

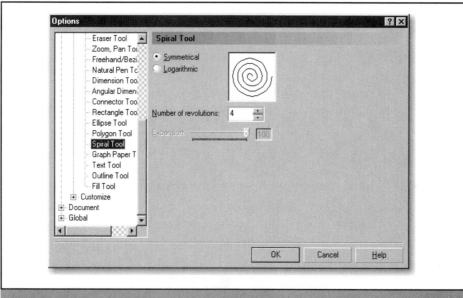

FIGURE 40-25   The Options Polygon Tool dialog box

FIGURE 40-26   The Options Spiral Tool dialog box

GRAPH PAPER TOOL

Select Graph Paper Tool from the tree structure of the Options dialog box to get the dialog box shown in Figure 40-27.

The options shown for the Graph Paper tool were discussed in Chapter 4. The values set here will be the defaults for any new graph paper you draw.

TEXT TOOL, OUTLINE TOOL, AND FILL TOOL

Select Text Tool from the tree structure of the Options dialog box to get the dialog box shown in Figure 40-28. Similar dialog boxes are shown if you select Outline Tool and Fill Tool.

Each of these dialogs contains a Goto button that will take you to the Tools | Options | Document | Styles dialog box discussed later in this chapter.

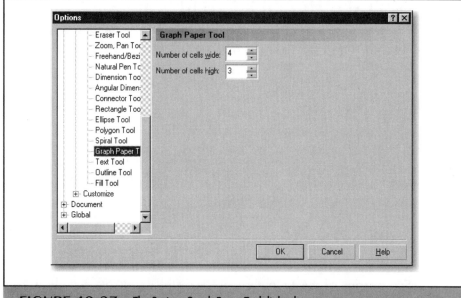

FIGURE 40-27   The Options Graph Paper Tool dialog box

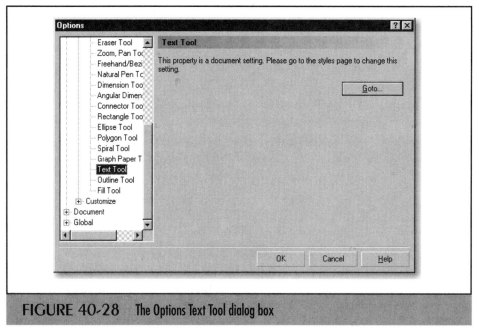

FIGURE 40-28　The Options Text Tool dialog box

CUSTOMIZING THE USER INTERFACE

CorelDRAW 6 ushered in a new era of customizability for Corel products. No longer are you forced to use only the tools in the format given to you. Now you can rearrange your toolbars, menus, and keystrokes and even write macros so you can work as productively as possible. CorelDRAW 8 takes customization even further.

When you select the plus sign next to Customize, you'll see a list of the available toolbars, as shown in Figure 40-29.

The toolbars with a check mark are currently displayed. You can easily display other toolbars or turn off one that is currently displayed by clicking its check box. To reset any of the toolbars to their default state, simply click the name of the toolbar in the list and then click the Reset button. You can create new toolbars by clicking the New button. This will add a new toolbar to the list and immediately highlight the name so that you can rename it by typing the new name.

In the Size portion of the dialog box are two slider controls that allow you to choose the size of the buttons that appear on the toolbars and the size of

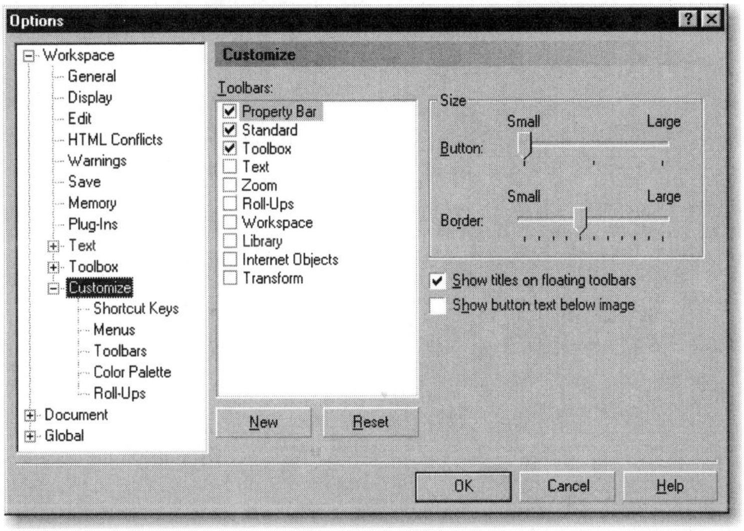

FIGURE 40-29 The Options Customize dialog box

the border surrounding the toolbars. If you enlarge the buttons, the toolbar may not be completely displayed on your screen. The border can be important because you can right-click it to access the list of toolbars without reentering this dialog box, but if you want to save space, feel free to make the borders smaller.

Last, you can choose whether to use the Show titles on floating toolbars option. By default, any toolbar that is not docked will have a title bar just like a normal dialog box, but since this takes up more room, you can turn this option off. Another option allows each button to have text below it so that it is easier to understand. To add this text, select Show button text below image. Note that this option does take up much more room than toolbars that show only the icons.

SHORTCUT KEYS

It seems that each new version of CorelDRAW uses different keyboard shortcuts. Relearning all new keystrokes with each new version can be

40

frustrating. However, now you can customize the shortcut keys to be anything you like. Select Shortcut Keys from the tree structure of the Options dialog box to get the dialog box shown in Figure 40-30.

On the left side of the screen is a list of all of the available commands, grouped into folders based on their functionality. Work your way through the command tree until you find a command you wish to change. When the command is selected, the Current shortcut keys window will display the shortcut, if any, that is currently assigned to that command.

To enter a new shortcut, place your cursor in the Press new shortcut key box and type the new keystrokes. When you've done this, the Assign button will become available. Click Assign to assign the new shortcut. If a conflicting shortcut exists, it will be listed. If you check the Navigate to conflict on assign check box, you'll automatically be sent to the conflicting command immediately after you click the Assign button. You can also select Delete conflicting shortcut if you want it removed.

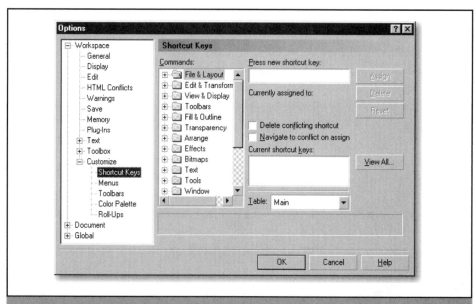

FIGURE 40-30   The Options Shortcut Keys dialog box

To see a list of all of the keyboard shortcuts, click the Vіew All button. The following dialog box will appear.

You can either look through the list of keystrokes on the screen, print it for future reference, or export it to an ASCII text file.

Since it is quite easy to make these changes, CorelDRAW also provides a way to get back where you started just in case you really mess things up. Click the Reset button to return the keyboard shortcuts to their default settings.

 At the bottom of the dialog box is a Table drop-down list. This list allows you to also change the Text Editing shortcut keys if you like.

MENUS

Select Menus from the tree structure of the Options dialog box to get the dialog box shown in Figure 40-31.

The left window displays a list of all the commands that can be included on a menu, grouped by the category of command. The figure shows the commands in the Arrange category. The right window shows the commands that are currently included in the drop-down menu. To add your own commands, simply click the command you want in the left window and then

40

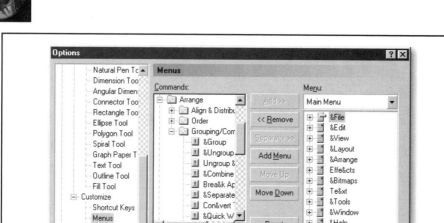

FIGURE 40-31　The Options Menus dialog box

click the Add button. To place the command where you want it, select the command you want it to appear below before clicking Add. If you happen to miss, the Move Up and Move Down buttons can help you to move the command into place.

You can add or remove separators as well. These are the little lines that appear in the drop-down menu to separate logically grouped commands.

One of the neatest uses of customization is to create your own menu for storing your favorite commands. The only problem with this is that your menu is on only your own computer, so using someone else's computer can get confusing! Don't forget that the Reset button will set everything back to the defaults if things get too crazy.

The drop-down list in the upper-right corner of the dialog box allows you to select the various pop-up menus within CorelDRAW. So you can customize them as well in the manner just above.

TOOLBARS

Earlier you saw how to select the toolbars that appear on the screen. You can also customize their contents so they contain only the buttons you want. There are many buttons that you may not use since they have easy shortcut keys. Other commands are strangely absent, and a button for these would be great.

Select Toolbars from the tree structure of the Options dialog box to get the dialog box shown in Figure 40-32. If the toolbar contains buttons that you don't want, drag them from the toolbar into the Options dialog box. They'll no longer be part of the toolbar.

To add buttons, you need to first select the category that you want from the categories list. As you select a command, the right side of the dialog box will display all of the available buttons for that category. If you click any of the buttons, a description of its functionality will be displayed at the bottom of the dialog box.

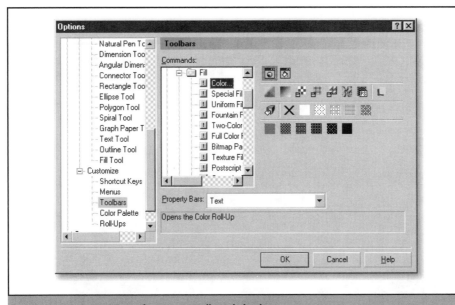

FIGURE 40-32   The Options Toolbars dialog box

Placing a button on a toolbar is as simple as dragging the button onto the toolbar you desire. If you don't drop it on a particular toolbar, CorelDRAW will create a new toolbar. You can even add buttons to a particular Property Bar. At the lower-left corner of the dialog box is the Property Bars drop-down list. Select the Property Bar to which you want to add a button, and the Property Bar on the main screen will change accordingly. Now just drag the desired button onto the Property Bar.

COLOR PALETTE

Select Color Palette from the tree structure of the Options dialog box to get the dialog box shown in Figure 40-33.

Selecting Wide Borders will leave a small amount of gray space between each color swatch on the palette. If you deselect this option, the colors are all placed next to one another so that you can fit more colors in one row. The Large swatches check box controls the size of each color swatch in the palette. By default, it is not selected so that the color wells are considered "small."

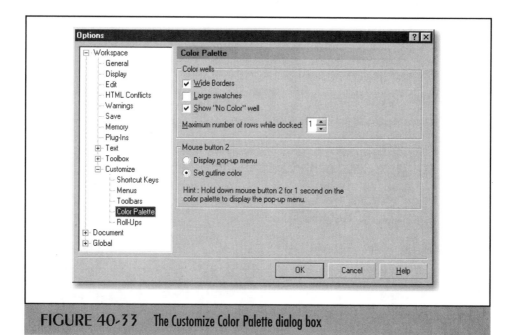

FIGURE 40-33   The Customize Color Palette dialog box

The Show "No Color" well option is one that creates a lot of confusion. The No Color well is the box with the X in it that signifies that you want to remove the color from a fill or outline. We sure couldn't imagine working without it, as it is used quite often. The Maximum number of rows while docked num box allows you to choose the number of rows of swatches that will be shown when the palette is docked. You may want to increase this number to show more colors on the screen.

You probably know that you can right-click the palette to set the outline color. You can change this so that right-clicking instead displays a pop-up menu. If you leave the right mouse button set to Set outline color, you can hold the button down for a second or two to display the pop-up menu. This gives you the best of both options.

ROLL-UPS

Select Roll-Ups from the tree structure of the Options dialog box to get the dialog box shown in Figure 40-34.

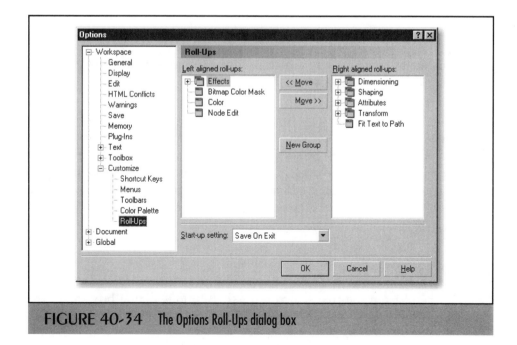

FIGURE 40-34 The Options Roll-Ups dialog box

The roll-ups listed in the left window will appear at the upper-left portion of your screen when they are rolled up, and those in the right window will roll up in the upper-right area of your screen. The grouping of the roll-ups is shown much like the directory structure in the Windows Explorer. You can drag and drop the name of a roll-up into another group, but this is easier to do with the roll-ups on the screen. You can also rename the groups by clicking twice (not double-clicking) on the name and typing a new name. To ungroup roll-ups, simply drag the name of the roll-up out onto the desktop. Grouping roll-ups is almost as easy. Select the roll-up you wish to add to a group, hold down the CTRL key, and drag the roll-up onto the group to which you want it added.

The Start-up setting drop-down list provides three options for working with roll-ups. Save On Exit will save the location of roll-ups so that the next time you start CorelDRAW, they will appear just as when you exited. No Roll-Ups will always start CorelDRAW with no roll-ups on the screen, and All Roll-Ups Arranged will display all the roll-ups rolled up.

Roll-ups is the last section included in the Workspace category. This means that any options discussed up to now can be saved as part of your workspace and shared with other users.

DOCUMENT

Select Document from the tree structure of the Options dialog box to get the dialog box shown in Figure 40-35.

The first checkbox asks if you want to Save options as defaults for new documents. When it is checked, the other options become available. Each of the options underneath Document in the tree structure within the dialog box is also repeated with check boxes. You are asked whether the changes you make in the other dialog boxes will apply to just the current document or to any new documents. Place a check mark in all categories that you wish to be defaults. Only those options set prior to entering the Options dialog box will be saved.

GENERAL

Select General from the tree structure of the Options dialog box to get the dialog box shown in Figure 40-36.

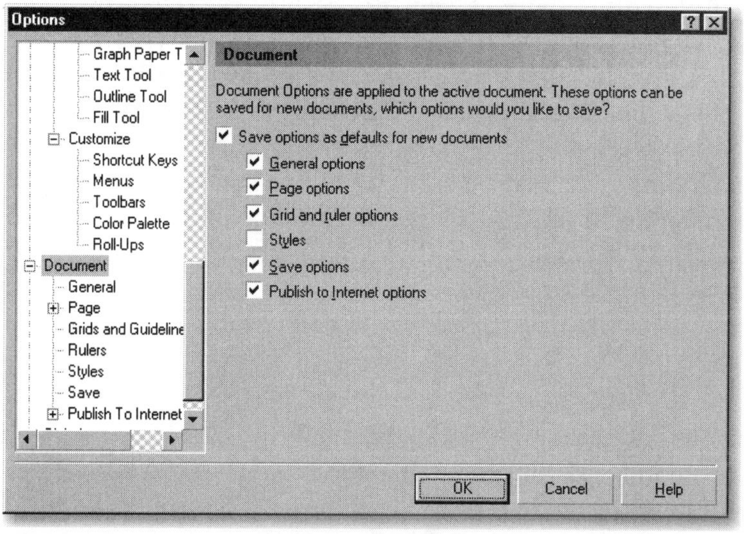

FIGURE 40-35   The Options Document dialog box

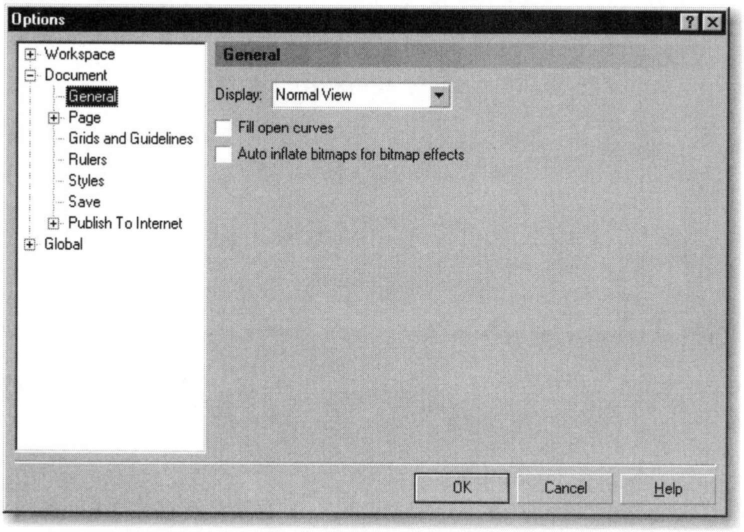

FIGURE 40-36   The Options General dialog box

The Display drop-down list includes each of the five display modes that were described in Chapter 12. Select the view that you wish to be the default. Initially, it is set to Normal View. A new option in CorelDRAW 8 is the ability to fill a curve that is not closed. By default, CorelDRAW 8 works just as previous versions. But by selecting Fill open curves you can change this behavior. Another new feature is the ability to increase the size of a bitmap when an effect needs to have a larger area than you currently have. If Auto inflate bitmap for bitmap effects is checked, you can increase the bitmaps in size as needed.

PAGE

All of the options in the Page dialog box and the subsections of Size, Layout, and Background are described in Chapter 28.

GRIDS AND GUIDELINES AND RULERS

All of the options in the Grids and Guidelines dialog box as well as the Rulers dialog box are described in Chapter 14.

STYLES

All of the options in the Styles dialog box are described in Chapter 33.

SAVE

All of the options in the Save dialog box are described in Chapter 27.

PUBLISH TO INTERNET

All of the options in the Publish to Internet dialog box and the subsections of Image, Text, and Links are described in Chapter 39.

GLOBAL

The options you select in the Global section of Options will affect not only CorelDRAW, but PHOTO-PAINT as well.

COLOR MANAGEMENT

All of the options in the Color Management dialog box and the subsections of General and Profiles are described in Chapter 24.

PRINTING DEFAULTS

Select Printing Defaults from the tree structure of the Options dialog box to get the dialog box shown in Figure 40-37.

The Print Preview mode drop-down list allows you select whether the preview is the Normal preview or Bounding box only. Normal will display the objects as they are drawn and is the default selection. But if you choose Bounding box only, you'll be presented with a gray box filled with a large X when you select Print Preview. Obviously this displays much quicker than the Normal setting.

Chapter 29 discusses the process of saving and using print styles. Here you can select which of all of the saved print styles will be used by default. Lastly, there is a check box for Print only current page by default. Normally, you'll

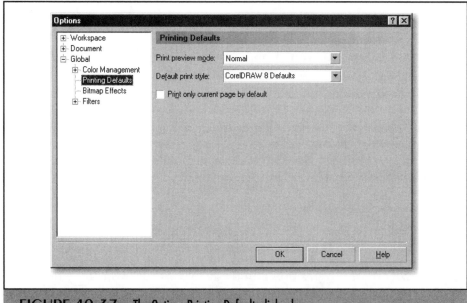

FIGURE 40-37   The Options Printing Defaults dialog box

40

want to print all of the pages in the document, but this check box will change
the default to only the current page.

BITMAP EFFECTS

All of the options in the Bitmap Effects dialog box are described in Chapter 23.

FILTERS

When you first installed CorelDRAW, you were asked which filters you
wanted to install. At the time, that list may have seemed mind boggling. You
may have just moved on because it was too confusing, or you may have
selected only a few filters to conserve hard drive space.

With earlier versions of CorelDRAW, you needed to reinstall the program
to change the filters installation, and if you didn't like their order in the
Open/Import or Export dialog box, you were forced to carefully edit an .ini
file. Now managing the filters is quite easy.

Select Filters from the tree structure of the Options dialog box to get the
dialog box shown in Figure 40-38.

Adding and Deleting Filters

When Filters is selected, you're presented with two lists of filters. The left
window shows all of the possible filters that can be installed. The right window
shows the filters that are currently installed, listed in the order in which they
appear in the Open/Import dialog box. Available filters are divided into the
categories Raster, Vector, Text, and Animation. Click the + sign next to any
category to expand the list. If the list is already expanded, click the - sign to
compress the list.

If you want to add a filter, find it in the list in the left window and select
it. Click the Add button in the middle of the dialog box, and the filter will
now appear in the list of active filters. Deleting filters is just as easy. Select the
filter in the left window and click the Remove button.

To reorder the filters, select a particular filter and use the Move Up and
Move Down buttons to position it in the list. The order you see in the list of
active filters is the order used in the Open/Import and Export dialog boxes.
Most people use only five to ten filters on a regular basis, so moving those

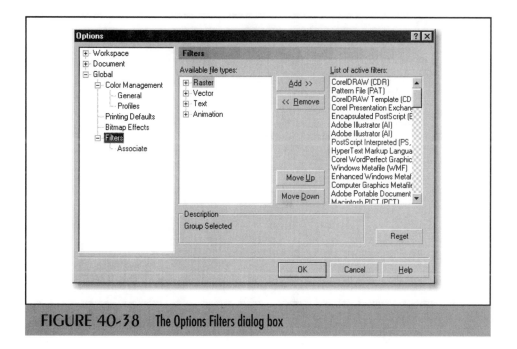

FIGURE 40-38 The Options Filters dialog box

you commonly use to the top of the list will save you the trouble of always scrolling through the list to find the filter you need.

With all of the customization features available, you can occasionally back yourself into a corner. Clicking the Reset button will put all of the filters back into the default configuration, so if you ever feel that you've messed up the filters beyond repair, just click Reset and start all over.

ASSOCIATE

Select Associate from the tree structure of the Options dialog box to get the dialog box shown in Figure 40-39.

When you view files in Explorer, each file is associated with a particular program. Sometimes, you don't want that association in effect for a particular file format, and other times you'll want to associate a file format with CorelDRAW. Here you can specify which formats are associated with CorelDRAW.

The file formats are listed in alphabetical order. To the left of the file format is a check box. Any format that is checked will be associated with CorelDRAW

40

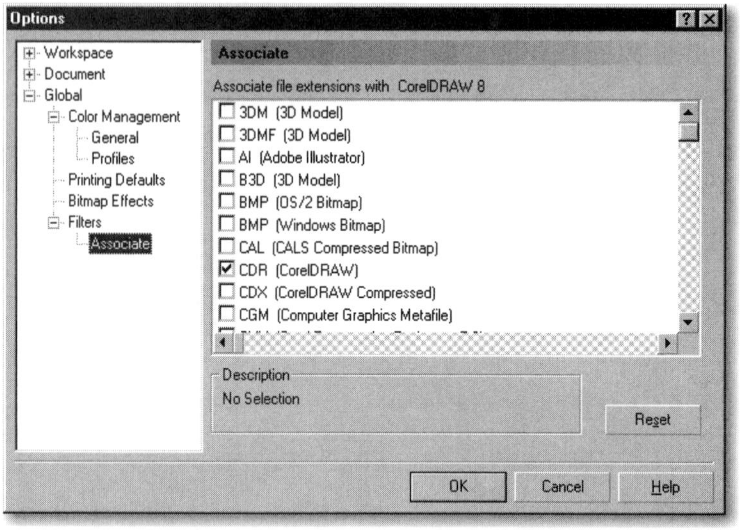

FIGURE 40-39 The Options Associate dialog box

8. You may want to add the formats that you use most often, but remember that any formats that are associated with CorelDRAW can't be associated with anything else. For example, you may use .tif files quite a bit and want them associated with CorelDRAW, but wouldn't you rather have them associated with Corel PHOTO-PAINT? The nice thing is that if you make a mistake, you can easily change the associations, which wasn't true in past versions.

MODIFYING THE SCREEN

When you first start CorelDRAW 8, you'll see a screen similar to the one shown in Figure 40-40. The Standard toolbar is along the top of the screen, with the Property Bar just below it. At the bottom of the screen is the Status Bar, which in CorelDRAW 8 defaults to only one line of information. The toolbox is docked along the left edge of the screen, and the palette is docked along the right side.

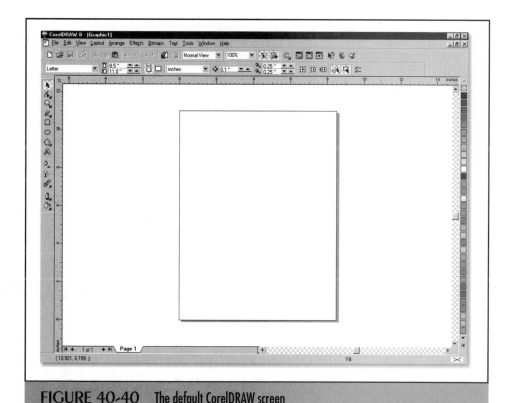

FIGURE 40-40   The default CorelDRAW screen

After making a series of changes, you can end up with a screen similar to that shown in Figure 40-41.

Right-click the Status Bar and choose Position | Top from the pop-up menu that appears. The Status Bar is extremely important in helping you use CorelDRAW, and it should be at the top where your eyes will focus on it more readily. Earlier versions placed it there, but pressure from Microsoft moved it to the bottom in later versions. Once you have the Status Bar at the top of the screen, move your cursor to the bottom edge until a double-headed arrow appears. Drag downward until the Status Bar expands to its full height of two lines.

Left-click the gray area around the Standard toolbar and drag this toolbar to the right side of the screen. It will automatically dock itself into place. Since

40

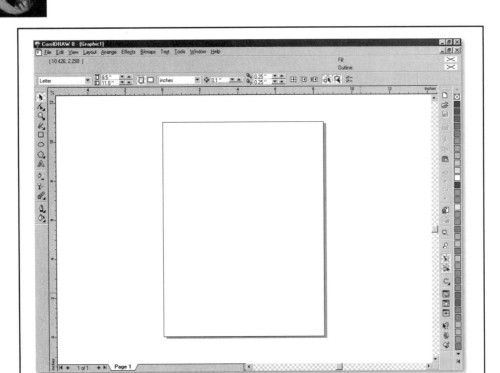

FIGURE 40-41 The CorelDRAW screen after several modifications

you'll most often have more extra space on the left and right sides of the screen, you may as well take advantage of it.

You may want to customize CorelDRAW even more by adding more toolbars or buttons, changing the menu structure, and even adding some custom keystrokes. What about changing the shortcut keys so they are the same as another of your favorite applications? You can do all of this by using the Customize options described earlier in this chapter.

AUTOMATION OF CORELDRAW

everal releases back, Corel added presets to CorelDRAW. Then CorelDRAW 6 brought scripts. Presets were easy, but very limited. Scripts could do lots of things, but you needed to be a programmer to write them. Now these features have been rolled together to provide a lot of power, and creating a script is now easy for all users. It's as simple as using your VCR, and certainly not as difficult as setting its clock!

USING SCRIPTS

To work with scripts, you'll need to get the Script and Preset Manager Docker onscreen. To do this, select Tools | Scripts | Script and Preset Manager. Initially, it will be displayed as a Docker. We've undocked it so that it takes up a little less room. You'll see two folders in the window, as shown next. One of them contains the presets that were included with CorelDRAW 6. The other contains the scripts that have been included with CorelDRAW 8. Note that the presets are scripts in this release; they are kept separate only for purposes of clarification.

Some of the scripts and presets require that an object be selected onscreen. Others require nothing at all. If something is required, you will receive an error message telling what you need to do to continue.

Just to get an idea of how scripts work, let's run one of the sample scripts.

1. Double-click the Scripts folder so you can see each of the scripts that are supplied with CorelDRAW 8.

2. Select the script called "Calendar" by clicking on it.

3. To run the script, double-click it or press the Play button (the rightward-pointing arrow).

This particular script is actually a wizard for creating a calendar, so once it starts, you'll see the dialog box shown in Figure 41-1.

The first screen doesn't really do anything. Click Next and you'll see the dialog box shown in Figure 41-2.

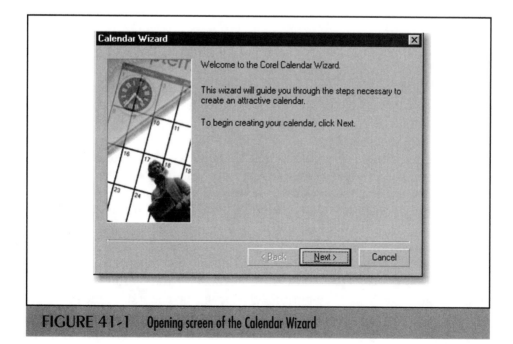

FIGURE 41-1   Opening screen of the Calendar Wizard

41

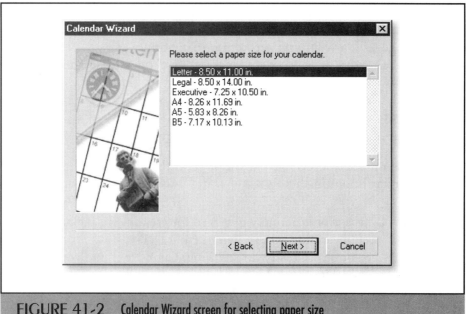

FIGURE 41-2   Calendar Wizard screen for selecting paper size

Now you are asked which paper size you wish to use for creating your new calendar. The list is very limited by comparison with the list that CorelDRAW provides, but you can always select another size later. So select a size and click Next to get the dialog box for selecting page orientation. You can choose either Portrait or Landscape. Once you've made your selection, click Next to get to the dialog box shown in Figure 41-3.

You can select three calendar styles. The Standard calendar puts the month and year at the top. Other choices allow you to place that information on the left or right side instead. Once you've made your selection, click Next. You'll now be asked if you wish to choose a font. This will bring up a common dialog box for font selection. When you've chosen a font, click Next to get to the dialog box shown in Figure 41-4.

There are two checkboxes here that will enable you to add either a picture or a border to the calendar. Click the checkbox for the option you want, if any, then press the Select File button. This brings up a standard file selection dialog box. Find the image you want and press OK. As the wizard informs you, it is probably not a good idea to add both a picture and a border, because

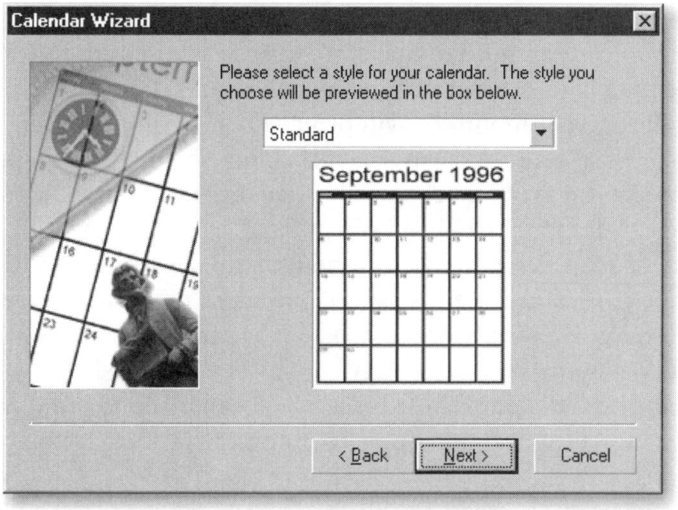

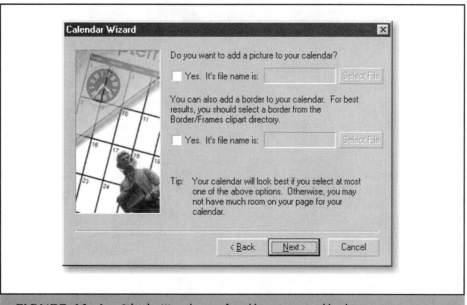

FIGURE 41-3   Calendar Wizard screen for selecting a style

FIGURE 41-4   Calendar Wizard screen for adding pictures and borders

41

there will be little room left for the calendar. When you've finished, click Next to get to the dialog box shown in Figure 41-5.

The last choices you need to make are the starting month for the calendar you are creating and the total number of months you need. The default selection is the current month (it will print only that month). But if you need a whole year, just select 12 months. Then click Finish and relax while the script goes to work creating your calendar. This may take a few minutes, depending on the speed of your machine. Just keep in mind how long it would have taken you to create it from scratch. The finished calendar is shown in Figure 41-6.

The script you've just seen is one of the most powerful scripts included with CorelDRAW 8. With CorelSCRIPT, you can automate just about any feature that is included in CorelDRAW or Corel PHOTO-PAINT. Creating a script such as the Calendar Wizard is a lot of work and is not a task for the average user. However, it is quite easy to automate tasks that you perform on a regular basis.

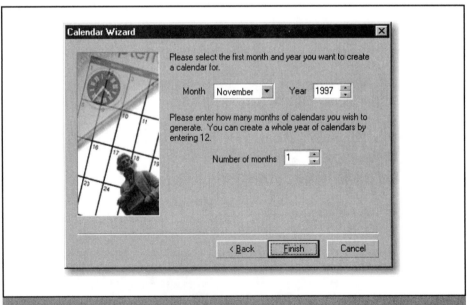

FIGURE 41-5   Calendar Wizard month selection screen

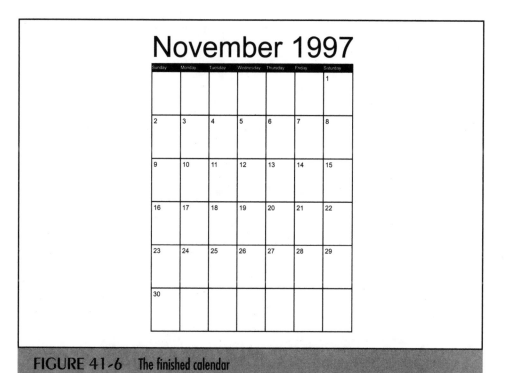

FIGURE 41-6   The finished calendar

RECORDING SCRIPTS

You've seen how to play back a script that has been already created. Now let's create a simple Drop Shadow script of our own so you'll see how easy it can be to create your own scripts.

1. Start with a large piece of Artistic Text.

2. With the text selected, click the red Record button at the bottom of the Script and Preset Manager window. (It's the one on the far right.)

3. Make a duplicate of the text with the CTRL-D shortcut key combination.

4. Color the new text black or whatever color you want for the shadow.

41

5. Select Arrange | Order | To Back and the new copy of the text will be placed in the back.

6. Use the Nudge arrows to move the shadow to exactly the place where you want it to be.

7. Click the Stop button. (The square one in the middle.)

You'll now be presented with the Save Recording dialog box shown here:

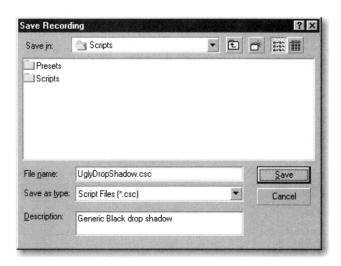

8. Give the new script a File name and a Description, then click Save.

The script you've just created should now be shown in the Script and Preset Manager window. Note that you may need to click the yellow folder button at the top of the window to back up one level. Play it back on another object if you like. This script is certainly not as elaborate as the Drop Shadow effect that comes with CorelDRAW, but you can see how easy it is to automate a task you perform quite often. All you have to do is perform the task manually once and it will then be recorded for future use.

Not all commands are supported by the scripting language. Two notable exceptions are moving the center of rotation and pasting from the clipboard.

EDITING SCRIPTS

So far, you've seen the kind of scripting that any user of CorelDRAW can work with. But those of you who wish to take scripting to another level can make some major modifications. Just be aware that these advanced scripting techniques may get your hands a little bit dirty!

Select Tools | Scripts | Corel Script Editor and you'll be presented with the Corel SCRIPT Editor program shown here:

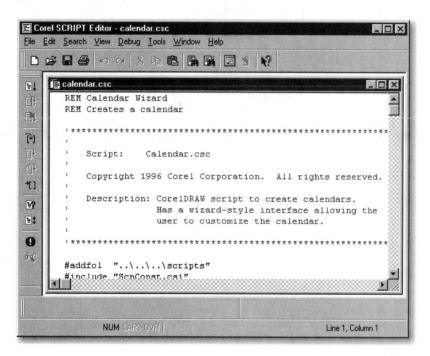

The Script Editor is used to work with the programming code directly and isn't nearly as friendly as the recording functions built into CorelDRAW. It is to be used for modifying the scripts you've recorded or to write a new script from scratch using the scripting language. The syntax used is very similar to that of Microsoft's Visual Basic.

This is a full-blown programming language, and we can't give full coverage to the programming aspects in this book, but every command, along with its syntax is described fully in the Help files. Another way to learn how the

41

commands work is to record the activities you wish to script and look at what the recorder creates for you.

When you've finished with your script, you'll notice several options in the File menu for creating .exe, .dll, .cao, and .csb files. These features give you a way to compile your script so that the code can be protected. To learn more about writing scripts, we strongly suggest that you study the Help files.

CREATING AN INTERFACE

If you really want to dress up your scripts, you can create dialog boxes to gather user input. To do this, we suggest you use the Dialog Editor. In CorelDRAW 6, it was a separate program, but now it is built into the Script Editor. Select Tools | Dialog (F2) to get to the Dialog Editor. The toolbar will change to give you the tools you need to draw various elements of the dialog box. You'll also see that a new window has opened to show you the dialog box you are designing, as shown below.

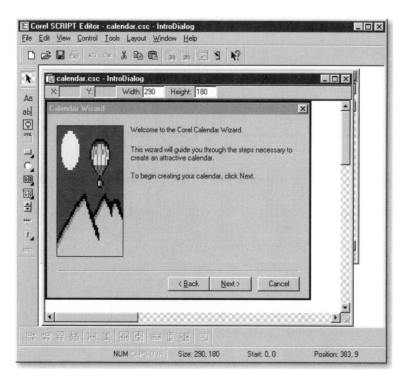

When you close the dialog window, you'll see that the programming code that describes the dialog box has been entered into your script. To make further changes, select Tools | Dialog with your cursor somewhere in the code that creates the dialog box.

To learn more about creating dialog boxes, we again suggest that you consult the Help files that accompany the program. They explain each of the tools and how best to use them.

In this chapter, you saw how you can automate your use of CorelDRAW. In some cases, a feature is provided to you as a script rather than an extra menu command or dialog box. You'll also find that third parties provide scripts that can further extend the capabilities of CorelDRAW.

If you've made it this far, you should be an expert at using CorelDRAW. We've covered most of the features within the program. And, while we feel that we've covered all of them, we don't assume that nothing has been overlooked along the way. Check the Help files to get information on anything that we may have missed or that was added in a maintenance release. If you're still having trouble, let us know and we'll see if we can help. We'll also regularly post updates on our Web page, so come and visit http://www.unleash.com. Happy drawing!

41

PART
6

APPENDICES

A

THIRD-PARTY RESOURCES

The uses of CorelDRAW are nearly endless, and a large number of companies make products to extend your use of CorelDRAW and Corel PHOTO-PAINT. Because many of these companies are small and hard to find, we've compiled a list of products and companies that we feel are useful to the CorelDRAW and Corel PHOTO-PAINT user.

The good news is that the list is very complete, but the bad news is that it takes many pages to print, and so we couldn't include the list in this book. Instead, we've made this information available on our Web site for downloading—so point your browser at **http://www.unleash.com** and enjoy the list!

Another benefit of keeping this list on our Web page is that we can update the contents on a regular basis, so if you know of a company or product that you feel would be of interest to other users, please let us know and we'll be glad to include it in the next Web site update.

B

PRODUCTION NOTES

This is the fifth CorelDRAW book we've authored, and we can happily say that this is the second book produced entirely on a PC.

We captured screens with Corel CAPTURE. These images were edited quite often utilizing Corel PHOTO-PAINT 7 or 8. This editing mainly consisted of cropping out an item or highlighting it with a filter. If you do notice a difference between the screens in the book and those on your system, it may be that the dialog box has changed since the previous release. Scanning was done using a Hewlett-Packard IIc and 4c.

The layout of the book was created in Corel VENTURA 7. The color pages were all created in CorelDRAW directly, with the most fantastic artwork being taken from winners of Corel's World Design Contest. We've credited the artist on images that were not created by the authors.

The fonts used in this book are Times, Latin Wide, Futura Condensed Light, and Futura Medium.

C

AUTHOR BIOGRAPHIES

We are often asked how we got to this point in our lives, so we've spelled out all the important details for you.

FOSTER D. COBURN III

Foster began using Ventura Publisher 1.0 to produce a programming magazine

while attending the University of Kansas back in the 1980s. He also started his own little company, Smart Typesetting, to produce various projects for clients.

As Smart Typesetting grew, a product called CorelDRAW 1.0 came along and did some incredible things that Ventura couldn't do. Soon Foster was doing a lot of work using this wonderful new package.

Along the way, he created some little shareware utilities and even helped create some fonts for inclusion in Microsoft's TrueType Font Pack 2. Then in 1993 the writing bug caught hold, and he created *CorelDRAW! 4 Unleashed*.

That first book led Smart Typesetting to morph into the current Unleashed Productions, Inc., which Foster co-owns with Peter McCormick. They teamed up to put on CorelDRAW seminars throughout the United States and even at a few international destinations. Foster also co-authored three more books, *CorelDRAW 5 Unleashed*, *CorelDRAW 6 Unleashed*, and *CorelDRAW 7: The Official Guide*.

The books and seminars led to a videotape series on CorelDRAW and Corel PHOTO-PAINT for versions 6 and 7 and a version 8 series should be available by the time you read this. In addition to the one-day seminars, Unleashed Productions now conducts three-day boot camps for those who want to learn CorelDRAW inside out.

Foster can be contacted by e-mail at foster@unleash.com; by mail at P.O. Box 7008, Cave Creek, AZ 85327; or by phone at (602) 595-0065. You may also want to visit the Unleashed Productions Web site at **http://www.unleash.com** for more information on Foster and Unleashed Productions, Inc.

C

PETER A. MCCORMICK

Peter McCormick became involved with art and computers relatively late in life.

At age 40 he discovered a latent talent for painting on canvas. This discovery eventually led him to the world of computer art. In 1992, at age 53, he discovered computers and CorelDRAW. It was love at first byte. He entered Corel's World Design contest that first year and was awarded Grand Prize in the Landmarks division for an image called Venice. That image appeared on the August 1992 cover of *PC Magazine* following the contest.

Peter then met and teamed up with Foster Coburn at a CorelDRAW users group and began creating ads for businesses in the Phoenix area. During this same period, Peter and Foster co-authored a series of books titled *CorelDRAW Unleashed* along with a third author, Carlos Gonzalez of Phoenix. The books were so popular that they have been translated into several languages. *CorelDRAW 7: The Official Guide* has been translated into several different languages as well.

Around this same time, Peter and Foster formed their current company, Unleashed Productions, Inc., and began teaching seminars throughout the United States. Together they have trained more than 7,000 CorelDRAW users. In November 1996 they traveled to London, where they were presenters at Corel World UK. Besides writing *CorelDRAW 8: The Official Guide* and conducting seminars across the country, Peter and Foster host CorelDRAW boot camps throughout the year at their training facility in Phoenix, Arizona. The boot camps are three days of intense training on the current version of CorelDRAW.

Besides writing books, Peter is a contributing editor for *Corel Magazine*. He also writes occasional articles for the *Corel User Magazine* in the UK. He will soon be writing articles covering Corel PHOTO-PAINT for the German version of *Corel Magazine*.

Peter writes for the real-world user of CorelDRAW. Rather than showing how to create complicated drawings, he wants readers to learn and understand the complexities and functionality of the program. Once readers learn how to use CorelDRAW's tools and effects, they can apply their own unique talents and become the World Design Contest winners of the future.

Peter can be contacted on the Web at pete@unleash.com; on Compuserve at 72172,1761; by mail at 13726 Aleppo Dr., Sun City West, AZ 85375; and by phone at (602) 584-8403. You may also want to visit the Unleashed Productions Web site at **http://www.unleash.com** for more information on Peter and Unleashed Productions, Inc.